# CONGRESS
# IN CONTEXT

# CONGRESS IN CONTEXT

John Haskell, Marian Currinder,
and Sara A. Grove

SECOND EDITION

WESTVIEW
PRESS

A Member of the Perseus Books Group

WESTVIEW PRESS was founded in 1975 in Boulder, Colorado, by notable publisher and intellectual Fred Praeger. Westview Press continues to publish scholarly titles and high-quality undergraduate-and graduate-level textbooks in core social science disciplines. With books developed, written, and edited with the needs of serious nonfiction readers, professors, and students in mind, Westview Press honors its long history of publishing books that matter.

Find us on the World Wide Web at www.westviewpress.com.

Every effort has been made to secure required permissions for all text, images, maps, and other art reprinted in this volume.

Westview Press books are available at special discounts for bulk purchases in the United States by corporations, institutions, and other organizations. For more information, please contact the Special Markets Department at the Perseus Books Group, 2300 Chestnut Street, Suite 200, Philadelphia, PA 19103, or call (800) 810-4145, ext. 5000, or e-mail special.markets@ perseusbooks.com.

*Designed by Cindy Young*

Library of Congress Cataloging-in-Publication Data
Haskell, John, 1959–
  Congress in context / John Haskell, Marian Currinder, and Sara A. Grove.—Second edition.
  pages cm
  Includes bibliographical references and index.
  ISBN 978-0-8133-4756-1 (pbk.)—ISBN 978-0-8133-4758-5 (e-book) 1. United States. Congress. 2. Legislative power—United States. 3. Representative government and representation—United States. I. Currinder, Marian. II. Grove, Sara A. III. Title.
  JK1021.H38 2014
  328.73—dc23
                                    2013036925
10 9 8 7 6 5 4 3 2 1

# CONTENTS

**PART 3.**
CONGRESS AND OTHERS

# LIST OF ILLUSTRATIONS

**TABLES**

## FIGURES

# LIST OF FEATURES

## EXHIBITS

# PREFACE

The unifying concept of this book is that Congress's central function in our separated system is to be, borrowing from James L. Sundquist, the "board of directors" of the federal government, empowered by the Constitution to authorize, fund, and supervise the activities of the government—that is, the executive branch agencies. As the lead author, I draw on my varied experiences as a college professor, a congressional staffer, and an instructor for federal agency personnel to produce a textbook that seeks to help people make sense of Congress in the context of its role in our separated system of government. The aim of *Congress in Context* is to convey my experiences working in government and with government officials, informed by the relevant political science literature, in a format that is lively and conveys a real-world sense of the first branch.

The journey that led to writing this book was a long one. I first taught a university-level course covering Congress—called Congress and the Presidency—as a graduate student in the fall of 1986. The sections on the two branches were clearly differentiated in the syllabus. Overall, the course was presented as a series of topics—the Congress in *The Federalist Papers*, congressional elections, leadership and committees in Congress, then the president in the Constitution, presidential personality, presidential elections, and so forth. As a grad student, I was too wrapped up in other more pressing matters to impose much organizational coherence on the course. To be honest, it never occurred to me to do that. The syllabus was handed down, as it were, and I did as I was told.

When I moved on to full-time teaching and a tenure-track job, my portfolio included separate courses on Congress and the presidency. I continued to teach Congress more or less as a set of differentiated topics, albeit with an introduction emphasizing that members have two roles, legislative and representative. Generally speaking, students seemed to enjoy the course, but I still did not impose the kind of structure or coherence that the material deserved.

One year I had the good fortune to work on Capitol Hill through the American Political Science Association Congressional Fellowship Program. From day one of my assignment, I was disturbed to find out how ignorant I had been about what members of Congress and their staff were up to on a day-to-day basis. I knew almost immediately that I had been stressing the wrong things in my Congress course, or at least had not been conveying to students what really mattered about the institution. At first I could not put my finger on exactly what I had missed. Eventually, my thinking began to crystallize: what members were doing was primarily aimed at changing government programs and agency policies and practices to the benefit of their constituents in particular, and sometimes to the benefit of broader groups across the country. I was in dozens of meetings involving a wide range of members and staff. Although a lot of these meetings were primarily "political," even those usually touched at least a little bit—and often much more than that—on what the members could do in law or by other means to change federal programs to the people's benefit.

This realization changed the way I taught Congress when I returned to the classroom. I covered the same main topics—elections, committees, party leadership, and so forth—but changed the focus to looking at congressional policy making in the context of the institution's role in the federal government. I began to stress that Congress *matters* . . . to the extent that what it does in law and through other methods alters or creates government programs that invariably have tangible effects on people's lives. Understanding how a bill becomes a law has intrinsic importance only insofar as a law may change, for example, Interior Department policies that affect the management of federal lands or the populations of endangered species, or as a law may involve funding one type of research instead of another at the National Institutes of Health (NIH).

In 2000 I landed a job at the Government Affairs Institute at Georgetown University. GAI has a unique mission among nonprofit educational institutions: it endeavors to explain how Congress works to executive branch officials. The notion is that the government functions better when the people who work in the two branches understand each other. Executive branch officials are in constant communication with members of Congress, and especially congressional staff, but most of them have trouble mastering the specialized lingo, understanding the complex authorization and appropriations processes, and grasping members' perspective on the world. This is where GAI comes in.

Teaching federal agency personnel about Congress brings into clear relief the most salient function of Congress: directing, through legislation and oversight, the work of the agencies and departments of government. It is tremendously important for executive branch officials, students at the undergraduate and graduate levels, and interested citizens to understand the legislative process and what drives members' decision making on Capitol Hill. After all, government programs as created by Congress and administered by executive branch officials have a profound effect on all of our lives. The federal government now constitutes well over 20 percent of the American economy, and it is unlikely to get smaller or less significant. It is Congress that provides the statutory basis for the work of the agencies. Understanding congressional policy making tells us a great deal about the kind of government we have now and will have in the future.

Gaining this understanding is what drives *Congress in Context* and its unique focus on exploring Congress as a board of directors. In addition to introducing this concept, the first four chapters of the book introduce the student of Congress to the institution, its constitutional underpinnings, the basic organizational units of the House and Senate, the importance of the bicameral structure, the impact of the representative role on the policy-making process, and the role and influence of campaigns and elections on everything the members do.

The book then turns to how Congress carries out its legislative duties. Chapters 5–10 cover the authorizing power, the funding power, and the conduct of oversight (the supervisory power), respectively. The aim is to give the reader a full understanding of the legislative process, Congress's role in establishing government agencies, how Congress directs the agencies through its funding power, and how the institution looks into the performance and conduct of agencies and programs and attempts to influence agency policy through oversight.

Chapters 11–13 are new chapters with this edition. Chapter 11 looks at the struggle over the direction of policy between the executive and legislative branches. We focus on the tools the two branches have to influence federal policy. We also consider carefully how the issue of context matters—domestic policy involves a far more even playing field than national security policy, where the executive has some clear advantages. Chapter 12 considers how the federal courts fit into the policy-making realm. And Chapter 13 covers the role of interest groups in the congressional policy-making arena.

In the last chapter, we assess the congressional board of directors in the 21st century. Ultimately, Chapter 14 addresses the question of whether the unwieldy institution of Congress is up to the great challenges of the years to come.

*John Haskell*
*November 2013*

# ACKNOWLEDGMENTS

The second edition has benefited tremendously from the work of coauthors Marian Currinder, senior fellow at the Government Affairs Institute, and Sara Grove, professor of political science at Shippensburg University. In particular, Marian is largely responsible for Chapter 4 and has aided the effort in various other ways. Sara took the lead on Chapters 12 and 13. The ideas of Ken Gold, the director of GAI, were integral to the national security sections of Chapter 11. In addition, Ken made sure GAI supported Marian, Sara, and me—which made this project possible.

Valerie Heitshusen, formerly a GAI faculty member and now with the Congressional Research Service, went through early drafts of Chapter 5 with a fine-toothed comb and otherwise helped me with the informal nuances of congressional procedure. In particular, her up-to-the-minute knowledge helped me capture some of the recent trends in how leaders in both chambers deal with complex legislation.

Several anonymous current Appropriations Committee staffers have helped with examples and details of the budget process. Former House Appropriations subcommittee staff directors Michelle Mrdeza and John Blazey provided insights into some of the uses of report language and general provisions in appropriations law. Jonathan Etherton, formerly of the Senate Armed Services Committee staff, has over the years shared vital insights into the role of hearings and the construction of authorization bills. Daniel Pearson and Doug Pasternak, investigators with the House Committee on Science and Technology, have shared their experiences conducting oversight of government programs and setting up hearings. Robert Dove and Alan Frumin, both former Senate parliamentarians, have been great resources on the ways of the "upper chamber." Mark Harkins, former chief of staff for Representative Brad Miller and now a senior fellow at GAI; Brenna Findley, former chief of staff for Representative Steve King; and Jean-Louise Beard, chief of staff for Representative David Price, have been very helpful in giving a flavor of the workings of the personal office. Cory Claussen, staffer with the Senate Agriculture Committee, assisted me in understanding the development and implementation of Dodd-Frank. We are very much indebted to Jonathan Degner, a campaign consultant who has been involved with several congressional campaigns and has run independent expenditure efforts, for sharing his knowledge of congressional politics on the ground.

Samuel Lovett, Nitt Chuenprateep, and Travis Forden designed the artwork and provided help on other high-tech matters that was desperately needed. The writing of the second edition of the book was made much easier with the research assistance of Tom Boerigter. He did exhaustive fact-checking and helped to select many of the new examples that appear in this edition. I am still indebted to Sarah Wohl, Amy Meyers, Daniel Fischer, and Chris Walker, all of whom worked on the first edition.

Westview Press editor Ada Fung deserves special commendation for taking the reins from Toby Wahl for the second edition. She is the reason the book has been enhanced with the addition of Chapters 11–13; it's a much better product as a result. We would also like to thank Cathleen Tetro, Brooke Smith, Melissa Veronesi, and Annette Wenda at Westview Press. We appreciate the dozens of ideas for improvement from reviewers of the first edition, including Peter Bergerson (Florida Gulf Coast University), Holly Brasher (University of Alabama at Birmingham), Dave Dulio (Oakland University), Alison Howard (Dominican University of California), Gary Lee Malecha (University of Portland), Hong Min Park (University of Alabama), John J. Pitney, Jr. (Claremont McKenna College), Pamela Schaal (Ball State University), and others who wish to remain anonymous.

This book would not have been possible without the help of every single person listed here as well as many others. But, unfortunately, we have to absolve them all of responsibility for any errors in its contents.

# THE NATURE AND ORIGINS OF CONGRESS

# 1

CHAPTER

# Congress as the Board of Directors

The US Congress is by far the least popular branch of the federal government. It is also probably the least understood. Even some high-ranking officials in the executive branch do not understand the basic dynamics of the institution and how it exercises its power. Amazingly, experienced professional staff members in Congress itself get confused from time to time about the intricacies of the legislative process. It is the aim of this book to demystify the institution—to give the reader a practical yet sophisticated treatment of Congress and the legislative process.

*Congress in Context* takes a different approach than most textbooks. Usually, Congress is treated in isolation from the rest of the government. But the framers of the Constitution explicitly intended for the branches of government to be interdependent. The aim here is to introduce readers to Congress's critical role within this interdependent system. Specifically, this book focuses on Congress in the context of its relationship with the executive branch.

## FIVE EXAMPLES OF THE FEDERAL GOVERNMENT IN ACTION

The initial focus of this chapter is counterintuitive. It is to look *away* from Congress itself and examine a few examples of the results of the policy-making process in Washington. These examples represent the federal government in action.

Some of what the government does appears on the front pages of the nation's newspapers every day—the president directs intelligence agencies to conduct drone attacks on suspected terrorists, agencies respond to Hurricane Sandy, a new health care entitlement is implemented, and so on. Although most government activities are far more mundane than these front-page headlines, make no mistake about it: the federal government is literally everywhere, involved in our lives and communities in innumerable ways, big and small. The scope of the government is almost impossible to fathom. It is a $3.5 trillion enterprise that accounted for more than 23 percent of the entire US economy in 2012—easily the largest single entity on the planet.

The following examples might not make headlines, but they do typify the federal government's ongoing involvement in the lives of its citizens.

## Example 1: Keeping Tabs on the Salmon Population

During his 2012 State of the Union address, President Barack Obama quipped: "The Interior Department is in charge of salmon while they're in fresh water, but the Commerce Department handles them while they're in saltwater. I hear it gets even more complicated when they're smoked."[1] The president was on to something. These fish have a complex life cycle, spanning periods spent in both freshwater and saltwater. They begin life inland and eventually find their way to the ocean. After maturing, they reverse course, heading back upriver to where they were born in order to reproduce and ultimately die.

Due to the ecological and economic importance of the salmon population, in 1965 Congress passed the Anadromous Fish Conservation Act, which assigned the Fish and Wildlife Service, part of the Department of the Interior, the main responsibility for the freshwater salmon habitat.[2] In 1973 the Endangered Species Act gave the National Oceanic and Atmospheric Administration (NOAA), an agency in the Commerce Department, jurisdiction over populations and conditions for salmon in saltwater.

If anything, the president downplayed the complexity of federal regulations regarding salmon.[3] In some circumstances, in the Columbia River Basin, for example, other agencies, including the Environmental Protection Agency (EPA) and the US Army Corps of Engineers, have a role. NOAA is also responsible for maintaining sustainable populations of other fish popular at restaurants and grocery stores, including tuna, swordfish, and halibut. The Sustainable Fisheries Act (1996) charged NOAA with balancing the sustainability of fish populations with the economic concerns of communities on the coasts and the interests of recreational anglers.

## Example 2: Funding Basic Science for Medical Purposes

The National Institutes of Health (NIH) in the Department of Health and Human Services conducts and supports through grants basic scientific research into a wide range of diseases, including cancer, mental illness, HIV/AIDS, addictive disorders, and many others. Scientists literally all over the country, at universities, hospitals, and other places, are conducting experiments with NIH grants. The agency was established in the Public Health Service Act of 1944, which gave it wide latitude to research illnesses and disabilities. It currently has 27 institutes covering nearly every imaginable area of medical science.

Although the NIH's programs are highly popular and often receive generous funding from Congress, approximately $32 billion in 2012, the agency is not without controversy. In particular, interest among NIH-funded scientists in studying the use of embryonic stem cells that could potentially be used to regenerate heart and lung tissue has drawn the sustained attention of Congress and recent presidents. A 1995 law severely restricted the latitude of the agency in the conduct of this research.

## Example 3: Planning for Cyber War

According to the *Washington Post*, the Department of Defense has a project called Plan X. "The five-year, $110 million research program will begin seeking proposals [in the summer of 2012]. Among its goals will be the creation of an advanced map that details the entirety of cyberspace. . . . Such a map would help commanders identify targets and disable them using computer code delivered through the Internet or other means. Another goal is the creation of a robust operating system capable of launching attacks and surviving counterattacks."[4]

The agency at the Defense Department (DOD) responsible for the program is the Defense Advanced Research Projects Agency (DARPA). It was established in law in 1958 following the Soviet launch of Sputnik (the first satellite), which produced concern that the United States was falling behind in science to our greatest foe. DARPA's mission was "to prevent technological surprises for the United States and maintain its technological superiority."[5]

Congress generally sees fit to allow the agency a great deal of discretion in what it does, given the speculative as well as secretive nature of its work. There are indications that DARPA will dedicate approximately $1.54 billion overall from 2013 to 2017 for projects broadly described under the heading "cyber offense."

## Example 4: SPOTting Suspicious Airline Passengers

Everyone knows that airline passengers have to go through intensive security before boarding a plane. This process was fully federalized following the attacks on September 11, 2001, after the creation in law of the Transportation Security Administration (TSA). But not everyone is aware of the Screening Passengers by Observation Techniques (SPOT) program. Congress first directed funds toward research related to behavioral observation and security in a 2005 Department of

Homeland Security (DHS) appropriations bill. In 2009 Congress designated $172 million specifically for screening programs such as SPOT and has continued to fund the program, in particular for the training and utilization of behavioral detection officers (BDOs).

When passengers pass through metal detectors, they are likely unaware they may be watched by a BDO. According to the TSA, BDOs are a nonintrusive way to "detect individuals exhibiting behaviors that indicate that they may be a threat to aviation and/or transportation security."[6] As of 2013, BDOs were stationed in 161 airports in the United States.

## Example 5: Helping Students Pay for College

A major thrust of President Lyndon Johnson's Great Society was to enhance the federal role in education at all levels—from elementary schools to universities. Since the passage of the Higher Education Act in 1965, the US government has been in the business of subsidizing student loans for college, principally through Stafford and Perkins Loans. These programs were administered by the then Department of Health, Education, and Welfare; the Department of Education Organization Act (1979) created a separate Department of Education, which took over responsibility in 1980.

In 2010 the Student Aid and Fiscal Responsibility Act (SAFRA) was passed into law. With SAFRA, subsidized loans would no longer be jointly administered by the government and private industry, but rather would be handled by the federal government alone. This was justified by studies indicating that the government would save some $68 billion over 10 years by taking private industry out of the equation.[7] In addition, in the aftermath of the Great Recession, Congress halved the interest rates on these loans effective until mid-2013 when compromise legislation put in place a variable rate system.

\* \* \*

As one might conclude from just these few examples, the federal government takes on an amazingly wide range of responsibilities. For our purposes, it is important to look a little more closely at exactly who is doing the work described in these examples.

In the first example, it is NOAA in the Commerce Department and the Fish and Wildlife Service in the Interior Department. The second involves an agency in the Department of Health and Human Services, the NIH. In the third case, it's DARPA in the Department of Defense doing the work. The fourth example shows us the TSA at the Department of Homeland Security at work, and in the fifth example, student loan programs, it is the Department of Education.

What all of these government agencies and departments have in common is that they are in the executive branch of government. The legislative branch, the US Congress, manages no federal programs and is not out there getting its hands dirty dealing with salmon and laboratory science. It is the vast executive branch that does the work of government. In a sense, Congress does not *do* anything at all. And the fact is that, perennial cynicism about a "do-nothing Congress" notwithstanding, in our federal system, the legislative branch was not *meant* to do anything.

## CONGRESS AS THE BOARD OF DIRECTORS

### Laying Down the Law

If Congress is not meant to do the work of government, then what exactly is its role? As political scientist James L. Sundquist put it, Congress operates as the "board of directors" of the federal government.[8] A board of directors can take many different forms, depending on the type of entity it governs in the business or nonprofit world. In a college or university, for example, a board of trustees holds ultimate power.

Congress's board-of-directors function more closely resembles that of a corporation. A corporation that issues stock is owned by its shareholders, who select the members of the board. In fulfilling its function—typically establishing the policies of the corporation and approving the corporation's budget—the board is answerable to those shareholders. The board gives wide latitude to those who are responsible for the day-to-day management of the corporation.

Congress's situation is very similar. The members are chosen by the voting public and are held accountable by regular and frequent elections. Congress sets forth in law the policies that guide the government, just as the corporate board sets forth company policy, and Congress is in charge of determining the budget for the government. Given the immense size and complexity of the government, Congress must usually give a great deal of discretion to the president and the lower-level executive branch agency officials in running day-to-day operations.

There is one major difference between Congress and its corporate counterpart: except in extraordinary circumstances, Congress does not get to choose the president, while the corporate board gets to choose the chief executive officer, who is fully answerable to it. An institutional rivalry between the legislative and executive branches was intentionally built into the federal government, a rivalry fostered by having members of Congress and the president separately elected.

Congress has tremendous leverage in the separated system of government. To put it succinctly, as the board of directors, it has three powers as set forth or implied in the Constitution:

1. Congress **authorizes** in law the activities of the government—which is to say the executive branch
2. Congress passes laws to **fund** what the executive branch does
3. Congress, when it sees fit, *supervises* the executive branch (a function usually referred to as **oversight**)

Congress was not designed to manage fisheries or conduct research on infectious diseases; it was designed to decide, based on its collective wisdom, whether the government will manage a particular fishery or conduct scientific research, to allocate money for these activities, and to check up on the executive branch agencies it has made responsible. Congress creates in law the agencies it assigns to perform government functions.

This authority comes from Article I, Section 1, of the Constitution, which explicitly gives Congress the lawmaking power: "All legislative powers herein granted shall be vested in a Congress of the United States, which shall consist of a Senate and a House." (Most of these legislative powers are specified in Section 8 of Article I.) Notably, the legislative power includes the power to appropriate money—also explicitly granted in Section 9 of Article I: "No money shall be drawn from the Treasury, but in consequence of appropriations made by law." In sum, Congress has the power to set up agencies and government programs, determine the policies carried out by those agencies, and establish the budgets for their operations.

The courts have always considered the supervisory or oversight function of Congress a legitimate extension of Congress's legislative power, for two reasons. First, Congress needs to be able to make sure the laws it passes are being faithfully executed. After all, what good would there be in having the power to authorize and fund the activities of the government if the executive branch agencies could ignore the law and carry out programs as they saw fit or spend money in ways that might be prohibited? Just as a corporation is answerable to its board of directors, Congress must have the authority to demand documents or otherwise investigate the executive branch to make sure the agencies are doing its bidding. Second, Congress needs to be able to conduct oversight in order to inform the legislative process. If a government program is not working, members of Congress need to be able to find out why so that they can consider making changes in the law to improve it. They may also choose either to fund the program at a higher level the next year, so that it can perform better, or to reduce and maybe even cut off its funding stream. Information is crucial to Congress's ability to legislate, and oversight is the main way in which Congress gathers data.

In all five of our examples of "government in action," executive branch agencies are carrying out responsibilities assigned to them in law. As noted in the first case, NOAA assesses the status of particular fish populations and balances various interests (recreational, economic, and so on) to promote the sustainability of fisheries—pursuant to the Endangered Species Act, in the first instance, and the Sustainable Fisheries Act, in the second. The Anadromous Fish Conservation Act gave the Fish and Wildlife Service authority over salmon in freshwater. Similarly, the NIH is authorized to conduct and support medical research because of the Public Health Service Act, and the 1958 Military Construction Act included the creation of DARPA to help the United States maintain its technological superiority. Just two months after the 9/11 attacks, the TSA was put in place by the Aviation Transportation and Security Act to protect against future threats. The Stafford Loan Program was overhauled in 2010 legislation; it had been initially authorized by the Higher Education Act of 1965.

## Holding the Purse Strings

It is important to note that in nearly all of these specific cases, Congress went a step further than what is described in the last paragraph. Although Congress often delegates a great deal of authority to executive branch agency officials, it is not always satisfied with simply providing broad guidelines and mission statements and leaving the details to the experts in the bureaucracy. Sometimes the members of Congress get into the specifics by detailing exactly where and how some of the money appropriated for government functions should be spent.

For example, in explanatory language accompanying a 2005 appropriations law—language that is not statutory, thus technically nonbinding—Congress told NOAA Fisheries how to break down its $90 million allotment for salmon recovery state by state. Furthermore, as can be seen in Exhibit 1.1 on page 11, members of Congress inserted sections urging the agency to spend the funds provided for salmon recovery in specific places for specific purposes: $100,000 for the United Fishermen of Alaska's subsistence program, $3.368 million for the Fairbanks hatchery facilities, $1 million for conservation mass-marking at the Columbia River Hatcheries, and so on.[9] Every single year, Congress determines in law exactly how much money goes to each of the 27 institutes and centers at the National Institutes of Health. Every year since 1995, Congress has also included language in an appropriations bill limiting what the NIH may do in the area of stem-cell research.

SEC. 509. (a) None of the funds made available in this Act may be used for—The creation of a human embryo or embryos for research purposes; or research in which a human embryo or embryos are destroyed, discarded, or knowingly subjected to risk of injury or death. (from the fiscal year 2012 Appropriation for Labor, Health and Human Services, and Education)

This issue has become the subject of great controversy within Congress and between the branches.[10]

Sometimes Congress micromanages the number of people who may be hired for a task. In the case of behavior detection officers, Congress provided money to train 145 new officers for fiscal year 2012—this despite President Obama's requesting funding for more than twice that many. The lesson is that agencies, in doing the work of government in pursuit of their respective missions, ultimately are answerable not just to the head of the executive branch, the president of the United States, but also to the board of directors on Capitol Hill. Congress may, if it chooses, give both general and specific instructions to those who do the work of government. If such instructions are signed into law by the president, the agencies are required to comply. When Congress, or some subset of members of Congress, conveys its wishes in less formal, nonstatutory ways (see Exhibit 1.1), agencies can be put in a very difficult spot: sometimes the instructions from the president and the congressional overseers are in conflict, and sometimes the instructions may not jibe precisely with the agency's mission as established in law.

Circumstances such as these lead to some of the most interesting clashes in our separated system of government. The constitutional design calls for Congress, with its particular perspective and way of doing business, to direct the executive branch, which is made up of dozens of agencies, with as many different corporate cultures. Unsurprisingly, as often as not, the two branches do not see eye to eye on the details of the work of government. The framers intentionally built this tension into our system of government: they believed that the way to protect the people's liberties was to ensure that the branches do not have the same perspective.

## CONGRESS IN A SEPARATED SYSTEM

As mentioned at the beginning of this chapter, Congress is often studied in isolation from the rest of the government. In this book, the aim is to understand Congress in context—specifically in the context of its role as the board of directors in a separated system of government. Although it is common to hear our institutions of government described as "separated powers," this is not a complete or precise characterization. In fact, as the framers made abundantly clear, ours is a system of *separate institutions sharing powers.*[11]

The genius of the checks and balances in the American political system is that each branch of government has been granted in the Constitution checks on the other branches. In fact, the idea was *not* to give branches truly separate powers. If one branch of government had truly separate, unchecked powers, the ambitious people in that branch of government (and the framers firmly believed that people in politics *are* ambitious!) would be tempted to run wild with that power, which

# EXHIBIT 1.1

## Congress Gives Specific Direction to NOAA in Language Accompanying Appropriations Bill

**PACIFIC COASTAL SALMON RECOVERY**

The conference agreement provides $90,000,000 for Pacific Coastal Salmon Recovery, instead of $80,000,000 as proposed by the House and $99,000,000 as proposed by the Senate. Language is included extending authorization for this program in fiscal year 2005 and authorizing participation by the State of Idaho.

Funds provided under this heading shall be allocated as follows: $24,000,000 for Alaska; $13,000,000 for California; $2,500,000 for Columbia River Tribes; $4,500,000 for Idaho; $13,000,000 for Oregon; $8,000,000 for Pacific Coast Tribes; and $25,000,000 for Washington.

With respect to the amounts for Alaska, the conferences agree to the following allocation: $3,500,000 is for the Arctic Yukon-Kuskokwim Sustainable Salmon initiative; $1,000,000 is for the Cook Inlet Fishing Community Assistance Program; $500,000 is for the Yukon River Drainage Association; **$3,368,000 is for Fairbanks hatchery facilities**; $250,000 is for an initiative to redefine optimum goals for sockeye, chinook, and coho stocks; $2,500,000 is for the NSRAA Hatchery; $500,000 is for Coffman Cove king salmon; $250,000 is for the State of Alaska to participate in discussions regarding the Columbia River hydro-system and for fisheries revitalization; **$100,000 is for the United Fishermen of Alaska's subsistence program**; $3,500,000 is to restore salmon fisheries in Anchorage at Ship Creek, Chester Creek, and Campbell Creek, including habitat restoration and facilities; $500,000 is for Alaska Village Initiatives to enhance salmon stocks; $800,000 is for Bristol Bay Science and Research Institute; $1,100,000 is for the Alaska Fisheries Development Foundation; $150,000 is for the State of Alaska for fishing rationalization research; $1,500,000 is for the State of Alaska for fisheries monitoring; $1,500,000 is for the Alaska SeaLife Center to restore salmon runs in Resurrection Bay . . .

. . . **Of the amounts provided to the State of Oregon, $1,000,000 is for conservation mass marking at the Columbia River Hatcheries.**

The conferees agree that NOAA shall report to the Committees by March 31, 2005, on final performance measures for this program, including an assessment of cumulative program effects on Pacific salmon stocks, and the identification of recovery needs of specific salmon populations as a resource for determining future funding allocations.

SOURCE: Explanatory "report language" attached to the fiscal year 2005 Appropriations bill for the Commerce Department.

NOTE: In this passage from nonstatutory report language, Congress strongly encourages NOAA Fisheries to spend its funds for salmon recovery in specific ways, including the three highlighted passages that are cited in the text. Agencies almost always follow the guidance given in report language even though they are not legally obligated to do so. This is because Congress's "power of the purse" gives it tremendous leverage.

was the situation the framers were trying to avoid. Their number-one priority was to prevent the central government from unnecessarily infringing upon the people's liberties. Pitting the branches against one another was thought to be the best way to accomplish this goal.

In particular, the framers were concerned about controlling the political branches, the executive and legislative. The judicial branch was thought to be the "least dangerous branch," since its pronouncements, to have any effect, would require the acquiescence of the political branches to fund them (Congress) and enforce them (the president).[12] In the parlance of the time, the judicial branch would have neither the "purse" nor the "sword," so it would be in no position to run away with its authority.

Whether the judicial branch has actually been constrained over the long course of American history is a matter of considerable debate. Many people feel that the lack of sufficient effective institutional checks on the Supreme Court and the lower federal courts led in the latter half of the 20th century to a runaway judiciary that has done more than just adjudicate the disputes brought to its attention. Even so, it remains the case that the judiciary does not usually participate in the day-to-day functioning of the government but most often serves as the referee. Chapter 12 covers the role of the judiciary in federal policy making.

The framers focused on balancing the checks the two political branches had on one another. As a result, those two branches are inextricably linked to each other by the Constitution. To get a sophisticated sense of what each branch does in the government, one must see it in the context of the other branch. In other words, what Congress does has tangible importance in our lives only insofar as its decisions are translated into the actions taken by officials in the executive branch agencies—whether they are tracking infectious disease, subsidizing public housing, prosecuting people accused of violating federal statutes, or patrolling the borders.

## Congress and the Execution of the Law

The relationship between the two political branches is not as simple as it might at first seem. Their interaction is not just a matter of one branch, Congress, creating laws and the other branch, the executive, implementing them.

Although members of Congress have to vote on every imaginable issue, including highly technical ones, it is impossible for them to be experts on everything. Members of Congress are generalists who have some knowledge of a lot of things but in-depth knowledge of very few. Because the laws written by the generalists in Congress are frequently—and often intentionally—broad, vague, or even ambiguous, there are almost always differing opinions on how to interpret and implement these laws. Furthermore, no law can anticipate all future circumstances.

Congress recognizes these facts of life and often leaves a great deal of decision-making authority to the discretion of experts in the executive branch agencies. In exercising their discretion, executive branch officials may not necessarily make decisions that correspond with the views of some current members of Congress.

This is especially common in times of divided government, when the president and congressional majorities have ideological differences. Confrontations between the branches, and even occasionally major headline news, may result. After the 2010 elections when Republicans gained control of the House of Representatives from the Democrats (the Democrats held on to the Senate), House Republicans made repeated efforts to alter and even repeal the Patient Protection and Affordable Care Act (PPACA) passed in 2010, one of the signature accomplishments of President Obama and Democrats in the 111th Congress. Much of the effort revolved around funding decisions. Because agencies' funding levels are reconsidered annually, members of Congress have a regular opportunity to poke around in executive branch business. Usually, the aim is to make sure money is being spent wisely and according to their wishes; sometimes, as in the case of the House Republicans and the PPACA, Congress can go so far as to try to eliminate funding for the implementation of government programs.

The branches are, in effect, in a continuous feedback loop. The implementation of Congress's broad statutes by the executive branch often attracts the attention of congressional overseers, who then may use various methods of persuasion and coercion (hearings, informal communications, and other types of oversight) designed to get the agencies to reconsider their decisions. Sometimes Congress reacts by introducing and passing new legislation with the hope of making its intentions clearer or changing the funding stream for government programs.

## The Executive Branch and the Legislative Process

Not only, then, is Congress sometimes an active player in the execution of the law, but, importantly, the executive branch is also a player in the legislative process. At the top of the executive branch, the president may veto a bill, which has the effect of putting him in the thick of any legislative activity in which he takes an interest. Congress has historically found it extremely difficult to achieve the two-thirds majority required by the Constitution to override a veto, and thus it is almost always necessary for it to take the president's views into consideration.[13]

In addition, the Constitution allows the president to recommend legislation to Congress (Article II, Section 3). Over time the White House has institutionalized its participation in the legislative process through the **Office of Management and Budget (OMB)**, an agency in the **Executive Office of the President (EOP)** that officially conveys the president's views on pending legislation. Furthermore, the agencies, where much of the expertise in government resides, often are the source of legislative proposals to fix government programs or address particular needs. In other words, although it is technically true that only members of the legislative branch may introduce legislation, Congress often finds itself considering bills suggested and written by the White House or executive branch agencies instead of writing the bills itself.

In summary, in our system of government, Congress is not just concerned with legislation but fully entitled to play a role in the execution of the law by checking up on how the agencies carry out its wishes; similarly, the executive branch is not limited to the implementation of the law but is fully entitled to play a role in the writing and even the interpretation of the law.

This relationship results in a constant struggle between the two political branches—just as the framers intended. In our conception of Congress as the board of directors of the federal government, we recall that it lacks one key power enjoyed by a corporate board: it does not get to choose the chief executive officer. Striving for businesslike efficiency was not the point of the constitutional arrangement; ensuring the liberties of the people was. The branches would share powers but have separate bases of support; it was understood that this arrangement would often lead to disagreement and a less-than-efficient legislative process.

Unlike legislatures in most countries, which play a subordinate role to the chief executive, the US Congress has retained its fundamental powers throughout American history. Congress remains powerful in many of the key ways in which a corporate board of directors is powerful; in particular, it establishes policy and determines the level of funding for government activities. It is not always a hands-on board; the government is way too big for Congress to delve into all the specifics. But no one can understand our system of government without grasping Congress's crucial role.

Congress is a complex institution arranged unlike any other organization, and this makes its ways subject to misinterpretation. Its internal workings are confusing, and it has its own vocabulary and rhythms. It is the aim of this book to interpret the institution of Congress, giving the reader a better understanding of the role of the legislative branch in our system of government.

## THE PLAN OF THE BOOK

The first objective is to establish a basic working knowledge of Congress. That is the aim of Chapters 2 and 3. The student of legislative branch policy making needs to understand the constitutional underpinnings of Congress's powers, the nature of the institution, and the roles and motivations of the members.

Congress's essential characteristics are shaped by the Constitution of the United States. One of these is the idea that Congress is both a lawmaking body and a representative institution, accountable and responsive to the public. The other is the fact that Congress is composed of two chambers, the House of Representatives and the Senate. The student of Congress needs to understand what it means for members of Congress to serve as both legislators and representatives, as well as how the two very distinct chambers operate.

Chapter 2 covers what is often referred to in political science literature as the "two Congresses." Congress's legislative and representative roles often prove extraordinarily difficult for members to reconcile. The tension between these roles may lead them at times in directions that they would not necessarily go if they had only to legislate. The chapter focuses in particular on the pressures that members face in their capacity as representatives. Members are on the front lines, hearing from all manner of groups and individual constituents. The reader will get a sense of the pressures members face and the motivations that drive their behavior; these pressures and motivations have a profound effect on their legislative work of authorizing and funding the activities of the federal government.

Congress's bicameral composition, the topic of Chapter 3, is, surprisingly, the source of much confusion. Few people—and not even all those who work on Capitol Hill—are fully aware of the ways in which the bicameral makeup of the institution drives the legislative process. The fact is that Congress is composed of two uneasily coexisting chambers that were created separate and distinct, yet must work together in order for the institution to enact law. Chapter 3 describes the dynamics of the relationship between the House and Senate and covers the organizational makeup of the two chambers, focusing on the two key organizational units: party leadership and committees.

Chapter 4 looks at the specific pressures the electoral environment puts on members of Congress. In this chapter, we lay the broader framework for understanding congressional elections, including eligibility requirements for office, the decision-making process involved in running for the House and Senate, the parties' efforts to recruit candidates, and the geographical context of congressional elections. The second part of the chapter focuses on the campaign itself—the advantages incumbents have, campaign finance, the role of outside groups and the political parties, campaign strategies, and the larger meaning of congressional election results.

Members of Congress face unrelenting pressure to campaign for reelection. In recent years, there simply have not been enough hours in the day for many members to give full attention to their legislative role. An essential takeaway of Chapter 4: the legislative work of Congress has been profoundly affected by what amounts to a continuous campaign for office—a theme we return to in the concluding chapter of the book.

In Chapters 5 through 10, we move to the main thrust of the book: how Congress directs the work of government through the exercise of its authorizing, funding, and oversight powers.

Chapter 5 looks at the nuts and bolts of the legislative process. The reader will gain a sense of how the process really works, not just how it appears to work "on paper." The chapter looks at how bills are developed, who decides which ones will be voted on, the procedures on the floors of the House and the Senate, and how the chambers go about trying to reconcile the differences between competing versions of a bill. Particular attention is paid to the creative—often referred to as "unorthodox"—methods that have been used in recent years to pass major legislation.

Chapter 6 discusses the institution's authorizing power. Congress is responsible for producing the legislation that gives agencies the authority to do their work—which might be preparing for war, cleaning a river, building a highway, and so on. In drafting the bills that set policy for federal agencies, congressional committees do most of the heavy lifting. We look at the different ways in which Congress exercises power over federal agencies and programs in law, even to the extent of producing legislation that reshapes and reorganizes whole departments and agencies. A case study of the 2004 restructuring of the federal government's foreign intelligence function illustrates the lengths to which Congress can go in asserting its powers. The chapter ends with a discussion of evolving trends in Congress's handling of its authorizing responsibility.

Once a federal program has been established, Congress has to decide whether and how much to fund it. Congress's funding role, the so-called power of the purse, is generally regarded as its most important function; after all, no agency can carry out a government program without money. The subject of Chapter 7 is the budget process in Congress, with the Appropriations Committees at the center of the action. We go through the appropriations process, from the president's budget request, to Congress's effort to look at the big picture with the budget resolution, to the appropriations bills themselves. The budget process is, year in and year out, the centerpiece of Congress's efforts to direct the work of government.

In Chapter 8, we look at federal budget issues that have come to dominate the political battles of the 21st century. First we look at the ramifications of Congress's inability to pass appropriations bills on time—or even close to that. Then we consider the problem of expanding entitlement programs and the projected growth of the national debt. Most observers think the government is on an unsustainable path, potentially leading to economic decline if nothing is done. We tackle the question of why it is so difficult for Congress to get its fiscal house in order and what lessons from the past might offer hope.

Once federal programs are put in place and funded, Congress has a responsibility to look into how they are operating. This is the supervisory or oversight function, the subject of Chapters 9 and 10. Chapter 9 focuses on the basics—where Congress gets its authority to conduct oversight, what the main purposes of oversight are, and what the institution has done to bolster its oversight capacity. In the end, we see that Congress views oversight as essential to its representative role. Members jealously guard their right to look into agency business on behalf of their constituents and the American people more broadly.

Chapter 10 gets into the methods Congress, principally its committees, uses to hold agencies accountable to it and, by extension, the American people. Congress's activities in this area take many forms. Committees may conduct full-fledged investigations of federal agencies or hold hearings to question federal officials. Individual members may simply make phone calls or write letters inquiring about particular programs. Sometimes oversight can be the main activity of Congress. In effect, the board of directors may substitute oversight activities for actual legislation in its efforts to influence what federal agencies do. At the end of the chapter, we discuss the political motivations that drive oversight.

Chapter 11 takes a step back to address the following question: does Congress or the president have the upper hand in influencing federal policy? In a system where the legislative and executive branches share powers, the direction of policy will always involve a struggle for power. To assess this question, we look at the "power tools" at each branch's disposal and consider how they are used in two specific cases: the implementation of financial regulatory reform (Dodd-Frank) and the federal school lunch program.

We also look in detail at the special case of national security policy. Here, unlike in the domestic sphere, the president has the clear advantage, although that may not have been the intent of the Constitution's framers. We look at why Congress's war powers role, as well as its role in national security more broadly, diminished dramatically after World War II. But that isn't the whole story: a web of accountability has built up over the past few decades that has constrained the president to some extent.

Laws passed by Congress often give executive branch agencies broad discretion. It is not uncommon for these agencies to run into controversy when implementing laws that may be broad to the point of vague or ambiguous. Sometimes this leads aggrieved parties to challenge agency actions in court. And taking a step back, the constitutionality of the laws themselves is occasionally challenged. Chapter 12 looks at the development of the federal court system charged with adjudicating these matters, as well as the evolution of the courts', especially the Supreme Court's, role. The chapter also covers the selection process for federal judges and, finally, the kinds of issues the courts will likely face in the coming years.

Chapter 13 develops a key element of the legislative environment affecting Congress as it attempts to direct the work of government through legislation and oversight—the role of interest groups. Going all the way back to the founding period, it was understood that in a free society, citizens would organize to "petition to redress grievances," as it is put in the First Amendment to the Constitution. That is 18th-century language for **lobbying**. Ever since, groups of Americans have attempted to exert pressure on members of Congress—today these efforts involve billions of dollars and highly sophisticated methods. Understanding congressional policy making requires a grasp of the impact of organized advocacy. The chapter covers the growth in advocacy in the past 50 years, methods of influence interest groups use, regulations that have been placed on lobbying, as well as what impact these groups actually have on federal policy making.

The last chapter, "Conclusion: Congress in the 21st Century," gives us an opportunity to take a step back to review what we have learned about the institution in its role directing the work of the federal government, as well as to assess the quality of that work. To a significant degree, the Congress of the 21st century is a product of the constitutional design. It is and always will be slow moving, parochial, and unfocused. But not everything about the institution is determined. Congress has changed in fundamental ways in response to the larger political and social environment. The party system, for example, did not exist in anything like its current form in the early days, and it has evolved in ways that affect the performance of the board of directors every bit as profoundly as the unalterable characteristics written into the Constitution. The pressures of the constant campaign and the ubiquitous influence of interest groups have changed the policy-making environment on Capitol Hill as well.

Our inquiry reveals that Congress is falling down on the job in important ways. Congress has a lot on its plate as it wrestles with all the problems of the 21st century. Laws will be required to get the nation's fiscal house in order, prepare the military for new challenges, and deal with climate change, among other things. Whether the board of directors is up to the task will say a great deal about the nation's future.

---

## Questions for Discussion

1. A corporate board of directors answers to the company's shareholders, whereas the members of Congress, as the board of directors of the federal government, answer to the voters. Are there similarities in the kinds of demands that shareholders and voters make of their respective boards? What are some key differences?

2.  In its capacity as a board of directors, how active should Congress be in providing specific direction to the agencies of government? Are there any general rules or principles it should follow in determining when to get involved in the execution or implementation of the laws it passes?

---

## Suggestions for Further Reading

Madison, James. *The Federalist Papers*. Nos. 47, 48, 49, and 51.

## NOTES

1. Quoted from: http://abcnews.go.com/blogs/politics/2011/01/obamas-salmon-joke-is-serious-business/.

2. See www.fws.gov/laws/lawsdigest/ANADROM.HTML.

3. See www.politifact.com/truth-o-meter/statements/2011/jan/26/barack-obama/obama-says-one-department-regulates-salmon-freshwa/.

4. Ellen Nakashima, "With Plan X, Pentagon Seeks to Spread U.S. Military Might to Cyberspace," *Washington Post,* May 30, 2012, A1.

5. See www.darpa.mil/About.aspx.

6. See www.tsa.gov/what_we_do/layers/bdo/index.shtm.

7. Congressional Budget Office cost estimate: www.cbo.gov/publication/20954.

8. James L. Sundquist, *The Decline and Resurgence of Congress* (Washington, DC: Brookings Institution Press, 1981), 38–39. Sundquist gives credit to W. F. Willoughby for first developing the board-of-directors analogy in the 1930s.

9. See "Conference Report for the Omnibus Appropriations Act for Fiscal Year 2005: Joint Statement of Managers (Pacific Coastal Salmon Recovery)."

10. For a good source of background on this topic, specifically the Dickey-Wicker amendment that established some limitations on stem-cell research, see http://embryo.asu.edu/view/embryo:128106. The current state of the debate can be found in Meredith Wadman, "High Court Ensures Continued U.S. Funding of Embryonic Stem Cell Research," *Nature,* January 7, 2013, www.nature.com/news/high-court-ensures-continued-us-funding-of-human-embryonic-stem-cell-research-1.12171.

11. See especially Charles O. Jones, *The Presidency in a Separated System* (Washington, DC: Brookings Institution Press, 2005); and Richard Neustadt, *Presidential Power and the Modern Presidents* (New York: Free Press, 1991).

12. Alexander Hamilton, *The Federalist Papers,* No. 78.

13. Historically, vetoes are overridden less than 5 percent of the time.

# 2

# The Two Congresses:
# Lawmaking and Representation

There is a common expression that people are "products of their environment." Even though there is obviously some truth to that claim, no one doubts that many of an individual's most important traits are heavily influenced by genetics. Similarly, the US Congress has certain characteristics and exhibits behaviors that have been shaped by the American political version of the genome: the seven articles, as amended, of the US Constitution. Article I of the Constitution establishes the powers and responsibilities of the legislative branch and, together with Article II, sets forth its relationship with the executive branch.

The Constitution gives Congress two distinct responsibilities: lawmaking and representation. Congress's essential nature is to a significant degree determined by the tension between these two roles. Lawmaking entails serving as the board of directors of the US government—authorizing, funding, and supervising its activities. The second responsibility is essentially political: each member of Congress represents and is accountable to a discrete group of people who make up the member's constituency.

The Constitution also established a bicameral legislature, with a House of Representatives and a Senate, to carry out these roles. The two chambers have different constituencies, fundamentally dissimilar rules, some different responsibilities, unequal stature, and, in sum, divergent perspectives on the political world—all of which makes them very hard to coordinate. Describing the two bodies is the subject of the next chapter.

This chapter describes Congress's legislative and representative roles and looks at the potential for conflict between them. The discussion begins with the seeming contradiction between the low regard the public usually has for the institution as a whole and the relative popularity of individual members. Even though members of Congress are often criticized for being "out of touch," in fact there is little grounds for that accusation. Their popularity derives from their responsiveness to constituents as they address citizens' public policy concerns and help them navigate the confusing government bureaucracy.

It is no mystery, then, why members of Congress are popular. They are good at the representative role—tending to the needs of the people back home. The representative role is priority number one for most members most of the time. What this means is that, in understanding the nature of Congress, one can never lose sight of the importance of members' district and state concerns as they make national policy and pass laws in their capacity as the board of directors.

The chapter ends by explaining why members' individual popularity does not necessarily translate into goodwill toward the institution as a whole. Congress has, to put it mildly, a public relations problem tied to its structure and the behavior of some members in their efforts at self-promotion.

## TWO DISTINCT RESPONSIBILITIES
### The Legislative Role

As mentioned in Chapter 1, Congress is given the lawmaking function at the beginning of the Constitution, in Article I. Subsequent sections of that article flesh out this role, and Section 8 spells out Congress's constitutional powers in setting policy for the government:

- To lay and collect taxes, duties, imposts and excises
- To pay the debts [of the nation]
- [To] provide for the common defense and general welfare
- To borrow money on the credit of the United States
- To regulate commerce [with foreign nations, among the states, and with the Indian tribes]
- To establish a uniform rule of naturalization
- To establish uniform laws on the subject of bankruptcies
- To coin money and regulate [its] value
- [To] fix the standard of weights and measures
- To provide for the punishments [for] counterfeiting
- To establish post offices
- To promote the progress of science and the useful arts by securing for limited times to authors and inventors the exclusive right to their respective writings and discoveries

- To constitute tribunals inferior to the Supreme Court
- To define and punish piracies and felonies committed on the high seas
- To punish offenses against the law of nations
- To declare war
- To grant marque and reprisal and make rules concerning captures on land and water
- To raise and support armies [and a navy] and make rules [for governing the armed forces]
- To provide for calling forth the militia to execute the laws of the union
- To suppress insurrections and repeal invasions
- To provide for organizing, arming, and disciplining the militia and for governing such part of them as may be employed in the service of the United States
- To exercise exclusive legislation over [the District of Columbia]
- To exercise . . . authority over [forts, depots, navy yards, and so on]
- To make all laws which shall be necessary and proper for carrying into execution the foregoing powers and all other powers vested by this Constitution of the United States

Section 9 of Article I establishes Congress's "power of the purse," the power that most regularly provides the leverage needed to direct the work of government. Section 10 establishes Congress's authority over the states in crucial policy areas, including tariffs and military affairs.

Furthermore, some of the most important amendments to the Constitution—including the one that established the constitutionality of a federal income tax in 1913 (Amendment XVI) and those that were meant to ensure equal rights and voting rights for all Americans (Amendments XIII, XIV, XV, XIX, XXIV, and XXVI)—further expanded the legislative reach of Congress, in some cases very dramatically. For example, Amendment XIX, giving women the vote (ratified in 1919), says: "The right of citizens of the United States to vote shall not be denied or abridged by the United States or by any State on account of sex. *Congress shall have power to enforce this article by appropriate legislation*" (emphasis added). In effect, Congress's authority was explicitly expanded to do what it deems legislatively necessary to protect women's suffrage. The 15th Amendment (1870) has an almost identical provision, giving Congress the power to act if the right to vote is denied based on "race, color, or previous condition of servitude."

The purpose of the Constitution was to establish a federal government strong enough to keep together a nation of far-flung states. The framers recognized that the first national governing document, the Articles of Confederation (1777–1788), was unable to do this. That document set up a confederation in which the states retained many important powers independent of the central government. The central government lacked critical enumerated powers, such as laying and collecting taxes, and there was no chief executive separate from the legislative body. (The president was the presiding officer for the legislative body.)

The framers' notion was that the legislative body needed to have clearly delineated powers that could not be nullified by the states. In the **Supremacy Clause**, Article VI of the Constitution states that federal laws take precedence over state laws. Most of the framers also felt that a separate chief executive was needed to enforce the laws of the land.

Essentially, the US Congress was given the responsibility to establish federal policy in law. As a practical matter, Congress was charged with creating programs to address the nation's needs and the departments and agencies of government to carry them out. As if this job was not big enough, the framers gave Congress another job every bit as important.

## The Representative Role

The framers of the US Constitution set up a **republic**. In a republic, sovereignty is vested in the voting citizenry instead of in a monarch. But because it is impractical for the voting citizenry literally to govern itself, the republican form of government gives power to the citizens' elected representatives. The elected representatives must face regular and frequent elections to retain their positions of authority.

To make the American republic operational, the original Constitution set up a popularly elected House of Representatives. All of its members would be up for reelection every even-numbered year. The Constitution stipulates that no bill may become law without passing both the House and the Senate in identical form, making it impossible for the government to impose anything on its citizens without the concurrence of their directly elected representatives. The provision in Article I that contains this stipulation is called the **presentment clause**:

> Every bill which shall have passed the House of Representatives and the Senate, shall, before it become a law, be presented to the President of the United States. If he approve he shall sign it, but if not he shall return it, with his objections to that House in which it shall have originated.

Originally, members of the Senate, who were given six-year terms, were not directly elected. The Constitution stated that they would be chosen by the state legislatures. This was changed in 1913 with Amendment XVII, which requires the direct election of senators in the states. Since that time, all members of Congress have been directly elected. However, unlike with the House, only one-third of the Senate seats are contested in each election cycle.

There is one exception to the rule that every sitting member must be directly elected: when a senator dies or retires in the middle of his or her term, most states give the governor the power to appoint a temporary successor until the next election cycle. On the other hand, when vacancies occur in the House, the seat may not be filled by appointment even temporarily; a special election must be held to fill the spot.

What was established in the Constitution was a system of *accountability*, which is the core principle of a republic. Citizens control the politicians they put in power by exercising the voting franchise. It is true that politicians may do what they want while in office, but if they intend to keep their jobs, they are unlikely to stray too far from voters' wishes. It is impossible to overemphasize the importance of accountability in a representative democracy. In such a system, it is extremely difficult for those who do not have the voting franchise to get the attention of the elected officials who wield power.

This is best illustrated by the situation of African Americans even after slavery was abolished. In much of the old Confederacy and the border states, African Americans were denied the vote for almost 100 years following the end of the Civil War in 1865, even though the 15th Amendment, ratified in 1870, was meant to ensure that the franchise could not be taken away based on race. When effective and forceful legislation in 1965 finally secured access to the voting booth for African Americans in these states, even the most dismissive of southern segregationist members of Congress became attentive within just a few years to the concerns of their newly enfranchised constituents. The example of Senator Strom Thurmond of South Carolina, described in Box 2.1, illustrates this point.

The American republic was arranged so that the elected representatives would be accountable to particular constituencies: to districts in the House and to states in the Senate. The House districts were to be apportioned to the states based on population, with the total number determined in federal legislation. (This number was set at 435 in 1911 and has not been changed since.)[1] Each state would get two senators.

This constitutional arrangement creates the *representative role* for members of Congress. Thus, all members of the institution must serve two functions—one primarily involving policy making for the government and the other being primarily political. A member's job is a complicated one: setting federal policy *and* looking after the interests of one's constituents is a lot of work. Moreover, the two roles are not necessarily always compatible. Understanding the tension between being a lawmaker and being a representative is one key to grasping the essential nature

# BOX 2.1

## Senator Thurmond Changes His Tune

Strom Thurmond was first elected to the Senate from South Carolina in 1954 after having served as the state's governor and as the presidential candidate of the "Dixiecrats" (officially the States Rights Party) in 1948, a breakaway group of southern Democrats disenchanted with a move by some prominent party leaders at the 1948 convention to embrace a civil rights platform. Thurmond took five southern states in the general election that year, capturing the vote of traditional Democrats who opposed any infringement on the states' right to maintain the racial status quo of legal segregation.

Thurmond achieved notoriety as a senator for his leadership in the promotion of the "Southern Manifesto" in 1956, a document signed by most southern members protesting the Supreme Court's *Brown v. Board of Education* desegregation decision of 1954. In 1957 he filibustered for more than 24 hours—a record for the Senate—in opposition to the 1957 civil rights bill. In short, he was a steadfast opponent of integrating schools and other public facilities and institutions in the South. He even went so far as to leave the Democratic Party when it became evident that the party was intent on moving more aggressively on the civil rights front, becoming a Republican in 1965.

That same year, the Voting Rights Act was signed into law, ending forever the disenfranchisement of the African American community in his home state and across the South. Thurmond's hard line started to change. His office began to provide constituent services for African Americans as it had for the white population in the state. He was one of the first southern senators to hire a black staff member, and many observers were stunned when he voted for the reauthorization of the Voting Rights Act some years later as well as the controversial establishment of a federal holiday commemorating Martin Luther King's birthday.

Although Thurmond never was able to secure consistent widespread support from South Carolina's African Americans in his reelection efforts, his constituent service operation in the state certainly contributed to a productive working relationship with the black community. And he did improve his percentage of the vote among African Americans as the years went by, usually besting the performance of other Republican southern senators.

SOURCE: Michael Barone and Richard E. Cohen, *The Almanac of American Politics, 2002* (Washington, DC: National Journal, 2001), 1367–1368.

of the institution, and ultimately to gaining a sophisticated sense of policy making in the US Congress.

## Reconciling the Two Roles: The Public's Mixed Feelings

One useful way to get at the interplay between the two roles of members of Congress is to look at how the public regards Congress.

Survey your friends, your work associates, your classmates, or almost any other group, and you will probably discover that there is general dissatisfaction with the performance of Congress. Scientific public opinion surveys regularly test this very issue, asking a random and representative sample of the public whether they approve of the performance of Congress. The results have varied a fair amount, depending on the circumstances. But as can be seen in Figure 2.1, a review of polling conducted by the Gallup organization over the past 30 years indicates a generally low level of approval of the institution. The ratings tend most of the time to range from about 20 to 40 percent. More often in recent years, the numbers have been in the lower half of that range. Many times in the past few years, the approval ratings have dipped below 20 percent. On the positive side, the months after the September 11, 2001, attacks yielded not only great popularity for President George W. Bush, whose approval ratings reached a high of 90 percent, but stratospheric (by historical standards) ratings for Congress of about 60 percent. Those ratings represent, as the saying goes, the exception that proves the rule.[2]

Interestingly, there is always a curious and sizable discrepancy between the paltry ratings the institution usually receives and the relatively favorable ratings given individual members. As can be seen in Figure 2.2, when polling organizations asked people whether their own member was doing a good job and deserved reelection, usually about half and often more gave the thumbs-up, and one-third or fewer thought their representative should not be reelected. Even in 2006, a year when Congress was held in especially low repute owing to lobbyist scandals and other factors, the majority of the public thought their representative deserved to be returned to Congress. In 2010 and 2011, things didn't look quite as rosy for incumbent members, although it is still the case by a large margin that people want their representative to be returned to office. (Of course, people would prefer to see *other* members defeated, a result consistent with the overall low approval ratings seen in Figure 2.1.)

Also telling are the reelection rates enjoyed by members. In the House in recent years, normally well over 90 percent of members seeking reelection succeed in their quest. It is not uncommon for that number to reach 98 percent or even higher. Even in 2010, when Democrats lost 63 seats and the majority, more than either party had lost since 1948, about 85 percent of incumbents were returned to

**FIGURE 2.1. Congressional Approval Rating**

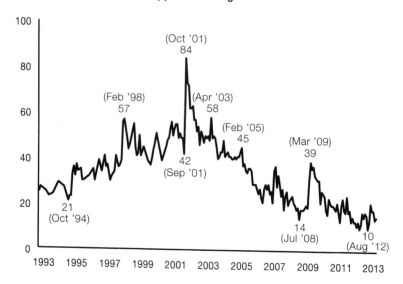

*Source:* Gallup Poll

**FIGURE 2.2. People May Disapprove of Congress, But They Approve of Their Representative**

GENERIC POLL QUESTION: "Does the US Representative in your district deserve to be re-elected?"

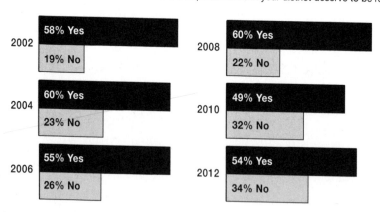

*Source:* 2004 and 2012 data is from Gallup poll. Others are from Pew Research Center poll.

**FIGURE 2.3. Typical House Member's Office Structure**

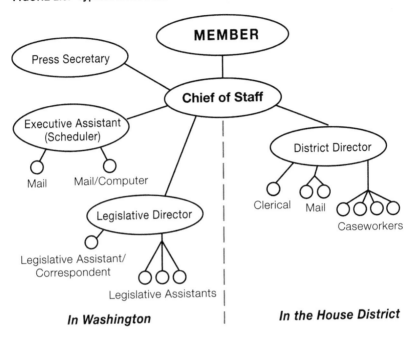

*Source:* Congressional Management Foundation

office. (See Figure 4.4 on page 99 for reelection rates in the House over the past 50 years.) In 2006, another year when public disgust with Congress led to a change in party power, more than 90 percent of those who sought reelection to the House of Representatives won.

In the Senate, usually over 80 percent of incumbents win reelection—91 percent won in 2012. The bottom line: individual members are much more popular than the institution in which they serve.

### What Explains the Seeming Contradiction?

What is going on here? How can there be such a discrepancy between the public's views of the institution and its views of the members of that institution?

Let's start with the favorable ratings of the members. How do they garner these good reviews? First and foremost, members of Congress take their representative role very seriously. Constituent service is the first priority for many if not most of them. In Figure 2.3,[3] one can see the most common staffing arrangements for members of the House. A full description of each aide's duties is included in note 3. (Senate offices have similar structures, but with more staff in most of the roles both in Washington and in the state.) Members' staffs are divided about equally between the district and Washington. Most have multiple offices in their districts or states, staffed by people whose exclusive duty is attending to constituents' problems with one or another government agency.

In this capacity, congressional offices are performing a function that can be traced back to classical antiquity—the **ombudsman** role, or serving as an intermediary between the citizen and the government. Members have staff in their district or state dedicated, for instance, to helping seniors cope with the complex Medicare prescription drug options, sorting out travelers' passport snafus at the State Department, and handling constituents' problems with Immigration and Customs Enforcement or with the Veterans Administration.

In fact, some members' staffs are legendary for their ability to untangle bureaucratic knots. Former New York senator Alfonse D'Amato, who served from 1981 to 1999, was affectionately nicknamed "Senator Pothole" because of his willingness to look into seemingly the smallest problems that New Yorkers had with government services. And the crack staff of five-term North Carolina senator Jesse Helms had a reputation as the "go-to guys" for constituents trying to get information from federal or even state and local agencies. Although it may be impossible to quantify precisely the effect that good ombudsmanship has on the popularity of a member of Congress, certainly it is safe to conclude that the overall effect is positive.[4]

Even in their Washington offices, members commit considerable staff time to dealing with constituents' concerns about issues they are following or pending legislation. In many offices, responding to constituent questions takes up more resources than any other single activity. Members receive thousands of e-mails, letters, and social media communications every month, not to mention the dozens of phone calls that come in every day, and most offices attempt to respond to all of these promptly. In fact, many members' public positions on emerging issues of the day are formulated in response to constituent concerns expressed in writing.

An informal poll conducted by the author of chiefs of staff and legislative directors for members of the House and Senate indicated that well over 50 percent of staff hours in the Washington office are spent either directly addressing constituent concerns or promoting the member of Congress back in the district or state. Members certainly believe that their ability to stay in office hinges on their responsiveness to constituents' concerns. They are probably right.

It is important to stress that **personal office** efforts extend well beyond ombudsman activities. More and more time and effort are placed on communicating not just with the press, but directly to voters through various forms of new media. From the youngest members in their 20s and 30s all the way to many of the older ones in their 70s and 80s, direct forms of communication through the official website, Facebook, Twitter, and other means are deemed vital to making sure constituents are aware of and understand what the House member or senator is doing on their behalf. These new modes of media of course give constituents multiple means to communicate views, requests, and questions. Managing all forms of media, new and old, is a more labor-intensive task than ever for member offices. Well-managed offices are able to convey a feeling of connection to their constituents.[5]

Another factor that explains the ability of members to cultivate good feelings is more organic. Members, with a few notable exceptions, are from the district or state they represent. They may have grown up there, and it may be their ancestral home; often they have relatives and friends in influential positions back home. As a result, they have an instinctive feel for the people and for their views, ambitions, and political leanings. Of course, many members, especially in the Senate, have diverse constituencies, or demographic shifts have changed their constituencies over time. These members must expend more time and effort to foster the trust and identification that are so crucial to effective representation and reelection.[6]

Members who do not originally hail from the district or state of their constituency, such as former New York senator Hillary Clinton, try extra hard to get to know the people they are representing. Clinton moved into the state to run for office in 2000. Not only did she win, but she markedly increased her margin of victory six years later, probably as a result of her persistence in getting to know the state and addressing the needs of her constituents.

## Are Members of Congress Out of Touch?

It would be amusing to members, if it were not so frustrating, that they are frequently accused of being "out of touch" with the people. Nothing could be further from the truth. In fact, scholars and journalists who study Congress are nearly unanimous in criticizing members for being *too* responsive, unwilling to take risks that threaten to put some distance between them and their constituents on controversial issues of the day.[7] Former members, such as Tim Roemer (D-IN), are sharply critical of today's members for their unwillingness to take controversial stands for fear of stirring up opposition back home. Roemer suggests that "members need to recognize that there are issues worth losing your seat for."[8]

Most members spend more time at home interacting with constituents than in Washington. Even members from as far away as California, or even Hawaii and Alaska, hop on a plane almost every week to get back for meetings, events, and perhaps a little time with their families—and these "weekends" are sometimes longer than the workweeks, lasting from Thursday afternoon until midday the following Tuesday. In 2009, as Congress attempted to process President Barack Obama's ambitious agenda, members spent a bit more time in Washington most weeks—often almost four full days. The 112th Congress saw Republicans in the House forcing members to spend longer weeks in Washington—but giving them more full weeks off in the bargain. In addition to weekends, members jealously guard the more extended recesses from legislative business—over most federal holidays Congress is out of session for at least a week—in order to go to town meetings, hold local office hours, give speeches at graduations, and spend time with their families.

Many congressmen, including 2012 vice presidential candidate Paul Ryan of Wisconsin, do not even rent an apartment in Washington. Former Representative Joe Walsh (R-IL) expressed a prevailing sentiment: "I sleep in my office for a number of reasons: one practical and one philosophical," he said. "I do not want to live in Washington, DC. I live at home. I believe [members] should be of their home district. They need to be home all the time, because if they're not, they forget what their district is all about. Philosophically, this is a statement that says I live in McHenry, IL. . . . I came [to DC] to do some work."[9]

It is a simple fact that many senators and representatives regard it as their responsibility to reflect the preferences of their constituents, not to vote based on their own independent views on the issues of the day. Another way to put that: most members are of the philosophy that they are in office to represent their constituents' views in Washington, not to represent Washington viewpoints back to their hometowns. They go to great lengths to gauge what is of salience to the people back home and keep tabs on voters' thinking through polling, social media, frequent meetings, and contacts with key community leaders. At the very least, members know that they must be able to provide a satisfactory explanation for any position they take that does not correspond neatly with the views of a majority of their constituents or those of a key group within the district or state.

The result of all these efforts is a happy one for most. In the House, most members have established so much credibility back in the district that they enjoy comfortable reelection margins. Typically, 15 percent or fewer of House races are decided by less than ten percentage points. And effective representation may pay another dividend: some members can weather embarrassing scandals—ethics violations, sexual peccadilloes—on election day and serve another term. Box 2.2 describes two interesting cases of members surviving despite misdeeds.

## Interest Groups and the Representative Role

Another common complaint about politicians in Washington is that they are in the pocket of the special interests that employ high-paid lawyer-lobbyists. Instead of looking out for the little guy, members of Congress are suspected of siding with interest groups, particularly those who "pay to play"—that is, those who contribute to their reelection campaigns. In effect, the complaint is that members, in directing

BOX 2.2

## Scandals Don't Necessarily Mean the End of a Career

Representative Charlie Rangel (D-NY) was first elected to Congress in 1970. Rangel rose through the ranks to eventually chair the House Ways and Means Committee, one of the most powerful posts in all of Congress, from 2007 to 2010. His career took a turn for the worse when he was accused of soliciting donations for a favored charity from corporations with interests before his committee, illegally holding four rent-stabilized apartments in Harlem, and failing to report income earned from renting out his private villa in the Dominican Republic. He was fined $23,000 for using one of the apartments as a campaign office and was found guilty of 11 ethics violations. He was stripped of his chairmanship in the process. Still, in the aftermath of the scandal he won the Democratic primary in the 15th District of New York, 51 percent to 23 percent, and the general election with more than 80 percent of the vote. His primary election in 2012—against the son of the long-serving member he defeated 42 years before to gain the seat—was close, but Rangel prevailed again, going on to win the seat in November that year.

Senator David Vitter (R-LA) ascended the political stepladder in typical fashion, winning a seat in the Louisiana State House and the US House of Representatives before being elected senator in 2004. As a conservative Republican with traditional stances on social issues, it was quite a scandal in 2007 when his phone number appeared in the records of a Washington, DC, prostitution ring run by the so-called DC Madam. *Hustler* was the first publication to break the story, which prompted the senator to apologize for "serious sins."* But he did not resign, and in fact decided to run for reelection. Despite a spirited challenge from the Democrats who saw an opening to pick up a seat, Vitter won reelection in 2010 by a convincing margin of 57 percent to 38 percent.

*"Senate Fields Are Set in West Virginia and Louisiana," *New York Times*, August 29, 2010, www.nytimes.com/2010/08/30/us/politics/30primary.html.

the work of the federal government, are beholden to those with access and power and consider their needs ahead of the interests of the general public.

In fact, the situation is much more complicated than that. Interest groups *are* influential, but not always in the way people think.[10] This will be looked at in depth in Chapter 13. For our purposes here, it is important to stress that interest groups' leaders and lobbyists recognize that the surest way to get members' attention is to show the *district and state effects* of the bills and policies under consideration, especially if jobs for constituents are at stake. In other words, members are especially attuned to groups that are well represented back home.

## Two Roles, One Field of Vision

Everything about a member of Congress's job involves some combination of the two essential roles—representative of the people back home and legislator crafting public policy for the nation. Although we can analytically distinguish between these two functions, in fact nothing a member does involves only one or the other.

Representatives and senators are constantly campaigning, especially those in the House, whose seats are contested every two years. As a result, their schedules are full of events back in their district or state staged for maximum political benefit. A Democrat might schedule a speech at the local union hall to energize labor support, encouraging active members to go door-to-door in his next campaign. A Republican might do the same thing at an exurban megachurch to motivate her base. Members advertise open town-hall meetings or try to attract local media to speeches—all with the aim of attracting positive publicity and ultimately active support and votes in the next election.

But none of these campaign activities occurs in a vacuum. The union gathering will be attended by people who want to ask the member what he is doing about making health care more portable. The most politically attuned church members will wonder whether their representative is using her membership on the Ways and Means Committee to alleviate the marriage penalty in the tax code. Speeches and town halls also have to include question time—a golden opportunity for community activists to get face time and question the member on the Middle East, or housing subsidies, or his or her latest vote on a controversial bill affecting small business. Even though members are primarily trying to promote their reelection prospects by appearing at public events, they always know that they have to be able to address the legislative side of their work. They cannot neatly detach one role from the other.

### *"Right-Eye Dominance"*

One consequence of serving two very different roles in one job is that at times, the two roles may come into conflict. This is an occupational hazard of being a member of Congress. Much of the time—perhaps most of the time—a member's sense of what is good public policy in the national interest is congruent with the views of his or her constituents. After all, members are elected at least in part based on their views on the major issues of the day, and the people tend to send the candidate to Washington who better reflects their positions. In addition, on matters of little concern to their constituents, representatives can exercise their judgment with little or no fear of retribution on election day.

Inevitably, however, conflicts emerge. How do members resolve strong differences of opinion on the merits of policy between themselves and key groups in their constituencies? How do members resolve conflicts between their own oft-stated principles or ideological predispositions and legislation that would adversely affect their state or district?

The best way to get at members' thinking is to understand how they see the world. Members understand, probably instinctively in most cases, that although they have two seemingly distinct roles, these roles are usually impossible to disentangle. As noted, nearly everything in their job involves *both* policy and political considerations.

To develop a useful metaphor, members may have one field of vision, but that field includes the perspective of their right eye, which sees the issues of the day in terms of the impact on constituents (the **representative role**), and the left eye, which sees issues in terms of the public policy merits (the **legislative role**). Most of the time, there is no conflict in the field of vision. But when there is, the member's dominant eye takes over. Most members are "**right-eye dominant**" most of the time, and some emphasize the representative role all of the time. Their careers depend on their ability to see district or state needs and preferences clearly. Box 2.3 describes some high-profile instances of members who lost their focus.

People are often critical of representatives and senators for their "right-eye dominance"—that is, for their focus on their representative role. But many members, maybe most of them, are strongly inclined to view their responsibilities in terms of being a delegate rather than a trustee in the traditional formulation. This difference has been debated in political theory since representative democracy was invented: should representatives in a republic exercise their own judgment (the trustee model), or is their responsibility to reflect the views of their constituents as best they can discern those views (the delegate model)?[11]

It is not the intention here to resolve the delegate-versus-trustee debate, but rather to explain the reality of representation in Congress. Although there are exceptions that illustrate the rule, the fact is that members tend to put their constituents first. The first two of the following examples are typical. The next two examples show members who charted their own, potentially perilous, course.

## Senator Kennedy, the Environmentalist

The late Edward Kennedy's (D-MA) tenure in the Senate was almost exactly coterminous with the environmental movement in this country, and that was not

# BOX 2.3

## Danger Lurks for the Inattentive Member

The fact that most members are easily reelected—most members win reelection by a wide margin—often leads to the following prescription from critics: because you have such a safe seat, perhaps you can render independent judgment on issues and, even more important, spend more time addressing the big and controversial issues of the day, such as promoting energy independence or addressing spiraling medical costs, instead of focusing on the narrow needs of your district or state.

But this advice misses the basic point: members are safe *because* they address the concerns of their constituents and interests important to their districts or states. Their careers are dependent on a district- or state-centered view of things. In fact, in each election cycle there are always a few members who lose touch with their constituencies and get punished at the polls. They become poster children for the remaining members, reminding them of first priorities.

In 2004 it was Democratic senator **Tom Daschle** of South Dakota, whose ascension to the top Senate leadership position in his party and his presidential ambitions led him in a direction counter to the views of too many constituents in his conservative state. He became the first Senate leader (he was minority leader at the time) to lose his seat in a half century. In 1994 the same thing happened to the Speaker of the House, Tom Foley of eastern Washington State, whose prominent national position with the Democratic Party was perceived as too liberal for his rural, conservative-leaning district.

In 2010 **Ike Skelton** (D-MO), chair of the Armed Services Committee, fell by the wayside after a 34-year congressional career. He had never won with less than 62 percent in his rural district, but was held to 45 percent by his Republican challenger, Vicky Hartzler. She won by linking Skelton to liberal congressional Democrats, citing statistics showing he supported his leadership 95 percent of the time. Skelton's rejoinder that he was endorsed by the National Rifle Association and other conservative groups was not enough.*

**Richard Lugar**, Republican senator from Indiana since 1976, was beaten in his party's primary in 2012 despite—or maybe in part because of—holding the lead Republican position on the Foreign Relations Committee. His focus on foreign affairs, his not-quite-conservative-enough voting record, and news that he had used a house he had sold in 1977 as his residence in the state showed he was "out of touch," according to his challenger, Richard Mourdock, Indiana's state treasurer.

Still, most members feel they can stray every so often, exercising their own judgment, and vote against the apparent views of the majority of their district or state, or even a key faction or interest group in that constituency. But in *every case,* they also recognize that they had better have a good explanation. Perhaps the most crucial part of crafting a position on an issue is explaining why you have taken that view. Voters want to know the reasoning—even if they disagree, voters are more likely to give their representative a pass on a controversial issue if they understand why he or she took that position, which entails making clear that they listened to and were open to all viewpoints when formulating the position.

*Karen Ball, "In Missouri, an Old Bull Goes Down," *Time,* November 3, 2010, www.time.com/time/politics/article/0,8599,2029219,00.html.

entirely a coincidence. Kennedy was first elected in 1962 when he won the seat once held by his then-president brother. At about this time, Rachel Carson (whose trailblazing book *Silent Spring* was published in 1962) and others were raising public awareness of the damage being done to the environment by various pollutants. As Kennedy became more influential in the Senate, he was an important congressional ally for the movement. In recent years, the major national, nonpartisan arm of the environmental movement, the League of Conservation Voters, rated Kennedy's voting record as high as 100 percent.

But Kennedy adamantly opposed an $800 million renewable-energy project proposed for the federal waters off of Nantucket Sound. The project, called Cape Wind, would have created the first offshore energy project in the United States, and the largest of its kind in the world. If completed, it would have provided a substantial amount of the power needed for Cape Cod and the nearby islands.[12] Cape Wind was enthusiastically embraced by major left-leaning interest groups, including the Sierra Club, the Union of Concerned Scientists, and US Public Interest Research Group.

In a May 2006 press release, Kennedy called for a "federal policy to be put in place before a project of this magnitude is given approval." He also expressed concern that the project might "[wreak] havoc" on "Massachusetts' fishing and tourism industries, the Coast Guard, navigation and national security."[13] Ultimately, the senator opposed comprehensive energy legislation on the Senate floor owing to special waivers he claimed were included for Cape Wind.

### Senator Bond Says No to Science

Former senator Christopher "Kit" Bond (R-MO) was always determined to fund water projects that provided jobs for the people of Missouri. In 2004 Bond advocated spending $1.7 billion to improve the Mississippi waterway connecting farmers in the Midwest with New Orleans and the open sea. Navigating this route requires passing through a series of locks; Bond pushed for longer locks to reduce congestion (and thus lower shipping rates). Bond's office estimated that the project would generate 48 million work-hours for carpenters.[14]

The problem, as good government advocates saw it, was that numerous studies going back to the early 1990s showed that the improvements were not even close to worth what they would cost. Furthermore, much less expensive innovations would suffice to reduce congestion.

The Army Corps of Engineers, which commissioned the original study and would be responsible for construction, sponsored other studies that proved more favorable to the idea. Unfortunately, these studies were criticized by the National Academy of Sciences for poor methodology. The original conclusion held: the lock expansion would cost far more than it would be worth, and it would make more sense to do much cheaper innovations, or even to do nothing at all. The senator did not budge; jobs, to be paid for by the nation's taxpayers, were at stake.[15]

* * *

We do not mean to pick on these two senators, both of whom had distinguished records and a long history of working productively on issues of national importance with members of the opposing party. Kennedy and Bond were in many ways model members of Congress. Rather, we mean to stress what is normal, expected, and even often necessary in most instances. Members must stick up for the people they represent, or they will not stay in Washington to make the contributions their experience makes possible in health care, defense, foreign policy, and other matters. There is a common saying in Washington that "you can't save the world if you don't save your seat." Political scientist David Mayhew put it this way in his seminal work *Congress: The Electoral Connection*: whatever a member's goals are in terms of solving the pressing problems of society, his immediate goal must always be to win reelection.[16]

Members by the dozen advocate tax reform and simplification, yet aggressively push for add-ons to tax legislation to provide tax breaks for groups or particular industries in their districts. Self-professed free-traders often turn around and support protections for industries that provide employment in their states. Scores of members from both parties voted for stringent spending limits in the Balanced Budget Act of 1997 and then turned around in 1998 to vote for a budget-busting transportation bill in order to have roads and bridges built or repaired in their districts or states.

Earmarking funds for spending on projects in a member's district or state presents a special problem. Representative Michelle Bachman (R-MN), like some other members, had long sworn off earmarks—even before the 2011 congressional prohibition of the practice. Yet in 2009, she submitted five earmark requests to the relevant committees for $40 million for projects in or near her district. Later, after the ban was in place, she said, "I don't believe that building roads and bridges and interchanges should be considered an earmark"[17]—although it was exactly these sorts of projects that were the source of much of the criticism of earmarking in the first place.

The bottom line: good government and ideological consistency are important, but not necessarily top priorities. One could charge members with hypocrisy—and it would be hard to quarrel with that interpretation—but there are other ways to look at this kind of behavior.

First of all, members do a faithful job of reflecting the views and preferences of their constituents. Most Americans want a simpler tax code, but they also want businesses in their hometowns to thrive in a competitive global environment—a goal that is enhanced by targeted tax breaks. Similarly, people want the cheaper goods and services that free trade brings, but they also want people in their community to keep their jobs; a stiff tariff can achieve the latter goal. And everyone thinks that the government should balance the books, but few seem able to identify major programs that should be cut to make this possible; certainly, few members will vote for cuts in transportation funding when their constituents complain about traffic and decaying bridges. And everyone knows that raising taxes is normally a political nonstarter. The fact is that the public has conflicting and contradictory desires that put cross-pressures on members of Congress.

Furthermore, doing what needs to be done to simplify the tax code, make Medicare solvent, or balance the budget is incredibly difficult. The political reality is that achieving these goals requires an extraordinary ability to cooperate and work with people with very different backgrounds and views. There is no place in life where it is easy to work with people whose priorities you do not share and whose outlook is opposed to your own. Congress is no different. There is a wide range of viewpoints and backgrounds among the membership. So if members cannot save the world in the near term, at least they can serve their people and save their seats.

Having said all of that, there are times when members go against the strongly held views of their constituents. Some members do it on a regular basis. Sometimes it costs them their seats, and sometimes they survive in spite of it.

*Congressman Rahall, Despite Several Controversial Votes,*
*Keeps on Winning*

Democrat Nick Rahall of West Virginia represents a 94 percent white, small town, and rural district—exactly the kind of district that has been trending Republican in recent years. Rahall is in his 19th term in Congress, having won reelection in 2012 with 54 percent of the vote in a district that went decisively for Republican presidential candidate Mitt Romney, this despite votes for the Troubled Asset Relief Program (TARP) and the 2010 health care overhaul that were not popular in his district. Not only that, Rahall voted to end mountaintop removal for coal, an extremely controversial position in coal-dependent West Virginia.

Rahall has managed to compensate for his more controversial positions by delivering for his district in other ways. In particular, he is the lead House Democrat on the Transportation and Infrastructure Committee, a perch from which he can bring good construction jobs to his district. Still, other members in similarly powerful positions on Capitol Hill have been defeated in recent years, including Rahall's predecessor as lead Democrat on the Transportation Committee, Congressman

Jim Oberstar of Minnesota. Oberstar's district, like Rahall's, was largely white and rural. Rahall will likely continue to be targeted by Republicans hoping to capitalize on the disconnect between his relatively liberal positions on high-profile issues and the views of many voters in the district.

## The Firebrand Survives, Time and Again

Iowa senator Tom Harkin, an uncompromising advocate for labor, civil rights, environmentalism, feminism, and similar causes, has been a leader of the liberal wing of the Democratic Party in Congress since the 1970s. Harkin has been in the Senate since 1984, representing a decidedly middle-of-the-road state—in fact, a state that seesaws between supporting Democratic and Republican presidential candidates. During this period, Iowa has almost always had a Republican-controlled House delegation, and Harkin's Senate colleague from the state is the moderately conservative Republican Charles Grassley.

Harkin has not taken the path of least resistance. And he has had to fight hard to keep his seat. Prominent House members have challenged him nearly every time, attracting national support and plenty of funds. Harkin has managed—though just barely one time—to beat every one of them. By comparison, Grassley, whose views seem to fit more neatly with the Iowa electorate, has not received a serious challenge for his seat in decades.

Harkin (like Rahall) does not ignore his constituents. He knows that, to have a chance at reelection, members have to address the needs of their constituents through targeted federal spending, good ombudsman work, and overall responsiveness. But neither does he trim his sails much on major national issues in order to ensure an easy path to reelection. He wins in spite of his positioning on some issues, not because of it.

This is a risky strategy, as Senator Rick Santorum (R-PA) learned the hard way in 2006. Much like Harkin, Santorum was often out of step with his state on major national issues. Far more conservative than the broader Pennsylvania electorate, which has trended Democratic in recent presidential elections, Santorum managed to win squeakers through hard work and spirited campaigning to secure two terms in the Senate, but in a year that was particularly unpropitious for Republicans, he could not withstand the tide, losing by a lopsided 18-point margin. Today another conservative, Pat Toomey, holds one of the state's Senate seats. He, like Santorum, is not inclined to trim his sails on fiscal and other issues and will face a challenge navigating his 2016 reelection run.

The lesson is clear: a "right-eye-dominant" perspective is the easy way to go for members of Congress, and most take that approach. The other strategy takes a lot more skill and carries greater risks. Members have to be able to explain to the satisfaction of their constituency any controversial positions they take. Even then, incongruent views may be costly.

## CONCLUSION: THE PRIMACY OF THE REPRESENTATIVE ROLE

To understand Congress as it carries out its duties as the board of directors of the federal government, it cannot be stressed too much how important it is to appreciate the motivations of the members. Their elected position makes them accountable to the people in their districts or states. Nearly every decision point that members face in the legislative process starts with a calculation of whether and how a given policy affects the people back home.

Probably the simplest useful way to think of Congress is to view it as an institution composed of 535 people scrapping furiously for the interests of the people they represent. Much of this battling is done in full view of the public on C-SPAN, on Twitter, and through various news outlets during floor speeches, press conferences, and committee hearings. Furthermore, members fight hard to enhance their party's chances of retaining or regaining the majority in their chamber, because majority status enhances members' ability to pursue the interests of their constituents and their policy or ideological goals. Majority status has its privileges: only the majority members chair committees and subcommittees, and the majority leadership controls the legislative schedule on the floor of the two chambers.

Often members' favored tactic to boost their party's electoral prospects is to tear down the other party, making theirs look better by comparison. The idea is that voters are cynical enough to find the argument that the other party is dastardly more persuasive than the contention that the member's own party will solve the major problems of the day. Although the evidence is far from conclusive,[18] a lot of politicians believe negative campaigning is more effective.

This reality does not make a pretty picture. No wonder the public dislikes Congress: 535 aggressive, district- and state-focused people fighting over public policy, with an overlay of partisan bickering, is not a good starting point for developing good public relations. In fact, Congress is *overly* engaged in public relations—all the members and committees have press people who promote individual members and their respective party's agenda, but almost never do they promote the institution.[19] In reality, self-promotion in Congress is often linked to the denigration of the institution, as in "Congressman Doe is fighting for the people against the evil forces in the Capitol that are in cahoots with corrupt lobbyists and special interests."

Compare that to the White House, which strictly controls the flow of information and has a sophisticated press relations shop dedicated to making the president look good. And don't forget the **Supreme Court**, which allows very little press access and shrouds its decision-making process in almost total secrecy, which gives it a certain mystique that cannot be matched.

The irony of the public's negative view of Congress is that *we, the people, want Congress to do many of the very things that make it look bad.* We want our members to fight for our interests. During reelection campaigns, members stress what they bring home to the district or the state because they know that these benefits and services are often exactly what makes them look good to us. Former senator Daniel Inouye (D-HI) became a legend in his state because of his ability to tend to local interests so effectively, as has Thad Cochran (R-MS) in his; Republican representative Frank Lucas has made looking out for the interests of Oklahoma his calling card as chair of the Agriculture Committee; Maryland congressman Steny Hoyer is credited for his tireless work on behalf of the federal workers and military families who populate his district; and the list goes on. Some voters may have high-minded expectations that their representatives should address major issues such as war, global warming, and the solvency of Medicare. But members know that they risk getting punished at the polls if they forget the particular needs of their district or state.

Strip away all the accoutrements of Washington and the intricacies of the legislative process, and we can see that this is the fundamental nature of Congress: a rough-and-tumble partisan arena, composed of 535 representatives drawn from a tremendously diverse country. The framers gave two jobs to the Congress they created: lawmaking and representing. In this book, we focus on the lawmaking side—Congress as the board of directors of the federal government. But the student of Congress must understand the ramifications of the representative role that looms so large for every member. *Members' representative responsibilities profoundly affect the institution's performance in directing the work of government. The political perspective of the representative role bleeds—and bleeds profusely—into the realm of policy making, whether in authorizing, appropriations, or oversight.*

---

## Questions for Discussion

1. Does Congress deserve its generally bad reputation? Or, given its structure, does it perform about as well as can be expected?

2. Members of Congress take their representative role very seriously and go back to their districts or states as often as possible to be in closer touch with voters. Would it be wise to require members to spend more time in Washington so that they could focus more on their legislative role?

3. A lot of people think that limiting members to a fixed number of terms in office, the so-called term-limits movement, would help to get members

to focus more on the legislative role, as they couldn't plan to make a lifetime career out of Congress. Are term limits a good idea? What are the pros and cons?

---

## Suggestions for Further Reading

Fiorina, Morris. *Congress: The Keystone of the Washington Establishment.* New Haven, CT: Yale University Press, 1989.

Hibbing, John R., and Elizabeth Theiss-Morse. *Stealth Democracy: Americans' Beliefs About How Government Should Work.* Cambridge: Cambridge University Press, 2002.

Madison, James. *The Federalist Papers.* No. 10.

Price, David E. *The Congressional Experience.* Boulder, CO: Westview Press, 2004.

## NOTES

1. The 111th Congress considered legislation that would add two seats to the House: one for the District of Columbia and one for Utah. Some critics of this proposal maintained that the Constitution permits only states, not the District of Columbia, to have voting representation in the House.

2. One of the best studies of public opinion and Congress is John R. Hibbing and Elizabeth Theiss-Morse, *Congress as Public Enemy* (Cambridge: Cambridge University Press, 1996).

3. The basic office structure depicted in the diagram is used, with some alterations, by most House members. Senators typically use a similar structure, but they will have more staff overall—anywhere from about 35–80 total staff depending on the state. (Senators representing states with larger populations get a larger operating budget than those representing sparsely populated states.) Senators employ more **legislative assistants (LAs)** and caseworkers, and they will have more people handling relations with the media. House members are restricted to 18 full-time staff and 4 part-time staff. The Senate does not have similar restrictions.

The district office is largely concerned with addressing specific problems constituents have with federal programs and agencies. Caseworkers focus on that sort of work under the direction of a district director or the **chief of staff** if he or she is in the district. Everyone—in the district and in Washington—is answerable to the chief of staff and ultimately the member of Congress.

In the Washington office, the **legislative director (LD)** oversees the office's legislative work. The LAs and the LD do a number of things. Each has a portfolio of issues to follow. They track any legislation in their portfolio that the member is interested in—remember members of Congress have to vote on every matter that comes before the body. LAs and the LD support the member in his or her committee assignments. They write speeches and talking points for the House or Senate floor and appearances back home. They draft or perfect existing letters that respond to constituent inquiries. Senate offices will always have **legislative correspondents (LCs)** to write first drafts. Some House offices also do. The central focus of the Washington office almost always is on legislation that has an effect on the district or state the member represents.

The press secretary (sometimes called the communications director) is in charge of handling media inquiries and polishing speeches and talking points. Most press secretaries are very aggressive in trying to place stories in the press back home and securing coverage by the local television news stations, all in the interest of burnishing the reputation of the member back home.

The executive assistant or scheduler has to deal with the hundreds and hundreds of requests that come into every office for face time with the member. Members are in constant demand to give speeches and meet with groups from back home or even individual constituents. A member's schedule will be loaded with short, usually 15- or 30-minute, meetings.

4. See George Serra, "What's in It for Me?," *American Politics Research* 22, no. 4 (1994): 403–420; and Albert Cover and George Serra, "The Electoral Impact of Casework," *Electoral Studies* 14, no. 2 (June 1995): 171–177.

5. See Brian Fogarty, "The Nature of Local News Media Issue Coverage of U.S. House Members" *Social Science Journal* 48, no. 4 (2011): 651–658; and Timothy E. Cook, *Governing with the News* (Chicago: University of Chicago Press, 2005).

6. See Richard Fenno, *Home Style: House Members in Their Districts* (Boston: Little, Brown, 1978); and William T. Bianco, *Trust: Representatives and Constituents* (Ann Arbor: University of Michigan Press, 1994).

7. Even a former congressman, Lee Hamilton (D-IN), suggests that members are too responsive; see his book *How Congress Works* (Bloomington: Indiana University Press, 2004), 54–55.

8. Tim Roemer, interview with the author, May 11, 2007.

9. http://news.medill.northwestern.edu/chicago/news.aspx?id:178076.

10. For important work on the impact of interest groups on congressional policy making, see F. R. Baumgartner et al., *Lobbying and Policy Change: Who Wins, Who Loses, and Why* (Chicago: University of Chicago Press, 2009); and Matt Grossman, *The Not-So-Special Interests* (Stanford, CA: Stanford University Press, 2012).

11. See *The Portable Edmund Burke* (New York: Penguin, 1999).

12. Elizabeth Mehren, "Cape Cod Wind Farm Project May Be Headed for Pasture," *Los Angeles Times,* May 5, 2006; Rick Klein, "Kennedy Faces Fight on Cape Wind," *Boston Globe,* April 27, 2006.

13. Office of Senator Edward Kennedy, "Floor Statement on the Cape Wind Project" (press release), May 9, 2006.

14. Sebastian Mallaby, "Kit's Caboodle," *Washington Post,* June 7, 2004, A23.

15. Michael Grunwald, "Army Corps Delays Study over Flawed Forecasts," *Washington Post,* October 5, 2000, A33.

16. David Mayhew, *Congress: The Electoral Connection* (New Haven, CT: Yale University Press, 1974).

17. Quoted in Steve Benen, "Political Animal," *Washington Monthly*, November 16, 2010, www.washingtonmonthly.com/archives/individual/2010_11/026666.php.

18. See, for example, Richard R. Lau, Lee Sigelman, and Ivy Brown Rovner, "The Effects of Negative Political Campaigns: A Mega-analytic Perspective," *Journal of Politics* 69, no. 4 (2007): 1176–1209.

19. In *Congress: Keystone of the Washington Establishment* (New Haven, CT: Yale University Press, 1989), Morris Fiorina argues that members appeal to their constituents for votes by criticizing Washington in general, and in particular the executive branch bureaucracy they in fact created and perpetuate.

# 3

# The House and Senate, Party Leadership and Committees

The Constitution set up a bicameral legislature to carry out the critical function of directing the work of the government. The decision to go with this arrangement was a tremendously important one; it affects virtually every aspect of the institution. In this chapter, we look in detail at the two chambers.

The first part of the chapter gives an overview of the constitutional debate and the key differences between the House and Senate. We look at what led to the bicameral legislature and how the framers defended the choice. The two chambers were established to serve different purposes—purposes that have in many ways remained constant over more than two centuries. Most important, the members of the chambers have different perspectives and operate under very different sets of rules.

After that we shift gears to look at how the two chambers organize themselves for business in the 21st century. The House and Senate have very similar structures, with majority party leadership taking responsibility for running each chamber, including determining the legislative agenda, and committees set up to do the serious work on legislation and oversight of the executive branch agencies. The chapter covers what majority and minority party leadership do, how top leaders are selected, how committees' jurisdictions are determined, and how members get on committees.

The two organizational units, party leadership and committees, are meant to help the chambers reconcile the inevitable conflicts and tensions that arise between the members' two jobs—representing their constituents and making policy for the nation. Ultimately, we see that the two chambers' activities are by and large not coordinated, which puts obstacles in the way of the efficient processing of legislation. But this inefficiency is not inconsistent with the intentions of the framers of the Constitution.

## THE GREAT COMPROMISE AND THE ORIGINS OF A BICAMERAL LEGISLATURE

The composition of the legislative body was a matter of great contention at the Constitutional Convention. Virginians put forward a plan that, among other things, proposed a single-chamber national legislature with representation based on population. Less populated states opposed the plan. Led by the New Jersey delegation, they proposed establishing a legislature that would be similar to the one set up in the Articles of Confederation, with each state receiving equal representation regardless of population.

Ultimately, Connecticut's Roger Sherman put forward what came to be called "the **Great Compromise**." It proposed a bicameral arrangement with one chamber's representation based on population and the other having equal representation for every state. It was this plan that was adopted.

Such a plan was defended by some at the time on the grounds that it would be much more difficult for unwise legislation to pass two such differently constituted chambers. With their very different perspectives, the members of the two chambers would have difficulty coming together on particular legislative solutions. The idea was that bad bills would be filtered out in the process.

More broadly speaking, the framers believed, based on their observations of what for most was their ancestral homeland, England,[1] that Congress as the branch with the electoral link to the people would be most prone to amass power and infringe on the liberties of the citizenry. The solution was described in the *Federalist Papers*:

> In republican government, the legislative authority necessarily predominates. The remedy for this inconveniency is to divide the legislature into different branches; and to render them, by different modes of election and different principles of action, as little concerned with each other as the nature of their common functions and their common dependence will admit.[2]

An inefficient legislative body was thought to be a virtue, because it would provide more time for careful consideration and identification of the public interest. It was feared that streamlined processes in a unicameral legislature would be more likely to result in laws that harmed the people.

The House and Senate were, at the end of the day, created for different purposes. The House was meant as the majority-rule institution—designed to reflect the passions of the people in the most fundamental sense of a democracy. The Senate was created to enshrine the idea of equality. The chamber gives exactly equal representation to each state. The Senate was not necessarily meant to reflect the views of the majority; instead, it would be possible for a minority to protect its interests in that chamber.

## Distinct Qualifications and Responsibilities

The two chambers were set up to give Congress a wider range of representative characteristics than would have been possible had there been only one chamber. Not only were the members of the chambers to be answerable to different constituencies, but they were given different time perspectives as well. The six-year term was thought to give senators the ability to take the long view. House members, it was thought, would be more likely to consider the immediate impact of legislation given the fact that they had to vie for reelection every two years. (In fact, a lot of people at the Constitutional Convention thought a two-year term was too long; fearing that members would not be tied closely enough to their constituents, they advocated annual reelection for representatives.)

In addition, as noted earlier, senators were not originally to be selected directly by the people. State legislatures selected them, making them more removed from the public than House members. While the Constitutional Convention recognized that it was necessary to make Congress directly accountable to the people, the prevailing view was that it would be better not to have the public, which might be prone to rash and ill-considered collective judgments, directly elect the entire Congress. A directly elected House was deemed sufficient to achieve an accountable lawmaking body.

The Senate was also given a higher age requirement: senators must be 30 years old, while House members may be as young as 25. Presumably with age comes wisdom. Again, the Senate was expected to be less impulsive and more statesmanlike in its decision making in order to check a more reactive House.

To reinforce this point, the Senate was made "more equal"—it was given some weighty responsibilities that the House does not have. For a treaty to become the law of the land, the Constitution stipulates that it must gain the Senate's approval. (Two-thirds of the Senate is required to ratify a treaty.) The House was given no such role, and as a result the Senate became a much bigger player in the realm of foreign affairs. The Senate's approval is also needed for the president's high-ranking executive branch appointments—now numbering about 800.[3] Again, the House has no role in this process. And nominations to the federal judiciary, all the way up to the Supreme Court, also require only Senate approval.

On the flip side, the House was given the responsibility to originate revenue bills. The seeming advantage, however, is really not all that significant: the Senate must also pass tax bills for them to become law, and senators are not constrained by the Constitution from amending House-passed revenue measures in any way they see fit.

There is another important way in which the Constitution insulates the Senate from immediate political pressures. The electoral cycle puts all House seats up for grabs every two years. The chamber as a whole is expected to be attuned and responsive to the political climate in the nation. In the Senate, on the other hand, only one-third of the seats are contested every two years. At any given time, then, most senators' jobs are not at stake in the next election cycle. The thinking was that the so-called upper body would be more likely to take the long view on legislation.

## The Key Difference Between the House and Senate? It's a Matter of Perspective

Many House members represent constituencies that are homogeneous in terms of some combination of partisanship, ideology, economic status, race, or other factors. Most senators, representing entire states, have more diverse constituencies in all or most of these respects. (Only seven states are so sparsely populated that they have only one House member.) When we remember that members of Congress are "right-eye dominant"—they look at the political world first in terms of their constituents' interests—we see that the relative homogeneity or heterogeneity of the constituencies leads to very different tendencies and approaches in the two chambers.

Many House members come to Washington with a strongly partisan or ideological take on their legislative work and the issues of the day because their districts are either strongly Democratic or Republican. (According to most analysts, about 80 percent of House districts are solidly aligned with one party or the other.)[4] A good number focus on a particular sector of the economy, as well, if the livelihood of their constituents is heavily dependent on it. On the other hand, most senators have to balance the needs of a wider range of economic interests and a more diverse set of views, backgrounds, and perspectives on the part of the people of their state.

For example, senators from North Carolina have to consider the views of different kinds of farmers (the state is one of the leaders in both tobacco and pork production), balance the needs of the banking industry in Charlotte with the high-tech and pharmaceutical industries in the Research Triangle as well as the furniture industry in the Greensboro area, advocate for a wide range of tourism and recreational interests from the mountains to the coast, and listen to the constituent needs of a diverse population that includes American Indians, a large African American population, and a growing number of Hispanics, as well as the majority who are white. The 13 House members from the state do not individually have to take into account anywhere near as many interests and viewpoints.

Essentially, the chambers have different styles and political contexts because of their different constituencies. As a rule, the House is a more partisan body that tends to focus on parochial, narrow concerns. The Senate, on the other hand, tends to be less bitterly partisan and is somewhat more apt to approach issues with a big-picture perspective. One can overstate these differences—for example, it is not uncommon for the Senate to have partisan struggles, and senators certainly look out for the particular economic interests of their states. But the two chambers do have distinct tendencies.

## The Prestige Gap

In part because of the Senate's enhanced legislative responsibilities in the Constitution, it is generally considered more prestigious than the House. There are additional reasons for the Senate's exalted position.

Senators tend to be more widely known, if only because of the fact that a senator is one of 100 and a House member is one of 435. Senators also are more likely to receive in-depth coverage in the media, both nationally and back at home. They often comment on major international issues (remember, they are the ones who handle treaties) and are frequently mentioned as presidential or vice presidential prospects. House members rarely make credible runs for the White House. In the past 50 years, 16 senators have appeared on major party presidential tickets, while only 3 sitting House members have been selected.

Back home, senators benefit from being one of only two in their chamber, while House members sometimes get lost in the shuffle among many other representatives. In addition, senators represent the whole state, while all but seven House members do not. Senate rules also give senators, as individuals, much greater power and leverage in the legislative process than House members have.

All of these factors contribute to the tendency of the Senate to attract interest from prospective candidates who have already accomplished a great deal politically or in the private sector. Governors or former governors often run for the Senate, but much less often the House. Famous athletes, such as Bill Bradley, a starter on two NBA championship teams, have made a run for the Senate as their first foray into electoral politics. John Glenn, the famous astronaut, also aimed first for the Senate. His initial effort was not successful, but he eventually served with distinction as a senator from Ohio. Al Franken, known for his appearances on *Saturday Night Live*, won a seat in Minnesota. Another actor, Fred Thompson, served Tennessee in the Senate. As one might expect, House members usually regard a run for the Senate as a potential upgrade.

## TODAY'S HOUSE OF REPRESENTATIVES: LEADERSHIP AND COMMITTEES

The House and Senate have parallel organizational units: party leadership and the committees. The party leadership in each chamber is responsible for organizing the chamber's legislative business, although the way that happens is quite different in the two bodies. The committees are specialized units that handle the details of legislation and oversight. This section describes these organizational units and looks at how they are meant to help the institution reconcile the tension between its legislative and representative responsibilities.

### Majority Party Leadership

The presiding officer of the House of Representatives is the *speaker,* or the **Speaker of the House**. The speaker is the only official position in the House listed in the Constitution; the Constitution does say that the House membership has the power to choose other officers. Federal law puts the speaker second in line for the presidency after the vice president.

The speaker is chosen from among the majority party in the House. This is not a constitutional requirement; in fact, the Constitution does not contemplate the existence of organized political parties. In practice, however, the two parties each choose a candidate for speaker, with a roll-call vote of the whole House membership determining the winner. This roll call is normally a formality.

The speaker, in a real sense, runs the House of Representatives. We will see in subsequent chapters how he or she does this, but the essential point is that the speaker determines the agenda of the chamber. In addition, the speaker appoints people to administrative positions to take care of the day-to-day operations of the House.

The speaker needs help in managing the legislative business of the House, so the majority party chooses other top leadership positions. The top leadership positions, employed by both parties when they are in charge, include:

*Speaker of the House.* Oversees the operations of the whole House and signs off on the agenda for floor consideration. The speaker also selects his or her party's members and the chairs for **select committees**, such as the Select Committee on

Intelligence. In addition, the speaker names the chair and all of his or her party's members on the Rules Committee.

*Majority leader.* Assigned by the speaker to develop the majority party's agenda for the floor of the House. The **majority leader** communicates that agenda to the whole House on the floor. Normally, the majority leader is charged with resolving differences among committee chairs on pending legislation that crosses committee jurisdictional boundaries.

*Majority whip.* Assigned by the speaker to canvass the opinions of the membership of the majority party on bills scheduled to come to the floor. As the official vote counter, the **majority whip** apprises the majority leader and the speaker when the party is likely to have the votes to move forward on its agenda.

*Caucus or conference chair.* Responsible for running the meetings of the majority party caucus or conference (including all party members), providing a formalized avenue of input on the legislative agenda of the House. In addition, the **caucus or conference chair** manages the public relations strategy for the majority party, keeping members informed about how the leadership would like for them to describe the issues of the day when speaking to the media and the public.

All of these top leadership positions, as well as some lower-level positions, are determined by a secret ballot vote in the party's *caucus* (Democrats) or *conference* (Republicans). Members running for these positions must secure a majority of 50 percent plus one to win the slot. If no candidate for a position receives the necessary majority, the last-place finisher is eliminated and a new balloting is held. Races for top leadership posts attract a lot of attention and can be rather suspenseful, as depicted in Box 3.1.

All the top leaders hire aides, called **leadership staff**, to help them with their duties. In addition, the leaders select deputies among the rank-and-file members in the party; in particular, the whip assigns trusted majority party colleagues to keep tabs on the thinking of other party members in their states or regions.

The leadership of both parties in the House also run *party committees*, composed of senior and some junior members of the party, to handle various important matters of party business.

These include a *Policy Committee*, which helps party leadership by doing research and polling on major issues of the day. This committee may also propose potential legislative solutions.

The parties also each have a **Steering Committee**. Charged with assigning members to committees and recommending committee chairs. Normally, this

## BOX 3.1

### Counting Votes in Leadership Races

Races for leadership in the parties can be very controversial, and close contests are not unusual. One of the most contentious in recent years was the February 2006 race for majority leader in the Republican-controlled House.

The opening came about due to the resignation of Tom DeLay of Texas, who had been majority leader since 2003. He was charged with money laundering in state campaigns. (He was convicted in 2011.) The minority whip and acting majority leader, Roy Blunt (R-MO), was the heavy favorite. But he had two challengers—John Boehner of Ohio and John Shadegg of Arizona. The first tally went 110 for Blunt, 79 for Boehner, 40 for Shadegg, and 2 write-ins for Jim Ryun of Kansas.

Blunt's 110 was 6 shy of the majority of votes required. Most observers expected Blunt to pick up the needed votes, but in a surprise Boehner prevailed, 122–109. It was seen as a sign that the party ultimately wanted to choose someone not in the leadership structure to signal a break from the scandal-tainted DeLay era.*

Former speaker Nancy Pelosi first won a major leadership position in 2001 when she was elected over Steny Hoyer to be minority whip for the Democrats. The campaign for votes was intense. Before the caucus was held, Pelosi claimed 120 commitments—12 more than the 108 needed for victory that year. Hoyer claimed 110 commitments. Someone had to be wrong. In the end, Pelosi won, 118–95, proving that she could count votes better than Hoyer.†

Because it was a secret ballot vote, no one really knows for sure who indicated support to *both* candidates. But clearly, some people did. Hoyer may have misinterpreted ambiguous comments as indications of support. Perhaps some members made it clear to both candidates that they were open to supporting them, but ultimately got what they wanted—a choice committee assignment, perhaps—from Pelosi. Or maybe Hoyer had exaggerated his support intentionally or unintentionally. It is unlikely we will ever know for sure.

*Jonathan Weisman, "In an Upset, Boehner Is Elected House GOP Leader," *Washington Post,* February 3, 2006, A1.

†Mark Sandalow, "Pelosi Breaks House Glass Ceiling," sfgate.com (*San Francisco Chronicle*), October 11, 2001, www.sfgate.com/cgi-bin/article.cgi?file=/chronicle/archive/2001/10/11/MN47587.DTL.

committee has most or all the committee chairs (or "ranking members" for the minority party) serving, plus a regionally representative sample of other party members. The leadership serves on the committee and gets a weighted vote in Steering Committee decision making.

The two parties have *campaign committees* as well—the Democratic Congressional Campaign Committee (DCCC) and the National Republican Congressional Committee (NRCC). These organizations, also made up of members of the party in the House, recruit candidates for potentially winnable races, coordinate campaign activities, and raise money. Their activities will be covered in much more detail in Chapter 5.

## Minority Party Leadership

The minority party has decidedly less influence in the House of Representatives. It serves essentially as the "loyal opposition," typically opposing the majority's agenda but without the ability to pursue an agenda of its own. The House is run by and for the majority party.

The minority party, like the majority, elects members to leadership positions by secret ballot. The top minority party leadership positions are:

*Minority leader.* Runs the minority party's operations in the House of Representatives and assigns members of his or her party to select committees and the Rules Committee; also names the **ranking members** (would-be chairs) of these committees. The **minority leader** usually takes on the responsibility of making the case to the American people for his or her party and against the majority agenda.

*Minority whip.* Assigned by the minority leader to canvass the opinions of minority party members on pending legislation that is under consideration by the majority. As the chief vote counter for his or her party, the whip tries to keep the party in line in opposition to majority party agenda items.

*Caucus or conference chair.* Given the task of running the meetings of all minority party members. In addition, the caucus or conference chair is in charge of managing the party's public relations strategy with an eye toward criticizing the majority party's legislative agenda and promoting minority party alternatives. This is the avenue for the rank and file to provide input on party strategy. As with the majority, the minority leadership has staff to help them with their duties, and they similarly deputize rank-and-file members for assistance.

## Leadership and the Media

It cannot be stressed enough how much time, energy, and staff hours party leadership, from the speaker and the minority leader on down, put into cultivating all forms of media and employing old and new techniques to reach out to the public, sometimes communicating ideas and approaches, sometimes soliciting comments and suggestions.[5] Building public support for a legislative agenda is a critical part of politics. Box 3.2 describes a technique used by Republican leaders in the past few years.

The public relations side of legislating is sometimes overlooked. Members of Congress are not comfortable voting for legislation that has not been thoroughly vetted. Party leaders know they have to sell what they think is a good policy option for fixing a problem. Bills of importance to leadership must be marketed, in effect, to the public and groups with a stake in the legislation—and to their rank-and-file membership at the same time, who need to understand its impact on key interests of relevance to their district or state.

Furthermore, parties know they have a continuous job reminding the public of the good they have done or, on the other hand, of the damage the other party has done or might do if it gets control of Congress. Not only that, but there is also a constant give-and-take, as one party advances its message on a major issue of the day, with the other party often ready with an immediate response, which, of course, must be responded to in kind, and so on.

## Committees in the House

The House of Representatives is not a continuous body. This means that the House, in effect, goes out of business at the end of a two-year Congress and must be "re-constituted" at the beginning of a new Congress. The chamber adjourns sometime late in the even-numbered election year (often in December after the election) and before the entire elected or reelected membership is sworn in for the new Congress on January 3. After the swearing-in, the House passes a resolution that organizes the chamber and establishes its rules for the upcoming two-year Congress. This document is prepared by the majority party leadership and ordinarily passes over whatever objections the minority may have.

One of the most important things this resolution does is establish the legislative committees, these committees' policy jurisdictions, and the number of members and the ratio of majority to minority members on each. For the most part, the committees, their jurisdictions, and even the ratio of members remain nearly the same from one Congress to the next. But when a new party takes power in the House, the changes are dramatic.

## BOX 3.2
### Eric Cantor Uses New Media

Then Republican majority whip Eric Cantor began exploiting new media in a big way in 2010, allowing the public to weigh in on what federal programs should be cut. The YouCut program on Cantor's website gave people the opportunity to cast a vote each week for federal budget cuts that Republicans would try to force Democrats to bring up for a vote. Once Republicans took over control of the House in 2011, the burden fell on them. Spending cuts endorsed by the public were sponsored by party members and introduced in the House. Citizens then could follow on the YouCut page the progress of the bill through the legislative process.

For Cantor, YouCut was part of a larger plan to connect with citizens. He told *Politico's* Mike Allen: "We will end up getting a better work product if we pay attention to the fact we have got to engage the public."[*] On his website, he promises to provide "a dynamic communications platform that creates a more open, visible and participatory legislative process. Built on Facebook, Citizen CoSponsor will enable you to follow legislation that you're interested in. You will then receive first-hand information and updates on the status of the bill as it moves through the legislative process."[†]

[*]John Rossomando, "Cantor Shows His Social Media, Tech Geek Side at Politico Event," *Red Alert Politics*, April 29, 2010, http://redalertpolitics.com/2012/04/19/cantor-shows-his-social-media-geeky-tech-side-at-politico-event/.

[†]www.majorityleader.gov/Citizens/.

The House currently has 21 committees in the 113th Congress, as listed here; most of them are authorizing committees charged with considering legislation that sets policy for the programs and agencies of the federal government. Some of the most prominent include the Energy and Commerce, Ways and Means, and Armed Services Committees. The House has one committee whose sole responsibility is to write bills to fund the functions of the government—the Appropriations Committee. All the authorizing committees as well as the Appropriations Committee conduct oversight over the executive branch agencies and programs in their jurisdiction. The Committee on Oversight and Government Reform is notable in that it has oversight jurisdiction over the entire government. The Rules Committee does not explicitly have any of the board-of-directors functions, but it is powerful nonetheless because it writes the rules that govern the consideration of much of the important legislation that reaches the House floor.

Here is a list of the committees in the House of Representatives (the authorizing committees appear in italics):

- *Agriculture*
- Appropriations (principal duty is funding)
- *Armed Services*
- *Budget*
- *Education and the Workforce*
- *Energy and Commerce*
- *Financial Services*
- *Foreign Affairs*
- *Homeland Security*
- House Administration (handles House administrative tasks)
- *Judiciary*
- *Natural Resources*
- Oversight and Government Reform (principal duty is oversight)
- *Permanent Select Committee on Intelligence*
- Rules (draws up rules for the consideration of legislation on the House floor)
- *Science, Space, and Technology*
- *Small Business*
- Standards of Official Conduct (handles ethics issues)
- *Transportation and Infrastructure*
- *Veterans' Affairs*
- *Ways and Means*

These committees, often called *standing committees,* normally remain in place from Congress to Congress. Very occasionally, a committee will be eliminated; more often, the party in charge will alter the name of a committee, such as Republicans did in 2011 when they changed Education and Labor to Education and the Workforce to highlight their more critical perspective on organized labor.

Most committees have several subcommittees that reflect further specialization of the committees' work. The House Armed Services Committee is a good example. It develops the bill that authorizes all activities of the Defense Department, including the US Army, Navy, Air Force, and Marine Corps. The vast jurisdiction of the House Armed Services Committee is divided up among seven subcommittees:

1. Emerging Threats and Capabilities
2. Military Personnel

3. Oversight and Investigations (of the Defense Department)
4. Readiness
5. Seapower and Projection Forces
6. Strategic Forces
7. Tactical Air and Land Forces

The Senate Armed Services Committee, with essentially the same jurisdiction, works in a similar way. The major difference is that the Senate has no subcommittee dedicated explicitly to oversight and investigations of the department. These are the six specialized subcommittees:

1. Airland
2. Emerging Threats and Capabilities
3. Personnel
4. Readiness and Management Support
5. SeaPower
6. Strategic Forces

The House Ways and Means Committee, which handles taxes, major entitlement programs, and trade, is another tremendously important committee. The Senate Finance Committee has a similar jurisdiction. The two also divide up their work similarly, although Senate Finance is a little more imaginative in the naming of its subcommittees. The Senate Finance Committee has jurisdiction over energy policy that the House committee does not have.

Below is a list of the six subcommittees of the House Ways and Means Committee:

1. Health
2. Human Resources
3. Oversight
4. Select Revenue Measures
5. Social Security
6. Trade

And here are the subcommittees of the Senate Finance Committee:

1. Energy, Natural Resources, and Infrastructure
2. Health Care
3. International Trade, Customs, and Global Competitiveness
4. Social Security, Pensions, and Family Policy
5. Taxation and IRS Oversight

As noted earlier, a new majority party adjusts the ratio of party members on each committee and determines the number of members serving on each. In 2011 Republicans put a majority of their party's members on each committee, a change from the Democratic majorities of the previous four years.

The understanding is that the ratios on the committees should mirror the ratio of the overall chamber. The 2012 elections gave the Republicans a 234–201 edge in the House—roughly a 54:46 ratio. In January 2013, Republicans established ratios on most committees closely approximating that overall ratio, although they did give themselves an added advantage on a few key committees, including Ways and Means (23–16, or 59 percent of the slots) and Appropriations (29–22, or 57 percent). The minority may complain but has no meaningful recourse, since the majority party gets its way on organizational matters and most other things in the House. The majority does feel constrained in giving itself lopsided committee majorities by the fact that they will someday, maybe sooner rather than later, be in the minority and would like to be treated fairly in that eventuality.

The largest committee in the House is Armed Services, with 62 members. The one committee that always has an overwhelming majority party advantage is the Rules Committee, which for 40 years has had a 9–4 edge for the majority party regardless of the chamber ratio. The majority party, Republican or Democrat, has found it essential to have a clear working majority on this committee because it has the all-important duty of structuring debate and the amendment process for legislation on the House floor.

## Committee Assignments

Getting good committee assignments is crucial for members of the House. Committees are where the serious legislative work of establishing and funding government programs, as well as writing tax law, is accomplished. To be a player in Congress, members must be on one or more committees that give them influence over government policy. The party's Steering Committees make the assignments. It is only in extremely rare cases, as can be seen in Box 3.3, that members are denied committee slots.

Most members of the House get two or three committee assignments. But members who serve on Energy and Commerce, Appropriations, Rules, or Ways and Means are, by both parties' rules, limited to one assignment. These committees are referred to as **exclusive committees**. Democrats include Financial Services in this category. However, exceptions are made, and many waivers are granted by the Steering Committees, more commonly on the Democratic side. This enables members not only to serve on an exclusive committee but also to serve on a committee

## BOX 3.3

### Representative Traficant
### Is Denied Committee Assignments

Members of Congress have to come to their party's steering committee to receive committee assignments. Even nominally independent members of Congress may receive assignments, even though independents are not guaranteed committee slots by House or Senate rules. They can show their allegiance, albeit unofficially, to a party by voting for that party's candidate for Speaker of the House and supporting that party's position on the organizing resolution in the House or Senate. Vermont's Bernie Sanders, an independent, has done just that in support of the Democratic Party. As a result, he received committee assignments from House Democrats while serving in that chamber and, since his election to the Senate in 2006, by Senate Democrats.

Democratic representative James Traficant of Ohio found himself in a highly unusual predicament in January 2001 after voting for Republican Dennis Hastert in the roll call vote for speaker. (Traficant had been siding with Republicans more and more often on issues over the previous several years, but had always run for reelection in northeastern Ohio as a Democrat.) Democrats proceeded to strip him of his committee assignments after the Hastert vote. He turned to the Republicans, who indicated no interest in giving him any assignments, either.

The reason? Traficant was under federal investigation at the time for misuse of the funds he was allotted to run his congressional office, and Republicans didn't want to be associated with him. He was the first member of Congress in more than 100 years not to serve on at least one committee.

---

that addresses the particular needs of their constituents. Democrat Earl Pomeroy of North Dakota enjoyed membership on both the Ways and Means and Agriculture Committees, a perk that his leadership hoped would solidify his electoral position in a strongly Republican state. In 2010 it was not enough, as he lost the seat to Republican Rick Berg.

Most members stick with the committee assignments they have when a new Congress convenes, although some may lobby for exclusive committee slots that open up owing to retirement or electoral defeat. New members nearly always lobby for assignments that enable them to serve their constituents' interests, but they also look for assignments that are intellectually interesting to them or where their professional expertise may be particularly useful.[6]

Exclusive committee assignments give representatives a considerable amount of leverage with their colleagues, but they are rarely awarded to freshman members. After the 2010 Republican landslide, however, the leadership-dominated Steering Committee saw fit to reward numerous new members with exclusive slots. Freshman Republican lawmakers were given roughly half of the new slots on those committees, including Appropriations. Republican leaders vowed to have that committee "make deep cuts to spending, and make them quickly," making the committee attractive to those new members intent on cutting the budget.[7]

In very rare cases, members may be stripped of committee assignments by leadership because of acts of egregious disloyalty to the party. In late 2012, Speaker John Boehner stripped four members not deemed "team players" from key committee assignments in an effort to consolidate his hold on power.

## Committee Chairs

The position of committee chair in the House is a very important one. Committee chairs set the agenda of their committees and are in charge of legislation in their areas of jurisdiction. Every chair is a member of the majority party. Chairs get to hire the committee's majority party professional (essentially "expert") staff—anywhere from 25 to approximately 80 people, depending on the committee's importance and jurisdiction—and direct their work. The *ranking member*, or top person from the minority party (who would be chair if his or her party were in control), gets the resources to hire about half as many professional staff. The majority needs the additional staff because it is responsible for setting up hearings, establishing an agenda, and moving legislation through the committee and to the House floor.

In decades past, the selection of a committee chair was automatic: the senior member in terms of service on the committee from the majority party would get the gavel. But in the 1970s, Democrats reformed the process by putting in place a mechanism by which the larger membership of the party—the party caucus—could make the determination in a secret ballot vote.[8] Although Democrats have usually kept to the seniority principle for chairs or ranking members, there has been competition for a chair position several times when an aggressive junior member of a committee would take on an elder. A few times, those challenges were successful. The ranking member of the Energy and Commerce Committee in the 113th Congress, Henry Waxman (D-CA), ascended to chair in 2009 when Democrats were in the majority after challenging and defeating John Dingell (D-MI) in a caucus vote. Dingell was senior in service on the committee to Waxman, and in fact has served in the House longer than anyone in history.

After taking over the House in 1995, Republicans took far less heed of seniority in making chair selections—a distinction between the parties that holds true today. Speaker Newt Gingrich employed very different criteria and for all intents and purposes handpicked the chairs. To him, what mattered were loyalty, an ability to raise large sums of money for the Republican Party, and a sophisticated understanding (as well as an ability to convey that understanding in public) of the major issues confronting the committee.

Gingrich's successor, Dennis Hastert from Illinois, who took over the speakership in 1999, installed a different process, although he seemed to use essentially the same criteria for selection as Gingrich did. Prospective committee chairs presented their case before the Republican Steering Committee, which voted to recommend its favorite to the Republican conference. The conference ratified the Steering Committee's recommendation every time. (In one instance, Hastert's weighted vote carried the day in the Steering Committee, giving Bill Thomas of California the helm at Ways and Means.) The Republican leadership in the 113th Congress employs similar methods, often overlooking seniority in favor of loyalty, effectiveness, and fundraising prowess.

This method of selecting committee chairs gives the leadership considerable control over the agenda of the chamber by putting only those people with a proven track record of loyalty in control of writing legislation. In addition, Republicans (but not Democrats) impose six-year term limits on their committee chairs or ranking members. Over the past 20 years, members who had served their limit often wanted to lead another committee. It helped their cause to have demonstrated loyalty and competence during the previous six years.

Subcommittee chairs and ranking members are generally determined on the basis of seniority and subject to the approval of the party caucus. However, both parties' leaders will deny these slots to members whose maverick tendencies undermine the party agenda. All subcommittee chairs, like committee chairs, are members of the majority party. No member may chair more than one. There are 104 subcommittees in the House in the 113th Congress. Most subcommittee chairs are recommended by the committees themselves; however, subcommittee chairs on Energy and Commerce, Ways and Means, Appropriations, and Financial Services must also be approved by the Steering Committee.

## Members' Offices

As noted earlier, members of the House may hire staff to assist them with constituent services and legislative work in Washington and in their **district offices**. Members all represent approximately the same number of constituents—about

720,000—and they get the same budget for setting up offices and hiring assistants. The average budget is about $1.45 million in total. There is some small variation to account for differences in travel expenses back to the district. To work in both their Washington and their district offices, House members may hire as many as 22 staff members, but only 18 may be full-time. Most members have between one and five district offices, depending on the geographical size of the district.

## TODAY'S SENATE: LEADERSHIP AND COMMITTEES
### Majority Party Leadership

The presiding officer of the Senate, as stipulated in the Constitution, is the vice president of the United States.[9] Rarely, however, does the vice president actually preside—in modern times, he has usually taken on that duty only when it looks as though a vote in the Senate may end up tied and the president has an interest in the outcome. In that eventuality, the vice president may cast a vote. Both Vice President Dick Cheney and Vice President Al Gore appeared in the Senate to break ties on crucial budget and tax bills. Otherwise, they generally stayed away from official duties.

The Constitution requires that the Senate select a *president pro tempore,* although that has become a largely ceremonial position held by the senior member of the majority party, who has no more interest than the vice president in the tedious work of presiding over endless debates and votes.

The person who really runs the Senate is the majority leader. By custom, the majority leader of the Senate has the right to be recognized first on the floor, which gives him or her the power to set the agenda in the chamber. The majority party has two top leadership positions in the Senate:

*Majority leader.* Determines the agenda on the floor of the Senate, usually after some consultation with the minority leader. The majority leader selects his party's members for select committees, including the Select Committee on Intelligence.

*Assistant majority leader.* Assists the majority leader in developing the agenda of the Senate. The **assistant leader** helps to negotiate agreements among committee chairs on complex legislation and is traditionally in charge of canvassing the party's membership on upcoming votes.

These positions are determined by secret ballot in a caucus of majority party senators.

As in the House, the majority party leaders hire staff to help them with their duties, managing legislation on the floor, counting votes, developing an agenda, and promoting the party agenda through the use of various forms of media, new and old.

Also as in the House, both parties have *party committees* to handle important business. Those committees and their main functions are listed below:

*Policy Committee.* Conducts research and polling on the major issues of the day. Also assists the majority leader in scheduling the floor agenda.

*Steering and Outreach Committee (Democrats); Committee on Committees (Republicans).* Assigns new senators to committees and makes any assignment adjustments in a new Congress.

*Campaign Committees (Democratic Senatorial Campaign Committee, or DSCC, and National Republican Senatorial Committee, or NRSC).* Helps recruit candidates for upcoming Senate races, coordinate campaign activities, and raise money.

*Democratic Technology and Communications Committee.* Assists the leadership in internal communications among members of the party and coordinates external messaging. Republicans have no counterpart.

## Minority Party Leadership

Every member of the Senate, including those in the minority party, has a great deal of power owing to standing rules, precedents, and customs. This fact enables the minority party to be a player in the establishment of the legislative agenda. (In the House, the minority is in a much weaker position.)

The minority party leadership is elected in a caucus of party members, just as the majority party leadership is. The top minority leadership positions are as follows:

*Minority leader.* Regularly negotiates with the majority leader over proposed legislative agenda items, representing the interests of his or her caucus. The minority leader's other responsibilities include naming members of his or her party to select committees, including the Select Committee on Intelligence.

*Assistant minority leader.* Assists the minority leader in dealings with the majority party in matters related to the agenda. The assistant leader's other responsibilities include canvassing his or her party's members on pending legislation.

Just as we have seen earlier with majority and minority leadership in both chambers, the minority party in the Senate hires staff to help with legislative duties—monitoring legislation, counting votes—as well as managing relations with the media.

## Committees in the Senate

Technically, the Senate is a continuous body, unlike the House, since two-thirds of its membership remains in place every election cycle. As such, the Senate does not have to be reconstituted every two years, as the House does. If there is a switch in party control, the new majority brings forward a resolution to reconfigure committee ratios. But even if the party control remains the same in the Senate after the election, senators are often interested in changing the makeup of the committees—especially if the majority has added or lost a significant number of seats. This happened after the 2008 elections, for example, when Democrats added eight seats to their majority.

The Senate, then, may either leave alone or adjust the committee structure, jurisdictions, and ratios for each new two-year Congress. The Senate has 20 committees in the 113th Congress, as listed here. In many respects, the committee structure of the Senate resembles the House's structure, but few committees match up exactly. (There is no official liaison between the two chambers to enforce corresponding committee and subcommittee arrangements.) Only the Appropriations Committees in the two chambers have exactly matching jurisdictions and subcommittees.

Here is a list of the committees in the Senate (the authorizing committees are italicized):

- *Agriculture, Nutrition, and Forestry*
- Appropriations (handles funding)
- *Armed Services*
- *Banking, Housing, and Urban Affairs*
- *Budget*
- *Commerce, Science, and Transportation*
- *Energy and Natural Resources*
- *Environment and Public Works*
- *Finance*
- *Foreign Relations*
- *Health, Education, Labor, and Pensions*
- *Homeland Security and Governmental Affairs*
- *Indian Affairs*
- *Judiciary*

- Rules and Administration (handles internal rules and administrative tasks)
- Select Committee on Aging (has no legislative jurisdiction)
- Select Committee on Ethics (handles ethics issues)
- *Select Committee on Intelligence*
- *Small Business and Entrepreneurship*
- *Veterans' Affairs*

There is one particularly notable difference between the two chambers that speaks to the profound variance in their operating environments: the Senate has no equivalent to the House Committee on Rules, which has tremendous power in structuring how legislation is handled on the House floor. In fact, no committee structures floor debate in the Senate; instead, formal and more often informal agreements are reached between the majority and minority leaders to move legislation along. (The Senate does have a panel called the Committee on Rules and Administration, but its main tasks are to handle administrative matters and internal Senate rules.)

As in the House, most Senate committees are authorizing committees—that is, they deal with bills setting policy for government agencies and programs. The Senate, too, has one committee that controls funding, the Appropriations Committee, just like the House. The Senate committee that focuses mostly on oversight of government programs and agencies is the Committee on Homeland Security and Governmental Affairs. Unlike its House counterpart (Oversight and Government Reform), it has authorizing jurisdiction over the Department of Homeland Security, as its name implies.

Also as with the House, most Senate committees have specialized subcommittees to carry out the committees' work. As a general rule, House subcommittees play a larger role in the legislative process than do Senate subcommittees. House members are typically on fewer committees and subcommittees than senators and are better able to turn their attention to narrower areas of policy. In a chamber with only 100 members, most senators are stretched very thin (many have multiple positions of authority in the chamber) and are unable to focus effectively at the level of subcommittee specialization.

The ratios between the parties on Senate committees always reflect very closely the ratio of the overall chamber. The prerogatives that all members have in Senate rules enable the minority to block attempts by the majority party to stack committees in its favor. As a result, at the beginning of the 113th Congress, with Democrats holding a chamber-wide 55–45 edge (including the two independents, Bernie Sanders and Angus King, who both sided with Democrats on organizational matters), most committees had a two-seat margin for the majority.

## Committee Assignments

Getting good committee assignments is crucial in the Senate, just as it is in the House. Senators develop expertise in their committee work, which usually results in considerable deference in their areas of specialty. Of course, senators try to get on committees that serve their constituents' needs and their own personal interests, as House members do, but senators are more likely to try to prioritize the Armed Services Committee or the Foreign Relations Committee in order to enhance their plausibility as a presidential candidate in the future.

All senators serve on multiple committees, usually four. There simply are not enough of them to make it feasible to establish exclusive committees, as the House does. But not all committees are created equal. The Senate has a long list of what it calls **"A" committees**:

- Agriculture, Nutrition, and Forestry
- Appropriations
- Armed Services
- Banking, Housing, and Urban Affairs
- Commerce, Science, and Transportation
- Energy and Natural Resources
- Environment and Public Works
- Finance
- Foreign Relations
- Health, Education, Labor, and Pensions
- Homeland Security and Governmental Affairs
- Intelligence
- Judiciary

Among these "A" committees, Appropriations, Armed Services, Finance, and Foreign Relations have exalted status and are referred to as **"super A" committees**. Democrats add one more committee to their "super A" list—Commerce, Science, and Transportation.

Returning members usually stick with the assignments they already have in order to accrue seniority. New members must lobby their party committee (the Committee on Committees for Republicans and the Steering and Outreach Committee for Democrats) for preferred assignments. Senate rules dictate that all members get one super-A slot.[10] Members are also entitled to another of the A committee slots, as well as at least one other assignment.[11] Assignments are doled out differently by the two parties.

The Republican Committee on Committees sticks to a seniority formula in determining committee slots. The Democrats' Steering and Outreach Committee also relies on seniority, but it considers several other factors, including the length of time since a particular state has been represented on a committee, the expertise of the new members, and their expected level of loyalty to the party.[12]

### Committee Chairs

As with the House, the rank of committee chair comes with many privileges. The chair determines the agenda of the committee and gets to hire the bulk of the professional staff who work for the committee. As with the House, the minority ranking member can also hire staff. Senate resources are usually more evenly divided between the parties than in the House. (In recent Congresses, while the resource ratio on House committees has been about two-to-one in favor of the majority, in the Senate the majority has gotten 55 to 60 percent of the funding.)

The majority party in the Senate gets all the committee and subcommittee chair positions. Both parties in the Senate still adhere to the seniority tradition in determining committee chairs and ranking members. It is not uncommon for a particular senator to be senior in service on more than one committee; in these cases, the senator may chair only one committee. In 2013 Senator Tom Harkin of Iowa, for example, is the senior Democrat on both the Agriculture and the Health, Education, Labor, and Pensions Committees. He has chosen the latter. Subcommittee chairs are also determined by seniority accrued on the subcommittee. There are 72 subcommittees in the Senate in the 113th Congress. Every Democrat chairs at least one.

The seniority tradition in the Senate has come under fire in recent years in the Republican Party. In 1995 the party put in place a mechanism in its rules, making it possible to challenge the senator in line to be chair or ranking member. While the senior Republican has never been denied the leadership role, the very threat that it could happen has had consequences. In 2005 Arlen Specter of Pennsylvania, in line to take over the Judiciary Committee, came under heavy scrutiny from conservative Republicans for his pro-choice stance on abortion. Specter was forced to promise not to get in the way of President Bush's nominees to the federal judiciary in order to get the position.[13] Later, in 2009, Specter switched parties, in part because of heavy Republican criticism of his vote for President Obama's stimulus package (he was one of only three Republicans in Congress to do so), and in part as a way to improve his chances of keeping his seat in the 2010 elections. (He ended up losing the Democratic primary that year.)

The fact that the seniority system remains in place—albeit tenuously on the Republican side—in the chamber gives committee chairs a measure of freedom from the dictates of the majority party leadership that their House counterparts do not always have. Republicans also enforce a six-year term limit on chairs and ranking members, as House Republicans do. Democrats do not have that policy.

## Members' Offices

Senators represent varied constituencies. Unlike the House, where the districts are all nearly the same size in terms of population, states range from Wyoming's approximately 560,000 residents to California's 38 million.

California senators do not get to hire 70 times as many staff members as Wyoming's senators do—which would reflect proportionally the populations of the two states—but they do get more resources than the senators from the sparsely populated states. (The Senate allotment ranges from $3 to $4.7 million.) The big-state senators usually hire 60 to 80 staffers to cover the Washington and state offices, while the smaller-state senators have the resources to hire 30 to 45 employees, depending on the state. Even with the larger allotment, California's senators are still not able to provide the kind of personalized service to their constituents that senators from sparsely populated states can deliver.

## HOUSE AND SENATE ORGANIZATION AND THE PRESSURES OF THE LEGISLATIVE AND REPRESENTATIVE ROLES

A useful way to think about the major organizational components of the two chambers—leadership and committees—is that they are meant to aid the institution and its members in balancing their legislative and representative responsibilities.

Committees, the workhorses of the institution, have the responsibility to study, formulate, and refine legislation in all areas of federal policy. In addition, these panels conduct oversight to keep track of how the executive branch agencies are implementing the laws passed by Congress and spending the money it provides. In short, congressional committees and subcommittees are the place where the serious work on national security, agriculture, taxes, and so forth goes on. As has been noted, the authorizing and appropriations committees all have delineated policy domains and jurisdiction over specific federal agencies and departments. If one had to point to one place in Congress where the board-of-directors role is carried out, it would be in the committees.

But committees are hardly immune from the political pressures inherent in the representative role. Members of the House serve on anywhere from one to three committees. Senators usually serve on four committees. As we saw, these assignments are not made randomly. Members lobby within their parties to secure desired committee assignments. In fact, for newly elected members, this becomes a preoccupation. To demonstrate back home that they are relevant players in Washington, it is crucial for new members to get on good committees. Naturally, members try to get on the panels most relevant to their constituencies—perhaps the Armed Services Committee for the representative who has naval bases in his or her district, or the Agriculture Committee if farming is important. Many members make concerted efforts to land a desired slot on the most prestigious committees (super-A committees in the Senate and exclusive committees in the House) when openings are available.

The upshot is that members, as they work on policy in committee, are carefully attuned to the political ramifications back home of the decisions they make and the bills they craft in their role as the board of directors. The job of legislator cannot be separated from the job of representative.

As the other main organizational unit in the two chambers, the party leadership decides what legislation to bring to the floor. The two parties embody distinct, if somewhat overlapping, philosophies of governance. The party that happens to be in the majority is in the advantageous position of being able to pursue its national policy goals in legislation, but to pursue that agenda successfully, party leaders must carefully consider their rank-and-file members' representative responsibilities. After all, they need to corral a sufficient number of votes to pass bills.

In other words, crafting as well as scheduling and passing legislation must be done with an eye toward the views and interests of members' constituencies. Congress cannot make law based solely on some abstract concept like "good public policy" or "the public interest"; nor can its members simply pursue their own ideological or philosophical agendas. Political considerations must be part of every calculation.

Both parties face conflicts. While the majority of Democrats support environmentally "green" policies, putting more regulations on industrial and auto emissions, for example, party leadership must be mindful of the members of the party whose districts include automobile or auto-parts manufacturing and coal fields whose electoral prospects will be negatively affected if the policies are viewed as too extreme. Similarly, Republicans face conflicts between the ardent desire of most party members to cut the size of government and those who, while interested in budget cutting, may want to see a generous federal farm-subsidy program continue because local economies depend on it. For congressional majorities, enforcing party loyalty and cohesion can be very challenging.

## CONCLUSION: CONSTITUTIONAL DESIGN AND THE MODERN HOUSE AND SENATE

The Constitution divided the board of directors into two very differently constituted chambers with different time perspectives and very different types of constituencies to represent. It is a branch of government that does not have a central organizing body. The two chambers of Congress are quite literally *uncoordinated*—unlike the human body, they do not have a central nervous system. And without a central nervous system, it is an institution that regularly has a great deal of difficulty coming together to make big decisions on directing the work of the government.

Still, the Constitution requires the House and Senate to work together to produce legislation. This is a tricky business and no easy task, nor was it meant to be. The two chambers were considered by the framers to be a key bulwark against the aggregation of too much power in one place. Power in the US system was divided in many ways—between the states and the federal government, among the three branches of government, and between the House and Senate. As we have seen, this last division was very important to many of the framers in view of the fact that they believed the popularly elected branch *should* have the most power. In fact, they gave Congress the power to make laws, the bedrock of all federal policy. That power was, to them, prone to abuse. Many of the framers wanted to protect against a proliferation of bad legislation that might emerge from a streamlined and smoothly functioning legislative process. Some would argue that Congress's deliberate pace and frequent inability to function efficiently approximate the framers' intentions.

---

### Questions for Discussion

1. If you had to identify one flaw in the design of the US Congress, what would it be?

2. Every committee in both chambers is controlled by that chamber's majority party. Is that fair when the minority party invariably has more than 40 percent of the overall representation?

3. If you were in party leadership, would you try to force all the members of your party to vote for what the majority of the party supported? What are the arguments for and against that practice?

4. The House and Senate committee chairs are selected by very different methods—heavily influenced by leadership in the House and dictated

by seniority in the Senate. What do you think of the seniority system? What are the advantages and disadvantages of the two systems from a member's perspective?

## Suggestions for Further Reading

Dodd, Lawrence C., and Bruce I. Oppenheimer. "The House in a Time of Crisis: Economic Turmoil and Partisan Upheaval." In *Congress Reconsidered,* edited by Lawrence C. Dodd and Bruce I. Oppenheimer, 27–58. 10th ed. Washington, DC: CQ Press, 2013.

Rohde, David. *Parties and Leaders in the Post-reform House.* Chicago: University of Chicago Press, 1991.

## NOTES

1. See chap. 2 of Charles Cushman's *Introduction to the U.S. Congress* (Armonk, NY: M. E. Sharpe, 2006) for an overview of the influence English history had on the framers' views of the Constitution.

2. *Federalist Papers,* No. 51.

3. The number stood at closer to 1,000 until August 2012, when President Obama signed The Presidential Appointment Efficiency and Streamlining Act into law, which reduced the number by 170.

4. Charlie Cook, "Wave Bye-Bye," *National Journal,* June 22, 2012, www.nationaljournal.com/columns/cook-report/the-cook-report-wave-bye-bye-20120621.

5. See Timothy E. Cook, *Governing with the News* (Chicago: University of Chicago Press, 2005); and Pat Sellers, "Winning Media Coverage in the U.S. Congress," in *U.S. Senate Exceptionalism,* edited by Bruce Oppenheimer (Columbus: Ohio State University Press, 2002).

6. The landmark study of members' motivations for serving on committees is Richard Fenno's *Congressmen in Committees* (Boston: Little, Brown, 1973). John Aldrich, Brittany Perry, and David Rohde reconsider Fenno's findings in light of the increased polarization in Congress in "Richard Fenno's Theory of Congressional Committees and the Polarization of the House," in *Congress Reconsidered,* edited by Lawrence C. Dodd and Bruce I. Oppenheimer, 10th ed. (Washington, DC: CQ Press, 2013), 193–220.

7. Erik Wasson, "New Appropriations Republicans Vow to Slash Spending Quickly," *Hill,* December 10, 2010, http://thehill.com/blogs/on-the-money/appropriations/133277-new-appropriations-republicans-vow-to-slash-spending-deeply-quickly. See also Molly Cooper's "Tea Party–Backed Freshmen win Plum Committee Assignments," *Hill,* December 12, 2010, 1; and John Aldrich, Brittany Perry, and David Rohde, "House Appropriations After the Republican Revolution," *Congress and the Presidency* 39 (2012): 1–25.

8. See David Rohde, *Parties and Leaders in the Post-reform House* (Chicago: University of Chicago Press, 1991).

9. The chief justice of the Supreme Court presides in the case of an impeachment trial, as stipulated in the Constitution.

10. The so-called Johnson Rule, named after Lyndon Johnson when he was the majority leader in the 1950s, established the precedent that all members would get one prestigious committee slot. Before that time, senior members were more inclined to hoard these assignments, at the expense of newer members.

11. Judy Schneider, *CRS Report for Congress: Senate Committees: Categories and Rules for Committee Assignments,* Congressional Research Service, January 18, 2005.

12. Judy Schneider, *CRS Report for Congress: Committee Assignment Process in the U.S. Senate; Democratic and Republican Party Procedures,* Congressional Research Service, November 3, 2006.

13. "Abortion-Support Threatens Arlen Specter's Political Future," November 9, 2004, www.lifesitenews.com/ldn/2004/nov/04110904.html; Andrea Stone, "Specter Pushes for Judiciary Chair," *USA Today,* November 8, 2004.

# 4

# Congressional Elections

In a political system based on the idea that public officials are to be regularly and frequently held accountable for their actions by the voters, the next election cycle always casts a long shadow. As a consequence, members of Congress are constantly concerned about the potential electoral consequences of their legislative actions, both setting government policy in the authorizing process and making decisions about funding in appropriations bills. Furthermore, members frequently try to use their supervisory or oversight power to their electoral advantage by shining a light on government programs that they believe are not delivering for their constituents or to take credit for those that are.

The time-consuming nature of the modern congressional campaign—especially the fundraising burden faced by members—has its own independent effect on the work of the board of directors. The bottom line is that one cannot understand how Congress does its work in directing the agencies of the federal government without understanding the electoral context.

The chapter starts with three vivid examples of what political scientist David Mayhew calls the *electoral connection* to the legislative work of members of Congress. Representatives and senators of both parties and across the political spectrum pursue specific legislative goals in order to impress upon their constituents the relevance of the work they do.

The next section looks at the fundamentals of the electoral context from the perspective of a potential candidate for the House or Senate. We look at the eligibility requirements for the job, what sorts of people choose to run, what motivates candidates, and the candidate recruitment efforts undertaken by the two parties.

The subsequent section looks at the geographical context of congressional elections. We cover the process of apportioning House seats among the states, as well as the rules governing the drawing of district lines. Of particular importance is the politics surrounding the drawing of these lines, which invariably involves partisan battles at the state level and sometimes brings up considerations of race and ethnicity.

Another key factor in understanding the context of congressional elections is the advantage held by incumbents. As noted in Chapter 2, members are reelected at very high rates and more often than not by comfortable margins. We look at why incumbents are so hard to beat, and what do they do to exploit their advantage.

We go on to examine the most crucial aspect of the incumbency advantage: campaign finance. Money is the building block to all aspects of a congressional campaign, including hiring staff, producing advertisements, and raising yet more money. We look at the pressures on all candidates to raise sufficient funds, either to squelch potential opposition or just to be competitive. Individual donors, political action committees (PACs), and the parties are the big players in campaign finance.

Then we turn to campaign themes and issues. Primary elections and general elections present distinct challenges for congressional candidates. Different issues may need to be addressed at each of these stages, requiring different strategies and themes—and always money. To a large degree, candidates rise or fall based on their campaigning abilities, fundraising, and strategy. But sometimes external events and national conditions can overwhelm even the best-laid plans.

Ultimately, we address the stakes in congressional elections. Every two years, every House seat and about one-third of the Senate seats are up for grabs. Congressional elections are tremendously consequential, not just because the immediate career interests of the members are on the line, but also because elections may portend shifts in national priorities. The party that captures a majority of seats gets to set the agenda for the next two years in that chamber, deciding the issues to focus on, the government programs that deserve more money, the new initiatives that should be considered, and so forth. What are the key factors that determine success for a political party? What do parties do to enhance their chances?

We conclude by looking at the impact of campaigns and campaigning on the legislative and oversight work of members of Congress. In the 21st century, running for Congress can be nearly a full-time job, cutting into the time needed to direct the work of government. The "continuous campaign" has tremendous consequences for Congress as an institution as it struggles to fulfill its legislative responsibilities.

## THE ELECTORAL CONNECTION
### Example 1: Representative John Murtha's Earmark Factory

As chairman of the House Appropriations Committee's Defense Subcommittee, former representative John Murtha (D-PA) secured 48 earmarks amounting to

$150.5 million in the 2008 military spending bill. Murtha's biggest earmark directed $23 million to the National Drug Intelligence Center, which is located in Pennsylvania's 12th District and employs hundreds of constituents.

The power that Murtha exercised over military spending, combined with his commitment to creating jobs for the people he represented, even prompted some defense contractors to relocate to his district. In addition to directing money to his defense-industry constituents, Murtha targeted federal funds for new roads, water projects, an airport, medical facilities, and federal offices in his district.

Taxpayers for Common Sense, a nonpartisan watchdog organization, estimated that Murtha channeled more than $2 billion to his district from his perch on the House Appropriations Committee. And he was proud of it! At a 2007 campaign fundraiser, Representative Murtha claimed that bringing federal dollars to his district "is the whole goddamn reason I went to Washington."[1]

Representative Murtha passed away in 2010, as did the long-standing tradition of earmarking appropriations bills. Upon taking control of the House after the 2010 elections, Republican leaders announced a moratorium on earmarks. As a result, House members must demonstrate their hard work on behalf of constituents in other, more conventional, ways.

### Example 2: A Senate Icon Looks after Mississippi

Senator Thad Cochran, Republican of Mississippi, doesn't get on the talk shows and rarely makes high-profile floor speeches. But he has been a force to be reckoned with over a 35-year Senate career.

Cochran has chaired both the Agriculture Committee and the Appropriations Committee during his time in Washington and helped shepherd through the process farm-bill reauthorizations and dozens of appropriations bills. In the 112th Congress, he was a leader in reauthorizing the National Flood Insurance Program. In the 113th Congress, he serves as ranking member of the Agriculture Committee (with another farm bill in the works) and ranking member of the Defense Appropriations Subcommittee.

Cochran has a conservative voting record but is respected by senators of both parties, having worked productively with Democrats on a wide range of legislation. He is also known for looking out for the home folks. Cochran can point to his efforts to promote shipbuilding in his state (with a lot of jobs to go with it), as well as using his perch on Appropriations to ensure continued funding for research at Mississippi universities on health, forestry, energy, and agriculture. His work on the National Flood Insurance Program was of particular interest to Mississippians who have been hard hit by hurricanes in recent years. The payoff for all this? The senator normally faces only token opposition for reelection.

## Example 3: Congresswoman Focuses on Issues of Importance to Sacramento

Congresswoman Doris Matsui (D-CA) has come a long way. She was born in an internment camp in Arizona during World War II and has now served the 6th District of California, which is composed of Greater Sacramento, for 10 years. For her entire time in Congress, Matsui has pursued a kind of twin strategy—look after the immediate needs of the district, but also help with Democratic Party priorities (she helped lead the push for funding stem-cell research and against the Central American Free Trade Pact)[2] in order to enhance her standing in efforts to secure powerful committee assignments. Those assignments in turn position her to better serve her constituents. She currently has a spot on the exclusive Energy and Commerce Committee. This is in fact her second exclusive committee assignment.

From the beginning of her time in Congress, she kept her eye on Sacramento's immediate needs, working with members of both parties from the state to ensure funding for transportation needs and flood protection. Until the earmark ban in 2011, she was unabashed in seeking funding for these and other district needs, including seed money for popular clean-tech companies. From her perch on Energy and Commerce, she continues to promote the clean-tech business as well as the health care concerns of her constituents.

* * *

It would be naive to think that electoral pressures do *not* influence the way members of Congress do their jobs in directing the work of government. After all, the republic was set up so that elected officials would be accountable to the public. Representatives and senators sponsor legislation that resonates with their constituents, secure federal funds for programs and projects that are important back home, and oversee the implementation of federal laws and programs that affect their district or state.

Representative Murtha's overriding focus on creating jobs in his district through earmarks in appropriations bills made him a tough candidate to beat. The unemployment rate in Murtha's hometown of Johnstown dropped from 24 percent in 1983 to around 5 percent in 2007, owing in part to his efforts. Voters knew that replacing Murtha with an inexperienced freshman member could be economically devastating for the district.[3] Senator Cochran has parlayed his positions of power on the Agriculture and Appropriations Committees to the benefit of his home state. It is almost impossible to quantify the range of federal support in agriculture, defense, health, and other areas that he has been responsible for. Congresswoman Matsui has, in a relatively short time, established herself as a power player in Washington, with friends in the highest places in the Democratic Party, which she has used both to deliver tangible benefits to the people back home and to solidify her hold on California's 6th District.

People get into politics for a lot of reasons—to address specific issues and problems, for instance, or to advance policy goals. But as these examples illustrate, members must focus on first principles—the needs of the people in their districts and states—to win reelection and give themselves the opportunity to pursue loftier ambitions.

## RUNNING FOR CONGRESS

### Eligibility

The laws governing who is eligible to run for Congress are established in the Constitution. Article I, Section 2, states that House members must be at least 25 years of age, US citizens for at least seven years, and inhabitants of the states from which they are elected (though not necessarily the districts they hope to represent). Article I, Section 3, requires that senators be at least 30 years of age, US citizens for at least nine years, and inhabitants of the states from which they are elected. Neither the states nor Congress can alter or expand upon these qualifications.

Interestingly, in the early 1990s, there was a major movement, spearheaded at the grassroots level by thousands of activists across the country, to change a key aspect of congressional representation by imposing term limits on service in Congress. Term-limit advocates proposed limiting congressional tenure to as little as six years in the House, although most supported a 12-year limit for both chambers. In a few cases, these activists succeeded in changing state laws or constitutions to put their plans in place. But in a 1995 case challenging state-imposed term limits on members of Congress, the Supreme Court established that qualifications for holding congressional office could be changed only by a federal-level constitutional amendment.[4]

In practice, voters have tended to hold congressional candidates to a higher standard than do the basic constitutional requirements. Voters, for example, seem to prefer the experience that typically comes with age. Table 4.1 provides a broad demographic profile of the 113th Congress. As can be seen, at the beginning of the 113th Congress, House members averaged 57 years of age, and senators averaged 62 years of age. There were only 23 House members under the age of 40. No senators under the age of 40 serve in the 113th Congress.

And while the Constitution does not require congressional candidates to reside in the districts or states they represent for a set period of time before running, voters have demonstrated a strong preference for candidates with long-standing connections to the places they wish to represent. Voters tend to shun so-called

**TABLE 4.1 The Demographic Makeup of the 113th Congress**

|  | HOUSE | SENATE |
|---|---|---|
| Women | 82 (19%) | 20 |
| African Americans | 44 (10%) | 1 |
| Hispanics | 29 (7%) | 3 |
| Asian Americans | 9 (2%) | 1 |
| Roman Catholic | 136 (31%) | 27 |
| Jewish | 22 (5%) | 10 |
| Protestant | 247 (57%) | 52 |
| Military experience | 88 (20%) | 18 |
| **PROFESSIONAL BACKGROUND** | | |
| Public service/politics | 184 (42%) | 42 |
| Business | 187 (43%) | 27 |
| Law | 156 (36%) | 55 |
| Average age | 57 | 62 |

Source: Congressional Quarterly.

carpetbagger candidates because they lack ties to the district or state—notwithstanding a few notable exceptions, such as Hillary Clinton's successful election and reelection efforts in New York.

## Deciding to Run

Individuals seek elective office for personal and political reasons. Ambition, a desire to help others, an interest in public policy, and pressure from party officials rank high on the list of motivating factors for those who decide to run for Congress. Whatever their reasons for running, the candidates themselves play a pivotal role in electoral politics. Make no mistake about it—running for federal office requires tremendous initiative and drive. The candidate must generate voter interest, be a tireless fundraiser, and know how to handle a range of media.

Before examining how parties select and recruit candidates, it is useful to consider more carefully the personal factors that motivate politicians. Political scientist Joseph Schlesinger argues that candidates are driven to a significant degree by their own ambitions. There are discernible patterns of officeholding, according to Schlesinger, and these patterns give direction to candidates' ambitions.

Some elective positions—namely, those that typically serve as stepping-stones to higher office—are more likely than others to attract candidates with what Schlesinger calls "progressive ambition." For example, serving on the city council is often a stepping-stone to serving in the state legislature. And serving in the state legislature is often a stepping-stone to serving in Congress. This kind of progression allows an individual to build contacts and credentials over time with key groups and the party organization.

Schlesinger suggests that by studying the political behavior of politicians who serve in these "stepping-stone" offices, we can make certain inferences about what they want to be next.[5] Seventy-eight of the 110 new members (94 representatives and 16 senators) who were elected to Congress in 2010 had held elected political office prior to running for Congress.

But naked ambition is not the only thing that matters, despite the prevailing stereotype of the career politician as someone purely seeking self-aggrandizement. Running for public office often appeals to individuals who see elective office as a way to help others. Members of Congress can assist constituents in obtaining their Social Security, disability, Medicaid, and veterans' benefits; expedite their passport applications; and respond to immigration and citizenship queries. Members from areas afflicted by floods or hurricanes can be instrumental in delivering federal assistance to relieve the suffering. Many members of Congress describe working with constituents as the most rewarding aspect of their jobs.

Former congressman Martin Frost, who represented Texas's 24th District from 1979 to 2005, says that "many of my colleagues either pursued or contemplated pursuing a career as a clergyman in their faith."[6] For many politicians, it is that urge to help people—just as a minister, priest, or rabbi does—that drives them into politics. Many politicians even use the same language commonly used with regard to clergy—they see politics as their "calling." Former congressman Tim Roemer of Indiana cites the drive to "serve the community," instilled in him by the Catholic Church, as the source of his motivation to run for elective office.[7]

In contemporary politics, congressional candidates are also frequently driven by a desire to shape the larger direction of public policy and the role of government in society. Many of the House Democrats elected in 1974—a year when many Democrats won office in the aftermath of President Nixon's Watergate scandal—were liberal activists who were highly critical of what they perceived as the chamber's conservative policy bias. Many of these members had not previously held elective office and ran for Congress to shake things up and accomplish their policy goals. In many respects, they did just that.

The House speaker at the time, Tip O'Neill of Massachusetts, said that senior House members referred to these new members as "outsiders" because "they had not come up through the state and local political systems." They had never "rung doorbells, or driven people to the polls, or stayed late stuffing envelopes at campaign headquarters." O'Neill was struck by how many of the newcomers had decided to run because of Vietnam, civil rights, or environmental and consumer issues. Many had been inspired by the civil rights movement in the 1950s and 1960s and by the presidential campaign of Robert Kennedy in 1968.[8]

Similarly, the 73 Republicans who were newly elected to the House in 1994—a landslide year for the party—were also interested in shaking things up and pursuing their big-picture policy goals. Many of them had been recruited for that very purpose by Republican leaders, especially then–minority whip Newt Gingrich of Georgia. They ran for office in the service of conservative goals, such as deregulating the economy, cutting tax rates, and reducing the size of government. Flash-forward to 2010, when 89 conservative Republicans were elected to the House on a wave of voter anger over burgeoning deficits.

Journalist Alan Ehrenhalt, in one of the most trenchant studies of political ambition in the United States, observes that there has to be a strong motivation for people to go through what they have to do to get elected to office, whether at the state legislative level or the federal level for the House or Senate. In the US system, so much depends on initiative to get a campaign going. In short, a candidate has to be a self-starter. Most of them have to put their careers on hold, spend a tremendous amount of time away from their families, and suffer the indignity of begging for campaign funds—all for a job that does not come with a lucrative paycheck.

What Ehrenhalt found was that people are motivated by the desire to make a difference—not just in the lives of people by serving as ombudsman but also by addressing bigger issues, such as the environment, taxes, government regulation, or health care. He notes that successful people in American politics in the late 20th century were good public speakers; often worked as teachers, lawyers, or salespeople; and were driven to get involved by the big issues of the day, just as O'Neill had noticed in the 1970s, Gingrich capitalized on in the 1990s, and John Boehner benefited from in 2010.[9]

## The Work of the Party Committees

The Democratic Senatorial Campaign Committee recruits Democratic candidates for the Senate, and the Democratic Congressional Campaign Committee recruits Democratic House candidates. The Republican counterparts are the National Republican Senatorial Committee and the National Republican Congressional Committee, respectively. These organizations dedicate their resources to locating qualified candidates, encouraging them to run, and often giving them a boost during the campaign. Most recruiting takes place during the electoral off-season (odd-numbered years). Recruiting scouts fan out all over the country, focusing on districts and states where party officials believe their candidates can be competitive, either against an incumbent of the other party or in an open-seat race to replace a retiring member.

The committee scouts interview local party officials, business and community leaders, and political activists, among others, in order to find talented candidates. What exactly makes a good candidate? The short answer usually is: experience in politics. A person who has won an election is more than likely to have the media savvy and fundraising skills that are needed in a run for Congress. In short, those with political experience know what they are getting into and what it takes to succeed. Former athletes, business leaders, celebrities, and hometown heroes may also fit the bill without necessarily having held elective office. They may bring instant name recognition or built-in fundraising networks to the table—both invaluable assets.

The issues of the day can also influence the kinds of candidates the party committees want to recruit. During the 2006 and 2008 election cycles, both parties focused on recruiting Iraq War veterans to run for Congress. They were better able to speak with authority on a key issue in voters' minds than some other potential candidates. By 2010 the economy, high unemployment, and big deficits dominated the political landscape, and Republicans recruited candidates who successfully gave voice to the anger many voters felt.

Locating strong candidates is one thing, but convincing them to run is quite another. After the campaign committee scouts have screened and interviewed their preferred candidates, they turn to their higher-profile colleagues for help in making the pitch. Prospective candidates can expect phone calls and meetings with national party officials, key fundraisers, sitting US representatives and senators, governors, and sometimes even the president or vice president.

The goal is to flatter prospective candidates, convince them that they can win, and assure them that they will have support at every stage of the campaign. Party operatives can also address any questions or concerns a prospect may have about the costs and benefits of running for office and what to expect during the campaign.

It is not at all easy to persuade someone to run. The main reason, as noted earlier, is that running for office is a grueling business that takes a person away from family and career, and the job is tenuous, requires yet more hard work (much of it unrewarding and often downright demeaning), and does not offer a fantastic salary. The recruiters strike out as often as not. Factors like the national political environment and the competitiveness of the seat come into play as well. A strong economy and a popular president can motivate potential candidates who share the president's party label, while the opposite conditions tend to shift the incentives to the out party's prospects.[10] Naturally, if a district or state is overwhelmingly Democratic or Republican leaning, it is considerably more difficult for the nondominant party to recruit candidates.

Put simply, candidates are rarely interested in running for office when they stand little chance of winning. When the president of the College of Charleston,

Alex Sanders, a Democrat who had served on the South Carolina Supreme Court, challenged Republican representative Lindsey Graham in 2002 for one of South Carolina's US Senate seats, he knew he faced long odds. Republicans dominate South Carolina politics, and Graham was the early favorite. Although just a House member, Graham had developed a statewide—indeed, nationwide—reputation for his leadership in the effort to impeach President Clinton. On the campaign trail, Sanders would frequently joke that he was the DSCC's eighth choice and became the nominee because the committee's top seven choices knew better than to waste their time running as a Democrat in South Carolina. Sanders's concerns were borne out—he lost to Graham by ten percentage points.

Sometimes the party's preferred candidate faces competition in the primary election. Traditionally, parties have not taken sides during primaries in order to avoid dissension within the ranks. More recently, however, the national organizations have gotten involved. Democratic and Republican operatives have occasionally gone to great lengths to discourage opposition to their favored prospect. This can take the form of actively discouraging local political and business leaders from contributing money to another candidate or even, in the extreme case, challenging the validity of signatures on petitions that would gain a spot on the ballot for the nonfavored candidate. Prior to the 2012 elections, House Majority Leader Eric Cantor (R-VA) took the highly unusual step of endorsing in a member-versus-member primary. In the Republican primary for Illinois's 16th District, Cantor backed newcomer Representative Adam Kinzinger, who went on to defeat Representative Don Manzullo, a 10-term member. Although many House Republicans found Cantor's willingness to publicly "choose sides" unsettling, others were not surprised. Representative John Campbell (R-CA) observed that "Eric tends to make his opinions known. He will err on that side rather than keeping it quiet."[11]

Republican Party officials tried desperately to persuade Representative Todd Akin (R-MO) to quit the race for Claire McCaskill's (D-MO) Senate seat after he caused an uproar with comments he made about rape and abortion. Heading into the 2012 elections, McCaskill was one of the most vulnerable Senate Democrats. But after Akin's gaffe, the seat became hers to lose. Karl Rove, a top Republican strategist, said, "I know Todd. He's a good man. He has a good heart. But he said a real stupid, indefensible thing from which there's no recovery. And if he really cares about the values of conservatism and pro-life, then he will not go down in defeat with the biggest loss of any Republican candidate for Senate in the modern history."[12] Ultimately, Republican Party operatives were unable to persuade Akin to step down. His decision likely cost Republicans the seat, as McCaskill handily defeated Akin in the general election, winning 58 percent of the vote.

How active the party organization should be at the primary stage (and, as in Akin's case, beyond) remains a matter of debate. The voter turnout rate for congressional primary elections typically hovers around 20 percent, and those who vote in congressional primaries tend to be highly motivated partisans.[13] While the party organization tends to favor candidates who they think have a more realistic shot at winning the general election, even if it means compromising on the issues, party activists want candidates who share their political ideologies.

## Protecting the Freshman Members

The work of the party committees is not over after a successful campaign. In fact, the campaign committees never rest. Immediately after the election, they work to persuade the congressional party leadership to give newly elected members from marginal districts plum committee assignments and help with finding someone to run their congressional office. Many new members have few Washington connections. And running a House or Senate office is nothing like running a state legislative office—or almost anything else, for that matter! The newly elected officials need to be able to hit the ground running because their constituents are going to be in touch from day one. Coping with the thousands of requests, e-mails, and letters that come in every week is no easy task.

Republican leaders, when they were in control of Congress in the 1990s and the first decade of this century, did everything they could to help their freshman members bring home tangible legislative achievements to aid in their reelection efforts. Newt Gingrich, the Republican speaker from 1995 to 1998, gave some new members exclusive committee assignments, and nearly all were rewarded with earmarked federal funding in their districts. Party leaders knew that their majority depended on the success of the freshmen.

When Democrats took over in 2007, their leadership took the unusual step of giving freshmen members subcommittee chairs—especially those who had been elected from districts that had historically gone Republican. In this way, the freshmen could influence legislation and demonstrate their effectiveness to their constituents right away. Speaker John Boehner continued this trend following the 2010 election and offered seats on the Appropriations Committee to a couple of newly elected Republicans that are usually reserved for much more experienced members.

These tactics are important because members are most vulnerable the first time they run for reelection. The opposing party is watching every move of the freshmen for missteps. New members not only must deliver the goods to their district but also need to spend time building up a war chest of campaign funds for the next cycle. If they stumble in either of these areas, look out! Elections expert Charles Mahtesian of *Politico* says that the parties' campaign committees are like lions tracking a herd of antelope. They look intently for the weaker members of the herd—usually from among the freshmen—to pick off.[14] They target the vulnerable ones and put the party machinery behind carefully selected challengers. In this way, the parties can add to their numbers in the next Congress and either solidify their majority or, if they are in the minority, make progress toward regaining control of the House or Senate.

# THE GEOGRAPHICAL CONTEXT OF CONGRESSIONAL ELECTIONS

## House Apportionment

In Article 1, Section 2, the Constitution mandates that a census of the population be taken every 10 years for the purpose of determining the allocation, or **apportionment**, of House seats. Following the first census in 1790, the number of House seats was set at 105, with each House member representing a constituency of approximately 33,000. As the population grew and new states were added, House membership increased. After the 1910 census, House members agreed to cap the number of seats at 435. In 2009 Congress considered legislation to add two seats— one for Utah and one for the District of Columbia. This was highly controversial, since the Constitution seems to limit voting membership in the House to the states. (The District of Columbia, Puerto Rico, Guam, the Virgin Islands, the Northern Mariana Islands, and American Samoa each send a nonvoting member to the House.) In general, attempts to increase membership beyond the states have been met with strong resistance. Some members have argued that a larger body would probably hinder legislative productivity, and no doubt there is also concern that a larger membership would only further dilute the power of individual members.

Today congressional districts average about 720,000 people. Every 10 years, the US Commerce Department's Bureau of the Census collects population data, and that information is used to reapportion the House's 435 seats among the 50 states. As the nation's population shifts, states may lose or gain House seats. The "method of equal proportions" is used to calculate how many seats each state is awarded once each state's population is determined.[15]

This system for allocating House seats was the result of a decade's worth of congressional debate and is designed to make the proportional differences between districts as small as possible.[16] The Constitution entitles each state to at least one representative, but districts are not always equal because of population disparities between the states. For example, Wyoming's entire population is about 500,000, so its single district is the least populous. Montana has a population of approximately 1 million, making its single district the most populous. It does not qualify for a second seat.

The politics of determining state population has in recent decades been a matter of considerable controversy. Members of Congress, as well as state and local officials, want the Census Bureau's population count to be as accurate as possible because the numbers are used not only for reapportionment but also for allocating federal aid for many government programs. However, counting the population is a massive, logistically challenging task. The homeless, people who rent, and the poor are typically undercounted because they are often difficult to locate. Critics of the Census Bureau's methodology argue that statistical adjustments should be made to correct for undercounting. The Supreme Court, however, has rejected using statistical projections to adjust the census figures and instead requires what amounts to a head count of the population.[17]

## House Districting

Every 10 years, after the census is taken and House seats are reapportioned, it is the individual state's job to reconfigure congressional districts. In 1964 the Supreme Court applied the "one-person-one-vote" principle to congressional districts and held that district populations must be roughly equal within the states.[18] Prior to 1964, district populations had varied enormously in size. For some states, these variances resulted when the state's population shifted internally (for example, people moved from the state's rural areas to the state's urban centers), but congressional district lines remained static. More often, however, the failure to adjust district lines in response to population shifts was quite intentional. Entrenched political interests associated with rural areas were intent on maintaining their power at the expense of urban centers.

The Court determined that unless all congressional districts have about the same number of people in them, one person's vote in one district may be worth more (or less) than one person's vote in another district. *Malapportionment*, as the justices called it, violates the constitutional principle requiring that representation in the House be apportioned according to population.

Although the Court's actions have nearly equalized each citizen's voting influence in the House, they have in some ways reinforced the political disconnect between citizens and their representatives. Rather than draw district lines in ways that encompass natural political communities, district mapmakers may cut across city and county lines to ensure that the district conforms to the "one-person-one-vote" principle. Some congressional districts thus become strange geographical conglomerations whose constituents have little in common, and members representing these districts can have a hard time communicating a coherent campaign message as they attempt to reach different constituencies within the district. Sometimes the sheer size of a district makes campaigning and constituent service extremely taxing. One former chief of staff reported that she drove as much as 1,200 miles in a long weekend attending events with or on behalf of her boss, the congressman.[19]

## The Politics of Redistricting

The **redistricting** process is handled in most states by the state legislature in the regular legislative process, and it normally requires the sign-off of the governor. But 14 states have turned the job over to nonpartisan boards or commissions. Even in those states, the elected politicians have to ratify the decision.

The party that controls the state legislature after the census is conducted initiates the redistricting for the US House seats. The new district lines usually hold for 10 years until after the next census is taken, although a high-profile exception occurred in Texas in 2003–2004.[20] The events surrounding the middecade redistricting in that state are described in Box 4.1. It matters a great deal in most states which party controls the state legislature and the governor's office in the year after the census, because they are the ones who determine the district lines. As a result, every 10 years, toward the end of a decade, both parties invest large sums of money in state legislative races and gubernatorial campaigns with the hope of controlling the redistricting process.

When states lose a seat or more in the reapportionment process after the census, **incumbent** members of the House get very jittery. Invariably, the new districts have to pit two incumbents against one another. For this reason, the number of members retiring from Congress tends to spike at the beginning of each decade. One of the most competitive—and most expensive—House races in 2012 pitted two Democratic incumbents against each other. California Representatives Brad Sherman and Howard Berman were drawn into the same congressional district following the 2010 redistricting cycle. The 2012 primaries were the first to take place under California's new nonpartisan, or "jungle," primary system. The new format sends the top two vote getters—regardless of party—to compete in the general election. Because Sherman and Berman took the top two spots in the primary, they faced off in November. Berman, who served 30 years in the House, lost to Sherman, who is now serving his ninth term. The two candidates spent a combined total of about $12 million fighting over who would represent California's 30th District.

## Partisan Gerrymandering

The practice of drawing district lines in ways that benefit certain individuals or groups is known as **gerrymandering**. The term originated in 1812, when the Massachusetts state legislature created a district that was shaped like a salamander.

# BOX 4.1
## Texts Redistricts Middecade

A recent exception to the redistrict-every-decade rule serves to illustrate the political stakes. Texas, a strongly Republican state in recent decades at least in terms of national politics, had, nonetheless, typically sent a majority of Democrats to Washington in their House delegation. This was partly due to the fact that Democrats were able to cling to a Democratic majority in at least one of the houses of the state's legislature. (The 1990 House districting had been established by a Democratic governor together with a Democratic legislature.)

In 2001, after the census, the Republican governor, Rick Perry, and the Democratic legislature were unable to come to a redistricting agreement. Ultimately, a federal court redrew the lines, maintaining the districts much as they had been in the 1990s. On that basis, Democrats won 17 seats to the Republicans' 15 in the 2002 elections.

But those elections brought Republican majority control to both houses of the state legislature, and Governor Perry secured a full term as well. (Perry had been the lieutenant governor under George W. Bush, taking the top job in 2000 after Bush was elected president.) Spearheaded by then–US House majority leader Tom DeLay, Republicans attempted to redraw the lines middecade for the 2004 election cycle.

This was not done without controversy. Democrats in the state senate went to great lengths—actually holing themselves up in another state in order to avoid capture by authorities—to deny Republicans a quorum and the ability to act in that chamber. DeLay was accused of various abuses in the matter, including illegal campaign contributions and intimidation of federal officials. In the end, Republicans gained that quorum and prevailed, although court challenges to the redistricting plan dragged on into 2006. The results were good for the majority. The Texas delegation to the House was 21–11 Republicans after the 2004 election, a gain of six seats for the party.*

Why don't states engage in middecade redistricting more often? After all, if the party control of the state legislature and the governor changes, as sometimes happen, why not engineer more seats for your party in Congress? The reason is that redistricting is a very labor-intensive and controversial task. Most legislatures meet for limited periods of time in a given year—many states consider legislative seats only part-time positions and pay accordingly. There is always plenty of pressing business on education, health, transportation, and other issues. There simply isn't the will or the time to revisit the House district lines. The legislatures normally act only when they have to, which is after the census.

---

*Charles Lane and Dan Balz, "Justices Affirm GOP Map for Texas." *Washington Post*, June 29, 2006, A1; "Republicans Take Four of Five Targeted Democratic Seats," USAtoday.com, November 2, 2004, www.usatoday.com/news/politicselections/vote2004/2004–11–02-tx-ushouse-redistricting_x.htm.

Elbridge Gerry was governor of Massachusetts at the time, so the salamander-shaped district (of which he approved) soon became known as a "gerrymander." Today the term *gerrymander* is used to describe the practice of drawing districts to benefit incumbents, political parties, or racial and ethnic minorities.

When the party in control of the state legislature wants to create districts that maximize the chances of its candidates winning, it can either *pack* the opposing party's supporters into as few districts as possible or *crack* the opposing party's supporters into a number of small clusters dispersed into more districts.

**Packing** minimizes the number of seats the minority party can win, while **cracking** disperses that party's supporters throughout the state. By packing the opposing party's supporters into a few districts, the controlling party ensures that its candidates will win by large, comfortable margins in most of the districts. Maryland's districts, as depicted in Figure 4.1, are a classic example of packing. Following the 2010 census, Democrats redrew the 6th District's boundary lines to favor their party. Republican representative Roscoe Bartlett represented the 6th District for ten terms before losing to Democrat John Delaney in the 2012 election. Prior to the post-2010 census redraw, Republicans were packed into Districts 1 and 6, which gave Democrats the advantage in Districts 2 through 5, 7, and 8. In 2008 Democrats were able to overcome the Republican advantage in District 1 along Maryland's Eastern Shore by electing Frank Kratovil in an open-seat race. Kratovil, however, lost to Andy Harris in 2010; Harris is now the only Republican member of Maryland's congressional delegation.

The idea of cracking is to introduce competition into more districts, which can make winning elections more challenging for the controlling party's candidates. But if the majority party's candidates win under a cracking scheme, the party can often claim control of a greater number of the state's House seats.[21]

In 1986 the Supreme Court ruled that partisan gerrymandering could theoretically be egregious enough to violate the *equal protection clause* in the 14th Amendment.[22] As of this writing, the Court has not identified any gerrymandering arrangements that violate this principle. The Court even upheld the 2003 Texas redistricting scheme (see Box 4.1) that was engineered by former US representative Tom DeLay. The Court found that although the Republican-controlled Texas state legislature had acted "with the sole purpose of achieving a Republican majority," it had not, they said, gone *too* far. The question of how much partisanship is too much remains unresolved.[23]

## Sweetheart Gerrymandering

Sweetheart gerrymandering can be driven by partisan interests, but its main effect is the protection of incumbent members of the House regardless of party.

FIGURE 4.1. Maryland "Packs" Republican-Leaning Voters into District 1

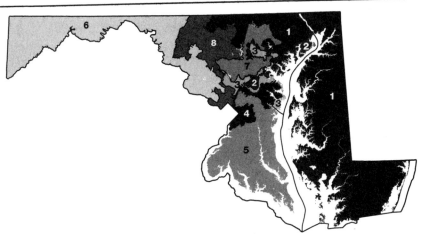

For example, many of the 2000 redistricting efforts across the country were aimed at protecting incumbents, and election results in 2002 and 2004 confirmed the success of this strategy. In the 2004 elections, for example, only 13 House seats switched parties, and only 7 incumbents lost in the general election. More than 85 percent of all House incumbents won with majorities greater than 60 percent—a whopping 20 points or more! California was the best case in point: not one of the 153 seats in the California state legislature or in its 53-seat US House delegation changed hands. And redistricting in 2010 had the cumulative effect of shoring up incumbents, according to Mike Maciag of *Governing*. Only about 64 of the 435 House races in 2012 were decided within a margin of ten percentage points; overall, only 7 seats shifted between the parties (from Republican to Democrat).[24]

The practice is quite common when divided government reigns at the state level. Like partisan gerrymanders, sweetheart gerrymanders may take unusual forms. Figure 4.2 depicts Illinois's 4th District, which is known as the "earmuff district" due to its shape. Created in the early 1990s, the district connects pockets of Hispanics on Chicago's North and South Sides with a strip of African Americans living on the perimeter of the 7th District. The district is a near lock for Democrats and was signed off on by then-governor George Ryan, a Republican. Democrats controlled the state legislature in the early 1990s, so the post-1990 redistricting process had to meet the approval of both parties. As a result, a number of safe districts were created for both parties. Following the 2010 census, Democrats controlled the state legislature, the governor's mansion, and therefore the redistricting process. Republicans challenged the Democratic redraw as unconstitutional, but

**FIGURE 4.2. Illinois's 4th District**

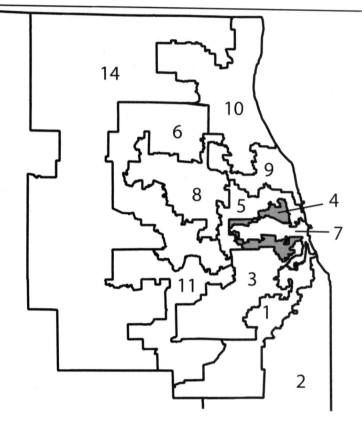

*Note:* Congressional districts in Chicago and vicinity.

the fact that they had accepted the 4th District gerrymander back in the 1990s made it difficult for them to protest the district's shape (which did not change).[25]

The egregious 2000 California gerrymander led Republican governor Arnold Schwarzenegger to respond by proposing that the responsibility for district mapmaking be turned over to a panel of retired judges in the state. Criticizing the system for its lack of accountability and competition, he asked, "What kind of democracy is this? The current system is rigged to benefit the interests of those in office and not those who put them there."[26] Schwarzenegger's proposal was placed on the ballot in a November 2005 special election but failed to win the support of voters.

Then in 2008, California voters approved Proposition 20, which gave a 14-person commission (the California Citizens Redistricting Commission) the authority to draw new boundaries for the state's 53 congressional districts. California thus became the first state to turn the redistricting process over to citizens. The commission created 11 new districts that contained two incumbents and one that contained three incumbents. New districts, combined with the state's new "jungle primary" system described earlier, made 2012 a particularly interesting year in California electoral politics. As a result of these changes, a number of members had to decide whether to stay put and fight for reelection, relocate, or retire. Californians elected 11 new members of Congress in 2012—more than one-fifth of its congressional delegation.

## Racial Gerrymandering

Redistricting in ways that deliberately dilute the vote of minority groups is forbidden by the Voting Rights Act of 1965 and its subsequent amendments. Beginning in 1980, the Supreme Court began to narrow the act's definition of what constitutes racially discriminatory intent in the drawing of district lines. In *Mobile v. Bolden* (1980), the Court held that the fact that an African American (or a person from another racial minority group) had never been elected under the particular system in question did not prove discriminatory intent. Congress responded by amending the Voting Rights Act to outlaw any practice that has the effect of discriminating, regardless of intent.

As a result, in 1986 the Court pivoted away from its *Mobile* decision and issued a ruling that required lawmakers to demonstrate that they had done all they could to maximize minority voting strength. In *Thornburg v. Gingles*, the Court determined that six of North Carolina's state legislative districts unlawfully diluted the voting strength of African Americans. Because few blacks had been elected from these districts, the Court reasoned that the system violated the law. The decision was widely interpreted to mean that mapmakers must design districts that include a majority of minorities wherever residence patterns make this even remotely possible.[27]

The 1990 census was followed by the creation of a number of "majority-minority" districts—districts in which the majority of the population was either black or Hispanic. As a result, in the 1992 elections African Americans gained 13 additional House seats and Latinos gained seven. But these newly created districts quickly came under scrutiny. North Carolina's Twelfth District, which patched together a number of heavily African American communities along Interstate 85 through the middle of the state, is perhaps the best known. It is shown as it was configured at the time in Figure 4.3.

The district was challenged in 1993 by five white North Carolinians who argued that it violated their right to equal protection under the law by diluting the strength of their votes. In *Shaw v. Reno*, the Supreme Court ruled that districts drawn for the purpose of enhancing minority representation might violate the constitutional rights of white voters. Three years later, in *Miller v. Johnson* (1995), the Court held

**FIGURE 4.3 North Carolina's Twelfth District**

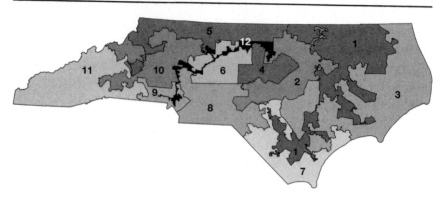

North Carolina's 12th District, as drawn in 1992 (depicted above) to improve the chances of an African-American getting elected, was ruled unconstitutional by the Supreme Court in1996. The district remains oddly shaped, snaking up Interstate 85 in the Piedmont region of the state.

that using race as the "predominant factor" in drawing districts is presumed to be unconstitutional unless there is evidence of a compelling government interest.

As one might expect, there was considerable confusion as to exactly what this meant. Throughout the 1990s, federal district courts responded to these decisions by ordering a number of states to redraw districts that were deemed unconstitutional racial gerrymanders. In 1999, just before the 2000 census, the Supreme Court heard another North Carolina case, *Hunt v. Cromartie,* and ruled that mapmakers could use race as a factor in drawing district lines if the primary motive was to achieve greater partisan balance rather than to ensure the election of a black or Hispanic representative.[28] The Court provided some clarification in *Bartlett v. Strickland* (2009), saying that legislatures did not have to go to great lengths to enhance the chances of a district electing a minority candidate if the minority population was below 50 percent.

Ironically, as a number of scholars have noted, while minorities elected in these districts have always been Democrats, the overall effect of packing African Americans or Hispanics may have been to increase the number of seats held by Republicans in the affected states. There is considerable disagreement, however, over the extent to which this is the case.[29]

## Senate "Districts"

The question of reapportionment does not arise in the US Senate because senators represent states with fixed boundaries. As we have seen, as part of the Great Compromise, the framers decided that seats in the House would be awarded by population and Senate seats would be awarded in accordance with the principle of equal representation—two seats per state.

The principle of "one-person-one-vote" simply does not apply in Senate representation. As political scientist Gary Jacobson has noted: "The nine largest states are home to 51 percent of the population but elect only 18 percent of the Senate; the smallest 26 states control 52 percent of the Senate, but hold only 18 percent of the population."[30] In effect, the votes of those who reside in populous states count for less than the votes of those who live in less populous states. A senator from California represents about 72 times more people than a senator from Wyoming.

* * *

While the parties put a great deal of effort into recruiting candidates who fit particular districts, at the same time they try to create districts that maximize their chances of winning seats. Partisan gerrymandering in particular helps the parties craft districts that are safe for their incumbents or that better fit their candidates.

In House districting, parties are pulled in two directions: on the one hand, the incumbent members of the House usually push the state legislatures hard for sweetheart arrangements that will make reelection easier for them; on the other hand, party leaders sometimes push "cracking" strategies to put more seats in play, with the hope of electing more members of their party to the House—even though those strategies may make life a little more difficult for some incumbents. It is interesting to note that Majority Leader DeLay's aggressive middecade redistricting plan was a classic and successful effort at cracking. (Republicans picked up six Texas seats in 2004.) He even put his own seat in jeopardy in order to put more conservative voters in neighboring districts to make them more Republican friendly. After his retirement in 2006, his district was held for one term by a Democrat.

## THE INCUMBENCY ADVANTAGE

Upon taking office, members of the House and senators immediately begin to accrue the considerable advantages of incumbency that contribute to high reelection rates. Not the least of those advantages is their effective participation as members of Congress. As we have already seen, members pass legislation and conduct oversight in ways that benefit their districts or states—funneling funds to specific needs and keeping agencies that deliver services to their constituents on their toes. It is only natural that incumbents highlight their accomplishments in Washington when they run for reelection.

Congressional scholar David Mayhew claims, "If a group of planners sat down and tried to design a pair of national assemblies with the goal of serving members' reelection needs year in and year out, they would be hard pressed to improve on what exists."[31] Indeed, members of Congress have significant advantages over those who challenge them for their seats. Generally speaking, these advantages can be broken down into two categories: institutional and political.[32]

## Institutional Advantages

As we saw in Chapter 3, members strive to get on committees that address the needs and interests of their constituents. The committees are where most of the detailed legislative work and oversight of government programs is done; effective members are able to get provisions into legislation that help back home. The key is to be able to plausibly take credit, for instance, for a tax break that enables more people to afford community college, or for funding to refurbish a levee that yields hundreds of jobs, or for a research grant for a new lab at the local university.

A typical tactic might be for a member to introduce a specific, limited bill to rebuild the levee system on a river in his district, and then, through his membership on the Transportation and Infrastructure Committee, making sure his idea is included in a much larger public works bill. The small bill itself probably would never go anywhere, but the larger bill has so many other similar projects that it will have broad support in the chamber. In this way, the member can point to a discrete bill with his name on it and, most important, deliver the goods.

All is not lost, however, if the member does not happen to serve on the committee that deals with the area of policy affecting his district or state. A member who serves on the Agriculture Committee is in a position to bargain with a member who serves on Armed Services. Members build alliances with their colleagues—there are always members on Armed Services who have farming interests in their districts, just as there are always members on Agriculture who have naval installations or air force bases back home. Once members show that they are effective legislators, they can become part of the deal making that can be used to their district's advantage. The bottom line in Washington is that committee work—the more powerful the committee, the better—is a member's key to being able to show constituents that he or she is effective.

Incumbents also benefit from an array of institutional resources. House members serving in the 112th Congress received an annual members' representational allowance (MRA) of approximately $1.4 million. Senators receive substantially more than House members; as noted in the last chapter, their allocations vary in relation to the population of the state they represent. The MRA is used to cover all of the office's non-campaign-related operating expenses, including staff and member salaries; equipment such as computers, fax machines, printers, and smartphones; the rent on district office space; and member and staff travel to the district. Although MRA funds cannot be used for campaign-related expenses, members obviously benefit electorally from having staff who respond to constituent requests and work on policy issues that matter to the district or state.

They also benefit from having the technical resources necessary to stay in constant touch with constituents. Both chambers have facilities where members can tape radio and television messages free of charge. Members also maintain interactive websites, and many have Facebook pages and Twitter accounts.

Members also benefit from the **franking** privilege, which allows them to send mailings to their constituents using their signatures (the "frank") instead of stamps. The frank is intended to provide members with a way to communicate legislative information to their constituents, but it also aids members in their reelection efforts. The essential point is that members do everything they can to connect their legislative work in Washington to the people back home. Most members use the frank to blanket their districts with newsletters or to send targeted information to specific groups, such as senior citizens, persons living in particular communities or neighborhoods, or constituents who have shown an interest in specific issues—the environment, deregulation, or other things.

Critics of the frank argue that it gives members a free way to advertise their work and to reach out to constituents, and there is undoubtedly some truth to the charge. Members maintain that they have a duty to apprise the people who sent them to Washington of their legislative and oversight activities. But the law does forbid them from directly soliciting political support with these mailings, and they cannot send mass mailings in the 90 days preceding an election.

Political scientist Morris Fiorina has argued that incumbents gain an advantage not only by advertising themselves but also by creating needs among their constituents, then catering to those needs. When Congress increased the size and scope of the federal government in the decades following World War II, it also created demand from citizens who wanted to take advantage of various federal programs. Members responded to this demand by expanding staff and increasing their capacity to communicate and work with constituents.[33] Today most—if not all—members believe that good constituency service is the key to getting reelected.

## Political Advantages

As previously discussed, most states give the job of congressional redistricting to the state legislature. This process frequently is deployed to protect incumbents.

When districts have to be substantially redrawn based on population shifts, the job of drawing safe-incumbent districts becomes more challenging. Running in such a district can present challenges for incumbents, as sometimes the member will find him- or herself with mostly new constituents. Nonetheless, incumbents almost always benefit from higher name recognition, a record of constituency service, and the adroit use of the board-of-directors powers to deliver projects to their districts and states as compared to a relatively inexperienced challenger.

When a state loses a district, the situation gets trickier. The competition is almost always extremely intense when two incumbents are pitted against one another. Such was the case in Iowa in 2012 after Republican Tom Latham and Democrat Leonard Boswell found themselves in the same district after the state lost a seat after the census. Latham ultimately prevailed after a hard-fought and expensive race.

Incumbent candidates are usually the ones who benefit from the various campaign services available to them through the parties' congressional campaign committees. Although all incumbents are entitled to baseline services from their party's congressional committees (policy talking points and campaign advertising templates, for example), at-risk incumbents are also provided with fundraising, advertising, and campaign staff assistance. At a minimum, congressional parties want to hold all of the seats they control in the chamber; providing campaign support for at-risk incumbents naturally is central to this goal.

Constituent voting behavior also tends to favor incumbent candidates. Voters are often criticized for their inattentiveness to the issues of the day and their inability sometimes to identify the major party candidates running for federal office. Data show that a sizable number of voters, especially in House races, recognize the name of only one candidate on the ballot—the incumbent. Presumably, they are thus more likely to vote for the incumbent.[34] But there is logic to keeping a House member or senator in office. Experienced incumbents, regardless of party or their position on hot-button issues, are more likely to be able to deliver tangible benefits in the form of federal dollars for their constituencies than a newcomer would be. A voter may be viewed as fully rational in supporting an incumbent, even when the voter is not of the same party or disagrees with the incumbent on some issues. An argument can be made that often even a scandal-plagued member would serve his or her district better than a newcomer.

## The Incumbency Advantage: The Bottom Line

Perhaps incumbents' most important advantage is the ability to discourage challengers from running. The bottom line is that incumbents are tremendously difficult to defeat. The average House incumbent reelection rate has been around 93 percent over the past six decades. The average reelection rate for incumbent senators has been about 80 percent in that time period.

Even in 2010, when majority control of the House switched from Democratic to Republican, 85 percent of all House incumbents won reelection. In 2012

**FIGURE 4.4. US House Reelection Rates, 1964–2012**

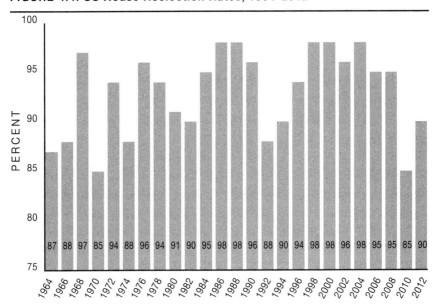

Republicans maintained control of the House, and incumbents were reelected at a 90 percent rate. Figure 4.4 shows the reelection rates of members of Congress.

These statistics confirm that challenging an incumbent is a daunting task that most potential challengers choose not to attempt. Almost all incumbents begin their general election campaigns with higher name recognition, more political experience, more money, and a better campaign organization than their challengers. They also benefit from the mere fact that constituents and political elites expect them to win.[35] These expectations influence media coverage of the campaign, donor contribution decisions (most donors want to give money to a winner), the likelihood of attracting campaign volunteers, and ultimately voter support.

## FINANCING THE CAMPAIGN

One of the most important—if not *the* most important—advantages that incumbents have over their nonincumbent challengers is campaign money. As elected officials in charge of directing the work of government, incumbents are positioned to help not only their constituents but also any interests that have policy concerns in their committees' jurisdictions. Their ability to attract campaign contributions is based in large measure on the influence they have in the legislative process and in their dealings with federal agencies.

For example, constituents are more likely to contribute to an incumbent who helped them secure Social Security benefits for their parents than to an unfamiliar challenger who has done nothing for them. Likewise, a trade association that worked closely with an incumbent to secure a policy that benefits association members is more likely to contribute to the incumbent than to his or her challenger. Giving money to a challenger is a speculative venture; the incumbent is more of a sure thing.

Put simply, incumbents are often rewarded financially through campaign contributions for the work they do in Congress. By constantly emphasizing their legislative and oversight powers, incumbents remind contributors (and potential contributors) of the power they exercise over the authorization, appropriations, and oversight processes. People often view campaign fundraising as little more than candidates begging for money from interest groups and citizens. But there is another side to it: incumbents are not shy about reminding potential contributors of the power they wield, implicitly suggesting that access to them is not a given and that continued financial support for their campaigns would be appreciated.

## The Fundraising Burden

Nonincumbent candidates face an upward battle when it comes to raising campaign money. As suggested earlier, in many ways they represent the unknown, and most investors prefer security and predictability. The high rate at which incumbents are reelected also convinces many contributors that money given to a challenger is money wasted.

In the 2012 elections, House incumbents raised an average of $1.6 million, while their challengers raised an average of $267,000. Senate incumbents raised an average of $11.8 million in 2012, while their challengers averaged $1.4 million.[36] But these numbers are deceptive. In an era when challengers going after more vulnerable incumbents are able to raise $1 million or more, House incumbents may have to raise two or three times the average in order to deter strong potential opposition. And the sky's the limit in potentially competitive Senate races.

Running for office requires that candidates campaign for both money and votes. As can be seen in Box 4.2, campaigns are complex and expensive undertakings; without money, candidates cannot pay for campaign staff, advertising, polling, consultants, direct mail, transportation, and various other campaign expenses. Independently wealthy candidates may choose to foot the bill for their own campaigns, but most candidates do not have that luxury.[37] (Campaign operatives report that independently wealthy candidates are often less successful than people think, usually because they prove unable to generate support among party activists who provide the crucial volunteer services that are necessary for a winning campaign.) Instead, they must spend countless hours on the phone, dialing for dollars. Representative David Price (D-NC) confesses that the cost of running for office the first time drove him and his wife to "shed our inhibitions and contact our Christmas card lists from years past, our professional colleagues at home and across the country, and far-flung family members." Price adds that he and his wife then did something they had said they would never do—they took out a $45,000 second mortgage on their home.[38]

## Reforming Campaign Financing: The New Rules

In 1974 Congress overhauled federal campaign finance laws in response to public outrage over recent scandals and the lack of strict reporting requirements and meaningful enforcement of the existing law. The **Federal Elections Campaign Act (FECA)** placed limits on campaign contributions and expenditures by individuals and groups, made political action committees legal, and created the Federal Elections Commission (FEC) to enforce the law.

About two months after FECA was enacted, its constitutionality was challenged in court. In *Buckley v. Valeo* (1976), the Supreme Court upheld the act's limits on contributions, but found its restrictions on total campaign expenditures unconstitutional. Limits on contributions were justified, according to the Court, because such limits prevented the appearance (and potentially the reality) of corruption. But limits on campaign expenditures, according to the Court, violated candidates' right to free speech guaranteed in the First Amendment. In effect, the Court said that by limiting how much money candidates could spend on their campaigns, the act also limited candidates' ability to express themselves. Congress responded to the Court's decision in 1976 by amending the portions of the act deemed unconstitutional.

Congress continued to tinker with federal campaign finance laws but did not pass another major reform package for almost three decades. The Bipartisan Campaign Reform Act (BCRA) of 2002, sometimes called "McCain-Feingold" owing to the sponsorship of Senators John McCain (R-AZ) and Russ Feingold (D-WI), was Congress's most recent attempt to regulate the money spent on federal elections. The act's central goals were to ban national parties and congressional campaign committees from raising and spending so-called soft money and to prevent outside groups from running issue ads before election day that mention candidates by name ("electioneering communications").[39]

Soft-money contributions—sometimes called nonfederal contributions—had not been subject to FECA restrictions. People could give any amount to the parties,

## BOX 4.2
### What Does a Congressional Campaign Look Like?

Challenging an incumbent, with all the institutional and political advantages they have, is no easy task for an aspiring politician. What some people don't realize is that setting up a political campaign is a lot like setting up a small business. Probably the biggest obstacle comes in the form of a very problematic catch-22: it is difficult for challengers to convince people to give them money for a likely doomed effort to take down an incumbent, while it takes a great deal of start-up money for a campaign to establish its credibility.

There is no one-size-fits-all campaign organization for either House or Senate races, because there is no one-size-fits-all district or state. Even though House districts all have about 700,000 people in them, they vary dramatically, from districts that cover all or nearly all of an entire rural state (the Third District of Nebraska covers most of the territory of the state and consists entirely of small towns) to suburban districts to compact districts in densely populated cities. What works for a campaign in Nebraska or Iowa is not going to work in Orlando, Florida, or northern New Jersey.

A competitive House race (there may be only 50 or fewer of these in a typical election cycle) may require a couple of hundred thousand dollars or more to start up. The campaign is typically going to need anywhere from four to eight paid staff—occasionally House campaigns will hire as many as ten staff. The *campaign manager* is the number-one person; the other two essential jobs are *finance director* and *field director*. The finance director heads the fundraising effort and will typically take on the duty of treasurer and also ensure that the campaign abides by federal guidelines in disclosing its contributions. The field director organizes the work in the district to contact voters, distribute campaign information, organize volunteers, and the like. In today's campaigns, an important part of the field director's job is done with social media.*

Additional paid staff in a rural or small-town district will likely include deputy field directors or, possibly, a press secretary. (Usually, one of the top three paid staff will double as press secretary.) Fieldwork is crucial in rural areas, because people tend to expect personal contact and because there is often no major media market.

In a typical House campaign, the candidate will rely heavily on unpaid informal advisors—a kind of "kitchen cabinet." These will be old hands knowledgeable about the district and, especially, people who have good fundraising networks. Most campaigns depend on local campaign contributions, but some

*See Robert Draper's "Can the Republicans Be Saved from Obsolescence?" in the February 14, 2013, *New York Times Magazine* for a discussion of some of the changes in campaigns due to heavy reliance on new media.

BOX 4.2 *(Continued)*

## What Does a Congressional Campaign Look Like?

candidates may, due to particular personal attributes, be able to tap into broader national sources of campaign cash. For example, a trial lawyer, a real estate agent, or a doctor may be able to make appeals through trade associations. A strong environmentalist may tap into national groups promoting those issues.

In addition, volunteers are crucial to almost every House campaign. Usually, candidates rely on volunteer help for scheduling, driving, managing the office, and canvassing. Candidates have to have the ability to inspire the sort of commitment required to get people to work for a cause for no pay.

There is still more to be done, much of which will need to be contracted out. Web page work as well as advertising and polling will often be done by outside firms. The urban or suburban district will often necessitate a great deal of money for advertising due to more expensive television time. Sometimes obtaining and analyzing voter lists will be handled by a consultant, although this depends on the experience of the campaign manager and others in the campaign.

For Senate races, depending on the state, paid staff will range from 10 all the way up to 50 people for the most populous states. The Senate campaign staff is an expanded version of the House campaign, with more paid people in the field, more paid people working on finance, and usually a paid communications director or press secretary. (There is normally much more media attention given to Senate races.) The need for outside expertise in the form of strategic and media consultants is usually greater, too. Social media outreach and organizing will be an even bigger undertaking than in the House campaigns.

For House races, it may be necessary to begin gearing up shortly after the last election. Some campaigns will start 20 months before election day, others closer to a year. The difference may come down to whether a candidate anticipates a primary election to determine his or her party's nominee. If so, an early start is crucial. Even if the candidate is home free to the general election, it may be necessary to begin building the campaign early if name recognition is a problem in major parts of the district, as it usually is in a House race.

For Senate races, the fundraising efforts will almost always have to begin much earlier. Building a statewide organization is also a painstaking task. Successful Senate challengers often begin organizing three or more years before the election.[†]

[†]The bulk of this box is drawn from an interview with Jonathan Degner, Democratic Party operative, September 25, 2008.

and many wealthy people had given tens or hundreds of thousands of dollars—a few even gave millions. These contributions were meant to be used only for so-called party-building activities (getting out the vote for the whole ticket, registration drives, infrastructure, and so on) rather than for the purpose of supporting particular candidates. But the practice of soliciting soft-money donations became controversial after the 1996 election when both parties exploited a gray area in the law in a big way. They used soft-money funds to pay for advertising that seemed clearly to benefit specific candidates rather than for promoting the party ticket more broadly. Compounding the problem, President Clinton was found to have been particularly aggressive in courting soft-money donors with deep pockets, having invited some to stay the night in the White House's Lincoln Bedroom. The practice appeared unseemly. BCRA ended the solicitation by the parties of big-money donors; the parties would instead have to rely on regulated contributions in much smaller amounts.

A 2010 Supreme Court case, ***Citizens United v. Federal Elections Commission***, took aim at the "electioneering communications" provision in BCRA. In 2008 Citizens United, a conservative nonprofit group, funded and filmed an anti–Hillary Clinton video. (Clinton was a candidate for the Democratic presidential nomination that year.) Citizens United deliberately paid for *Hillary: The Movie* with general treasury funds and ran the video within thirty days of a Democratic primary so that the violation would serve as a test case. In arguments before the Supreme Court, the FEC held that the video was a form of electioneering communications, while Citizens United claimed that it was a form of free speech.

In a 5–4 decision, the Court struck down the electioneering communications provisions of BCRA, thereby allowing corporations and unions to use their treasury funds to pay for independent expenditures and issue advocacy. As a result, corporations and unions can legally spend unlimited amounts of money on behalf of federal candidates, as long as they do not coordinate their efforts with candidate campaigns.[40]

The contribution limits set by BCRA, however, have not been challenged. The law doubled and indexed to inflation contribution limits for individuals (the limits had not been adjusted for inflation since the 1970s) and placed new limits on individual contributions to national, state, and local party committees. Table 4.2 lists the federal contribution limits for the 2013–2014 election cycle.

Candidates for federal office must fully disclose to the FEC the sources of their campaign contributions. The national party committees and federally registered PACs also must report to the FEC the sources of their contributions. The FEC makes this information available to the public through its website.

**TABLE 4.2 Federal Contribution Limits, 2013–2014**

| | To Each Candidate or Candidate Committee per Election | To National Party Committee per Calendar Year | To State, District, and Local Party Committee per Calendar Year | To Any Other Political Committee per Calendar Year[a] | Special Limits |
|---|---|---|---|---|---|
| Individual may give | $2,600[b] | $32,400[b] | $10,000 (combined limit) | $5,000 | $123,200[b] overall biennial limit: $48,600[b] to all candidates $74,600[b] to all PACs and parties[c] |
| National party committee may give | $5,000 | No limit | No limit | $5,000 | $45,400[b] to Senate candidate per campaign[d] |
| State, district, and local party committee may give | $5,000 (combined limit) | No limit | No limit | $5,000 (combined limit) | No limit |
| PAC (multicandidate)[e] may give | $5,000 | $15,000 | $5,000 (combined limit) | $5,000 | No limit |
| PAC (not multicandidate) may give | $2,600[b] | $32,400[b] | $10,000 (combined limit) | $5,000 | No limit |
| Authorized campaign committee may give | $2,000[f] | No limit | No limit | $5,000 | No limit |

*Source:* Federal Elections Commission.

[a] A contribution earmarked for a candidate through a political committee counts against the original contributor's limit for that candidate. In certain circumstances, the contribution may also count against the contributor's limit to the PAC. 11 CFR 110.6. See also 11 CFR 110.1(h).

[b] These contribution limits are indexed for inflation.

[c] No more than $48,600 of this amount may be contributed to state and local party committees and PACs.

[d] This limit is shared by the national committee and the national Senate campaign committee.

[e] A multicandidate committee is a political committee with more than fifty contributors that has been registered for at least six months and, with the exception of state party committees, has made contributions to five or more candidates for federal office. 11 CFR 100.5(e)(3).

[f] A federal candidate's authorized committee(s) may contribute no more than $2,000 per election to another federal candidate's authorized committee(s). 11 CFR 102.12(c)(2).

## Political Action Committees

Federal law prevents corporations, federal contractors, and labor unions from contributing money directly from their treasuries to candidates. These groups can, however, encourage their employees, stockholders, or members to support particular candidates. They can also engage in independent spending and recommend the election or defeat of particular candidates, as long as they do not coordinate their efforts with candidate campaigns.

More commonly, these groups participate in the electoral process by forming **political action committees**. A PAC is best understood as the electoral arm of a corporation, labor union, interest group, or some other organized entity.[41] Although federal law prohibits these groups from giving directly from their treasuries to candidates, it allows them to establish separate, segregated accounts from which campaign contributions and other political expenditures can be made. PACs can solicit contributions from individuals affiliated with the sponsoring organization, then make contributions to political candidates. For example, a corporation cannot give directly to political candidates, but its PAC may do so. The important thing is that PACs rely on *voluntary* contributions from the organization's membership, employees, or supporters. It is against federal law to compel employees to give to the PAC.

Beginning in 1974, PACs were required to register with the FEC and report their receipts and contributions. There were 89 corporate PACs in 1974, 201 labor PACs, and trade association, membership, and health care industry PACs totaled 318. As of 2009, the FEC counted 1,598 corporate PACs, 272 labor PACs, and 995 trade association, membership, and health care PACs. Overall, there were 4,611 PACs registered with the FEC that year. PACs contribute to candidates for a variety of reasons, including partisanship, ideology, incumbent voting records, and influence in the House or Senate. The candidates to whom PACs contribute vary in accordance with a given PAC's political and policy goals.

PAC contributions, contrary to popular belief, are not primarily intended to sway members' votes on the floor or influence their legislative work, although it is certainly helpful to give to an open-minded member of Congress, since a contribution may give an organization the opportunity to make its case. More commonly, such contributions are made to help keep like-minded legislators in office (or to help a like-minded challenger get elected).

Members know that adding a provision to a bill that benefits a contributor and has no connection to their constituency can generate very bad publicity and may in some circumstances even violate the law. Congressman Don Young of Alaska did just that with a provision in a 2006 transportation bill that aided the interests of a Florida-based campaign contributor. (The so-called Coconut Road earmark was actually added to the bill *after it passed the House and Senate* and before it appeared on President Bush's desk. Young acknowledged this irregular process, contending that the earmarked addition was a correction.)[42] This incident was front-page news, put Young's seat in jeopardy, and led to a congressional ethics investigation.

Political action committees can give up to $5,000 per candidate, per election. For this reason, their contributions are especially attractive to House incumbents, who have to run for office every two years. During the 2012 election cycle, House members collected 40 percent of their total contributions from PACs, while their Senate counterparts took in 22 percent of their total contributions from PACs, according to the Center for Responsive Politics. FEC data show that total PAC contributions to all congressional candidates topped $433 million in the 2012 election cycle. Political action committees can also bundle contributions from supporters, then present them all together to candidates. (Individuals may do this as well.)[43] This strategy can help PACs show their clout and gain influence with the candidates they favor.

**Leadership PACs,** which are established by politicians (independent of their campaign committees), are a form of the traditional political action committee. Like other PACs, leadership PACs can contribute up to $5,000 per candidate, per election. Funds can be used to pay for travel, political consultants, overhead, meals, and other activities that can benefit the member's political fortunes.

Members use their leadership PACs to give money to their colleagues, to candidates, and to their party committees. By "spreading the wealth," members can build support for their parties as well as their own ambitions. Those interested in pursuing positions in elected leadership, committee chairmanships, or higher office can gain support by giving generously. Senators and representatives who are contemplating a run for the presidency often use their leadership PAC money to travel in key presidential primary states on behalf of local candidates. Leadership PACs were relatively rare throughout the 1970s and 1980s. But by the mid-1990s, the number of registered leadership PACs began to expand as more rank-and-file members sought to increase their power and influence in the chamber. There were 54 registered leadership PACs in 1994, 86 in 1996, 338 in 2006, and 447 in 2012.[44] Leadership PACs contributed just over $43 million to federal candidates during the 2012 election cycle—$18 million more than they contributed to federal candidates 10 years earlier, in 2002, according to the Center for Responsive Politics.

## Super PACs and 501(c)(4) Groups

Shortly after the 2010 *Citizens United* decision, the US Court of Appeals for the District of Columbia issued a decision that legalized a new player in the campaign finance game: the super PAC. In *SpeechNow.org v. Federal Election Commission*, the court ruled that contributions to PACs that make only independent expenditures cannot be limited. Most PACs make direct contributions to candidates, party committees, and other PACs and can accept up to $5,000 per year from individuals, party committees, and other PACs. Super PACs can accept unlimited contributions from corporations, unions, and individuals, and then use that money to advocate on behalf of federal candidates. Like regular PACs, super PACs have to disclose their contributions and expenditures to the FEC. And because super PACs operate in the realm of independent expenditures, they cannot coordinate with candidate campaigns.

Super PACs are an extremely efficient campaign vehicle because there are no limits on what they can raise and spend. Some donors, however, are reluctant to give to a committee that is required to disclose all contributions. Fortunately for these donors, there are 501(c)(4) groups. The Internal Revenue Service, rather than the FEC, regulates these "nonprofit social welfare" groups, and they do not have to disclose donors. The IRS says these groups "must be operated exclusively to promote social welfare," but they are allowed to spend money on electioneering and lobbying activities, provided that is not their "primary activity."

Because 501(c)(4) groups can give unlimited amounts of money to super PACs, they in effect provide donors with a way to "launder" their contributions en route to super PACs. For this reason, contributions from these groups are often referred to as "shadow money" or "dark money" because the source of the money is not transparent. Republican operatives Karl Rove and Ed Gillespie, for example, founded American Crossroads, one of the wealthiest, most active super PACs in 2012 election. They also founded Crossroads Grassroots Policy Strategies, a 501(c)(4) that could (and did) contribute millions to their American Crossroads super PAC. But where GPS's money comes from is a mystery.[45] Similarly, on the Democratic side, the well-known super PAC MoveOn.org is supported by a 501(c)(4) called MoveOn.org Civic Action.

## Party Committees

We have seen how the four congressional campaign committees—the Democratic Congressional Campaign Committee, the Democratic Senatorial Campaign Committee, the National Republican Congressional Committee, and the National Republican Senatorial Committee—are involved in recruiting candidates for federal office. They, together with the national party bodies (the Democratic National Committee [DNC] and the Republican National Committee [RNC]), also assist congressional candidates in crucial ways during campaigns.

First, they *give money directly to candidates*. The two Democratic congressional campaign committees raised a total of $326 million for the 2012 election cycle, and their Republican counterparts raised just over $270 million.[46] The national and congressional party committees can give House candidates $5,000 per candidate, per election. The law currently allows the national and senatorial party committees to give Senate candidates a combined total of $45,400 per election cycle (see Table 4.2).

Increasingly, the congressional campaign committees have called on their own to give for the good of the whole. Both parties now require incumbents who are not in competitive races to pay dues to the committees—those filling a more prestigious committee chair (or even in some cases a subcommittee chair) or holding a ranking-member position may be assessed in the hundreds of thousands of dollars. For example, an Appropriations Committee subcommittee chair in the House is expected to give at least $250,000 to the DCCC for efforts in electing and reelecting more vulnerable Democrats. An exclusive committee chair can be assessed up to $500,000 per election cycle. The party committees set different fundraising targets for different members depending on factors like seniority and electoral vulnerability.[47]

Although this dues system is meant to encourage "team spirit," it also provides party leaders with a way to gauge member support for the party. Safe incumbents who do not "pay in" are much less likely to be rewarded with key committee assignments or other positions of power. These contributions are of the highest priority to the leadership of both parties and are considered a crucial component of a strategy to either maintain or gain power in the House or Senate.

Second, party committees can *make coordinated expenditures to pay for the campaign-related services, such as advertising, consultants, and polling,* requested by the candidate. When expenditures are coordinated, the candidate has a say in how the money is spent. For example, a candidate can request that the party committee purchase television airtime or pay for a series of polls. These expenditures, which can be made only during the general election, were capped at $45,600 for House candidates in the 2012 election cycle.[48] Party committees can coordinate with Senate candidates to spend two cents (adjusted for inflation) for every person of voting age in the state.

Third, the party committees may also make uncoordinated **independent expenditures (IEs)** on behalf of candidates. The committees can pay for campaign ads and direct mail, sponsor get-out-the-vote efforts, and underwrite phone banks. As long as they do not coordinate with the candidate—and that means no connection whatsoever between the party apparatus and the candidate's campaign—the parties can spend an unlimited amount in independent expenditures.

It is not uncommon for the party committees to spend $1 million or more on a competitive House race or many millions on a Senate campaign. In 2012 party committees spent more than $5 million on independent expenditures in each of 26

House races. And independent spending topped $20 million in at least six Senate races.[49] IEs usually consist of various forms of negative advertising (leaflets, television, radio, and so on). This is advantageous for the candidate for whom the effort is made, as he or she can plausibly deny any direct connection to the attacks made on the opposing party's candidate.

Often these independent efforts come in the form of massive infusions of money in the last two or three weeks of the campaign. The parties wait to see which of their challengers are gaining traction and which of their incumbents are losing ground. And then they pull the trigger. These crucial late-in-the-day decisions often determine winners or losers in tight races. Two weeks before election day in 2012, the party committees were dumping money into the too-close-to-call Virginia Senate race at a rate of about $9 million every seven days! And party spending in the tight race between Democrat Tammy Baldwin and Republican Tommy Thompson for a Wisconsin Senate seat topped $8 million per week in the final weeks of the campaign. Sometimes the party committees have been known to pull the plug when a candidate appears to be losing ground. The Republicans initially invested heavily in the 2012 Missouri Senate race of Representative Todd Akin, but as soon as he made a major gaffe and lost ground in his race against Democrat Claire McCaskill, the committees decided to redirect their money to other more competitive races.

Sometimes the party committees invest in campaigns against candidate wishes. When Senator Russ Feingold ran for reelection in 1998, the DSCC spent vast amounts of money in independent expenditures on his race. Feingold, who built his reputation in the US Senate on the issue of campaign finance reform—especially the importance of limiting money in politics—and other "good government" issues, strongly objected to the party's efforts on his behalf. He did not accept money from special interests, but the DSCC does; therefore, he did not want the committee's money being spent on his behalf. The committee was more concerned with holding his seat for the Democrats and chose to ignore his protests. Feingold went on to narrowly win reelection.

## Putting It All Together

Candidates have a number of sources they can turn to for campaign money, including individuals, political action committees, and party committees. It comes as a surprise to some people that most contributions to federal candidates come from individuals. As shown in Table 4.3, House Democrats and Republicans collected almost 60 percent of their total contributions from individuals in the 2010 election cycle. Senators amassed more than two-thirds of their total contributions from individuals.

**TABLE 4.3 Sources of Campaign Contributions to House and Senate Candidates, 2004–2010**

| | Average Contributions | PERCENTAGE OF CONTRIBUTIONS FROM | | | | |
| | | Individuals | Parties | PACs | Candidates | Unknown |
|---|---|---|---|---|---|---|
| **House** | | | | | | |
| 2004 | $766,752 | 57 | 0.6 | 36 | 4 | 3 |
| 2006 | $953,044 | 54 | 1.0 | 35 | 5 | 5 |
| 2008 | $1,031,148 | 54 | 0.02 | 34 | 7 | 5 |
| 2010 | $1,160,870 | 8 | 0.2 | 34 | 6 | 2 |
| **Senate** | | | | | | |
| 2004 | $5,418,860 | 76 | 0.6 | 17 | 4 | 2 |
| 2006 | $7,943,700 | 68 | 0.3 | 13 | 13 | 5 |
| 2008 | $5,698,551 | 64 | 0.02 | 20 | 5 | 11 |
| 2010 | $7,555,000 | 64 | 0.3 | 14 | 14 | 8 |

*Source:* Gary C. Jacobson, The Politics of Congressional Elections, 8th ed. (New York: Pearson Longman, 2013), 68–69 (drawn from FEC data).

Under current law, individuals can contribute up to $2,600 per candidate, per election. Candidates who run in both primary and general elections thus can collect up to $5,200 from individual contributors. The majority of individual contributors, however, do not "max out" their contributions to candidates but instead give in smaller amounts. Candidate campaign committees keep track of which contributors have maxed out and which have not; those who can legally give more are typically contacted by the campaign (often repeatedly!) and encouraged to give again.

Running a competitive campaign requires that candidates constantly be on the lookout for new sources of money and campaign assistance. With the brief two-year election cycle they face, many House members stay in an almost constant campaign mode. But senators, too, expend a great deal of time and effort on fundraising throughout their terms. Raising anywhere from $5 million to $20 million or more in small denominations, as most need to do, is no easy task. Most members view fundraising as a "necessary evil"—something they loathe but must do.

As the cost of running a viable campaign continues to climb, members devote more and more time to fundraising. More than anything else, the pressures of fundraising cut into the time that members can devote to their legislative and oversight work. We return to this critical issue in the chapter's conclusion.

## CAMPAIGN THEMES AND ISSUES

Many different factors influence the kind of campaign run by candidates for the House or Senate. When people decide to throw their hat into the ring, they presumably have a good sense of *why* they are running for office. Perhaps the candidate believes that the incumbent is doing a poor job, or that important issues are being ignored. Perhaps the candidate is driven by a sense of public duty or by personal ambition. Whatever the reasons, most candidates enter a campaign with a game plan for winning. The best-laid plans, however, can be shattered by unforeseen events. Scandal, a terrorist attack, skyrocketing gas prices, or local events can force candidates to adjust their message in midcampaign. Indeed, a campaign that encounters no unexpected bumps and bruises along the way is rare.

### Primary and General Elections

Primary campaigns tend to be quite different from general election campaigns. During the primaries, candidates of the same party are pitted against each other. Whoever wins the primary goes on to run in the general election against the opposing party's candidate.[50]

Election specialists have traditionally depicted the dynamics that shape elections in terms of a bell curve.[51] The middle of the curve represents the median voter—most voters, the theory goes, reside here—and the outer edges of the curve represent partisan, ideologically driven voters. This sort of configuration of the electorate is depicted in Figure 4.5. Voter turnout for primaries is typically low, and the people who do participate tend to be the party's "true believers" or "the base"—highly motivated partisans who have strong policy preferences. To win the primary, candidates must appeal to these voters. Conventional wisdom says that Democrats have to prove they are liberal enough, and Republicans have to prove they are conservative enough. As a result, primary candidates tend to campaign out on the edges of the bell curve. They frame their messages to appeal to primary voters, emphasizing their partisan credentials.

The bell-curve model presumes that candidates will moderate their messages in the general election to appeal to the largest proportion of voters—those who reside in the middle. Turnout rates are much higher in the general election, and a broader spectrum of voters participates. Candidates sometimes reframe their primary campaign messages accordingly, to attract moderate support. During the general campaign, the theory goes, candidates typically meet with more diverse groups of voters, expand the range of issues they discuss, and continually travel the district or state.

**FIGURE 4.5.** Median Voter Hypothesis

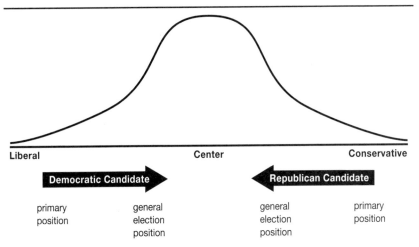

But to the extent that a House seat is safe for a particular party, appealing to the center of the political spectrum may not be necessary. Districts may have been gerrymandered to achieve one-party dominance. Or a district may be dominated by one party without gerrymandering, perhaps because it includes a contiguous group of counties or a city with generally like-minded voters. For example, Nebraska's Third District consists of most of the state's landmass and the lion's share of its counties. Nebraska 3 is strongly Republican. Most of California's Twelfth District is the city of San Francisco; its voters are overwhelmingly liberal and Democratic. The distribution of voters in these sorts of districts might look something like Figures 4.6 and 4.7.

Incumbents who hold seats from such districts tend to worry more about primaries than general elections. With a district heavily skewed to favor one party, that party's candidate almost always wins the general election. Surviving the primary, then, is often the key to reelection.

Although House incumbents do not want to offend moderate voters, if the primary is the only potential stumbling block in the path toward reelection, the incumbent needs to play only to the base. Democrats from overwhelmingly liberal districts discourage opposition in the primary by taking liberal issue positions down the line, just as Republicans from conservative districts are consistently and strongly conservative to achieve the same end.

In 2012 thirteen House members (six Republicans and seven Democrats) were defeated in primary elections. In most of these races, the incumbent candidate was challenged from the more ideological wings of the party. Representative Jean Schmidt (R-OH) was the first incumbent to lose a primary in 2012. Her opponent,

**FIGURE 4.6  District with Democratic Skew**

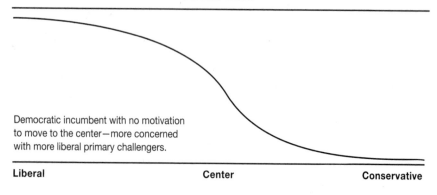

Democratic incumbent with no motivation
to move to the center—more concerned
with more liberal primary challengers.

| Liberal | Center | Conservative |

**FIGURE 4.7  District with Republican Skew**

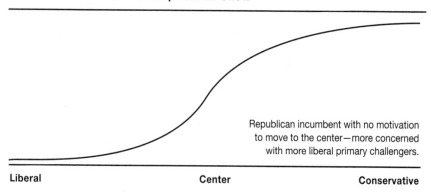

Republican incumbent with no motivation
to move to the center—more concerned
with more liberal primary challengers.

| Liberal | Center | Conservative |

Brad Wenstrup, was a political newcomer who successfully challenged her from the right, highlighting her votes to raise the debt ceiling. Republicans did not expect Schmidt to lose, so the race was not even on the party's radar. The party also thought that Representative John Sullivan (R-OK) was safe, but he lost to Jim Bridenstine, a museum director who ran as an outsider and as the more conservative candidate.[52] For both Schmidt and Sullivan, emphasizing their accomplishments in Congress seemed only to highlight their "insider status" to activist primary voters attuned to ideological distinctions.

Because senators represent entire states, they usually must appeal to a broader spectrum of voters than their House counterparts in districts dominated by one party. States tend to have something more closely resembling the bell-curve distribution of voters in Figure 4.5. As a result, many senators have to look both ways—to their flank to avoid a primary challenge as well as to the center for the general election in order to defeat any serious opposition that may have materialized in the opposing party.

Senators who assume that they will face a well-funded opponent in the general election often try to build a record of moderation in the first few years of their term; if a primary opponent gains traction, however, the incumbent senator must take more ideological stands as the primary approaches. Finding the right balance is tricky and takes a great deal of political and rhetorical skill.

Senator Richard Lugar of Indiana, a six-term member and one of the Senate's leading experts on foreign policy, lost his 2012 bid for reelection to Richard Mourdock, a Tea Party conservative who vowed to bring more partisanship to Washington. "The moral of the story is: Don't play defense, play offense—one of the fundamental rules of elections," said Senator John McCain (R-AZ), who endorsed Lugar.[53] A number of Republicans claimed that Lugar ignored their advice to run a more vigorous primary campaign. Having served in the Senate for 35 years, Lugar was not overly concerned about beating back a primary challenge. After defeating Lugar, Mourdock went on to lose the Senate seat to Democratic candidate Joe Donnelly, showing that the candidate who attracts the most votes in a primary does not always appeal to the broader swath of voters who turn out for the general election.

Six-term Democratic senator Max Baucus of Montana has walked this tightrope very effectively in recent years. Montana is a Republican state, but in recent election cycles Baucus has managed to stave off serious primary and general election opposition by developing a record of independence on major issues of salience to his state. He has won his last two terms, in 2002 and 2008, against weak Republican general election candidates after little or no primary opposition. Baucus decided not to seek reelection in 2014.

## The Emerging National Factor in Congressional Elections

Congressional candidates must make strategic decisions about the issues or themes they will emphasize in their campaigns. These decisions are driven to a great extent by the political environment and, as noted, are also subject to change over the course of a campaign. Incumbents naturally focus on their accomplishments in office and run on themes that emphasize their experience, popularity, and constituency service. The evidence shows that incumbents are on safe ground to the extent that the campaign stays focused on these themes.

Keeping the focus on district and state concerns, however, is not as easy as it used to be. Although it is important to stress that incumbency is still an advantage, for all the reasons already covered, and state and local issues often still predominate, national issues, party differences, and the president's popularity are now much more likely to creep into the equation.

In 1994 congressional Republicans undertook a novel approach to winning the House by, in effect, nationalizing their campaign message. Democrats had controlled the chamber since 1954, and many Republicans viewed themselves as a permanent minority. Minority whip Newt Gingrich convinced his colleagues that they would never win majority control if they continued to run localized, "every man for himself" campaigns. Gingrich argued that if voters understood what the Republican Party stood for nationally, they would vote Republicans into the majority. Perhaps more important, he spent several years contrasting the Republicans with Democrats. The Republicans were the "party of reform," while the Democrats were depicted as scandal-plagued, corrupt, "inside the Beltway" operatives who were out of touch with the real concerns of the people. Gingrich had led the campaign to force Speaker Jim Wright's resignation based on ethics charges in 1989. And he hammered mercilessly on Democrats for their overall arrogance in running the House—including their attempt to raise congressional salaries by more than 50 percent in the dead of night and their permitting check-kiting through the House bank. He even criticized the free ice deliveries that every Capitol Hill office got every day at taxpayer expense.

On the positive side, he created the "Contract with America." The Contract was a ten-point platform that served as the campaign centerpiece for many Republican congressional candidates in 1994. It clearly stated the party's common principles and legislative goals—ending corruption, doing away with wasteful spending, cutting taxes, and so on. Republicans pledged to enact the items outlined in the Contract if they were elected to the majority. Although the themes were national, Republican leaders encouraged their candidates to emphasize those that were most relevant to their constituents. Ultimately, the combination of hitting Democrats where they were weak while also pointing to a policy agenda in the Contract proved successful, and Republicans won majority control for the first time in 40 years.

One of the Republicans' greatest triumphs that year exemplifies this approach. Longtime Democratic congressman Neal Smith of central Iowa found himself in a tough general election race for the first time in many years. Smith, a highly influential subcommittee chair on the Appropriations Committee, had brought back millions of dollars to the district for everything from recreational facilities to university research centers. Although scandal free, he could be depicted as the consummate Washington insider simply because he had served for so long. Out of the woodwork came a self-funded Republican challenger, plastic surgeon Greg Ganske. He drove around the central Iowa district in a 1958 automobile symbolizing the year Smith was first elected. His ads attached Smith to what Ganske depicted as the corrupt pork-barrel activities of the Appropriations Committee and claimed that, as a newcomer to politics, he would be the kind of congressman needed to clean up the nation's capital and save taxpayer money. Smith didn't know what hit him, and Ganske won an upset victory.

Democrats took note and waited for their opportunity, which finally arrived in 2006. The party had been in the minority since the 1994 Republican takeover and, until 2006, had lacked an overarching national message on which to run. But in 2006, a number of bribery scandals involving Republican members of Congress and an increasingly unpopular war gave them the national themes they needed. The Democratic Party committees encouraged their candidates to focus their campaign messages on Republican corruption (and to stress their support for ethics reform) and the unpopular Iraq War. Democratic candidates also repeatedly tied Republican candidates to President Bush, whose approval ratings hovered around the 30 percent mark. The message worked: Democrats picked up more than enough seats to take over the House and just enough to take the Senate.

But ultimately the fallback position for an incumbent is to stress what he or she has done by way of constituent service and delivery of federal funds. Heading into the 2008 elections, Republican leaders advised their candidates to run localized campaigns. Tom Davis, former NRCC chair and at that time a Republican congressman from northern Virginia, circulated a 20-page memo to his House colleagues stating that "the political atmosphere facing House Republicans this November is the worst since Watergate and is far more toxic than the fall of 2006 when we lost 30 seats and our majority, and came within a couple of percentage points of losing another 15 seats."[54] Because the Republican brand name was "in the dirt," Davis suggested that candidates would be better off focusing their campaign messages on local issues and constituent services. By emphasizing national themes, Republican candidates risked reminding voters of their affiliation with an unpopular Republican president, the Iraq War, and a faltering economy. Davis's strategy may have saved some seats; however, Democrats still gained an additional 21 seats in the election. They also picked up seven Senate seats on election day.

By 2010 the tides had turned. Democrats had controlled the House and Senate for four years, and President Obama was two years into his first term as president. Sensing a "liberal backlash," Republican leaders targeted moderate-to-conservative Democrats, linking them to the policies of liberal House Speaker Nancy Pelosi and President Obama. By hammering repeatedly on this theme, Republican Vicky Hartzler managed to unseat Representative Ike Skelton (D-MO), the 78-year-old chairman of the House Armed Services Committee. Skelton, a military expert and social conservative, had represented his Republican-leaning district for more than 30 years; he had never won with less than 62 percent of the vote, but in 2010 he captured just 45 percent. The 2010 wave election that handed majority control of the House back to the Republicans also knocked out John Spratt, a moderate Democrat from South Carolina who chaired the House Budget Committee, and Virginia Democrat Rick Boucher, who chaired a powerful Energy and Commerce subcommittee in the House. By painting even the most moderate Democrats with a liberal brush, Republicans were able win back majority control of the House.

\* \* \*

Incumbents hold significant advantages over their challengers, but it has always been the case that they are vulnerable if they lose touch with their constituencies. A generation ago, the prevailing view was that incumbents should stress, almost to the exclusion of everything else, their individual qualities and their ability to deliver for the district. In the 21st century, the situation is different. The examples cited here suggest that parties and their candidates now need to be more cognizant of the larger political environment in which they are working and campaigning, especially in marginal districts. If national conditions are bad for a party, major investments need to be made to shore up its incumbents and other candidates in close races; conversely, parties need to put themselves in a position to take advantage of good national conditions by recruiting strong challengers and raising a lot of money. In today's environment, losing sight of national factors—the economy, the president's popularity, and so forth—can have catastrophic consequences for parties and candidates on election day.

## THE STAKES IN CONGRESSIONAL ELECTIONS

Every two years, congressional elections involve 435 House races and at least 33 Senate races. (One-third of the Senate is up every cycle, but there are usually a few elections to fill out the remainder of the term of senators who died or resigned from office.) The outcome of each race is determined to a significant degree, as we have seen, by the quality of the individuals running as well as by local or state issues. But the cumulative effect of these races is national: because the overall results determine which party controls each of the chambers, *the majority party's leadership gains the opportunity to shape the congressional agenda and drive national policy for the next two years.* In other words, the views and policies of the board of directors of the federal government is at stake on election day, potentially affecting which government programs will be enhanced or created and which agencies will suffer cuts in funding, what changes will be made to the tax code, and so on.

### The Landscape

As noted earlier, not all congressional races are close. In fact, the overwhelming majority of House seats are won easily by incumbents—in 2012 only 15 percent of House races were decided by fewer than ten percentage points. (The definition of a **marginal district** is usually one in which the race is within that ten-point differential.) Many incumbents have no opponent, and many others have only token, underfinanced, and unknown challengers. By contrast, in the Senate, about one-third of the seats are judged to be competitive in most cycles. Box 4.3 explains why Senate races tend to be more competitive than House races.

Majority control of the two chambers—power in Congress—usually comes down to 25 to 50 tight House races and 5 to 12 competitive Senate races. The two parties' committees focus tremendous attention each cycle on these campaigns

---

## BOX 4.3
### Competitiveness in House and Senate Races

Senate races are on average much more expensive to run than House races for obvious reasons—more media markets, more constituents to reach, more territory to cover, and so forth. At first glance, one might assume, then, that Senate incumbents might be safer than House incumbents. After all, raising $10 million or so to put up a serious challenge to a sitting member would seem to be almost impossible to do.

But in fact the opposite is true—a much higher percentage of Senate races are competitive than House races (30 percent as compared to 10 percent is typical), and senators are more vulnerable to defeat. Why is this so?

There are a number of factors. First, consider some key differences between the typical House district and a Senate "district." In a populous state, it is next to impossible for a senator to be able to deliver the level of service that an energetic House member and his or her staff can in a relatively compact 700,000-person district. As a result, senators seem more remote and inaccessible to constituents. In addition, the Senate constituency itself is likely to be much more diverse, in terms of partisanship, racial composition, economic status, ideology, and every other way, than the typical House constituency. It is harder for a senator to connect with constituents and keep most of them reasonably happy with his stances on the issues of the day. All of this means that there is a greater proportion of voters open to supporting a challenger.

Second, Senate races attract a lot more media attention than House races, giving challengers the potential for more free publicity than House challengers can get. It is also the case that a Senate seat is more prestigious than a House seat. Because of this, Senate seats frequently attract the interest of ambitious politicians who have already made a name for themselves—former governors, celebrities, professional athletes, and others. These types of people don't have to get over the hurdle of name recognition, can often raise a lot of money, and may even have a network of supporters in place.*

*Gary C. Jacobson, *The Politics of Congressional Elections,* 7th ed. (New York: Longman, 2009), 101–103.

because the stakes are so high. They pay particular attention to competitive *open-seat* races. Open seats have no incumbent. If the district demographics do not skew strongly toward one party or the other in an open-seat district, no candidate has a built-in advantage.

## National Trends

Observers have noted a fairly regular trend in the results of House elections. In a presidential election year, the party of a newly elected or reelected president almost always picks up seats. In the midterm election, when the presidency is not contested, the president's party almost always loses seats.

Table 4.4 shows the results of House races since 1950. Although the party swings are not always dramatic—and in fact President Clinton's Democrats *picked up* seats in 1998, as did President Bush's Republicans in 2002—the trend is clearly in favor of the president's party in a presidential election year and against his party in the off-year.

Political scientists believe that the winning presidential candidate helps his party pick up seats, although the level of that assistance from a strong presidential candidate may be exaggerated in journalistic circles. A good turnout for a presidential candidate may add 3 to 5 percent to the vote for a House or Senate candidate of his party.[55] These additional votes, of course, can be crucial at the margin.

In midterm elections, the president's popularity is often mentioned as a factor in his party's fortunes. Another key factor is the performance of the economy. A strong economy helps the incumbent president's party, at least at the margin. But the fact is that presidents are not always unpopular in the middle of their terms, nor is the economy always performing poorly. So why does their party tend almost always to lose seats?

One key factor that tends to work against the president's party in the midterms is that the president's very success in energizing his party's voting base the presidential year may have brought into office candidates of his party who, in a sense, should not have won. Some may have squeaked by in districts that tend to favor the opposition. The result: the president's party has more vulnerable incumbents in a midterm election, while at the same time the opposing party has had its most vulnerable members weeded out. (Analysts say that the president's party has greater "exposure.") The party out of the White House sees opportunities and may be able to persuade strong candidates to run and contributors to contribute. It is rare, as can be seen in Table 4.4, for a party to pick up seats in consecutive electoral cycles; double-digit gains like those made by Democrats in House races in 2006 and 2008 are unusual. A successful party is usually busy protecting its vulnerable incumbents and may not have the resources to go after incumbents of the opposing party.

## TABLE 4.4 House Election Swings, 1950 to the Present

| ELECTION YEAR | NET PLUS OR MINUS FOR PRESIDENT'S PARTY[a] | PRESIDENTIAL RESULT |
|---|---|---|
| 1950 | -28 | (midterm for Dem. President Truman) |
| 1952 | +22 | Eisenhower (R) 55–44% over Stevenson |
| 1954 | -18 | |
| 1956 | -1 | Eisenhower 58–42% over Stevenson |
| 1958 | -48 | |
| 1960 | -20 | Kennedy (D) elected (50–50% over Nixon) |
| 1962 | -4 | |
| 1964 | +37 | Johnson (D) 61–38% over Goldwater |
| 1966 | -48 | |
| 1968 | +4 | Nixon (R) 44–43% over Humphrey |
| 1970 | -12 | |
| 1972 | +15 | Nixon 61–38% over McGovern |
| 1974 | -48 | Watergate and Nixon resignation |
| 1976 | +1 | Carter (D) 50–48% over Ford |
| 1978 | -15 | |
| 1980 | +33 | Reagan (R) 51–42% over Carter |
| 1982 | -26 | |
| 1984 | +17 | Reagan 59–41% over Mondale |
| 1986 | -5 | |
| 1988 | -1 | Bush (R) 53–46% over Dukakis |
| 1990 | -8 | |
| 1992 | -9 | Clinton (D) 43–37% over Bush |
| 1994 | -54 | GOP Revolution/Contract with America |
| 1996 | +3 | Clinton 49–41% over Dole |
| 1998 | +5 | |
| 2000 | 0 | Bush II (R) elected (50–50% over Gore) |
| 2002 | +6 | |
| 2004 | +3 | Bush 51–48% over Kerry |
| 2006 | -31 | |
| 2008 | +21 | Obama (D) 53–46% over McCain |
| 2010 | -63 | |
| 2012 | +8 | Obama 51–47% over Romney |

Source: Adapted from Norman J. Ornstein, Thomas E. Mann, and Michael J. Malbin, *Vital Statistics on Congress, 2008* (Washington, DC: Brookings Institution Press, 2009). Updated from contemporaneous news accounts.

[a]In a presidential election year, the figure represents the president-elect's party's net gain or loss in House seats.

As political operatives and political scientists alike know, the biggest factors in any congressional race are the quality of the candidates running for competitive seats and the candidates' ability to raise the funds to compete effectively. A "high-quality" candidate is usually defined as one who has experience in politics—for example, in state legislative politics, on county commissions, as a mayor—and thus has a network of supporters and knows how to do what needs to be done to put together a campaign.

The lesson is that aspiring politicians think strategically, as political scientist Gary Jacobson stresses. Talented ones are unlikely to run for office when the prospects do not look good. (Open seats always attract a lot of attention.) Because candidates have to pull the trigger for their campaign effort a year or more before the election, the key is to look at the political environment at that time. If the economy is poor and the president is unpopular a year or more before the election, the party out of the White House will be more successful in persuading ambitious, high-quality, experienced politicians to run. Those politicians know they can raise money and make a good go of it. But if the president is popular and the economy is strong, the prospects for the out party are not so good, and it will be less successful in recruiting and fundraising.

In today's congressional election environment, as noted before, national political conditions are a larger factor than they were decades ago. These national factors affect campaigns indirectly through the strategic decisions made by politicians thinking about starting up a campaign. National factors also enter into campaigns more directly through advertisements tying candidates to national political figures, party platforms, or major issues.

## CONCLUSION: THE BOARD OF DIRECTORS AND THE CONTINUOUS CAMPAIGN

In Chapter 2, the argument was put forward that senators and representatives are "right-eye dominant"—meaning that they see their legislative and oversight work as members of the board of directors through the prism of the needs and priorities of their constituents.

The representative role puts a lot of pressure on members. Constituent groups constantly demand face time with members. Most members feel very strongly that they need to spend time back in the district or state or risk being portrayed as out of touch and uninterested in the people. Such a charge was partially responsible for bringing down the otherwise popular Indiana senator Richard Lugar in the 2012 primary elections. Lugar was defeated by a more conservative challenger who painted him as an "inside the Beltway" politician.

The requirements of running for office in the 21st century have their own independent effect on members of Congress. Raising the kind of money it takes to build up a war chest to compete in the next electoral cycle (or to scare away potential competition) is extremely time-consuming, and time spent fundraising may come at the cost of time working on complex policy issues in Washington. Even while in Washington, some members find themselves shuttling back and forth to party committee offices during the day to make fundraising calls—some practically camp out at the party offices. (It is illegal for them to make those calls from their congressional offices.)

For those in competitive districts, running for office is nearly a full-time job. The demands for contact back home with constituents are intense. Moreover, the explosion of high-tech media makes members more accessible and more vulnerable to attack than ever. They tread carefully as they carry out their official duties—someone is always watching, recording, or videotaping.

It should be noted that electoral pressures affect different members in different ways. Most have relatively safe seats, but some do not. Although even the members with safe seats expend a great deal of time and effort keeping their seats safe, the pressures on those who come from marginal districts and competitive states can be all-consuming.

All of this effort takes time away from legislative and oversight duties. During the 1960s and 1970s, an average two-year Congress met for 323 days. During the 1980s and 1990s, the average dropped to 278 days. Today the average hovers around 250 days. In addition, the number of committee and subcommittee hearings during a two-year session has declined significantly.[56] As a result, members have less time to examine legislative proposals, less time to look over agency officials' shoulders to make sure they are carrying out the law in the way intended, and less time to forge the difficult and necessary compromises with their colleagues to address pressing national issues.

Representatives and senators have a complex and tremendously difficult task juggling and meshing their twin responsibilities as legislators and representatives in this era of the continuous campaign. The bottom line is this: fulfilling their representative role, especially as it involves addressing the pressures of the modern campaign, affects everything members do as they direct the work of the federal government.

## Questions for Discussion

1. What would be the advantages and disadvantages to having the government finance congressional campaigns? Would it make sense to have

federally financed television time for the major party candidates? Why or why not?

2. Following the 2010 census, California voters tried to take the politics out of drawing congressional and state legislative district lines by giving that power to the 14-person Citizens Redistricting Commission. Is this a good idea? How do you think members of Congress view this idea?

3. What are the pros and cons of a "jungle primary" system like the one California instituted in 2012?

4. Experts see social media as a huge factor in congressional elections in the 21st century. Can you identify specific ways this might be true? How might a campaign less adept at social media be at a disadvantage?

## Suggestions for Further Reading

Currinder, Marian. *Money in the House.* Boulder, CO: Westview Press, 2009.

Erikson, Robert S., and Gerald C. Wright. "Voters, Candidates, and Issues in Congressional Elections." In *Congress Reconsidered,* edited by Lawrence C. Dodd and Bruce I. Oppenheimer, 91–116. 10th ed. Washington, DC: CQ Press, 2013.

Herrnson, Paul S. *Congressional Elections: Campaigning at Home and in Washington.* 6th ed. Washington, DC: CQ Press, 2012.

Jacobson, Gary. *The Politics of Congressional Elections.* 8th ed. Boston: Pearson, 2013.

Pitney, John J., James W. Ceaser, and Andrew E. Busch. *Epic Journey: The 2008 Elections and American Politics.* Lanham, MD: Rowman and Littlefield, 2009.

## NOTES

1. John R. Wilke, "Murtha Inc.: How Lawmaker Rebuilt Hometown on Earmarks," *Wall Street Journal,* October 30, 2007.

2. Michael Barone and Richard Cohen, *The Almanac of American Politics: 2010* (Washington, DC: National Journal Group, 2009), 157.

3. Wilke, "Murtha Inc."

4. *U.S. Term Limits v. Thornton* (1995). In this case, the Court ruled that an Arkansas term-limit law did not create an additional requirement for holding office.

5. Joseph A. Schlesinger, *Ambition and Politics* (Chicago: Rand McNally, 1966).

6. Martin Frost, interview with the author, September 12, 2006.

7. Tim Roemer, interview with the author, March 26, 2009.

8. Robert V. Remini, *The House* (Washington, DC: Smithsonian Books, 2006), 446–447.

9. Alan Ehrenhalt, *The United States of Ambition* (New York: Three Rivers Press, 1992).

10. Gary C. Jacobson, "The Congress: The Structural Basis of Republican Success," in *The Elections of 2004*, edited by Michael Nelson (Washington, DC: CQ Press, 2005), 163–186.

11. Jessica Brady and John Stanton, "Eric Cantor Uses 'Real Bullets' in Primary Endorsement," *Roll Call*, March 22, 2012.

12. Jennifer Haberkorn, "Karl Rove Predicts Historic Loss for Todd Akin," *Politico*, August 27, 2012.

13. According to statistics compiled by the Committee for the Study of the American Electorate.

14. Charles Mahtesian, interview with the author, October 23, 2007.

15. US Bureau of the Census, "Congressional Apportionment: How It's Calculated," www.census.gov/population/www/censusdata/apportionment/calculated.html.

16. For more detail, see *Guide to U.S. Elections*, 5th ed. (Washington, DC: CQ Press, 2005), 849.

17. Ibid.

18. *Wesberry v. Sanders* (1964).

19. Brenna Findley, chief of staff to Congressman Steve King (R-IA), interview with the author, April 5, 2009.

20. Erik Engstrom describes aggressive redistricting efforts in the late 19th century in "Stacking the States, Stacking the House," *American Political Science Review* 100, no. 6 (2006): 419–427.

21. Cracking can also refer to drawing district lines in such a way as to dilute the concentration of a minority group, thereby denying that group a reasonable chance to elect one of its members.

22. *Davis v. Bandemer* (1986).

23. *League of United Latin American Citizens v. Perry* (2006).

24. Mike Maciag. "Analysis: Redistricting Mostly Protected Incumbents in 2012 Congressional Races," *Governing Magazine* (November 16, 2012), www.governing.com/blogs /by-the-numbers/redistricting-gerrymandering-effect-2012-congressional-elections .html.

25. Bob Benenson, "Why the Courts Punt of Gerrymandering," www.centerforpolitics .org/crystalball/articles/why-the-courts-punt-on-gerrymandering/.

26. *Guide to U.S. Elections*, 853–854.

27. Gary C. Jacobson, *The Politics of Congressional Elections*, 8th ed. (Boston: Pearson, 2013), 16.

28. *Guide to U.S. Elections*, 866.

29. See David Lublin, *The Paradox of Representation* (Princeton, NJ: Princeton University Press, 1999); and Carol Swain, *Black Faces, Black Interests* (Oxford: Oxford University Press, 1995). Erik Engstrom has a somewhat different view, suggesting that racial redistricting has not helped the Republican Party as much as some people have asserted; see "Race and Southern Politics: The Special Case of Congressional Redistricting," in *Writing*

*Southern Politics,* edited by Robert P. Steed and Laurence W. Moreland (Lexington: University Press of Kentucky, 2006).

30. Gary Jacobson, "Modern Campaigns and Representation," in *The Legislative Branch,* edited by Paul J. Quirk and Sarah A. Binder (Oxford: Oxford University Press, 2006), 113.

31. David Mayhew, *Congress: The Electoral Connection* (New Haven, CT: Yale University Press, 1974), 81–82.

32. See Steven D. Levitt and Catherine D. Wofram, "Decomposing the Sources of Incumbency Advantage in the U.S. House," *Legislative Studies Quarterly* 22 (1997): 45–60.

33. Morris P. Fiorina, *Congress: Keystone of the Washington Establishment,* 2nd ed. (New Haven, CT: Yale University Press, 1989).

34. See Jacobson, *Politics of Congressional Elections,* chap. 3.

35. Paul S. Herrnson, *Congressional Elections,* 6th ed. (Washington, DC: CQ Press, 2012), 250–251.

36. Marian Currinder, "Campaign Finance: Fundraising and Spending in the 2008 Elections," in *The Elections of 2008,* edited by Michael Nelson (Washington, DC: CQ Press, 2009), 179.

37. The law permits candidates to spend an unlimited amount in personal funds on their own campaigns.

38. David E. Price, *The Congressional Experience,* 3rd ed. (Boulder, CO: Westview Press, 2004), 16.

39. Marian Currinder, "Campaign Finance: Funding the Presidential and Congressional Elections," in *The Elections of 2004,* edited by Michael Nelson (Washington, DC: CQ Press, 2005), 113.

40. Marian Currinder, "Campaign Finance," in *The Elections of 2012,* edited by Michael Nelson (Washington, DC: Sage/CQ Press, 2013).

41. Herrnson, *Congressional Elections,* 137–139.

42. David D. Kirkpatrick, "Campaign Funds for Alaskan; Road Aid to Florida," *New York Times,* June 7, 2007, available at: www.nytimes.com/2007/06/07/washington/07earmark.html.

43. Most individual "bundlers" are federal lobbyists. Although members of Congress undoubtedly appreciate the fundraising help that bundlers can provide, they also understand that such relationships between members and lobbyists may be perceived as corrupt. A lobbyist who delivers 20 $1,000 contributions to a candidate might be viewed by some as finding a way around the $2,300 federal contribution limit. To address this potential problem, Congress passed legislation in 2007 requiring the disclosure of bundling activities by registered lobbyists. The law requires candidates to report to the FEC the name and contact information for each registered lobbyist "known (or 'reasonably known') to have made at least two bundled contributions totaling more than $15,000 during specified six-month reporting periods." See Sam R. Garrett, "Campaign Finance Developments in the 110th Congress," Congressional Research Service, September 28, 2007, 2.

44. Herrnson, *Congressional Elections,* 140. See also www.opensecrets.org/pacs/industry.php?txt=Q03&cycle=2012.

45. Marian Currinder, "Campaign Finance," in *The Elections of 2012,* edited by Nelson.

46. www.opensecrets.org/parties/index.php.

47. Josh Lederman, "Many Dems Haven't Paid Party Dues," *Hill,* March 21, 2012.

48. Candidates in states with only one representative can receive up to $91,200 in independent expenditures.

49. See www.cfinst.org/Press/PReleases/12-11-02/CFI_s_2012_Independent_Spending_Update_for_November_2nd.aspx.

50. Though most congressional elections feature a Democrat and a Republican in the general election, third-party candidates can also compete, as long as they qualify for a place on the ballot.

51. See, for example, Anthony Downs, *An Economic Theory of Democracy* (New York: Harper & Row, 1957).

52. Nathan L. Gonzales, "Oklahoma House: Incumbent Sullivan's Unexpected Loss," *Rothenberg Political Report,* June 27, 2012.

53. Paul Kane, "Richard Lugar Loses Primary Nomination to Conservative Challenger Richard Mourdock," *Washington Post,* May 8, 2012.

54. Chuck Todd et al., "GOPer Compares Brand to Bad Dog Food," May 14, 2008, http://firstread.msnbc.msn.com/archive/2008/05/14/1022156.aspx.

55. Ibid., 167–168.

56. Norman Ornstein, "Part-Time Congress," *Washington Post,* March 7, 2006.

# INSIDE CONGRESS | 2

# 5

# Understanding the Legislative Process

The first four chapters are meant to provide a foundation for understanding how Congress exercises its powers as a board of directors for the federal government. As described in the first chapter, those powers include the authorizing power, the so-called power of the purse, and the implied power of supervision or oversight of government programs. The key idea in the first part of the book is that Congress doesn't exercise those powers in a vacuum; policy-making decisions are affected by the pressures members face in their representative role, in particular the electoral connection covered in the last chapter, and the bicameral nature of the institution.

Congress's importance in the federal system stems from its lawmaking power. Passing a law establishes government policy by giving an agency the legal authority to do things, which may involve building a road, giving a loan to a college student, purchasing a vehicle to patrol the border, collecting a tax, or cleaning up a river. Normally, an agency will need *two* laws actually to do something, one that provides the authority to, say, clean up a river, and a second to provide funding for carrying out that task. But that is jumping ahead.

This chapter deals with something more basic. If a law is what is required before the government—federal executive branch agencies, to be specific—can do something, it is important first to understand how Congress goes about passing a law. In this chapter, we look at the legislative process. Subsequent chapters deal with the substance of how Congress exercises its authorizing, funding, and oversight powers.

The legislative process is anything but simple; in fact, most people find it extremely confusing. The aim here is to understand how the process works in practice. To that end, we start by establishing a couple of "first principles" that practitioners—members of Congress and staff, plus lobbyists and other interested parties—all know form the basis of grasping what is going on.

Then it's time to get to the details. But we do not approach our examination of "how a bill becomes a law" with the introduction of a bill, as one might expect; instead, we look at the decision party leaders make concerning what bills they will schedule for a vote on the floor. The reason we do this is that the legislative process from beginning (bill development and introduction) to end is conditioned by that leadership decision. The process can best be understood by considering high-level decisions before getting down to the nitty-gritty.

After considering agenda setting from the leadership perspective, we move through the process step by step, beginning with committee consideration in the House, the development of the rule for floor consideration, then the debate and vote on the bill on the floor. After that, we look at the Senate, with a special eye to its unique and often laborious approach to processing legislation.

Of course, getting similar bills through the House and Senate is not enough; bills must pass both chambers in identical form in order for a policy idea to become law. We describe the main ways the chambers attempt to reconcile their differences so that a bill can be sent "down Pennsylvania Avenue" to the president for his signature. Of course, the president isn't required to sign anything; we'll look at the role of the president at the end of the process.

The legislative process as practiced today says a lot about Congress and the political system more broadly. Perhaps the most perceptive take on the legislative process comes from political scientist Barbara Sinclair, who for a couple of decades has described a system of "unorthodox lawmaking."[1] We look at the creative lengths Congress may go to pass bills, with a close look at the process used to pass the 2010 Patient Protection and Affordable Care Act, and consider what recent trends in the legislative process say about the contemporary Congress.

## FIRST PRINCIPLES OF THE LEGISLATIVE PROCESS

Almost everyone at some point in their lives has been exposed to the "how a bill becomes a law" chart, whether in an American government textbook or on *School House Rock*. The legislative process in the US Congress is a complex system that, if all the stages in the chart are strictly followed, takes about a dozen steps, occurring at different times and involves different groups of representatives and senators.

Figure 5.1 shows how the process is typically depicted. Note that a bill may start either in the House or in the Senate. The one exception is revenue bills, which the Constitution stipulates must start in the House. It is also possible to have two similar or identical bills start at the same time in both chambers. A bill may make it through the process in one chamber and never receive consideration in the other. Of course, such a bill will never become law.

**FIGURE 5.1. The Legislative Process**

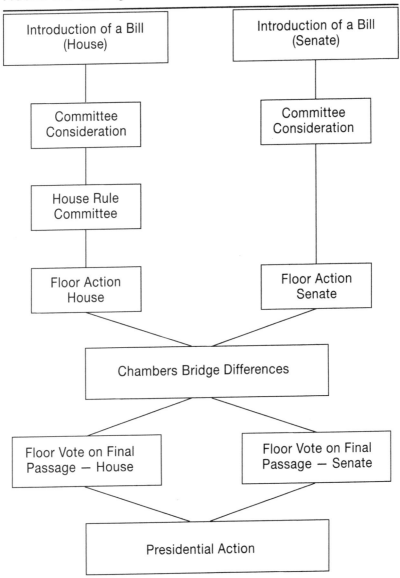

The process is cumbersome. Following the chart, a bill must first be examined and voted on by the relevant committees in both the House and the Senate. (Often, subcommittee consideration precedes the full committee stage, especially in the House.) A majority vote of the panel moves the bill along. At that point in the House, many major bills make a stop at the Rules Committee for a rule-governing debate on the chamber's floor. Then a vote is taken involving all members on the rule for debate and, subsequently, on the substance of the bill. A floor vote is also required in the Senate on its version of the bill. Normally, with important legislation, the two chambers' versions differ, necessitating negotiations to bridge those differences. A conference committee composed of both a House and a Senate contingent may be used to do this. (Conference committee members from each chamber vote separately on the bill.) Finally, the House and the Senate must vote on the final version of the bill. Another vote may still be required in each chamber if the president decides to veto the bill. A two-thirds vote, not a simple majority, is needed in each chamber to override a presidential veto.

One way to think about the process is to recognize that there are as many as a dozen points at which potential legislation may be killed. Not surprisingly, the legislative process is almost always lengthy and involves considerable negotiation and compromise at most or all of the stages.

To get a real sense of the process and how it actually works, however, it is important to recognize that *almost every stage of the legislative process as it appears on the chart is optional.* In other words, bills do not have to follow the route in the chart. No law—and certainly not the Constitution—requires that the chambers go through all these steps. The steps were devised by members of the two bodies over the past 220 years as they settled on rules and precedents based on what they thought was a good way of developing public policy. The idea is that legislation should receive careful consideration by the expert members and staff on the subcommittees and committees, to be followed by a public debate on the floors of the two chambers. In a republic, the legislative process provides a method by which the elected representatives, coming at the issues from the different perspectives of the House and Senate, carefully and deliberately transform the people's relatively raw opinions and views into public policy that directs the work of the government agencies.

But the only part of the process that is absolutely required is that the House and Senate present to the president a bill that has passed both chambers in identical form. This requirement is based on the presentment clause of the Constitution, which is in Article I, Section 7: "Every Bill which shall have passed the House of Representatives and the Senate, shall, before it become a Law, be presented to the President of the United States."

In other words, only the last stage—the House and Senate voting on identical versions of the bill—must happen. A majority of both the House and the Senate must agree to its passage on the floor—and that's it. All the actions of the authorizing committees and their subcommittees, the Rules Committee, and any conference committee are, in a sense, optional.

As a result, understanding the legislative process in a relevant way begins with *the Rule of 218 and 60.* This means that the legislative process always boils down to the vote on final passage of a bill in the two chambers. Although technically passage requires only the vote of a majority of the members present in both chambers, in the Senate in this day and age, with the constant threat of a filibuster, 60 votes are almost always required to move significant legislation instead of the 51 that would constitute a simple majority. In the House, 218 votes constitute a majority if all 435 members are present and voting. Everyone on the Hill knows that if they want to get anything into law, the Rule of 218 and 60 ultimately is the key.

## It's Never Over 'til It's Over

It is important to be familiar with the legislative process as depicted in the chart, but it is not the best way to understand its essence. The Rule of 218 and 60 comes closer. A sports analogy is also helpful.

In a football game, if one team builds an early two-touchdown 14-point lead, maintains that lead, and then extends it by scoring two more touchdowns in the fourth quarter while holding the other team scoreless the whole game, the game is for all intents and purposes over. The reserves come in for both teams, and the fans start heading for the exits. The idea is that at some point it becomes impossible for a team that's well behind to catch up.

Baseball is different. No matter how far behind a team falls, it always has the ninth inning. Even with two outs in the ninth and a significant deficit, if a team keeps hitting it has a chance. It is better to be the team that is ahead, of course, whether by one, two, or ten runs, but the trailing team always has a chance.

The legislative process is like baseball, not like football.

Imagine that a member of the House wants to enact a law that will affect an agency's activities. That bill might amount only to a short paragraph that prevents the agency from doing something or that requires the agency to take a particular action, or it might be a full-fledged overhaul of a program or the establishment of a new program. The member's best strategy is to get the desired bill language incorporated into a larger bill on a similar topic that the committee of jurisdiction is working on. (Committees may not have the time to deal with each and every little idea in a piecemeal fashion.) If the regular order of the legislative process is followed, the member will work with the relevant committee to get the language added. If he or she succeeds in getting the language included at the committee stage and the committee approves the bill, the member is probably in good shape, since the committee members are likely to close ranks to protect their legislative product as the process goes along. But there is never any guarantee.

All the way to the very end, at any stage, that provision might be removed. Even toward the end of the game, when the two chambers negotiate to bridge their differences, it is possible to make significant changes to the legislation, even to the point of taking out provisions that were included in both chambers' versions of the bill. If that happens to our representative's favored provision, it will be like losing a baseball game in the bottom of the ninth. By the same token, even if the representative fails to get the language into the committee version and does not succeed in attaching it to the larger bill during floor votes, he or she could be extremely clever and get a colleague to insert the provision in the legislation at the very end (a conference committee or informal late-stage negotiations)—which is analogous to a dramatic, game-ending grand-slam home run in the last of the ninth inning.

The bottom line here is that persistent and skilled members know how to exploit the process. Bill language, whether relatively minor and particular or much more substantial, can be attached to legislation that is moving at any stage. The process on paper—sometimes called "regular order"—almost seems like a relic of the past. Stages on the "how a bill becomes a law" chart are regularly skipped. Even committee consideration is sometimes circumvented, though traditionally it has been assumed that giving experts a chance to weigh in on legislation is essential. Sometimes one chamber or the other cannot find the time or the political will to take on something controversial at any stage and may, at the end, accept the other chamber's version in a floor vote.

Everyone on Capitol Hill now knows that the "how a bill becomes a law" chart has limited utility. It has been skirted so often that **unorthodox lawmaking** is regarded by some as the norm. It is useful to think of the process as a game in which 535 people are trying to direct the actions of government in law by manipulating procedures so that their favored provisions and legislation are somehow inserted in a larger bill in time for final passage.

It is important to stress, using the baseball analogy, that it is better to build an early lead—that is, to have one's bill language in as early as possible and ideally in both the House and the Senate versions. Sometimes, however, that may be neither the best strategy nor even possible, so a representative or senator may have to rely on power hitting in the last of the ninth before the vote on final passage.

We now move to the legislative process in the two chambers. Instead of proceeding chronologically from start to finish, we begin with the way legislation is scheduled for consideration on the floor of the House and Senate. As we shall see, *the decision by party leadership whether to bring a bill to the floor conditions all of the earlier stages of the legislative process.*

## Scheduling Legislation

Who determines which bills get a vote on the floor of the House and Senate? And what criteria are used to make that decision? Answering these two questions goes a long way toward gaining a sophisticated understanding of the legislative process.

The answer to the first question is easy: the majority party leadership of the chamber in question determines which bills get to the floor. Specifically, in the House the speaker, who is the head of the majority party's leadership team, has the final say. The speaker also has considerable influence over the conditions under which bills will be considered. In the Senate, the gatekeeper is the majority leader, although the Senate majority leader has considerably less control over the conditions of debate and consideration than the speaker does in the House.

The implications of this authority are tremendously consequential. A great many bills—thousands every Congress—are introduced by the members, and most don't pass into law.[2] Many of the bills are on trivial matters, such as renaming a post office, and many times members introduce bills just to make a statement or draw some attention to an issue in the near term. Hundreds receive varying levels of consideration at the subcommittee or committee level. But it is only those that the leadership wishes to schedule for floor time that have a chance to become law. A great deal of time and effort is expended at earlier stages in the process on legislative proposals that will never see the light of day. All in all, the party leadership has no greater power than that of controlling access to the floor.

The answer to the second question is quite a bit more complicated. What are the criteria that influence the decision to bring bills to the floor?

It stands to reason that the majority party leadership will try to pursue an agenda that promotes the interests of their party. Specifically, they wish to pass bills in their chamber (and ideally laws that pass both chambers) that will impress the American people enough so that they will retain power after the next electoral cycle. Also, as strong partisans, the top leaders believe that what their party stands for is good for the country. Thus, the majority leadership has an agenda driven by a desire to do what is best for the country, based on their party's ideological perspective, as well as a desire to pursue this agenda in such a way that the party will be rewarded with two more years in power after the next election. Here is how the leadership attempts to do this, starting with the House.

## Scheduling Legislation in the House

As we saw in Chapter 3, the top House leadership consists of the speaker, the majority leader, the majority whip, and the caucus or conference chair. This leadership team enlists the aid of rank-and-file members who are interested in contributing to the party's success. The speaker runs the entire operation, and he or she assigns to the rest of the team particular duties related to running the House and determining the legislative agenda.

First, the party needs to identify a legislative agenda. What issues do party members need to address? How should they address those issues? In what order should they take on these issues? How should these issues be marketed to the larger public and to influential groups? The last question is crucial: a good public relations or "messaging" operation is an important part of passing legislation and maintaining a legislative majority.

The speaker typically names the House majority leader as the chief strategist in charge of putting together the legislative agenda. The majority leader consults with a wide range of people and also speaks with the president, if he is of the same party, to see which direction he wants to go on the issues. The majority leader talks to pollsters hired by the party to see what is salient to the public and why, consults with members of the party in the House to see what they are hearing about the intensity of feeling on certain issues back home in their districts, coordinates with the White House if the president is of the same party, and keeps tabs on what is percolating up through the various committees.

Numerous meetings are held with other top leaders, key members of the party in the House, and influential people outside the House. Ultimately, the speaker and the majority leader settle on an agenda that serves the party and the country in their view. This might mean, for example, scheduling energy independence legislation for floor consideration that week, a tax reform bill the following week, and the budget resolution shortly thereafter.

Lying in wait, however, are some pretty significant stumbling blocks to being able to follow through on the type of energy, tax, and budget bills they want. First, are the relevant committees working on legislation that fits into the plan? Are bills ready and out of committee? What do they look like? Do they fit with what the leadership deems to be "good for the party and good for the country"?

It is primarily the job of the majority leader to deal with these problems. He is in constant communication with committee chairs and has formulated agenda ideas in a reciprocal process in which they tell him what they want to do and what they can pass out of committee, and he tells them what the leadership would like to see. Ultimately, anything at odds with leadership goals is unlikely to be scheduled for floor consideration, and the committee chairs know this. If leadership is desperate to move on a particular area of policy and the relevant committee chair is not cooperating (or cannot due to internal committee friction), the leadership may circumvent the committee process and put together a bill by other means. This is not always popular, and it is fairly rare, but it does happen. More often in these circumstances, the committees do what they can or want to do, and then leadership takes over, incorporating their ideas into a bill and making what are called **post-committee adjustments** before the bill is taken to the floor.

Another second stumbling block is a purely practical consideration. Do the leaders have the votes to pass the bills on their agenda, in the form they want to pass them and when they want to pass them? The majority whip is in charge of gathering intelligence. The whip begins well ahead of the time when the leadership is contemplating having the vote by canvassing members, with the help of the "whip team" composed of loyal party members, to see whether they will vote for the bills coming up. The whip asks a variety of questions of the rank and file in the party. Are they firm supporters of this legislation? If not, are there changes they would like to see made? What would it take to change their minds, if anything? If they are undecided, will they hold their vote to see whether it is needed for passage?

The bottom line is that the whip needs to find out whether the majority has the votes—218 to be precise—to pass the legislation on its agenda. If so, they can get anything they want through the chamber. If not, they need to know whether they can change the minds of wavering members by making adjustments in the bill. The leadership team does have a great deal of leverage; after all, members' legislative goals can be realized only if the leadership schedules a vote on their bills. (Leadership also has considerable control over the committee assignment process.) But in the end, even an ideologically homogeneous party as the Republicans have become in recent years can have a great deal of trouble getting members to toe the party line to get to 218, as the experience of Republican whip Kevin McCarthy showed in the 112th Congress (see Box 5.1).

It should be noted that getting to 218 votes may include some members of the minority party. But that is not always a desirable path for the majority—plus it is difficult to get information as to minority members' intentions when contentious bills are coming up. There are times when they are strongly encouraged by their leadership not to support the majority's high-priority legislation.

The process of establishing the legislative agenda of the House has undergone significant changes in recent decades owing to the increased assertiveness and power of party leadership. Several decades ago, House leadership essentially acted as glorified clerks: they processed legislation as it came from the committee chairs, who were in many respects the real powerhouses in the chamber.[3] Today the leadership in the House really leads. The change began in the 1970s, although the real quantum leap in party leaders' power and assertiveness came with the Republican takeover of the House in 1995. Republican speakers Newt Gingrich (1995–1998) and Dennis Hastert (1998–2007) asserted their prerogatives successfully, and their Democratic successor, Nancy Pelosi (2007–2011), followed suit.[4]

Today leadership in the House is prepared to ignore the process as spelled out in the "how a bill becomes a law" diagram if, in their view, the greater good of the party and the country is at stake. And they have the means to do it. The fact is that the process before floor consideration, especially at the committee and subcommittee

## BOX 5.1

## Running the House Isn't Easy:
## Republicans Struggles with Internal Divisions

Republicans took charge of the House of Representatives after the 2010 midterm elections. The leadership team—Speaker John Boehner, Majority Leader Eric Cantor, Majority Whip Kevin McCarthy, and Conference Chair Jeb Hensarling—were ready to wield their majority to move an agenda through the chamber to challenge the priorities of President Barack Obama and the Democratic Senate.

But it didn't prove easy at all. Republicans have adhered to a "majority of the majority" policy in bringing bills to the floor since early in the 21st century. The idea is that leadership doesn't want to pass any bills that most Republicans don't support. In practice, for a lot of controversial bills, the majority may have to rely entirely or nearly entirely on their own members to pass bills, since the minority may not see it in their interest to provide votes for the legislation.

Traditionally in Congress, the task of rallying votes for a transportation bill doling out money for roads and bridges across the country is one of the less difficult ones. Members of both parties are normally eager to support such legislation. However, with the prohibition on earmarking funds to specific districts put in place in 2011, in early 2012 Majority Whip McCarthy (whose job it is to count votes for the Republicans) had to report to the Speaker Boehner that he simply didn't have the votes. Many Republicans were against the spending in principle, and others couldn't be persuaded without the lure of earmarks. And many Democrats were disinclined to support a bill that they thought shortchanged essential infrastructure.

During other key votes in the 112th Congress, McCarthy found himself scrambling. Of the 240 Republicans in the House, 60 were in the Tea Party Caucus. These members (plus 5 others) didn't support a measure to increase the debt limit—even with the imminent threat of a first-time in US history default on debt—in 2011. To pass this essential legislation, Republicans had to rely on Democratic support to put them over the top. Similarly, in the waning days of the 112th Congress, Republicans in the House were unable to come together on legislation staking out their position to prevent the so-called fiscal cliff of automatic spending cuts and tax increases that took place in January 2013.

stages, is conditioned and driven to a large extent by big-picture agenda concerns as developed by the majority party leadership.

## Scheduling Legislation in the Senate

In the Senate, the majority leader has scheduling power, but his situation is much more difficult to manage than the speaker's. The Senate majority leader is limited by Senate rules and precedents that result in a de facto 60-vote requirement for most bills of any consequence to come to a vote (thus, the majority party almost always needs some minority party cooperation to move forward on bills), by the need to move much Senate business by unanimous consent, and by the right each senator has to offer amendments on any bill.

Just as in the House (with the speaker), the Senate majority leader would like to move a legislative agenda that enshrines the party's principles in a way that will enhance its chances at maintaining power in the next election cycle. But to move an agenda, the majority leader almost always has to coordinate with the minority party leadership. All senators have the prerogative to hijack the floor for extended periods of time, and, as a result, even minority party senators' concerns on almost any significant piece of legislation must be heard.

In the Senate, following any sort of regular procedure is sometimes not an option. Delicate negotiations between Democrats and Republicans are always going on, and all senators, *whether they serve on the committee of jurisdiction or not*, may weigh in on any particular issue. If acrimonious partisanship rules the day, as has sometimes been the case in recent years, little can be accomplished. Having said that, creative approaches to the legislative process have made the majority party notably stronger in the Senate than it used to be.[5]

\* \* \*

The point of the above discussion is not to dismiss the early stages of the legislative process. Fortunately, since most of the policy expertise in Congress is with the **committee staff**, subcommittee and committee consideration of bills is still the norm. But there are many variations on a theme. Committee consideration in one or the other chamber may be short-circuited, bills are often altered in significant ways after committees have had their say, bills that struggle in one chamber or the other may be tacked on to legislation at the very end of the process (in a conference committee or during informal negotiations between the chambers), and both chambers are extremely imaginative in how they package legislative products for the floor and how they structure debate. All of this unorthodox lawmaking needs to be put in today's context: in this era of partisan politics, party leaders have taken a much more prominent role, especially in the House, in controlling floor access for the greater good of their party, and the committee chairs have had to accommodate the leadership in order to remain relevant. *The legislative process is driven by the interests of the majority party, not by adherence to established rules of order.*

## KEY STAGES IN THE LEGISLATIVE PROCESS: THE HOUSE
### Introducing a Bill

Only members may introduce a bill in Congress, but as mentioned earlier, introducing a bill does not guarantee anything—not even consideration in a committee, much less consideration on the floor of the chamber.[6] If a bill does not pass into law in any given two-year Congress, it needs to be reintroduced in the next Congress to receive consideration.

Members have a lot of different motives in introducing bills. Many times they do so for strictly political reasons—perhaps as a favor to a group in their constituency—but do not have the time or even the inclination to do everything possible to move the bill along in the legislative process. Often, members may not be in a position to move the bill along because they do not serve on the relevant committee or otherwise have the necessary clout. Most members of the minority party in the House, and even many in the majority party, are not going to get the attention and support of party leaders, without which their idea stands no chance.

An important but often overlooked aspect of bill introduction is the origin of the idea for a bill. Interest groups and constituents are sometimes the source, and of course members and their staff develop bills to address policy concerns and the needs of districts or states. As often as anything else, ideas for legislation come from the government itself—that is, from executive branch agencies. Members of Congress, in their role as the board of directors, solicit ideas on how to fix problems in the performance of government programs from agency officials, who are often the ones in the best position to know what will work. Furthermore, many agencies aggressively push ideas that the administration would like to see implemented and look for sympathetic members to introduce their bills for them. They try to work with members who are in a better position to move bills through the process, especially party leaders and committee and subcommittee chairs.

### Referring a Bill to a Committee

The first step in the legislative process is **committee referral**, which is usually a routine step. The committees have established jurisdictions in House rules and precedents; the nonpartisan parliamentarian of the House analyzes the bill in question and makes the appropriate referral. The situation gets much more complicated—and much more political—when legislation is introduced that does not fit neatly into any single existing committee's jurisdiction.

Over the past three decades or so, House leadership has exercised a great deal of power in the referral process when a piece of legislation can be construed as falling under the jurisdiction of more than one committee. Indeed, many of the most important issues of the day do not fit neatly into one or another committee's jurisdiction. In these cases, the referral process may become an important tool for the House leadership in driving its agenda.

House leadership has a few different ways of referring a bill once it is established that the bill does not entirely fit into one committee's jurisdiction. The most common method is probably best described as a type of **split referral**. The leadership identifies the committees that should be involved in considering the bill and refers the bill to them with instructions as to the portion of the bill they should work on and a date when they should finish consideration (also known as *reporting out* the committee's version of that part of the bill). When there is a primary committee of jurisdiction that is instructed to work on the bulk of the bill, as is often the case, that committee is less likely to be given a reporting deadline.

Producing legislation that makes sense for the party in power can be very tricky. The leadership (with the majority leader typically taking the lead) must be very skilled. Committees may have different views on important aspects of a given piece of legislation, and the exact lines of jurisdiction may not be perfectly clear. Committees must work together to produce legislation that makes sense. The majority leader's role is to broker the deal, looking out for the larger interests of the party as important legislation moves through the process. Committee leaders are likely to be the most knowledgeable people in the chamber on the issues in question and may have the best sense of what can be passed. But the leadership has the keys for access to the floor. The negotiations between the leadership and the committee chairs may be intense. Sometimes leadership may need to wrest control of a bill from one or more of the committees if the chairs are not sufficiently cooperative.[7]

In these cases, a bill may be put together independent of the committee or committees of jurisdiction. This is not usually a popular move, but issues of particular sensitivity may require such action. Congressional procedure specialist Walter Oleszek suggests several possible motivations for bypassing committees, including avoiding contentious hearings and markups in committees that have sharp partisan disagreements, the need to pass an agenda item in a timely fashion, avoidance of intraparty gridlock in a committee, and a consensual understanding with the committee chair.[8]

More commonly, postcommittee adjustments are made to legislation before it makes the floor. Political realities often dictate that bills have to be changed from the version that emerged from committee in order for them to pass on the House floor. Changing circumstances may also make it necessary to adjust a bill.

## The Rules Committee

There are four House of Representatives calendars on which bills are placed to await floor consideration: the House Calendar, the Private Calendar, the Discharge Calendar, and the Union Calendar. But for most consequential matters, the House takes up issues in an order determined by the majority party leadership, paying no heed to the order in which they appear on the relevant calendar.

This is done by securing what is known as a **special rule** from the Rules Committee, which allows bills to, in effect, jump the queue. If leadership thinks it is time to bring up the energy bill, for instance, it requests a special rule. The **Rules Committee** has 13 members, 9 of whom are selected by the speaker and 4 of whom are selected by the minority leader, and its importance cannot be overstated: *the Rules Committee provides the means by which the majority party runs the House.*

One way to think about the Rules Committee is to see it as a rule-*waiving* committee. If the standing rules of the House call for a certain order of business or disallow certain types of provisions in a bill that the leadership wants to move, they can ask the Rules Committee to draw up a special rule to have those rules waived.

Here is how it works: The leadership brings a favored bill that has just been reported out of a committee before the Rules Committee. The bill is quite controversial and may even contain provisions unrelated to the bill's main purpose, a violation of the House's **germaneness** rule. The Rules Committee's job is to draw up the guidelines for the consideration of this bill on the House floor. For one thing, because the bill is important to leadership (and since the overwhelming majority of the Rules Committee was handpicked by the speaker), the special rule will prohibit anyone from raising a point of order on the House floor challenging the existence of nongermane provisions in the bill. More important, the special rule will also structure the debate and amendment process on the floor.

It was once more common for the special rule to permit unlimited amendments subject to the standing rules of the House. This sort of rule is called an **open rule**. As politics in Congress has become more partisan, open rules are used less and less. It can be seen in Table 5.1 that the use of open rules fell dramatically between the 103rd Congress in 1993–1994 and more recent Congresses.

Ten years ago, open rules were commonly applied to more than half of the bills brought before the Rules Committee; more recently, that number has dropped to one-quarter or even less, although they made something of a comeback in the 112th Congress, most notably on some appropriations bills. (The data include the **modified open rule**, which typically either allows any amendments to be offered

**TABLE 5.1 The Increase in the Use of Closed and Structured Rules for Consideration of Legislation on the House Floor, 1997–2012 (105th–112th Congresses)**

| RULE TYPE | 105th | | 106th | | 107th | | 108th | |
|---|---|---|---|---|---|---|---|---|
| | # | % | # | % | # | % | # | % |
| Open/modified open | 74 | 53 | 91 | 51 | 40 | 37 | 34 | 26 |
| Structured/modified closed | 42 | 30 | 49 | 27 | 44 | 41 | 62 | 47 |
| Closed | 24 | 17 | 39 | 22 | 23 | 22 | 37 | 28 |

| RULE TYPE | 109th | | 110th | | 111th | | 112th | |
|---|---|---|---|---|---|---|---|---|
| | # | % | # | % | # | % | # | % |
| Open/modified open | 24 | 19 | 23 | 14 | 1 | 1 | 25 | 19 |
| Structured/modified closed | 61 | 49 | 81 | 50 | 72 | 65 | 64 | 47 |
| Closed | 40 | 32 | 59 | 36 | 38 | 34 | 46 | 34 |

*Source:* House Rules Committees and Donald Wolfensberger of the Woodrow Wilson Center.

as long as they have been preprinted in the *Congressional Record* or puts some limit on the time allotted for amendments.) Use of the open rule has declined because allowing all members the opportunity to amend a bill leaves open the possibility that the minority party will offer amendments for the sole purpose of embarrassing majority party members, forcing them to make tough votes that weigh party loyalty against their potential electoral interests. Essentially, in this scenario, the majority party leadership loses some control of the agenda, which they are loath to let happen.

On the other hand, as Table 5.1 shows, **closed rules** have become more common. The pure closed rule allows no amendments. Usually, however, the leadership gets the Rules Committee to develop some sort of restrictive rule, often called a **structured** or **modified closed rule.** Such a rule permits only certain types of amendments to be offered (structured rule) or allows only a single substitute amendment (modified closed rule). Members who wish to amend an important bill often appear before the Rules Committee with their amendment in hand to plead their case.

Exhibit 5.1 shows examples of a structured rule and a closed rule from the 110th Congress. The structured rule specifies amendments for the Coast Guard Authorization Act of 2007. The closed rule, forbidding amendments, is for the Renewable Energy and Job Creation Act of 2008.

The leadership cannot always afford to be too restrictive. After all, they need to keep a majority of members happy in order to move their agenda, and rank-and-file members may insist on having a chance to amend some section of a bill.

Once the Rules Committee agrees to and reports a special rule, the rule must be adopted by the House by a majority vote. An hourlong debate on the special rule precedes the vote to adopt the rule. In other words, the leadership cannot literally dictate their preferences for the nature of the debate on the floor on the

---

## EXHIBIT 5.1

### STRUCTURED AND CLOSED RULES FOR DEBATE ON THE HOUSE FLOOR

---

**STRUCTURED RULE: HR 2830—COAST GUARD AUTHORIZATION ACT OF 2007**

1. Provides one hour of general debate, with 40 minutes equally divided and controlled by the chairman and ranking minority member of the Committee on Transportation and Infrastructure and 20 minutes equally divided and controlled by the chairman and ranking minority member of the Committee on Homeland Security.

2. Waives all points of order against consideration of the bill except those arising under clause 9 or 10 of rule XXI.

3. Provides that, in lieu of the amendments in the nature of a substitute recommended by the Committees on Transportation and Infrastructure, Homeland Security, and the Judiciary now printed in the bill, the amendment in the nature of a substitute printed in part A of the Rules Committee report accompanying the resolution shall be considered as an original bill for the purpose of amendment and shall be considered as read.

4. Waives all points of order against the amendment in the nature of a substitute printed in part A of the Rules Committee report accompanying the resolution except those arising under clause 10 of rule XXI. This does not affect the point of order available under clause 9 of rule XXI (regarding earmark disclosure).

5. Makes in order only those further amendments printed in part B of the Rules Committee report accompanying the resolution.

6. Provides that the amendments made in order may be offered only in the order printed in the report, may be offered only by a Member designated in the report, shall be considered as read, shall be debatable for the time specified in the report equally divided and controlled by the proponent and an opponent, shall not be subject to amendment, and shall not be subject to a demand for division of the question in the House or in the Committee of the Whole.

7. Waives all points of order against the amendments printed in part B of the Rules Committee report except for those arising under clause 9 or 10 of rule XXI.

8. Provides one motion to recommit with or without instructions.

bill itself; they need to gain the assent of a majority of the House. These are usually party-line votes. Members of the majority party may need, for political purposes, to vote against a bill. But in the interest of maintaining control over the agenda, the majority party leadership will expect its rank and file to support the special rule crafted by the Rules Committee.

One very important tool the majority party leadership sometimes uses is to include a **self-executing provision** in the rule. The special rule says that, upon its

---

## EXHIBIT 5.1 *(Continued)*

### STRUCTURED AND CLOSED RULES FOR DEBATE ON THE HOUSE FLOOR

---

9. Provides that in the engrossment of HR 2830, the text of HR 2399, as passed the House, shall be added at the end of HR 2830.

10. Provides that, notwithstanding the operation of the previous question, the Chair may postpone further consideration of the bill to a time designated by the Speaker.

11. Authorizes the chairman of the Committee on the Judiciary to file a supplemental report on HR 2830.

**CLOSED RULE: HR 6049—RENEWABLE ENERGY AND JOB CREATION ACT OF 2008**

1. Provides one hour of debate equally divided and controlled by the chairman and ranking member of the Committee on Ways and Means.

2. Waives all points of order against consideration of the bill except those arising under clause 9 or 10 of rule XXI.

3. Provides that the amendment in the nature of a substitute recommended by the Committee on Ways and Means now printed in the bill shall be considered as adopted and the bill, as amended, shall be considered as read.

4. Waives all points of order against provisions of the bill, as amended. This waiver does not affect the point of order available under clause 9 or rule XXI.

5. Provides one motion to recommit with or without instructions.

6. Provides that, notwithstanding the operation of the previous question, the Chair may postpone further consideration to a time designated by the Speaker.

*The House leadership often chooses to limit members' ability to amend legislation that the leaders bring to the floor. With the structured rule, House leadership permits certain amendments, as specified in points 6 and 8. For HR 6049, a closed rule is in place so no amendments are permitted.*

**SOURCE:** House Rules Committee, as suggested by Donald Wolfensberger of the Woodrow Wilson Center.

adoption by the House, certain legislative provisions will be automatically added to the bill that emerges from the committee or committees of jurisdiction. This is the mechanism by which leadership makes postcommittee adjustments to legislation. Such additions do not require a separate vote as amendments to the bill on the House floor, which could jeopardize their inclusion.

But special rules may go even further. The majority party leadership can arrange for the marriage of what are in effect two separate bills in a special rule. This is done when leadership believes that joining the bills before the vote would lead to its defeat. Such a rule stipulates that each bill will get a separate vote but that, by virtue of the adoption of the rule, the bills will then be joined before being sent over to the Senate or to the president for his signature if the Senate version has already passed the Senate as a single measure.

Speaker Pelosi arranged just such a marriage in 2007 when President Bush requested more funding for the Iraq War. The majority of Democrats did not want to give the president the money without a timetable for the withdrawal of US troops—something the president adamantly opposed; in addition, Democrats wanted to add money for domestic priorities, including an increase in the minimum wage.

Any bill requiring the troop-withdrawal timetable would have been vetoed, as would also have been the fate of a stand-alone bill that provided funding for domestic priorities opposed by the president. The solution: bring a war-funding bill without the troop-withdrawal requirement to the floor, where it would pass with more Republican than Democratic support, then separately bring the domestic spending and minimum wage bill to the floor, where that bill would pass with mostly Democratic support. The rule governing the floor consideration of these bills brought them together as one, which was the version the Senate had already passed, before sending them to the president. The president was happy enough with the war funding that he chose not to veto the entire package even though he opposed the additional domestic spending.

In an extreme example, for many years a self-executing provision in the special rule governing debate on the Budget Resolution in the House stipulated that the House approved an increase in the **debt ceiling** with the passage of the resolution (whose purpose is to provide a blueprint for spending and tax policy). This enabled the House to escape a separate vote on raising the debt ceiling. This tactic is no longer in use.

## Suspension of the Rules

Another tactic the leadership uses to move legislation is the *suspension procedure*, or the **suspension of the rules**. In fact, most bills come to the floor by this procedure.[9] In this case, the leadership bypasses the Rules Committee in moving bills to the floor. Under the suspension procedure, only 40 minutes of debate are permitted (divided equally between supporters and opponents), the bill is not amendable, and a two-thirds vote is required for final passage. Technically, that vote does double duty, both suspending the normal rules and passing the bill.

The suspension procedure has been used primarily for noncontroversial matters, but increasingly the leadership has employed it to pass important matters, including major reauthorizations (the reauthorization of the National Aeronautic and Space Administration [NASA] was handled this way in 2008), public lands bills, and even some budget legislation. The limited debate and the prohibition on amendments have led to a great deal of criticism of this practice, but its utility is clear. The leadership, provided it can round up the supermajority support, can move things much more quickly and cleanly in this fashion than it can even through the use of special rules. Of course, it should be noted, the two-thirds requirement cannot be met if the leadership does not have support from the minority party, which it must have in order to use suspension procedures successfully.

## Floor Consideration

To the best of its ability, the majority leadership tries to make floor consideration of the legislation on their agenda as anticlimactic as possible. But there are too many uncertainties involving wavering members and changing circumstances for them always to know for certain that they can attain the outcome they want if the vote is close.

As we have seen, the main mechanism the leadership uses to structure floor consideration and move their legislative agenda toward the desired result is through the creation and adoption of a special rule. Normally, in fact, the rule is adopted and the majority gets its way. The minority party may try to amend the rule, but such efforts rarely succeed. It does happen, slightly less rarely, that the rule itself is defeated. When that happens, it is a major embarrassment for the leadership, who must go back to the drawing board.

By adopting the rule, the House resolves itself into something called the **Committee of the Whole**. This "committee" includes all the members of the House. In fact, the Committee of the Whole is a parliamentary tactic to facilitate a manageable debating and amending process.

The Committee of the Whole requires that only 100 members be present for a quorum, instead of the 218 required to conduct business when the "actual" House convenes. (In fact, the quorum requirement is enforced only on the infrequent occasions when a member insists upon it.) Also, there are strict limits on debate during the amendment process, including a "five-minute rule" (five minutes for each side to make its case) for each amendment.

Most of the business of the House is conducted in the Committee of the Whole. First, there is general debate on the bill. The member managing the bill on the floor, usually the chair of the committee with preponderant jurisdiction, divvies up the time he or she has been allotted (a half hour, an hour, or more, as granted by the rule) among those who wish to speak in support of the bill. Opponents of the bill receive an equal amount of time (typically managed by the ranking member of the main committee of jurisdiction) to have their say.

After general debate, the amending process begins as allowed under the special rule. (Of course, no amendments are permitted under a closed rule.) Technically, those offering amendments have five minutes to explain them, followed by the floor manager, who has five minutes for rebuttal, unless more time is allowed for that amendment under the provisions of the special rule. Any other member may also speak for five minutes by offering an amendment to "strike the last word [of the amendment]." This is not a change that the member really wishes to enact; rather, the member is complying with a parliamentary requirement in the Committee of the Whole that, once general debate is finished, only those offering amendments may speak. Really, then, what the member is doing is commenting on the substantive amendment in question, not saying that he or she wishes to remove a word from it. In point of fact, members are rarely permitted to take the full five minutes to comment on the pending amendment. Nor is enough time usually allotted to give anywhere near all the membership the opportunity to speak. With 435 members, the majority feels the need to impose restrictions in order to streamline the process.

After the debate on the substantive amendment is complete, a recorded vote may be requested. The call is put out to all members, wherever they may be on Capitol Hill, to come to the House chamber. They cast their vote by inserting a card into one of the voting stations on the floor of the chamber, indicating a vote of yea, nay, or present. Members have 15 minutes to cast their vote. More commonly, the rule stipulates that debates will be held on all the amendments, one after the other, before the call is put out to cast a vote. Fifteen minutes are allotted for members to get to the chamber and vote on the first amendment, after which five minutes are allotted for each of the other amendments. This arrangement is called **stacking votes**. The advantage of stacking is that members do not have to run back and forth from their offices or a hearing all day to vote on each individual amendment.

When the Committee of the Whole finishes its business, it reports the bill back to the full House, which then convenes to consider that business. Usually, the amendments that have been passed in the Committee of the Whole are voted on packaged together, a way of voting referred to as *en bloc*. Ordinarily, that package succeeds, since the full House is, after all, the same body of people who voted on the amendments in the first place in the Committee of the Whole. Amendments that were closely contested in the Committee of the Whole may be separated out and voted on individually.

Next, the bill itself, as amended, comes up for a vote. Normally, 15 minutes are allotted for this vote. In particularly contentious matters, the speaker may leave the vote open longer, but doing so invites considerable controversy. Box 5.2 describes an extreme case of leaving the vote open. Obviously, the majority would rather have the votes easily in hand and conclude business in a timely fashion. The fact is that the majority controls the House floor and will go to great lengths if necessary, even violating long-established norms of conduct, to move its agenda.

Opponents of a bill have little recourse. If they have been shut out of any opportunity to amend it or to bring their favored approach up for consideration, they may make their point by offering a **motion to recommit**. Such a motion expresses the minority's discontent with what has happened and calls for specific changes in the bill. Usually, opponents use a motion to recommit as a last-ditch effort to scuttle the bill, but sometimes a successful motion to recommit effectuates changes in the legislation that the minority favors.

In 2007 Republicans stymied a Democratic agenda item with a cleverly crafted motion to recommit. That year the Democratically controlled US House was poised to pass a bill that would give the residents of the District of Columbia a full-fledged voting House member. (Currently, the District has a delegate, who has all the privileges of a member of Congress *except* voting rights on the House floor.) In an effort to score political points at the expense of Democrats representing progun constituencies, the Republicans offered a motion to recommit with instructions to repeal the gun ban in the District. Speaker Pelosi did not want these Democrats to have to vote against the gun-ban repeal, so she pulled the DC voting bill from the floor rather than have some of her more vulnerable members cast a controversial vote.[10]

## KEY STAGES IN THE LEGISLATIVE PROCESS: THE SENATE
### Bill Introduction and Committee Referral

The process for bill introduction is essentially the same in the Senate as it is in the House, but the committee referral process is different. According to Senate rules, the majority leader cannot exert the kind of influence over referral that the speaker of the House can through the various types of multiple referrals available in that chamber.

The parliamentarian of the Senate—a nonpartisan office, as it is in the House— refers the entire bill to the committee with preponderant jurisdiction based on the content of the legislation.[11] The rules do not include the option of a multiple referral.

## BOX 5.2

## Prescription Drug Coverage Passes in the Wee Hours

One of the most dramatic moments in the recent history of Congress occurred in the early-morning hours of November 22, 2003. President Bush
and the Republican Congress were determined to pass their version of a massive new Medicare entitlement program to provide prescription coverage for seniors. They ran into major stumbling blocks on the House floor from Democrats
*and* Republicans.

Intent on getting out of town for Thanksgiving, the House was working late
to complete important business. Finally, at 3:00 a.m., a vote was called on the
Medicare prescription drug bill. Members had 15 minutes to register their votes.
The outcome seemed clear: by a 219–215 vote, the plan had failed. But this was
an unacceptable outcome for the Republican leadership of the House headed by
Speaker Dennis Hastert, as well as for the president, who intended to campaign
for reelection in part on the basis of this accomplishment.

It is not uncommon for House votes to be kept open to give members more
time to get to the floor, or even to do a little persuading to change what looks like
the wrong outcome from the perspective of the majority party. But in this case,
it was taken to extremes. The president got on the phone to talk to some members. He had instructed the secretary of Health and Human Services, Tommy
Thompson, to hang around the Capitol to lobby for the bill. And, of course, the
House leadership, including the speaker himself and Majority Leader Tom DeLay,
was active.

One Republican, Jo Ann Emerson of Missouri, was called at home; leaders
were told by her husband that in fact she was still at the Capitol—she had been
hiding among a group of Democrats on the House floor and had gone unseen
after casting a nay vote. Another Republican opponent of the legislation, Nick
Smith of Michigan, initially claimed to have been illegally threatened by powerful
Republicans for his vote against the legislation. (He later recanted the charge.)

Ultimately, after holding the vote open for a record two hours and 51 minutes, the leadership managed to change three minds, and the bill was passed.
Many Democrats have still not forgotten what they regarded as an abuse of the
legislative process—even some Republicans remain bitter at the tough tactics
of their party's leadership. In any case, this, admittedly extreme, case exemplifies the kind of control that the majority party can exert in the House of
Representatives.*

*A good description of the vote can be found in many journalistic sources. A longer
description can be found in Norman Ornstein and Thomas Mann, *The Broken Branch*
(Oxford: Oxford University Press, 2006), chaps. 1 and 4.

The reality, however, is that complex bills often do receive consideration in more than one committee in the Senate. The difference from the House is that consideration of a bill by multiple committees is not handled by a split referral engineered by the majority leadership. Instead, the Senate divides up legislation in informal ways. Committee chairs talk to one another. Often, the chair of the committee of jurisdiction agrees to allow other committees to deal with certain provisions of a bill. Chairs do not do this to be magnanimous; they recognize that in the Senate, they will need the support of other key members down the line if they want the bill to become law.

As in the House, it is possible for the Senate leadership to bypass the committee process altogether. Then–Senate majority leader Tom Daschle of South Dakota did exactly that with comprehensive energy legislation in 2002. The committee chair handling the bill, Max Baucus of Montana, intended to include a provision permitting drilling for oil in the Arctic National Wildlife Refuge, a policy that Daschle and many other Democrats opposed. The leader bypassed the committee and brought the bill to the floor without the drilling provision.[12]

The leadership often works to develop postcommittee adjustments to enhance the chances of legislation on the floor and to move forward a favored agenda item. But as with the committee referral process and every other aspect of Senate procedure, the actions of the majority leader in setting and pursuing an agenda are highly constrained compared with what the speaker can do in the House. Assuming the votes are in hand, the Speaker of the House may impose his or her agenda, streamlining the committee and floor consideration process to that end. The majority leader of the Senate is in no such position.

The Senate operates under a supermajority principle. The Senate leader must respect the rights of the minority because every senator has a wide range of prerogatives that can be used to delay floor action, sometimes even indefinitely. This precludes the kind of tight control over the agenda that is possible in the House. The upshot is that the leadership rarely is able to pursue a partisan agenda with any consistent success. The majority leader must take into account not only the views of the minority party but very often those of every single senator. So engineering postcommittee adjustments on legislation, for example, must to a significant degree be a cooperative activity.

## Floor Consideration

In the Senate, every member has equal stature, and thus every member has an equal right to recognition on the Senate floor. The majority leader, however, is slightly "more equal." If the majority leader asks to be recognized, he or she may trump the rest of the membership of the body. It is this simple right of first recognition that gives the majority leader the ability, by tradition, to establish the agenda.

The majority leader's agenda-setting power, however, is much more constrained than the House speaker's. Not only may any of the other senators take the floor, but they may hold the floor for as long as they want (often called a **filibuster**), raise any issues they want, and offer any amendments they want.[13] By contrast, members of the House must stay on topic, have a limited time to speak, and usually operate under restricted amending procedures.

All of this stems from the fact that, in the House, a simple majority can establish the rules (including the amending process) and bring a measure to a vote. In the Senate, a simple majority is not able to "call the previous question," parliamentary-speak for bringing a bill to a vote. Either *every senator* must agree to allow a vote, or, alternatively, a supermajority of 60 is required.

The implication of these differences with the House is that the agenda of the Senate can become very fluid. The leader has great difficulty moving legislation in a timely fashion, and because members can offer any amendments they wish, the very nature of the agenda can very easily be turned on its head. Whole bills that the leader wants to see disappear can theoretically reappear on the floor at any time in the form of an amendment.

How can the leader move his agenda, serving the interests of his party and the country? Only with the greatest difficulty, as we shall see.

### Unanimous Consent: Passing the Simple Stuff

The best way to move toward floor consideration and a vote in the Senate is to achieve **unanimous consent** from the whole membership to do so. When non-controversial matters are counted, *most* Senate business is not only brought to the floor by unanimous consent but also *passed* by unanimous consent—with little or no debate.

Keep in mind that the Senate docket is considerably longer than the House's. The Senate, unlike the House, must approve of judicial nominations as well as hundreds of nominations to high-level executive branch positions.

The majority leader uses a technique called **hotlining** to deal with the heavy workload. What happens is that the majority leader and the minority leader send a message to their respective senators, delivered to a dedicated phone and e-mail account in each office. The message says that the majority leadership intends to pass by unanimous consent certain bills or nominations for executive branch positions or district court nominations at some point—say, the next day. Any senator who objects is expected to notify his or her leadership. If no senator communicates an

---

## BOX 5.3

### The Federal Election Commission Is Put on Ice

As of December 31, 2007, the Federal Election Commission was, for all intents and purposes, forced to close its doors by the US Senate. The independent agency, charged with enforcing the federal election and financing laws, is governed by a six-member commission. A vote of at least four commissioners is required to enforce the complex and controversial campaign laws. As the 2008 campaign got into full swing, three openings on the commission were unfilled. These slots require Senate confirmation. Unfortunately, some senators objected to one of the president's nominees. As a result, through much of the 2008 election cycle the commission failed to have a quorum and was unable to rule on important campaigning financing matters, including one especially sticky matter involving Senator John McCain's decision to opt out of public financing for his campaign for the Republican nomination.*

*Martin Kady II, "FEC Nominations on Hold Until After Memorial Day," Politico.com, May 21, 2008, www.politico.com/blogs/thecrypt/0508/FEC_nominees_on_hold_until_after _Memorial_Day_.html.

---

objection, the leader can anticipate that no opposition will arise the next day when he or she makes a unanimous consent request to pass the measures or approve the nominations.

The catch is that any one senator, by objecting, derails the process. By objecting to a unanimous consent request, a senator places a **hold** on legislation or a nomination. In effect, the senator is threatening to delay the process—which could involve speaking at great length (a filibuster) or, more commonly, using less strenuous available tactics to tie up the Senate floor. For minor and noncontroversial matters, it is simply impracticable for precious floor time to be used. (And it takes quite a long time to quash even a single senator, as we shall see shortly.) So a senator who places a hold (essentially, objecting to a unanimous consent request) stops a bill or a nomination from going forward. At times such a tactic can have major ramifications, in the extreme even effectively shutting down a federal agency (see Box 5.3).

The hold process gives each senator tremendous leverage. A clever member can often find a priority matter to object to that will force the majority leader to come calling—even if that senator doesn't care one way or another about the nomination or bill itself. In this way, every member is in a position to bargain with the leadership and can exert influence on almost any legislation he or she wants.

## Unanimous Consent: Major Legislation

Even much substantial legislative business is brought to the floor only after *every member* agrees to proceed. That does not mean that all members *support* the legislation in question; it does mean that they agree to permit debate to move forward without engaging in a filibuster or other delaying tactic.

Members will agree to let the majority leader go forward, even if they oppose the bill, for a lot of reasons. They may simply wish to have their say and get on record opposing the bill. They may want the opportunity to bring up amendments for a vote. They may want a concession or two or a provision added to another bill later in the year. They may just want to have some predictability in their schedules, which can be facilitated only by ceding some control over the agenda to the majority leader. All members recognize that the leader can be helpful in the future with some matter of particular importance to them.

For complex legislation, the majority leader may negotiate something called a **unanimous consent (UC) agreement**, or *time-limitation agreement*. Getting to a UC agreement is a very delicate matter. Persuading 100 strong-willed individuals to agree to anything is difficult.

The UC agreement is basically a version of a House special rule, with the obvious exception that it needs to have everyone on board, not just the support of a majority. The agreement structures floor consideration, perhaps by limiting amendments and debate time. Usually, many amendments have to be permitted in the Senate, and much more time for debate allowed (often multiple days), than in the House, since all members are in a position to bargain.

## Holds, Filibuster, and Cloture

Just as with the relatively minor or noncontroversial matters discussed earlier, any senator may place a hold by objecting to a unanimous consent request for a major bill or nomination. It is then necessary to invoke something called **cloture** in order to bring the matter to the floor for an eventual vote. Invoking cloture is the forceful way, as opposed to getting unanimous agreement, to put a limit on debate and come to a vote in the Senate. Because cloture requires 60 votes, it almost always involves members of both parties. (Even when a party has 60 senators, as Democrats enjoyed for about a year during the 111th Congress, rarely can all 60 be held together.) After cloture is invoked—which takes two days—consideration of the bill is limited to thirty hours and all amendments must be prefiled and germane to the subject of the bill.

What is astonishing is that this often underestimates the time it takes to move toward a vote. This is because even recently streamlined Senate procedures provide more than one opportunity for members to filibuster on any given bill.[14] It may take a week or so to come to a vote.

The cloture process is so cumbersome that it is reserved for major bills or nominations—let's say energy or transportation legislation, an overhaul of defense policy, or a contentious nomination to the Supreme Court. The days it takes to invoke cloture and come to a vote are generally not wasted on minor matters.

Invoking cloture is useful to the majority leadership for another reason: it provides protection against nongermane amendments. After cloture, members are limited to amendments that are related to the bill. Minority party senators, in particular, value their right to bring up extraneous matters for a few reasons: because they may care a great deal about an issue that the majority doesn't want to raise; because the amendment, if adopted, would tend to undermine support for the larger legislation; or to score political points at the majority's expense even if the amendment fails. The source of most disagreements and tension between the majority and minority in the Senate is amendments—the majority wants to limit the minority's ability to offer controversial amendments, and the minority insists on its right to bring up its issues.

In today's Senate, the majority leadership often begins consideration of a bill by invoking cloture (if they can) or by including 60-vote requirements for all or most provisions covered in a unanimous consent agreement.[15] Because gaining 60 votes requires the cooperation of some minority party members, the Senate majority leader and minority leader communicate regularly, even daily at times. Compromise is the only way forward, if a way can be found at all. This distinguishes the Senate from the House in a critical way. The House majority leadership may move an agenda as quickly as it would like without consulting the minority (as long as they have the votes). In the Senate, when the majority leader indicates a readiness to move forward with a particular bill, he or she needs to know who from the rank and file *of both parties* might have objections.

* * *

The Senate is characterized by seemingly endless deliberation and delay and almost always by compromise on substance. It is certainly in the interest of all the members to complete important business—and they have a lot of it to do; however, nearly all senators have strong feelings on certain issues, and all resolutely defend the interests of their respective states. Negotiations can thus be slow and painstaking, and often it is impossible, given time constraints, to move an ambitious agenda. Certainly, the Senate tends to lag behind the House.

In the end, in the case of complex legislation the majority leader usually feels his or her way along on the floor. A UC agreement may not cover the whole bill, with the leader getting agreement to move forward only on selected parts. Negotiations continue as certain provisions are disposed with. As the bill proceeds, members may insist on more floor time or more amendments. The leadership of the two parties are in constant contact and rely on each other's good faith. Ultimately, the aim is to get something passed and to move toward reconciling the Senate bill with what may already have passed the House.

## RECONCILING THE DIFFERENCES

As we have seen, the presentment clause of the Constitution requires that legislation sent to the president be passed in identical form in each chamber. This is no easy task, as senators and members of the House almost always have very different perspectives on issues. As a result, the versions of a bill that emerge from each chamber—whether it is an appropriations bill, the defense authorization bill, or a bill to authorize funding for roads and bridges—will differ, usually in significant ways, even when the same party controls the House and Senate.

It is important to point out that the two chambers do not always strike a deal, and lack of a deal means the death of a bill. But it is also true that once the two chambers have passed complex legislation, there is a great deal of buy-in, and many members do not want to see all the effort they have put in wasted. Having said that, important matters have in fact languished in limbo—sometimes for years—as the chambers tried to hammer out a compromise. Recently, legislation to reform the credit industry took several years of negotiation, stretching over more than two Congresses to be finalized. The most recent comprehensive energy legislation, signed into law in 2005, followed a similar years-long path to final passage and law. Sometimes the sticking point is the president, whose veto threat can complicate the process. Because the president is a player in the legislative process, it is necessary to consider his concerns on major legislation.

There are three ways in which the chambers can come to an agreement on legislation. The easy way is for one chamber simply to pick up what has passed the other and then pass that bill unaltered. This is rare for consequential matters, but quite common for less controversial ones, although the bulk of the health care overhaul passed in 2010 was achieved that way in a classic case of unorthodox lawmaking (see Box 5.4). Alternatively, in a process often called **amendments between the chambers**, the House and Senate may pass legislation back and forth, amending the legislation as they go along until both sides' needs are met and one chamber adopts whatever the other chamber has passed. The third option is to form a **conference committee**, an ad hoc panel made up of the relevant players in the House and Senate, to hammer out the differences. We focus on the latter two approaches, as they are the ones normally used for important legislation.

## Conference Committee

One common way to bridge the differences between bills passed by the House and Senate is to form a conference committee (or simply a *conference*) made up of members from each chamber. One chamber or the other requests a conference, and the other may follow up by agreeing to the request. The speaker is in charge of appointing the House conferees. He or she is bound by what are fairly flexible rules in making these appointments. At least a majority of members must be supportive of the House version of the bill, and there must be minority party representation. Typically, the speaker appoints members from the committee or committees who worked on the bill from the beginning, on the theory that they are the most qualified to deal with the complex questions that will come up in negotiations with the other chamber.

In the Senate, the committee chair or chairs who worked on the bill and the majority leader choose their party's delegation to the conference, and the minority leader and the committee's ranking member choose the remainder of the conferees. It is most important to note that the Senate process of agreeing to go to conference with the House is complex, requiring three steps. Because it is relatively easy for determined senators to block the effort with dilatory tactics, the process of amendments between the chambers is used more often than a conference committee as the method of bridging differences on major legislation by a ratio of about two to one.[16]

The conference committee approach to bridging differences is logical for complex legislation, on which there are often many differences between the two chambers' versions. Difficult negotiations are required to handle all the problem areas in the bill. On appropriations bills, for example, there are often hundreds of differences between the two versions. (Appropriations bills were traditionally handled in conference committees, but that is no longer true.) The 2010 reform of the financial regulatory system known as "Dodd-Frank" was handled in a conference committee. It involved members from multiple committees in each chamber and dozens of highly contentious issues on which the two chambers differed.

Often, the thinking is that the best way to handle the negotiations is behind closed doors, where hard decisions can be made more easily and simple "split the difference" compromises can be hidden from view. In addition, conference committees are made up of those members who are most knowledgeable on the particular issues in question.

Technically, conference committees meet in public; in reality, they hold very few public sessions—usually only one pro forma session—while handling the real work behind the scenes. The public session is often reserved for officially ratifying

# BOX 5.4

## Reforming Health Care

The passage of the Patient Protection and Affordable Care Act in 2010 did not follow "regular order" in Congress. Not only was there no conference committee, but special procedures bypassing the filibuster were used to amend parts of it, and the bill was used as a vehicle to pass major unrelated legislation that had not been debated fully in either chamber.

The bill (and the ancillary matters) was a huge priority for Democrats, who decided that they would use almost any means necessary to meet their policy objectives when they had the levers of power. A closer look at the process is instructive of the way the contemporary Congress works—a leadership-controlled environment where regular order matters a lot less than results.

### EARLY EFFORTS

Senator Max Baucus led Senate negotiations on health care reform through much of 2009, culminating in the Finance Committee reporting out S 1796, America's Healthy Future Act of 2009, on October 19. The bill as S 1796 went no further.

Meanwhile, Representative John Dingell introduced HR 3200, America's Affordable Health Choices Act of 2009, on July 14. It was referred to several committees for examination, including Energy and Commerce, Education and Labor, and Ways and Means. These committees reported out their respective portions of the bill on October 14, 2009. The bill as HR 3200 went no further.

However, it resurfaced after negotiations and numerous changes as HR 3962, the Affordable Health Care Act for America, on October 29. It was referred to several committees that day, all of which immediately ratified it. It was scheduled for floor action on November 7 and passed, 220–215. This bill went no further.

### NOW IT GETS TRICKY

HR 3590, the Service Members Home Ownership Tax Act, was introduced in the House (sponsored by Representative Charles Rangel) on September 17, 2009. This bill extended the first-time home owners' tax credit for military people and some other federal employees. It was referred to the Ways and Means Committee. On October 8, it passed the House under Suspension of the Rules, 416–0, and was sent to the Senate.

HR 3590 underwent a makeover in the Senate. Baucus's health care bill, with some substantial alterations, was attached to the simple tax measure. (The Constitution says revenue measures must start in the House. The health care

# BOX 5.4 *(Continued)*
## Reforming Health Care

bill had tax provisions and thus needed to be attached to a House-passed tax bill. Essentially, HR 3590 served as a shell for the larger reform bill.) The bill was renamed the Patient Protection and Affordable Care Act. Cloture was invoked on November 21, and ultimately the Senate's version of health care was passed as HR 3590 by a vote of 60–39 on Christmas Eve. Only Democrats voted for it.

### THE ELECTION OF SCOTT BROWN, AND A NEW END GAME

While the two Democratically controlled chambers intended to come together in conference to iron out the very significant differences between their two versions of health reform, a wrench was thrown into the works when a special election was held for the late senator Edward Kennedy's Massachusetts seat in January 2010. Surprisingly, Republican Scott Brown secured the seat, denying Democrats their 60-vote filibuster-proof majority that would be needed for final passage of a compromise version.

After a period of handwringing, House Democrats recognized that they would have to accept the Senate version or there would be no health reform at all. HR 3590 was brought to the House floor in March 2010, passing in exactly the form it passed the Senate back in December, 219–212. The Patient Protection and Affordable Care Act was signed into law by President Obama on March 23.

### MINOR FIXES, AND SOME NEW GOODIES

But because the House wasn't entirely happy with HR 3590, they had forged a deal with the Senate to immediately address some of those misgivings. The "fixes" were designed to take advantage of the Senate's fast-track reconciliation procedure that eliminates the filibuster and requires only 51 votes instead of the usual 60 that was needed for HR 3590. HR 4872, the Health Care and Education Affordability Reconciliation Act of 2010, was introduced in the House on March 17. It passed on March 21, shortly after HR 3590, by a vote of 220–211. Four days later, the Senate passed it 56–43—with a few minor changes to comply with parliamentary rulings. The House concurred with the version as amended by the Senate.

It was signed into law on March 30. Interestingly, the Reconciliation Act included a major provision not related at all to health care: a total restructuring of the federal student loan program and significant increases in Pell Grants. Both were regarded as major accomplishments by Democrats.

the work done behind closed doors. The final version of the bill agreed to in the conference committee is called the **conference report**.

Conference committees are required by the rules of both chambers to keep the negotiations within the scope of the bills as passed by the two chambers. Thus, new items that were not in the House or Senate bill are not allowed to appear magically in the final version; negotiations must stay within the parameters of the two bills. (If one bills says the government should buy 50 missiles and the other says 100, the final version must have a number somewhere between 50 and 100.) Moreover, items that appeared in both the House and the Senate versions must stay in the final version.

In the real world, members sometimes stray from these rules (which are treated more like guidelines). Each chamber has methods that can be used to get around the rules prohibiting extraneous provisions, staying within the parameters of the two bills, and removing agreed-to items in the final product. The decisions in conference are not always premised on abiding by the technical rules of the chambers.

Instead, conference negotiations are premised on the Rule of 218 and 60. What really guides behavior is the question, what do we need to do to put together a conference report that can pass both chambers? If new provisions need to be added, given changing views or changing circumstances, then new language is inserted. If the president threatens a veto based on something he opposes that is in both versions, then every effort is made to find a way to waive the relevant chamber's rule once the conference report is sent back to the House and Senate floors. The larger point is that so much is at stake at this point, so many members have put in so much time and effort, that everything possible will be done to produce a final version that can pass both chambers.

When the final version is completed, the delegation from the House and the delegation from the Senate vote separately. If both chambers' delegations vote in favor by a majority vote, the conference report is sent back to the House and Senate for a vote on final passage. The conference report may not be amended on the House or Senate floor—a real advantage of using the conference process—but it may be filibustered in the Senate. Thus, 60 votes are often required to get a vote on final passage in the Senate.

## Amendments Between the Chambers

Sometimes it is impossible to form a conference committee, particularly if senators block the formation of one. Or it may be easier, or deemed preferable, to avoid a conference. In these cases, differences can be resolved by sending a bill back and forth in the process called amendments between the chambers, with each chamber making changes until one chamber agrees with the whole version as sent to it from the other.

Although it is true that amendments between the chambers may sometimes be the only option for arriving at agreement, it is also the case that the majority party leadership in the two chambers may prefer this method. The reason: it can give them more control over the process than a conference committee.

Conference committees bring into the same room many of the committee members who have worked on the bill in both chambers—with complex legislation, these are often members from three or more congressional committees. Although leadership is almost always asked to help broker the negotiations in these cases, the fact is that a conference committee is run by one of the committee chairs and the work is driven to a great degree by the interests of the committee members. The bottom line is that the leadership may lose control over the final legislative product to committee chairs who do not necessarily see eye to eye with them on all the major substantive issues involved.

By ping-ponging the bill back and forth between the chambers, the leadership retains control over the negotiations and scheduling. Unlike in a conference committee, where rank-and-file congressional negotiators make the changes, the leaders determine the parameters for changes in the bill through the amendment process on the floor of the two chambers. These negotiations between the top leaders of the two chambers can be highly delicate, as one would imagine, especially in the Senate, where leadership operates under more constraints than House leadership.

Negotiations using the amendments between the chambers method are entirely informal and can be limited to just a few prominent players, all to the benefit of leadership trying to push through an agenda advantageous to their party. Still, the complexity of the issues at stake on many bills and the desire of the rank and file to have a conference committee can trump the leadership's desire for more control.

## The End of the Process: The White House

With most major legislation, the president and his closest aides and cabinet members have been involved in the negotiations on Capitol Hill. The administration is likely to have an interest in every major piece of legislation that affects the work of the executive branch of government. If Congress wants the final version of a piece of legislation to become law, and the members cannot override a presidential veto, they will have to address the president's concerns. In effect, the administration becomes part of the legislative process to the point of lobbying aggressively for its viewpoint.

Of course, if the president does not like the final product, he may also veto it. When he does that, he explains his reasons and sends the bill back to Congress.

Both houses must muster a two-thirds vote to override a veto and make a bill law over the president's objection. In the past 20 years, only seven presidential vetoes have been overridden, and only four of those were on substantial legislation.

The president may also allow a bill to become law without his signature. If he does not act on a bill within ten days, it becomes law. He may also "**pocket veto**" a bill by refusing to sign it in the last ten days of a two-year Congress. In this way, Congress has no opportunity to override the veto, and the bill does not become law.

But ordinarily, as already mentioned, Congress wants a result for all the hard work that went into navigating the legislative process and so compromises with the president to produce a bill he will sign. Sometimes, however, Congress passes legislation, knowing the president will veto it and knowing it cannot override that veto, simply to make a point. This is most common when the government is divided and Congress is intent on demonstrating what it could pass into law if a president of the other party were elected. Democrats did this in the 1980s and early 1990s with the Family and Medical Leave Act, which was passed three times in that period, but Congress was unable to override presidential vetoes. Finally, in 1993, Democratic president Bill Clinton signed it into law.

## CONCLUSION

The legislative process in review:

- There are multiple "veto points"—places where bills can be stopped, making the system inefficient, but probably in keeping with the intentions of the constitutional framers.
- The legislative process "on paper" is not a requirement; the only requirement for a bill to become law is that it passes both chambers in identical form.
- Party leadership determines the legislative agenda on the House and Senate floor, thus conditioning the early stages (development of bills and committee consideration) of the legislative process.
- The House is run by simple majority rule, which may mean little or no consultation on some matters with the minority party.
- The Senate comes to a vote only by unanimous consent or by a 60-vote supermajority threshold; as a result, compromise between the parties is almost always required on significant legislation.
- In the House, the legislative process may be streamlined and efficient; this is almost never the case in the Senate.

Critically important to understanding Congress in the 21st century is the concept of *unorthodox lawmaking*. The parties will go to great lengths to pass their agenda *when they want to pass it,* even if it means ignoring some of the stages of the "how a bill becomes a law" chart. Party priorities trump a regularized and predictable process. The process for passing the health care overhaul described in Box 5.4 is an excellent example, as is the case of the prescription drug bill from 2003 (Box 5.2).

The House was forced to hold its nose and vote for the Senate's version of the health care bill in 2010, having very little say in its contents. Not only that, the companion reconciliation bill that addressed a few of the House's concerns included comprehensive reform of the student loan program and major changes to the Pell Grant program, both unrelated to the issue at hand and accomplished without hearings or markups by the committees of jurisdiction. But both were high priorities for the Democratic majority, which was intent on accomplishing its ends even if it meant disregarding regular processes. Similarly, the prescription-drugs-for-seniors bill—a major priority for Republicans at the time—would never have made it into law without flaunting House rules in ways that had never been seen before.

It is also important to note that the routine business of Congress, such as passing annual agency budgets, is increasingly impossible to do without resorting to legislative legerdemain—packaging multiple bills together and skipping important stages of the process, especially any vote on the Senate floor for individual bills. We look carefully at this development in Chapter 8.

An increasingly partisan Congress paradoxically leads both to a desire of the parties to do whatever they can to pass their top agenda items and at the same time to a situation in which the complex legislative process is next to impossible to negotiate for ordinary annual business. We will revisit this topic in depth in the last chapter of the book.

## Questions for Discussion

1. A lot of people think Congress is an archaic body better suited to an earlier time when the pace of change, socially and economically, was much slower. Would you argue for or against the proposition that a legislative process as inefficient as Congress should be overhauled? If you think so, what might those reforms look like?

2. The Speaker of the House has a great deal of power through the Rules Committee in structuring debate and determining the legislative agenda. What are the pluses and minuses of such a system?

3.  What would be gained by doing away with the tradition of extended debate in the Senate? What would be lost, if anything?

---

## Suggestions for Further Reading

Cox, Gary W., and Matthew D. McCubbins. *Legislative Leviathan: Party Government in the House.* Berkeley: University of California Press, 2007.

Koger, Gregory. *Filibustering: A Political History of Obstruction in the House and Senate.* Chicago: University of Chicago Press, 2010.

Sinclair, Barbara. *Unorthodox Lawmaking: New Legislative Processes in the U.S. Congress.* 3rd ed. Washington, DC: CQ Press, 2008.

Smith, Steven S., and Gerald Gamm. "The Dynamics of Party Government in Congress." In *Congress Reconsidered,* edited by Bruce Oppenheimer and Larry Dodd, 167–192. 10th ed. Washington, DC: CQ Press, 2013.

## NOTES

1.  Barbara Sinclair, *Unorthodox Lawmaking: New Legislative Processes in the U.S. Congress,* 3rd ed. (Washington, DC: CQ Press, 2008).

2. Usually, more than 10,000 bills and resolutions are introduced over a two-year Congress. For example, in the 112th Congress (2011–2012) about 12,000 bills and resolutions were introduced. Only 2 percent of that total ended up as enacted law, and 7 percent succeeded as concurrent resolutions of Congress. The latter involve statements on world affairs, the use of the Capitol Rotunda, internal matters, and many other things. These do not go to the president and do not have the force of law. Comprehensive statistics can be found at www.govtrack.us/congress/bills/#statistics.

3. An excellent resource on the evolution of Congress, covering the changing role of committee chairs, their relationship to party leadership, and other related matters, is Nelson Polsby, *How Congress Evolves: Social Bases of Institutional Change* (Oxford: Oxford University Press, 2004). See also John H. Aldrich, Brittany N. Perry, and David W. Rohde, "Richard Fenno's Theory of Congressional Committees and the Partisan Polarization of the House," in *Congress Reconsidered,* edited by Bruce Oppenheimer and Larry Dodd, 10th ed. (Washington, DC: CQ Press, 2013), 193–220.

4. See Gary W. Cox and Matthew D. McCubbins, *Legislative Leviathan: Party Government in the House* (Berkeley: University of California Press, 2007); and Steven S. Smith and Gerald Gamm, "The Dynamics of Party Government in Congress," in *Congress Reconsidered,* edited by Oppenheimer and Dodd, 167–192.

5. See Nathan W. Monroe, Jason M. Roberts, and David W. Rohde, *Why Not Parties? Party Effects in the United States Senate* (Chicago: University of Chicago Press, 2008).

6. This summary of the legislative process in the House and Senate draws heavily from three principal published sources: Sinclair, *Unorthodox Lawmaking;* Walter Oleszek, *Congressional Procedures and the Policy Process,* 8th ed. (Washington, DC: CQ Press, 2010);

and Valerie Heitshusen, *CRS Report for Congress: The Legislative Process on the Senate Floor, an Introduction,* Congressional Research Service, November 28, 2012. It also draws from numerous e-mail correspondences and in-person interviews with congressional staff and analysts at the Congressional Research Service.

7. In the 110th Congress, Speaker Pelosi found herself at odds on important matters of policy with Energy and Commerce Committee chair John Dingell. Because he was unwilling to move legislation of the sort the party leadership preferred, Dingell's committee was frequently bypassed and legislation was brought to the floor without his having weighed in. Dingell was challenged for the committee chair post by Henry Waxman of California at the beginning of the 111th Congress, and Waxman won a close vote in the Democratic caucus.

8. Oleszek, *Congressional Procedures and the Policy Process,* 127–128.

9. Valerie Heitshusen, *CRS Report for Congress: Introduction to the Legislative Process in the U.S. Congress,* Congressional Research Service, November 30, 2012, 8.

10. Don Wolfensberger, "Democrats' DC Vote Fix Backfires in Gun Law Blowup," *Roll Call,* April 9, 2007.

11. There is an exception to this in Senate rules. Any bill with tax provisions is referred to the Senate Finance Committee regardless of whether Finance is the committee of preponderant jurisdiction.

12. For an excellent description of this debate and Majority Leader Daschle's use of Senate rules in this instance, see the American Geological Institute's "Arctic National Wildlife Refuge Update (11-19-02)," www.agiweb.org/gap/legis107/anwr.html.

13. The Senate, unlike the House and most other legislative bodies around the world, has no means to "call the previous question"—that is, make a motion to end debate and bring a bill or amendment to a vote. Essentially, then, a debate has to run its course before a matter can be voted on. As a practical matter, informal agreements are made to limit debate in the Senate. Invoking cloture on a lengthy debate has the effect of limiting debate but does not bring the bill or amendment to an immediate vote. Two of the best books on the filibuster and unlimited debate are Gregory Koger's *Filibustering: A Political History of Obstruction in the House and Senate* (Chicago: University of Chicago Press, 2010); and Sarah Binder and Stephen Smith's *Politics or Principle: Filibustering in the United States Senate* (Washington, DC: Brookings Institution Press, 1997).

14. A description of the 2013 reform of the filibuster procedures can be found in Elizabeth Rybicki, *CRS Report for Congress: Changes in the Senate Procedures in the 113th Congress Affecting the Operation of Cloture (S.Res. 15 and S.Res. 16),* Congressional Research Service, March 19, 2013.

15. See Megan Suzanne Lynch, *CRS Report for Congress: Unanimous Consent Agreements Establishing a 60-Vote Threshold for Passage of Legislation in the Senate,* Congressional Research Service, May 12, 2009.

16. See Elizabeth Rybicki, *CRS Report for Congress: Going to Conference in the Senate,* Congressional Research Service, February 18, 2011.

# 6
CHAPTER

# Authorizing the Work of Government

In this chapter through Chapter 10, we get down to the business of how Congress exercises its legislative and oversight powers. These activities follow a logical progression:

First, Congress passes *authorizing* statutes that establish agencies and federal programs for one year, multiple years, or indefinitely. These statutes detail, with varying levels of specificity, the aim of the programs and the policies that agency officials must follow when implementing the law. Basically, these laws give agencies the legal *authority* to take actions. In addition, most authorizing statutes set a funding ceiling for the agencies and programs *but do not provide the actual funding* for those programs. (Important exceptions to this last rule are covered later in the chapter.)

Second, Congress passes *appropriations* laws to fund the agencies and programs within the parameters set in the authorizing statutes. Appropriations for the vast majority of government programs are provided on an annual basis. Congress is supposed to appropriate money only for those programs that have a current authorization for appropriation established in law. The appropriations process is covered in Chapter 7.

Third, once programs have been established, funded, and then implemented by the executive branch agencies, members of Congress, usually through the committees of jurisdiction, may choose to check to see whether federal officials are carrying out those programs in the way intended. This is the supervisory power of the Congress, usually called *oversight*. Congress conducts oversight not just to make sure its wishes are being carried out but also to inform the process of *reauthorizing* (or reconsidering and updating) programs and the next annual round of appropriations. Oversight is covered in Chapters 9 and 10.

The vast majority of bills making their way through Congress at any given time are authorizing bills. These bills may be very long and detailed, establishing policies for enormous government departments such as the Department of Defense. They may cover an important area of policy within a department or agency. For example, the Elementary and Secondary Education Act covers a substantial portion of the activities of the Education Department, but not all of them. A bill may also target a particular program for changes, or even just a particular part of a program.

Through the authorization process, members of Congress are interested in affecting the ongoing work of government by establishing new programs, changing policies, or extending or tinkering with existing programs. Given the size of the government, the possibilities are endless. For a range of reasons, most of these efforts come to nothing—as we have seen, only a small fraction of the thousands of bills introduced every year in Congress make it through the legislative process to become law.

We start the chapter where most of the real work is done. Woodrow Wilson, in his days as a political scientist in the late 19th century, once wrote: "It is not far from the truth to say that Congress in session is Congress on public exhibition, whilst Congress in committee rooms is Congress at work."[1] Things have not changed all that much: the serious business is still done in committee and subcommittee. The first section looks at the authorizing committees in Congress, and in particular at how the work of directing the government is divided among them.

We then get into more detail about the policy work of these committees. How do they go about their business? Most important, exactly what sort of direction do the authorizing statutes produced by these committees give to executive branch agencies? How does the work of authorizing committees relate to the funding responsibility of Congress? In addition, to get a sense of the lengths to which the board of directors can go in exercising its authorizing power, we examine the case of the reorganization of the 16 government agencies charged with collecting and analyzing foreign intelligence. Congress, with prodding from the 9/11 Commission and the public, passed legislation in 2004 that created the Office of the Director of National Intelligence to oversee and coordinate the intelligence agencies; this reorganization fundamentally changed many of the long-standing roles and relationships among these agencies.

Next we look at the special case of authorizing legislation that results in what is called *direct spending*. Normally, authorizing legislation gives instructions to agencies as to how they will go about their work implementing government programs. The legislation recommends a funding amount for agencies and programs, but does not actually give agencies the authority to get money from the Treasury to conduct their programs. Subsequent appropriations bills provide that authority, thereby enabling the agencies to implement authorized government programs.

Direct spending legislation does double duty, in effect doing an end run around the normal process. It both sets agency policy and determines spending levels. Direct spending legislation has become increasingly important in recent decades.

In authorizing the work of government, Congress is expected to consider carefully what the agencies are doing and to update laws to keep up with changing times and new technologies, revise or eliminate programs that are not fulfilling their original purpose, and create new programs or agencies to address emerging problems. These days Congress is beset with a backlog of expired and outdated authorizations. The last section of this chapter considers the impact of the institution's failure to handle its workload in a timely fashion.

Another critical issue examined in the last section is the practice of including direct spending provisions in authorizing legislation. This practice in effect muddies the division of labor in the institution between those committees that write legislation authorizing the work of government and those that handle the bills that determine funding levels for agencies and programs. This trend has had a tremendous impact on how Congress handles its budgeting responsibility.

## THE AUTHORIZING COMMITTEES

Most committees in Congress are **authorizing committees**. Each committee has jurisdiction over certain departments and agencies in the executive branch. Listed here are all the House and Senate authorizing committees, together with brief summaries of their jurisdictions. Bills that would affect the work of an agency in a particular committee's jurisdiction are referred to that committee, and often subsequently to one or more subcommittees, for more in-depth consideration. The members of a committee are the ones who work on and frequently develop the legislation that affects the agencies in their purview. Such legislation may do everything from tinker with an individual program to reorganize large swaths of the federal government. The committees also have oversight power over the agencies in their jurisdiction (the subject of Chapters 9 and 10). It is important to stress that Congress's ability to look into the work that agencies are doing to implement government programs is closely linked to the authorizing process. Committee members need to know how government programs are working in order to make informed decisions when they update authorizing laws.

### House Authorizing Committees and Their Jurisdictions

*Committee on Agriculture.* The dairy industry; human nutrition; inspection of livestock, poultry, meat produce, seafood, and seafood produce; forestry; rural development; crop insurance

*Committee on Armed Services.* General defense issues; ongoing military operations; all the armed services; some energy programs

*Committee on Education and the Workforce.* All federal education programs, including elementary and secondary education and higher education; school lunch and nutrition programs; pensions and retirements for workers; job training; wages and hours of labor; worker health and safety

*Committee on Energy and Commerce.* Biomedical research and development; health and health facilities; exploration, production, storage, supply, marketing, pricing, and regulation of energy resources; travel and tourism; public health (including Medicaid)

*Committee on Financial Services.* Housing and financial services sectors (banking, insurance, real estate, public and assisted housing, and securities); the Federal Reserve System; consumer protection laws

*Committee on Foreign Affairs.* Foreign affairs, establishment of boundaries; the diplomatic services; UN policy

*Committee on Homeland Security.* Homeland security issues, including customs

*Committee on the Judiciary.* Federal judiciary proceedings; civil and criminal law; bankruptcy; counterfeiting; subversive activities affecting the security of the United States; presidential succession

*Committee on Natural Resources.* Fisheries; wildlife; military parks and battlefields; national cemeteries; national parks; mining interests; petroleum conservation

*Committee on Oversight and Government Reform.* The federal civil service; federal paperwork reduction; federal holidays and celebrations; oversight and reorganizations of the executive branch

*Committee on Science, Space, and Technology.* Energy research; astronomical research and development; standards; science education

*Committee on Small Business.* Assistance for and protection of small business, including financial aid and paperwork reduction; small business enterprises and government contracts

*Committee on Transportation and Infrastructure.* Coast Guard activities; management of emergencies and natural disasters; roads, bridges, and other infrastructure, such as water projects

*Committee on Veterans' Affairs.* All issues pertaining to veterans; life insurance issued by the federal government for service in the armed forces; service members' civil relief and pensions

*Committee on Ways and Means.* The tax code; Medicare programs; trade policy; Social Security programs (old age and disability)

*Permanent Select Committee on Intelligence.* All intelligence-related activities, including the organization of the intelligence-related agencies in several departments

## Senate Authorizing Committees and Their Jurisdictions

*Committee on Agriculture, Nutrition, and Forestry.* Farm programs; forestry and logging; nutrition and health; farm viability; food and agriculture research; inspection of plants, animals, and products

*Committee on Armed Services.* Aeronautical and space activities related to national defense; the armed services; the benefits and privileges of members of the armed services

*Committee on Banking, Housing, and Urban Affairs.* Banks and financial institutions; housing; nursing home construction; urban development

*Committee on Commerce, Science, and Transportation.* The activities of the Coast Guard; fisheries; water projects; aviation; interstate commerce; science, engineering, and technology research and development and policy; highway safety

*Committee on Energy and Natural Resources.* National energy policy; territorial policy; federal lands issues

*Committee on Environment and Public Works.* Pollution and other environmental issues; nuclear power; highways and other infrastructure

*Committee on Finance.* The tax code; Social Security programs; Medicare and Medicaid programs; trade policy

*Committee on Foreign Relations.* The diplomatic service; the boundaries of the United States; foreign economic, military, technical, and humanitarian assistance; UN policy

*Committee on Health, Education, Labor, and Pensions.* Federal education policy (elementary, secondary, and higher); US labor policy, including wages, pensions, and work conditions; health policy and public welfare

*Committee on Homeland Security and Governmental Affairs.* Many homeland security issues; the federal workforce; postal issues; oversight of the executive branch

*Committee on Indian Affairs.* Matters related to Indian populations and land

*Committee on the Judiciary.* Bankruptcy; federal penitentiaries; the federal civil and criminal code; the federal judiciary, including nominations

*Committee on Small Business and Entrepreneurship.* Small business activity

*Committee on Veterans' Affairs.* Compensation of veterans and other veterans' issues, including vocational rehabilitation; national cemeteries

*Select Committee on Intelligence.* All intelligence-related activities, including the organization of the intelligence-related agencies in several departments[2]

* * *

As noted in Chapter 3, at the beginning of each Congress (in the January immediately after congressional elections), the House and Senate decide how and whether to restructure the committee system that was in place in the previous two years. Each chamber may create new committees, rename existing ones, and change the panels' jurisdictions.

There is a great deal of variety in the workloads and prestige of the committees. But the key to committee power is jurisdiction. How important are the agencies and programs under the panel's control? These jurisdictions have evolved a great deal over the years. The establishment of committee jurisdictions is fundamentally a political decision in the sense that, as noted earlier, the full membership in each chamber votes to establish committee jurisdictions.[3] In the House, the majority leadership controls the process. In the Senate, the minority party may play a major role as well. Any jurisdictional changes reflect some combination of purely political considerations and policy concerns. Box 6.1 tells the story of significant jurisdictional changes engineered by the House Republican leadership for the Financial Services and Energy and Commerce Committees in the 107th Congress.

One could argue that the most powerful authorizing committee in Congress—the one with jurisdiction over more important government functions than any other—is the Senate Finance Committee, which has the major entitlement programs in its jurisdiction, the agencies that administer these programs (the Social Security Administration [SSA] and the Centers for Medicare and Medicaid Services), the tax code and the Internal Revenue Service, some energy programs, and

---

## BOX 6.1

### Politics Drives Changes in Committee Jurisdictions

Back in 1865, the House of Representatives first established the Committee on Banking and Currency. Before that, the Ways and Means Committee had jurisdiction over banking issues. The *committee's jurisdiction* was adjusted only incrementally over the years to adjust to changing times. By the mid-1990s, after several name changes but only relatively minor jurisdictional changes, it was called the Committee on Banking and Financial Services.

Bigger changes lay ahead in the 107th Congress in 2001. A fight erupted within the Republican Party over the chairmanship of the powerful Energy and Commerce Committee. Representatives Billy Tauzin of Louisiana and Michael Oxley of Ohio angled for the coveted job. They lobbied the leadership and raised hundreds of thousands of dollars for the Republican Party to prove their loyalty. Both appeared in front of the Republican Steering Committee to make their case. It was a close call for the party. Both Tauzin and Oxley were respected members who had demonstrated knowledge of the issues and a commitment to the party's principles.

Ultimately, a deal was struck. Tauzin would get the Energy and Commerce chairmanship, but his committee would lose a key aspect of its jurisdiction—control over securities and exchange issues. Those matters would be handled by the old Banking and Financial Services Committee, which would be renamed the Financial Services Committee. Oxley would get to be chair of that committee.

Thus, a significant change in two committees' jurisdictions was borne of a political compromise. Oxley would probably have preferred the Energy and Commerce position, but the leadership settled on giving him the chairmanship of a rival committee with additional policy turf. Committee jurisdictions are as likely to be drawn based on political considerations such as these as on substantive policy questions.*

*"Tauzin Tapped to Chair House Commerce Panel," *Mediaweek*, January 8, 2001, www.allbusiness.com/services/business-services-miscellaneous-business/4818358–1 .html.

trade policy. The House Ways and Means Committee has an almost identical jurisdiction, minus Medicaid. The Commerce, Science, and Transportation Committee in the Senate and the Energy and Commerce Committee in the House also have very broad authority over government agencies and the economy.

Perhaps the busiest authorizing panels are the Armed Services Committees in the House and Senate. Every year the entire Defense Department, an approximately $600 billion organization in 2012,[4] comes under review—its authorizing legislation covers only one year. These committees perennially produce and pass legislation that determines the policies of the Defense Department and the armed services of the United States for the upcoming fiscal year. On the authorizing side of Congress's duties, the work of these committees is probably the most demanding given the scope of the Defense Department and the imperative to produce a product every year.

Other committees have nowhere near the same exacting schedule as the Armed Services Committees or the vast jurisdictions of Ways and Means; Finance; Commerce, Science, and Transportation; and Energy and Commerce. All of the authorizing committees have authority over important parts of the government, but not all committees are created equal.

## AUTHORIZING LEGISLATION: EXERTING CONTROL OVER GOVERNMENT POLICY

The role of most authorizing legislation is to determine the policies of the US government. Agencies are directed in law to carry out certain programs, abide by certain restrictions, and achieve certain objectives.

In simple terms, what Congress does as a board of directors in authorizing legislation is to codify its thinking as to what the government should do. The staffs and members of these committees are charged with developing national policy on controlling immigration, managing fisheries, regulating banks, defending the nation, and so forth. They put together bills designed to carry out their thinking. The members and their staffs are responsible for attempting to shepherd those bills through the legislative process with the aim of delivering a product to the president's desk that he will agree to sign. The realities of legislative politics dictate, however, that the architects of the bills will nearly always have to accept changes and negotiate compromises along the way. Skillful legislators realize, as the saying goes, that "the perfect should not be the enemy of the good." In other words, it is impossible in the legislative process to achieve the ideal, but a good solution is better than no solution at all. Box 6.2 takes a glimpse at the work of committees, and especially the staff, as they research the issues of the day with an eye to creating legislation to direct the work of government agencies.

## The Authorization-Appropriation Connection

For the most part, authorizing bills do not enable agencies to get money from the Treasury to carry out the programs set forth in legislation. It is subsequent appropriations bills that plug money into agency accounts so that agencies are able to do what is required in authorizing statutes.

In Congress, *thinking,* in effect, is separated from *spending.*[5] Most members and staff serve on committees that are charged with thinking through what the government does, or should do, in a particular policy domain; others—the Appropriations Committees' members and staff—determine how much money will be available for those aims based on current priorities and the constraints of the overall budget.

From almost the beginning of the republic, Congress has seen merit in the idea of dealing with authorizing and funding in separate bills. This is reflected in the rules of both chambers. There are a few reasons for this separation.

First, merit has been found in the argument that it makes sense to think through what government *should* do before making a decision on what government can *afford* to do. In fact, the nature of many authorizing bills makes it impossible to consider budgetary constraints with any precision. Some authorizing bills are major undertakings, establishing and altering policies in huge government departments. These bills may cover several years, laying out a road map for what the government should do, for instance, in higher education, transportation, space exploration, or energy. In effect, for much of the federal government, Congress lays out a plan with projected spending needs but with no idea whether the objectives can be fully funded. The **Appropriations Committees** follow up every year by looking at budgetary constraints, considering new priorities and unforeseen exigencies, and finally making funding decisions based on these and other criteria. The division of labor makes sense: make a plan for what Congress would *like* to see done, and then follow up by deciding on an annual basis what it is that *can* be done.

Allen Schick, a leading expert on the federal budget process, notes two other reasons Congress decided on this division of labor. If authorizing issues were linked with funding decisions in the same bill, extended debates and intractable disagreements over policy questions would "impede the flow of funds to federal agencies."[6] Or, at the other extreme, Congress might hastily pass unwise policy in its eagerness to make sure that essential government activities were funded and a potential government shutdown was avoided. In short, as a practical matter, the overriding importance of keeping agencies running makes it important to divorce policy decisions from funding decisions. In reality, appropriations bills rarely get passed on time anyway. One of the reasons is that policy issues have intentionally been injected into (and in fact are very difficult at times to separate from) the appropriations process.

# BOX 6.2

## The Inner Workings of Congressional Committees

The serious lawmaking work in the US Congress is usually done by committees and subcommittees. Committees are run by a chairman or chairwoman (or, generically, chair) from the majority party. That person controls the bulk of a committee's resources (in the 113th Congress it was about two-thirds in the House and at least three-fifths in the Senate) and sets the committee's agenda. The ranking minority party member controls the remainder of the resources.

These resources enable committee chairs and the ranking members to hire expert staff in their area of jurisdiction. Depending on the committee and the scope and importance of its jurisdiction, total staff range from about 25 all the way to 100 or so. (Of course, the chairs can afford to hire many more than the ranking members.) Expert staff on congressional committees go by all sorts of different titles, including *clerk, counsel, staff lead, staff director,* and *professional staff*. This last title, *professional staff*, is the one most widely used. The key distinction on Capitol Hill is between the committee's professional staff (subject-matter experts in public policy) and the *personal staff* who work in members' personal offices, attending to the immediate concerns, often political in nature, of members in Washington and back in the district or state. Personal staff cover policy, too, but usually in less depth than professional staff.

Professional staff come from a lot of different places. Some have worked on Capitol Hill their entire careers and have developed subject-matter expertise in a personal office covering issues for a particular member. Some come from academic specialties that relate to particular policy jurisdictions. Others come from the executive branch agencies. In the case of the Armed Services Committees in the House and Senate, many professional staffers are retired military officers.

Although nearly all staff are hired by members for their expertise, generally they have ties to one party or the other and are certainly expected to be loyal to the chair or ranking member. After all, they can be fired with no notice for insubordination, incompetence, or almost any other reason. They work at the direction and pleasure of the chair or ranking member who hired them.

What do the staff do on a daily basis? That depends. Often, they are researching issues of interest to the members of the committee and especially the chair or ranking member or subcommittee chairs or ranking members. They may be working on constructing legislative solutions to new problems or putting together a bill to update an authorization for an agency and its programs.

# BOX 6.2 *(Continued)*

## The Inner Workings of Congressional Committees

However, the process for moving forward on legislation involves much more than research. It involves constant communication with interested parties in the public as well as executive branch officials. As bills are being prepared, the chair will want to hold *hearings* to get key people (from interest groups, agencies, and academe) to testify in public and take questions on the issues involved. The idea is get certain things on the public record that will help the committee as it puts together the bill and moves it through the legislative process. Staff are given the task of setting up hearings, which involves finding and interviewing potential witnesses, preparing the members, and crafting questions for them to ask.

When a bill has been developed to the chair's liking, it will be marked up at the subcommittee and full committee level. The subcommittee stage may be skipped, but for many major bills this is an important part of the process—especially in the House. Subcommittees are composed of a subset of the members of the committee and focus on specific areas of the full committee's jurisdiction. House members generally have more time to get into issues at the subcommittee level of specialization than senators do. As a result, the subcommittee stage is more commonly skipped in Senate authorizing committees.

A *markup* is an open meeting of the subcommittee or committee during which the members go through the bill, line by line if necessary, amending it as they go along. At this stage, the bill is often called the *chairman's mark*, which essentially means that it is the version crafted by staff as directed by the chair. Ultimately, the bill is voted on and moved along the process to the next stage.

For example, the Armed Services Committees in the House and Senate each begin the work on reauthorizing the activities of the Defense Department early each year. They divide this massive undertaking among the committee's six subcommittees. (The House Armed Services Committee has a seventh subcommittee that focuses mostly on oversight.) After hearings in the winter, most at the subcommittee level, the subcommittees mark up their portion of the bill in late winter or early spring. At that point, the full Armed Services Committees take up the whole Defense authorization bill and conduct a markup that can last the better part of a day or sometimes even longer. Ultimately, in a typical year, the bill is reported out of committee after receiving majority support among the committee's membership at a markup. This is called a *favorable report*. Bills that do not receive committee support rarely go any further in the legislative process.

## What Authorizing Bills Do

The typical authorizing bill may accomplish one or more of the following:

1. establish an agency
2. establish or change substantive aspects of a government program (or set of programs) and direct to agency officials
3. authorize agency funding levels
4. reorganize an agency or department

### Establish an Agency

Authorizing bills are the board of directors' means of establishing new agencies, and programs to be managed by those agencies, to perform certain functions. In certain periods of our history, Congress has set up myriad programs and agencies to address pressing problems.

In the 1930s, Congress, with President Franklin Roosevelt's prodding, established an "alphabet soup" of new agencies to address the immediate needs of the citizenry during the Great Depression as well as to arrest the downward spiral of the economy. The National Recovery Administration (NRA), the Public Works Administration (PWA), the Civilian Conservation Corps (CCC), the Federal Deposit Insurance Corporation (FDIC), the Works Progress Administration (WPA), and many others were created for those purposes.

The years 1964 to 1971 saw another spate of activity inspired initially by President Lyndon Johnson's Great Society agenda. Medicare, Medicaid, the National Endowment for the Arts (NEA), the National Endowment for the Humanities (NEH), and many other agencies and programs were established in 1965. Also that year, the Higher Education Act (HEA) established new agencies within the existing Department of Health, Education, and Welfare (HEW). Numerous new programs were created to support certain colleges and universities as well as individuals who might not be able to afford postsecondary schooling.[7] For the first time, the federal government was a major player in university and college life in the United States. In 1970 the Environmental Protection Agency (EPA) was established on the basis of a proposal by President Richard Nixon that was approved by Congress.

The year 2002 saw the establishment in law of a major new government department. The Department of Homeland Security consolidated several existing government agencies to the end of protecting the nation against terrorist attacks. Exhibit 6.1 shows the operative section of the Homeland Security Act, the law passed that year that established the new department. More recently, in 2010, the **Dodd-Frank** Financial Regulatory bill developed a creative approach to protecting people's assets by setting up the Consumer Financial Protection Bureau (CFPB)—a new agency within the Federal Reserve that was given considerable authority to enforce consumer protection laws.

## Establish or Change Substantive Aspects of a Government Program and Direct Agency Officials

Authorizing bills get right to the heart of what the federal government does, setting forth policies that agencies are bound by. Congress, in its role as the board of directors, may give almost any sort of direction it likes.

---

## EXHIBIT 6.1

### Congress Establishes a New Government Department

**TITLE I—DEPARTMENT OF HOMELAND SECURITY**

**Sec. 101. Executive Department; Mission.**

(a) ESTABLISHMENT—There is established a Department of Homeland Security, as an executive department of the United States within the meaning of title 5, United States Code.

(b) MISSION—

(1) IN GENERAL—The primary mission of the Department is to—

(A) prevent terrorist attacks within the United States;

(B) reduce the vulnerability of the United States to terrorism;

(C) minimize the damage, and assist in the recovery, from terrorist attacks that do occur within the United States;

(D) carry out all functions of entities transferred to the Department, including by acting as a focal point regarding natural and manmade crises and emergency planning;

(E) ensure that the functions of the agencies and subdivisions within the Department that are not related directly to securing the homeland are not diminished or neglected except by a specific explicit Act of Congress; and

(F) ensure that the overall economic security of the United States is not diminished by efforts, activities, and programs aimed at securing the homeland.

SOURCE: Homeland Security Act of 2002.

NOTE: Congress has the power to establish in law a new department or agency of government. In this case, in the Homeland Security Act of 2002, Congress brought together several agencies under the new department with the aim of improving the government's ability to prevent terrorist attacks and otherwise protect the homeland.

Working on an authorizing bill gives Congress the opportunity to reconsider and tinker with existing government programs or establish new ones. The No Child Left Behind Act has been the commonly used name for the extension of the Elementary and Secondary Education Act (ESEA) of 2002, originally passed in 1965. Among other things, it instituted the Reading First Program, which provides state-of-the-art reading instruction to needy children in the early grades, and the Charter Schools Program, a competitive grants program designed to provide more school choice for parents. It also recommended increased funding for some existing programs.[8] ESEA, like HEA, was authorized for five years. Congress starts revisiting major sets of programs like these at about the time the authorization expires.

Other authorizing bills have traditionally specified projects that the agency leadership must undertake, often providing explicit instructions. The Water Resources Development Act of 2007 outlines in great detail the navigation, dam, and flood-control projects that need to be tackled by the secretary of the army. A few of the hundreds of projects in the bill are shown in Exhibit 6.2.

In the 112th Congress, rules were put in place in both the House and the Senate ending this practice, often called **earmarking**. Now Congress passes laws that give agencies much more discretion in the specific use of funds for such things as roads, water projects, and grants for such things as community centers or scientific research. For example, the 2012 reauthorization of surface transportation projects (roads, bridges, bike lanes, and mass transit) stipulated how states may spend money in terms of broader categories and general locations, but did not earmark for individual projects. For example:

CALCULATION .—Of the funds apportioned to a State . . .
- (A)  50 percent for a fiscal year shall be [used] . . .
  - (i)  in urbanized areas of the State with an urbanized area population of over 200,000;
  - (ii)  in areas of the State other than urban areas with a population greater than 5,000; and
- (B)  50 percent may be [used] in any area of the state[9]

This section of the bill goes on to stipulate that states must consult with regional transportation planning organizations in the use of the funds made available, if such an organization exists.

Instructions for agencies in authorizing bills vary a great deal and can cover just about anything. Normally, they dictate the objectives of a government program, but they may also require the agency to contact Congress on certain matters, to promote and advertise certain programs, to interact with other agencies that have

# EXHIBIT 6.2

## Project Authorizations for the Army Corps of Engineers

### SEC. 3005. SITKA, ALASKA.

The Sitka, Alaska, element of the project for navigation, Southeast Alaska Harbors of Refuge, Alaska, authorized by section 101(1) of the Water Resources Development Act of 1992 (106 Stat. 4801), is modified to direct the Secretary to take such action as is necessary to correct design deficiencies in the Sitka Harbor Breakwater at Federal expense. The estimated cost is $6,300,000.

### SEC. 3007. RIO DE FLAG, FLAGSTAFF, ARIZONA.

The project for flood damage reduction, Rio De Flag, Flagstaff, Arizona, authorized by section 101(b)(3) of the Water Resources Development Act of 2000 (114 Stat. 2576), is modified to authorize the Secretary to construct the project at a total cost of $54,100,000, with an estimated Federal cost of $35,000,000 and a non-Federal cost of $19,100,000.

### SEC. 3009. TUCSON DRAINAGE AREA, ARIZONA.

The project for flood damage reduction, environmental restoration, and recreation, Tucson drainage area, Arizona, authorized by section 101(a)(5) of the Water Resources Development Act of 1999 (113 Stat. 274), is modified to authorize the Secretary to construct the project at a total cost of $66,700,000, with an estimated Federal cost of $43,350,000 and an estimated non-Federal cost of $23,350,000.

### SEC. 3010. OSCEOLA HARBOR, ARKANSAS.

(a) In General—The project for navigation, Osceola Harbor, Arkansas, constructed under section 107 of the River and Harbor Act of 1960 (33 U.S.C. 577), is modified to allow non-Federal interests to construct a mooring facility within the existing authorized harbor channel, subject to all necessary permits, certifications, and other requirements.

(b) Limitation on Statutory Construction—Nothing in this section shall be construed as affecting the responsibility of the Secretary to maintain the general navigation features of the project at a bottom width of 250 feet.

SOURCE: The Water Resources Development Act of 2007.

NOTE: Congress may act in authorizing law to require specific agency actions, such as the various projects shown here from the Water Resources Development Act of 2007. In this way, Congress leaves no doubt what the agency—in this case the Army Corps of Engineers—must do.

overlapping concerns, and everything in between. The board of directors is in a position to dictate as much or as little as it wishes to federal agencies.

But the fact is that the federal government is involved in such an incredible range of activities, many of which are highly technical, that Congress almost always leaves a great deal to the discretion of agency officials. There is simply too much to keep track of in some areas of government. In effect, Congress delegates authority to executive branch officials. Much like a corporate board of directors, members of Congress defer to the experts in the field—the agency officials who were hired because of their knowledge in a particular area. Of course, Congress, again like a corporate board, retains the ultimate authority to overrule the actions of agency officials by changing the law.

The National Institutes of Health, an agency within the Department of Health and Human Services, provides a good example of congressional delegation to the experts. The institutes are set up for scientific research on a wide range of health issues, often conducted through grants to scientists at universities or labs. The agency has persuaded Congress to minimize its meddling by arguing that scientific grant decisions should be made strictly on the merits without regard to any political considerations. Even so, agency officials are wise to be wary of awarding grants to controversial entities or for controversial purposes, since members of Congress are well within their rights to restrict the agency's discretion in future legislation.[10]

### Authorize Agency Funding Levels

As we have seen, authorizing bills set policy for federal agencies. But they often do another crucial thing: they authorize funding levels for government programs.

Most authorizing bills have an **authorization of appropriations** section. The time frame of an authorization of appropriations may vary widely. Defense Department authorizations cover only one year. Others, such as the authorization for the wide range of programs covered in the Higher Education Act or the Elementary and Secondary Education Act, cover five years. For an example of an authorization of appropriations that was part of a larger reauthorization of NASA, see Exhibit 6.3. This authorization of appropriations covered three years. (When an agency authorization or a set of programs like HEA is said to "expire," that usually means that the authorization of appropriations has reached the end of its time.)

Authorized funding levels do not, however, give an agency the authority to spend the money; rather, the authorization merely reflects the considered view of the policy makers on the relevant committee and the larger Congress about the funding that ought to be provided for a program or an agency. It is more like a hunting license. A license does not get a hunter any game; he or she has to go find it

# EXHIBIT 6.3

## Authorization of Appropriations for NASA

**TITLE I—AUTHORIZATION OF APPROPRIATIONS**

**Sec. 101. Fiscal Year 2011.**

There are authorized to be appropriated to NASA for fiscal year 2011 $19,000,000,000, as follows:

    (1) For Exploration, $3,868,000,000 . . .

    (2) For Space Operations, $5,508,500,000 . . .

    (3) For Science, $5,005,600,000 . . .

    (4) For Aeronautics, $929,600,000 . . .

    (5) For Education, $145,800,000 . . .

    (6) For Cross-Agency Support Programs, $3,111,400,000 . . .

    (7) For Construction and Environmental Compliance and Restoration, $394,300,000 . . .

    (8) For Inspector General, $37,000,000.

**Sec. 102. Fiscal Year 2012.**

There are authorized to be appropriated to NASA for fiscal year 2008 $19,450,000,000 as follows:

    (1) For Exploration, $5,252,300,000 . . .

    (2) For Space Operations, $4,141,500,000 . . .

    (3) For Science, $5,248,600,000 . . .

    (4) For Aeronautics, $1,070,600,000 . . .

    (5) For Education, $145,800,000 . . .

    (6) For Cross-Agency Support Programs, $3,189,600,000 . . .

    (7) For Construction and Environmental Compliance and Restoration, $363,800,000 . . .

    (8) For Inspector General, $37,800,000.

**Sec. 103. Fiscal Year 2013.**

    (1) For Exploration, $5,264,000,000 . . .

    (2) For Space Operations, $4,253,300,000 . . .

    (3) For Science, $5,509,600,000 . . .

    (4) For Aeronautics, $1,105,000,000 . . .

    (5) For Education, $145,700,000 . . .

    (6) For Cross-Agency Support Programs, $3,276,800,000 . . .

    (7) For Construction and Environmental Compliance and Restoration, $366,900,000 . . .

    (8) For Inspector General, $38,700,000.

SOURCE: Reauthorization of the National Aeronautics and Space Administration, 2011.

NOTE: Most authorizing legislation provides a spending ceiling for the agency in question in the "authorization of appropriations" section of the bill. In this case, NASA is reauthorized for fiscal years 2011–2013. This reauthorization does not give the agency money—that comes in subsequent annual appropriations law that may not exceed the ceiling in the authorizing bill.

and kill it. For government programs, the hunting grounds are the Appropriations Committees, and appropriations bills provide the actual game (money).

Typically, the authorization levels in the first year (or the only year in the case of Defense bills) are met or nearly met in appropriations bills because the appropriations decision is made so soon after the authorization decision is made. Similar political circumstances pertain: an overwhelming floor vote for an authorizing bill that contains a particular funding ceiling in the spring or summer will usually be supported by adequate funding later in the year when the appropriations bill is voted on. But when the authorization of appropriations covers multiple years, what the authorizing committee envisions for later years may well not jibe with future political and budgetary realities, many of which cannot be anticipated.

This has been the case for ESEA programs in this decade. As can be seen in Table 6.1, as time passes since the original No Child Left Behind legislation was passed in 2002, the disparity between the authorized funding levels and the actual funding provided in the appropriations bill each year for the Education Department to implement the programs becomes greater. Funding levels have increased for the programs, but the generous funding increases envisioned in 2002 for the next several years were by and large unrealized.

It should be noted that authorizations of appropriations frequently expire before Congress can put together and pass into law a comprehensive reauthorization of a program, a set of programs, or an agency. In most cases, Congress still appropriates funds for the programs with the expired authorization of appropriations. Technically, this practice violates rules of both chambers of Congress, but the programs may be essential, popular, or both. To members of Congress, the only alternative is to figure out a way to waive the rules against unauthorized appropriations and include funding in the appropriations bills.

Table 6.1 shows that ESEA funding continued after the authorization of appropriations expired in 2007. In fact, the best funding year by far for ESEA was 2009, when the American Reinvestment and Recovery Act added more than $10 billion to these programs as part of an effort to mitigate the effects of the severe recession.

When Congress chooses to fund programs whose authorizations of appropriations have expired, in most cases the substantive policy guidelines for the conduct of those programs as set forth in the authorizing bill are still in effect. In other words, although a program's authorization of appropriations expires, the policy provisions for it usually do not. What happens is that Congress intends to reconsider and update the old legislation—both the substantive provisions and the funding levels—but the members get bogged down by controversies and disagreements about what direction to go with the programs. They fail to pass the legislation on time but want to keep the funding stream going. Later we look at some of the ramifications of this failure.

**TABLE 6.1 Appropriations for Elementary and Secondary School Programs Fail to Keep Pace with No Child Left Behind Targets, Plus Funding Continues without Reauthorization (in millions of dollars)**

| FISCAL YEAR | AUTHORIZED LEVEL | APPROPRIATED FUNDS[A] | APPROPRIATED. AS % OF AUTHORIZED[A] |
|---|---|---|---|
| 2002 | $26,417 | $22,195 | 84 |
| 2003 | 29,217 | 23,837 | 82 |
| 2004 | 32,017 | 24,463 | 77 |
| 2005 | 34,317 | 24,520 | 71 |
| 2006 | 36,867 | 23,504 | 64 |
| 2007 | 39,442 | 23,658 | 60 |
| 2008 | not reauthorized | 24,597 | N/A |
| 2009 | not reauthorized | 39,030[b] | N/A |
| 2010 | not reauthorized | 25,144 | N/A |
| 2011 | not reauthorized | 29,154 | N/A |

[a]In millions of dollars.

[b]Includes supplemental funding from the American Recovery and Reinvestment Act (2009).

*Source:* National Education Association

*Note:* It is not unusual for annual appropriations to fail to match the multiyear spending ceiling in authorizing laws, as shown here for federal elementary and secondary education levels. Additionally, Congress chose to continue funding for these programs even though the Elementary and Secondary Education programs were not reauthorized for funding (and still haven't been at this writing).

## *Reorganize an Agency or Department*

Taking its power to the extreme, Congress may pass authorizing legislation that radically alters the roles and relationships of existing government agencies. As the board of directors, Congress can restructure and refocus the government in any way it sees fit.

Defense policy expert Charles Cushman calls the reorganizing power Congress's "nuclear weapon."[11] If the members think that agencies are not addressing important matters, they can blow them up and start again from scratch, reshuffling chains of command, creating new entities, and moving authority and power from one position or agency to another. Congress's power to do this stems from the **necessary and proper clause** in Article I, Section 8, of the Constitution. The Congressional Research Service summarizes the authority this clause gives the Congress:

> [Congress] has the power to organize the executive branch. Congress has the authority to create, abolish, reorganize, and fund federal departments. . . . It

has the power to assign or reassign functions to departments and agencies, and grant new forms of authority and staff [to executive officials] . . . [and] exercises ultimate authority over executive branch organization and . . . policy.[12]

The most ambitious example of the use of this power was the restructuring of the defense establishment in 1947. Before that, the War Department, consisting of the US Army and the Army Air Force, had been completely separate from the Navy and the Marine Corps. The new configuration consolidated all the services (the Air Force was separated from the Army) under the Defense Department. The various rivalries and turf battles among the services made for an awesome bureaucratic task for the department's civilian and military leadership. Most experts believe that major problems in achieving anything resembling a cohesive whole remained until 1986, when new legislation streamlined the chains of command, bridging the service rivalries in a reasonably effective way.[13] It took nearly 40 years to make substantial progress in reorganizing the essential national security function.

A true work in progress is the Department of Homeland Security, created by Congress in 2002 as a response to the September 11, 2001, attacks. It consists of 22 federal agencies with a wide range of rather disparate missions, from the Coast Guard to Immigration and Customs Enforcement to the Secret Service, which investigates financial crimes in addition to providing protection for major political figures, to the Transportation Safety Administration. At least all the major components of the Department of Defense had the same objective: defending the nation and killing adversaries in time of war.[14]

Many observers are not sanguine about the prospects of the DHS becoming anything resembling a unified and smoothly functioning whole in the near term given the various potentially incompatible missions and corporate cultures that have been forced together to create a new department. With both Defense and Homeland Security, legislation made wholesale changes in roles and relationships.

## Case Study: Congress Restructures the Intelligence Community

The events of September 11, 2001, were to have yet another major impact on the way the US government does business. As news emerged of lapses within the intelligence agencies leading up to the attacks, Congress created a bipartisan commission, headed by Lee Hamilton, former Democratic congressman from Indiana, and Thomas Kean, former Republican governor of New Jersey, to investigate and make recommendations.

The National Commission on Terrorist Attacks upon the United States—the so-called 9/11 Commission—released its findings in July 2004. Central to these findings was a recommendation to reorganize the way the government collects and analyzes foreign intelligence, a task that had been undertaken by 16 agencies across the government.[15]

Specifically, the 9/11 Commission recommended creating a new position to oversee and direct intelligence activities. Previously, the director of the Central Intelligence Agency (DCI), who was responsible for setting intelligence-gathering priorities for the government and bringing together intelligence information for the president, had been what amounted to the head of intelligence. The problem was that most intelligence activities were not housed in the Central Intelligence Agency (CIA), an independent agency, but rather were in the Defense Department.

The Defense Department's intelligence-gathering activities are extensive, constituting about 85 percent of all spending on intelligence. Three agencies within the Department—the National Reconnaissance Office (NRO), the National Security Agency (NSA), and the National Geospatial-Intelligence Agency (NGA)—are involved in gathering information through satellites and communications systems. In addition, the department has extensive intelligence-gathering and -analyzing capabilities that support specific military activities. The CIA is involved only in the gathering and analysis of human intelligence—generally intelligence gathered by humans from humans.

The problem was that the DCI would invariably get frustrated in his efforts to direct the actions of Defense Department intelligence agencies. In fact, the CIA director's statutory authorities were vague vis-à-vis Defense agencies.[16] The DCI would end up choosing to focus more of his efforts at the CIA. The bottom line: no one in government had the ability or authority effectively to coordinate and carry out a comprehensive intelligence plan.

A lot of ideas about how to address this problem had been percolating on Capitol Hill, particularly since the attacks. The 9/11 Commission report proved a tremendous catalyst. The commission members fanned out over Congress and, with the help of a group of people who had lost loved ones in the attacks, lobbied the rank-and-file membership hard. In December 2004, Congress passed and sent to President Bush a bill that he was prepared to sign: the Intelligence Reform and Terrorism Prevention Act, which restructured the community. It passed both chambers with massive bipartisan majorities, in the House 336–75 and in the Senate 89–2.[17]

For the second time in just over two years, Congress had used, in Cushman's term, the nuclear bomb. It created a fully new entity, the Office of the Director of National Intelligence (ODNI), which would be separate from any of the clandestine service agencies and in fact be independent of any larger department. Its job would be to direct all foreign and domestic intelligence operations. Within it would be the National Counterterrorism Center, an agency created by executive order and given the task of supporting ODNI on intelligence coordination.

The person named as director (the DNI) would take over from the CIA director the responsibility of directing the entire intelligence community and would report directly to the president. Unlike the situation that had pertained for the DCI when he headed the larger community, the DNI would have enhanced statutory authority over all the intelligence agencies, including those in the Defense Department.

Most important, the Intelligence Reform Act gave the DNI authority over intelligence budgets across the government that the DCI had not had. The DNI is now in a position to exert control over the funds going to all the intelligence agencies in government. (There is one major exception: the agencies involved in providing tactical intelligence for military operations are largely free of the DNI's control.) The DNI also is required by law to set intelligence priorities for the government. The bill says that the DNI shall "manage and direct the tasking of, collection, analysis, production, and dissemination of national intelligence by approving requirements and resolving conflicts."

Whether the DNI can really exert the sort of influence and control envisioned in the law remains to be seen. Government intelligence agencies do a wide range of tasks, and some of the government's intelligence agencies now have multiple masters. Furthermore, the processes set forth in the legislation to give the DNI the power to coordinate intelligence are still untested.[18]

One major question involves the three major intelligence-gathering agencies in the Defense Department—the National Reconnaissance Office, the National Security Agency, and the National Geospatial-Intelligence Agency. Many members of Congress wanted to see these agencies remain at least partly under the control of the Defense Department. They made sure to include language in the bill that prohibits the DNI from abrogating existing Defense Department authorities.

The lesson is that even radical legislation like the Intelligence Reform Act is not immune to the congressional tendency to split the difference in order to get a final product. The main thrust of the intelligence bill was to create a workable system of coordination and control over government intelligence activity, but there were people in powerful places on Capitol Hill who believed that some aspects of the status quo should be retained.[19] In the end product, not all of the lines of authority are crystal clear; much depends on the character of the DNI and the secretary of defense. Can the DNI's priorities for key intelligence agencies prevail over the secretary's when conflicts exist? The president is, of course, the ultimate arbiter. Another question is how much influence the DNI can have over the proud and insular CIA, an agency with a long history and proven track record in bureaucratic trench warfare.

Nevertheless, the point is that Congress responded to a devastating attack on American soil by reorganizing government functions. In 2002 the board of directors created the Department of Homeland Security in an effort to coordinate a great variety of government activities ranging from border protection to transportation safety to first responders to controlling counterfeiting. Then, two years later, the board restructured the intelligence community. Broad and extensive authorizing statutes were put together and passed with surprising speed, proving that Congress, even in an era of partisan bickering and stalemate on many matters, is capable of carrying out the most far-reaching of its powers. Whether the restructuring will prove both lasting and effective remains to be seen.

## AUTHORIZING DIRECT SPENDING

Although Congress normally exercises its authorizing power separately from its funding power, there is a major exception to the general rule. Authorizing bills may be written so that they do more than merely authorize programs and subsequent appropriations; they can do double duty by giving an agency, in effect, direct access to the US Treasury.

**Direct spending** legislation is an authorizing bill that both sets up a program (establishing policies and so forth) and mandates funding, based on a formula or criteria set forth in that bill, without the need for a separate appropriation. Government programs set up in this manner are generically called **mandatory programs** and sometimes **entitlements**. Well-known examples include Medicare programs that provide health care for the elderly and the Department of Agriculture's Supplemental Nutrition Assistance Program (SNAP, sometimes called "food stamps") that gives vouchers to the needy for the purchase of groceries.

Unlike programs that arrange to build and buy things (say, a spy plane or a bridge), or clean up a river, or pay civil servants to monitor the nation's borders, a typical mandatory program, such as Medicare and food stamps, sends money directly to individuals or in support of services that benefit those individuals. It should be noted that funding for most programs that provide financial support to individuals—like the Pell Grant Program, which provides support for lower-income college students—cannot be delivered without two legislative decisions, an authorization and an appropriation. Mandatory programs that bypass the appropriation step are the exception—but a few of them are very, very big exceptions.

To get a sense of what Congress is thinking when it sets up a mandatory program, consider the following scenario in which the process of creating a program in the normal two-step way is compared with the direct spending approach.

### Addressing Poverty Among the Elderly as a Two-Step Process

Let's imagine that Congress decides that it needs to write a law to establish an agency and a program to address the problem of rampant poverty among the elderly. In the normal two-step process, congressional committees would write, and then pass, an authorizing bill that sets forth the objectives and policies of the agency. We can imagine that the agency would be instructed to administer a program to provide financial support, probably at varying levels depending on need, to people who meet certain qualifications. This bill would have within it an authorization of appropriations section setting a funding ceiling (probably with a ceiling increase each year) for, say, each of the next five years. Funding for the programs would not be ensured but instead would be dependent on subsequent annual action on an appropriations bill. That appropriations bill would determine how much of the authorized funding level is plugged into the agency's accounts for these programs. Full funding might not be forthcoming some years, depending on economic conditions and other national priorities.

## Addressing Poverty Among the Elderly with Direct Spending

Alternatively, Congress might structure the legislation to *mandate* a payment to people who qualify based on certain criteria. Instead of leaving the support of the elderly up to the annual discretion of the Appropriations Committees, Congress might deem widespread poverty among the aged as too important a problem to leave to chance. To make the program politically irresistible, members could write legislation to guarantee a monthly check from the government for *any elderly person,* rich or poor, who meets a set of basic criteria—an age threshold, a documentable history of regular employment, and so on.

The level of the payment to each individual would be set in the authorizing statute. Anyone meeting the criteria would be entitled, in law, to receive a payment from the government. He or she would get that money indefinitely, or until Congress chose to rewrite the authorizing statute.

The key differences between direct spending and the normal two-step funding process are that *the payment level is set by formula in the authorizing law*—there is no role for the Appropriations Committees to step in and fund below the recommended level—and *the total amount spent on the program is not actually controlled by anyone.* That total is entirely dependent on how many people reach the right age and meet the other criteria. In effect, the authorizing bill would do an end run around appropriators, who write the laws that control the funding for most programs.

* * *

Of course, a real-world entitlement, Old Age and Survivors' Insurance (what is usually called "Social Security"), administered by the Social Security Administration, resembles the program in the second scenario. It is the largest single program established and funded in an authorizing statute. The authorizing language puts no end time on the program: qualifying citizens can continue to collect benefits from the Treasury indefinitely or until Congress acts to end or alter the program.

In the earlier years of the program, the government's year-to-year financial liability was fairly stable and predictable. After all, demographers and statisticians can estimate pretty accurately how many people will qualify and how many will die off. But the program eventually took on a life of its own. First, politicians amended the original legislation that created the program to increase the payment levels, sometimes dramatically; eventually, in the early 1970s, the payments were tied to a cost-of-living index. In years with rampant inflation, overall spending on the program soared uncontrollably.

Medicare programs, administered by the Centers for Medicare and Medicaid Services, have also grown dramatically. First established in 1965, Medicare has been altered numerous times. In 2003 prescription drug coverage for senior citizens was added. Medicare programs provide medical care for those age 65 and older by paying hospitals and other health care providers for services rendered based on criteria set forth in law and in subsequent regulations outlined by the agency—sometimes by assisting seniors with premiums in private plans and also by providing prescription drug coverage. As with Social Security programs, the total money spent in a given year on Medicare is not set in appropriations legislation; instead, it is determined by the number of qualified beneficiaries who submit claims that must be paid out of the Treasury. Total spending may vary unpredictably, depending on inflation in the health care field and other factors.

The 2010 health care reform bill, the Patient Protection and Affordable Care Act, made significant changes to Medicare that are designed to shore up the programs and save the government money. An independent board was set up to make recommendations for savings when the programs exceed projected costs—recommendations that would go into effect absent congressional action to stop them. In addition, high earners ($200,000 for single filers and $250,000 for joint filers) will pay more payroll taxes to support the program.[20] We will look at federal budget issues related to Medicare and other mandatory programs in more depth in Chapter 8.

## Nonpermanent Direct Spending

Not all mandatory programs are like Social Security and Medicare programs, which are set to continue on a permanent basis unless altered in the future. Congress may establish a program that goes around the Appropriations Committees while still setting an effective end time to the program.

For example, the so-called Farm Bill establishes subsidies for certain commodity farmers as well as funding levels for the Supplemental Nutrition Assistance

Program. According to the law, government payments to farmers could vary in any given year, and sometimes by a great deal, depending on market conditions, and SNAP payments would vary as well depending on how many people qualified for assistance. But the subsidy structures governing Farm Bill programs are typically set to expire in five years.

When the expiration of these programs looms as the five-year period nears an end, the Agriculture Committees go into overdrive to try to update the existing criteria based on new conditions and the policy ideas of the party in power, as well as those of the influential committee members. Farm groups representing the different commodities that receive support are in constant contact with key staffers and members of Congress, offering ideas for enhancing subsidies and improving the processing of payments.

Ideally, Congress accomplishes a comprehensive overhaul of the farm subsidy programs before the five years are up, establishing new and updated payment schedules for the next five-year period and new criteria for SNAP. As often as not, however, farm issues are controversial, and the committees are unable to shepherd a new farm bill through the legislative process in time. When that happens, the existing criteria are temporarily extended by an act of Congress, usually for a period of a few months, to give Congress time to finish the new bill.

## Comparing Mandatory and Discretionary Programs

There is an important distinction to note here between the funding for the vast majority of government programs that require an appropriation separate from the authorization bill in order to get money from the Treasury and the mandatory programs, just discussed, that give agencies direct access to the Treasury to fund their programs. In the first instance, when the authorization of appropriations expires, the Appropriations Committees, in crafting their annual bills, may go ahead and provide the agencies with funding to keep their programs running. *Budget authority*—the ability to draw money from the Treasury to run a program—is provided to the agencies in that appropriations bill. *But with nonpermanent mandatory programs, the agency in effect loses its budget authority when the authorization statute expires.* For that reason, that statute needs to be extended if the programs are to continue.

This is also true with an agency like the Federal Aviation Administration, which among other things provides for air traffic control. The FAA depends on authority from Congress to collect fees from airlines and airports to support its programs. If its authorization expires, it loses its authority to collect the fees and may have to curtail air traffic control and other essential services. (Normally, the FAA authorization, like the Farm Bill, is temporarily extended so that there is no disruption in air travel.)

The bottom line is that mandatory programs are set up to ensure funding based on provisions set forth in authorizing legislation. The vast majority of federal programs are funded only if the Appropriations Committees annually provide for funding in their bills. Programs dependent on action by the Appropriations Committees are called **discretionary programs**. Members of Congress often try to turn discretionary programs subject to appropriations into mandatory programs in order to guarantee their funding. Rarely is there interest in Congress in taking a program in the other direction. In fact, only one major mandatory program has ever been converted into a discretionary program: Aid to Families with Dependent Children (AFDC) was converted into Temporary Assistance to Needy Families (TANF) in 1996 (see Box 6.3).

## The Spending Continues—Sometimes Without the Thinking

In directing the work of the government, Congress relies heavily on the expertise of its authorizing committees. The staff and members of these committees are among the top "policy wonks" on Capitol Hill in each jurisdiction. Congress can direct the agencies to do its bidding, at whatever level of specificity it wants, by passing authorizing bills. These bills bind the agencies to the will of Congress as expressed in law. Congress normally plans to revisit agency and program authorizations on a regular basis—to "reauthorize" those functions, in the parlance of Capitol Hill. Times change, circumstances change, new issues arise, and congressional committees invariably wish to leave their mark on the government in a timely fashion by updating existing laws governing programs and agencies.

But as a general rule, these committees have been getting a bad reputation. One congressman put it this way: "Most authorizing committees are just debating societies; they rarely put in the serious work and effort required to pass legislation."[21] (This member excluded the Armed Services Committees and the House Transportation and Infrastructure Committee from his analysis.) He pointed to the frequency with which Congress fails to complete timely reauthorizations for agencies and programs for which the authorization to appropriate has expired. He rued the fact that authorizing committees are losing stature to the Appropriations Committees, which *must* finish bills to keep the government funded and functioning.

What seems to happen is that agencies and outside groups with an interest in a particular policy end up focusing some of their attention away from the authorizing committee of jurisdiction if that committee cannot come together to pass a bill updating an agency or programs. Some agencies report that they focus almost all

## BOX 6.3

### A Rare Occurrence: The Termination of an Entitlement

Aid to Families with Dependent Children was a mandatory federal program established in 1935 in the Social Security Act. Its purpose was to create a grant program that would allow states to make welfare payments for needy children in one-parent families—in those days, a significant portion of the payments went to single mothers whose husbands had died.

Originally, states were able to define what constituted "needy" families and set their own standards for payments. The federal government would reimburse one-third of the cost. However, by the 1960s the federal government had expanded its role, taking on the program's entire cost and setting the relevant criteria for receiving payments.

By the 1980s, the program had become much more controversial. Instead of widows receiving the bulk of the payments, unwed and often never-wed single mothers were getting most of the money. Some critics alleged that the program was a disincentive to marriage, as intact two-parent families were not eligible for payments. By the 1990s, the cost of the program had skyrocketed to more than $6 billion a year.

In 1995 the first Republican Congress in a generation began work on an overhaul of the program. With AFDC, anyone eligible to receive payments would receive them and could receive them indefinitely as long as they qualified. In bad economic times, mandatory payments to needy families put an additional burden on the federal budget. The solution: terminate AFDC and replace it with a discretionary program, Temporary Aid to Needy Families, which would be controlled annually in the appropriations process and would have guidelines in law making people ineligible for aid after three years. President Clinton signed these changes into law in the summer of 1996, marking the first and only time a major mandatory program had been eliminated.*

*See Ron Haskins, *Work over Welfare: The Inside Story of the 1996 Welfare Reform Law* (Washington, DC: Brookings Institution Press, 2006).

of their attention on the Appropriations Committees if they need a change in law to enable them to do their work more effectively in a changing world.

Why do the authorizing committees often fail to complete the essential work of reconsidering government programs in a timely manner? After all, there is a reason the Congress includes in, for example, its NASA authorizing bill a two-year authorization to appropriate: it believes that NASA programs need to be comprehensively reevaluated on a biennial basis.

First, many sticky, controversial, or politically charged issues come up when a congressional committee takes up a major overhaul of an agency, such as NASA, or a set of programs within an agency, such as the farm program. Simply put, it can be difficult or impossible to come to the agreements necessary to move the bill through the legislative process in a timely fashion. As we have seen, the process is complex and time-consuming: sometimes it is impossible to get 218 House members and 60 senators to agree on something.

Second, the congressional calendar is jammed, especially in the Senate, where the rules permit unrestricted debate and amendments and, with the responsibility of approving hundreds of presidential nominations, the docket is longer than in the House.

## The Root of the Problem

The historical roots of the problem explain a great deal. Prior to the 1960s, not only was the government smaller, but there was a much more trusting relationship between the executive and legislative branches than there is now. This was reflected in the fact that in decades past, Congress tended to give very broad statutory discretion to the agencies when it set up programs. Congress basically trusted the bureaucrats to do what was laid out in law and to exercise their discretion in a reasonable way. And many of the authorizing laws were open-ended, with indefinite authorizations of appropriation and no so-called sunset provisions that could effectively close down programs after a certain time. Congress had far fewer staff, and many members did not think they needed more. If they wanted to redirect the work of the agencies by changing an existing authorization, they could, but they felt no urgency about it. As a result, the calendar for legislative activity was nowhere near as overwhelming as it is today.

Then, in the 1960s, a spasm of legislation stemming from the social and political upheaval of the era greatly expanded the scope of government. The period from 1964 to 1971 was especially intense. A lot of these new programs were experimental and controversial. At the same time, Congress was becoming more professionalized as it acquired many more expert staff and a generally more sophisticated membership. Many people on the Hill believed that too much discretion had been given over the years to unelected executive branch agency officials. The upshot was that Congress, in creating new programs, often established sunset dates for agency and program authorizations.

As Congress "bulked up" even more in the 1970s—more staff, a new support agency with the establishment of the Congressional Budget Office (CBO), new self-imposed oversight requirements—it became increasingly willing to meddle in areas that it had delegated to agency officials in the past. Legislatively, Congress wanted to keep the agencies on a short leash. Government programs and federal money touched every constituent and practically every entity in society by this time, and members were eager to exercise their authority over the government's work in order to serve the people in their districts or states.

The problem was that there just wasn't time to do everything they needed to do. Congress found itself unable to keep up with many of the authorizing responsibilities it had given itself, despite its good intentions. The situation was made worse by an increase in the level of partisanship, which complicated efforts to pass many bills. Ironically, just as Congress decided that it was best to keep the government on a short leash, either the politics were too contentious or they simply did not have the time to update authorizations as needed or required.

As noted earlier, the consequences were not necessarily catastrophic—it was not that programs were unable to get money appropriated for their continuation. It is relatively easy to get around the rules of the House and Senate prohibiting unauthorized appropriations. Even if Congress could not update the authorization for NASA, for instance, it surely was going to keep the agency going. Jobs at the agency and government contracts were at stake, and the agency was doing vital and popular work. There are exceptions to this rule, however, that can have real consequences—note the impact of an expiration of the FAA authorization, which has the effect of denying the agency the ability to collect fees from airports and airlines and can lead to the curtailing of air traffic control.

The upshot of all these changes was that the authorizing committees that could not update the laws affecting their areas of jurisdiction became less relevant. If a change in law needed to happen, the most effective tactic was to turn to the Appropriations Committees and get something inserted in a bill there. The budget experts at Appropriations ended up being the gatekeepers for important policy changes—a situation that was not what Congress intended with the division of labor between authorizers, who are supposed to think through policy issues, and appropriators, who are meant to consider the budgetary implications of government program spending.

Ultimately, we get back to the congressman's comment noted earlier. Many authorizing committees do not wield the same kind of power they did in the past. They conduct oversight, and they try to do the authorization updates, but if no one is confident that they can produce a passable final product, the authorizing committees may lose the attention of their stakeholders and the public. Conversely, the appropriators gain in power and prestige.

In today's Congress, observers know that the Armed Services Committees in both chambers are relevant; they reauthorize the work of the *entire Defense*

*Department every year.* All the other authorizing committees could be that relevant, so no one with something at stake can safely ignore them. But they are inconsistent, making progress on legislative changes some years, but not in others. Many do finish reauthorizations, but quite often this happens years behind schedule.

Most programs and agencies should be carefully reevaluated and reauthorized on a regular basis—and the failure to do so has real costs. The experts on the authorizing committees, both members and staff, do the important thinking about what the federal government should do. This thinking is translated into law through the authorization process. Because the programs are mostly either essential or popular or both, Congress goes ahead and funds their continuation without the kind of thorough examination needed.

## Authorizers Usurp Their Rivals: The Increase in Mandatory Spending

While the foregoing discussion might lead one to believe that the Appropriations Committees have the clear upper hand over the authorizing committees, this is not entirely the case. Appropriators *have* usurped authorizers when authorizers have let their bills lapse, as we have seen. But it is also true that authorizers have managed to undermine appropriators' control of the purse strings by including the legal authority for agencies to get money from the Treasury in their authorizing legislation.

Over the past 40 years, the amount of federal money spent directly through authorizing legislation has outstripped that controlled by the appropriators in their bills. The spending on the big entitlements, such as Social Security and Medicare—which are put on automatic pilot for all intents and purposes—does an end run around the Appropriations Committees.

Members of Congress, in an effort to establish a program that the appropriators cannot touch, can offer legislation to fund a program by direct spending in authorization legislation. Naturally, appropriators resist this, pointing out that direct spending programs put more of the budget outside of the annual control of the Congress. They say that these programs often become sacrosanct and in lean times have put an incredible burden on the budget, contributing to deficits. Furthermore, with the retirement of the baby-boom generation beginning in the 2010s, entitlement programs are putting tremendous stress on the nation's finances. The appropriators argue that it is better for Congress to keep as much of the government under control as possible by subjecting it to yearly review.

In recent years, a few members of Congress have made a big push to turn federal support for students with learning disabilities (a program established by the Individuals with Disabilities Education Act in 1975) into a mandatory program, protecting it from the yearly whims of appropriators.[22] So far the Appropriations Committees have successfully resisted this gambit, preserving their influence over the funding of the program. But it is a classic example of a struggle, four decades in the making, that pits budget watchers on the Appropriations Committees against policy experts on the authorizing committees who want to make sure that more resources are guaranteed for their favored programs.

* * *

In sum, the influence of the authorizing committees is in flux. Their failure to complete timely updates of agencies and programs has left an opening for appropriators to exploit. The Appropriations Committees are happy to decide what changes will be made in agency policy in the funding bills they write.

On the other hand, in the past few decades authorizers have succeeded at funding programs outside of the appropriations process. Programs whose funding is for all intents and purposes on automatic pilot have proven hard to control. They tend to grow in popularity and often are enhanced over the years. Nonetheless, the direct spending strategy has allowed authorizers to regain some of the power they lost to the appropriators.

## CONCLUSION

A great deal of legislative activity revolves around the authorizing process. Thousands of bills are introduced every year aimed at changing, enhancing, or creating government programs, sometimes altering the roles, relationships, and responsibilities of government agencies and even on occasion establishing entirely new departments. In 2009 alone, Congress evaluated authorizing bills to address global warming and other aspects of the nation's energy policy, the health care system, food safety policy, policies on the procurement of weapons, the regulatory structure of the financial system, and a great many other issues. Some (health care, weapons procurement, food safety, and financial regulations) resulted in legislation in 2010. In 2012 authorizing committees looked at federal transportation policy, farm programs, education programs, and other matters.

In this chapter, we looked at the scope of Congress's power to authorize the work of government. As we saw in the last chapter, House and Senate party leaders today play crucial roles in determining the agenda for their respective bodies. Nevertheless, most of the serious policy work happens in the committees and subcommittees, where the specialized expertise resides. In the end, the interaction between the leadership and the committees determines what Congress authorizes the government agencies to do on the people's behalf.

## Questions for Discussion

1. Does it make sense to have mandatory funding for certain government programs? If so, what kind of programs should be handled this way? Which ones should not be mandatory? What is the downside to making program funding mandatory?

2. Congress in general tries to avoid getting into reorganizing whole agencies and departments. Why is this? There was a time when presidents were basically given the power to reorganize departments and agencies as they saw fit. Is that a good idea?

3. One of the results of Congress's inability to complete many authorizations on a timely basis is ceding more authority to the heads of agencies and the president to make decisions in changing times. Is this a good thing, given the expertise that resides in the executive branch? Why or why not?

## Suggestions for Further Reading

Binder, Sarah A. *Causes and Consequences of Legislative Gridlock*. Washington, DC: Brookings Institution Press, 2003.

King, David C. *Turf Wars: How Congressional Committees Claim Jurisdiction*. Chicago: University of Chicago Press, 1997.

## NOTES

1. Quoted in Jean Reith Schroedel, *Congress, the President, and Policymaking* (New York: M. E. Sharpe, 1994), 121.

2. All of the committee websites, most with complete descriptions of their jurisdictions, can be found at www.house.gov and www.senate.gov.

3. See David C. King, *Turf Wars: How Congressional Committees Claim Jurisdiction* (Chicago: University of Chicago Press, 1997).

4. This figure includes what is called "overseas contingency operations," which is another way of describing costs associated with war and some intelligence operations. These are not included in the Defense Department's so-called base budget. Overseas contingencies have ranged from nearly $100 billion to about $200 billion since the beginning of the war in Afghanistan.

5. The idea of calling the authorizing committees the "thinking committees" and the appropriations committees the "spending committees" comes from Michael Robinson, former professor of government at Georgetown University and currently a scholar at the Pew Research Center for the People and the Press.

6. Allen Schick, *The Federal Budget,* 3rd ed. (Washington, DC: Brookings Institution Press, 2007), 191–194 (quote on 194).

7. In 1980 the name of the department was changed to Health and Human Services (HHS). The Education Department was created to administer HEA programs and other programs in the education area that had been handled by HEW.

8. Wayne C. Riddle, *CRS Report to Congress: No Child Left Behind—an Overview of Reauthorization Issues for the 110th Congress,* Congressional Research Service, December 14, 2006.

9. This is from the Surface Transportation Extension Act of 2012, 39.

10. One example of politics entering into the realm of government grants for scientific research was noted by Christine M. Marra, "Syphilis and Human Immunodeficiency Virus," *Archives of Neurology* 61 (2004): 1505–1508: "In 2003 . . . Representatives Patrick Toomey (R, Pa) and Chris Chocola (R, Ind) proposed an amendment to defund five peer-reviewed, approved NIH grants. Four of these grants had sexual themes as determined by their 'key words,' such as 'abortion,' 'condom effectiveness,' 'commercial sex workers,' and 'men who have sex with men.' The measure was defeated by only 2 votes (212 to 210). Subsequently, Congress directed NIH to defend 190 funded studies that dealt with human sexuality."

11. Charles Cushman, interview with the author, September 8, 2008.

12. Frederick M. Kaiser et al., *CRS Report for Congress: Congressional Oversight Manual,* Congressional Research Service, October 21, 2004, 5.

13. This was the Goldwater Nichols Department of Defense Reorganization Act of 1986, named after Senator Barry Goldwater (R-AZ) and Representative William Flynt Nichols (D-AL).

14. Cushman, interview with the author.

15. See the 9/11 Commission website, www.911commission.gov/. The complete report is available at http://govinfo.library.unt.edu/911/report/index.htm.

16. Richard A. Best Jr. et al., *CRS Report for Congress: Director of National Intelligence; Statutory Authorities,* Congressional Research Service, April 11, 2005, 2.

17. Charles Babington, "Senate Passes Intelligence Reform Bill," *Washington Post,* December 8, 2004, A4.

18. Best et al., *CRS Report for Congress,* 5.

19. Babington, "Senate Passes Intelligence Reform Bill," A4.

20. See Patricia Davis et al., *CRS Report to Congress: Medicare Provisions in the Patient Protection and Affordable Care Act,* Congressional Research Service, November 3, 2010.

21. Then-Representative Mark Kirk (R-IL), speech, March 18, 2004. Kirk was elected to the Senate in 2010.

22. A description and criticism of congressional efforts to make the Individuals with Disabilities Act a mandatory program is Krista Kafer and Brian Riedl, "Comments on the Harkin Amendment to the Elementary and Secondary Education Act," Heritage Foundation, November 30, 2001, www.heritage.org/research/education/WM61.cfm.

# 7

# The Power of the Purse

For Congress, no power is more crucial than the so-called power of the purse. The agencies cannot function without money—they cannot fight wars, build bridges, patrol borders, or anything else.

The vast majority of government programs (which have been established in authorizing statutes) require an appropriation in order to be implemented. In simple terms, what happens when an appropriations bill becomes law is that Congress gives the executive branch agencies the legal authority to spend money—that is, **budget authority**. To draw an analogy, budget authority puts money in a given agency's bank account, which enables it to draw funds from the US Treasury and commit those funds for a particular purpose. Committing to spend money is called **obligating** funds, which might entail, for example, entering into a contractual arrangement with a construction company to build an interstate highway or repair a bridge. Payments made to a contractor in exchange for work that is completed are called **outlays**.

The appropriations process is tremendously important just by virtue of the fact that it funds most of what government does. After all, holding the purse strings gives Congress a lot of leverage to force an agency to do one thing or not to do another. The board of directors determines which programs receive funding and how much they get. But that is only part of the picture.

In the last chapter, we saw that agency authorizations are not always updated on schedule. Congress cannot keep up with its workload because government has gotten so big and the policy issues that come up during the authorizing process are usually too complex and controversial to resolve easily. But an agency does not necessarily shut down if its authorizing legislation is not passed on time. As long as the agency receives funding, its programs will continue functioning.

So what can the board of directors do if it wants to change the policies of agencies that do not have an updated authorization? One common method is through the oversight process. But congressional oversight of agency performance, as we shall see in Chapters 10 and 11, has limitations. First, it is not systematically performed, and second, it can be used only as a means to persuade agency officials to do things as certain members of Congress would want them done. As a tool of the legislative branch, it cannot *compel* action in the same way that a law can, whether that law is an authorizing or an appropriations statute.

Invariably, members of Congress look to the appropriations process when they wish to force agencies to do certain things or prohibit them from doing certain other things. Appropriations bills are *must-pass legislation*—these bills need to be completed every year to keep the essential functions of the federal government up and running. While appropriations bills are meant only to provide funding and not to establish policy, members of Congress include provisions in appropriations bills telling agencies what they can and cannot do. In many years, the annual appropriations process is the primary way in which Congress flexes its muscle in directing the actions of the federal agencies.

The first step in understanding the budget process on Capitol Hill is to get a sense of the tremendous scope of the federal budget and the different categories of spending—the subject of the first section of the chapter. After taking this bird's-eye look at the federal budget, the next step is to look at how that budget is developed each year.

We begin by looking at how the president puts together his budget. The president's budget is his request for what he would like to see passed into law, in terms of both spending and taxes, in the coming year. (Congress refers to the president's budget as the budget request.) The February delivery of the president's budget effectively kicks off the legislative season on Capitol Hill.[1] Congress immediately begins digesting the request with an eye to its impact on both the economy and their own particular priorities insofar as they may differ from the president's. Their aim is to produce their own budget blueprint by April 15 each year. This blueprint is called the Concurrent Budget Resolution. It presents Congress's big-picture goals, but it is not law and thus does not commit the government to any actions any more than the president's budget request does.

The appropriations process begins in earnest after the **budget resolution** is passed. We look first at how the appropriations bills are put together and passed. The Appropriations Committees in the two chambers, primarily at the subcommittee level, assess carefully, through hearings and other means, what the executive branch agencies are requesting in terms of funding for the coming fiscal year. On the basis of input from the agencies and many other sources, the subcommittees then begin the process of writing appropriations bills and moving them through the legislative process.

Then we look at the appropriations bills themselves—the meaning of the different sections of the bills and, most important, how Congress uses these bills in various ways to direct the work of the agencies. As we saw in Chapter 6, the theory is that the authorizing committees, which are staffed by policy experts, decide in the legislation they write what it is that the government ideally should be doing to address the needs of the nation, and then the appropriators follow up by funding authorized programs as close to the maximum level allowable given budget constraints and other factors of their choosing. The reality is that authorizations frequently lapse or are extended without a thorough examination of the programs and agency policy. In these instances, appropriators "fill the gap" by including policy provisions in the funding bills. As we shall see, Congress is more than willing to meddle in agency affairs in the appropriations process, both by specifying what agencies must do with their funds as well as by limiting what they may do.

In recent years, the appropriations process has not proceeded smoothly, to say the least. In fact, from 1997 to 2013, Congress did not once do its work on time—and most years it was not even close. This has led to charges that the congressional budget process has "broken down." In Chapter 8, we look at why Congress has failed in recent years to complete arguably its most essential function and what it does to avoid a government shutdown.

## UNDERSTANDING THE FEDERAL BUDGET

The federal government is a massive entity; in fact, it is the single largest entity on the face of the earth. In fiscal year 2012, the government spent about $3.5 trillion, an amount that constitutes about 23 percent of the entire US economy and is larger than the economies of all but a few countries in the world. The actions of something as big as the federal government, then, not only affect every American individually in terms of the reach of government programs and policies, but can also significantly affect the overall performance of the economy. Economists acknowledge that the impact of something so large is often unpredictable, but there is no denying its significance.

There are a lot of ways to break down federal spending, but if the goal is to understand how Congress directs the actions of the government, the most useful way is to look at it the way the board of directors does. On Capitol Hill, spending is broken down into three broad categories, discretionary spending, mandatory spending or direct spending, and spending to pay for the interest on the accumulated national debt.

## Discretionary Spending

This category refers to spending on government programs (known as *discretionary programs*) that are dependent on budget authority in yearly appropriations acts for their funding. **Discretionary spending** is often called *controllable* spending, because appropriations acts are in effect for only a single year, so Congress retains more control over agency programs that are covered in these acts. Most of what the government does fits into this category—including providing for the defense of the nation, protecting the homeland, funding most education and research programs, providing foreign aid, caring for the national parks, tracking infectious diseases, inspecting the food supply, regulating the nuclear industry, implementing environmental laws, and on and on. The operating budgets of all the agencies are included in the discretionary spending category, including those that administer mandatory programs.[2]

## Mandatory Spending, or Direct Spending

This category refers to spending on programs that is determined by formulas or criteria set forth in authorizing legislation. This sort of spending is often referred to as *uncontrollable* because the spending levels are not set from year to year in appropriations bills, as with discretionary programs, but rather depend in most cases on the number of people who meet eligibility criteria for the subsidies or payments. If the economy takes an unexpected downturn, more people will qualify for Medicaid (medical assistance to the poor) and unemployment insurance—both mandatory programs—and federal spending will increase in ways sometimes not anticipated by economists and budget experts. Many mandatory programs are called *entitlements* because citizens who qualify through age, disability, employment status, poverty, or other criteria are *entitled* to payments from the government by law. The biggest mandatory programs include those administered by the Social Security Administration, especially Old Age and Survivors' Insurance, the Medicare programs, and Medicaid; others include unemployment insurance and food stamps.[3]

## Interest on the National Debt

This category is exactly what it sounds like: Congress authorizes the Treasury Department to borrow to finance the activities of the government that are not covered by taxes and other revenue sources. Ordinary citizens, banks, and foreign governments in effect lend the Treasury money by buying US bonds. Like any credit account, this debt must be serviced. Sometimes people confuse the national debt with the **deficit**. The deficit is any annual shortfall, which will add to the

**FIGURE 7.1. Mandatory Spending Consumes a Growing Share of the Federal Budget**

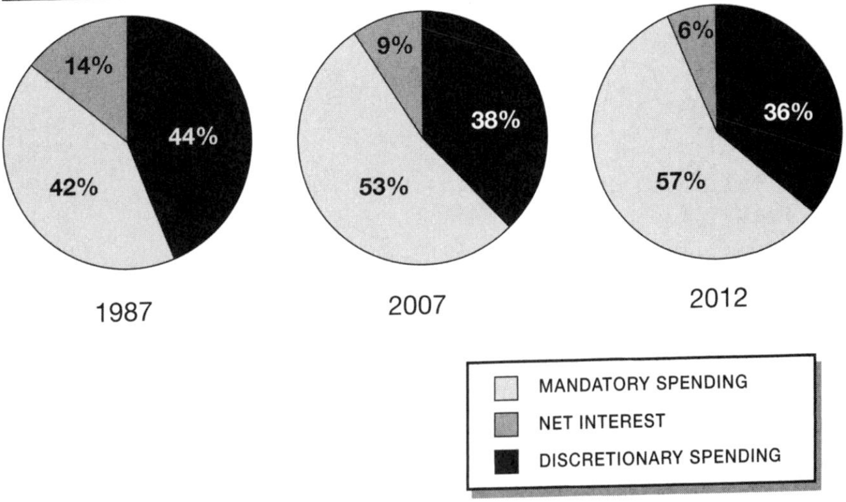

1987          2007          2012

☐ MANDATORY SPENDING
▨ NET INTEREST
■ DISCRETIONARY SPENDING

*Source:* Congressional Budget Office.

nation's total accumulated debt. In 2012 about 70 percent of the total debt of $16 trillion was owed "publicly," that is, to citizens, banks, and foreign governments; the remainder was owed internally to government trust funds, mostly the Social Security trust fund.

The breakdown of the federal budget has changed dramatically over the past 40 years. Figure 7.1 shows the preponderance of **mandatory spending** in the 2012 budget—only since the 1980s has mandatory spending outstripped discretionary. The discretionary part of the federal government is, however, tremendously important; as mentioned earlier, it includes most of the essential government services that Americans rely on every day. But in sheer dollar terms, the major mandatory programs have swamped the discretionary side of the budget. Most of the change is due to the growth of Medicare, Medicaid, and Social Security, although there was also a significant uptick in spending on Supplemental Nutrition Assistance and Unemployment Insurance—both mandatory programs—during the recent severe recession. As can be seen in the more detailed agency-by-agency breakdown of federal spending in Table 7.1, the amount of money spent by the Social Security Administration in fiscal year 2011 was greater than that spent by the Defense Department. (More than $600 billion of SSA spending was on mandatory programs.) In addition, almost 90 percent of the spending at the US Department of Health and Human Services is for mandatory Medicare and Medicaid programs.

## TABLE 7.1 Spending (Outlays) by Agency, Fiscal Year 2011

| AGENCY OR DEPARTMENT | OUTLAYS[a] | % OF TOTAL OUTLAYS |
|---|---|---|
| Agriculture[b] | $139,396 | 3.59 |
| Commerce | 9,930 | 0.26 |
| Defense | 678,074 | 17.48 |
| Education | 65,484 | 1.69 |
| Energy | 31,371 | 0.81 |
| Health and Human Resources[c] | 891,247 | 22.98 |
| Homeland Security | 45,741 | 1.18 |
| Housing and Urban Development | 57,002 | 1.47 |
| Interior | 13,519 | 0.35 |
| Justice | 30,519 | 0.79 |
| Labor[d] | 131,975 | 3.40 |
| State | 24,354 | 0.63 |
| Transportation | 77,301 | 1.99 |
| Treasury[e] | 536,740 | 13.84 |
| Veterans' Affairs | 126,918 | 3.27 |
| Corps of Engineers (civil) | 10,138 | 0.26 |
| Other Defense (civil programs) | 54,775 | 1.41 |
| Environmental Protection Agency | 10,772 | 0.28 |
| Executive Office of the President | 484 | 0.01 |
| General Services Administration | 1,889 | 0.05 |
| International Assistance Programs | 20,583 | 0.53 |
| National Aeronautics and Space Administration | 17,618 | 0.45 |
| National Science Foundation | 7,146 | 0.19 |
| Office of Personnel Management | 74,090 | 1.91 |
| Small Business Administration | 6,163 | 0.16 |
| Social Security Administration | 784,194 | 20.22 |
| Other Independent Agencies | 18,265 | 0.47 |

*Source:* Office of Management and Budget.

[a]In millions of dollars.

[b]Includes mandatory spending on farm subsidies and food stamps.

[c]Includes mandatory spending on Medicare and Medicaid programs.

[d]Includes mandatory spending on unemployment insurance and other things.

[e]Outlays to service the national debt constitute most of the total.

## THE PRESIDENT'S BUDGET: KICKING OFF THE CONGRESSIONAL BUDGET PROCESS

Each year Congress eagerly awaits the delivery of the **president's budget** on the first Monday in February. Its arrival serves as the kickoff for the congressional budget season.

In a nutshell, the president's budget is a detailed description of the president's agenda for the coming fiscal year beginning on October 1. It also tracks the long-term implications of that agenda. This is because presidents often propose new programs and changes in tax law that would take years to implement. The budget includes exactly what the president wants each and every agency of the government to do, how much money the executive branch would need appropriated to carry out its agenda, and, on the revenue side, any tax laws the president would like to see enacted or changed.

A lot of work goes into this document. Budget offices in every federal agency and department, together with the Office of Management and Budget, an agency in the Executive Office of the President responsible for coordinating the development of the president's budget, spend a good part of the year putting together the documents. Literally thousands of federal workers spend a major part of their day on this task.

It is not uncommon for congressional leaders to declare the president's budget "dead on arrival" the moment it arrives in February, especially if the presidency and Congress are controlled by different parties. Members of Congress invariably point out that it is the legislative branch that decides in law what the government will do and, more to the point, how much it will spend.

But the president's budget request *does* matter, regardless of which party is in control or if control is divided. The claim that the comprehensive presentation of the president's vision for the upcoming year is irrelevant—or "dead on arrival"—is just political rhetoric. There are two reasons the president's budget matters when the final policies are put into law.

First of all, the president has the power to veto laws passed by Congress, which, as we have seen, makes the president a player in the legislative process. It is a rare day when Congress overrides a presidential veto. If Congress wants to put something into law, the president's preferences almost always have to be a part of the equation. Because the president's budget is, in effect, the official statement of his agenda, it is a consequential document, and Congress invariably must incorporate at least some of the president's priorities into appropriations law. The separated system of government is a power-*sharing* arrangement, and it applies to the budget as much as anywhere else.

Second, the federal government is an incredibly vast entity with an incredibly complex budget. It is literally impossible for the relatively limited congressional staff to have intricate, detailed knowledge of the vast range of government programs. There are thousands of employees in the budget offices of the federal government putting together the president's budget, yet there are only a couple of hundred professional staff on the congressional Appropriations Committees. Congressional staff rely on the experts in the executive branch to a significant degree. As a practical matter, Congress uses the president's budget request as a starting point each year when putting the budget into law in the appropriations acts. The federal budget is simply too big for Congress to start from scratch each year in deciding what to fund.

## Putting the President's Budget Together

Putting together the president's budget is a fairly orderly process that takes place in the year before the budget is presented to Congress on the first Monday in February. The order of events for the budget process, beginning with the presidential budget submission and ending with the completion of appropriations legislation, is depicted here. The dates are for the fiscal year 2014 (FY 2014) federal budget. The federal **fiscal year** starts on October 1—for FY 2014, October 1, 2013—and ends on September 30, 2014.

The following is the timetable for the formulation of the budget for fiscal year 2014 (FY 2014):

- *March 2012 through January 2013*—Federal agencies and departments formulate the president's budget under the guidance of the Office of Management and Budget.
- *First Monday in February 2013*—The OMB delivers the president's budget to Congress.
- *Winter and early spring 2013*—Congressional committees examine the president's budget request.
- *April 15, 2013*—Congress passes the Concurrent Budget Resolution to set forth its budgetary priorities.
- *May through the end of September 2013*—Congress begins and completes work on appropriations bills and other budget-related legislation.

The Office of Management and Budget supervises this process for the president,[4] setting guidelines for each department and agency, according to the priorities of the president. As indicated earlier, agencies begin work on a particular fiscal year budget about 18 months before the relevant fiscal year begins, usually in March of the previous calendar year. Through the spring and summer, agencies work with their parent departments (for example, the US Fish and Wildlife Service and the Bureau of Land Management are part of the Interior Department, and each branch of the armed services works with the Defense Department) to put together a detailed budget, which they submit to the OMB around Labor Day. Independent agencies, such as NASA, the National Endowment of the Humanities, and many regulatory agencies, work directly with the OMB without the supervision of a parent department.

The OMB then goes through a comprehensive review of the submissions of the various departments and independent agencies of government, checking carefully to see whether they are staying within the OMB budgetary guidelines reflecting the priorities of the president. During the fall, OMB is in constant contact with officials at the departments and agencies. Ultimately, the OMB completes a full draft of the president's budget by around Thanksgiving and returns the relevant portions to the departments and independent agencies. This is called the **passback**. If the departments and agencies do not like what they see in the passback, they may appeal the decisions made by the OMB up the executive branch chain of command all the way to the president himself. In practice, the president usually hears only a few appeals; top-ranking White House officials handle most of the work for him. This practice can differ a great deal, however, from one president to the next.

Ultimately, the OMB and the agency and department budget offices throughout the government work through the holidays and into January finishing up the complex budget documents that will be transmitted to Congress. The OMB also writes descriptive material providing an overview of the president's goals and priorities, which is intended to sell the budget to Congress and the American people. The president, as tradition dictates, delivers his prime-time State of the Union address in late January, which is in many ways a preview of and initial sales pitch for his comprehensive budget request.

The OMB stays very busy the rest of the year, monitoring the progress of the president's agenda on Capitol Hill and submitting official statements—called *statements of administration policy* (or *SAPs*)[5]—on the president's position on bills as they make their way through the legislative process. At the same time, the OMB must manage the whole budget preparation process all over again for the next fiscal year.

## CONGRESS RESPONDS: THE CONCURRENT BUDGET RESOLUTION

Congress's first order of business, once it receives the president's budget on the first Monday in February, is to establish its own priorities. That is what the **Concurrent Budget Resolution** (or the **budget resolution**) is meant to do.

**FIGURE 7.2. Congressional Budget and Appropriations Process**

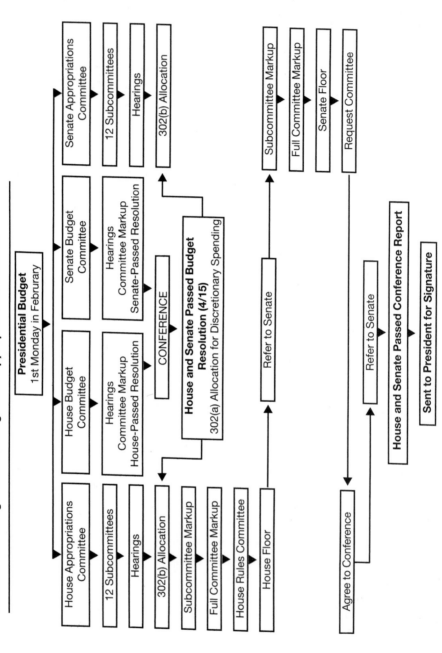

The budget resolution establishes the priorities of the majority party in Congress—or in the case of a House and Senate controlled by opposing parties, a compromise set of priorities. It is meant to put in place the framework for building the federal budget for the next fiscal year on the spending and revenue side, setting budget rules to guide the work of Congress in the ensuing several months as it attempts to pass appropriations bills, authorizing bills that affect mandatory programs, and tax bills on the revenue side before the new fiscal year starts on October 1. In and of itself, the budget resolution is not law and never goes to the president. As can be seen in the congressional budget process chart in Figure 7.2, it is supposed to pass both houses of Congress in identical form by April 15.

## What Does the Budget Resolution Do?

Putting together the budget resolution is like sitting down at the kitchen table on January 1 and trying to establish a reasonable framework for your personal or family budget for the next year. You would probably estimate what your income will be and decide what sorts of expenditures you are stuck with (rent or the mortgage, student loan payments, and the like) and what other expenditures you would have more control over (vacations and travel, new clothes, eating out, and so on). In the more controllable area, you would decide whether you could spend more or whether it would be wise to cut back. You might consider whether you would like to take on any more long-term obligations, such as purchasing a new car or buying a first home if you are a renter. You might entertain the idea of increasing your revenue stream by working harder, taking on a second job, or trying to find a new, more remunerative, one.

Setting out a personal budget like this is, in many respects, a goal. You might aim to cut back on spending, or you might aim to work harder and make more money, but you would have to take real, concrete actions during the year to accomplish those things. Similarly, Congress's budget resolution puts it on record for a set of priorities on spending and taxes, but it does not actually accomplish those goals. You probably would hope that your actions during the year will closely coincide with the personal or family budget you established on the first day of the year; in the same way, the majority party in Congress would like for the bills it passes during the year establishing the actual federal budget and revenue stream to resemble its budget framework as voted on in the budget resolution.

In our personal or family budget, many of us do relatively little tinkering with big, fixed expenses (often because we cannot), such as the mortgage, college tuition for the children, insurance costs, and health care premiums. And increasing the revenue stream by taking another job, working harder, or getting a new job might not be feasible, either. As a result, in most years our most important financial decisions boil down to the ones we have more control over. Will we cut back on controllable spending—by spending fewer nights out, taking a less extravagant vacation, and buying fewer clothes—or will we leave room in our budget to increase those discretionary types of expenditures?

The same is true for Congress. The members often leave the revenue stream alone, making no major changes in the tax code. And typically they leave in place long-term obligations such as mandatory spending for Social Security and Medicare programs, which take up so much of the budget (much as your personal budget may be dominated by mortgage, tuition, and car payments). Attention ends up being focused on the controllable part of the budget, the part Congress has to look at every year—the discretionary spending accounts. These costs happen to be extremely important (national defense, research, border security, education, and so on) but are less expensive in terms of sheer dollar amounts than mandatory programs, as we have seen. The congressional budget resolution always establishes an allocation for discretionary spending, which becomes the focus of a great deal of attention every year.

## The Budget Process Is Created

The budget resolution and the Budget Committees were a creation of the 93rd Congress in 1974. Up until that time, Congress had no institutionalized way to coordinate taxing and spending policy—in other words, *to budget*. The Ways and Means (House) and Finance (Senate) Committees set tax policy, and the Appropriations Committees took care of spending policy. The problem was that by this time, the appropriators were rapidly losing control of much federal spending, entitlement programs having been dramatically expanded and enhanced in the mid-1960s and early 1970s. As large deficits were becoming chronic, the federal budget seemed to be out of control.

The Budget and Impoundment Act of 1974 was passed in part to address the problem. One committee, the Budget Committee (each chamber would have one), would look at both sides of the ledger—taxing and spending—and develop a blueprint to guide lawmaking in those areas. This would be the Concurrent Budget Resolution.

The idea was to have members of the Budget Committees take a big-picture view of the federal budget that would not be linked to arbitrary jurisdictional categories as reflected in the congressional committee structure and the departments and agencies of the government. The new law broke down federal spending into 21 **functional categories** or areas of government activity not strictly tied to those jurisdictions. The committee members would recommend how much money needed to be spent on health, or on education, training and employment, or on science and technology, and so on, given existing federal programs. They might envision new programs as well. They would add up that spending and then be in a position to compare it to revenue as received by the Treasury, based on current tax law. Or alternatively, the committee could envision tax cuts to boost the economy or tax increases to balance the budget or for other purposes.

The budget resolution coming out of committee would, in effect, be a recommendation on spending and taxing priorities for the next fiscal year (and usually projected out for five years) to the rest of Congress. It would also provide information on the deficit or surplus situation, frequently offering the committee's judgment on what kind of deficit the government could prudently handle. Although not legally binding, the concurrent passage in the two chambers of the resolution would put Congress—or at least the majority party, which normally dictates the terms of the resolution—on record as keeping to a certain level of overall spending and a specific deficit figure. It could also, in certain circumstances, provide a special streamlined process to make it less difficult for Congress to do unpopular but necessary things, such as raising taxes or cutting spending on mandatory programs.

It is most important to stress the political implications of the budget resolution. It is not binding, but it does represent a public statement by the majority party of its priorities in the federal budget—essentially what the majority party in Congress wants the government to spend and what tax levels and deficit it deems appropriate. Failing to follow through with legislation consistent with those goals can have political repercussions.

The reason the budget resolution can be a relatively pure expression of the majority's preferences is that by law it cannot be filibustered in the Senate, unlike almost every other kind of bill. Thus, the majority in the Senate does not need to consult and compromise with the minority, as it normally must do with other legislation. When the same party controls both chambers, the resolution usually passes with little or no minority party support.

## The Early Stages of the Process

Immediately upon receipt of the president's budget in early February, the Budget Committees in the House and Senate commence with hearings to examine the president's request. These usually take the form of looking at the president's big-picture goals as laid out in his spending and taxing priorities.

Budget Committee hearings are often high-profile affairs, with members of the committee grilling the chairman of the Federal Reserve, the secretary of the Treasury Department, the secretary of the Defense Department, and the president's chief budget adviser, the OMB director. If the party in control of Congress is different from the president's party, nationally known experts outside of government who will take the side of the congressional majority are called on to highlight the differences between the two parties.

Ultimately, each Budget Committee chair in the House and Senate will direct his or her staff to write up the resolution itself. The chair normally does not consult very much with the minority party in the development of the resolution. If the presidency and Congress are controlled by the same party, there is considerable cross-fertilization between the branches, and the resolution is likely to enshrine most of the president's priorities. But even in the case of unified government, it can be difficult at the end of the process for the House and Senate to agree to the same blueprint. Twice during the two-term administration of George W. Bush when Republicans controlled the levers of power in Congress, and in 2010 when President Obama and the Democrats were in charge, House and Senate negotiators were unable to agree on a budget blueprint.[6] The perspectives of the two chambers can be so different as to preclude agreement, even with unified party control. When the House and the Senate are controlled by different parties, agreement is next to impossible, as has been seen in 2011, 2012, and 2013.

## The Components of the Budget Resolution

The budget resolution is essentially a big-picture view of what Congress (usually the majority party) thinks the government should do in the next fiscal year. Normally, it has five key components:

1. It adds up the total spending envisioned, including the discretionary area, mandatory programs, and anticipated debt service.
2. It establishes a target for all tax revenues.
3. It establishes spending limits, the so-called 302(a) allocations, for congressional committees—most important, for the Appropriations Committees, which handle the discretionary part of the federal budget.
4. It calculates the expected deficit (or surplus) in the coming fiscal year.
5. If the majority party wishes to make significant changes to a tax law or mandatory program, the resolution *may* include **reconciliation instructions**. These instructions are the means by which the Budget Committees expedite the consideration of such changes. The reconciliation instructions give broad guidance to the authorizing committees that deal with tax matters or mandatory programs. When those committees finish their work (they are given a target date), they send the results to the Budget Committee in their chamber. The Budget Committee packages all the component parts into a *reconciliation bill* for floor consideration. *That bill may not be filibustered on the Senate floor.* The term

*reconciliation* is used because the budget resolution gives instructions to the relevant committees to *reconcile* current tax law with the revenue target set forth in the budget resolution, or to *reconcile* the law governing mandatory programs with the spending totals in the budget resolution.

The budget resolution covers all aspects of the federal budget. In looking at the tax side, it may call for changes, or it may merely calculate revenue based on existing law and economic conditions. The resolution looks at the spending side and always sets the level of the more controllable discretionary spending for the next fiscal year, the 302(a) allocation, which is then parceled out to government agencies by the Appropriations Committees in appropriations laws. It may merely calculate mandatory spending based on current law, or it may call for changes. It calculates the expected debt service based on the yearly deficit projected to be added to the national debt. (Of course, if the resolution anticipates a budget surplus, the debt service may well decrease as the national debt decreases.)

The more ambitious budget resolution that calls for tax or mandatory program changes (or both) may handle these in one of two ways. It may simply put forth a budget that calls for, let's say, a new Medicare prescription drug program or tax increases to close the deficit and then allow the relevant committees to go about their work putting the change into effect through the normal legislative process. Or the resolution may use reconciliation instructions that require authorizing committees to send their tax or mandatory program changes back to the Budget Committee for approval and packaging for floor consideration. Reconciliation instructions can work to streamline the legislative process in the Senate, but they have certain disadvantages.

## Passing the Budget Resolution

The budget resolution is typically rammed through the House and Senate committees on party-line votes. On the floors of the respective bodies, however, the process differs in significant ways.

In the House, the minority party is not permitted to amend the majority's budget resolution on the floor, but it is typically allowed a full-fledged alternative resolution to be brought up for consideration (technically called an **amendment in the nature of a substitute**, or simply a *substitute*). It is normally voted down on a party-line vote, followed by the affirmative vote, also party line, for the majority's resolution. Occasionally, a rump group from one or the other party is permitted to offer a full alternative resolution. In recent years, the Republican Study Committee (a conservative caucus within the party), the Blue Dog Coalition (a group of moderate Democrats interested in deficit reduction), and the Congressional Black Caucus have been allowed to offer alternatives.[7]

In the more freewheeling Senate, no filibuster is permitted (and in a rare departure in Senate procedure, debate is limited to 20 hours), but amendments are allowed. Within the debate time limit set in law, dozens of amendments are brought up, often on specific spending proposals that are not usually a part of the original resolution document. Some of these pass; most do not. Those that do pass usually do not survive the subsequent conference negotiations to produce a Concurrent Budget Resolution. More often than not, senators offer amendments in order to appease certain interested parties and to indicate publicly their support for a particular program or agency. In other words, most of these amendments are for political consumption only and have little or no effect on subsequent spending or tax legislation.

In the end, a relatively simple and clean resolution is agreed to by the bodies after the conference committee meets. It states the spending and revenue levels for the government in the coming year, sets the discretionary allotment for the Appropriations Committees, calculates whatever deficit or surplus is likely to result, and sometimes includes reconciliation instructions for any controversial and high-priority matters for the majority party.

The agreement is not usually made by the April 15 deadline—the resolution falls behind schedule by a month or more in most years if it is finished at all. *The impact of failure is considerable*: the processing of appropriations bills for discretionary spending is delayed, and major changes in mandatory programs or tax policy are much more difficult to enact.

## The Reconciliation Process

In 2003, when the Republican Congress wished to institute several tax cuts, including a large reduction in the capital gains tax rate, it chose to go the reconciliation route. The reason? If a tax bill is produced pursuant to reconciliation instructions in the budget resolution, that bill, like the resolution itself, may not be filibustered in the Senate. As we saw in Chapter 6, the Senate usually requires 60 votes to pass consequential legislation; with reconciliation, the tax bill would be *fast-tracked* and require only 51 votes. This worked to the Republicans' advantage because there was substantial Democratic opposition to this particular provision and the GOP did not have the working 60-vote margin to pass the bill in the normal way.

As can be seen in Figure 7.3, a separate procedure is followed when reconciliation instructions are included in the budget resolution.

As noted earlier, these instructions may pertain only to tax law and mandatory programs. (Discretionary spending is covered by the 302[a] allocation.) The

**FIGURE 7.3. Budget Reconciliation Process**

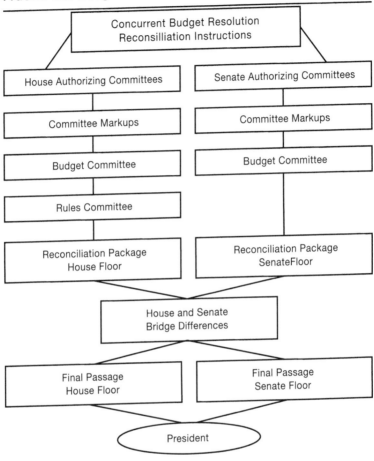

relevant authorizing committees are given instructions to produce tax or manda-tory program changes to meet certain revenue or spending targets. When these committees have completed their work, it is packaged together by the Budget Com-mittees before floor consideration.

For the Republicans in 2003, the downside was that, according to Senate rules, if a reconciliation bill will increase the deficit or reduce the surplus after a five-year period, its provisions must expire at that point.[8] So the capital gains provision, as well as several others passed with it, had to be set to expire at the end of the five-year period. This would *not* have been the case if the bill had passed in the normal legislative process without the filibuster protections afforded by reconciliation.

Contrast that to the Medicare prescription drug plan, a mandatory spending program that Republicans budgeted for and that passed the same year. It, too, increased the deficit after five years, but Republicans chose to pass it in the normal way, unprotected from the filibuster by reconciliation procedures. They calculated that they could probably quash any attempted filibusters by picking up some Democratic votes. As a result, when the Medicare prescription drug plan passed, it was not set to expire in five years.

It should be noted that changes put into effect by reconciliation procedures—specifically, cuts in mandatory programs and tax increases—do *not* have to expire after five years, since such changes would tend to *decrease* the deficit. The reconciliation process was put in place to make it somewhat easier to do unpopular things that go against the grain in Congress—namely, tax more and cut popular mandatory programs. Sometimes these sorts of actions are needed if deficits threaten economic growth. (Parts of the controversial Affordable Care Act passed in 2010 were passed in the reconciliation process, but these provisions were not set to expire, as the nonpartisan Congressional Budget Office calculated that the overall impact of the bill would not add to the deficit.)

\* \* \*

The budget resolution is often criticized as toothless—a "New Year's resolution"—and easily ignored once Congress gets down to the real business of passing laws. But in fact the resolution does put constraints on discretionary spending in the form of the 302(a) allocation, an important part of fiscal discipline, and has been the vehicle, through reconciliation, for putting into place most of the major changes in tax law in the past 30 years, as well as many significant changes in mandatory programs. It was used in 1996 that ended the federal welfare entitlement. But it is also true, as noted, that Congress has in recent years found it very hard to agree on a resolution.

## THE APPROPRIATIONS PROCESS

From year to year, no committees direct government action more than the Appropriations Committees. These panels have funding jurisdiction over the operations of the entire government and most government programs, excepting the mandatory programs, the funding levels for which are determined in authorizing legislation. From the moment the president's budget request arrives on Capitol Hill the first Monday in February, the Appropriations Committees are hard at work examining the funding that the agencies want in the coming fiscal year and developing the legislation that they believe will enable the agencies to serve their missions. This is the so-called power of the purse, the board of directors' most important tool in directing the work of government.

There are 12 appropriations bills that determine discretionary spending levels for the next fiscal year, and all are truly "must-pass" legislation. In fact, the US government could operate satisfactorily if Congress did nothing more in a given year than pass these 12 bills. Because of the centrality of these bills, the appropriations process typically becomes the center of attention for Congress. As efforts by authorizing committees to create new programs or make changes in existing ones are either passed into law or, more commonly, run into insuperable obstacles in the legislative process, the focus turns to the appropriations bills.

The fact that these bills must be passed does not make them *easy* to pass; in fact, the opposite is true. Appropriations bills can be extremely difficult to complete and often require highly creative approaches to the legislative process in order to become law.

## The Appropriations Committees

The Appropriations Committees first came into existence in the 1860s. Before that time, spending and taxes were handled by the Ways and Means and Finance Committees. The two responsibilities were separated in 1865, leaving Ways and Means and Finance with jurisdiction over the tax code and giving the new Appropriations Committees control over funding legislation.[9]

For much of the history of the Appropriations Committees, nearly all federal spending was discretionary, and thus under their control. Beginning in the 1930s and especially in the 1960s, the tide began to turn with the creation of mandatory programs through authorizing legislation. Still, to this day, even though only about 35–38 percent of federal spending is discretionary, this category includes most of the essential work of the government. These committees do not have quite the overarching control they had in their heyday, but they remain the most important committees on the Hill year in and year out—largely because they must act to keep the government operating.

Today, in both chambers, the Appropriations Committees have 12 subcommittees, as listed here. Funding jurisdiction over the executive branch of the federal government is divided among 11 of them. One subcommittee handles funding for the legislative branch. The following is a list of the appropriations subcommittees in both the House and the Senate:

1. Agriculture, Rural Development, Food and Drug Administration, and Related Agencies
2. Commerce, Justice, Science, and Related Agencies
3. Defense (includes funding for intelligence agencies)

4. Energy and Water Development and Related Agencies
5. Financial Services and General Government
6. Homeland Security
7. Interior, Environment, and Related Agencies
8. Labor, Health and Human Services, Education, and Related Agencies
9. Legislative Branch
10. Military Construction, Veterans' Affairs, and Related Agencies
11. State, Foreign Operations, and Related Agencies
12. Transportation, Housing and Urban Development, and Related Agencies

Each of the 51 House members (in the 113th Congress) who serve on the committee gets two or three subcommittee assignments. Most of these members serve only on the Appropriations Committee. Members traditionally clamor to get on Appropriations because it deals with "real money"; authorizing committees, on the other hand, may be relatively less appealing because they do not actually dole out money in most cases. In recent years, as discretionary spending has faced cuts instead of increases, the appeal of the committee for some members (especially on the Republican side) has waned.

In the Senate, the 30 members of the Appropriations Committee may have as many as five subcommittee assignments, but unlike in the House, all Senate appropriators have other committee assignments.

Not only does the majority party control the chair position for the full committee, but all the subcommittees are chaired by majority party members as well. These 12 slots are some of the most sought-after positions in Congress—the group of subcommittee chairs is sometimes called the "college of cardinals." The cardinals write the first drafts of appropriations bills, a task that effectively gives them substantial influence over billions of dollars of federal spending each year. The majority leadership of the committees also hires the bulk of the expert committee staff, many of whom have been with the committee for a long time and have far more detailed knowledge of the federal budget than the members themselves. Of the approximately 200 staffers on Appropriations in the House and Senate, more than 70 percent are hired by the majority. Having said that, Appropriations staff operate in a more bipartisan fashion than those on most other committees.

## The Subcommittee Hearings

Much like the members of the Budget Committees, who begin examining the president's budget the moment it reaches Capitol Hill, the Appropriations subcommittees begin holding hearings and initiating meetings with executive branch agency officials in early February. But unlike the Budget Committees, with their bird's-eye view of the federal budget, the Appropriations Committees—at the subcommittee level—get into the specific details of government programs at all the agencies.

From February through April every year, a parade of agency heads and other high-ranking officials, as well as the top brass in the armed services, march up to Capitol Hill for formal and informal meetings with Appropriations staff and members. The agency personnel have one task: to defend the president's budget request to their congressional overseers. Although agency officials might have had bitter disagreements with the OMB and the president over funding matters and other policies, once the president's budget is delivered, they all must be on the same page. Disagreements within the executive branch are regarded as internal matters, and all executive branch personnel are required to support the final decision as handed down by the OMB for the president.

Subcommittee hearings are the most public of the interactions between appropriators and the agencies. While Appropriations staff have done in-depth research into the agency budget requests and have usually been in constant contact with top agency personnel throughout the year, hearings are the opportunity to get high-ranking officials on the public record on the key issues facing the agency and its funding levels.

Often, agency heads and the members of the subcommittee understand each other well and have long-established relationships. They may collaborate on the questions to be asked and the answers to be tendered during the hearings in order to advance common goals. Sometimes members of Congress try to get agency people to admit that they disagree with the president's spending priorities. Such prodding can lead to very uncomfortable moments for high-ranking people, who must stay true to the president's priorities as expressed in the president's budget in all official interactions. (Most agency officials serve at the president's pleasure.) Politics and opposing priorities in the two branches or between the two parties are almost always behind these sorts of clashes. Agency officials need to be on their toes while testifying. A well-stated case in public may make it tougher for members to cut agency funding or otherwise tie agency officials' hands if they are so inclined.

In the larger picture, hearings are a chance for any interested group to gauge what is happening with the federal budget in a given year (in fact, many nongovernmental groups are brought in to testify at hearings) and for members of Congress to advance a case for their priorities. Hearings amount to a public vetting of the views of the relevant parties.

## The All-Important 302(a) and 302(b) Allocations

The day Congress passes the Concurrent Budget Resolution is a big one for appropriators. The resolution contains the **302(a) allocation**, which represents the total sum of funds that Congress intends to allocate to discretionary spending for the next fiscal year. The appropriators take over from there. The Budget Control Act (BCA) passed in 2011 set ceilings for discretionary funding each year through 2021 in an attempt to rein in spending. (These ceilings represent an approximately 2 percent increase per year—less than what would be needed to maintain current government services in most cases.) It is unlikely future budget resolutions will permit funding in excess of the limits, especially since it would require a law—not just a concurrent resolution—to do so. In cases when no Concurrent Budget Resolution can be achieved, it is likely that Congress will fall back on these ceilings to function as the 302(a) allocation for discretionary spending.

It is up to the Appropriations Committees in the two chambers, in internal deliberations controlled by the respective full committee chairs, to divide the 302(a) allocation among the 12 subcommittees. This subdivision of the larger pot of money is called the **302(b) allocation**. Each subcommittee gets one. Ideally, the budget resolution passes by April 15, giving the committees ample time to set the 302(b) allocations and the subcommittees time to complete their bills. But with the budget resolution more commonly being tardy, the appropriations process begins to fall behind schedule.

Typically, the House Appropriations chair moves more quickly than the Senate chair in establishing 302(b) allocations for each subcommittee. Table 7.2 shows the 302(b) allocations in the House and Senate for fiscal year 2013.

Senators on Appropriations are stretched so thin that it is harder for them to find the time to come to a speedy agreement. They serve on other committees, and some have twice as many subcommittee assignments as House appropriators. Some senators are also chairs of both an Appropriations subcommittee and another full authorizing committee. This amounts to two full-time jobs! Most House appropriators have the advantage of being able to focus exclusively on their committee work while doing legislative business in Washington.

The 302(b) allocation determines, for example, how much money the Subcommittee on Homeland Security has to distribute in its bill to the 22 agencies in the Department of Homeland Security. The chair of the Subcommittee on the Interior, Environment, and Related Agencies finds out the total sum he has to work with for the Interior Department and its agencies, the Environmental Protection Agency, and related smaller agencies. As can be seen in Table 7.2, the Senate 302(b) allocations are usually slightly different from the House ones, since senators are bound to have some different priorities in the distribution of discretionary spending even if the two chambers are controlled by the same party.

One cannot exaggerate the importance of the 302(b) allocations. It is at this stage that the relative priority of defense spending versus social spending—or more specifically, for example, spending on the Commerce Department, science,

**TABLE 7.2 302(b) Allocations for Fiscal Year 2013**

| APPROPRIATIONS SUBCOMMITTEES | HOUSE ALLOCATION[a] | SENATE ALLOCATION[a] |
| --- | --- | --- |
| Agriculture | $19,405 | $20,785 |
| Commerce, Justice, Science | 51,131 | 51,862 |
| Defense | 519,220 | 511,161 |
| Energy and Water | 32,098 | 33,361 |
| Financial Services and General Government | 21,150 | 22,991 |
| Homeland Security | 39,117 | 39,514 |
| Interior and Environment | 28,000 | 29,662 |
| Labor, HHS, Education | 150,002 | 157,722 |
| Legislative Branch | 4,289 | 4,420 |
| Military Construction/ Veterans' Affairs | 71,747 | 72,241 |
| State and Foreign Operations | 40,132 | 49,843 |
| Transportation & HUD | 51,606 | 53,438 |
| **Total** | **$1,027,896** | **$1,047,000** |

[a]In millions of dollars.

*Source:* House and Senate Appropriations Committees

and space (the Subcommittee on Commerce, Justice, Science, and Related Agencies) versus spending on foreign aid and diplomacy (the Subcommittee on State and Foreign Operations)—is determined. This sets up potentially bitter zero-sum games among the agencies covered in the same appropriations bill. The Interior Department is pitted against the EPA in their bill, the Defense bill pits the armed services against one another, and the Homeland Security bill forces Customs and Border Protection, the Secret Service, and 20 other agencies to squabble over the same pot of money.

## Marking Up the Appropriations Bills

The Appropriations subcommittee chairs have one job: to write a bill to fund the agencies in their jurisdiction that can ultimately pass into law after the legislative process runs its course. Ideally, that final bill, with all the inevitable changes and compromises along the way, will resemble the priorities of the chair and his or her party. The first task is to get the subcommittee members to go along.

The bills almost always move first in the House since, again, Senate appropriators have trouble focusing the way House members can because of the multiplicity
of their legislative duties.[10] The goal in the House, in keeping with the chamber's
rules, is to get all 12 appropriations bills passed on the floor and sent to the Senate
before the July 4 holiday break. In recent years, the House has sometimes done this,
but more often several of the bills are not passed until mid- to late July.

The Appropriations Committees are under more pressure than many other
committees to produce a product that can make it through the process and become
law. After all, the functioning of the federal government depends on the successful
completion of the appropriations bills. Subcommittee chairs, as a result, are carefully attuned to the legislative realities, especially the need for bipartisanship due to
the ability of the minority party to block action in the Senate—appropriations bills
can be filibustered. It is chiefly for this reason that the Appropriations Committees are characterized by more bipartisanship than almost all other congressional
committees.

House subcommittee chairs schedule a markup as soon as they and their staff
put together a bill. Most chairs consult carefully with all subcommittee members,
including minority party members, and try to assemble a consensus product—that
is, one that is more likely to make it through the entire legislative process and to the
president's desk relatively intact.

As soon as the bill passes the House subcommittee—it is not uncommon to
have a unanimous bipartisan vote at this stage—it is scheduled by the full committee chair for a markup involving the entire committee. Although it is relatively easy
to get a consensus among the 12 to 15 subcommittee members, the full committee
can be a different matter. The hearing room is jammed during the markup with
members, staff, and a standing-room-only crowd of interest group representatives
and others who have a stake in the particular government funding decisions being
made. The chair goes through the bill line by line, with committee members offering amendments that change wording or funding levels. Eventually, a vote is taken
on the bill as amended, and it is then in a position to move toward floor consideration in the full House.

The completion of the bill at the committee stage in the House is a key point in
the funding process for agencies and government programs. House Appropriations
Committee members and their staff are among the most knowledgeable people
on the Hill regarding the particulars of agency funding. They not only establish
a benchmark for the rest of the appropriations process but produce a **committee
report** (written by the subcommittee staff that originally worked on the bill) explaining in plain language what they want the agencies to do to comply with the
committee in the next fiscal year. This so-called **report language** is not statutory,
but as a clear statement of the wishes of the appropriators, it is closely followed by

agency heads. Even if Congress does not put something into law, it is wise for the agency heads to abide by committee report language—after all, they have to come before the committee members each and every year to plead their case for more funding or different priorities. There is no point in needlessly irritating these key players and their staff.

## The Rules Committee and the House Floor

As can be seen in Figure 7.2 on page 212, appropriations bills, like other legislation, make a stop at the Rules Committee before going to the House floor. Technically, this step is unnecessary. House rules give appropriations bills privileged status, which means that they may move to the head of the queue for consideration on the floor. In reality, however, appropriations bills always make the obligatory stop at the Rules Committee for a special rule before being scheduled for the floor by leadership.

The reason is simple: although appropriations bills are traditionally kept open to amendment on the floor of the House (unlike almost all other controversial and important measures) and thus do not require a closed rule, they always run afoul of at least a couple of House rules. The Appropriations Committee, as a result, needs protections for its bill on the floor that can be granted only by the Rules Committee. Two House rules in particular are always violated in appropriations legislation.

First, in theory, appropriations bills are supposed to provide funding only for programs that have current authorization of appropriations. But authorizing committees often fail to update authorizations, for the reasons discussed in Chapter 6. However, members of Congress (and the public for that matter) insist that key government programs continue operating, whether or not they have a current authorization for appropriations. Every year hundreds of billions of dollars are appropriated for programs whose authorizations have expired. As indicated in Table 7.3, in FY 2012 more than $261 billion of discretionary spending—more than 20 percent of the total—was for programs whose authorization of appropriations had expired. In addition, because of Congress's difficulty in reauthorizing agencies and programs, some policies on the books are out of date. As a result, members of authorizing committees often request that key provisions they were unable to pass as part of a larger authorization be included in the appropriations bill as considered in the Appropriations Committee. If they really want their pet provisions in law, the appropriations bill is a good vehicle to achieve that end, since those eventually must pass. This practice also violates a House rule—appropriations bills are only supposed to provide funding and are not supposed to establish agency policy.

Appropriators may try to resist doing this for controversial policy provisions. Anything controversial will make it tougher to round up the necessary votes for

**TABLE 7.3 Fiscal Year 2012 Appropriations with Expired Authorizations, by House Authorizing Committee**

| HOUSE COMMITTEE | NUMBER OF LAWS[a] | AMOUNTS APPROPRIATED[b] |
|---|---|---|
| Agriculture | 8 | $      37 |
| Education and the Workforce | 27 | 42,594 |
| Energy and Commerce | 55 | 47,156 |
| Financial Services | 16 | 31,238 |
| Foreign Affairs | 25 | 39,585 |
| Homeland Security | 7 | 189 |
| House Administration | 4 | 81 |
| Judiciary | 28 | 27,584 |
| Natural Resources | 54 | 2,677 |
| Oversight and Government Reform | 10 | 92 |
| Science, Space, and Technology | 16 | 5,718 |
| Small Business | 2 | 535 |
| Transportation and Infrastructure | 31 | 12,527 |
| Veterans' Affairs | 11 | 51,014 |
| Ways and Means | 4 | 131 |
| **Total** | **259** | **$261,158** |

*Source:* Congressional Budget Office

[a] Number of laws under the jurisdiction of the committee with expired authorization of appropriations. This column includes laws with expired authorizations of appropriations for definite or indefinite amounts. The total is less than the sum of the entries because public laws containing authorizations that are under the jurisdiction of more than one committee are counted only once in the total.

[b] In millions of dollars.

passage of the bill. It should be noted that appropriators sometimes inject favored policy provisions of their own if they feel strongly about directing an agency to do something.

The upshot is that appropriations bills almost always violate the prohibitions against unauthorized appropriations and policy language in an appropriations bill. Violation of these rules may make a bill subject to a point of order on the floor. The enforcement of a point of order for a rules violation strips the offending provision from the bill. To avoid that, the Rules Committee must be consulted to obtain a waiver. If the special rule containing that waiver passes, the bill may not be challenged on the floor based on those rule violations.

That special rule, while permitting unauthorized appropriations and policy language in the underlying bill, *will not permit amendments on the floor that violate those rules.* So even though the bill that comes out of committee is almost always considered under some version of an open rule, amendments must abide by the rules of the House regardless of the fact that the bill itself does not.

One type of amendment that is permissible is one that increases or decreases funding for an agency. However, appropriations bills must stay within the 302(b) allocations given to each subcommittee. The bill reported from the committee is almost always at the 302(b) limit. If a member wishes to offer an amendment giving more money to a particular agency or program, that amendment must have an offset within the bill that cuts funding for something else. It is difficult for members to get support for amendments of this nature because they irritate other members who support the agency or program that would receive the cut. These amendments fail more often than they pass.

The other sort of amendment that is allowable on the House floor contains what is called **limitation language**, which restricts what an agency may do with appropriated funds. (Appropriations bills are loaded with limitation language even before they make it to the floor.) Limitation language is one of Congress's favorite tools for meddling with federal agencies. Telling an agency what it *cannot do* with its funds may be just as effective as telling the agency in an affirmative way what it must do. Limitation language has been used in recent years to prevent agencies from implementing regulations on the concentration of media ownership (the Federal Communications Commission), enforcing environmental standards (the EPA), and other matters. (Examples of limitation language can be seen in Exhibit 7.2 on page 234.)

Although limitation language can have a significant impact on agency policy, it is technically not a violation of the House rule that prohibits policy language. Policy language is defined as wording that affirmatively directs an agency to do something, as opposed to wording that prohibits *using appropriated funds* for a particular activity.

## Appropriations Bills in the Senate

The Senate lags behind the House most years in dealing with appropriations bills, owing to an overloaded schedule, the tradition of extended debate, and the overburdened membership. With these funding bills, the Senate normally waits for the House to pass a bill before it marks up its version. When the House begins passing bills in May and June, the markup process in Senate subcommittees is effectively jump-started.

For example, let's say that a House-passed appropriations bill—call it HR 2000, "Appropriations for Homeland Security"—is referred to the Senate Subcommittee on Homeland Security. As the Senate subcommittee chair and his or her staff prepare for markup, they retain the House number (HR 2000) but remove all House-passed language (with policy provisions and dollar figures for the agencies) and substitute their own version of the bill that they have been working on through the winter and spring.

After the subcommittee passes its version of the Homeland Security funding bill, the bill moves to the full committee for a typically more contentious markup, just as in the House. The Senate Appropriations Committee will produce its own nonstatutory committee report—written by the relevant subcommittee staff as in the House—expressing its instructions for the department in plain language.

The Senate floor amendment procedure for appropriations legislation is more freewheeling than in the House. The majority leader in the Senate usually tries to negotiate a unanimous consent time agreement so that there will be an end time to debate on this must-pass legislation. But to get such an agreement, he has to make allowance for dozens of amendments. Senators will offer amendments that change funding levels (they, too, have to find offsets to stay within the 302[b] limits, just as House members do), and they will inject policy matters into these bills through limitation language, just as in the House.

When all goes smoothly in the Senate, the subcommittees and the full Appropriations Committee move bills along as soon as the House sends its finished product over, so that many appropriations bills will get to the Senate floor in July. Ideally, more than half are finished and moved on to conference committee before the traditional August recess, when subcommittee staff from the two chambers try to iron out the differences between the two versions of the bill in question. The aim is to have the remaining bills move through the Senate in September.

The reality is that the process rarely proceeds on schedule—in fact, in recent years the Senate has brought precious few appropriations bills individually to the floor, which makes it next to impossible to get these bills passed into law before the new fiscal year.[11] The next chapter looks into the breakdown of the appropriations process and the methods used to get money to the agencies in lieu of regular appropriations.

## The Conference Committee Stage

Appropriations bills are complex and detailed pieces of legislation and, as such, always require lengthy and intense negotiations to resolve the substantial differences between the two chambers' versions of a bill. (The chambers are technically working on the same bill—HR 2000 in our example—although the language of each bill differs.) Unlike with some authorizing bills, conference committees are the method of choice for bridging the differences when both chambers are able to pass a bill.

The conference committee is composed of the relevant subcommittee members as well as the full committee chair and ranking member from each chamber. Subcommittee staff meet for hours at a time to iron out the differences in dollar amounts and substantive policy language. The idea is to produce one consensus product. Staff resolve the vast majority of these differences in ways they are confident will satisfy the subcommittee leadership, the committee leadership, and the party leadership. They consult with the committee chair, the ranking member, the subcommittee chair, and the ranking subcommittee member on any controversial sticking points.

The finished version, the conference report, is agreed to by the majority of the senators and representatives in the conference and returned to the chambers for final approval. At that point, the bills are normally not amendable on the floor of either chamber.[12] In the House, to the extent that standing rules have been violated, a special rule may be needed to protect the bill from points of order. In the Senate, cloture may need to be invoked. Naturally, since these are must-pass bills, the president's strongly felt views have to have been considered in the negotiations in order to stave off the possibility of a veto.

## Looking at Appropriations Bills

Appropriations bills are detailed pieces of legislation, but their structure is surprisingly simple and straightforward. There are only two components to an appropriations bill—**accounts** and **general provisions**.

Accounts are the main units of appropriations law. There are about 200 accounts in the 12 appropriations bills that encompass broad categories of activities in the agencies or departments. Some agencies have numerous accounts; smaller agencies may have only one account. The account is recognizable as an unnumbered paragraph containing dollar amounts and giving an agency budget authority. The paragraph usually includes only a very general and broad description of the purpose for the money, and it cites the relevant authorizing statute that governs the use of the funds. Examples of accounts from the fiscal year 2012 appropriation for the Defense Department are shown in Exhibit 7.1, including military personnel funding for the different armed services.

General provisions are located at the end of the accounts for a particular agency or department and at the end of each bill. They are consecutively numbered, as can be seen in Exhibit 7.2. General provisions most commonly take the form of so-called limitation language, which restricts how money in the accounts may be spent. It is often stated: "None of the funds made available in this act may be used [for a particular purpose]." Some general provisions require agencies to report back to Congress on a regular basis on the status of a program (known as *report requirements*), serving as a means of conducting oversight of the executive branch; some include instructions for agencies on how to get permission in the new fiscal year to move money from one program to another in response to unforeseen developments (*reprogramming instructions*); and sometimes they contain policy direction for the agencies. In effect, general provisions are used by Congress to

---

## EXHIBIT 7.1

### Accounts in Appropriations Law from the FY 2012 Appropriation for the Department of Defense

---

**DIVISION A—DEPARTMENT OF DEFENSE APPROPRIATIONS ACT, 2012**

That the following sums are appropriated, out of any money in the Treasury not otherwise appropriated, for the fiscal year ending September 30, 2012, for military functions administered by the Department of Defense and for other purposes, namely:

**TITLE I**

**MILITARY PERSONNEL**

**Military Personnel, Army**

For pay, allowances, individual clothing, subsistence, interest on deposits, gratuities, permanent change of station travel (including all expenses thereof for organizational movements), and expenses of temporary duty travel between permanent duty stations, for members of the Army on active duty, (except members of reserve components provided for elsewhere), cadets, and aviation cadets; for members of the Reserve Officers' Training Corps; and for payments pursuant to section 156 of Public Law 97–377, as amended (42 U.S.C. 402 note), and to the Department of Defense Military Retirement Fund, $43,298,409,000.

**Military Personnel, Navy**

For pay, allowances, individual clothing, subsistence, interest on deposits, gratuities, permanent change of station travel (including all expenses thereof for organizational movements), and expenses of temporary duty travel between permanent duty stations, for members of the Navy on active duty (except members of the Reserve provided for elsewhere), midshipmen, and aviation cadets; for members of the Reserve Officers' Training Corps; and for payments pursuant

manage—some critics would say "micromanage"—the agencies. In recent years, there have been somewhere between 1,100 and 1,200 general provisions in all the appropriations bills—a dramatic increase from the congressional practice a generation ago.[13]

Appropriations bills, when finalized by the conference committee, are called conference reports. This term can be confusing, because, as noted earlier, nonstatutory instructions from the appropriations committees (attached to the bill at an earlier stage of the process) are called committee reports. (The term *report language* is generically used to describe these nonstatutory instructions.) To further complicate

---

### EXHIBIT 7.1 *(Continued)*

## Accounts in Appropriations Law from the FY 2012 Appropriation for the Department of Defense

to section 156 of Public Law 97–377, as amended (42 U.S.C. 402 note), and to the Department of Defense Military Retirement Fund, $26,803,334,000.

**Military Personnel, Marine Corps**

For pay, allowances, individual clothing, subsistence, interest on deposits, gratuities, permanent change of station travel (including all expenses thereof for organizational movements), and expenses of temporary duty travel between permanent duty stations, for members of the Marine Corps on active duty (except members of the Reserve provided for elsewhere); and for payments pursuant to section 156 of Public Law 97–377, as amended (42 U.S.C. 402 note), and to the Department of Defense Military Retirement Fund, $13,635,136,000.

**Military Personnel, Air Force**

For pay, allowances, individual clothing, subsistence, interest on deposits, gratuities, permanent change of station travel (including all expenses thereof for organizational movements), and expenses of temporary duty travel between permanent duty stations, for members of the Air Force on active duty (except members of reserve components provided for elsewhere), cadets, and aviation cadets; for members of the Reserve Officers' Training Corps; and for payments pursuant to section 156 of Public Law 97–377, as amended (42 U.S.C. 402 note), and to the Department of Defense Military Retirement Fund, $28,096,708,000.

NOTE: Each of these paragraphs effectively plugs money into the account of one of the armed services. The money is for the coming fiscal year and must be spent according to existing authorizing law (cited near the end of each paragraph—42 U.S.C. 402 note). Other stipulations may be placed on the use of the money later in other parts of the bill.

matters, a third version of report language—the **joint explanatory statement (JES)**—is contained within the conference report. The term *conference report*, then, encompasses the whole package—the final version of the bill plus the JES.

The JES explains how the two chambers reconciled their differences; in addition, it reiterates some suggestions that the House and Senate Appropriations Committees made in their committee reports. These suggestions frequently involve criticism of agency management practices, as can be seen in the sharp language directed at the Department of Homeland Security and the Transportation Security Administration in Exhibit 7.3. As noted above, the JES also often includes report

---

## EXHIBIT 7.2

### General Provisions in Appropriations Law from the FY 2004 Appropriation for Military Construction

---

**GENERAL PROVISIONS**

SEC. 107. None of the funds appropriated in Military Construction Appropriations Acts for minor construction may be used to transfer or relocate any activity from one base or installation to another, without prior notification to the Committees on Appropriations.

SEC. 108. No part of the funds appropriated in Military Construction Appropriations Acts may be used for the procurement of steel for any construction project or activity for which American steel producers, fabricators, and manufacturers have been denied the opportunity to compete for such steel procurement.

SEC. 109. None of the funds available to the Department of Defense for military construction or family housing during the current fiscal year may be used to pay real property taxes in any foreign nation.

SEC. 110. None of the funds appropriated in Military Construction Appropriations Acts may be used to initiate a new installation overseas without prior notification to the Committees on Appropriations.

SEC. 111. None of the funds appropriated in Military Construction Appropriations Acts may be obligated for architect and engineer contracts estimated by the Government to exceed $500,000 for projects to be accomplished in Japan, in any NATO member country, or in countries bordering the Arabian Sea, unless such contracts are awarded to United States firms or United States firms in joint venture with host nation firms.

SEC. 112. None of the funds appropriated in Military Construction Appropriations Acts for military construction in the United States territories and possessions in the Pacific and on Kwajalein Atoll, or in countries bordering the Arabian Sea, may be used to award any contract estimated by the Government

requirements that instruct agencies to update Congress on the performance of government programs. It is important to note that the JES does not necessarily render the committee reports irrelevant to the agencies. If the JES does not contradict direction from the two chambers' committee reports, it is understood that the agencies should do what they're told by the committees.

In the past, the JES also gave specific earmarked instructions to agencies on how to spend the money in an account. Exhibit 7.4 contains a few of the hundreds of earmarks for the Justice Department's Edward Byrne Discretionary Grants in the "Fiscal Year 2005 Appropriation for Commerce, Justice, and Science." Earmarking

---

## EXHIBIT 7.2 (Continued)

### General Provisions in Appropriations Law from the FY 2004 Appropriation for Military Construction

to exceed $1,000,000 to a foreign contractor: Provided, That this section shall not be applicable to contract awards for which the lowest responsive and responsible bid of a United States contractor exceeds the lowest responsive and responsible bid of a foreign contractor by greater than 20 percent: Provided further, That this section shall not apply to contract awards for military construction on Kwajalein Atoll for which the lowest responsive and responsible bid is submitted by a Marshallese contractor.

**SEC. 113. The Secretary of Defense is to inform the appropriate committees of Congress, including the Committees on Appropriations, of the plans and scope of any proposed military exercise involving United States personnel 30 days prior to its occurring, if amounts expended for construction, either temporary or permanent, are anticipated to exceed $100,000.**

**SEC. 114. Not more than 20 percent of the appropriations in Military Construction Appropriations Acts which are limited for obligation during the current fiscal year shall be obligated during the last 2 months of the fiscal year.**

NOTE: In this particular bill, many general provisions limit the use of funds. All those from Sections 107–112 fit into the category of so-called limitation language. In addition, Sections 108, 111, and 112 give clear instructions to agencies to favor US firms when awarding contracts. The highlighted portions provide other sorts of specific guidance to the Department. In Section 113, the Appropriations Committees require notification in the case of deployment of military personnel requiring the use of $100,000 or more of construction funds. In Section 114, the committees are stipulating that the department may not spend a disproportionate part of the appropriation in the last part of the fiscal year.

funds in this way was discontinued in the 112th Congress beginning in 2011. Some observers believe the practice may make a comeback.

## The Purpose of Appropriations Bills

Appropriations bills have many purposes. The most obvious is to dictate how much money agencies are going to get for particular purposes. Accounts determine the amounts of money that agencies will have with which to work. Sometimes within the accounts and more commonly in the general provisions and the report

---

### EXHIBIT 7.3

**Excerpt from Joint Explanatory Statement in the FY 2005 Appropriation for Homeland Security Conference Report**

---

**FINANCIAL MANAGEMENT OF THE DEPARTMENT**

The conferees are concerned with the Department's execution of its financial responsibilities after numerous budgetary and management crises over the 18 months of the Department's existence, notably with the Bureau of Immigration and Customs Enforcement and the Transportation Security Administration. The Department and senior agency management are coping with major changes in the organizational environment, resources, and communication networks of new and radically expanding or changing agencies. It is, therefore, to be expected that the Department will experience direct and indirect costs and management problems as it integrates its agencies. The conferees also acknowledge that reconciling different systems and legacy accounting bureaucracies is difficult. **Nonetheless, the conferees will not assent to a repeat of recent experience of shifting and multiple, last minute requests for funding relief, particularly when the Department and agencies can neither explain nor even fully understand their own financial condition. Such a level of uncertainty is inexplicable, and adversely affects the Department's ability to fulfill its missions and carry out Administration and Congressional policy.**

**The conferees direct the Secretary and Department agency heads to devote the resources and managerial energy required to ensure that basic financial control and transparency in accounting are achieved, and avoid the waste and disruption caused by failure to carry out this fundamental management function.**

**TRANSPORTATION SECURITY ADMINISTRATION REPROGRAMMINGS**

The conferees are concerned that the Department of Homeland Security has submitted numerous reprogramming for the Transportation Security Administration

language (or JES), Congress may specify how some of the money it gives the agencies should be spent. When Congress does this, in effect it is telling the agencies what they should do *that differs from what the agencies stated they would like to do in the president's budget documents.* Congressional specifications in the accounts and the general provisions are legally binding on the agencies.

Specifications in report language—the JES and the committee reports—are not legally binding, but agencies almost always do Congress's bidding as expressed there for fear of biting the hand that feeds them.[14] Agencies are mindful that they have to plead their case every year before the appropriators. Failure to abide by

---

## EXHIBIT 7.3 *(Continued)*

### Excerpt from Joint Explanatory Statement in the FY 2005 Appropriation for Homeland Security Conference Report

(TSA) to the House and Senate Committees on Appropriations that TSA cannot fully explain and justify. In fiscal year 2004, three TSA reprogrammings were submitted. For each of these reprogrammings, TSA was unable to provide timely and consistent data to answer specific questions about the need for these actions. **For instance, when the Department's reprogramming letter states that . . . $42,200,000 will be used to fund screener professional development to increase retention, and to cover higher benefit costs and increased supervision costs', the conferees expect TSA to readily explain the dollars for each of these three items. Similarly, TSA has been unable to provide an accurate annual estimate for a variety of requirements, such as maintenance costs, and salaries and expenses, which has led to repeated reprogramming requests for additional funds to cover these activities throughout the year, at the expense of other TSA or Department programs. This causes the conferees to question the competency of TSA's estimating capabilities. Therefore, the conferees direct that the Department institute financial controls to enable TSA to live within its resource limitations to negate or minimize the need for reprogrammings.**

NOTE: The highlighted portions indicate Congress's views of the management of the Department of Homeland Security and the Transportation Safety Administration (an agency within the Department). Congress's pointed views as expressed in nonstatutory language are usually carefully considered by the agencies. The board of directors' leverage over the agencies derives in large measure from its power over funding levels. Failure to follow explicit guidelines set forth in the JES can have dire consequences for an agency in future legislation.

238

---

## EXHIBIT 7.4

### Earmarks in the Joint Explanatory Statement

*Edward Byrne Discretionary Grants*—The conference agreement includes $170,027,000 for discretionary grants under this account.

**Within the amounts provided, [Office of Justice Programs] is expected to review the following proposals, provide grants if warranted, and report to the Committees on Appropriations regarding its intentions:**

$700,000 for the New Orleans, LA, Police Department for crime fighting initiatives;

$200,000 for the Orleans Parish, LA, District Attorney's Office for crime fighting initiatives;

$500,000 for the Paul and Lisa Foundation;

$2,000,000 for the Northern Virginia Regional Gang Task Force;

$587,000 for the Northwest Virginia Regional Drug Task Force;

$3,000,000 for the State of Virginia for anti-gang coordination;

$2,500,000 for Mothers Against Drunk Driving including the continuation of Spanish language public service announcements;

$1,500,000 for the National Institute of Justice and Bureau of Justice Statistics to conduct a study of conditions of confinement in Indian country correctional facilities and the factors that exacerbate those conditions;

$150,000 for the Obscenity Crimes Project to provide citizens with an online tool to report Internet obscenity crimes;

$350,000 for Gospel Rescue Ministries;

$300,000 for The Women's Center in Vienna, VA

SOURCE: The FY 2005 Commerce, Justice, and Science Appropriations Conference Report—Joint Explanatory Statement.

NOTE: In this case, the account providing the funds for the Byrne Discretionary Grants gave no specific instructions to the agency as to the use of the money. Nor did the general provisions in the law. But the report language (JES) that we see here did. In fact, the list of earmarks goes for several pages and proposes to use all of the appropriated funds ($170,027,000). The highlighted portion shows that Congress is only suggesting the agency fund the entities listed, but, like most agencies, the Office of Justice Programs took these suggestions seriously and funded them all.

suggestions in report language may result in unpleasant public hearings, less money in future bills, or more restrictive requirements in those bills.

Instructions in report language have one key advantage for the agencies: because they are not set in law, agencies have the flexibility to make the case to the Appropriations Committees that following certain suggestions would have adverse consequences. Agencies develop relationships with the appropriators and staff in order to be able to have these kinds of discussions. If they can persuasively argue that the agency mission will be best served by giving them more flexibility, members and staff may well relent.[15]

## Supplemental Appropriations

Nearly every year, the government runs into some unexpected and unaccounted-for expense. Massive flooding in the Midwest cannot be anticipated, and when it occurs government agencies such as the Federal Emergency Management Agency (FEMA) may not have enough money to respond effectively. Jet fuel prices can be so volatile that the US Air Force and the Navy may be unable to afford to fly their planes with the money they were provided in the regular appropriations process. The president may intervene in an escalating international crisis, as President Clinton did in Bosnia in the 1990s. Extra money that was not provided in the regular appropriations process the previous year is needed in the current fiscal year.

In these situations, Congress receives a request from the president for supplemental appropriations for emergencies like these. Because time is often of the essence, the Appropriations Committees will drop everything to consider the request and, if warranted, report out legislation. In the 1990s, the amounts were not too large—in the neighborhood of $5 billion or less.

Supplemental appropriations became more controversial when they were used to fund not just the first year or two of the wars in Afghanistan and Iraq in the early 2000s but were continued for nearly 10 years—an unprecedented development.[16] Eventually, as war costs escalated, supplemental appropriations of nearly $200 billion had been used by decade's end—roughly 20 percent of the entire discretionary budget of the United States. The practice of funding our involvement in the wars in Iraq and Afghanistan by this method was scaled back in FY 2010 and finally halted in 2011.

## CONCLUSION: THE IMPORTANCE OF THE POWER OF THE PURSE

Congress's funding power is without a doubt its most important tool in directing the work of the federal government. The power of the purse gives it the leverage to get agencies to do things, or not do things, as key members and the institution as a whole see fit.

In the budget process, Congress looks at what the government does both in the big picture and at a more granular level. The Concurrent Budget Resolution is the board of directors' way of setting forth priorities for the government. It is passed as an answer to the chief executive's statement of priorities, as detailed in the president's budget. But the budget resolution is only a broad brushstroke. If Congress is particularly ambitious and resolves to make major changes in the tax code or the mandatory spending programs, the relevant authorizing committees get to work to put those goals into effect.

Every year Congress must work on appropriations bills to fund the vast majority of programs that fit into the discretionary spending category. It is in these bills, and in the appropriations process more broadly, that Congress regularly does the bulk of its most important work directing government agencies and programs. In appropriations bills, agencies are given budget authority to operate, and they are often given explicit instructions as to how to manage and implement government programs. As often as not, these instructions appear in nonstatutory report language, which agencies normally choose to follow given the annual leverage that Congress has over their budgets.

Sometimes the appropriators go so far as to, in effect, stand in for the authorizers by specifying agency policy formally in appropriations law. Appropriators may also influence agencies in much less formal ways through letters, phone calls, or other communications. In addition, they conduct investigations, require reports on ongoing agency activities, and hold hearings that shine a spotlight on agency actions, whether strictly related to funding or not. The effectiveness of these tactics in changing agency behavior is based on the implied threat that failure to comply may result in cuts in funding or limitation language in future bills.

The power of the purse comes down to this: *the appropriations process involves all three of Congress's powers—authorizing, funding, and oversight.* And it takes place every year, unlike most agency reauthorizations. Year in and year out, the appropriations process is the number-one way in which Congress directs the work of the federal government.

---

## Questions for Discussion

1. Congress frequently fails to pass a budget resolution. What impact does that have?

2. The use of reconciliation to pass certain measures goes against Senate tradition in important ways. How so? Do you think it is good to have a

mechanism to force important policy changes through the Senate? Why or why not?

3. Why does Congress rely so much on the appropriations process—more so than on the authorizing process or oversight—to direct the work of the federal agencies?

4. What are the drawbacks of Congress's practice of using the appropriations process to set agency policy?

## Suggestion for Further Reading

Noah, Timothy. "Romancing the Parliamentarian." *Slate,* September 2, 2009. www .slate.com/articles/news_and_politics/prescriptions/2009/09/romancing _the_parliamentarian.html.

Schick, Allen. *The Federal Budget.* 3rd ed. Washington, DC: Brookings Institution Press, 2007.

## NOTES

1. This century presidents (both Barack Obama and George W. Bush) have delivered the budgets later than the first Monday in February. President Obama's budgets have come as late as mid-April. Although the law mandates the February date, there is no penalty for lack of compliance. It should be noted that presidents are given a pass in their first year, seeing that they take the oath of office only about two weeks before the budget is due.

2. This definition is drawn from that used by Allen Schick in *The Federal Budget,* 3rd ed. (Washington, DC: Brookings Institution Press, 2007), 327.

3. Ibid.

4. For a description of the process by which the agencies put together their budgets, see www.whitehouse.gov/omb/. In particular, the *A-11 Circular* details what the agencies and departments must do; see www.whitehouse.gov/omb/circulars/a11/current_year/ a11_toc.html.

5. For examples of SAPs, see www.whitehouse.gov/omb/legislative/sap/index.html.

6. In recent years, Congress has found it very difficult to pass the budget resolution, sometimes even when the same party controls both chambers. In fact, seven times in the past 14 years, Congress has been unable to pass it, a failure whose implications will be examined in Chapter 8.

7. More information on the Republican Study Committee can be found at http://john-shadegg.house.gov/rsc/about.htm. The Blue Dog Coalition website and the Congressional Black Caucus website are found, respectively, at www.house.gov/ross/BlueDogs/ and www .thecongressionalblackcaucus.com/.

8. The Senate's so-called Byrd Rule applies to this situation and puts other stipulations on what may be in a reconciliation bill; for example, it forbids cuts in Social Security

programs. More on the Byrd Rule can be found in Robert Keith, *CRS Report for Congress: The Budget Reconciliation Process; The Senate's Byrd Rule,* Congressional Research Service, April 7, 2005.

9. See Charles H. Stewart, *Budget Reform Politics: The Design of the Appropriations Process, 1865–1921* (Cambridge: Cambridge University Press, 1989).

10. House Appropriations Committee staff and members often claim that the Constitution requires that appropriations bills move first in the House. The Constitution says that *revenue* bills must move first through the House. This stipulation obviously applies to tax bills and probably does not apply to spending bills. In addition, the Senate did in fact pass an appropriations bill before the House a few times as recently as the late 1990s.

11. According to the thomas website at the Library of Congress (http://thomas.loc .gov), only one appropriations bill was brought to the Senate floor in 2010, two in 2011, and none in 2012.

12. The Senate added a rule in 2007 that makes it easier to strip provisions in the conference report that were added during the conference committee deliberations. This was to prevent so-called air-dropped earmarks that were not considered earlier in the process.

13. Schick, *The Federal Budget,* 266.

14. Some report language in the JES is legally binding, according to the Government Accountability Office, a support agency of Congress that among other things has the final word on the interpretation of appropriations bills. The GAO says this is the case when the bill itself, in either the account paragraph or the general provisions, refers to sections of the JES. When the bill refers to the JES, the specific language is "incorporated by reference" into the statute, which means for legal purposes it is made statutory. It is also true that report language that is not technically binding is almost always followed by agency officials.

15. It is also the case that some report language provisions amount to "throwaway" language that is inserted to assuage certain constituencies but is of no real concern to members.

16. By comparison, in America's last extended conflict, in Vietnam, supplemental appropriations accounted for the bulk of war costs only in the first two years (fiscal years 1966 and 1967). Subsequently, they were used sparingly or not at all through the end of US involvement in 1975. See Stephen Daggett, *CRS Report for Congress: Military Operations; Precedents for Funding Contingency Operations in Regular or in Supplemental Appropriations Bills,* Congressional Research Service, June 13, 2006.

# 8

# Federal Budget Issues in the 21st Century

Budget issues are always important in American politics. But they are particularly so now, as the nation, coming out of a severe recession that contributed to a dramatic increase in national indebtedness, is at the same time facing the retirement of the baby-boom generation. That generation's huge numbers are putting tremendous pressure on the government's largest mandatory programs. Most budget experts conclude that the nation literally cannot continue on its current path and must make major changes in its fiscal policies. Congress's legislative responsibilities put it at the center of policy making on these matters.

This chapter looks at a wide variety of budget challenges Congress faces in the new century. First, we consider a problem that has plagued Congress since the late 1990s: an inability to keep the government funded and fully functioning in a timely manner. Completing appropriations bills on or nearly on time is the board of directors' first responsibility, it could be argued, and it has been difficult for Congress to meet it. Instead, agencies are usually funded in fits and starts as the fiscal year begins, with the full budget instructions coming well into the new fiscal year or, occasionally, not at all. Numerous continuing resolutions and annual omnibus acts have become the norm. There seems to be almost an annual threat of major functions of the government shutting down.

Next we look at the big issues that the nation faces in the upcoming years and decades. Foremost among these are the commitments to seniors and other groups in the population written into authorizing law as mandatory programs. Medicare programs, Medicaid, and Old Age and Survivors' Insurance (administered by the Social Security Administration) are the big three areas of concern. Projections show that the United States cannot meet its obligations within the next couple of decades, and the pressures on the budget are severe beginning this decade. In this

**FIGURE 8.1. Appropriations Bills Approved on Time by Fiscal Year**

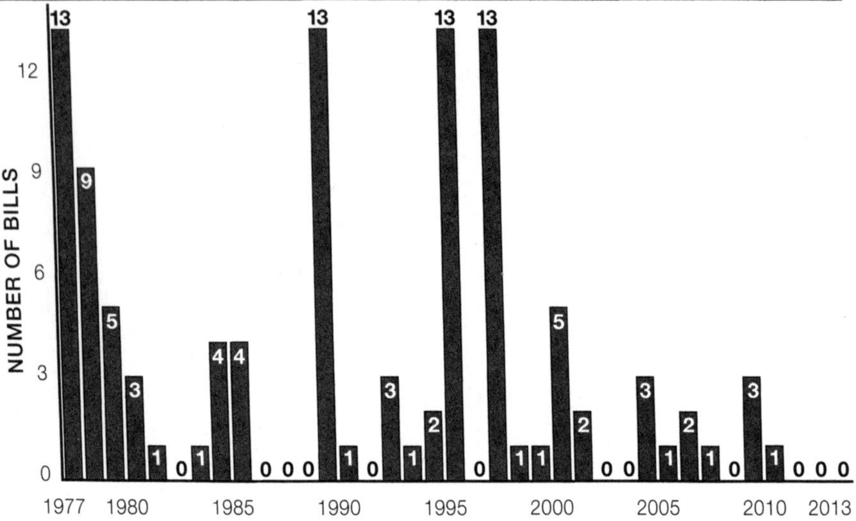

*Note:* There were 13 appropriations subcommittees from 1977 to 2005. There were 11 bills in 2007 and 2008. The House had 11 subcommittees and the Senate had 12. Both chambers have had 12 subcommittees since FY 2008.

chapter, we look at these issues, what it would take for Congress to address them in a meaningful way, and why it is so difficult for Congress to act as the problems fester. In the end, we consider any lessons from the past as a guide to what might be done to put the nation on a sustainable fiscal path.

## THE BUDGET PROCESS: KEEPING THE GOVERNMENT RUNNING

No description of the congressional budget process would be complete without noting that, even though appropriations bills fall into the category of *must-pass legislation*, they rarely pass on schedule. Figure 8.1 documents the recent history of Congress's efforts to fund the federal government in a timely fashion. In the 16 years from fiscal year 1998 through fiscal year 2013 (fiscal year 1997 was the last time all the bills passed on time), an average of only slightly more than one appropriations bill has passed before the beginning of the new fiscal year—or even close to it.

The dysfunction has become chronic. Agencies end up being able to budget only in the very short term. This can make it impossible to start new programs or make significant changes to existing ones, affecting the continuity of essential government operations in a profound way. It is instructive to see why the board of directors fails to accomplish its most essential function year after year and what it must do to keep the government running on a temporary basis.

Of course, efficiency in processing legislation was never meant to be Congress's hallmark. As we have seen, the Senate was set up more for delay than for action, and it is always going to be difficult for the two chambers to come to a meeting of the minds given their different perspectives. Divided government can throw another wrench in the works, making agreement on controversial matters harder still. And Congress's legislative workload is tremendous. All of these factors, together with the demands of constant campaigning and fundraising, trips home, shortened schedules, and other factors, sometimes make it difficult to find floor time—especially in the Senate—to deal with legislation, even must-pass legislation.

In the case of appropriations bills, two specific factors impede the process: scarce funds and policy debates usually stemming from partisan differences.

## Not Enough Money

Members of Congress are invariably under political pressure to keep spending down as a general principle, and that is especially true in the one area that is more controllable: discretionary spending in appropriations bills. As spending soars on the major "untouchable" mandatory programs like Social Security and Medicare, pressure to control spending and reduce deficits increases in the discretionary areas.

Early in the year, as we have seen, the party in power sets a top-line number for discretionary spending in the budget resolution. Although party leaders pay lip service to funding all their key priorities in the resolution, there is usually movement among key players on the Budget Committees and the party leadership (who want to portray their party as "fiscally responsible" in preparation for the next election cycle) to limit the growth of spending in the 302(a) allocation. In fact, as we have seen, to enforce this point Congress passed the Budget Control Act in 2011 to put a statutory lid on the allocation.

Problems arise when the Appropriations subcommittees find out what this tight figure means for their 302(b) allocations. If the country is at war, spending on defense will be up, so subcommittees that cover domestic spending will often get little or no increase to fund health research, education, environmental cleanup, and other popular priorities. Unfortunately, the full consequences of the "fiscal conservatism" message are not internalized by all members of Congress, most of whom, regardless of party, clamor for more spending for the programs that are important in their districts or states.

The upshot is that the subcommittee chairs often have trouble putting together bills that can move quickly through their chamber because, when it comes to voting, members invariably object to belt-tightening for popular government programs, especially those that serve the people in their districts or states. This is more of a problem in the Senate. Because the House moves first on appropriations, members usually decide to pass something that is not perfect, knowing that corrections can be made later. And House rules may streamline debate, thus limiting the amount of time it takes to pass the bills. In the Senate, streamlining debate is next to impossible, so there is often resistance to moving bills to the floor that might not pass and will crowd other matters off the agenda.

In recent years, Senate subcommittee chairs have generally succeeded in getting their bills adopted by the full committee, but the full Senate is a different matter. In 2010 only one appropriations bill made it to the Senate floor, in 2011 the number was two, and none made it to the floor in 2012. The trend goes back about 10 years and has occurred under both Republican and Democratic leadership. Obviously, the appropriations process bogs down when this happens. After all, a bill cannot reach the conference stage if it doesn't pass the Senate. As a result, bills do not get to the president's desk before the beginning of the fiscal year on October 1.

### Policy and Politics

In addition to money woes, appropriations bills become magnets for controversial policy provisions. Many members view must-pass bills as a great opportunity to raise controversial issues that are not being addressed to their satisfaction in the authorization process. Although appropriations bills are not supposed to have policy language in them to start with, and policy amendments are not technically permitted in either chamber, these restrictions can be overcome relatively easily.

One of the most common ways of introducing policy into appropriations legislation is to offer an amendment to prohibit spending funds for a particular purpose—the so-called limitation language that appears in the general provisions section of appropriations bills (see Chapter 7). The bill provides the agency with the funds it requested, but ties its hands by specifying what it may *not* spend money on. This is a handy way to set agency policy, because telling an agency what it *cannot* do usually does not, for technical reasons, run afoul of rules restricting the addition of policy language.

In recent years, immigration policy, abortion, the closure of the Guantánamo Bay prison, and offshore drilling restrictions, to name a few issues, have been brought into the debates about funding government agencies. The principal objective of these efforts is not to resolve the issue in question, but instead to score political points against the opposing party. In fact, it is the desire of Senate majority party leadership to avoid controversial amendments, mostly from minority party members, that more than anything else leads them to refuse to bring individual appropriations bills to the floor.

Appropriations decisions have always been separated from authorizing decisions to the extent possible (see Chapter 6) to keep the process of funding the government on track. The fear was that contentious policy debates would hamper the flow of money for essential government programs. As it has turned out, that fear has been realized.[1] As the authorizing process has proven unable to resolve divisive policy debates, those debates have increasingly moved to the appropriations process, slowing down the processing of those bills.

### The Specter of a Government Shutdown

There are consequences when appropriations bills don't pass. If funding for the operations and programs of an agency is not signed into law by the time the new fiscal year starts on October 1, the agency often has to shut its doors. National parks may close if the Interior Department spending bill is not passed. The State Department may be unable to process passport requests if there is no funding provided.[2]

In the winter of 1995–1996, the government did shut down for about three weeks. President Clinton and the Republican Congress were at loggerheads on spending priorities, and neither side would give in. All they could agree on was to fund critical functions such as defense, border security, the Social Security Administration, and a few other areas. Much of government was allowed to shut down, including hundreds of programs affecting the lives of millions of Americans. The failure of the two sides to reach a timely compromise was decidedly unpopular.

A similar dynamic occurred in April 2011, when a Republican House of Representatives dead set upon big cuts in discretionary spending was at loggerheads with a Democratic president and Senate. The government had been on temporary funding since the beginning of the fiscal year that had started more than six months earlier. Finally, as budget authority was about to expire, the two sides compromised to keep the government funded through the fiscal year (see Box 8.1).[3]

### Continuing Resolutions and Omnibus Appropriations

To avoid a government shutdown Congress has to pass, and the president sign, a **continuing resolution**. A CR is normally a simple piece of legislation that serves as a stopgap to fund the functioning of the government at the previous year's level for a specified period into the new fiscal year. The CR may be set to fund the government for any length of time, from a day to a year. Typically, no changes are made from the previous fiscal year in the distribution of money and no major changes to

## BOX 8.1

### Case Study in Congressional Dysfunction:
### Debating the Debt Ceiling in 2011

A little more than 100 years ago, Congress had to act every time the US Treasury needed to borrow money to cover any shortfall when revenues failed to pay for all government obligations. Due to our involvement in World War I and other legal obligations, increasingly the Treasury needed to go out in the marketplace to find funds so the government could make ends meet. And every time Congress had to act to permit it, which became tremendously burdensome. The concept of a "debt ceiling" was developed in 1917 whereby Congress set a dollar figure above which the Treasury could not go, requiring the Treasury to come to Congress only when that ceiling was reached in order to get new authority to borrow.

More often than not, Congress's vote to raise the debt ceiling has been uncontroversial. After all, the need to borrow money is just a function of the accumulation of other fiscal decisions Congress has made—to create and fund government programs and to pass tax laws to generate revenues. In effect, the need to borrow is entirely derivative of other legislative actions on spending and revenue generating, which is how most political systems look at it and why most countries don't require their equivalent of the Treasury Department to get legal borrowing authority in a separate law. But in the United States, it is still the case that when the ceiling has been reached, new authority must be granted in law by Congress.

Although the vote to borrow money is never a favorite for members of Congress, majorities have ultimately agreed to grant new authority before any crisis would happen.* And the failure of the United States to meet its obligations to its creditors, which today include a diverse group including individuals, pension funds, banks, foreign governments, and other entities, would lead to widespread financial panic. The reason? US Treasury bonds have historically been considered the safest possible investment; defaulting on obligations to creditors would rattle international markets in potentially unprecedented ways.

The year 2011 ushered in a "new normal" in the treatment of the debt ceiling vote. The previous year, Republicans had secured a sizable House majority, gaining 63 seats in a landslide. This new majority energized an already solidly antispending, antitax Republican membership. Many members, both old and new, were eager for a confrontation with congressional Democrats and President Obama over fiscal matters.

Treasury secretary Timothy Geithner had informed Congress that the debt ceiling then established in law, $14.29 trillion, would be reached in May. He did, however, say that taking extreme measures involving shifting around federal

## BOX 8.1 *(Continued)*

### Case Study in Congressional Dysfunction:
### Debating the Debt Ceiling in 2011

pension funds and other accounts could keep the government running for a few more months—until August 2, 2011, to be precise.

The battle over what to do raged well into the summer. Vice President Joe Biden tried to broker a deal on spending and taxes that might be agreeable to both parties on the Hill. As those efforts seemed to founder, President Obama and Speaker of the House John Boehner convened secret negotiations with the aim of achieving a "grand bargain" that would couple tax increases with spending cuts mostly in mandatory programs, resulting in some $4 trillion in deficit reduction over ten years (the changes would be weighted in favor of spending cuts). As part of the deal, the debt ceiling would be raised at least through the end of 2012.

In the end, these high-level negotiations did not succeed. Instead, on July 31—just two days before the Treasury said it would have to default on US obligations—a more modest deal was reached that would raise the debt ceiling in the immediate term by about $900 billion in exchange for spending caps on all discretionary programs that would rein in their growth through 2021 by approximately the same amount. It passed the House on August 1, 269–161, and passed the Senate the next day by a 74–26 vote. Other provisions were put in place to raise the debt ceiling an additional $1.4 trillion to carry the Treasury at least through the 2012 election campaign season.

In the end, default was averted, but only at the last minute. Most observers believe waiting until the 11th hour had a negative effect on markets; at the very least, coming to the brink showed a new willingness on the part of Congress to take risks when it comes to the debt ceiling. At best, the process of coming to the brink was the first of a series of baby steps toward dealing in a serious way with the major budget issues the nation faces—the subject of the next section of the chapter.[†]

*For many years, Democrats engineered a way, with creative use of House rules, to vote to increase the debt ceiling without actually having to specifically vote to do so. Essentially, by voting for a budget resolution (which cannot itself become law) that envisioned future borrowing needs in excess of the debt ceiling, a special rule would deem that the House had adopted a debt ceiling increase. This method, the so-called Gephardt Rule, is no longer in existence. The Senate was never able to figure out a way to do something similar.

[†]For a fascinating overview of the negotiations leading up to the Budget Control Act, see Matt Bai, "Who Killed the Debt Deal?," *New York Times Magazine,* March 28, 2012.

existing programs are permitted, but at least the government agencies can continue operating until an appropriations bill is finally agreed to, however late that happens. Sometimes several CRs are required before bills can be completed. The average in recent years has been about five CRs. Three times in recent years, fiscal years 2007, 2011, 2013, much of the government was eventually placed on a continuing resolution for the entire year.

The impact of yearlong CRs is considerable. As just noted, agencies may not easily be able to adjust funding allocations among programs even if circumstances would suggest doing so. And it is difficult to enter into new contracts or start new programs. Certainly, long-term planning for complex government projects is severely hampered when the government limps along on short-term CRs until a larger deal can be signed. This is not a recipe for good government!

The common solution to budget gridlock involves the use of **omnibus appropriations**. They are the go-to legislative vehicle when individual bills are too controversial or do not have enough funding in them to pass on their own. What happens is that House and Senate leaderships find a single appropriations bill that is in conference, having passed both chambers, and attach several other bills to it (which are not in conference, having failed to pass one or both chambers) and bring the whole package up for a vote as an omnibus conference report, usually months into the new fiscal year. In 2003 the government was on CR for five months before the eleven unfinished bills were packaged together as an omnibus act. For FY 2012, eight bills were joined to the Military Construction and Veterans Administration bill nearly three months into the fiscal year.

The advantage of the omnibus approach is that members can usually find something they desperately want in the huge package, thus justifying a vote even though they may think some programs or agencies are underfunded. The disadvantage is that an omnibus conference report does not permit amendments and is too large for members to be able to digest in the short period of time they are given to consider it.[4] It undercuts the responsibility of all the membership to consider with some care what they are funding the government to do.

Despite those problems, Congress now regularly relies on omnibus appropriations bills to finish its essential work on the discretionary part of the federal budget. In this era of intense partisan wrangling, it has proved impossible to process the 12 bills through the normal process in anything resembling a timely fashion.

## Failure to Pass the Budget Resolution

As we saw in the last chapter, the two houses have more regularly in recent years (including every year since 2010) failed to agree to a concurrent budget resolution—the nonbinding document that lays out spending and tax priorities for the next fiscal year and beyond. This has a couple of significant consequences.

First, the lack of a budget resolution contributes to the delay in processing appropriations bills. The resolution includes the 302(a) allocation for discretionary spending. When the two houses cannot agree to a resolution, they usually cannot agree to a common cap for discretionary spending, which means the two chambers are not starting from the same place as they mark up the bills. This makes it that much harder to come to agreement on those measures in a timely fashion.

Second, the budget resolution may include reconciliation instructions that can expedite Senate consideration of major changes in the tax code and mandatory programs. Without a resolution, it is much harder to legislate comprehensively in those areas. As we shall see in the rest of the chapter, that is exactly where major changes need to be made.

## THE MAJOR ISSUES CONGRESS FACES: DEFICITS AND BALANCING THE BUDGET

The most common complaint about the federal budget from informed observers is concern about the persistent and potentially destabilizing deficits the government runs. Nearly every year, the president proposes a budget that assumes insufficient revenue to pay for what the government does, and nearly every year Congress, while changing the president's request at the margins, goes along. Ambitious proposals to upset the status quo by cutting or eliminating major programs or raising taxes in order to balance the budget rarely see the light of day.

There is a lot of debate and disagreement about the wisdom of deficit spending, but one thing can be said for sure: deficit spending adds to the accumulated national debt, which puts a burden on the federal budget in terms of debt service. (As noted on page 214 in the last chapter, *deficits* refer to annual shortfalls when government spending exceeds revenue. These add to the total accumulated national *debt* the federal government carries over from year to year.) The question is whether the government can sustain the debt it is accumulating without causing significant harm to the economy.

Most economists think that deficit spending is not necessarily bad. For instance, it may be wise policy to spend more or cut taxes in order to reinvigorate the economy in times of recession. In the fall of 2008, economists of all stripes agreed that the government needed to borrow large sums of money to stave off a potentially disastrous meltdown in the credit markets. In addition, just as with one's household budget, government does make some productive investments. (Going into debt to pay for college tuition will pay off, one hopes, in the long run.) Up to a point, deficit spending can be defended in the interest of long-term productivity. Improved roads and waterways help commerce, funding research can lead to important innovations, and spending on education to better equip the workforce can also have a positive effect on the economy and, ultimately, living standards.

But just as it is not wise for a person to go into debt for immediate gratification (more clothes, another car, an expensive vacation), the government places a burden on future generations when it runs a deficit to fund unproductive programs. And no one seriously questions the fact that the government's current deficit spending is largely focused on addressing the immediate needs and desires of the population rather than on productive investments.

## Identifying the Problem: Growing Deficits

In recent years, annual deficits have reached unprecedented levels. Figure 8.2 shows deficits in the new century, from FY 2000 through FY 2012, then projected out from 2013 through 2023. The government, beginning in FY 2002, coming off four years of surpluses, began to sustain significant deficits through FY 2008. Beginning in 2009, the deficit numbers grew to more than $1 trillion for the first time. Why did the government go into deficit in 2002 and continue on a generally worsening path through 2012?

First, it is interesting to note that projections by the nonpartisan Congressional Budget Office (CBO) in early 2001 anticipated *larger and larger surpluses through the first decade of the new* century if current law went unchanged.[5] The 107th and 108th Congresses (2001–2005) passed tax laws and made spending decisions, some proposed by President Bush, that changed that trajectory. Some of the spending decisions were in response to the September 11, 2001, terrorist attacks (Homeland Security, the war effort in Afghanistan, increases in special operations budgets, and other things); some involved domestic spending that was unrelated to the attacks (education spending and prescription drugs for the elderly, for example). Tax cuts made in 2001 and 2003 deprived the Treasury of considerable revenue, adding to imbalance.[6]

All in all, discretionary spending increased in real terms in the first decade of the new century by about 50 percent, after having been kept under control for most of the last two decades of the 20th century. Discretionary spending trends over the past few decades are depicted in Figure 8.3. The recent explosion in this category of spending happened under unified Republican control (part of 2001, 2003–2006), unified Democratic government (2009–2010), and with divided government (part of 2001, 2007–2008). Mandatory spending continued its steady rise of about 30–50 percent a decade, before and after the new century. With the severe recession beginning in 2008, spending on countercyclical mandatory programs—programs

FIGURE 8.2. Deficits Grow in the New Century

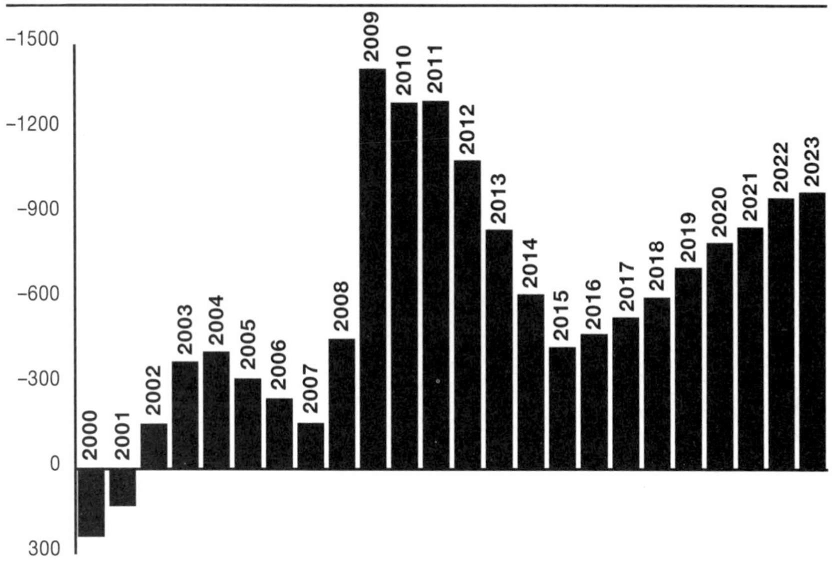

Note: Measured in billions of dollars.

Source: Data before 2013 is from the Congressional Budget Office historical tables. Data for 2013 and after is from Congresional Budget Office projections.

such as Supplemental Nutrition Assistance, Medicaid, and unemployment insurance that millions more qualify for in times of recession—shot up, as did spending designed to prop up the financial industry. In addition, tax revenues tanked, as happens in recessions when fewer people are working and making money (Figure 8.4). When taken as a whole, the first decade of the 21st century added trillions of additional dollars to the national debt.

At the end of the day, as the country works its way out of the recession, revenue numbers improve, the spending for the wars in Iraq and Afghanistan dwindles, and discretionary spending caps take effect, the deficit numbers will begin to fall in the mid-2010s. But if nothing is done, that situation is only temporary, as intense pressure is placed on the budget later this decade and into the 2020s and beyond with the retirement of the baby-boom generation.

## Identifying the Problem: Entitlements and Debt Service

Although government revenue is clearly not keeping up with current demands for government services as reflected in chronic annual budget deficits, the single most important long-term problem is the seemingly uncontrollable growth of mandatory programs (or "entitlements") that provide services and benefits mostly to the

254

FIGURE 8.3. Discretionary Spending in Constant Dollars, 1983–2011

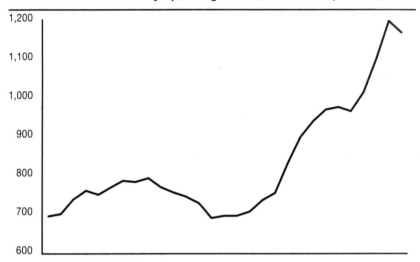

*Note:* Measured in billions of (FY 2005) dollars. From the Congressional Budget Office.

*Source:* Congressional Budget Office.

FIGURE 8.4. Tax Revenue Craters in the Great Recession

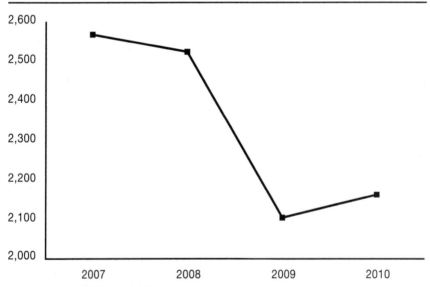

*Note:* Measured In billions of dollars.

*Source:* Congressional Budget Office Historical Tables.

large and growing elderly population. The popularity of these programs makes addressing the problem all the more difficult. They are often called the "third rail of American politics," a reference to the electrified rail that powers trains and subways. Anyone who touches that rail will almost certainly die. Many politicians fear a career-ending electoral defeat if they propose cuts in Medicare, the portion of Medicaid that funds nursing home care for middle-income Americans, or Social Security. Tax increases may be a part of the solution to the problem, but taxes cannot be raised enough to cover the long-term Social Security, Medicaid, and Medicare liabilities. A way to restrain the growth of the popular entitlements has to be found.

Mandatory spending begins to dominate the federal budget as the demographic bubble known as the baby boom—people born from 1946 to 1964—retires in larger and larger numbers and begins to receive full benefits. The figures are stark. In 2012 all mandatory spending plus **interest on the debt** totaled about 62 percent of federal spending. By 2023, under CBO projections, mandatory and debt service jump to 76 percent of all spending, a portion that continues to expand later that decade and beyond.[7]

The important thing is that these programs are not only wildly popular but set on "automatic pilot"—they grow in perpetuity unless Congress and the president act to cut them. The fact is that politicians find it a lot easier to leave these programs alone (or even to enhance them, as was done in 2003 with the addition of prescription drug coverage to Medicare and in 2010 when the Affordable Care Act expanded Medicaid) than to cut them back in some way. In this sense, the mandatory programs are very different from discretionary programs, which are not on autopilot, coming under scrutiny every year in the annual appropriations process.

Policy makers in Washington face a serious conundrum. If the nation continues to tax at a similar level to what it does today, annual deficits will remain high (and start to shoot up later this decade) to pay for the growing entitlement programs as well as whatever other basic services that can be afforded, including national defense, education, health research, environmental controls, air traffic control, border protection, and so on. These deficits will add to the already huge national debt. The effect: the portion of the federal budget committed to debt service will rise to levels never before seen.

As shown in Figure 8.5, in 2013, debt service costs totaling $224 billion constituted a little more than 6 percent of the federal budget. By 2023, if nothing is done to change the trajectory of spending and the revenue stream, debt service of $857 billion would make up more than 14 percent of spending. The situation only gets worse going forward. To pay that kind of debt service and maintain current levels of government services would mean a much larger federal government in the 2020s and beyond, with the effect of putting the brakes on economic growth. This

**FIGURE 8.5.** The Projected Debt Service Explodes, 2013–2035

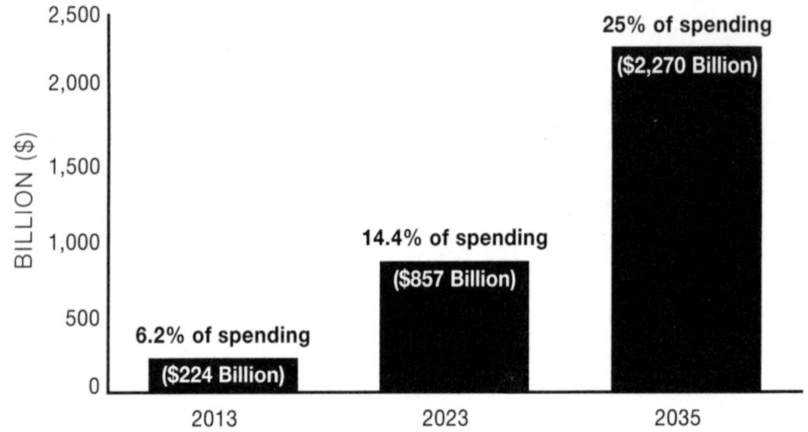

*Source:* Congressional Budget Office.

scenario—a "fiscal train wreck," in the words of former comptroller general of the GAO David Walker[8]—is literally unsustainable. In the future, as it became clearer that the United States could not get its budget under control, it would no longer be able to borrow money at reasonable rates. The US economy—and the global economy for that matter—would likely suffer severe consequences.[9]

### Congress First Faces Entitlement Growth in the 1970s

Mandatory programs did not always take up so much room in the budget. Discretionary spending used to dominate the federal budget. Before new major mandatory programs were adopted in the 1960s, most federal spending was addressed every year in appropriations bills. Congress had much smaller appropriations committees, and the few members lucky enough to be on them were usually fiscal conservatives who were determined to come as close to balancing the budget every year as was possible given economic conditions and whether the country was facing exigencies—wars, natural disasters, and the like. And these members were in a good position to exercise influence since almost all federal spending had to be approved by them. In those days, appropriators were known as the "watchdogs of the Treasury" and accorded prestige and respect for taming the irresponsible and free-spending habits of the rest of the membership. In effect, leadership made sure that someone minded the store, while the rest of the members went their merry way proposing this or that new program.

Everything changed in the 1970s. The new Medicare and Medicaid systems began to grow and expand, and Social Security payments, once adjusted on a yearly basis, were first increased sharply by bipartisan agreement, and then tagged to inflation automatically. Suddenly, the federal budget was under no one's control. Furthermore, a movement by young Democrats took hold in the House to expand and democratize the Appropriations Committee so as to make it responsive to the larger membership of the party (many of whom were dedicated to expanding federal programs) and the whole House.

As deficits soared, Congress recognized that it had no watchdog at appropriations anymore, and so what it did, with the Budget and Impoundment Act of 1974, was create the Budget Committees to produce a budget resolution to inform the rest of the membership of the budgetary consequences of their taxing and spending decisions (see Chapter 7). The problem was that the popularity of the mandatory programs was too great to confront, and to complicate matters a tax revolt was brewing in the country. Republicans, joined by many Democrats, supported and put in place tax relief, first in the late 1970s, then more dramatically in 1981 as part of President Reagan's agenda. For the most part, both parties at first turned a blind eye to the potential for exploding deficits.

To the extent that there are still "watchdogs of the Treasury" in Congress today, they are usually to be found on the Budget Committees. But the Budget Committees only have the authority to bring nonbinding resolutions to the floor. These can include reconciliation instructions, which were meant to make the hard decisions (increasing taxes and cutting spending) easier to pass by prohibiting the filibuster in the Senate. But the reconciliation process has been used more often in recent years to put in place tax cuts (2001 and 2003) or implement far-ranging health care reform (2010) than specifically to reduce deficits.

## A Novel Approach to Cutting the Deficit: The Gramm-Rudman Act

The budget deficit problem we now face is nothing new. In the 1980s, concerns about deficit spending and a rising national debt became front-page headlines, as annual deficits nearly quadrupled from $60 billion in 1980 to $220 billion in 1986. In that span, the national debt more than doubled. Congress and President Reagan could not agree on a way forward, even if they could basically agree on the nature of the problem. The consensus was that, while discretionary programs could be cut, it was the "autopilot" entitlements that needed to be changed to find sufficient savings, and revenues would have to be looked at as well.

But, in what is familiar to 21st century Americans who are following contemporary budget debates, neither party was terribly enthusiastic about the unpopular business of cutting benefits or raising taxes. The solution? Pass a bill that would make very, very unpopular cuts in basic services (national defense, transportation, science research, and so forth) on an indiscriminate basis every year whenever

Congress could not find the will to raise revenue and cut entitlement benefits to meet a certain deficit target. This indiscriminate budget-cutting exercise was termed **sequestration**.

The Gramm-Rudman Deficit Reduction Act of 1985 called for exactly that. It required budget deficits to decline every year until, in 1990, the budget would be balanced. Any year the target wasn't met because of congressional inability to achieve deficit reduction, painful across-the-board cuts would be made in discretionary programs including defense (while the Cold War was going on!). The theory was that no one could stand for these cuts to happen—members would not want to weaken defense or deprive their constituents of Pell Grants or roads or bridges—so they would make the necessary changes in tax law and entitlements.

In fact, the "meat cleaver" approach to deficit reduction did not work. One year the Gramm-Rudman Act's constitutionality was challenged, putting off the sequestration. Other years Congress employed budget gimmicks of various kinds to get around the requirements as deficits continued at about the same levels and the chambers were no closer to coming to an agreement on a larger deficit-reduction plan.

## Discretionary Caps and PAYGO: 1990–2002

Ultimately, Congress threw its hands up in the air, giving up on Gramm-Rudman as large deficits persisted at the beginning of the 1990s. Members decided to try a new approach. Instead of putting forth arbitrary deficit targets that might be hard or impossible to meet, whether because of a lack of will or because of an unanticipated national emergency or economic downturn, they would enact a law that would aim to rein in natural congressional tendencies that led to deficit spending. Those problem tendencies? Spending more on popular programs, creating new ones, and cutting people's taxes.

This approach, passed into law in 1990 (the Budget Enforcement Act), involved putting in place tight statutory caps on discretionary spending for three years and a pay-as-you-go policy (PAYGO) for changes in tax law and mandatory programs. The whole budget was covered. For discretionary spending, appropriators had legal limits in place that would be harder to evade than allocations in the budget resolution that amounted only to internal rules. And anyone who wanted to enhance a mandatory program or offer a tax cut had to offset it by an equal or greater amount involving either more revenue, a cut in a mandatory program, or some combination of the two. (The act also raised taxes on higher-income taxpayers.)

In the end, this approach worked much better than Gramm-Rudman. Statutory caps and PAYGO were renewed twice, eventually through 2002, which for most of that period meant that major tax cuts and new mandatory programs were off the table (since finding the required offsets was politically too difficult), and discretionary spending was kept at levels that didn't even keep up with inflation. The impact of all this, together with strong economic growth in the mid-1990s leading to revenue windfalls for the Treasury, was huge: the budget was balanced in 1998 and large surpluses were realized from 1999 to 2001. Large surpluses were expected for many years after that.

As described before, things changed beginning in 2001. A major tax-cut bill passed that evaded the still-in-effect PAYGO law (by passing a bill waiving PAYGO late in the year) and many other factors contributed to a lower surplus in FY 2001 and deficits ever since.

## The Budget Control Act of 2011

As shown earlier, the problem Congress faces is a burgeoning national debt, exacerbated by huge annual deficits in recent years and the continuing retirement of the baby-boom generation, putting more strain on major entitlement programs. Congress's most recent attempt to get a handle on the problem was the Budget Control Act, passed in August 2011. Tied together with the need to raise the debt ceiling (see Box 8.1), the BCA was an attempt to make a down payment of sorts on the national debt, using a combination of methods employed before.

First, the BCA reenacted statutory caps on discretionary spending to put a stop to the run-up in this area in the previous decade.[10] The caps amounted to keeping discretionary programs below an inflationary growth trend, mimicking the successful efforts in the 1990s. It would have the effect of reducing deficits over the next 10 years by nearly $1 trillion, given reasonable projections of economic growth and revenue collection. Second, the BCA created a "supercommittee" composed of 12 select members of the House and Senate charged with finding an additional $1.2–$1.5 trillion in deficit reduction over those same 10 years. The assumption was that the bulk of these savings would be from trimming mandatory programs, with some coming from changes in tax law that would enhance revenues. In order to facilitate action in the balky Senate, the supercommittee's proposal could not be filibustered, similar to reconciliation bills in the normal budget process. The hitch: the supercommittee had only until the end of 2011 to come up with a plan that could be fast-tracked in the Senate.

If the panel failed (which it did) and if Congress didn't act during the next calendar year (2012) through normal processes (it didn't), about $1.2 trillion in across-the-board cuts would be implemented by sequester beginning in 2013 through 2021. These would come overwhelmingly from discretionary programs and be nearly equally divided between defense and domestic programs. The idea, just as with Gramm-Rudman in 1985, was that the sequester would be so unpalatable to members of Congress, with essential defense and domestic programs cut indiscriminantly, that Congress would act to find deficit reduction in bigger mandatory programs and by raising revenue. As with Gramm-Rudman, the deficit reduction was not found; unlike Gramm-Rudman, in 2013 sequestration went into effect.

But only so much can be done on the discretionary side of the budget. Sequestration is at best a partial answer and at worst a process that will undercut national security and the productive investments the government makes, virtually all of which are discretionary. With the moment of truth on the debt coming closer, the question became: why can't Congress find the will to do what it needs to do to fix the problem?

## What Is So Hard About Budget Issues?

Budget decisions in Washington—as reflected in the actions of both the president and Congress—are driven by politics. This should not surprise anyone—we are, after all, talking about politicians! And politics makes balancing the budget difficult for a simple reason: voters like more government services and prefer to pay less in taxes. And the politicians are nothing if not responsive to voters.

Figure 8.6, taken from a Pew Research Center poll, illustrates the level of support for spending cuts in major issue areas—in short, not much. And this is especially true for some of the biggest programs, such as Medicare and Social Security. Pew finds that people are in favor of raising taxes—but only on a tiny percentage of top earners, those making $250,000 and above.

As we have seen, influential interest groups are important to politicians in myriad ways, from providing helpful advice on legislative strategy and public policy to funding campaigns to getting out the vote. Interest groups, among other things, are organized around the goal of channeling the views of the public in an effective way to Washington policy makers. This usually involves advocating for more spending on government programs or for tax breaks that benefit particular groups of citizens. Industry is also heavily invested in lobbying for tax breaks and subsidies. And companies always make the case that tax breaks are necessary in order to maintain productivity and jobs. To say it is difficult for politicians to resist the force of the lobbyists when they speak for the strongly held views of their constituents and the job-creating industries in their districts is an understatement.

Dealing with budget deficits and the debt crisis by extension involves some combination of cutting spending (especially mandatory) and raising taxes. This is the conclusion of outside observers as well as key members of Congress of both parties who are deeply involved in the issues. In a sense, *everyone knows what needs to be done*. Bipartisan commissions seem always to come to the same conclusion.[11] Usually, the commissions have the following components in varying proportions:

**FIGURE 8.6. Americans Side with More Spending, Not Less**

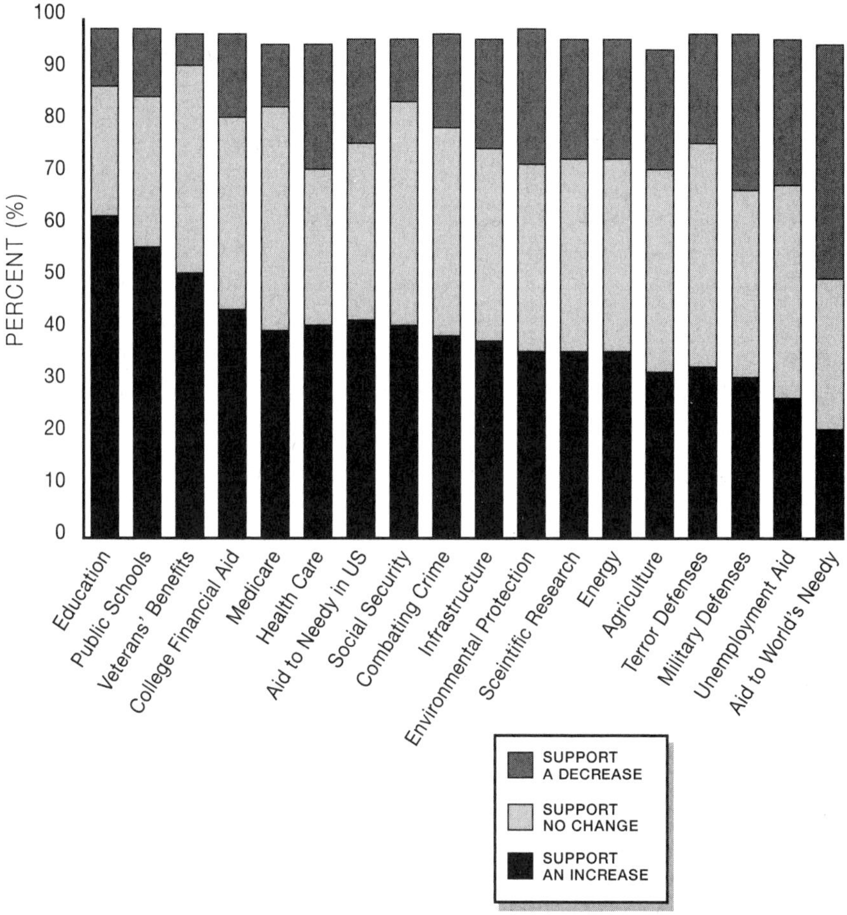

*Source:* Pew Research Center.

1. reducing Social Security costs long term by raising the retirement age slightly and changing the way the annual cost-of-living adjustment is calculated to reflect more accurately what people pay for a typical "basket" of consumer goods[12]

2. broadening the tax base from which the government collects revenue by removing so-called tax expenditures—essentially provisions that exempt portions of income from taxation—and some tax breaks for corporations

3. forcing wealthier seniors to pay more premiums for government subsidized health care (in Medicare) and continuing efforts to rein in costs in the health care system

It is generally agreed that these sorts of changes are needed at least to begin to address the problem. It should be noted that arguably the biggest problem—reining in health care costs long term—is the toughest one to address with any certainty.

Invariably, though, cutting spending for almost any program raises the ire of some interested party that represents real flesh-and-blood voters. Increasing taxes does the same thing, sometimes for a much broader segment of the electorate. No wonder the president and members of Congress find it hard to balance the budget!

Politicians who go against the grain and try to address deficits in a serious way rarely get any traction. And if they do, they often pay a big price. President George H. W. Bush agreed to discretionary spending caps and substantial tax increases in the controversial 1990 Budget Enforcement Act with the Democratic congressional leadership. In 1992, despite having led the country to a decisive and highly popular victory in the first Persian Gulf War, presiding over a rebounding economy, and having a virtually spotless reputation, Bush garnered only 38 percent of the vote against then-governor Bill Clinton and the independent candidate, Ross Perot. Republicans believe strongly that his willingness to raise taxes doomed him, and the party has taken a consistent position resisting any tax increases (the party normally advocates tax cuts) ever since.

The 1990 Bush deal did not produce immediate results in terms of the federal budget picture. President Clinton faced an even more dire deficit predicament when he took office in 1993. He proposed still more tax increases and significant spending cuts. He could get only Democrats in Congress to go along with his plan, with just enough votes to pass it. Then the party paid a heavy price in 1994 (Clinton was lucky he was not up for reelection), and Congress went to the Republicans for the first time in 40 years in a landslide. Similar to the situation for Republicans, the prevailing view among many Democrats was that taking responsibility for dealing with the deficit by raising taxes and cutting spending was a huge political loser.

Typically, even suggesting changes to sacrosanct programs is a nonstarter. In 2005, after winning reelection, President George W. Bush suggested privatizing portions of Social Security and changing the formula for cost-of-living increases, in order to put the program on a sustainable path for the long haul. Predictably, Democrats opposed the plan, but more instructively the *Republican-controlled Congress* refused even to take it up legislatively.

More recently, Republicans have put forth a budget plan to find major savings by restructuring Medicaid and Medicare. Essentially, the plan envisions putting more of the Medicaid burden on the states and capping Medicare spending, as opposed to the current open-ended entitlement arrangement. The proposal was spearheaded by House Budget Committee chair (and 2012 vice presidential nominee) Paul Ryan. At the same time, President Obama and congressional Democrats have proposed raising taxes, mostly on higher-income Americans making $250,000 and higher.

The political upshot of these efforts was predictable. Democrats relentlessly attacked any electorally vulnerable Republicans for advocating changes to Medicare; in particular, in Florida, home to millions of retirees, the 2012 Republican presidential ticket was accused of cutting health care for seniors. At the same time, Republicans claimed Democrats and President Obama in particular would undermine the economy by proposing to take money from small business owners and other productive citizens by raising their taxes. Democrats believe that old-age entitlements are their best issue, which makes them loath to compromise on them. Republicans define their party brand by resistance to any tax increases, which in turn is central to their electoral success.

## Is There Any Hope?

There is no denying the obvious: addressing the government's long-term budget problem is very difficult. It is not easy to get politicians to raise taxes or cut spending. But a great deal is at stake. Economic growth is affected by chronic deficits and the debt crisis, and, as we have seen, the situation will get much more serious in future years. Increasing expenditures on retirement programs will also crowd out spending for other crucial government activities, including national defense, infrastructure, research and development, and education.

The politics of the situation does not seem to hold much promise. Republicans believe strongly in cutting taxes and oppose any effort to raise more revenue. At the same time, while they might be inclined to support cuts in the major mandatory programs, many live in fear of what Democrats will do to them during campaigns if they propose changes in Medicare or Social Security. Democrats, for their part, believe in the major mandatory programs and will abide no substantial changes in them. They would be willing to think about increasing revenues through the tax code, but some in their ranks are terrified of the "tax-and-spend" label that Republicans would hit them with during the election season.

Some encouragement can be found in tough decisions that were made in the not too distant past. From about 1983 through the 1990s, it was not at all uncommon for serious proposals to be put forward to cut spending, raise taxes, or do both. Sometimes legislation was enacted to do these things (the 1990 and 1993 bills in particular, signed by Presidents Bush and Clinton, respectively), although the political consequences of these actions tended to depress any future enthusiasm for belt-tightening.

Two of the most dramatic instances were in 1983 and 1997. In 1983 Social Security was bankrupt; incoming payroll taxes could not cover the growing commitment for old-age insurance payments. Congress and the president were at a loss. What to do? A bipartisan commission was formed. Headed by Alan Greenspan (before he became chair of the Federal Reserve) and including leading players in Congress, the commission was charged with coming up with a consensus solution.[13]

The solution would guarantee a funding stream for the program for at least 50 years. It was strong medicine, with a tax increase and some benefits made taxable for the first time, as well as a benefit cut in the form of increasing the retirement age. Congress, with Democrats in charge of the House and Republicans controlling the Senate, adopted the proposal. Republican president Ronald Reagan signed on.

In 1997 it looked like a balanced budget was in sight—if only entitlements and discretionary spending could be brought under control. President Clinton and Speaker Gingrich provided the impetus, and Congress put together a plan that extended and tightened statutory caps on discretionary spending over the next five years and found roughly $250 billion of savings in Medicare.[14] The Balanced Budget Act of 1997 was passed. It aimed to balance the budget by 2002. As we saw, the budget achieved balance ahead of schedule, in 1998, owing to an unexpected flood of tax revenues.

These two landmark agreements are instructive in a couple of ways. In 1983 Congress and the president decided that it would be politically wise to charter a commission, which would meet out of the public eye, to work on the details of a plan rather than to have Congress do it out in the open. If wise old hands struck a reasonable deal that both parties in Congress agreed could not be picked apart on the floor of the House or Senate with amendments, then it would have a better chance of passing. Congress often deals with sticky issues this way. Making deals in secret makes it a little less clear exactly who is to blame for the controversial or unpopular aspects of a plan, enhancing the chances for passage.

Maybe more important is that in each case, government was divided, with Democrats and Republicans alike having some control over the levers of power. In 1983 it was a Democratic House and a Republican-controlled Senate and White House. In 1997 Clinton, a Democrat, was dealing with Majority Leader Trent Lott and Speaker Gingrich representing the Republican Congress. It is likely that neither side, if they had been in control of both branches, would have wanted to face the voters to accept full responsibility for the unpopular aspects of these bills. As noted, both sides believe they will get killed at the polls when they advocate tax increases or spending cuts, especially in popular mandatory programs.

But if responsibility for the needed actions can be shared, there may be room for agreement. In 1997 the bill was sweetened by including some tax cuts to appease Republicans and some social spending for Democrats. This might be the model for addressing the difficult budget issues the country faces.

## CONCLUSION

This chapter has focused on two overarching criticisms of how Congress handles the power of the purse vested in it in the Constitution. First was the evident breaking down of the regular budget process.

The theory behind the process on the Hill is simple: the Budget Committees put together a blueprint for a budget—the Concurrent Budget Resolution—that is (ideally) economically sound and addresses the priorities of the majority party in all areas of spending and revenue, after which the Appropriations Committees and some other panels move bills through the legislative process to fill in the details.

The problem: Congress hasn't processed all the appropriations bills on time since 1996, and most years they haven't even been close. (Of course, this isn't helped by the common failure to agree on the budget resolution.) Members of Congress do not necessarily want to leave large swaths of the federal government on a continuing resolution months into the fiscal year, hampering the operations of agencies that need new budget authority to make critical hires, enter into contracts for services, and put in place needed programs. But as we have seen, the bills are delayed when politicized policy debates get injected into the process. In addition, although members want to show themselves to be wise stewards of the taxpayers' money in the larger picture, it does not always add up when nearly all of them fight hard for more money for programs affecting their own constituencies. These fights over scarce resources also make it very hard to move bills through the process.

In 2007 and 2011, the situation became so dire that Congress ended up putting most of the federal government on a continuing resolution for the whole fiscal year. Agencies had to spend countless staff hours looking into what they could legally do with the money they had, since no full-fledged appropriations bill had been passed to make clear what new priorities could legally be addressed. New circumstances call for reallocations of funds, but continuing resolutions normally include little more than the authority to spend for ongoing programs at the previous year's level. Americans complain about inefficient practices at government agencies, but some of them are surely caused by Congress's failure to get the funding bills done on time.

The second problem is the so-called fiscal train wreck that is visible on the horizon. The institution does not appear to be well equipped to make the hard decisions necessary to rein in spending on entitlement programs for seniors and pay for all the government services the public demands. The situation as it stands now, with the retirement of the baby-boom generation, is literally unsustainable, promising severe economic dislocation if not addressed in a more responsible fashion.

In the past, Congress has found a way to address difficult fiscal issues, sometimes by circumventing the regular legislative process. In 2011 Congress passed the Budget Control Act, which employed a variety of methods to force action on deficits and debt. To date, the results are not conclusive, and, in fact, it is clear much more must be done. The question is when and where the political motivation to do so will be found.

## Questions for Discussion

1. Both a corporate board and Congress have the responsibility to budget. What makes it harder for Congress to perform this task efficiently than it might be for a corporate board or, say, a board of trustees at a college or university?

2. Some people think a two-year budget cycle—appropriations bills covering two years instead of one—would make it easier for Congress to handle its power of the purse responsibly. Can you see anything wrong with this plan? Do you think it likely that Congress would adopt it? Why or why not?

3. What aspect of the legislative process that you have learned about—from Chapters 6 or 7—do you think could be reformed to make it easier to make hard decisions on the budget? Or is the budget problem caused by factors largely unrelated to process?

4. If everyone knows what must be done, at least in principle, to deal with the budget crisis, what is stopping Congress from taking action?

## Suggestions for Further Reading

Bai, Matt. "Who Killed the Debt Deal?" *New York Times Magazine,* March 28, 2012.

Government Accountability Office. "The Federal Government's Long-Term Fiscal Outlook: Fall 2012 Update." December 3, 2012. www.gao.gov/assets /660/650466.pdf.

Rudder, Catherine E. "Tax Policymaking and Fiscal Responsibility: Is Congress Capable of Doing Its Job?" In *Congress Reconsidered,* edited by Bruce Oppenheimer and Larry Dodd, 347–375. 10th ed. Washington, DC: CQ Press, 2013.

Thurber, James A. "The Dynamics and Dysfunction of the Congressional Budget Process: From Inception to Gridlock." In *Congress Reconsidered,* edited by Bruce Oppenheimer and Larry Dodd, 319–345. 10th ed. Washington, DC: CQ Press, 2013.

# NOTES

1. Allen Schick, *The Federal Budget*, 3rd ed. (Washington DC: Brookings Institution Press, 2007), 194.

2. In areas that affect national security, exceptions are made whereby emergency funds keep at least minimal staffing intact at, for example, Customs and Border Protection in the Department of Homeland Security or at the Federal Aviation Administration in order to keep air traffic controllers in place.

3. See Brad Knickerbocker, "Government Shutdown 2011 Avoided with 11th Hour Budget Deal," www.csmonitor.com/USA/Politics/2011/0409/Government-shutdown -2011-avoided-with-11th-hour-budget-deal.

4. Sometimes the omnibus bills are not technically "conference reports." This happens when there is no available appropriations bill in conference, as none has passed both chambers. Still, the bills are cobbled together into one large package. The problem is that because the package is not a conference report, the omnibus does not have automatic protections against amendments on the floor. This is particularly problematic in the Senate, where individual members are in a better position to insist on the opportunity to offer amendments.

5. The CBO operates under a projection model that assumes no change in current tax law or mandatory programs and assumes an inflation rate increase in discretionary spending. This is meant to provide members of Congress with a baseline to inform decision making on bills that would spend or cut programs or change the tax code. Philip G. Joyce's *The Congressional Budget Office: Honest Numbers, Power, and Policymaking* (Washington, DC: Georgetown University Press, 2011) provides the best description and analysis of the CBO.

6. An analysis of the disappearance of the projected surpluses was made by Charles Blahous in "How Did Federal Surpluses Become Huge Deficits?," August 20, 2012, www .economics21.org/commentary/how-did-federal-surpluses-become-huge-deficits. Blahous concludes, largely using CBO data, that spending increases accounted for about half the change, tax cuts about one-quarter, and the rest were due to modeling errors.

7. See the CBO's "Budget and Economic Outlook: 2013–2023," www.cbo.gov/sites/ default/files/cbofiles/attachments/43907_Outlook_2012-2-5_Corrected.pdf.

8. Walker starkly laid out the situation on *60 Minutes* on March 4, 2007. The interview can be read and seen at Daniel Schorn, "U.S. Heading for Financial Trouble?," *60 Minutes*, July 8, 2007, www.cbsnews.com/stories/2007/03/01/60minutes/main2528226.shtml.

9. See Government Accountability Office, "The Federal Government's Long-Term Fiscal Outlook: Fall 2012 Update," December 3, 2012, www.gao.gov/assets/660/650466.pdf.

10. An excellent overview of the BCA and its potential implications at the time of passage can be found at www.ombwatch.org/files/budget/debtceilingfaq.pdf.

11. See, for example, the report of the president's commission usually called the Simpson-Bowles Commission, "The National Commission on Fiscal Responsibility," December 2010, www.fiscalcommission.gov/sites/fiscalcommission.gov/files/documents

/TheMomentofTruth12_1_2010.pdf; and another effort by the so-called Domenici-Rivlin Task Force, "Restoring America's Future," November 2010, http://bipartisanpolicy.org/sites /default/files/BPC%20FINAL%20REPORT%20FOR%20PRINTER%2002%2028%2011 .pdf.

12. The idea is that to gauge more accurately the impact of inflation on the typical consumer, we should assume that consumers, when faced with, say, a dramatic increase in the price of oranges, will often find a replacement item that has not gone up in price—say, bananas. This leads to a lower consumer price index than if it were assumed the consumer would stay with the suddenly more expensive oranges.

13. See Paul Light, *Artful Work: The Politics of Social Security Reform* (New York: McGraw-Hill, 1985).

14. In fact, Congress has for the most part seen fit not to let the 1997 Medicare cuts (which would have affected medical service providers) go into effect. This was not particularly controversial at the time, as the government was soon to realize balanced budgets and the surpluses. In recent years, as the debt crisis has become a bigger issue, efforts to find savings in Medicare have gathered steam.

# 9

# The Oversight Power

In previous chapters, we have looked at how Congress establishes and funds government agencies and programs in authorizing and appropriations law. Once programs are established and funded, it is up to the executive branch agencies to implement the law. But that does not mean the board of directors loses interest.

Quite to the contrary—Congress has a legitimate interest in how the laws it passes are executed by government agencies, and members are well within their rights to look into how programs are administered. After all, what use would the legislative power be if the chief executive—the president—or the head of an agency or department could administer a program and spend federal funds in ways that contradicted what was set in law? (In fact, executive branch officials run the risk of impeachment, a lawsuit, jail time, or some combination of these sanctions if they contravene the law.)

Furthermore, as Congress begins the annual appropriations process and the periodic reauthorizations of government programs and agencies, it needs a great deal of information in order to make considered decisions. Much of that information must come from the agencies. Congress looks into what is working and what is not working to see whether changes in the law need to be made. The board also needs to see whether funds are being put to good use, whether funds should be shifted to other priorities, or perhaps whether more money might be required for an agency to serve its mission effectively. In short, conducting oversight—looking into how agencies carry out programs—is an integral part of the legislative process. Oversight is every bit as much the regular business of Congress as actual legislating; neither can be done effectively without the other.

Oversight is a tough job for members of Congress and their staff. The government is huge and complex, and agencies do not always make it easy to get information.

Presidents, cabinet secretaries, and agency heads have an interest in protecting their prerogatives and running programs in ways that they feel reflect well on their stewardship of the government. From the executive perspective, Congress can seem to be meddling when members ask for information that seems only to advance a cause that matters to a particular district or state or the interests of one political party.

Congress has a very different perspective. It sees an executive branch run by unelected people—cabinet secretaries, agency heads, and other high-ranking officials. (The president and the vice president are the only elected officials in the executive branch.) As the representatives of the people, members of Congress see oversight as a key means to hold powerful officials accountable for government activities that were put in place and funded through legislation by Congress.

The idea of the US government as a codependent system is most evident in the area of congressional oversight of government agencies and programs. Every day the legislative branch initiates inquiries into program performance, calls powerful cabinet secretaries and agency heads to Capitol Hill for public hearings on major issues, and sits down with agency policy experts to work on legislative solutions for problem programs. For their part, the agencies report back on the progress they are making and sometimes initiate communication in an effort to influence the legislative process in the interest of agency missions and the president. It is a wary interaction. Each side has leverage to further its goals, and each side has a distinct role. At the end of the day, neither branch can perform its duties without the other—the essence of codependency

This chapter focuses on the sources of Congress's oversight power. This power stems from specific aspects of the Constitution. Congress has found the need over the years to bolster its ability to conduct oversight by passing laws clarifying the power, in some cases, and adding capacity to help it keep track of the proliferation of agencies and federal programs, in others. This power extends well into the private sector when nongovernmental entities—businesses, colleges, and so forth—are regulated by law or receive subsidies.

The main aim of this chapter is for the reader to grasp exactly the purpose of oversight, *why* it is such an important tool for Congress in its efforts to direct the federal government, and understand the various legislative branch agencies involved in the oversight process. In Chapter 10, we will look at *how*, and *when*, Congress conducts oversight.

## THE CENTRAL PURPOSE OF OVERSIGHT: PROTECTING THE PEOPLE'S LIBERTIES

In creating separate branches of government, the framers of the Constitution put in place instruments for each branch to check the others. One of the most influential of *The Federalist Papers* states that "the constant aim is to divide and arrange [the branches of government] in such a manner that each may be a check on the other."[1] The notion that one branch needs to be able to dip into the territory of another was thought to be a key, if not *the* key, to ensuring that the people's liberties would not be trampled on by a central government that was being given substantial powers.[2]

James Madison, who wrote *The Federalist Papers* just quoted, did not think that the act of writing down the essential liberties—freedom of speech, freedom of the press, freedom of religion, right to jury trial, and so on—in what became the Bill of Rights would be nearly sufficient to protect them. In his view, a carefully structured government was the only hope for securing the people's freedoms. A threat to liberty could certainly arise from an executive branch that wielded unchecked authority under the control of the president. Administering the laws of the land could be done in capricious and dangerous ways. Keep in mind that the president was to be the one who could call the state militias into service and otherwise have the responsibility of maintaining domestic tranquillity. The executive had "the sword," in the manner of speaking at the time, and thus was a potential threat to the people's liberties.

To keep the executive from running wild, Congress, which contained the representatives of the people, would need to be able to check up on the executive. First and foremost, this would be done by *monitoring executive actions to make sure that the laws were obeyed and the liberties of the people were not infringed upon.*

As noted in Chapter 6, Congress was given the power to "create, abolish, reorganize, and fund federal departments."[3] Congress, then, as the representative of the people, needed to be able to protect these prerogatives in the separated system; only by being able to "look over the shoulder" of executive branch officials could it do this. How else could Congress make sure that the president was spending money in accordance with the law? How else could it make sure that legally required programs to give educational grants to the needy were being administered properly? After all, Congress had been given the legislative power, which the Constitution spelled out as the power of the purse and the authority to establish federal program guidelines. The executive would be required to follow clearly stated legislative intent, and Congress would be entitled to make sure it was doing so.

Probably most important for Congress, as the framers believed and which is still applicable today, is its "power of the purse . . . [its] most complete and effectual weapon . . . as the immediate representatives of the people."[4] Naturally, it is necessary to be able to look into how money is spent by the agencies if that power is to mean anything.

### Ensuring Good Government

This gets to Congress's other main objective in pursuing oversight, which is *to ensure good government.* The power of the purse carries with it a tremendous responsibility: the efficient, wise, and honest stewardship of taxpayers' money. The US government has become, as we have seen, the single largest entity in the world, spending close to $4 trillion yearly on everything from spy satellites to farm subsidies to social work. It is a big job to make sure that this kind of money is being spent wisely.

The executive branch has some mechanisms in place to do its part. It has monitors in every department and agency charged with ferreting out waste, fraud, and abuse (the inspectors general offices, for example). The Office of Management and Budget has the responsibility to manage budget activity throughout the government. Under the George W. Bush administration, the OMB evaluated every government program to see whether it was being carried out efficiently and whether it addressed the intended problems or achieved the intended results.[5] This evaluation was such an ambitious undertaking that it took much of Bush's two terms in office to complete.

But ultimately it is Congress, as the people's elected representative, that is responsible for evaluating government activities, and in this capacity Congress is often wary of the messages coming from the president or top department and agency officials appointed by the president. Executive branch leaders may have a political motivation to downplay internal management problems, and they may not want malfeasance to come to light. As a result, Congress has a responsibility to make its own judgments as to the efficiency or effectiveness of any given program. And members and staff on Capitol Hill try to be particularly attuned to waste, fraud, and abuse in a program or in the contracting process. In a forward-looking sense, Congress needs information about current programs in order to inform the legislative process as to changes and enhancements that may need to be made in law to meet new circumstances.

## The Constitution and the Courts

The Constitution does not specifically enumerate the oversight power. The absence of debate at the Constitutional Convention on this question did not mean that the framers did not want Congress to be able to supervise the executive branch; quite the opposite was true. As historian Arthur Schlesinger wrote, "It was not considered necessary to make an explicit grant of such authority. The power to make laws implied the power to see whether they were faithfully executed. The right to secure needed information had long been deemed by both the British Parliament and the colonial assemblies as a necessary and appropriate attribute of the people to legislate."[6]

In addition to being a necessary component of the lawmaking power generally and, specifically, the power of the purse, oversight is implied in at least a couple of other ways in the Constitution. The fact that the Senate must confirm top executive branch officials suggests that the leadership of government agencies has a responsibility to answer to Congress when asked for information. Also, Congress's ability to impeach and remove high-level executive branch officials implies a wide-ranging power to investigate potential wrongdoing.

Many times over the course of US history, federal courts have upheld Congress's right to look into the business of the agencies, as well as private citizens' business, in a wide range of circumstances. While the courts have restricted Congress occasionally, usually when oversight efforts threaten individuals' liberties as found in the Bill of Rights,[7] the grant of authority is rather broad. A 1927 case, *McGrain v. Daugherty,* said that Congress's ability to investigate the administration of a government agency did not necessarily need to pertain to specific proposed legislation. If it was reasonable to assume legislation "could be had," then Congress had a right to information. Furthermore, the Supreme Court gave Congress wide latitude to conduct what some have described as "fishing expeditions" when it said, "To be a valid legislative inquiry there need be no predictable [legislative] end result."[8]

## WHAT ARE THE LIMITS TO CONGRESS'S OVERSIGHT POWER?

There is no debate regarding Congress's right to check to see how programs are running, particularly when Congress is considering pending legislation in conjunction with conducting oversight. With appropriations, of course, Congress is annually looking into how agencies are spending money and determining what funding levels should be provided for the next fiscal year. The administration recognizes that when Congress requests information in the course of exercising its legislative duties, those requests must be answered. It is unusual for agency witnesses to refuse to testify or fail to produce at least some of the requested documents.

The sticking point today between the branches often crops up when Congress goes beyond simply looking into the performance of government programs and gets into investigations of alleged wrongdoing by agency officials or the president himself. In those circumstances, the presidents have sometimes invoked **executive privilege**, which is commonly defined this way: the doctrine that allows the president and other high officials of the executive branch to keep certain communications private if disclosing those communications would disrupt the functions or decision-making processes of the executive branch.

The very first president, George Washington, maintained that the executive should "communicate [to Congress] such papers as the public good would permit."[9] He seemed to imply that, while the executive should cooperate with legitimate congressional inquiries, for the executive to function effectively within the constitutional framework, he needed space for privileged internal deliberations.

Today presidents often assert their prerogatives over against Congress regarding so-called predecisional deliberations. The view is that the White House and the agencies should be able to shield from view the details of the decision-making processes, although not, of course, the decisions they make in the executive capacity.

Congress does not agree—over the course of history there has been considerable overlap between what presidents regard as privileged internal deliberations and what Congress believes it should have access to in disposing of its legislative and oversight responsibilities. No hard and fast rule has ever been laid down by the Supreme Court; it much prefers to stay out of the issue of exactly which internal deliberations in the executive branch can be shared with Congress and which cannot. They regard these disputes as "political questions" that are better left to the executive and legislative branches to work out.[10]

## Congressional Subpoenas

It is not uncommon for Congress to find itself thwarted in conducting an investigation of a federal agency. In those instances, Congress may issue a *subpoena* to top executive branch officials, requesting documents and perhaps their testimony. Subpoenas are issued by committees to officials serving in agencies in their jurisdiction.

The president may claim executive privilege to deny access to documents or refuse testimony. Failure to comply with a subpoena may in the extreme case lead to Congress issuing a citation of contempt (requiring the vote of one of the houses of Congress) against the official who is holding back. The case is then referred to the Justice Department for potential prosecution. A conviction for contempt of Congress can lead to fines or imprisonment.

However, it is much more common in cases involving executive privilege claims for the two sides to reach an accommodation that respects the prerogatives of both branches before things go too far. Congress usually gets the information it is seeking from the executive, but not always everything and not always in open proceedings or in sworn testimony. Congress is generally successful because of the leverage it can wield, particularly its power of the purse.[11]

## Bush and Obama Push the Limits

Both the George W. Bush and Obama administrations attempted to push the limits of executive privilege—in Bush's case to the point of asserting that presidential advisers and agency officials have immunity from congressional subpoenas. But in

August 2008, a federal district court disagreed with the administration, ruling that former White House counsel Harriet Miers would in fact have to appear in front of the House Judiciary Committee to entertain questions concerning her role in the controversial firings of several US attorneys.[12] Obama's attorney general, Eric Holder, faced an unprecedented contempt of Congress charge in 2012, as depicted in Box 9.1.

Both of these situations show the differences in viewpoint between the two branches. The courts have not resolved—and probably never will—the specific limits of executive privilege, on the one hand, and congressional investigatory power, on the other. *U.S. v. Nixon* (1974) suggested that only a very narrow range of direct interactions between advisers and the president could be protected. The circle of executive privilege would not extend to presidential interactions with agency officials, even at the cabinet level. Certainly, the Bush and Obama administrations have looked to expand the scope considerably.

One rule of thumb applies to many situations: Congress wins out when the information in question is needed for a specific legislative decision, but if, for example, "national security is directly implicated," then the balance tips in favor of the executive branch's desire not to disclose the information.[13] The president has sources of authority in the national security realm (the commander-in-chief role and others, as we shall see in Chapter 11) that he does not have in the domestic sphere.

## BOLSTERING OVERSIGHT THROUGH STATUTE

Though the Constitution grants Congress the power to "create, abolish, reorganize, and fund federal departments," it does not spell out exactly how Congress should do this, or how it should make sure that these agencies remain responsive to the needs of the American public. To fill in these gaps, Congress has passed legislation over the years to bolster their oversight capacity. Some of this legislation created legislative branch agencies that are responsible, in whole or in part, for augmenting Congress's ability to supervise the executive.

### Congressional Support Agencies: The GAO and CBO

In 1921, Congress created the General Accounting Office, later renamed the Government Accountability Office, which was given the power to audit agencies' use of funds.

In effect, the creation of GAO was a cry for help by Congress—the board was saying it needed help, and a lot of it, keeping tabs on everything it is supposed to oversee in government. To that end, as noted earlier, it has created three independent legislative branch support agencies.

## BOX 9.1

### House Republicans Charge
### Attorney General Holder with Contempt

On June 27, 2012, for the first time in US history, the attorney general of the United States was charged with contempt of Congress for failing to provide internal documents subpoenaed in an Oversight and Government Reform Committee investigation. The vote took place in the House of Representatives, with 255 members, 238 Republicans and 17 Democrats, in support. Contempt of Congress is a misdemeanor punishable by a maximum $1,000 fine and 12 months' imprisonment.

The background was this: In 2006 the Bureau of Alcohol, Tobacco, and Firearms, an agency in the Justice Department, initiated a program called Operation Fast and Furious. It involved tracking firearms sales to illegal "straw purchasers," who would not initially be apprehended. Instead, the firearms in question would be tracked—the eventual objective being to identify and arrest key figures in major drug cartels. Some 2,000 weapons were tracked from the program's inception until 2011. It turned out that two of the weapons were bought by someone suspected of killing a border patrol agent, Brian Terry, in late 2010.

A congressional investigation into Terry's death led by Representative Darrell Issa (R-CA), chair of the Oversight Committee, brought matters to a head. Attorney General Eric Holder claimed he knew little or nothing of Fast and Furious in early 2011, and in fact denied any major flaws in the program. Ultimately, it became a matter of what Holder knew and when he knew it when it came to light that he may have been briefed on the program as far back as mid-2010. Issa subpoenaed reams of administration documents. Although some documents were provided, President Obama eventually claimed executive privilege over much of the material.*

In the end, House Republicans were unsatisfied with what they got and initiated the unprecedented contempt charge. The criminal citation in these cases is referred to an office in the Justice Department, which is extraordinarily unlikely to move forward against the attorney general (the cabinet official in charge of the department). A separate civil citation was also brought by the House. This will not be resolved quickly, but could be a chance for the courts to take a stand on the president's expansive executive privilege claim.

*Jonathan Weisman and Charlie Savage, "House Finds Holder in Contempt in Inquiry on Guns," *New York Times*, June 28, 2012, www.nytimes.com/2012/06/29/us/politics/fast-and-furious-holder-contempt-citation-battle.html?pagewanted=all&_r=0.

The GAO describes its responsibilities this way:

> [The GAO's] work is done at the request of congressional committees or subcommittees or is mandated by public laws or committee reports. [The agency] also undertake[s] research under the authority of the Comptroller General [the director of the GAO]. [The GAO] support[s] congressional oversight by
> - auditing agency operations to determine whether federal funds are being spent efficiently and effectively;
> - investigating allegations of illegal and improper activities;
> - reporting on how well government programs and policies are meeting their objectives;
> - performing policy analyses and outlining options for congressional consideration; and
> - issuing legal decisions and opinions, such as bid protest rulings and reports on agency rules.
>
> [The GAO] advises Congress and the heads of executive agencies about ways to make government more efficient, effective, ethical, equitable and responsive.[14]

The agency has about 3,000 employees and is headed by the comptroller general, who is insulated from political pressures by a 14-year term of office. (The comptroller general may be removed only for cause.) The GAO's investigations into government programs are respected as fair and impartial, even if the objects of the investigations are not always happy with the conclusions.

The GAO takes requests for investigations into federal programs from any member of Congress, but in practice it is usually able to handle only higher-priority matters coming from party leaders and committee and subcommittee chairs and ranking members. Members of Congress know that to get a GAO investigation into a program of interest, they need to go through the committee with jurisdiction over the agency in question. Better yet, require regular audits by the GAO in law. As mentioned earlier, the comptroller general also has the authority to initiate investigations into matters of pressing importance without a specific congressional request.

The GAO investigators write up a report of their findings after completing an investigation. The investigations may take anywhere from months to a year or more to complete. The agency gets a chance to see the report and comment on it before it is made public. (The report may include a rejoinder from the agency in question.) All reports on nonclassified matters are immediately made public via the GAO website.

Sometimes these reports can be tremendously embarrassing to federal agencies, creating major publicity problems. In 2005 the GAO was made aware of lapses in the process by which the Nuclear Regulatory Commission awarded licenses to companies to purchase radioactive materials for legitimate scientific or medical purposes.[15] In 2006 GAO investigators created two fictitious companies, both of which were able to obtain licenses from the NRC without much difficulty. The agency never checked to see whether the companies had a legitimate purpose or even whether they actually existed. (Of course, they did not.) No site visits were made to check whether the material could be safely stored. Not only that, but the GAO investigators found that the licenses the agencies gave the GAO investigators (posing as fictitious company executives) were so unsophisticated that they could be tampered with to enable the "companies" to buy almost unlimited quantities of radioactive material.

Members of Congress may do what they wish with a GAO report. A report may be ignored if the results do not square with the agenda of the requester, or it may end up being the focus of hearings to further publicize the issues it highlights. Congressional staff regularly use GAO reports in their oversight efforts, and GAO investigators and agency officials are frequently asked to testify about their findings.

If the GAO finds problems in the conduct of a program, it makes recommendations to the agency and keeps track of agency compliance in order to inform Congress. In the long run, some reports influence changes in law and funding priorities. In the nuclear materials case, the GAO report prompted major changes in the licensing processes at the agency. We will look at a GAO audit of for-profit universities in the next chapter.

In 1974 Congress created the Congressional Budget Office, another support agency for Congress, with a different mandate from the GAO. The CBO can "secure information . . . directly from various departments" to aid Congress in understanding the budgetary implications of legislation it is contemplating.[16] It adds value by providing Congress estimates of administration proposals for new programs and projected budget deficits—essentially "second opinions" that the board can use to challenge the president. In the 1980s, Reagan administration budget numbers were called into question by the CBO as underprojecting future deficits. In 1993, and then again in 2009–2010, the CBO played a big role in providing Congress independent analysis on the cost of health care reform proposals put forward by Presidents Clinton and Obama

## Staff Capacity and Oversight Requirements

Congress has also put into law provisions that require committees to be watchful of agencies in their areas of jurisdiction. Of particular note was legislation in 1946 that authorized staff for the committees. Before that time, work on the Hill was handled by members and a staffer or two in their personal office. By the 1940s, after the expansion of government in the New Deal, the growth of the defense establishment during World War II, and the need to maintain a large military after the war, Congress was overwhelmed. Washington was not a sleepy little town anymore, and the board of directors needed some help. As seen in Box 9.2, then-senator Harry S Truman showed what a senator fortified by strong staff support could do in the public interest.

In recent decades, particularly since the explosion in government programs in the 1960s and early 1970s, the House and Senate have gone further by putting in place explicit oversight responsibilities in their respective bodies of rules. In the House, the Oversight and Government Reform Committee takes the lead in supervising government agencies and programs. In the Senate, the Homeland Security and Governmental Affairs Committee has that responsibility. The authorizing committees in both chambers, as well as the Appropriations Committees, are given specific responsibilities to conduct oversight in their jurisdictions. In the House, each authorizing committee must establish an oversight subcommittee to keep tabs on the agencies in its jurisdiction.

## Whistleblower Laws

Congressional staff conducting oversight often rely on information they receive directly from the civil servants who run government programs. Because the executive branch has prerogatives of its own that it feels it must protect, it sometimes resists congressional meddling in executive affairs. It is not always sure of members' motivations, which could be driven by narrow, district-specific interests or by partisan politics. As a result, agency heads and presidents have tried to close the lines of communication from executive branch personnel to Congress, putting up a wall between the branches. In Congress's view, however, the divide between the branches must be permeable in order for the system to function.

To combat this, legislation introduced over the years has provided legal protections for executive branch personnel, and often people in the private sector, who pass information to members of Congress. These so-called **whistleblower** laws are meant to shield people from reprisal when they share information with Congress about a potential violation of the law or other abuse in an agency or business.[17] The first law was passed in the 1860s. Its objective was to protect people who reported on contracting fraud during the Civil War. Many other laws protect whistleblowers in other specific circumstances. Of particular note, the 2010 Dodd-Frank Financial Reform Act included protections and even incentives for people to report firms that do not comply fully with Securities and Exchange Commission regulations. A

# BOX 9.2

## Senator Truman Shows the Value of Congressional Staff

As a member of the Senate in the 1930s and into the early 1940s, Harry Truman had the typical skeletal staff for that time, consisting of clerical assistance plus one or two professionals to help him handle his legislative duties.

After getting reelected in 1940, Truman set his sights on the government contracting process in the defense area as the nation geared up for the massive rearmament required to fight a world war. He had received considerable correspondence in his Senate office alleging widespread "waste and favoritism" in government contracts.

In March 1941, the Special Committee Investigating National Defense, which came to be known as the Truman Committee, was established. Its charge was to look into the methods by which contracts were awarded, the geographic distribution of contracts, the effect of the rearmament program on labor, the accounting practices of contractors, and other matters. Initially, President Franklin Roosevelt opposed the investigation, alleging that it would undermine morale for the war effort. Truman assured the president that his aim was not to criticize the military but rather to focus on contracting and contracting alone. Ultimately, the Truman Committee was credited with uncovering considerable waste and saving the government billions of dollars.

How did Truman do it? Initially, the committee was given only $15,000 to conduct its business. This enabled Truman to hire a full-time investigator and relatively little else. In the end, Truman was able to prevail upon the Senate to give him far more resources, and at its height the committee had 18 investigators and other support.

The Truman Committee was a precursor to the greater expansion of congressional staff in 1946 and in later years. Congress came to recognize that, after the tremendous growth of government in the 1930s and '40s in response to the Depression and war, it needed to bulk up in order to be able to keep up with everything going on in the executive branch.*

*Donald H. Riddle, The Truman Committee (New Brunswick, NJ: Rutgers University Press, 1964).

high-profile recent case involved reprisals against Food and Drug Administration scientists who communicated to Senator Charles Grassley (R-IA) on internal matters at the agency. It is described in Box 9.3.

## The Government Performance and Results Act

In 1993 Congress passed into law the Government Performance and Results Act (GPRA). The purpose of the law was to institute a new regime of strategic planning in federal agencies. Drawing from the business world, Congress required the agencies to assess every program they run by stating the program's purpose and the results the agency expects it to achieve and to provide a method to measure those results. Annual reporting to Congress in all of these areas is required.

In 2010 the GPRA Modernization Act was passed. It enhanced the original version by requiring more frequent performance reports to congressional committees of jurisdiction—quarterly instead of annually. Experts in the private sector recommend that Congress go further by aligning congressional committee jurisdictions to agency responsibilities. The EPA and Department of Homeland Security both report to multiple committees on the Hill, undermining Congress's ability to address performance results systematically.[18]

Presidents have probably made better use of GPRA reports than Congress. The chief executive has a greater interest in streamlining government; after all, it is good politics for the president to show (or claim) that more is being done on his watch with fewer government workers and less taxpayer money. In fact, President George W. Bush took particular interest in measuring performance and pushing agencies to assess programs from top to bottom. He instituted a thorough examination of every program as part of his management agenda, which took years to complete. These evaluations had a significant impact on the funding requests he made to Congress.

## The Inspectors General

As the federal government expanded in the 1960s and 1970s and more instances of malfeasance came to light in the conduct of federal programs, Congress decided to institutionalize internal controls in the agencies. The Inspector General Act of 1978, as amended in 1988, created offices ("the IGs," for short) across the government in almost every agency and department. (A few government departments already had an IG.) They were given a mandate to ferret out waste, fraud, and abuse in the conduct of government programs.[19]

IGs for all the government departments and most major subcabinet-level agencies are appointed by the president and must receive Senate approval. IGs at some

BOX 9.3

**Whistleblowers at FDA
Have Their Computers Monitored**

The Food and Drug Administration is the agency responsible for assessing medical devices and approving them for use. Senator Chuck Grassley (R-IA) has long taken an interest in the agency on a whole range of matters, from over-the-counter glucose monitors to the drug-approval process. Recently, he became concerned about the approval of a device meant to identify breast cancer.

The matter came to a head in 2012 when six former and current FDA employees filed suit in federal court for infringement of their freedom of speech and the right to petition Congress. Some of these officials had been involved in providing information to Senator Grassley as well as the incoming Obama administration in January 2009 concerning what they regarded as improper actions on the part of the agency in the approval of the device. They claimed the agency retaliated by systematically monitoring their computer usage.

Grassley stated that whistleblowers are treated "like skunks at a picnic" by their agencies.* In this particular case, the senator was drawing attention to the matter for a long-term project of his: to put in place a much more rigorous legal system of protecting whistleblowers. Current law *does not provide protections from retaliation for federal public health officials who contact Congress,* the press, or the White House with potentially damaging information. Grassley hopes the spotlight he has helped to shine will lead to stronger protections.

*Ellen Nakashima and Lisa Rein, "Grassley Opens Investigation into FDA Surveillance," *Washington Post,* February 1, 2012, http://articles.washingtonpost.com/2012–02–01/politics/35442448_1_fda-spokeswoman-erica-jefferson-fda-commissioner-fda-scientists-and-doctors.

smaller agencies as well as at independent agencies are appointed by the agency head. The law requires that IGs be chosen based on experience in auditing and investigations and without regard to political affiliation. This requirement is not always adhered to.[20] Presidentially appointed IGs may be removed by the president for cause; others may be removed by an agency head.

The idea was that these offices, though situated within the agencies and hence part of the executive branch, would be given a measure of independence by being required to report directly to the legislative branch on a regular basis. (Agency officials other than IGs normally must clear their communications with Congress through the Office of Management and Budget in the president's Executive Office.) Congress felt that it could not trust the president to make internal investigations a high priority, owing to the potential political fallout for the president from the expo-sure of illegal or wasteful activities by his appointees in executive branch agencies.

The law gives IGs a great deal of latitude in looking into agency business. They have access to agency records and can exercise subpoena power. In addition, the law provides some protection to any agency employee who comes to the IG with a complaint involving mismanagement of funds or other illegalities.

IGs refer suspected violations of federal law to the attorney general of the United States for potential prosecution. They also submit reports of their activities twice a year, both to their agency head or department secretary and directly to the congressional committees of jurisdiction for the agency. These reports typically highlight programs that the IG believes are wasting taxpayer money and often include recommendations to improve program performance. The purpose is to gain the attention of the agency head, who may implement administrative changes to remedy the situation, and Congress, which may hold hearings or act through legislation to improve program performance.

IGs bring returns for the taxpayer dollar. Based on available data, in fiscal year 2009 IGs reported potential savings government-wide of more than $43 billion. This comes to close to $20 for every $1 appropriated to support IG activities. That year IGs initiated approximately 5,900 criminal actions, 1,100 civil actions, 4,400 government suspensions and disbarments, and 6,100 indictments.[21]

## WHY OVERSIGHT HAPPENS

As noted here and in earlier chapters, Congress has in effect built a government over the years, through authorizing and appropriations statutes, that is massive and complex. Agencies handle all the work that goes into measuring the impact of pollutants, testing medical devices and new military hardware, ensuring the safety of nuclear reactors, and conducting research on all sorts of social phenomena and medical problems. And that of course is a short list.

It is simply impossible for Congress to anticipate in law exactly how to do those things, especially when one considers the fact that laws are normally meant to be flexible enough to allow agencies to adjust to changing circumstances. The bottom line: if the federal government is going to be involved in every aspect of our lives and make strides in improving life in this country, Congress has to delegate respon-sibilities to agency officials. Agency officials are given the ability to implement the laws, which often involves giving them the power to make binding decisions that carry the force of law. The fact is that any law of any consequence defers to the executive branch.

We saw that in Chapter 6 with the Intelligence Reform Act of 2004 involv-ing the restructuring of the entire 16 agency intelligence function of the US government—activities including gathering information and analyzing that information to support troops in the field or to anticipate the next moves of adversaries and potential adversaries all over the world. The bill had to be written with ambiguous language just to pass Congress. The strongest supporters of reform wanted the new overarching agency, the Office of the Directorate of National Intelligence, to be able to influence the budgets of all the intelligence programs; others wanted department heads to continue to have control over how their agencies went about their business. The solution: bill language that said that the ODNI would have influence over all intelligence agency budgets, but not in such a way as to *"abrogate the statutory responsibilities of the heads of the departments of the United States Government."* In other words, whether or not the ODNI had the ability to fully coordinate and control intelligence gathering was left unclear. It would, in effect, be resolved in practice instead of in law.[22]

The Clean Air Act (1972, since amended), giving authority to the EPA to regulate greenhouse gas emissions, has been variously interpreted by different administrations. It would have been impossible to put in law exactly how to regulate emissions, which are highly complex to measure; in addition, the exact source of some emissions might be subject to dispute; and then taking the next step to finding a workable solution is far from an easy task. The disputes have been so intense that the federal judiciary has been called in to adjudicate. Massachusetts brought suit against the Bush administration early this century, culminating in a 2007 court ruling that EPA regulations under President Bush were so lenient as not to be in keeping with the law. More stringent regulations put in place by the Obama administration were upheld at a federal appeals court in 2012.[23]

Perhaps the two most consequential laws to come from the 111th Congress were the Dodd-Frank financial reform legislation and the Affordable Care Act that aimed to broaden health care coverage by a variety of means, both passed in 2010. In these cases, extensive deference was given to the executive. Key decisions on all sorts of specific areas of health coverage were delegated to the secretary of health and human services (who, of course, works for the president). In fact, the bill could be characterized most accurately by saying it set up only a broad outline of a reformed health care system, leaving most of the important details to the executive branch.

The same is true of Dodd-Frank. In an interview with the authors, a lead congressional staff member for the financial derivatives section of the bill (roughly 20 percent of the whole) described whole sections that left to the Treasury Department and some independent agencies the responsibility of defining key terms and in effect determining exactly what to regulate.[24]

What should one make of this? For one thing, with broad delegation comes congressional oversight. In the intelligence example, congressional committees of jurisdiction (and many members not on these committees) are and will continue to be very interested in how this unfolds. Every year, as a part of the reauthorization of the intelligence programs, these committees will judge the results of this ambiguous delegation of authority and consider potential legislative fixes if needed.

The key point: just because Congress delegates authority to executive branch agencies does not mean that Congress loses interest. Just the opposite is true. By writing expansive laws, Congress gets the federal government involved in more things and, especially, more involved in the lives of American citizens. When people—constituents—are affected by government, members of Congress pay attention. When something goes wrong with a program, invariably people contact their representative or senator. So why does oversight happen? *Oversight happens because Congress wants to know about the programs that affect the people that voted them into office and have the power to unseat them, or vote them back in.*

Implementation of the Clean Air Act has for decades drawn the attention of a range of committees that can claim some jurisdiction over the EPA. Regulatory decisions in this realm have a tremendous impact on business and ordinary citizens; as a result, members pay attention, whether they are pushing a pro- or antiregulatory agenda. Similarly, the implementation of Dodd-Frank and the Affordable Care Act are front-burner issues on Capitol Hill, given their wide scope affecting the economy and individual citizens.

An analogy helps to wrap up the point. If you came into a lot of money or won a huge lottery jackpot, you might decide to use some or all of the money to build a state-of-the-art home. It might include all the latest in green features so as to leave as little carbon footprint as possible. If you have a large family, it might have multiple rooms. In any case, you could now afford the best entertainment equipment, recreational facilities, and lavishly appointed features all over.

Naturally, you would develop a blueprint and hire a contractor, who would subcontract the work to specialists in the various amenities you envision. As you periodically check in on the work, you might come across a subcontractor who is doing something you don't want. The subcontractor might point to his or her instructions and claim to be "following orders." You, of course, own the property and will assert your prerogative to get things done right. (You might also simply have changed your mind once you see how something is being done. You are still the owner and of course are within your rights to demand that the house be built to your [revised] specifications.)

Congress looks at the federal government in a similar way. It is a "house"—incredibly complex and expansive—that it arranged to build. It has the right—because members are the representatives of the sovereign, which is the American people—to demand the project be carried out to its specifications. And the specifications may change as elected representatives change their minds or new members take their place. Congress's view: it has the right to look into any government program, into any agency's business, because it "owns" the government on behalf of the American people.

## CONCLUSION

Oversight is part and parcel of the legislative power granted to Congress in the Constitution. The authority given the board of directors to write law creating a federal program and subsequently to fund that program does not mean anything unless it has the power to look into whether the program is running properly. Oversight is an implied constitutional power, a power understood to exist from the beginning of the republic and normally challenged only on the narrowest of margins. Congress has seen fit numerous times to bolster its oversight power both by creating support agencies (the GAO and CBO) and by passing laws that enable it to keep better tabs on the agencies.

Congress conducts oversight because its members are very interested in how the implementation of the laws is affecting their constituents. It is a representative institution, and members are strongly incentivized to monitor what the agencies are doing, potentially taking action when things go awry.

## Questions for Discussion

1. Do you think the framers' main purposes for congressional oversight are being realized? If not, why not?

2. Congress's laws are frequently vague (see the case with the intelligence reform), often giving very broad authorities to federal agencies. Are there dangers in leaving so much policy-making discretion to unelected federal officials in the agencies? Why might it be that Congress avoids being more specific when it puts things in statute?

## Suggestions for Further Reading

Kriner, Douglas. "Can Enhanced Oversight Repair the 'Broken Branch'?" *Boston University Law Review* 89 (2009): 765–793.

Rozell, Mark J., and Michael Sollengerger. "Executive Privilege and the Unitary Theory in the George W. Bush Administration." In *Rivals for Power,* edited by James A. Thurber, 209–228. 4th ed. Lanham, MD: Rowman and Littlefield, 2013.

Schlesinger, Arthur M., and Roger Burns, eds. *Congress Investigates: A Documented History, 1792–1974.* New York: Chelsea House, 1975.

## NOTES

1. James Madison, *The Federalist Papers,* No. 51.

2. Frederick M. Kaiser, *CRS Report for Congress: Congressional Oversight,* Congressional Research Service, January 3, 2006, 2.

3. Frederick M. Kaiser et al., *CRS Report for Congress: Oversight Manual,* Congressional Research Service, May 1, 2007, 5.

4. *The Federalist Papers,* N. 58.

5. The Bush administration conducted the Program Assessment Rating Tool (PART) to evaluate government programs. For more information on this initiative, see www .whitehouse.gov/omb/part/.

6. Arthur Schlesinger and Roger Burns, eds., *Congress Investigates: A Documented History, 1792–1974* (New York: Chelsea House, 1975), xix.

7. Ibid., introduction.

8. From *Eastman v. United States Servicemen's Fund* (1975).

9. Quoted in Louis Fisher, *CRS Report for Congress: Congressional Investigations; Subpoenas and Contempt Power,* Congressional Research Service, April 2, 2003, 2.

10. Generally speaking, to the extent the courts have weighed in, Congress is on solid ground requesting predecisional materials if these are related to pending legislation.

11. Ibid.

12. Jon Ward, "Federal Judge Rejects Executive Privilege for Miers, Bolten," *Washington Times,* July 31, 2008, www.washingtontimes.com/news/2008/jul/31/federal-judge-rejects -executive-privilege-two-whit/.

13. Chris Schroeder, "*Cheney v. United States District Court*: Liberal Civil Discovery Rules Versus the Separation of Powers," Supreme Court Online (Duke Law), www.law .duke.edu/publiclaw/supremecourtonline/commentary/chevuni.

14. See US Government Accountability Office, "About GAO," http://gao.gov/about/ index.html.

15. David de Sola, "Government Investigators Smuggled Radioactive Materials into U.S.," CNN, March 27, 2006, www.cnn.com/2006/US/03/27/radioactive.smuggling/.

16. Kaiser et al., "Oversight Manual," 7–10.

17. Ibid., 6–7.

18. John Kamensky, "GPRA Modernization Act Explained," *IBM Center for the Business of Government,* January 6, 2011, www.businessofgovernment.org/blog/business-government /gpra-modernization-act-2010-explained-part-1.

19. Frederick M. Kaiser, *CRS Report for Congress: Statutory Offices of Inspector General; Establishment and Evolution,* Congressional Research Service, July 1, 2003.

20. For a summary, see Oversight and Government Reform Committee chair Henry Waxman's study on the politicization of the inspector general's office, "The Politicization

of Inspectors General," October 21, 2004, http://oversight.house.gov/story.asp?ID=726. Waxman found that some IGs chosen by President Clinton did not have the requisite background, but that a far greater percentage of Bush appointees did not.

21. See Susan Ragland, "Inspectors General: Reporting on Independence, Effectiveness, and Expertise," Government Accountability Office, September 2011, www.gao.gov/new.items/d11770.pdf.

22. Richard A. Best Jr., *CRS Report for Congress: Intelligence Reform After Five Years; The Role of the Director of National Intelligence,* Congressional Research Service, June 22, 2010; Best, *CRS Report for Congress: Director of National Intelligence Statutory Authorities; Status and Proposals,* December 16, 2011.

23. Neela Banerjee, "U.S. Court Upholds EPA's Authority to Regulate Greenhouse Gases," June 26, 2012, http://articles.latimes.com/2012/jun/26/business/la-fi-epa-court-20120627.

24. Interview with Cory Claussen, professional staffer, Senate Committee on Agriculture, December 5, 2012.

# 10

# Methods of Congressional Oversight

In the last chapter, we focused on *why* Congress does oversight. In this chapter, we consider *how* oversight is conducted and get into the slipperier area of *when* oversight happens. In other words, *when* do overscheduled and thinly stretched members of Congress turn the spotlight on agencies and government programs?

As suggested in the last chapter, most oversight is instigated by congressional committees. These panels have oversight responsibility for the agencies in their jurisdiction. Committees employ a range of methods to look into the actions of executive branch agencies.

Although the methods of oversight are various, the most public face of oversight happens when committees and subcommittees hold hearings. Hearings can help inform the development of authorizing and appropriations legislation, but members of Congress use hearings for a range of other purposes that also fit into the category of "oversight." Commonly, hearings are part of a process to nudge executive branch officials in a certain direction—that is, to get them to change the way they are implementing government programs. Essentially, hearings are often used by committees and subcommittees in lieu of actual legislation that would compel agency actions. The legislative process can be extremely difficult to navigate, so influential members of Congress may decide that hearings and other forms of oversight will achieve the results they want more surely and quickly.

Congressional investigations into agency actions are a crucial component of oversight. We look at a specific case in the late 1990s when congressional committees investigated the Internal Revenue Service. High-profile hearings forced the

IRS commissioner to change some agency policies immediately and eventually led to a full-fledged reform bill that was signed into law by President Clinton in 1998.

Congress may also oversee the executive branch by putting into law, or in accompanying report language, explicit directions for agency officials to follow. Sometimes this effectively takes the form of a **legislative veto**, an approach that has been ruled unconstitutional but, curiously, is still very much in use.

Congress also relies on so-called extracongressional sources for some of its oversight—in particular the Government Accountability Office. It acts on congressional requests to look into the performance of government programs. The GAO's nonpartisan stature and its experienced staff lend credibility to its findings. Here we take a close look at a GAO study of for-profit universities that provided Congress some interesting results to consider in the development of legislation.

The last section, in addressing the "when" question, looks at the politics of congressional oversight. Congress is often criticized for failing to conduct oversight in a comprehensive and systematic manner, a charge that undoubtedly is true. While the board has a crucial responsibility to make sure government programs are not wasting taxpayer money, the task is daunting. There are too few members and not enough staff and other resources to conduct truly thorough oversight of the activities of a government that is so big.

Instead, members of Congress rely on an imperfect "fire-alarm" system to alert them when something important goes wrong that might merit their attention.[1] Congressional staff monitor all sorts of sources. They receive reports from agencies, the GAO, and the offices of the inspector general; they try to keep up with academic studies; and they are bombarded with information from interest groups, journalists, and sometimes even agency whistleblowers—all in an attempt to keep tabs on everything going on in their jurisdiction. If deemed warranted, they use the appropriate oversight tool and possibly introduce legislation. Ultimately, the key question becomes: is there a pattern to the conduct of oversight, and if so, what is that pattern?

## CONGRESSIONAL OVERSIGHT COMMITTEES AND HEARINGS

Although individual members of Congress are well within their rights to make inquiries about the conduct of government programs, it is the committees and subcommittees of Congress that are officially sanctioned by House and Senate rules to supervise the vast federal bureaucracy. Members acting on their own may be able to focus attention on problem areas in the government, but it is the committees and subcommittees that have the expertise and the wherewithal to be the most aggressive and effective overseers of the agencies.

## Congressional Oversight Committees

Most committees in Congress have fully sanctioned oversight responsibilities. Two committees in particular are intended primarily to conduct oversight, the House Committee on Oversight and Government Reform and the Senate Committee on Homeland Security and Governmental Affairs.

The subcommittees in the House Committee on Oversight and Government Reform are:

1. Federal Workforce, Postal Service, and Labor Policy
2. Government Organization, Efficiency, and Financial Management
3. Health Care, District of Columbia, Census, and National Archives
4. National Security, Homeland Defense, and Foreign Operations
5. Regulatory Affairs, Stimulus Oversight, and Government Spending
6. TARP, Financial Services, and Bailout of Public and Private Programs
7. Technology, Information Policy, Intergovernmental Relations, and Procurement Reform

And the subcommittees in the Senate Committee on Homeland Security and Governmental Affairs are:

1. Contracting Oversight
2. Disaster Recovery and Intergovernmental Affairs
3. Financial Management, Government Information, Federal Services, and International Security
4. Oversight of Government Management, the Federal Workforce, and the District of Columbia
5. Investigations (Permanent Subcommittee on Investigations)

These committees and their subcommittees are intended, among other things, to look into the effectiveness of government programs as well as to investigate potential malfeasance in the agencies. Their jurisdiction is the *entire government*. House rules require the Oversight and Government Reform Committee to provide the information it collects from the agencies to the relevant authorizing committees to inform their consideration of legislation. In the Senate committee, the Permanent Subcommittee on Investigations was created to look into criminal matters and abuse of power in the executive branch.

Both of these committees take their mandate quite a bit further than just looking into executive branch activities; sometimes they look into malfeasance in the corporate world, professional sports, and other areas. On the Senate side, the

Permanent Subcommittee on Investigations shined a concentrated spotlight in 2009–2010 on some of the practices of the major investment banking firms, in particular Goldman-Sachs. A high-profile hearing was credited with helping rally support for the passage of the Dodd-Frank legislation aimed at reining in those practices.

More controversially, a few years ago the House Oversight and Government Reform Committee took a special interest in the use of steroids in Major League Baseball. While it raised more than a few eyebrows to expend so much effort hounding baseball players, the committee noted that some performance-enhancing drugs are federally controlled substances, and thus subject to congressional scrutiny, and that baseball has an antitrust exemption in federal law.

To aid in looking into executive branch activities, these two committees have also been accorded enhanced subpoena power. Congress may subpoena government officials (and documents they may have produced in their official capacity) in an effort to compel testimony. Most congressional subpoenas require a majority vote to be enforced by the committee making the request for testimony or information. Only the Oversight and Government Reform Committee and the Homeland Security and Governmental Affairs Committee may issue a subpoena based on the decision of only the committee chair. In the case of the Permanent Subcommittee on Investigations, the subcommittee chair may issue the subpoena.

Authorizing committees also have oversight responsibilities in their areas of jurisdiction and thus, in effect, have two roles: they authorize the existence of government programs in law, and they are responsible for looking into whether these programs are being carried out according to congressional intent. Their oversight function is meant to inform the development of new authorizing legislation.

The Appropriations Committees in the House and Senate also get into the act. They are expressly responsible for looking into how government moneys are being spent as a means of informing the annual appropriations process. The House Appropriations Committee has a special investigations unit to look into potential illegalities in the expenditure of government funds.

## Congressional Hearings

Congressional hearings are the public face of oversight on Capitol Hill. Many hearings serve both to probe the conduct of government programs and to inform Congress about pending authorizing or appropriations legislation. They may serve other purposes as well. Here are descriptions of the different types of congressional hearings.[2]

*Legislative hearings.* The purpose of legislative hearings is to look into legislation that a committee is considering. A legislative hearing typically involves testimony from some combination of executive branch officials, interest group leaders, and outside experts with an interest in the legislation.

*Oversight hearings.* Oversight hearings primarily involve testimony from executive officials about the conduct of government programs. Other people representing groups with a stake in the programs may also be asked to testify. Oversight hearings often serve the dual role of informing the reauthorization process for agencies and programs.

*Investigatory hearings.* In investigatory hearings, which are a type of oversight hearing, the committee or subcommittee is looking to expose improper conduct on the part of government officials in the implementation of government programs. Some investigatory hearings probe into private-sector activities, sometimes with an eye toward enhancing the regulatory role of the government.

*Confirmation hearings.* Only the Senate conducts confirmation hearings. The Senate has the responsibility to consider and then vote to approve or reject presidential nominees—in other words, provide advice and consent—for high-ranking executive branch positions and federal judgeships. Hearings are often held to question nominees.[3]

Hearings are meetings of a congressional committee or subcommittee that are called by the chair of that panel for a specific purpose. They are almost always held in public, with the exception of hearings that involve classified information. (The House and Senate Intelligence Committees, for example, usually conduct their hearings in closed session in a special room that is regularly swept for listening devices.) Hearings bring government officials, interest group representatives, and other private citizens to Capitol Hill to answer questions from the members of the committee or subcommittee. Occasionally, members of Congress request a chance to give testimony—or are asked to—and to take questions from members of a committee on which they do not serve.

Oversight hearings are rarely called to pat agency officials on the back for a job well done. Often the committee members are at odds with the agency representative and trying to press their case as to how things should, in their view, be done in the implementation of a government program. An implicit or sometimes explicit threat may hang in the air: *If you do not accede to our wishes, we will begin work on requiring you by law to do things our way. Perhaps you can make it easier for everybody by simply changing how you implement this program.*

There are literally hundreds of these types of hearings every year. Why is it so common that Congress and the executive branch are at odds about the conduct of government programs?

First of all, those who are asked to carry out the law—the government bureaucrats—frequently have a different view on how to do their work than the elected representatives who wrote the law. At one level, the clash between the branches boils down to a difference of perspective. Members of Congress answer to their constituents; they are driven by reelection concerns as well as the needs of their party. Executive branch officials, on the other hand, receive direction from the president and view themselves as working for the nation as a whole. Divergent perspectives may lead to different interpretations of the same law.

This is especially apparent when one understands something about the ambiguity that is intentionally built into most major legislation. The board of directors passes laws that leave a great deal to the discretion of the experts in the agencies. It is also true that no law can anticipate the future events to which those carrying out the law may have to respond. In some cases, ambiguous legal language may have been necessary to gloss over strong differences of opinion among members and enable the leadership of Congress to secure the necessary majorities for final passage, as in the case of the intelligence reform legislation discussed in Chapters 5 and 9.

The bottom line is that there is a lot of potential for disagreement in the implementation of a federal program. Hearings provide a convenient public venue for Congress to publicize and hash out these differences of opinion. This venue is particularly convenient for Congress because members stage the hearings to put the agency officials at a distinct disadvantage. Of course, sometimes differences can be negotiated in private, but even then Congress may see some advantage in bringing a matter to the public's attention.

### The Way to Think About Hearings

Anytime a member of Congress goes public in official proceedings, it is safe to assume that the event or the speech is scripted, or at the very least that the member intends to influence the course of events in a particular way. This is certainly true with hearings.

To develop an analogy, hearings resemble election campaigning in that they often boil down to a question of marketing.

When influential people in a political party decide that they want to field their most qualified candidate in a race that looks promising for their party—say, the incumbent candidate of the other party has been involved in a scandal, or a retirement opens up a seat—they usually begin by doing what they can to market their candidate. Marketing congressional candidates involves, more than anything else, advertising in a variety of media (television, the Internet, and the like). Marketing experts, or campaign consultants, do a tremendous amount of research on behalf of political candidates to determine what to say in the advertising and how to describe and depict the candidate publicly. Candidates prepare speeches, use teleprompters, carefully stage backdrops, and depict themselves in strategic ways in ads. Experts recognize that a good advertising campaign is crucial to winning votes. This is true even though voters recognize that there is nothing spontaneous about advertising or even about most campaign appearances.

These same marketing elements of political campaigning apply to hearings. Committee chairs direct their staff to research the issues and programs to which they want to draw attention. The staff find witnesses inside and outside of government who will help the chair make his or her case in public session. The staff also come up with questions and other preparatory material for the members of the committee. In other words, members hold hearings in order to advance a particular agenda. Often they are trying to expose a poorly functioning government program, while trying to persuade agency officials to alter policies. Or in a legislative hearing, they are trying to put a good first foot forward in selling a pending piece of legislation to the public and to other members of Congress. Even the most brilliant piece of legislation starts the legislative process with far fewer than the 218 (in the House) and 60 (in the Senate) supporters it ultimately needs.

Hearings are essentially the public face of a great deal of research that has been done ahead of time to advance the committee chair's agenda. (Box 10.1 shows what committee staff do in preparing and strategizing for hearings.) They are only *ostensibly* fact-finding exercises. In reality, the facts have been found; committee and subcommittee chairs are trying to place those facts in the context that best serves their interests and the interests of their party. They are using the public forum of the hearing as a way to *market* their legislative and oversight agendas, just as campaign advertising serves to market candidates.

*Bringing Attention to Issues*

If hearings are not fact-finding exercises, but rather are fact-*exposing* exercises, how do members of Congress set up hearings to maximize this role?

As their first and most important goal, members want to gain the attention of the target audience, which may be a specific interest group or groups, other members of Congress, the general public or some targeted segment of it, or some combination of these. There are different ways for hearings to find their audience, but in all cases publicity—through the mass media, specific media outlets, or trade publications—is the key (see Box 10.1). The target audience has to be drawn in. For example, if a hearing is meant to criticize administration policy regarding funding research on Parkinson's disease, will more media attend if the committee brings in major university researchers who can explain in scientific detail why more money is needed or if a movie and television star like Michael J. Fox, who suffers from the disease, appears in a public session? Asking the question itself almost serves to answer it.

Congressional committee staff will have talked to scientists and are likely to have one or two testify at some point in order to get their views on the record, but the main thrust of the hearing is bringing in the celebrity so that the media will

---

## BOX 10.1
### Staff Preparation and Hearing Follow-Up

Congressional committee staff are responsible for putting on hearings. They try to leave as little to chance as possible. To the extent possible, the hearing is meant to convey a specific message, and it takes a lot of work to make that happen. Experienced House oversight staffers provided the following before-during-after summary of what they do.

**PREHEARING**
- basic research and discovery
- formal and informal interviews (agency officials, private sector)
- identifying and, in some cases, preparing witnesses
- formal and informal document requests from agencies (or the private sector)
- pitches to the media to cover the hearing
- developing the staff report
- brief and prepare committee members, write statements and questions

**DURING THE HEARING**
- chair's or ranking member's statement
- member questions and follow-up
- documents for the record
- staff report made public
- gain commitment from the witnesses for specific follow-through

**POSTHEARING**
- press release
- questions for the record (requiring agency responses)
- requests for additional documents from agencies (or private sector)
- letter to the Appropriations Committee regarding program in question (possibly recommend increase or cut in funds)
- possible follow-up request to the GAO to audit program in question

cover it more broadly and people—members of Congress as well as the general public—will be aware of the issue. In this way, the chair hopes public pressure will be brought to bear to rally support for his or her objective.

Congressional committees have brought in Michael J. Fox to advocate for more Parkinson's research money, Sheryl Crow to talk about copyright issues, and Ben Affleck to inform them about the genomic revolution. Each of these celebrities had an interest in the issue at hand, even if he or she was not a technical expert. And in all these cases, the portion of the hearing that featured them got a great deal more attention than the testimony from subsequent panels of witnesses that included scientists, lawyers, interest group advocates, and technical experts from the agencies.

The same principles apply when committee chairs request the testimony of a cabinet official—say, the secretary of defense—who oversees a vast bureaucracy with a multibillion-dollar budget and thousands of employees. The cabinet secretary will garner far more attention from the media, and in turn shine a light on the issue in question, than the anonymous technical experts in the agency. The technical person will certainly have been consulted or even deposed, but he or she may not be valuable as a witness. If technical matters come up in the hearing that the top official cannot answer, he or she is required to provide the committee with answers within a short period of time. The committee can thus add technical details to the official record without necessarily having to summon the experts in person.

The idea is to draw attention and advance an agenda, and actors, athletes, models, and cabinet officials usually seem to do this better than experts. It is not always necessary to have a celebrity witness, especially if the target audience is narrow and requires only local or specialized coverage. But in any case, hearings may have little more substance than most election campaign advertising, and they are often almost as scripted. The simple lesson is that public relations and marketing are every bit as important in moving policy priorities forward in the US Congress as they are in winning over voters in an election campaign or selling beer to consumers.

## Scheduling Hearings

It is up to the discretion of the committee or subcommittee chair to decide when and whether to hold hearings. Having said that, certain hearings are scheduled on a fairly regular basis every year, although their content varies depending on circumstances. As we saw in Chapter 8, the Appropriations subcommittees in the two chambers must work on funding bills each and every year. A given subcommittee may handle the funding for two or three cabinet-level departments and a dozen or more agencies. Invariably, from February to May every year, agency heads and

other important officials march up to the Hill to appear in front of the subcommittees to defend the president's budget request and answer questions about how
they are implementing existing programs.

In the defense world, not only must the armed services defend their budgets to
the appropriators on Capitol Hill, but the top brass are subjected each year to authorization hearings. The Armed Services Committees on the Hill work on annual
comprehensive authorizing legislation; US Army, Air Force, Navy, and Marine leadership expect to appear in front of the Armed Services subcommittees (and often
the full committee) every year. Similarly, departments or agencies whose multiyear
authorizations expire in a given year can also plan on being summoned to appear
at hearings to have their work examined.

On any given day, however, many of the hearings on Capitol Hill are much
more discretionary. All agencies have to be on their toes, particularly when things
go awry with their programs, because the committees with jurisdiction are likely
to be interested in bringing problems to light. Box 10.2 provides a good example of a congressional response to headline-making news that affected a federal
agency—the Consumer Product Safety Commission. In this case, we can see Congress using oversight as a way to inform both its authorizing and its appropriations
processes.

An agency head knows that an article in the *Washington Post* exposing wasteful
spending or malfeasance of some sort in his or her agency is likely to elicit an invitation to appear in front of a congressional committee. For example, the breakout
of hostilities in Syria led to a congressional response, including a request to have
the secretary of state and other high-ranking official explain the administration
policy. When the General Services Administration spent lavishly at a conference (as
was in the news in 2012), congressional committees put top agency officials on the
hot seat, just as they did with the director of the Secret Service when agents were
found to have been soliciting prostitutes in Colombia.

The aftermath of Hurricane Katrina led to dozens of hearings, most involving
an almost inquisition-like atmosphere for the top officials at the Federal Emergency Management Agency whose responses were considered insufficient. The
Senate Committee on Homeland Security and Governmental Affairs alone held 22
hearings (and deposed more than 300 people) on the matter and produced a highly
critical 737-page report that recommended wholesale changes in the management
of FEMA and other agencies involved.

So, as we have seen, hearings are often held in response to events, but they may
also simply be driven by the whims of the chairs. If an issue interests a chair, he or
she will try to draw attention to it. Hearings are a good way to accomplish that end.
Chairs who do not like administration policy or program implementation in their
area of jurisdiction can call a hearing.

## What Do Hearings Look Like?

A great deal may be at stake for an agency at a committee or subcommittee hearing. In probing into a program, Congress may be contemplating a funding cut or other legal restrictions on agency actions. Members may also be intent on embarrassing witnesses in order to get them to change their behavior. It is a high-pressure environment, and the playing field is not level.

"The witness is not in the driver's seat at a hearing," one committee staffer said.[4] Although agency people have an opportunity to share what they know, the hearing is really not about the witnesses; it is about what the members of the committee want and what they have to say, whether in prodding the witness or in acting on behalf of constituents. Remember, the point of the hearing is to promote the agenda of the chair and often the interests of his or her party.

Given all of this, it is surprising that hearings often have a fairly informal flavor. Most hearings do not have Michael J. Fox or a well-known cabinet secretary testifying; more often a lesser-known agency official or interest group representative is testifying. As a result, even though every hearing is important to some members of Congress or some agency or some group in society affected by a government program, most hearings do not attract the attention of the general public or the mass media.

Members stroll into and out of hearings. Sometimes they ask a question and then leave before the answer is completed. Or they ask a question and turn to whisper to a staff member sitting behind them or another member while the witness nervously responds. The attending public must be quiet, but people do shuffle in and out of hearings whenever they want. This environment can be rather unnerving for the inexperienced witness.

It should be noted that the absence of members from hearings does not mean they are being lazy. In fact, the opposite is usually true. Their schedules are chock-a-block with fundraising events and meetings with key constituent groups, administration officials, and congressional leaders—and other hearings. Sometimes a member has two or more hearings to go to *at the same time*. Not every hearing rises to the top of the priority list, and sometimes it can be impossible for a member to stay the whole time.

Hearing procedures vary from committee to committee, but they tend to be fairly uniform in the House and to follow a similar overall framework. The committee or subcommittee chair opens the proceedings by announcing the purpose of the hearing, after which the witness delivers his or her testimony, usually a summary of detailed testimony submitted to the committee before the hearing. Sometimes several witnesses appear at one time—a "panel." These witnesses all briefly summarize their testimony. Members then have the opportunity to ask questions.

BOX 10.2
## CPSC Head Gets Grilled

Members will almost always demand to hear from an agency head when things go wrong—especially when the issue hits home with constituents, as in this case concerning the safety of children's toys. This article, published on the ombwatch.org website on September 25, 2007, provides a good description of how hearings can fit into all facets of the board of directors' activities—funding, authorizing, and oversight. And, in this case, committees in both chambers get into the act.

### CONGRESS HEARS PLEAS FOR EXPANDED AUTHORITY AND RESOURCES AT CPSC

A proliferation of children's product recalls due to potentially dangerous exposure to lead has left many turning to the federal government for answers. The Consumer Product Safety Commission (CPSC) has borne much of the brunt for the regulatory failures. Congress is considering solutions including new federal standards for lead, expanding the agency's regulatory authority and increasing agency resources. Currently, CPSC regulations ban the use of lead paint in many products, including toys. Children may also be exposed to lead in jewelry. CPSC has initiated a rulemaking which would ban lead in jewelry. While that rule moves through the regulatory pipeline, CPSC has begun a campaign of voluntary recalls focusing on reducing lead exposure in children's products.

However, neither CPSC regulations nor enforcement practices have kept up with a changing marketplace dominated by Chinese imports. Subsequently, a large number of children's products containing lead have found their way into American households. In these cases, CPSC has had to resort to voluntary recalls, in which the agency works with toy manufacturers and distributors in order to publicize a recall and work to remove tainted products from the market.

In 2007, CPSC has negotiated at least 43 recalls of children's products—from toys to school supplies to jewelry—containing lead, according to CPSC recall announcements. Those 43 recalls have involved approximately 10.8 million products, 84 percent of which were manufactured in China.

The product failures have spurred congressional oversight. Both the House and the Senate have held hearings focusing on children's exposure to lead from toys, jewelry and other products.

The Senate Appropriations Committee Subcommittee on Financial Services and General Government held a hearing on Sept. 12. One panel of witnesses included CPSC Acting Chairman Nancy Nord. Subcommittee members questioned Nord on a new agreement CPSC has negotiated with its Chinese counterpart. Under the agreement, the Chinese agency, the General Administration of Quality Supervision, Inspection and Quarantine, has pledged to work to eliminate lead in toys manufactured in China.

Senators inquired as to whether the agreement would yield actual benefits in the form of safer toys. Nord could not provide a straightforward answer. On multiple occasions, Nord instructed the subcommittee to "ask the Chinese."

Another panel included Mattel chairman Robert Eckert, Toy Industry Association president Carter Keithley, and Consumers Union counsel Sally Greenberg. Eckert was forthright in acknowledging his company had allowed lead-tainted products on the market and

BOX 10.2 *(Continued)*
## CPSC Head Gets Grilled

apologized for the mistakes. All witnesses expressed full-throated support for a strong and well-resourced CPSC.

During the hearing, ranking member Sam Brownback (R-KS) urged CPSC to "pull out the heavy club" and do a better job enforcing current regulations. Sen. Richard Durbin (D-IL), chairman of the subcommittee, closed the hearing by saying that China, the CPSC and Congress had failed, and he encouraged greater federal involvement: "There are moments when we need government, when we need someone to make certain that the products on the shelves are always going to be safe for our families and our kids. We need to step up to that responsibility."

On Sept. 19 and 20, the House Energy and Commerce Committee Subcommittee on Commerce, Trade and Consumer Protection held a two-day hearing on lead paint in children's toys. Congressmen from both parties were critical of CPSC and the toy industry. Committee Chair John Dingell (D-MI) scolded Nord for being too trustworthy of China, saying, "We have a fistful of promises from China."

Congressmen and witnesses also discussed legislative solutions. One proposed solution would require toys be certified for safety by an independent third party before the products could be sold. Gary Knell, president of the Sesame Workshop, announced his company would begin the process voluntarily.

Sen. Mark Pryor (D-AR) has introduced the CPSC Reform Act of 2007 (S. 2045). The bill would mandate third-party certification for children's products. It would also ban the presence of lead in children's products and tighten the standard for lead in all paints to 0.009 percent from the current 0.06 percent standard. The legislation goes beyond children's products and lead issues and addresses some of the broader problems plaguing CPSC. Pryor's legislation would also provide CPSC expanded ability to assess civil penalties for parties in violation of CPSC standards. The legislation would also mandate an expansion in appropriations for CPSC.

CPSC's eroding resources have been cited as a reason for the agency's inability to properly ensure product safety. The agency's budget is half of what it was in the 1970s when accounting for inflation. CPSC's staff, once near 1,000, is now 420.

President George W. Bush's proposed budget for FY 2008 would exacerbate this problem. CPSC's budget for FY 2007 was $62,728,000. Bush has proposed a new funding level of $63,250,000 for FY 2008, a cut when taking inflation into account. Bush's budget proposes a cut in staff down to 401.

Congress is attempting to counter the president on his proposed cuts. In their respective versions of the Financial Services and General Government Appropriations bills, the House proposed $66,838,000 for CPSC, and the Senate proposed $70,000,000 for FY 2008. Bush has repeatedly indicated he will veto appropriations bills exceeding his requests.

Pryor's legislation would mandate an increase in staff to at least 500 full-time employees by the beginning of FY 2014. It would also mandate an increase in appropriations to $141,725,000 by FY 2015. The legislation has not yet been considered by the Senate Commerce, Science and Transportation Committee.

The chair starts, often with a statement followed by questions for the witness or witnesses. The ranking member follows. After that, each member, either in order of seniority alternating between parties or in order of attendance at the hearing if some members arrive late, are given five minutes to ask questions. In the Senate, some committees have slightly different rules, and the enforcement of the time limits is often more relaxed.

Most hearings last only two or three hours, with one or two panels of witnesses. Most witnesses will be chosen by the majority party. Some that deal with more controversial topics and more complex issues require more witnesses and last longer. Some hearings may go on for days or weeks—although this is rare. Extended hearings are usually the result of investigations into major scandals or allegations of extensive malfeasance. Occasionally, controversial nominations to the Supreme Court or to cabinet-level positions result in multiday confirmation hearings.

### Testifying at Hearings

As suggested earlier, hearings are important regardless of the surrounding atmosphere. Of course, some attract worldwide attention, such as the hearings into the Watergate break-in in the 1970s, the Iran-Contra scandal in the 1980s, or the impeachment of President Clinton in the 1990s, but even relatively casual and ill-attended hearings are likely to be very significant to particular groups or agencies.

For a given agency, *every* hearing involving its business is momentous. Certainly, if the hearing is about an agency's budget or a pending reauthorization bill, anything is fair game and the agency officials who testify need to be thoroughly briefed. Funding levels and key provisions in the authorization law may hang in the balance. Preparation for a hearing is a significant undertaking at an agency. The witness, either the agency head or other supervisory personnel, does not necessarily know every detail of the programs under examination. As a result, the briefing process spearheaded by the agency's congressional affairs staff is often intense.

Furthermore, and most important, because hearings are a stage for the representatives or senators, witnesses need to be mindful of the political climate. Members may be examining programs for a host of reasons. Though issues may be technical in nature, members are more often interested in programs that affect their constituents or have larger political ramifications. Remember: the chair is calling the hearing for a reason. Even hearings that are conducted regularly, such as those by appropriations subcommittees, go in the directions that the chair and other members want. Witnesses need to be aware of issues such as what is going on with each member on the committee or subcommittee, what the two parties are fighting about at the time, and what kinds of questions each member tends to ask.

Ideally, experienced agency heads and their legislative affairs officers have developed good relations with key congressmen and staffers that enable them to anticipate better the line of questioning. Often friendly staff alert witnesses to the sort of questions that will be asked or even solicit potential questions from the agency. Although most oversight hearings are not particularly friendly confrontations between the branches, good relationship building with staff and members can help an agency mitigate congressional criticism and possible negative legislative ramifications down the road.

## The Many Faces of Hearings

The bottom line is that hearings are an important part of all three of Congress's main responsibilities—funding, authorizing, and oversight. Even though most hearings are carefully structured and orchestrated by the committee staff, the performance of the witnesses is crucial. The chair is trying to advance a legislative or oversight agenda by shining a light on a particular agency activity. As a result, government officials need to be aware of what is going on and be ready to defend their position or offer possible solutions to problems that Congress identifies.

In effect, hearings are a way for the people's elected representatives to hold powerful *unelected* people—cabinet secretaries, agency heads, top military brass—accountable to the public. Because of the complex nature of so much of what government does, Congress gives the executive branch tremendous discretion. One way for Congress to try to change how agencies exercise their discretion is to hold a hearing that puts their decision making in a bad light. Public embarrassment can be enough to force an agency to change its ways or to be more careful about consulting with Congress in the future before moving forward on major initiatives.

Hearing transcripts—the verbatim records of what officials say in response to congressional questions—are very useful for Congress as well. Congressional staff report that they sometimes consult hearing transcripts and other official agency documents to see what the experts wish to see in law as they put legislation together.[5]

Congressional committee staff who become interested in addressing certain aspects of government programs often work hard to persuade their boss to hold a hearing on the subject. This is how they force at least some members of the committee or subcommittee to focus on the matter. (No members want to look uninformed in a public setting, so they will agree to spend time learning the issue.) Getting members to focus on something is very important—it puts agency officials and other interested parties on the alert and can pay real dividends in terms of good public policy and legislative changes down the road.

\* \* \*

Hearings should be thought of as part of the ongoing communication between the executive and legislative branches. Congress directs the executive through legislation, but in so doing must give it a great deal of leeway. It has an interest in checking up on the agencies, just as the agencies have an interest in checking in with the legislative branch. Agencies would like to stave off unfriendly hearings so that their funds will not be cut or their hands will not be tied in restrictive legislation. Disagreements inevitably arise, and Congress will wish to dig deeper and use hearings to publicize its findings. Good relations with Congress can help agencies reduce the frequency and impact of the often adversarial and unfriendly hearing environment.

## CONGRESS INVESTIGATES: THE SENATE AND THE IRS

In the fall of 1997 and spring of 1998, the Senate Finance Committee conducted an aggressive investigation of the Internal Revenue Service, the largest agency in the Treasury Department, and that investigation culminated in a series of hearings. It is instructive to look at Congress's actions at this time, as these hearings exemplify the range of motivations that drive congressional oversight.

Congress has always had a complicated relationship with the IRS. On the one hand, the agency's tax-collecting responsibility gives it one of the most essential of government functions. After all, the government cannot provide the services it does without revenue from individual income taxes, corporate levies, and other forms of taxation. Because the overwhelming majority of Americans faithfully pay their taxes, Congress is motivated to give the IRS the authority to track down those companies and individuals who cheat. On the other hand, no one likes to pay taxes, so complaints from constituents about overzealous IRS agents resonate with the board of directors. The result is that Congress wavers between pushing for more aggressive enforcement of tax laws and pressuring the agency to take it easy on taxpayers when complaints of IRS abuses are frequent.

In 1997 the pendulum seemed to have swung far over to the side of taxpayers and against the IRS. Conservative Republicans were feeling their oats after having taken over Congress in the 1994 elections. It was time, in their view, to show that they were serious about radical reform of the tax code, which they criticized as a drag on economic efficiency for being overly complex and much too burdensome and costly to comply with.[6]

It had come to the Senate Finance Committee's attention through complaints from private citizens and from agency whistleblowers that the agency was too often heavy-handed in its tax-collection practices.[7] The Finance Committee's chairman, Senator William Roth of Delaware, thought it was about time to hold some hearings exposing what his staff had found. This would be good politics, he felt, for Republicans (the administration was Democratic at the time, and the IRS commissioner was a Clinton appointee), it might motivate better behavior on the part of agency officials, and it might lay the groundwork for a larger legislative overhaul of the agency and the tax code. There were even some prominent Republicans, including then–House majority leader Dick Armey of Texas and House Commerce Committee chair Billy Tauzin of Louisiana, who were trying to generate interest in a movement to eliminate the IRS and replace the existing tax code wholesale.

## September 1997: The Hearings Begin

> It was, as theater, reminiscent of those great old mob trials—back when the mob really meant something. Wearing black cotton hoods, six witnesses filed into a Senate chamber last week to tell an astonishing tale of corruption and abuse of power. But this wasn't about the Mafia; this was about mainstream America. It was all the more frightening that the witnesses weren't colorful thugs like Jimmy the Weasel or Sammy the Bull, but solid citizens who, acting as Internal Revenue Service agents across the nation, had wives, kids, well-tended yards. And, it seems, scruples. Seated behind a screen, their voices altered electronically—most sounded like Munchkins with Deep South accents—the whistle-blowers heaped dirt on their employer. They told of an IRS that is a virtual police state within a democracy, a Borgia-like fiefdom of tax terror at the heart of the U.S. economy.[8]

This was how *Newsweek* reported the proceedings. Agency witnesses went on at length about IRS agents framing innocent taxpayers in order to meet "production" quotas. They talked about supervisors waiving multimillion-dollar tax liabilities for companies they hoped would hire them at lucrative salaries when they left the agency. The whistleblowers told of the agency policy of hounding poorer taxpayers while auditing only a tiny percentage of wealthier people. These witnesses were concerned for their own safety.

Ordinary citizens testified too. They told of being hounded for a decade or more to pay taxes that they did not actually owe. One woman told of being forced into bankruptcy and divorce. Tom Savage, a Delaware builder, had an illegal lien placed on his property by the IRS, which ultimately cost him hundreds of thousands of dollars.[9]

The acting IRS commissioner at the time, Michael Dolan, was placed on the stand as well, and he had no defense.[10] He apologized effusively and immediately communicated his displeasure to agency supervisors in IRS offices around the country. According to contemporaneous reporting, he suspended several managers the day the hearings ended. The agency acknowledged that the quota system in place in some offices (with supervisors receiving bonuses for tax collections) was against the law and promised to correct its procedures.

Some congressional critics noted that the Finance Committee was not able to document with any precision how widespread the abuses were.[11] Were these isolated instances? Or was this behavior epidemic in the agency? No one kept or could find complete statistics. In any case, the effect was immediate. Aggressive congressional oversight based on more than a year of investigations by committee staff yielded an immediate response from the agency. But the committee was far from done.

### Spring 1998: More Hearings and Legislative Action

In the winter, a new IRS commissioner, Charles Rossotti, was installed, replacing acting head Dolan. Drawn from the business world, Rossotti promised a new, updated, consumer-friendly approach to tax collection. He said he wanted the public to believe that the IRS took seriously the word *Service* in its name.[12]

But Senator Roth's staff had done a lot more digging, and the goals of the chairman and other top Republicans, including Majority Leader Trent Lott, were far from realized. As the *Washington Post* reported: "Some Republicans apparently hope to parlay voter dislike of the tax agency into support for an entirely new tax system, and in the meantime are finding bashing it a helpful campaign tool. House Majority Leader Richard K. Armey (R-TX) and the National Republican Senatorial Committee say last fall's hearings boosted contributions."[13]

A week of hearings was scheduled for late-April 1998. More whistleblowers came forward. This time Yvonne D. DesJardins, chief of employee and labor relations at the agency, testified openly. She said executives at the agency broke the rules and protected each other. The agency's director of equal employment opportunity had pending sexual harassment claims against him. In one case, an agent had threatened a state trooper with an audit when subjected to a routine traffic stop.[14]

Numerous tales of gun-toting agents, sometimes in groups of a half dozen or more, were related, suggesting that the agency used the most severe form of physical intimidation. Democratic senator Patrick Moynihan of New York said, "We have to be much concerned about the paramilitary performance of the IRS."[15] Tax preparers and other small businesspeople told of being targeted by the IRS because of complaints apparently lodged by competitors and vengeance seekers.

In the most dramatic testimony of the week, former Senate majority leader Howard Baker (R-TN) was brought forward to tell of how a rogue IRS agent tried to frame him and other Tennessee politicians on money-laundering and bribery charges. That agent did not lose his job initially—he was relieved of his duties only after an arrest for suspected possession of cocaine years later.[16]

The hearings were handled with "gotcha" tactics. Normally, congressional committees inform an agency ahead of time who its witnesses will be in oversight hearings; in this case, no heads-up was given. The agency was left scrambling. Commissioner Rossotti held an impromptu press conference after the second day of hearings, promising to get to the bottom of some of the allegations.[17] He immediately formed an independent task force to look into agency procedure and protocols. At the end of the hearings, he asked Congress for new laws giving him more authority over agency personnel.

## Legislative Action Resulting from the Hearings

The impact of the hearings was considerable. In 1997 the House had passed reform legislation, but it had not been acted on by the full Senate. In 1998, after the second round of hearings, impetus developed for much wider-ranging reforms. The *Washington Post* reported, "Using uncommonly derisive language against an agency run by his own administration, [President] Clinton showed in his weekly radio address that he is determined not to be outdone by Republicans in voicing scorn for out-of-bounds tax collectors."[18] Clinton had originally opposed Republican reform efforts; the hearings seemed to bring him into the negotiations on the Hill.

The bill did not do everything some Republicans had wanted; certainly, it did not abolish the agency and the tax code along with it. But those who wanted those sorts of changes cited progress toward their goal. The reform law, signed by President Clinton on July 22, 1998, contained several service-related changes, including bolstering the Office of the Taxpayer Advocate, limiting interest charges on outstanding tax liability (which some believed to be exorbitant), changing the burden-of-proof standard in some court cases, and establishing an independent agency oversight board.[19]

In the end, Senator Roth was able to bring about some significant changes at the IRS. The committee continued to receive a great deal of criticism for its selective use of witnesses and its inability to substantiate every charge with accuracy or to demonstrate the pervasiveness of the abuses it alleged were happening. But no one doubted the brilliance or effectiveness of the political theatrics. The senator had a story to tell, and he told it well. He believed that the culture of the agency needed an overhaul, and the point was well taken. The agency took some voluntary actions to address committee concerns, and it asked for certain legislative remedies. The theatrics helped to jump-start the legislative process, with the president signing on to the most far-reaching legislation affecting the agency in decades.

## OTHER METHODS FOR GETTING RESULTS THROUGH OVERSIGHT

As we mentioned at the beginning of this chapter, there are a few different means of congressional oversight. We have already discussed the most public face of congressional oversight—hearings. In the following section, we outline a few of the other methods, like including specific explicit directions for agency officials to follow in legislation; using so-called extracongressional sources for some of its oversight, in particular the Government Accountability Office; and other more informal methods of oversight used by some members of Congress.

### Oversight in Legislation and Report Language

Like a board of directors might do with business initiatives, if Congress wants to make sure that government programs are carried out the way it wants, it can make administrative details clear in law. Although presidents often bristle at what they

---

### EXHIBIT 10.1

**Oversight in Legislation: Instructions to Customs and Border Protection**

---

**BORDER SECURITY FENCING, INFRASTRUCTURE, AND TECHNOLOGY**

For expenses for customs and border protection fencing, infrastructure, and technology, $400,000,000, to remain available until September 30, 2014: *Provided*, **That of the total amount provided under this heading, $60,000,000 shall not be obligated until the Committees on Appropriations of the Senate and the House of Representatives receive a detailed plan for expenditure, prepared by the Commissioner of U.S. Customs and Border Protection, and submitted not later than 90 days after the date of the enactment of this Act, for a program to establish and maintain a security barrier along the borders of the United States of fencing and vehicle barriers, where practicable, and other forms of tactical infrastructure and technology.**

SOURCE: FY 2012 Appropriations Act for Homeland Security.

NOTE: The Appropriations Committees put teeth in their request for administrative details by "fencing off" a large portion of the money ($60 million) pending approval of the plan for the border fencing. This sort of arrangement, as described in the text, constitutes an unconstitutional legislative veto, but is unlikely to be challenged by the agency or department.

regard as infringements on the flexibility they claim to need to carry out laws in the most effective and efficient manner, if they sign a law that includes specific instructions, they are left with little choice but to do what Congress says.[20]

Exhibit 10.1 shows a provision in appropriations legislation for fiscal year 2012 in which Congress stipulates that Customs and Border Protection (CBP), an agency within the Department of Homeland Security, must provide for approval a "detailed plan for expenditure" planning for and implementing border fencing. This is a classic example of the legislative branch delving into details of the execution of law that it normally would leave to the agencies. At the time, the Department of Homeland Security had been under heavy fire for its unresponsiveness to congressional criticisms of the way it was administering its programs, and it was in this climate that the requirements seen in Exhibit 10.1 were put on it.

Usually, Congress's actions in this area are relatively mundane, as shown in Exhibit 10.2, taken from the fiscal year 2012 appropriation for the National Endowment for the Arts. It contains administrative detail, to be sure, but not a full-fledged blueprint for a major program, as with the CBP and the border-fencing plan.

---

## EXHIBIT 10.2

### Oversight in Appropriations Law for the National Endowment for the Arts

---

**ADMINISTRATIVE PROVISIONS**

None of the funds appropriated to the National Foundation on the Arts and the Humanities may be used to process any grant or contract documents which do not include the text of 18 U.S.C. 1913: *Provided,* **That none of the funds appropriated to the National Foundation on the Arts and the Humanities may be used for official reception and representation expenses:** *Provided further,* **That funds from nonappropriated sources may be used as necessary for official reception and representation expenses:** *Provided further,* **That the Chairperson of the National Endowment for the Arts may approve grants of up to $10,000, if in the aggregate this amount does not exceed 5 percent of the sums appropriated for grant-making purposes per year:** *Provided further,* That such small grant actions are taken pursuant to the terms of an expressed and direct delegation of authority from the National Council on the Arts to the Chairperson.

SOURCE: FY 2012 Interior, Environment, and Related Agencies Appropriation.

NOTE: The highlighted area typifies the normal oversight instructions given agencies in appropriations law. Most administrative detail is left to the agency.

Far more often, Congress relies on nonstatutory suggestions in report language attached to legislation to influence the administration of the law. Exhibit 10.3 shows two examples of what agencies consider to be congressional efforts to micromanage program administration. The first involves the Office of the Federal Detention Trustee, an agency within the Department of Justice. The second involves NASA. In both cases from FY 2012 appropriations bills, Congress through the appropriations committees is looking to keep very close tabs on how agencies account for the spending of appropriated funds.

When agencies resist the instructions in report language, the committee sometimes comes back the next year and makes the requirements statutory (sometimes using the legislative veto technique described below), leaving no room for the flexibility or dialogue between the agency and Congress that can arise from nonstatutory provisions.

## The Legislative Veto

The micromanagement of the CBP shown in Exhibit 10.1 is an example of what is often described as a "legislative veto." Congress put into law provisions that gave the Appropriations Committees the ability to reject the administrative actions proposed or taken by the agency. The legislative veto is used when Congress acknowledges an agency's prerogative to run government programs, but retains the power to veto the actions taken by the agency. The veto may be exercised by a committee or by one or both of the houses of Congress (depending on how the legislation is written). Political scientist Michael John Berry describes three types of legislative vetoes:

> The legislature empowers an executive agency with certain discretionary policy-making responsibilities. Following this legislative authorization, the agency has latitude in terms of how it chooses to implement policies within its jurisdiction. Negative legislative vetoes allow the policies delegated to administrative agencies to be implemented unless Congress takes some action to veto a specific action. . . . Affirmative legislative vetoes require certain administrative actions or decisions to be first submitted to Congress for congressional approval. Absent the approval of Congress, administrative agencies are not permitted to continue making policy with respect to the functions requiring congressional consent. . . . Deliberative legislative vetoes require congressional notification of proposed administrative actions . . . prior to their execution.[21]

Legislative vetoes were commonly put into legislation in the middle decades of the 20th century and generally served the interests of both branches. The executive

# EXHIBIT 10.3

## Oversight in Report Language

### THE OFFICE OF THE FEDERAL DETENTION TRUSTEE

The conference agreement includes $1,580,595,000 for the Office of the Federal Detention Trustee (OFDT).

The conferees are aware that OFDT's resource needs are directly impacted by law enforcement and prosecutorial priorities, such as increases in immigration enforcement by [DHS] and efforts to combat drug and gun smuggling along the Southwest Border. However, the conferees remain concerned about the Department's ability to anticipate the true funding needs for this account. **The conferees expect OFDT to keep the Committees on Appropriations apprised of changes in average daily population forecasts so that resource requirements for fiscal year 2012 and beyond can be verified and refined, particularly with regard to the impacts of law enforcement initiatives on the Southwest Border.** The conferees direct OFDT to resume providing quarterly reports to the Committees on Appropriations, which shall include the actual number of individuals in the detention system and the annualized associated costs.

### NATIONAL AERONAUTICS AND SPACE ADMINISTRATION

**Adjustments to [Multipurpose Crew Vehicle] and**
**[Space Launch System] Funding**
**Funds provided in this Act for MPCV and SLS are intended for the actual design and development of the vehicles themselves.** Therefore, the conferees direct that the charging of related expenses to these program lines be kept to a minimum. Any funds deducted from the total to pay for civil service labor, [NASA] headquarters program support, program integration, mission operations, extravehicular activities or other related expenses must be separately delineated both in the spending plan . . . and in all future requests. The conference agreement provides a statutory set-aside for SLS ground operations; therefore no additional charges to SLS funding for this purpose is permitted. All activities funded with ground operations set-aside shall primarily serve the SLS program.

SOURCE: FY 2012 Appropriation for Commerce, Justice, and Science—Joint Explanatory Statement.

NOTE: Congressional oversight instructions are more commonly found in report language attached to appropriations bills and often get into the nitty-gritty of agency funding requirements, particularly in an era of scarce resources. In the first instance, the committees require the OFDT to report on the number of people detained so that they have a better sense of what to appropriate. In the second, the committees are requiring NASA to spend appropriations in this account for the specific vehicle projects themselves and as little as possible for associated expenses.

got the delegated authority it wanted, and Congress had a relatively easy way, if so inclined, to meddle with subsequent agency policy making.

The problem was that the legislative veto was ruled unconstitutional in 1983 (*Chadha v. U.S.*). The Supreme Court said that when Congress delegates authority in law to the agencies, it must go through the full-fledged legislative process (passage in both houses and the president's signature) to retract that delegation of power. It cannot "veto" executive actions just by a vote of the House or Senate or a single committee.

Still, Congress continues to put what amount to legislative vetoes into law—more frequently than ever before, in fact.[22] Probably the most common sort of legislative veto in the 21st century appears in appropriations bills. Typically, the wording is like that seen in the first paragraph of Exhibit 10.1:

> For expenses for customs and border protection fencing, infrastructure, and technology, $400,000,000, to remain available until September 30, 2014: *Provided, That of the amount provided under this heading, $60,000,000 shall not be obligated until the Committees on Appropriations of the Senate and the House of Representatives receive a detailed plan* for expenditure, prepared by the Commissioner of Customs and Border Protection, and submitted not later than 90 days after the date of the enactment of this Act.

The aim of the italicized section is to accomplish what appropriators describe as **"fencing off" funds**. Congress is, in law, providing the agency with $400 million, but giving itself the ability to deny $60 million of that amount simply by a decision of the Appropriations Committees to reject the agency's administrative plan of action.

As noted, this is probably unconstitutional—technically, Congress needs to go through the legislative process in order to reject an administrative plan. But in reality, the agency has little choice.[23] It must square its plan with a particular subset of Congress or risk losing a great deal of its funding.

## The GAO and Oversight: The Case of For-Profit Higher Education

As noted in the last chapter, the GAO is a critical part of Congress's efforts to keep track of what is going on in the federal government. For the most part, the GAO does longer-term audits of the performance of government programs after receiving requests from committee chairs or ranking members. They also do a lot of work mandated in law by Congress.

In the larger oversight picture, GAO reports are used to highlight issues that members, usually committee chairs, are interested in. GAO personnel often testify in hearings about their findings. A recent example of an influential GAO report occurred in 2010. It involved a request for an investigation by Senate Health, Education, Labor, and Pensions Committee chair Tom Harkin. The report is excerpted in Box 10.3.

Harkin held numerous hearings highlighting the incendiary findings about the practices of some for-profit colleges. He brought a 29-year-old divorced mother of twins to the committee to testify about the $21,000 in debt she accrued from one college—before she learned it wasn't accredited. In the end, in 2011 the Education Department responded by revising existing regulations that would cut off federal money to schools whose graduates too often cannot make enough money to pay back loans.[24]

## Informal Methods of Oversight

Putting requirements into law is most effective way to try to influence executive branch agencies as they go about their business of implementing government programs, but that is not always possible for all sorts of reasons; first and foremost among these reasons is that the legislative process is often too cumbersome to navigate. Nonstatutory report language in an appropriations bill also sends a very clear message to the agencies: if you do not do what we say, we may cut your funding or tie your hands in law next year.

And as we have seen, hearings can be effective in getting agencies to change policy without having to "go the distance" and produce legislation, which would not be able to anticipate all eventualities anyway. But members have all sorts of policy preferences, receive an enormous number of requests from constituents, and are always trying to get agencies to do more for their districts and states. Even hearings involve a great deal of heavy lifting, and often members' needs cannot wait. If this is the case, they may try more informal means of moving things along in an agency.

Members will sometimes act on their own to try to get results. Iowa Republican senator Charles Grassley's office focuses on oversight like no other on Capitol Hill. When the senator catches wind of what he regards as poor program implementation, a waste of taxpayer dollars, or shoddy regulatory practices, he does everything he can to shine a light on the problem, even if he is not on the committee of jurisdiction. He is famous for his efforts to ferret out waste and fraud at the Defense Department, for instance, even though he is not a member of the Armed Services Committee. We noted last chapter (see Box 9.3) Grassley's interest in the Food and Drug Administration, the agency responsible for approving drugs and keeping the food supply safe; its chief overseer in the Senate is the Health, Education, Labor, and Pensions Committee—a panel, once again, on which Grassley does not serve.

314

---

## BOX 10.3

### The GAO Digs into the World
### of For-Profit Colleges

In response to a request from the Senate Health, Education, Labor, and Pensions Committee, the GAO looked into the practices of for-profit colleges. The final product, "Undercover Testing Finds Colleges Encouraged Fraud and Engaged in Deceptive and Questionable Marketing Practices" (by Gregory D. Kutz), was made public in August 2010. The summary of the audit is reproduced below:

> Enrollment in for-profit colleges has grown from about 365,000 students to almost 1.8 million in the last several years. These colleges offer degrees and certifications in programs ranging from business administration to cosmetology. In 2009, students at for-profit colleges received more than $4 billion in Pell Grants and more than $20 billion in federal loans provided by the Department of Education. GAO was asked to 1) conduct undercover testing to determine if for-profit colleges' representatives engaged in fraudulent, deceptive, or otherwise questionable marketing practices, and 2) compare the tuitions of the for-profit colleges tested with those of other colleges in the same geographic region. To conduct this investigation, GAO investigators posing as prospective students applied for admissions at 15 for-profit colleges in 6 states and Washington, D.C. The colleges were selected based on several factors, including those that the Department of Education reported received 89 percent or more of their revenue from federal student aid. GAO also entered information on four fictitious prospective students into education search Web sites to determine what type of follow-up contact resulted from an inquiry. GAO compared tuition for the 15 for-profit colleges tested with tuition for the same programs at other colleges located in the same geographic areas. Results of the undercover tests and tuition comparisons cannot be projected to all for-profit colleges.
>
> Undercover tests at 15 for-profit colleges found that 4 colleges encouraged fraudulent practices and that all 15 made deceptive or otherwise questionable statements to GAO's undercover applicants. Four undercover applicants

BOX 10.3 *(Continued)*

## The GAO Digs into the World
## of For-Profit Colleges

were encouraged by college personnel to falsify their financial aid forms to qualify for federal aid—for example, one admissions representative told an applicant to fraudulently remove $250,000 in savings. Other college representatives exaggerated undercover applicants' potential salary after graduation and failed to provide clear information about the college's program duration, costs, or graduation rate despite federal regulations requiring them to do so. For example, staff commonly told GAO's applicants they would attend classes for 12 months a year, but stated the annual cost of attendance for 9 months of classes, misleading applicants about the total cost of tuition. Admissions staff used other deceptive practices, such as pressuring applicants to sign a contract for enrollment before allowing them to speak to a financial advisor about program cost and financing options. However, in some instances, undercover applicants were provided accurate and helpful information by college personnel, such as not to borrow more money than necessary. In addition, GAO's four fictitious prospective students received numerous, repetitive calls from for-profit colleges attempting to recruit the students when they registered with Web sites designed to link for-profit colleges with prospective students. Once registered, GAO's prospective students began receiving calls within 5 minutes. One fictitious prospective student received more than 180 phone calls in a month. Calls were received at all hours of the day, as late as 11 p.m. To see video clips of undercover applications and to hear voicemail messages from for-profit college recruiters, see http://www.gao.gov/products/GAO-10–948T. Programs at the for-profit colleges GAO tested cost substantially more for associate's degrees and certificates than comparable degrees and certificates at public colleges nearby. A student interested in a massage therapy certificate costing $14,000 at a for-profit college was told that the program was a good value. However the same certificate from a local community college cost $520. Costs at private nonprofit colleges were more comparable when similar degrees were offered.

Massachusetts Democrat Ed Markey is famous for hounding the Nuclear Regulatory Commission, forcing the agency to answer questions about safety arrangements at plants and the new reactor-license approval process.

Individual members can be effective by themselves in drawing attention to inefficiencies or malfeasance in government programs. The unfortunate fact for high-profile agencies is that they have to be prepared for inquiries not just from their committees of jurisdiction and the overarching oversight committees, but also even from aggressive individual members.

## CONCLUSION: THE POLITICS OF CONGRESSIONAL OVERSIGHT

Of the three ways in which Congress wields influence in its role as the board of directors, oversight is the most contentious. For one thing, Congress has the responsibility to make sure that programs are executed as intended, but it does not always make its intentions clear in legislation. For another, Congress has a legitimate need to look into how laws are being administered, although the line where Congress is inappropriately encroaching on executive prerogatives has never been defined precisely (see Chapter 9). And Congress, when exercising oversight, often uses imprecise and blunt nonstatutory methods—hearings, informal communications, report language, and so on—that leave a lot of wiggle room for executive discretion and interpretation and ongoing disagreement. It is also often the case that different members of Congress send conflicting signals to federal agencies.

But oversight is an effective tool for Congress, and for several reasons it is not only pervasive but sometimes the most useful or even the only way Congress can get the executive branch to do what it wants.

- First it is not practical, or even possible, for Congress to write laws that are precise enough to direct the executive in every detail, and members certainly cannot anticipate future events when passing a bill. As a result, Congress always gives the executive branch a measure of leeway to carry out a program as it sees fit. If Congress is unhappy with how that delegation of authority is managed, it may use its oversight tools to try to redirect executive action.
- Second, the members of the board are faced with a profound conundrum: Congress is not a fast-moving institution by its nature, *but the public still expects the members to respond effectively and quickly to events.* Often the only feasible way for Congress to respond is to communicate its concerns to the relevant agency handling an immediate crisis, such as a natural disaster, by means of hearings, letters, and floor speeches and

in this way pressure the agency to do what Congress wants in response to the event.

- And third, following from the second point, it is very difficult and sometimes nearly impossible for Congress to come to an agreement on important bills, to overcome a presidential veto, or even to find time to schedule floor consideration. In lieu of legislation, Congress may only be able to resort to its ability to shine a spotlight on a program in a hearing or by some other means in order to effect policy change and direct the work of government. Often there is an implied or even explicit threat that the agency may face more restrictive legislation or a funding cut down the line if it does not heed the members' wishes. In other words, oversight can be a substitute for legislative solutions when the legislative process proves too difficult to navigate. But the key is that Congress's power to compel through the law makes it impossible for agencies to ignore.

## Members and Program Efficiency

Everyone has an interest in the efficient operation of government programs. After all, who wants to see their tax money wasted? That goes for members of Congress too, especially if they can take some credit for the streamlining of a program or for improved agency responsiveness to citizen complaints and needs.

But program efficiency is not priority number one for most members. Watchdog groups in Washington as well as the GAO and the inspectors general may regard it as their primary duty to monitor government programs for poor performance, inefficiencies, and even fraud and abuse. (In fact, this is the primary duty of IGs and the GAO.) But members of Congress have other competing concerns. First and foremost is the reason they were sent to Washington in the first place: to look after the needs of their constituents. Most of them are making a career out of politics, and that requires getting reelected every two years in the House or every six years in the Senate.

As congressional scholar David Mayhew has noted, spending time looking over the shoulder of government bureaucrats and getting into the mind-numbing details of the operations of specific government programs are not tasks that usually contribute very much to the members' goal of reelection.[25] Of course, exposing egregious waste and malfeasance is good for a member's reputation and can enhance his or her prospects of reelection, but these sorts of opportunities are rare. The fact is that most voters are not interested in the detailed workings of government programs.

The bottom line is that members' precious time, as well as the time of their staff, is better spent communicating directly with voters, working on high-profile issues and issues of particular salience in the district or state, and ensuring the district's or state's fair share of federal funding on infrastructure. Auditing government programs does not usually provide the same kind of political reward.[26]

Advocating for more resources for a district or state, as almost all members do, is not necessarily consistent with the drive to ensure the most efficient conduct of government programs. If studies indicate that the addition of one lane to a highway bypass will alleviate traffic congestion in a particular city, a member of Congress may still argue for federal funds to build *two* lanes; after all, constructing two lanes would provide twice as many good-paying jobs for his or her constituents, even though the second lane would be unnecessary and would cost the taxpayer a good deal more money.

## Discerning a Pattern to Congressional Oversight

The bottom line is that focused oversight of government programs is sporadic. But there are some discernible patterns.

- If a program touches a member's district or state, he or she is much more likely to keep tabs on it. The member will try to be absolutely sure that the agency is responsive to the needs of his or her constituents and that money is going where it needs to go. As we have seen, this member will not necessarily be concerned about saving money. If jobs are involved, the member may want to see more money funneled in, even if the project could be completed with a lower expenditure.
- Major events in the world or the nation prompt congressional oversight. The Federal Emergency Management Agency came under intense scrutiny in the aftermath of Hurricane Katrina in 2005 and in the years following. Citizens and members were appalled at the agency response. Members score political points when they respond with hearings that put an agency on the hot seat, as well as when they propose legislation that addresses the weaknesses that are exposed.
- If oversight can enhance the stature of a member's party, he or she will be more aggressive in pursuing it. In times of unified government, there is typically less oversight and many fewer hearings investigating agency business. But in times of divided government, oversight increases. In 2007, when Democrats took over Congress and President Bush was still in the White House, they dramatically bolstered the oversight capacity of key committees. Republicans did the same in 2011 when they retook the House during the Obama administration. In 2012, for example, the

Oversight and Government Reform Committee and others focused on the Fast and Furious Program in the Justice Department's Bureau of Alcohol, Tobacco, and Firearms, as noted in the discussion in Chapter 9 of the contempt charges against Attorney General Eric Holder. The Energy and Commerce Committee spent much of 2011 and 2012 looking into Recovery Act loans to Solyndra, a solar-power company. The company eventually went bankrupt, costing the government hundreds of millions of dollars. Republicans believed President Obama had received a free ride from Democrats in Congress from 2009 through 2010, and they wanted to settle some scores by exposing agency misdeeds and win political points at the Democrats' expense in the process.

## The "Fire-Alarm" System

Ultimately, it is impossible for Congress to supervise every government program and uncover every instance of agency mismanagement. Having said that, a great deal of very careful and systematic oversight is done by congressional staff, the GAO, and the IGs, often behind the scenes and out of the limelight. This kind of oversight is institutionalized: it is carried out yearly by appropriations staff as they work on their annual bills, by authorizing committee staff, and by the oversight committees.

At the same time, in a free and open society such as ours, reporters looking for a good story explore what government agencies are doing, interest groups continually monitor agencies that do work that affects their issues, and academics conduct research on government programs in their realm of expertise. Congressional staff reach out and are contacted by these various sources. In the end, a sort of **"fire-alarm" system** prevails, according to political scientists, in which, however haphazardly, Congress is able to keep tabs on what government does.[27] When something goes wrong, congressional staff are likely to hear about it.

But many important matters fail to rise to the surface. It is hard to get the attention of members of Congress. Our elected representatives have complicated jobs, incredibly crowded schedules, and dozens of issues to keep track of. It is hard even for some of their staffers to get their attention. Members have to pick and choose what to give highest priority. Getting into the details of most programs to save a few dollars or to make minor improvements is not on the top of the list for most of them. What does make it to the top of their list, however, is oversight to highlight major failures, particularly when the opposing party can plausibly be blamed. Oversight in response to constituent complaints about agency responsiveness or overbearing IRS agents also rises to the top. The key when it comes to oversight, according to Mayhew, is whether members can claim credit for better program performance in a way that resonates with their constituents. For better or worse, most members find their time better spent in other ways.

---

## Questions for Discussion

1. What are the shortcomings of the so-called fire-alarm system? Why must Congress rely on it?

2. What would it take to get Congress to do oversight more systematically? Why do you think it has become so much rarer for a member to conduct oversight of a president of his or her own party, as Harry Truman did back in the 1940s?

3. Why must the board of directors often depend on oversight to get the agencies to do what it wants them to do?

---

## Suggestions for Further Reading

Kutz, Gregory D. "For-Profit Colleges: Undercover Testing Finds Colleges Encouraged Fraud and Engaged in Deceptive and Questionable Marketing Practices." Testimony Before the Committee on Health, Education, Labor, and Pensions, US Senate. Government Accountability Office, August 4, 2010. www.gao.gov/assets/130/125197.pdf.

McCubbins, Matthew, and Thomas Schwartz. "Congressional Oversight Overlooked: Police Patrol Versus Fire Alarms." *American Journal of Political Science* 28, no. 1 (1984): 165–179.

Oleszek, Walter. *Congressional Procedures and the Policy Process.* 7th ed. Washington, DC: CQ Press, 2007.

## NOTES

1. See Matthew McCubbins and Thomas Schwartz, "Congressional Oversight Overlooked: Police Patrol Versus Fire Alarms," *American Journal of Political Science* 28, no. 1 (1984): 165–179.

2. For an excellent overview of the role of hearings, see Walter Oleszek, *Congressional Procedures and the Policy Process,* 7th ed. (Washington, DC: CQ Press, 2007), chap. 3.

3. Richard Sachs, *CRS Report for Congress: Types of Committee Hearings,* Congressional Research Service, March 8, 2001.

4. Paul M. Feeney, "Crouching Hearing, Hidden Legislation," *Journal of Public Inquiry* (Spring–Summer 2002): 29.

5. Jonathan Etherton, former professional staff member on the Senate Armed Services Committee, interview with the author, April 19, 2007.

6. David Cay Johnston, "Behind IRS Hearings, a GOP Plan to End the Tax Code," *New York Times,* May 4, 1998.

7. Thomas H. Moore, "IRS Nightmares Get Senate Hearings," CNN, September 24, 1997, www.cnn.com/ALLPOLITICS/1997/09/24/irs.hearing/; Albert B. Crenshaw, "IRS Hearings to Focus on Alleged Improper Conduct," *Washington Post,* April 28, 1998, A4.

8. Michael Hirsch, "Behind the IRS Curtain," *Newsweek,* October 6, 1997, www.news week.com/id/97087/.

9. Ibid.

10. Ibid.

11. "Phantom Rogues at the IRS" (editorial), *New York Times,* August 19, 2000, http://query.nytimes.com/gst/fullpage.html?res=9E0DE5DD133EF93AA2575BC0A966 9C8B63; Albert B. Crenshaw, "An IRS Under Siege Walks a Fine Dotted Line," *Washington Post,* February 6, 1998, A1.

12. Crenshaw, "An IRS Under Siege Walks a Fine Dotted Line."

13. Crenshaw, "IRS Hearings to Focus on Alleged Improper Conduct."

14. Albert B. Crenshaw and Stephen Barr, "IRS Official Reports Agency Double Standard," *Washington Post,* April 29, 1998, A4.

15. Albert B. Crenshaw, "Alleged Victims Tell of IRS Raids That Hurt Businesses," *Washington Post,* April 30, 1998, A4.

16. Albert B. Crenshaw, "Witnesses Say IRS Agent Tried to Frame Ex-Senator," *Washington Post,* May 1, 1998, A1.

17. Crenshaw, "Alleged Victims Tell of IRS Raids That Hurt Businesses."

18. John F. Harris, "'Outraged' Clinton Vows IRS Overhaul," *Washington Post,* May 3, 1998, A1.

19. Peter Baker, "Clinton Signs IRS Overhaul into Law," *Washington Post,* July 23, 1998, A1.

20. The George W. Bush administration instigated a firestorm when it began aggressively using the presidential signing statement to assert the right to ignore parts of laws that the president believed encroached on his executive prerogatives. (Signing statements, which are commonly issued by the White House after signing a bill into law, had most frequently been used in previous administrations to explain, for example, how a president planned to implement the legislation.) Although Bush attracted a great deal of attention with his claim that he did not need to abide by everything in the laws he was signing, neither the GAO nor the CRS has found evidence that he followed through on the more controversial of his threats. The GAO's views can be found in Gary Kepplinger, "Presidential Signing Statements: Agency Implementation of Select Provisions of Law," testimony before the House Subcommittee on Oversight and Investigations, March 11, 2008, www .gao.gov/new.items/d08553t.pdf. The CRS's T. J. Halstead wrote about them in "Presidential Signing Statements: Constitutional and Institutional Implications," Congressional Research Service, September 20, 2006.

21. Michael John Berry, "Beyond Chadha: The Modern Legislative Veto as Macropolitical Conflict," paper delivered at the annual meeting of the American Political Science Association, September 2007, 11.

22. Louis Fisher, *CRS Report for Congress: Committee Controls of Agency Decisions*, Congressional Research Service, November 16, 2005.

23. The House Appropriations Committee staff aided in the development of the CBP legislative veto example.

24. Tamar Lewin, "Education Department Increases Its Regulation of For-Profit Colleges," *New York Times*, June 2, 2011, www.nytimes.com/2011/06/02/education/02gainful.html.

25. David Mayhew, *Congress: The Electoral Connection* (New Haven, CT: Yale University Press, 1974), 110–140.

26. See Terry Moe, "The Politics of Bureaucratic Structure," in *Can the Government Govern?*, edited by Jon E. Chubb and Paul E. Peterson (Washington, DC: Brookings Institution Press, 1989), esp. 278.

27. McCubbins and Schwartz, "Congressional Oversight Overlooked."

# CONGRESS AND OTHERS | 3

## 11

CHAPTER

# Congress and the President:
# The Struggle over
# Directing Public Policy

The last five chapters of this book focused on Congress's powers to direct what the federal government does. We saw that for agencies of the government to do things, they need legal authority—authority that can come only from an act of Congress. Similarly, they need Congress to give them the funds to do the work they are authorized to do. And Congress relies on the implied power of oversight to encourage agencies to "do the right thing," at least as key members of Congress see it.

The interesting thing about our system of government is that these agencies and the officials who work in them do not for the most part answer directly to the legislative branch. The chain of command in the executive branch goes from the people in the agencies running federal programs on a day-to-day basis up to the top leadership of those agencies and departments (most of whom were appointed by the president, some requiring Senate confirmation) to the president himself. And to be clear: the president certainly likes to think of himself as having a say over the direction of federal policy.

And in fact, the president would be right—he has a good many tools to influence federal policy in any area, such as education, health, defense, transportation, space, and so on. It is most certainly *not* the end of the story when a law is passed. After all, Congress has to depend on an executive branch agency to implement that law.

Federal policy is most accurately thought of as the result of a struggle between the two political branches, with Congress as the board of directors pressing its case through lawmaking and oversight and the president maneuvering within the wide range of discretion he is given in law. Sometimes, when Congress passes a particularly far-reaching law or the president exercises his prerogatives in controversial ways, the federal courts are brought into the action either by people in the government or by interested parties in the public. We will look at the courts' role in federal policy making in the next chapter.

Here, the focus is on the political branches. In the end, with regard to almost any issue—education, workplace, safety, land management, and all the rest—one can reasonably ask: which branch is more influential in setting the direction of policy as carried out by the agencies and departments of government? In short, who is the boss of those agencies? Is it the president, who literally *presides* over the executive branch agencies, or is it Congress, the institution that is the source of the authority by which the agencies act?

The answer is really: both. In some areas, one branch will have an advantage, at least for a time; in others, the other branch will. At the end of the chapter, we assess which branch might be said to have more lasting impact on the direction of policy. But first, we will look at the development of the relationship between the branches in directing federal policy. The history of the relationship involves a period in the middle decades of the 20th century when Congress delegated a great deal of authority to the president. Congress pushed back in the 1970s, reclaiming some of its prerogatives. We are at a time when, in domestic policy, the two branches each have the resources to influence policy in important ways, if those resources are exploited effectively.

The next section provides a review of what each branch has going for it in the struggle for control over public policy. Here we call them "toolkits,"[1] which are essentially those resources—or "power tools"—the branches have for influencing the direction of policy.

After that, we see how the struggle plays out in a couple of important areas of public policy. Two good examples of how the political branches employ the tools at their disposal are federal policy on regulating the financial sector of the economy and the nutritional components of federally subsidized school meals.

We finish the chapter by looking at national security policy, where the relationship between the branches is different. For a long time, presidents have had the clear upper hand, dating back to the end of World War II. National security is a kind of exception to the rule that the branches struggle on a more or less equal basis over the direction of policy. But it is not true that presidents are entirely unaccountable in the pursuit of their policy aims in this realm. We will see the ways in which the law constrains presidents, even regarding covert operations such as the predator drone program conducted by the Obama administration.

# THE RELATIONSHIP BETWEEN THE BRANCHES IN THE 20TH CENTURY: A HISTORY OF DELEGATION

Congress has always delegated authority to the president. But this tendency went to a new level with the 1921 Budget and Accounting Act, which created the Bureau of the Budget (BOB), later renamed the Office of Management and Budget.

Prior to this act, each agency of government went directly to Congress to appeal for money to fund its programs.[2] The president simply did not have the staff to manage the relationship between the agencies and Congress. Long-standing relationships had developed between agency personnel and members of Congress, often leaving the president out of the equation. In this way, it was Congress that had its hooks in the agencies, effectively driving policy through the power of the purse. This power dynamic generally held true even though presidents had the power to nominate agency heads who served at their pleasure.

Prior to 1921, the executive branch spoke with many voices, and to say there was a coherent presidential agenda was a stretch. This began to change with the creation of the BOB. Its charge was to provide Congress a comprehensive look at the federal budget every year—essentially bringing together all the agency requests into a coherent whole on behalf of the president. This gave the president the wherewithal potentially to press for an agenda, to have his branch of government effectively speak with one voice.

It is reasonable to wonder why Congress would willingly have provided the president this potentially powerful institutional tool, which could be wielded against it in the struggle over the direction of policy. But the federal budget was under great stress, and had been since the end of World War I in 1918. Debt had exploded because of the war effort and seemed uncontrollable. Congress was under tremendous pressure to do something about it. The idea to pass off some responsibility to the executive seemed appealing at the time.

## The New Deal and the National Security State

Another crisis, in this case the Great Depression, drove calls for dramatic and rapid federal action. The election of Democrat Franklin Roosevelt and an overwhelmingly Democratic Congress in 1932 put in place the political conditions that made this possible. Given the severity of the Depression, Congress was moved to pass almost anything Roosevelt wanted. New agencies were created to address the banking crisis, the farm crisis, unemployment, and myriad other things. These agencies were often given very broad authorities to deal with the crisis at hand.[3]

The most notable example was the establishment of the National Recovery Administration in the National Industrial Recovery Act of 1934. Its charge: keep the economy from spiraling further out of control by regulating all sorts of economic activity, including wages, production levels, and prices in certain industries. By 1935 the so-called NRA codes, which spelled out the regulations, were under scrutiny in the courts. The Supreme Court ruled that year that congressional delegation of authority to executive branch agencies that were regulating production in the poultry industry was unconstitutional.[4] The Court said that regulating commerce in this way was tantamount to lawmaking and was the proper purview of Congress, not unelected agency officials. Under pressure in the next few years, the Court reversed course, permitting agencies to exercise these sorts of powers as long as they were rooted in some way in statutory authorities.[5] (We look more closely at the relevant cases in the next chapter.)

As the federal government assumed more and more responsibilities for the welfare of the citizenry as a response to economic hardship, the complexity of managing all the new programs and agencies became increasingly apparent. President Roosevelt was driven to ask for broad authorities to reorganize the executive branch. Included in his request was the need for more assistance at the White House in the form of an Executive Office of the President (EOP), essentially a layer of bureaucracy to help the president make sense of everything the government was doing. It would ideally give him the ability to deal with jurisdictional disputes and overlapping responsibilities among the agencies.

The Reorganization Act of 1939 gave the president much of what he wanted. The sprawling new government was rationalized to an extent under cabinet departments, and the EOP was formed.[6] Presidents were given the ability to reshuffle the agencies, with Congress able to weigh in only after the fact.

After World War II, presidential power was further enhanced by the National Security Act of 1947, which (especially after it was amended in 1949) gave the president the tools to bring together the big picture in foreign policy, military policy, and intelligence gathering. The National Security Council was created at the White House, and the armed forces were brought under one umbrella at the Department of Defense. We will look more at this development later in the chapter.

## The Great Society

What had been created in the New Deal was a much bigger federal government, active in ways it had never been before in regulating the economy, providing social insurance, and directing agricultural policy. But the federal presence in other important aspects of American life—civil rights, the environment, education, health, sciences, and transportation—was still rather modest. But this changed, beginning in the 1950s and escalating in the mid-1960s.

The 1950s saw the development of the interstate highway system and the beginnings of major investments in science with the Space Act of 1958 that created NASA. But progressive forces saw their efforts come to full fruition in the mid-1960s, during Lyndon Johnson's **Great Society**. In 1964 the Civil Rights Act was passed into law, outlawing racial segregation and providing legal protections against discrimination based on race and sex; 1965 saw the Voting Rights Act, which led to a federal takeover of voter-registration policy in large swaths of the country to guarantee the right to vote to African Americans; and also in 1965 the federal government became a major player in education policy at all levels. In addition, Medicare and Medicaid were passed into law that year, giving seniors and the poor federally subsidized medical coverage. In the 1960s and into the early '70s, environmental and consumer protections were enacted, the National Endowments of the Arts and Humanities were created, and science funding skyrocketed. Pretty much any area of American life the federal government had not been involved in was federalized to a significant extent in that era.

The upshot of all this was an even bigger executive branch with ever more responsibilities, usually involving considerable delegation of authority to agency officials and by extension the president. Congress was rapidly being overshadowed. Its staff was overwhelmed keeping up with everything it had created, and presidents such as Democrat Lyndon Johnson (1963–1969) and Republican Richard Nixon (1969–1974) were more than happy to step into the breach and direct agencies according to their respective agendas.

## The 1970s: Congress Pushes Back

Congress found itself in a tricky situation. While it was a practical necessity to delegate authority to the president if it wanted the government to do all the things it had put into law, members found themselves getting more and more communications from their constituents who were now virtually all touched profoundly by federal programs, seemingly on a daily basis. The members *had to be* more interested in the work of the agencies as their constituents pestered them for answers, but they did not have the resources to keep up.

The 1970s saw Congress trying to get back into the power game, to reinvigorate its ability to direct the work of the agencies as it, Congress, saw fit. After all, the members were the ones writing the laws and believed to a man and woman they had a right to direct the agencies.

Around this time, Congress appropriated itself resources for more staff, especially at the committee level, to keep track of the agencies. The House began requiring every committee to put together annual agency oversight plans. In addition, Congress began requiring agencies in law or in accompanying report language to update the committees of jurisdiction on the progress and performance of programs of particular interest. New laws scheduled **legislative sunsets** on agency authorities, essentially Congress forcing itself to reconsider what the agencies were doing. Congress put inspectors general into every agency and department in 1978 to report directly to Congress on waste, fraud, and abuse in the executive branch. The president's legal authority to reorganize agencies and departments was allowed to lapse. The Ethics in Government Act put in place a system that would give tremendous powers to independent counsels (sometimes called special prosecutors) to look into abuses of power in the agencies and the White House.[7]

One of the motivations of all of this was political survival: an enhanced capacity to monitor the executive branch would enable members to better serve their constituents. Some political scientists came up a more cynical interpretation, namely, that members could exploit the vastly complex government their branch had created by "saving the day" for constituents confused by red tape and at the same time scoring political points by chastising agency officials in public.[8]

Whatever the motivation, Congress felt itself at too great a disadvantage in the early 1970s and needed to bolster its ability to influence the direction of federal policy. In doing so, it made itself a more serious player in contending with the president over the direction of federal policy.


## THE TOOLKITS OF EACH BRANCH

### Congress's Toolkit

In the 21st century, both the executive and the legislative branches have considerable means to influence the direction of public policy. In virtually every imaginable area, particularly in the domestic realm, there is a struggle for the upper hand; today you could say it is a struggle between two fairly evenly matched heavyweights.

This book, specifically the last several chapters, is about Congress's powers vis-à-vis the federal agencies. What follows is a summary of the "power tools" available to the board of directors to shape policy. After that, we look at the president's toolkit. Then we see the power tools in action in two key areas of public policy. At the end of the chapter, we try to answer this question: which branch is more powerful in influencing the direction of federal policy?

*Legislative direction.* As we have seen, Congress may be as specific as it wants to be in legislation—authorizing or appropriations—in giving direction to agencies. *Particularly in appropriations bills* (see Chapter 8), Congress gives specific administrative instructions to the agencies. If the president signs the bill, he has for all intents and purposes agreed to Congress's micromanaging of a program.

*Legislative sunsets.* Whereas it was once common for Congress to give indefinite authorizations to federal programs, beginning in the 1960s it rarely did anymore.

THE TOOLKITS OF EACH BRANCH 331

Now, many agencies come up for reauthorization on a regular basis. As covered in Chapter 6, it is true that most expired authorizations apply only to the authorization of appropriations—the actual agency programs continue to be authorized to exist (and usually receive funding in spite of the expiration date on funding authorization). Even so, the fact that Congress sunsets agency authorizations gives them real or at least implied power to redirect what the agency does in law. Needless to say, agencies are wary.

*Spending limitations.* Congress is effective in directing agency policy by prohibiting the use of funds for certain purposes in what is called limitation language in appropriations bills. It also sometimes "fences off" portions of agency appropriations until the Committees on Appropriations sign off on a spending plan. This enables even a small subset of Congress—these committees—to have immense influence. (See Chapter 7.)

*Direction in report language.* Appropriators exert their influence in nonstatutory ways as well, giving explicit direction to agencies, sometimes in very forceful language, in the committee reports and the joint explanatory statements that are attached to appropriations bills. Although agencies are not legally bound in these cases, ordinarily they follow these instructions to the letter, as they have to come back to the Appropriations Committee every year for money. It is unwise to make enemies of the members of that committee!

*Investigative authority and threat of subpoena.* The power Congress has to investigate wrongdoing in the agencies and issue subpoenas for testimony and documents (see Chapter 9 and 10) enables it to get executive branch officials' attention. Even just the idea that Congress can dig around in agency business, forcing the commitment of considerable resources, means that agencies have to pay attention to even informal suggestions made by key members of Congress, especially committee chairs and party leaders.

*Hearings and using the media.* Congress is in a position to draw attention to issues it cares about by holding hearings and planting stories in the media. Normally, agencies try to avoid controversy and will do their best to address the wishes of key members. For this reason, even the *threat* of a hearing—or the *threat* of legislative action, for that matter—can be an effective tool in directing public policy.

*The fire-alarm system.* As discussed in Chapter 10, Congress attempts to monitor agencies through GAO audits, inspectors general reports, and regular reporting requirements. In addition, many interested parties with a stake in federal policy—academics, interest groups, and advocates of all stripes—have contacts on congressional staffs. And the media, especially investigative journalists, are a crucial resource. Taken together, this so-called fire-alarm system is a valuable tool, bolstering Congress's ability to keep tabs on executive branch agencies. When their constituents are affected, or when they can score points against the other party, or when a special policy concern is involved, chances are that some sort of action will be taken.

All in all, then, Congress has ways to influence agency policy even when it has given agencies wide latitude in the law itself. New laws can always be more specific, and especially annual appropriations bills can wield the all-important power of the purse for policy ends. But as often as not, it is the implied or threatened use of legislative tools that gives Congress the ability to affect public policy.

## The Presidential Toolkit

This book has not been about the executive branch explicitly, although the theme is that one cannot understand the two political branches in isolation. As a result, we have frequently touched on the agencies and the president in relation to the powers wielded by Congress. One thing we have stressed in this chapter and earlier: the executive branch by necessity has been delegated a great deal of wiggle room in implementing the aims of legislation passed by Congress. *In fact, perhaps the most important thing to remember about any law passed by Congress is that it does not accomplish anything in the real world without subsequent action, which includes interpretation and implementation by executive branch agencies and sufficient appropriations provided by Congress.*

In short, crucial to understanding the direction of federal public policy is how the objectives of Congress are put in place by the agencies. The president, atop the executive branch, has a lot of power tools at his disposal to make a difference.

*Executive orders.* Perhaps more important than anything, presidents may issue **executive orders** to provide direction to agencies in the implementation of the law.[9] These orders may either require specific action by an agency official (usually a department secretary or agency head) or give that official broad authority to act as he or she sees fit. Laws normally lay out fairly broad objectives to, for example, make progress in cleaning the air or regulating a specific market. Within these confines, the president has a great deal of latitude to direct policy. Executive orders have legal force when the president has been given delegated authority in law, as noted above. Presidents can go further and "fill in the blanks" by issuing orders to agency officials in areas that Congress has not specifically legislated in. This can be controversial and may lead to congressional reaction. Presidents can go even further and provoke confrontation by issuing an order that could be construed as contradicting what the law says. In those situations, the federal courts are often asked to intervene and settle the matter.

Some areas of public policy shift dramatically from president to president, almost from day one of a new administration. For example, recently presidents have put forward dueling executive orders on US funding for international health groups that perform abortions. As the *Washington Post* reported in early 2009:

> President Obama yesterday lifted a ban on U.S. funding for international health groups that perform abortions, promote legalizing the procedure or provide counseling about terminating pregnancies.
>
> Obama issued a memorandum rescinding the Mexico City Policy, also known as the "global gag rule," which President Ronald Reagan originally instituted in 1984, President Bill Clinton reversed in 1993 and President George W. Bush revived in 2001.
>
> The memorandum revokes Bush's [executive] order, calling the limitations on funding "excessively broad" and adding that "they have undermined efforts to promote safe and effective voluntary family programs in foreign nations." In an accompanying statement, Obama said he would also work with Congress to restore U.S. funding support for the United Nations Population Fund "to reduce poverty, improve the health of women and children, prevent HIV/AIDS and provide family planning assistance to women in 154 countries."[10]

*Appointment power.* Presidents appoint thousands of agency officials, including the top tier of about 800 people subject to Senate approval. These people serve at the president's pleasure, which gives him a way to exert authority over the direction of policy.

*Agency management.* The day-to-day operations of the agencies are performed largely by career civil servants who cannot be fired by the president. These people have the experience and know-how to make the agencies work. However, they do answer to the top so-called political appointees who manage the agency in the service of the president's objectives.

*The president's budget.* As covered in Chapter 7, every year the Office of Management and Budget puts together a comprehensive budget for the entire government, detailing what the president would like to accomplish and what funding that would require. It is essentially a blueprint for federal public policy. Of course, Congress may choose to alter that blueprint legislatively, usually by funding different priorities. But the fact is the president has a significant tool as the "contractor," the guy who actually has people working for him who know all the details of the thousands of federal programs. Congress is comparatively *very* thinly staffed. To the extent Congress does not get into the details of government programs, the direction laid out in the president's budget carries the day.

*Veto power.* The veto power is the president's most effective tool in influencing what gets passed into law. But, if not handled deftly, it is a rather blunt one. Presidents cannot veto parts of bills; they have to accept the whole thing or nothing at all. It is, then, the *threat* of vetoing a bill (very few vetoes are overridden) that is the key to wielding power vis-à-vis Congress. The OMB's Statement of Administration Policy (SAP) is the official conveyance of a veto threat. It is used at different stages of the legislative process to signal to Congress what parts of a bill, if any, are unacceptable. The language in an SAP can be opaque. Sometimes presidents *suggest* that they will veto a bill because of a certain provision without saying it outright. Essentially, the veto power is the president's entrée into the legislative process, giving him the potential to influence the shape of legislation.

*The Office of Information and Regulatory Affairs (OIRA).* The executive branch's *rulemaking* process is managed by the Office of Information and Regulatory Affairs, an agency within the OMB. The rulemaking process is of paramount importance; essentially, it is the way agencies put legislative authority and direction into effect. Congress's typically broadly stated legislation gives authorities to executive branch agencies to do countless things, from securing the Internet to cleaning up rivers to ensuring the safety of air travel. To put the law into effect agencies develop regulations through the rulemaking process that companies, local governments, and private citizens have to abide by.[11] These regulations have the force of law, as they are rooted in statutes passed by Congress.

While the agencies themselves develop the regulations through processes that are open to public input, OIRA reviews those regulations before they are put into effect.[12] OIRA is headed by a presidential appointee, giving the president considerable leverage over the specifics of federal regulations, which might mean a more or less strict rule on land use or a more or less inhibiting regulation on what financial instruments a bank may use.

*The bully pulpit.* The president has an unequaled ability to draw attention from the media, giving him the potential to marshal public opinion in the interest of influencing the direction of legislation or policy more broadly. Also, unlike Congress, the president can speak with one voice. Congress can be a cacophony of voices that are not necessarily on the same page, a disadvantage when trying to influence agency policy.

# PUTTING THE TOOLKITS TO WORK: TWO CASE STUDIES

In the words of a prominent congressional staffer:

> In American Government class I learned that when a major law was passed—say, to secure voting rights or to clean the nation's rivers—policies were immediately in place to make those goals happen. When I actually worked in government, I found out that it doesn't work that way. Laws have to be interpreted and implemented. Those things take time. And of course funds are needed to make them happen. In fact, the passage of a law is just the beginning of the fight.[13]

The development of public policy on any issue is ongoing. All three branches may get into the act; the executive and legislative always do. What follows are two examples that illustrate this staffer's point that the actual direction of public policy at any given moment is the result of a struggle between the branches. The first case is the implementation of the Dodd-Frank bill. After that we look at the National School Lunch Program after passage of the Healthy Hunger-Free Kids Act of 2010.

## Financial Regulation

In the fall of 2008, following the demise of Lehman Brothers (a major investment banking firm), it appeared that the financial system was bound to implode without drastic action. Many firms had made a lot of bad bets, and some banks were so large that if they followed Lehman, the consequences would be a depression of a magnitude not seen since at least the 1930s. The Emergency Economic Stabilization Act proposed to bail out some of the nation's major banks—even and it seemed especially those that had not handled their assets responsibly. Although there was a lot of opposition, and passage wasn't easy, President Bush signed the bill into law on October 3, 2008. It set up the Troubled Asset Relief Program, which was authorized to bail out banks to the unprecedented tune of $700 billion.[14]

Politicians and policy experts were chastened by the experience as the economy began to recover ever so slowly from the financial crisis. What could be done to prevent repeating the mistakes made by financial institutions that had been deemed "too big to fail"? Ultimately, there was considerable momentum to restructure the entire federal regulatory apparatus for the financial system, particularly after Democrats won the presidency and padded their margins in the House and Senate in the 2008 elections.

The path to legislation was long, however, as the problems themselves were incredibly complex and the debate increasingly took on a partisan tone, with

Republicans opposing what they regarded as reform ideas that would tend to hinder the free movement of capital. In the end, the Dodd-Frank Wall Street Reform and Consumer Protection Act (named after Senator Christopher Dodd of Connecticut and Representative Barney Frank of Massachusetts, both Democrats and the principal sponsors of the legislation) was signed into law by President Obama on July 21, 2010. It envisioned a strengthened Securities and Exchange Commission (SEC) and Commodity Futures Trading Commission (CFTC), both of which had seen dramatic reductions in key areas of funding in recent years. Broadly speaking, Dodd-Frank mandated that those agencies pursue "securities fraud, reviewing public company disclosures and financial statements, inspecting the activities of investment advisors, investments companies, broker-dealers and other registered entities, and [maintain] fair and efficient markets." The law also created the Consumer Financial Protection Bureau (CFPB)—an agency that would be part of the Federal Reserve and have funding independent of Congress—to have broad authority to police a wide range of lenders and debt collectors, as well as some activities of credit unions and banks.

The law gave wide latitude to these key agencies to put the broad objectives of the law into effect through the federal regulatory process. They were given one year to accomplish that. President Obama appointed heads of these agencies (Chairwoman Mary Schapiro at the SEC and Chairman Gary Gensler at CFTC, who lead five-person bipartisan commissions, as well as the single director of the CFPB, Richard Cordray), giving him some influence over the direction of the policies. All the agency heads, however, serve fixed terms, giving them substantial independence.

The problem for implementation: the regulatory process is long and involved, requiring agencies to give the public (especially the entities subject to regulation and consumer advocate groups) ample opportunity to weigh in on proposed regulations. Experts acknowledge that putting the law into effect through regulations that explain what is and is not allowed was simply impossible in such a complex area of policy in only one year's time. Furthermore, the agencies were simply not staffed sufficiently to be able to make it happen. At the end of 2012, two and a half years after passage, only one-third of the needed regulations were in effect, one-third were proposed and in the pipeline, and fully one-third were not even proposed yet.[15]

There are a lot of factors to consider, not just in the completion of the task but in the actual policies being implemented. Some were internal to the executive branch agencies. As mentioned, the agencies simply did not have the staffing to get the job done, and the process itself was cumbersome. Furthermore, the agencies themselves have not always agreed on what to do in keeping with the law and even which agency is meant to take the lead in particular areas. The so-called Volcker

Rule, a requirement of Dodd-Frank that aims to restrict banks from doing anything too risky with their money, is supposed to be the product of the work of the Federal Deposit Insurance Corporation and other banking agencies, with the CFTC playing a role. The SEC, too, has seen fit to join the policy-making process.[16] At this writing, no final rule has been put forth.

Struggles like these attract attention from members of Congress. Those critical of the delays or the direction of proposed regulations will bombard the agencies with letters demanding answers. Those critical of proposed regulations will, for their part, work behind the scenes lobbying the regulators furiously to narrow their force. Senator Scott Brown (R-MA) made it clear in various ways to officials at the Federal Reserve that he would fight on behalf of financial firms in his state for broad exceptions to the Volcker Rule.[17] And regulators have to listen to the politicians on Capitol Hill—after all, what good is a regulation that proves to be such a lightning rod that its implementation is not funded or it is overturned by subsequent legislation? All the hard work would be for naught.

Key members of Congress, especially committee chairs, use various tactics to influence the direction of policy. In the case of Dodd-Frank, these members send letters to the agency heads as proposed regulations are publicized, making it clear what they intended when they passed the legislation. Most of the efforts are more subtle than that—calls from committee staffers to make sure agency officials know they are paying attention: "My boss (the senator) is starting to get anxious about the pace of your work."

In fact, two Senate committees (Banking and Agriculture—the two in that chamber most involved in Dodd-Frank) have conducted hearings on the severe liquidity problems and eventual bankruptcy of derivatives broker MF Global. These drew attention to the very problems Dodd-Frank was meant to address with the hopes of encouraging agencies not to water down regulations. The threat of new refined legislation is always in the background—or even an unpleasant hearing involving the regulators themselves.

For opponents of Dodd-Frank, the 2010 midterm elections were a boon. An antiregulatory Republican House gave these members much more leverage over the agencies' processes. They held hearings on the negative impact of the regulations, as they saw it, putting pressure on the regulators. More important, in the annual appropriations process Republicans had the newfound leverage to reduce the growth of the agencies, making it impossible to do everything they were required to do under the time constraints laid out in Dodd-Frank. Sometimes limitation language restricting the scope of regulations was added to the House version of the Financial Services and General Government appropriations bill. These almost never made it into law, but they were effective bargaining chips in negotiations with the Democratic Senate and the president—chips that were cashed in for cutting funding for the relevant agencies. Slowing the regulatory process can be part of a long-term strategy for legislation down the road to change or even repeal the law.

### Healthy School Lunches . . . with Tater Tots?

Congressional passage of the Healthy Hunger-Free Kids Act of 2010 gave the Food and Nutrition Service (FNS), an agency in the US Department of Agriculture, the tools to make systematic change to the National School Lunch Program, among other things. This bill was near to the Obama administration's heart, in fact a pet project of the first lady, Michelle Obama.

The School Lunch Program had been in place by one name or another since before the 1940s, even though it never had specific statutory authorization. Its aim was and is to ameliorate hunger among the nation's needy children. It was given full-fledged legal authorization in 1946 and was amended in the 1960s in part to update nutritional standards in the meals.

The 2010 act gave the FNS the new authorities it needed to bring school lunches, breakfasts, and other similar programs in line with the latest nutritional science— something private-sector experts and nonprofits had advocated since the last revision in 1995. As with the authorities given to the financial regulatory agencies in Dodd-Frank, the FNS was given a lot of running room to put forward regulations to improve school meals.

The FNS tapped into the expertise of the Institute of Medicine, a widely respected independent organization. The IOM had put out a report, "School Meals: Building Blocks for Children," in 2009 that was an important source for the legal authorities provided in the 2010 Hunger-Free Kids legislation.[18] In 2011 the FNS made it known that it planned to put in place a new regulation pursuant to that law that would remove starchy vegetables, including corn, peas, lima beans, and potatoes, from school breakfasts and reduce them to one cup per week at lunch. In their place would be more fresh leafy vegetables and other nonprocessed foods.[19] This would go into effect in 2012. The evidence showed that the changes would improve the nutritional value of the federally subsidized meals in keeping with the spirit and letter of the law.

The oversight fire-alarm system went off in the halls of Congress in the fall of 2011—especially loudly in the office of Senator Susan Collins (R-ME). The lead outside group bringing attention to the issue appeared to be the National Potato Council. Collins went the floor of the Senate with an amendment to the agriculture appropriations bill to prohibit implementation of the new rule. In an interview with *Politico,* she said, "To improve the quality of school lunches and breakfasts is something I have always supported. But either my amendment becomes law, or the department will decide it needs to cut its losses and rewrite the rule without waiting for it to become law. At the end of the day, the result is going to be the same."[20]

The administration entered into negotiations with the senator almost immediately. FNS head Kevin Concannon said, "Our proposed rule will improve the health and nutrition of our children based on sound science. . . . [W]e will work with Congress to ensure the intent of this rule is not undermined."[21]

Collins's opposition as publicly stated emphasized the considerable additional costs associated with preparing fresh vegetables in place of processed foods— french fries, tater tots, and so on. Of course, potatoes are an important product in Maine, which didn't escape her attention.

In the end, the administration put into effect its new rule in early 2012, and in fact the school lunch menus did undergo major changes.[22] But Congress had pressured the administration into considering its concerns. In this case, a single powerful senator forced the administration to negotiate with her.

## CONGRESS AND THE PRESIDENT: DOMESTIC VERSUS NATIONAL SECURITY POLICY

In Chapters 6–10, we have detailed the various ways in which Congress directs the work of government—through statute (both authorizing and appropriations) and various forms of oversight. As we have seen, there are often serious disagreements between the branches because of their different outlooks and perspectives. When one branch is charged with *directing* the work of government, and the other charged with *doing* the work of government, there are bound to be differences of opinion in the interpretation of congressional intent, as expressed in law or otherwise. This tension was built into our system quite intentionally to serve as a check on the power of the federal government; it could be described as part of the normal relationship between the branches. Each branch was given the ability to invade, as it were, the sphere of the other branch in order to serve as a check on its power.

In national security policy and especially war powers, however, the system of checks and balances does not work in the same way. In the past several decades, presidents have resisted efforts by Congress to intervene in policy decisions in this realm (especially those involving the commitment of troops to battle and covert operations); in fact, presidents are frequently downright dismissive of legislative branch efforts in ways rarely seen on the domestic side of policy. The past half century and more has been a period of existential threat and vigorous activism by the United States in world affairs. The nation faced the possibility of full-scale nuclear war and attempted to contain the spread of Soviet-style communism; attempted to promote democracy, human rights, and capitalism around the globe; confronted international terrorism; and shouldered the host of responsibilities that went along with its position as, eventually, the world's only superpower.

Every post–World War II president has initiated or overseen some form of American military action abroad. In a number of administrations, foreign wars have been the dominant focus of attention. Over the same period in this area of policy, Congress has become increasingly less effective, sometimes seemingly to the point of complete subordination to the will of the president.

The relationship between the branches is extraordinary in the area of war powers in part because there is no consensus over the meaning and implications of the relevant constitutional language. What are Congress's prerogatives? What exactly are the president's? The debate has gone on without interruption ever since World War II, with no end in sight in the 21st century. In fact, the Iraq War highlighted the clash between the branches. Former senator Robert Byrd of West Virginia, a vigorous proponent of congressional prerogatives, succinctly summarized the presidential position on the matter in the days leading up to the beginning of that conflict in 2003: "The Bush Administration thinks that the Constitution, with its inefficient separation of powers and its cumbersome checks and balances, has become an anachronism in a world of international terrorism and weapons of mass destruction."[23]

## The Constitutional Provisions

Congress has essentially the same sources of power in determining the national security policy of the nation that it has in all other policy areas—those provisions in Article I that give the institution the power to authorize and fund the actions of the government. However, there are four constitutional provisions that are at the heart of the continuing debate over the two branches' prerogatives in the specific realm of war powers.

The first is the power to declare war, granted, in Article I, Section 8, to Congress:

> Congress has the power . . . to declare war, grant letters of marque and reprisal, and make rules concerning captures on land and water; to raise and support armies, but no appropriation of money to that use shall be for a longer term than two years; to provide and maintain a navy; to make rules for the government and regulation of the land and naval forces.

The second provision, in Article II, Section 1, refers to the general grant of executive power to the president:

The executive power shall be vested in a president of the United States of America.

The third, in Article II, Section 2, gives the president the commander-in-chief power:

The president shall be commander in chief of the army and navy of the United States, and of the militia of the several states, when called in the actual service of the United States.

The fourth, also in Article II, Section 2, confers a more general power over foreign affairs to the president:

[The president] shall have power, by and with the advice and consent of the Senate, to make treaties, provided two thirds of the senators present concur; and he shall nominate, and by and with the advice and consent of the Senate, shall appoint ambassadors.

Many scholars and politicians believe that the framers of the Constitution placed the power to commit the country to war in the hands of Congress and Congress alone. They see this as the most logical reading of Article I, Section 8. This perspective maintains that the president's commander-in-chief power, or any other constitutionally granted executive powers, cannot usurp Congress's authority to decide whether to go to war. As such, the power to declare war is not a shared power except insofar as a declaration of war, to be legally in effect, requires the president's signature.

Those in favor of congressional prerogatives say that the framers of the Constitution placed the war power exclusively in the hands of Congress in direct reaction to the existing European model, which placed the war power exclusively with the monarch. According to scholar Louis Fisher: "The framers broke decisively with that tradition. Drawing on lessons learned at home in the American colonies and the Continental Congress, they deliberately transferred the power to initiate war from the executive to the legislature. The framers, aspiring to achieve the ideal of republican government, drafted a Constitution 'that allowed only Congress to loose the military forces of the United States on other nations.'"[24]

Following this line of thinking, some Congress partisans suggest that the president's commander-in-chief power does not kick in until war is declared. This idea is backed up by a literal reading of the Article II, Section 2, provision stating that "the president shall be Commander in Chief of the Army and Navy of the United States, and of the militia of the several States, *when called into the actual service of the United States*" (emphasis added). A declaration of war would constitute the most obvious "call into the actual service of the United States." Presumably, this interpretation might also mean that the president has to relinquish the commander-in-chief power when the war is over.

But declarations of war have gone out of fashion. The United States has had dozens of military engagements, both major and minor, since the last congressional declaration of war in 1942. Is Congress's constitutional claim on the power to commit the nation to war even relevant anymore?

## The President and the War Power

By designating the president the "commander in chief," in Article II, Section 2, the framers empowered him to do at least two things: one, to conduct military operations pursuant to declared or authorized wars; and two, to repel attacks on the homeland. Beyond that, there is no consensus as to what the framers intended.

Recent presidents and some scholars certainly do wish to extend the president's powers beyond those basics. They believe that the **commander-in-chief power** requires no trigger from a congressional authorization or declaration of war to take effect—instead, they maintain, it is always in place. Furthermore, although no president has attempted to lay claim to the power to declare war, numerous presidents and proponents of presidential war power have pointed to the commander-in-chief clause in the Constitution as, at least in part, a legitimate basis for sending US forces into battle irrespective of any action by Congress.

The most expansive interpretations of presidential power in the past 60 years include the contention that the Constitution gives the president the authority to commence and conduct virtually any military action that he sees as being in the interest of the nation.[25] *Presidents of both parties, even when they have received or sought congressional authorization, now maintain that they do not need that congressionally granted authority to commit American troops.* What has caused this rather dramatic and consequential change from an often restricted view of the president's prerogatives to a greatly expanded view of his commander-in-chief role? And how is it justified?

### World War II, Communists, and the Standing Army

World War II saw a massive mobilization of the nation's industry and populace for war. The nation, together with its allies, fought the three notorious dictators from

Japan, Italy, and Germany on multiple fronts around the globe. The scale of it easily exceeded the mobilization efforts required for World War I.

For the Second World War, American forces were based on multiple continents, as they had been for World War I, but there was a major difference in the American posture in the years after the war. Instead of "standing down"—dramatically scaling back the armed forces at the end of a war—the United States retained an international posture by maintaining bases all over the world and, in effect, keeping all the branches of the armed services on ready alert.

The reason? It was recognized very soon after the end of the war that a US ally in World War II, the Soviet Union, might constitute a threat to the Western European allies, and perhaps even the United States itself. The Soviets had rapidly solidified their position by exerting control over much of Eastern and central Europe. This development—the establishment of what were called the Warsaw Pact or Eastern-bloc nations—concerned Western Europeans, who feared further Soviet expansion into their countries. With the prodding of Britain's Winston Churchill and under the leadership of President Harry Truman, a bipartisan consensus developed in the United States around the idea that the Soviet Union needed to be contained within its sphere of influence.

The Soviets, for their part, made little effort to hide their intention to exert influence on other continents. It appeared that the Soviet Communists were on the move, and the only conceivable obstacle to them would be the United States, which, despite the considerable sacrifice of its citizens during the war, was relatively intact and economically vital compared to its other allies. Politically, the containment of the Soviets became an imperative supported enthusiastically by most Democrats and Republicans alike. The 45-year Cold War had begun.

This became only more of an imperative when the Soviet Union tested its first atom bomb in 1949. The United States no longer had a monopoly on nuclear weapons. The race to build more and more lethal bombs began in earnest. The competition with the Soviet Union affected American politics and its institutions profoundly. By the late 1940s, covert operations to counter Soviet influence in Europe and, in fairly short order, across the globe had escalated. The United States did not dare scale back its military posture for fear of encouraging the Soviets' ambitions. American interests were considered threatened in Asia, the Middle East, Africa, Central and South America, and, of course, Europe.

## Post–World War II America and the Commander in Chief

In earlier times, American presidents, even if they had wanted to, would have had a great deal of difficulty unilaterally and precipitously committing the nation to a major foreign entanglement. The nation did not maintain the type of military posture necessary for sustained, large-scale military ventures. Considerable mobilization, necessitating appropriations for the armed services and other actions of Congress to harness industry, would have been required.

After World War II, the president had a lot more to work with. As noted, he had armed forces positioned at far-flung bases that were easily deployable anywhere around the world. It would take longer to mobilize a force for a large-scale war, but such a force was available at bases in the United States. The president also had the ability to inflict massive damage anywhere on earth with the rapidly growing nuclear arsenal, over which he had unquestioned authority. Most important perhaps, postwar presidents had what amounted to explicit bipartisan support to do what needed to be done—to contain the spread of communism by any means necessary.

It was not a huge stretch for presidents to conclude that they could get away with acting unilaterally to engage American troops or conduct covert operations whenever and wherever American interests were threatened. In fact, every single president since the end of World War II, Democrats and Republicans alike, has claimed the authority to do so. But how did presidents justify this rather radical departure from the long-established constitutional interpretation that Congress has control over the decision to commit troops to battle?[26]

Truman's 1950 decision to send troops without congressional authorization into the Korean conflict, a major front in the Cold War, precipitated a series of justifications. In 1951 Secretary of State Dean Acheson, testifying before the Senate Foreign Relations and Armed Services Committees, said, "Not only has the president the authority to use the armed forces in carrying out the broad foreign policy of the United States and implementing treaties, but it is equally clear that this authority may not be interfered with by the Congress in the exercise of power which it has in the Constitution."[27] Notably, some years later, a Johnson administration State Department official, Leonard Meeker, stated, "The grant of authority to the president in Article II of the Constitution extends to the actions of the United States currently undertaken in Vietnam."[28]

Practically speaking, the argument was that Congress had spent the money to put the armed forces on ready alert all over the globe for a reason. And that reason was that our interests and our very existence were perceived to be threatened in the Cold War. To presidents, there was no longer any debate: the nation was in a precarious situation that constituted something like a permanent emergency. The commander in chief had the authority unilaterally to commit troops to war if need be.

Advocates of presidential prerogatives have grounded this power in more than the commander-in-chief clause in Article II. Rather, they put forth a broader argument rooted in all three of the Article II provisions noted earlier.[29] The president is said to be solely responsible for representing the nation in foreign relations based on the primary role that presidents are given in the Constitution in treaty negotiations and the receiving of ambassadors. The Supreme Court essentially took this position in 1936.[30] The Court has also cooperated by not standing in the way of executive agreements and other unilateral diplomatic actions taken by presidents. And most broadly, the executive power vested in the president in the very first words of Article II is said to give him the exclusive power to act in the interest of the nation during a time of crisis. The centuries-long debate over the interpretation of "executive power" is described in Box 11.1.

The argument from this perspective is that the modern-day need for quick action (or "dispatch," in the words of the framers) necessitates a change in the way we should think about the constitutional provisions affecting presidential power. In the Cold War period from the late 1940s to 1991, when the Soviet Union collapsed, the Soviets' intercontinental nuclear capability, as well as their incursions and influence around the world affecting American interests, put the nation's security permanently at risk.

After the Cold War, Presidents George H. W. Bush and Bill Clinton still viewed the world as a dangerous place for American interests. Bush, in particular, identified American economic and strategic interests in the Middle East as a reasonable justification for unilateral presidential action in the First Gulf War. (He got the authority in law to remove Iraq from Kuwait, but claimed that he did not need it to act, given the UN resolutions and the clear threat to American interests.) And Clinton went further, arguing that instability and human rights violations in south-central Europe, as well as North Atlantic Treaty Organization commitments, justified unilateral presidential actions in the Kosovo conflict. It is interesting that US membership in NATO and the United Nations explicitly *does not* legally commit it (or any other nation for that matter) to war. The charters of the organizations leave it up to member states to make that determination. Having said that, these two presidents' political case for committing American troops was surely bolstered by our participation in those bodies.

Clinton and his successor, George W. Bush, also faced the threat of international terrorism. Again, the need for speed was used to justify presidential action, even to the point of committing the nation to war.

Ultimately, the consensus view among presidents, if not among scholars or members of Congress, is that waiting for Congress to weigh in before any commitment of American troops is an antiquated and downright dangerous idea in this day and age. (Some would add that, on the international front, a nation has more flexibility with less formal mechanisms of committing its military to war—specifically, statutes authorizing the use of force.) The view is that, unlike in previous eras, the nation's vital interests are so extensive and, in many cases, vulnerable, and the capabilities of America's enemies so diabolical and sophisticated, that the

# BOX 11.1

## The Curious Case of Executive Power

One of the most intriguing and controversial passages in the Constitution of the United States is the one right at the beginning of Article II: "The executive power shall be vested in a president of the United States of America." The framers did not define fully what they meant by that sentence, which may have been intentional. After all, they were dipping their toes into a touchy subject so soon after the nation escaped the yoke of the English monarch, and they needed to tamp down controversy in order to get the Constitution ratified.

Many of the framers believed that the executive, while kept in check for obvious reasons, needed to have much more power to act decisively and make the government work than the impotent one that was set up in the ill-fated Articles of Confederation. The articles were an overreaction, they thought. The Constitution would put in place checks, but the executive needed "energy" and needed to be able to act with "dispatch" and authority. One of the reasons they settled on establishing a single executive instead of an executive council was in the interest of "energy" and "dispatch."*

But the executive's powers were not defined in Article II at anywhere near the level of specificity that Congress's were in Article I. What were the limits of this "executive power"? The legislative powers "herein granted" were exhaustively listed, especially in Article I, Section 8. The *executive power* seemed to be a more general grant of authority. (Gouverneur Morris was the delegate who actually penned the document. It is widely believed, given his sentiments on the matter of executive authority, that he was responsible for making sure executive powers were not circumscribed in the way legislative powers were by the inclusion of the words *herein granted* in the first sentence of Article II.)

The issue of what executive power meant became a political football. An entire political party movement, the Whigs, was organized around the idea that the president should limit himself to simply executing Congress's wishes (except in the most dire emergency) in order that the office would not endanger the liberties of the people. Others, especially Thomas Jefferson and Andrew Jackson, felt that the Constitution permitted them to exercise more discretion if done in the interests of the nation. Teddy Roosevelt in particular was famous for asserting that the president should act aggressively in the national interest as the "steward" of the nation, as long as he did not run afoul of the Constitution or the laws passed by Congress. There were plenty of gray areas for presidents to exploit, he said, and he meant to do so.

But there has been, since the beginning, an even more expansive interpretation of "executive power" that has been used to bolster controversial unilateral presidential actions. John Locke, a 17th-century English philosopher, was the source of something called the *prerogative view* of executive power. Locke had written that the executive needed "to act according to [his] discretion for the public good, without the prescription of the law, and *sometimes even against it.*"† What he meant was that the executive could or even should break the law if that was necessary to serve the public in a crisis.

*Alexander Hamilton, *The Federalist Papers,* No. 70.

†John Locke, *Second Treatise of Government* (1690) (emphasis added).

BOX 11.1 *(Continued)*

## The Curious Case of Executive Power

Abraham Lincoln seemed to have Locke's view in mind when he wrote a famous letter to A. G. Hodges in 1864, defending some of the actions he had taken as president in the period leading up to and during the Civil War:

> Was it possible to lose the nation, and yet preserve the Constitution? By general law life and limb must be protected; yet often a limb must be amputated to save a life; but a life is never wisely given to save a limb. I felt that measures, otherwise unconstitutional, might become lawful, by becoming indispensable to the preservation of the nation. Right or wrong, I assumed this ground, and now avow it.[‡]

President Nixon used the same justification, citing Lincoln's letter, in defense of some of his actions—many of which were plainly illegal—to quell protests and infiltrate what he regarded as potentially subversive domestic groups during the Vietnam War.[§] Thomas Jefferson was familiar with Locke's arguments and seemed to subscribe to them as well.[∥]

President George W. Bush was extremely assertive regarding the president's executive prerogatives. His Administration put forth the *unitary theory* of executive power, which argues for strict limits on Congress's power to encroach on the president's turf.[#] Specifically, adherents of this view maintain that the president must have full control over subordinate officers in the executive branch and that the Constitution, through the commander-in-chief and foreign-relations clauses as well as executive power, gives the president the authority to move unilaterally in the realm of foreign and military affairs. (One former high-ranking Bush administration official suggested that the president's assertions of prerogative provoked such a fierce reaction from the other branches that, ironically, the institution of the presidency was weakened while he was still in office.)[**]

The exact meaning of "executive power" will never be established to everyone's satisfaction. The Constitution is far too opaque on the subject for a final answer to be discerned. But certainly, presidents have occasionally relied on the idea of an "undefined residuum" of executive power to bolster their case for an expanded interpretation of the commander-in-chief role.[††]

[‡]Lincoln's full letter can be found at http://showcase.netins.net/web/creative/lincoln/speeches/hodges.htm.

[§]Nixon publicly espoused this position in the famous Nixon-Frost interviews of 1977. The relevant passages can be found at www.landmarkcases.org/nixon/nixonview.html.

[∥]Jack L. Goldsmith, *The Terror Presidency* (New York: W. W. Norton, 2007), 80–83.

[#]A full examination of the unitary executive theory can be found in Stephen G. Calabresi and Christopher S. Yoo's book *The Unitary Executive* (New Haven, CT: Yale University Press, 2008).

[**]Goldsmith, *The Terror Presidency*.

[††]William Howard Taft used the "undefined residuum." He was an opponent of the expansion of presidential prerogatives advocated by his contemporaries, Teddy Roosevelt and Woodrow Wilson.

requirement of dispatch legitimizes the invocation of, in effect, an umbrella of constitutional authority (encompassing the commander-in-chief clause, executive power, and the Article II, Section 2, provisions covering foreign relations) to commit the country to military and covert action irrespective of congressional authorization.

## Two Key Dimensions of the Presidential Advantage

There is no doubt about who the winner is in the struggle between the branches over the direction of national security policy: it is the executive in a landslide. Simply put, over the past several decades, Congress has not exerted the same kind of influence over national security policy, especially committing the country to war, as it has over domestic policy. Even its vaunted "power of the purse" has a diminished impact when it comes to influencing the president in the conduct of war. There are a couple of principal, overarching, reasons for the ascendancy of the executive branch.

First, there is a very strong *political dimension* to Congress's inability to weigh in on foreign or military affairs as effectively as it does on domestic policy. A long tradition of depoliticizing foreign and defense policy is encapsulated in the saying that "politics stops at the water's edge." This notion, articulated by Republican senator Arthur Vandenberg in 1952, meant, in his words, that it is important "to unite our official voice at the water's edge so that America speaks with maximum authority against those who would divide and conquer us."[31] He said this in the particular context of the Cold War at a time when he and some other Republicans were working with Democratic president Harry Truman to present a united front. Such a viewpoint gives the president extra leverage, as he always speaks with one voice—something that is virtually impossible for Congress to do. Presidents become much harder for other politicians to challenge when they are understood to be speaking for the interests of the nation in foreign relations.

The president's political advantage has not, however, enabled him always to dictate what America's proper role in world politics will be. In fact, during the Vietnam War era the debate about war and foreign policy was extremely heated, and during the Reagan years Congress was unusually assertive in opposing the president's policies in Latin America. That said, in the spirit of Arthur Vandenberg, a tradition of bipartisanship and unity in support of the president generally dominates in the most relevant congressional committees (the Senate Foreign Relations Committee and the Armed Services Committees in both chambers). And certainly, it is politically difficult or impossible for members of either party to support pulling the plug on funding for an ongoing military operation.

The second reason Congress has become weak on national security policy is the *informational dimension*. Although it is true that Congress depends on information from the executive branch to exercise its authorizing, appropriations, and oversight powers in the domestic arena, the situation is more problematic in the defense sphere. Information related to national security is controlled to a greater degree by the executive branch. The president has a tremendous built-in advantage vis-à-vis Congress when troops are stationed in or patrolling potentially hostile territory or seas. Presidents are able to use their access to military intelligence to portray events in such a way as to make it very difficult for Congress to oppose decisions in the national security area, including the march to war, when time is of the essence.

Perhaps the most famous example of this sort of information management was the controversial Gulf of Tonkin incident, which led to Congress passing a resolution that granted a broad authorization for military activity in Southeast Asia. Two ambiguous engagements in Southeast Asian waters in 1964 between American destroyers and North Vietnamese torpedo boats were portrayed by the Johnson administration as unprovoked attacks on the American ships. Congress had no ability in this time of crisis to gain access to all the available information (in fact, it took decades for all of it to become public) and had little recourse other than to respond affirmatively and quickly to the president's request for action. The resulting authorization for war was, as Johnson said privately, "like grandmother's nightshirt; it covers everything."[32] It should be noted that only two members of Congress opposed that authorization, and they were both defeated for reelection in the next electoral cycle.

President George W. Bush's administration was also criticized for how it managed ambiguous information in 2002 and 2003 concerning Iraq's program for developing and acquiring weapons of mass destruction. Ultimately, Secretary of State Colin Powell made the case to the United Nations in early 2003 that the United States had irrefutable evidence of the program. The closely controlled information—much of it highly classified—was nearly impossible to challenge, giving a decided advantage to the administration in its case for war. The conventional wisdom a decade later: the Bush administration took the country to war with Iraq based on faulty or misinterpreted intelligence.

In a broader sense, access to information related to defense and national security is limited by the sheer volume generated by the Department of Defense, the armed services, the intelligence agencies, the Department of State, and all the other departments and agencies that have some level of involvement with national security policy (including the Federal Bureau of Investigation (FBI), the Department of Homeland Security, and the Energy Department). Members of Congress, their staffs, and the institution's support arms—the Congressional Budget Office,

Government Accountability Office, and Congressional Research Service—simply do not have the staffing and other resources to access or analyze the vast quantity of information in a systematic way. Congress is at a distinct disadvantage.

Although there are areas of domestic policy where the sheer volume of information presents problems, there are some important differences in the national security area. First, much of the information is collected outside the United States. Second, information related to national security is analyzed, cataloged, and stored by the defense and intelligence agencies and is often not available in the public domain (as opposed to domestic policy areas, where stakeholders, reporters, and others can get access to the information and provide Congress "outside help"). And last, a significant portion of that information is always going to be classified or sensitive and therefore may not be shared on a regular basis with Congress. Although members of Congress automatically have top security clearance, most congressional staff do not, and practical limitations are placed on sharing classified or sensitive information even with the members themselves.

In fact, through a combination of laws, report language, and interbranch understandings, the president shares some intelligence information with just the so-called Gang of Eight, a group that includes the Speaker of the House, the House minority leader, the Senate majority and minority leaders, and the chairs and ranking members of the two chambers' Intelligence Committees.[33] Gang of Eight notifications are supposed to be limited to covert operations—an area where information is held especially tightly by presidents for fear of leaks or the exposure of potentially risky activities. Such exposure could put operatives overseas in immediate mortal danger and could also be highly embarrassing, both diplomatically and politically.

One example of an operation that came to light and created political fallout is the National Security Agency surveillance program, which stirred great controversy in 2006. The NSA, an intelligence agency under the auspices of the Defense Department, was collecting information on terror suspects via wiretapping and other methods. The program's legality was dubious, and its existence was shared only with the Gang of Eight. When a few details of the program were leaked, some in Congress asserted that its existence should have been shared with a much broader range of members.[34]

In general, Congress's efforts to assert its oversight authority over covert operations have been sporadic and often thwarted. And despite the establishment of a congressional oversight regime beginning in 1979 with the creation of the House Intelligence Committee—the first systematic congressional oversight of the intelligence agencies in the nation's history—it took only a few years before Congress was again left out of the loop by the president and the CIA director regarding important covert operations.[35] In such matters, *sharing information with Congress depends on the cooperation and good faith of the president.* Congress has a great deal of difficulty locating or gaining access to information it might want in a timely fashion if the president chooses not to share it.

The result of both the political and the informational dimensions is that presidents have the upper hand, given their control of the flow of information, and the political dynamics militate strongly in favor of congressional deference in national security policy. Members of Congress do not necessarily dislike this arrangement—after all, when left out of the loop, they may be in a position to avoid accountability for botched intelligence or military ventures that bog down and may even be in a position to score political points at the president's expense.

## Congress and National Security Policy: Accountability Before the Fact

Just because the president can take the initiative and determine the direction of national security policy does not mean that Congress has stood idly by. In fact, presidents are held accountable in a variety of ways in the 21st century that did not pertain prior to the 1970s.

In the '70s, Congress's push against executive overreach included angling for some influence in national security policy. The first notable effort was the War Powers Act of 1973, a reaction to presidential warmaking in Southeast Asia. In it, Congress required presidents to inform them in a timely fashion when troops were put in harm's way and put in place a mechanism by which troops would have to be withdrawn from hostilities within 90 days absent congressional approval. The first provision has been generally heeded by presidents, the second not at all, as presidents have regarded it as an unconstitutional infringement on their prerogatives.

In addition, Congress instituted the aforementioned oversight regime over covert operations, with the institution of permanent intelligence committees in both chambers. Notably, the Foreign Intelligence Surveillance Act of 1978 put in place a mechanism of required judicial approval for domestic wiretappings and other methods of eavesdropping when espionage or plans for terrorist acts are suspected.

Jack Goldsmith, a Harvard scholar and former high-ranking official in the Justice Department during the George W. Bush administration, makes the case for what are essentially before-the-fact constraints on presidential action in national security:

> Presidents used to wiretap at will in the name of national security, but now they must comply with complex criminal laws and get the approval of a secret court. Presidents used to conduct covert operations without any accountability, but now they must comply with elaborate restrictions and

report all important intelligence activities to Congress in a timely way. Presidents used to have carte blanche in interpreting or ignoring international human rights law and the laws of war, but now these laws are embodied in complex regulations and criminal statutes that touch on every aspect of military and intelligence operations. Presidents used to hide information easily, but now they must take extraordinary steps to maintain records and give the public broad access to internal documents. Quasi-independent inspectors general that were viewed as unconstitutional during the Reagan revolution are now well-established auditing and investigatory thorns in the president's side.

There are many other examples, but perhaps the best indicator of the impact of law on the presidency is that the CIA has well over one hundred lawyers, and the Department of Defense has over ten thousand, not including reservists. These lawyers—and many tens of thousands of other lawyers in other agencies—devote their days and many of their nights to ensuring that the extravagantly regulated executive branch complies with the law and with numerous forms of ex post accountability—inspector general audits, congressional investigations and queries, reporting requirements, and testimony before Congress—that influence executive behavior before the fact.[36]

It is hard to exaggerate the increase in the legal restrictions on various military actions in this era. As Goldsmith points out, the National Defense Authorization Act in 1977 was 16 pages long; in the new century, these bills are many hundreds of pages.[37] And international law has changed, too, putting in place other restrictions. At literally every stage of military action, lawyers are there to sign off on commanders' decisions. This is especially true when the armed services engage in peacekeeping, humanitarian assistance, and enforcement of economic sanctions—which is much of what is done nowadays. These situations are much more delicate, and legally appropriate actions are more circumscribed than they are in combat.

The predator drone program has gotten a great deal of attention in recent years, as President Obama has dramatically increased attacks on suspected terrorist targets in Pakistan and other places. These unmanned aircraft, directed by pilots 7,000 miles away in places like Nevada and Virginia, have the capacity to pinpoint targets and deliver lethal blows. Military lawyers literally sit with the pilots to assess the potential collateral damage, including civilian deaths, that might have an impact on the legality of a particular strike.

In the highest-profile cases, things move up the chain of command. The targeted killing of Anwar al-Awlaki, an American citizen living in Yemen who was alleged to have planned the so-called underwear bomber's efforts to blow up an airliner with 289 people on board in late 2009, was signed off by lawyers at the very highest levels of the Justice Department. Al-Awlaki was killed in September 2011 by a predator drone.

These targeted killings are controversial for another reason. A long-standing executive order makes it illegal for the United States to carry out an assassination: "*No person employed by or acting on behalf of the United States Government shall engage in, or conspire to engage in, assassination.*"[38] As a result, it is incumbent on the administration to have a legal justification for targeted killings. The Bush and Obama administrations have balked from sharing their thinking in the interest of concealing methods used in highly sensitive covert operations. But as more publicity has surrounded the drone campaign, total avoidance has become impossible. The Obama administration has leaned on the 2001 Authorization for the Use of Force Against al-Qaeda, claiming that eliminating the leadership of the group—even its offshoots almost anywhere in the world—is sufficient justification.

\* \* \*

As we have seen, Congress cannot conduct oversight in many aspects of national security policy as easily or as thoroughly as it can in the domestic sphere.[39] The amount of information is almost too vast to easily digest and can be next to impossible to extract. Furthermore, presidents have independent constitutional authorities in national security that they do not have in the domestic realm. With modern weapons systems as they are, the commander in chief can do a great deal before anyone even has a clear picture of what happened.

But, at the same time, the system of accountability that has developed is not insignificant. It is an imperfect system, to be sure, and barely constitutes "oversight" strictly understood,[40] but it is a far cry from the 1950s and '60s, when Congress had few mechanisms in place for monitoring executive actions in war and national security before or after the fact.

## CONCLUSION: WHO'S THE BOSS OF THE FEDERAL AGENCIES?

The relationship between the president and Congress was constitutionally established to invite struggle.[41] It was meant to give each political branch the leverage to challenge the other's prerogatives in order to prevent either one from abusing its power. For the most part, the relationship between the branches involves a shared and relatively balanced exercise of power. Of course, the relationship has tensions built into it. This involves wrangling over the interpretation and implementation of authorizing and appropriations laws, with the federal judiciary sometimes adjudicating disputes.

As a result, the direction of federal policy is typically determined in a tug-of-war between the two political branches. The exception is in the area of national security policy, where the president has real advantages. Congress relies on a nebulous system of what we call "accountability before the fact" for influence. In the day-to-day formation of policy in this realm, Congress is normally reactive to presidential initiative taking.

It is an open question which branch has more influence over the direction of federal policy in the domestic sphere. In effect, this is a fight over who runs the federal agencies who must implement public policy.

In this chapter, we looked at the "power tools" at Congress's and the president's disposal. At first blush, the president appears to have the upper hand, especially in issuing executive orders to implement broad statutory guidance. Congress simply does not have the capacity to track regularly every area in which it delegates authority. And data indicate that Congress does not do anything to nullify the overwhelming majority of executive orders.[42] Furthermore, recent trends show an increased willingness on the part of Congress to delegate. Dodd-Frank aspires to regulate the financial industry in very ambitious ways. The Affordable Care Act gives great power to the secretary of the HHS to put in place broad-ranging reforms in health care delivery. Even in the relatively narrow area of earmarking specific spending, Congress has in recent years refrained from directing federal dollars to specific districts or states, instead giving the agencies and the president more latitude in deciding on specific projects.

However, arguably the foremost expert on rulemaking and regulatory policy in the agencies, Cornelius Kerwin of American University, has a different take, which stresses the strengths Congress has in directing federal policy:

> The question of who runs the bureaucracy is by no means settled; Congress and the president have long struggled to gain the hearts and minds of [agency officials]. Both have formidable powers at their disposal to influence the course of bureaucratic decision-making. The president prepares budgets, appoints senior officials, and issues executive orders that profoundly affect how agencies manage their work. Congress is the ultimate decision maker on budgets and appointments, conducts oversight and investigations, and engages in casework on behalf of constituents. In the battle for influence over the [agencies], congressional powers are at least as substantial as those of the president. Congressional power to define an agency's mission and fix its budget is more determinative than the transitory and fragmented sources of presidential influence. Therefore, when delegating the power to interpret and prescribe law, Congress does it in the secure knowledge that it retains

sufficient power and opportunity to redirect [bureaucratic decision making] that go[es] astray.[43]

Which perspective—the commonly held one that presidents have the edge or Kerwin's view of congressional advantage—is right? There is no easy answer. In fact, the direction of federal policy may be influenced differently in one area than another depending on the priorities of presidents and members of Congress. For example, at this writing in 2013, President Obama has a great deal of running room in prescribing the direction of federal policy at the elementary and secondary school level due to acquiescent congressional committee leadership. But as far as the direction of space policy and federal land management, Congress is far more assertive and influential.

The fact is that Congress does not have the resources to keep up with everything, but when key members focus or when it can pass a law requiring a new direction, it can really be the driver. Congress put a lasting mark on the direction of health care with the passage of the Affordable Care Act (while also delegating a great deal to the executive at the same time) and in food safety with the Food Safety Modernization Act of 2010, for example. And there is the case noted earlier of Senator Susan Collins almost single-handedly changing federal policy on school meals in the fall of 2011. Even a single member, if her actions are strategic enough, may have a great deal of impact.

Congress is well within its rights to push for its views after it has given the executive wide statutory latitude. Obviously, it can always pass a new law to make policy clearer. But even when the executive is working within its legislative mandate—as was the case with the Food and Nutrition Service above—members of Congress may try to affect what happens in that space. They have the tools to prevail at least some of the time. After all, the agencies have to come to Congress for money every year; it is the power of the purse that gives it the most leverage. At the end of the day, it is Congress that has the direct electoral link to the sovereign public; members feel very strongly about keeping powerful *unelected* agency officials accountable to the people.

## Questions for Discussion

1. No one doubts that the president can act unilaterally to commit troops to combat if the nation is under imminent threat. But when there is time for full debate, should Congress or the president have the right to decide whether to commit troops to battle? More generally, should Congress

assert itself in the area of foreign policy and war powers? Why or why not?

2. Pick an interesting area of federal domestic policy and try to identify whether it is the president or Congress that is currently more influential.

3. Whose power tools do you think are typically more effective, the president's or Congress's? Why do you take that position?

## Suggestions for Further Reading

Cooper, Joseph. "The Modern Congress." In *Congress Reconsidered,* edited by Bruce Oppenheimer and Larry Dodd, 401–436. 10th ed. Washington, DC: CQ Press, 2013.

Goldsmith, Jack L. *Power and Constraint: The Accountable Presidency After 9/11.* New York: W. W. Norton, 2012.

Howell, William G. *Power Without Persuasion.* Princeton, NJ: Princeton University Press, 2003.

Kerwin, Cornelius. *Rulemaking.* 3rd ed. Washington, DC: CQ Press, 2003.

## NOTES

1. The "toolkit" metaphor is borrowed from phraseology used by William G. Howell in *Power Without Persuasion* (Princeton, NJ: Princeton University Press, 2003).

2. Allen Schick, *The Federal Budget,* 3rd ed. (Washington, DC: Brookings Institution Press, 2007), chap. 2.

3. A good overview of the politics surrounding New Deal legislation can be found in Stephen J. Wayne's *The Legislative Presidency* (New York: Harper Row, 1978).

4. *A.L.A. Schechter Poultry Corp. v. United States,* 295 U.S. 495 (1935).

5. The beginning of the end of restraint on Congress's powers to regulate commerce was in 1937. Legal scholars point to the *West Coast Hotel Co. v. Parrish,* 300 U.S. 379 (1937), case as a key turning point.

6. The White House Office itself, housing the president's closest advisers, and the Office of Management and Budget spearhead the Executive Office of the President. Other agencies in the EOP attempt to manage complex policy areas that span several agencies, including the Council on Environmental Quality, the National Security Staff, the Office of Science and Technology Policy, and several others.

7. Independent counsels were often highly controversial, especially Lawrence Walsh, who looked into wrongdoing in the Reagan administration, and Kenneth Starr, who led investigations concerning President Clinton. Eventually, both parties agreed that it would be wise to let the law that established the office expire. This happened in 1999.

8. The classic work on this topic is Morris Fiorina's *Congress: Keystone of the Washington Establishment* (New Haven, CT: Yale University Press, 1989).

9. See Howell, *Power Without Persuasion;* Phillip J. Cooper, *By Order of the President* (Lawrence: University Press of Kansas, 2002); and Kenneth R. Mayer, *With the Stroke of a Pen* (Princeton, NJ: Princeton University Press, 2002).

10. Rob Stein and Michael Shear, "Funding Restored to Groups That Perform Abortions, Other Care," www.washingtonpost.com/wp-dyn/content/article/2009/01/23/AR20 09012302814.html.

11. Cornelius Kerwin, *Rulemaking,* 3rd ed. (Washington, DC: CQ Press: 2003).

12. Many independent regulatory agencies are given the authority in law to put forth regulations without OIRA review.

13. Interview with Cory Claussen, professional staff, Senate Committee on Agriculture, December 8, 2012.

14. The authorization was subsequently lowered to less than $500 billion, and this aspect of the bailout ended up costing taxpayers very little money once the banks got on their feet. The program was expanded to assist other entities.

15. Davis Polk, "Dodd-Frank Progress Report, January 2013," www.davispolk.com/files /Publication/7191edca-f4ed-4460-a514-01ca9d3cf8b9/Presentation/PublicationAttach ment/63d52126-7e7f-477a-b47c-08e8acfe145e/Jan2013_Dodd.Frank.Progress.Report .pdf.

16. Danielle Douglas and Dina ElBoghdady, "Regulatory Criticized for Delay in Finalizing 2010 Volcker Rule," *Washington Post,* October 26, 2012, A15.

17. Ben Protess, "Behind the Scenes, Some Lawmakers Lobby to Change the Volcker Rule," http://dealbook.nytimes.com/2012/09/20/behind-the-scenes-a-lawmaker-pushes -to-curb-the-volcker-rule/.

18. See www.iom.edu/Reports/2009/School-Meals-Building-Blocks-for-Healthy -Children.aspx.

19. David Rogers, "Susan Collins Triumphs in Spud Fight," *Politico,* October 18, 2011, www.politico.com/news/stories/1011/66304.html.

20. Ibid.

21. Ibid.

22. This chart shows the pre-2012 and current school lunches as developed by the Food and Nutrition Service at the Department of Agriculture: www.fns.usda.gov/cnd /Governance/Legislation/cnr_chart.pdf.

23. Robert C. Byrd, "Preserving Constitutional War Powers," *Mediterranean Quarterly* 14, no. 3 (2003): 2.

24. Louis Fisher, *Presidential War Power* (Lawrence: University Press of Kansas, 1995), 1, quoting Edwin B. Firmage, "War, Declaration of," in *Encyclopedia of the American Presidency,* edited by Leonard Levy and Louis Fisher (New York: Simon & Schuster, 1994), 1573.

25. In the past couple of decades, an argument has been made in some quarters that Congress's power to declare war means that Congress has the power to recognize the existence of a war already in progress. The argument is that the commander-in-chief power and other Article II provisions were always meant to give the president the power

to assess the international situation and commit the nation to war and to have Congress follow up with an official "declaration." Taking this position is Albert Jenner, "Fixing the War Powers Act," *Heritage Lectures*, no. 529 (May 22, 1995), www.heritage.org/research /nationalsecurity/hl529.cfm.

26. David Gray Adler, "The Constitution and Presidential Warmaking: The Enduring Debate," *Political Science Quarterly* 103, no. 1 (1988): 1–36.

27. Quoted in Edward Keynes, *Undeclared War* (State College: Pennsylvania State University Press, 2004), 2.

28. Quoted in ibid.

29. John Yoo, *The Powers of War and Peace* (Chicago: University of Chicago Press, 2006).

30. See *United States v. Curtiss-Wright Export Corporation* (1936).

31. Quoted in Richard Benedetto, "Remember When Partisan Politics Stopped at the Water's Edge?," *USA Today*, November 18, 2005, www.usatoday.com/news/opinion /columnist/benedetto/2005-11-18-benedetto_x.htm.

32. Quoted in *The American Experience: The Presidents*, PBS special, www.pbs.org/wgbh /amex/presidents/36_l_johnson/l_johnson_foreign.html.

33. Alfred Cumming, "Statutory Procedures Under Which Congress Is to Be Informed of U.S. Intelligence Activities, Including Covert Actions," Congressional Research Service, January 18, 2006.

34. Ibid., 7–8.

35. Fox Butterfield, "Casey Said to Have Failed to Follow Arms Rule," *New York Times*, April 3, 1987, http://query.nytimes.com/gst/fullpage.html?res=9B0DE1D6103DF930A3 5757C0A961948260.

36. Jack L. Goldsmith, "The Accountable Presidency," *New Republic*, February 1, 2010.

37. See Jack L. Goldsmith's *Power and Constraint: The Accountable Presidency After 9/11* (New York: W. W. Norton, 2010), 129.

38. Executive Order 12333, first signed by President Ronald Reagan in 1981.

39. Jennifer Kibbe, in "Congressional Oversight of Intelligence: Is the Solution Part of the Problem?," *Intelligence and National Security* 25, no. 1 (2010): 24–49, does a great job of explaining why it is so much more difficult to conduct oversight on intelligence matters given the classified nature of much of the information.

40. E-mail exchange with Dickinson College political scientist Andrew Rudalevige. See his book *The New Imperial Presidency* (Ann Arbor: University of Michigan Press, 2006).

41. On the relationship between the branches in foreign policy, see Cecil Van Meter, *Invitation to Struggle: Congress, the President, and Foreign Policy*, 4th ed. (Washington, DC: CQ Press, 1992).

42. See Howell, *Power Without Persuasion*, chap. 5.

43. See Kerwin, *Rulemaking*, 30.

# 12
CHAPTER

# Congress and the Courts

During his confirmation hearings in January 2006 for a vacancy on the US Supreme Court, federal appellate court judge Samuel Alito was subjected to intensive questioning by Democratic senators on the Judiciary Committee. He had been nominated for the opening by President George W. Bush. An excerpt of his exchange with Senator Patrick Leahy (D-VT) about his association with Concerned Alumni of Princeton University (CAP) provides insight into the tensions and high stakes involved in the confirmation process.

> SENATOR LEAHY: [CAP] is a group that received attention because it was put together but it resisted the admission of women and minorities to Princeton. They were hostile to what they felt were people that did not fit Princeton's traditional mold: women and minorities. . . . And yet you proudly, in 1985, well after—well after the criticisms of this—in your job application proudly put that you were a member of it, a member of Concerned Alumni of Princeton University, a conservative alumni group. Why in heaven's name, Judge, with your background and what your father faced, why in heaven's name were you proud of being part of CAP?
>
> JUDGE ALITO: Well, Senator, I have wracked my memory about this issue, and I really have no specific recollection of that organization. But since I put it down on that statement, then I certainly must have been a member at that time. But if I had been actively involved in the organization in any way, if I had attended meetings, or been actively involved in any way, I would certainly remember that, and I don't. And I have tried to think of what might have caused me to sign up for membership. And if I did, it must have been around that time.

LEAHY: But, Judge, with all due respect, CAP was most noted for the fact that they were worried that too many women and too many minorities were going to Princeton. In 1985, when everybody knew that's what they stood for, when a prominent Republican like Bill Frist and a prominent Democrat like Bill Bradley both had condemned it, you, in your job application, proudly stated this as one of your credentials. Now, you strike me as a very cautious and careful person. And I say that with admiration, because a judge should be. But I can't believe that at 35, when you're applying for a job, that you're going to be anything less than careful in putting together such a job application. And, frankly, I don't know why that was a matter of pride for you at that time.[1]

As the transcript from the hearing illustrates, senators are concerned about the background, experience, and associations of nominees to the federal bench. Although once there was a commonly held notion that judges would be neutral and simply apply the law to the case at hand, federal judges now are widely viewed as players in the policy-making process whose judgments often have a profound impact on society. As a result, the factors that drive their thinking are of great interest to elected officials.

Curiously, the framers of the Constitution spent relatively little time debating the creation of a federal court system in Philadelphia in 1787. The main focus there was on establishing the powers of the preeminent branch of government, Congress, and to a significant extent, the presidency. In fact, the Constitution placed decisions about the specific structure and jurisdiction of the federal court system into the hands of Congress, and they did not even address the question of the proper qualifications for members of these courts.

This chapter will examine the interplay between Congress and the federal court system in four sections. First, we consider the creation of the federal courts by Congress from the broad guidelines provided in the Constitution. At the beginning, a three-tiered system was established, with a district or trial level and an appellate level to go with the Supreme Court—the only component explicitly specified.

Next we look at how the courts became major players in the federal system by establishing the power of judicial review of laws passed by Congress. After judicial review was established in *Marbury v. Madison*, 5 U.S. 137 (1803), federal courts have weighed in periodically on the constitutionality of laws passed by Congress. We track some of the major pronouncements of the Supreme Court, including during the late 19th century, the New Deal period, and more recently, when more conservative courts have occasionally struck down provisions of law that pushed the boundaries of Congress's power to regulate commerce and campaign activity.

Federal courts have also delved into the regulatory process, making determinations as to whether agency decisions are in keeping with their organic laws.

In the third section, the selection and approval process for federal court judges is discussed. As we saw at the very beginning of the chapter, the qualifications and viewpoints of Supreme Court justices have become a point of great contention. The same sometimes holds true for lower-court nominees. This is because, although the federal courts serve as referees instead of players in the policy-making process—weighing in when cases are brought to their attention—the cases that do come before them involve tremendously important matters. Furthermore, the courts' pronouncements, though not always supported by all parties, are routinely enforced. As a result, the judicial philosophy and ideological orientation of prospective judges become key factors.

At the end of the chapter, we look ahead to the types of issues that the federal courts will be called upon to adjudicate in the coming years—covering controversial areas in social and regulatory policy. In Congress, this means an intense interest in both the types of judges nominated by presidents as well as the decisions they make while serving on the bench.

## THE CREATION OF THE FEDERAL COURT SYSTEM

The provisions of Article III of the US Constitution do not portend the importance of the federal courts in the United States today. Article III, Section 1, merely provides that "the judicial Power of the United States shall be vested in one supreme Court, and in such inferior Courts as the Congress may from time to time ordain and establish." When the First Congress convened in 1789, one immediate task was to organize the structure for the federal judiciary.

The members of the new Congress were uncertain about the creation of lower federal courts, largely because of the existence of state-level courts that had been in operation since as early as 1691. Additionally, as was the case with many of the decisions of the founding conventions and the early congresses, state boundaries were important to respect in the new federal system. After all, there would have been no Constitution had the states not chosen to ratify it.

When the First Congress passed Senate Bill 1, now known as the **Judiciary Act of 1789**, it created a federal judicial system that had three tiers. At the trial level, Congress established a system of **district courts**, *one in each state,* presided over by one district judge each. At the intermediate appellate level (where district court decisions could be appealed), three **circuit courts** were created to span the whole country as it stood at the time; the panel of judges to decide appeals was composed of one district court judge and two justices from the Supreme Court. No one actually served only at the intermediate appellate court level. Finally, at the apex, was the Supreme Court, as established by Article III of the Constitution. Over the course of the nation's history, the basic three-tiered structure of the federal courts has remained as formed in the Judiciary Act of 1789.

But as the nation industrialized and grew, so too did litigation in the federal court system. The workload of the US Supreme Court, in particular, was shifting as questions about national policies were moving to the forefront. The growth of the nation's physical landmass also increased the amount of time district judges had to serve on the appellate circuit. Following the Civil War, Congress addressed the need for reorganization of these circuit courts. This reorganization in 1869 increased the number of circuits to nine, gave the circuit courts greater control over appeals, created positions at the circuit level, and also "free[d] the Supreme Court to concentrate on the key cases."[2]

Responding to further increases in litigation, Congress created the Circuit Courts of Appeals with the passage of the Evarts Act in 1891, named after its sponsor, New York senator William Maxwell Evarts. The nine regional appellate courts further insulated the US Supreme Court—which would not have to handle the circuit caseload. Within two years of this expansion, Congress created an additional circuit to cover the District of Columbia; this appellate court would address cases that arose from conflicts associated with the growth of the federal bureaucracy.

Although the structure of the courts of appeals has remained intact since 1891, the boundaries of the courts have shifted as Congress recognized the expansion of the nation's population and the concomitant increase in caseloads. Also, two additional Circuit Courts of Appeals were created in the 20th century, bringing the total to 11 (not counting the DC Circuit). In 1982, Congress added an appellate court, the US Court of Appeals for the Federal Circuit, with a jurisdiction unrelated to geography, but instead based on specific cases involving patents, customs, and some other matters.

Today, there are 94 district courts that still conform to the idea from 1789 of retaining jurisdiction within a state's boundary (some states have more than one); these district courts have 677 federal judgeships, all created by Congress to address a myriad of questions associated with the ever-growing body of federal law (see Table 12.1). Within the US Courts of Appeals, today, there are 179 judgeships. As it has done throughout our nation's history, Congress continues to evaluate the amount of litigation and the need to adapt the number of federal circuits and judgeships.

As for the Supreme Court, while Article III of the Constitution put it in place, its size was not specified. In the beginning, the Court was composed of a chief justice and five associate justices. The lack of prestige in serving on this new federal court was evident, with President Washington having the opportunity to replace four of the six justices, including the chief justice. The Court's size varied some in the

**TABLE 12.1  The United States Federal Courts**

| | |
|---|---|
| SUPREME COURT | The United States Supreme Court |
| | 9 Judgeships |
| APPELLATE COURT | United States Courts of Appeals |
| | 179 Judgeships |
| | 11 Regional Circuit Courts |
| | US Court of Appeals for the District of Columbia Circuit |
| | US Court of Appeals for the Federal Circuit |
| TRIAL COURT | United States District Courts |
| | 677 Judgeships |
| | 94 Judicial Districts |
| | US Bankruptcy Courts |
| | US Court of International Trade (9 Judgeships) |
| | US Court of Federal Claims |
| | 874 Total Judgeships |

19th century, before its present size—nine justices including the chief justice and eight associate justices—was established in 1869. Despite the continuity, the very size of the Supreme Court has been vigorously contested, as we shall see later in the chapter.

## CONGRESS AND THE SUPREME COURT: A HISTORY OF JUDICIAL REVIEW

Just as the Constitution was vague on the question of the structure of the federal court system, it did not discuss the Court's ability to serve as a check on the power of Congress or the executive. The Constitution does provide in Article III, Section 2, both original and appellate jurisdiction for the US Supreme Court—which means that certain types of federal cases would be taken up first by the Supreme Court (original jurisdiction), while others would be brought to the Court by appeal (appellate jurisdiction). Under its original jurisdiction, the Court would act as a trial court "in all cases affecting ambassadors, other public ministers and consuls, and those in which [one of the states] shall be party." The question of what types of cases would come to the Supreme Court on appeal would be established by Congress. Wanting to establish the balance between the already existing state and the newly minted federal courts, the First Congress provided the Supreme Court with appellate jurisdiction in cases involving decisions by state courts that overturned a federal law or treaty or upheld a state law that was potentially in conflict with the Constitution or treaties.

However, unlike modern constitutions, notably those written in the 20th and 21st centuries for new and emerging democracies, the Constitution is silent on the Supreme Court's ability to exercise the power of **judicial review**, that is, the power to determine that acts of the legislative and executive branches are unconstitutional.

Under Chief Justices John Jay (1789–1795), John Rutledge (1795), and Oliver Ellsworth (1796–1800), the Court conducted little business and confronted relatively little controversy about the scope of its jurisdiction. The work of the early Court did not raise constitutional issues; from 1793 until 1800, nearly half (47.5 percent) of the Court's workload focused on admiralty or maritime issues.[3] One case of note during the tenure of Chief Justice Ellsworth that was a harbinger of major change was *Hylton v. United States*, 3 U.S. 171 (1796). In this case, the Court upheld an act of Congress that levied a duty on carriages.

The transition between the presidencies of John Adams and Thomas Jefferson in 1801 was a major event in American history, as Jefferson represented a different political party (the Democratic-Republicans) and a very different perspective on the role of the federal government from the first two presidents. This produced a good deal of bad blood and ultimately changed the shape of the relationship between the three branches of the national government.

In the election of 1800, the Federalists (Adams's party) lost control of the presidency and Congress. Attempting to retain control of at least one branch of government, the lame-duck Federalist-controlled Congress passed the Judiciary Act of 1801, with its stated purpose to reorganize the federal judiciary. As part of the act, Congress created six judicial circuits and new judgeships to replace the need for Supreme Court justices to "ride the circuit"—or sit on cases at the appellate level above the district courts. With less than three weeks until the end of his presidency, Adams signed the bill into law and began the process of nominating individuals who supported the Federalist agenda to the new positions. Alternately called the "Midnight Judges Act," the law precipitated the constitutional crisis at the heart of *Marbury v. Madison* (1803).

Under the leadership of newly appointed chief justice John Marshall (1801–1835), the Supreme Court was asked to hear the case of William Marbury, one of the midnight appointees, who did not receive his commission—essentially the official documents enabling him to take office as justice of the peace for the District of Columbia—even though his nomination had been approved by the Senate. After President Jefferson took office, he instructed the secretary of state not to accept the commissions that arrived late, so Marbury was denied the position. (Marbury was an ardent Federalist and supporter of Adams.) Marbury brought his case directly to the US Supreme Court under Section 13 of the Judiciary Act of 1789, which provided for the use of a **writ of mandamus**, which would compel the secretary of state to deliver Marbury's commission to the federal bench.

In crafting the opinion for the Court, Chief Justice Marshall and his colleagues answered not only the question at hand (Marbury's claim to the justice of the peace position), but also made a power grab. Marbury should be given the position because his nomination was approved by the Senate, they wrote; however, they also ruled that the mechanism through which Marbury sought relief, coming directly to the Supreme Court by the process laid out in the Judiciary Act, was unconstitutional. In effect, this particular provision of the Judiciary Act of 1789 had changed the language and intent of the Court's original jurisdiction in Article III of the Constitution. Congress was within its constitutional powers to determine the scope of the Court's appellate jurisdiction (as set out in Article III), but not its original jurisdiction. Marbury never received his commission.

Reaching its conclusion in *Marbury,* Chief Justice Marshall relied on Article VI, the Supremacy Clause, to take power for the Court and away from the legislative and executive branches:

> It is also not entirely unworthy of observation that, in declaring what shall be the supreme law of the land, the Constitution itself is first mentioned, and not the laws of the United States generally, but those only which shall be made in pursuance of the Constitution, have that rank.
>
> Thus, the particular phraseology of the Constitution of the United States confirms and strengthens the principle, supposed to be essential to all written Constitutions, that a law repugnant to the Constitution is void, and that courts, as well as other departments, are bound by that instrument.

This ruling established the power of judicial review—the role of the Court as the arbiter of the language and intent of the Constitution. The exercise of this power has placed the Court at odds with Congress on many highly charged issues through the years.

## Exercising Judicial Review: Slavery and Taxes

The second occasion when the Court struck down an act of Congress was in the infamous *Dred Scott v. Sandford,* 60 U.S. 393 (1857) decision. *Dred Scott* invalidated the so-called Missouri Compromise of 1820, the law that had settled for decades the question of the extension of slavery to the territories, balancing the interests of free and slave states. Interpreting the Constitution, Chief Justice Roger Brooke

Taney (1836–1864) determined that Congress did not have the authority to prohibit the ownership of slaves in any territory, which had been part of the Compromise.[4] The delicate balance on the slave question was eroded, and the nation moved to civil war.

The relationship between Congress and the Court faced another significant test in *Pollock v. Farmers' Loan and Trust Co.,* 158 U.S. 601 (1895). Tax policy had become an important topic, as the Civil War's cost placed demands on the national treasury. In the post–Civil War era, populists and progressives advocated for an income tax in order to fund more programs and redistribute wealth that was associated with increased industrialization.

In 1894 Congress passed the Wilson-Gorman Tariff Act that levied a 2 percent tax on personal income and corporate profits in excess of $4,000. With some reservations, President Grover Cleveland signed the bill. Charles Pollock, an investor in the Farmers' Loan and Trust Company, filed suit, challenging the right of Congress to levy what was a "direct" tax. He maintained that under Article I, Section 9, of the Constitution, Congress was not permitted to levy direct taxes unless they were in proportion to the census.

On appeal, the US Supreme Court heard the views of corporate interests and the US government over five days of oral argument in March 1895. These arguments mirrored the debates on taxation at the Constitutional Convention in 1787 and the views of the authors of *The Federalist Papers* (James Madison, Alexander Hamilton, and John Jay). The conclusion of the March arguments and subsequent discussions among the justices produced a four-to-four deadlock because Justice Howell Jackson was not present for the vote, being bedridden with tuberculosis. The Court granted five hours of reargument in early May 1895.

On May 20, 1895, in a five-to-four opinion authored by Chief Justice Melville Fuller (1888–1910), the Supreme Court struck down the provision of the Wilson-Gorman Tariff Act that taxed personal income and corporate profits. In writing for the narrowest of majorities, Fuller noted, "The power to lay direct taxes apportioned among the several States in proportion to their representation in the popular branch of Congress, a representation based on population as ascertained by the census, was plenary and absolute; but to lay direct taxes without apportionment was forbidden." The Court concluded with an explicit statement: "We are of the opinion that taxes on personal property, or on the income of personal property, are likewise direct taxes."

According to Peter Irons, "The *Pollock* decision provoked little denunciation [in the near term] from labor and 'progressive' groups, but they had little influence" at the time.[5] Eventually, progressive forces gained more power in Congress and began efforts to revive a national income tax. Ultimately, the 16th Amendment to the US Constitution was ratified in 1913. It read: "The Congress shall have power to lay and collect taxes on incomes, from whatever source derived, without apportionment among the several States, and without regard to any census or enumeration." Ironically, the amendment was originally proposed by *opponents* of a federal income tax—they believed it would never be ratified, thereby settling the issue once and for all. Like political maneuvers sometimes do, the strategy backfired.

After the tempest surrounding the *Pollock* decision, the Court invalidated only a handful of statutes over the next three decades, including two acts regulating the use of child labor.[6] When progressives in Congress attempted to use the same strategy of adding an amendment to the US Constitution on that issue, the effort failed.

## Congress and the Supreme Court During the Great Depression

The Great Depression and the election of Franklin Delano Roosevelt in 1932 marked the start of a period where a contentious relationship developed between the Supreme Court and the president, with Congress in the middle of the brawl.

Coming into office, FDR championed a package of legislation that would provide a **New Deal** for citizens. The legislative package consisted of proposals that were wide ranging and designed to get the nation's economy back on its feet. The first piece of legislation, the Emergency Banking Act, was signed into law only five days after Roosevelt gave the inaugural address in which he essentially declared war on the Depression. From March 9 through June 16, 1933, with the help of an overwhelmingly Democratic Congress, 16 pieces of legislation were passed and sent on for FDR's signature. The New Deal included the Agricultural Adjustment Act to address the sorry state of the farm economy; the Tennessee Valley Authority Act, which provided power to millions; and the National Industrial Recovery Act (NIRA), which was meant to address a wide range of economic ills.

Because of the fundamental change that was implicit in the passage of the New Deal, including a huge surge in federal regulations, challenges mounted and eventually reached the Supreme Court. The first two cases—consolidated in *Panama Refining Company v. Ryan,* 293 U.S. 388 (1935)—dealt with the NIRA. In these, the Court ruled that Section 9(c) of the NIRA represented an unconstitutional delegation of power to the executive branch by Congress and invalidated executive orders that affected the oil companies, as well as regulations issued by the Department of the Interior.

Writing for the Court, Chief Justice Charles Evans Hughes (1930–1941) noted that:

> Such regulations become, indeed, binding rules of conduct, *but they are valid only as subordinate rules and when found to be within the framework of the policy which the legislature has sufficiently defined.* . . . Thus, in every case in

which the question has been raised, the Court has recognized that there are limits of delegation which there is no constitutional authority to transcend. We think that § 9 (c) goes beyond those limits. . . . If § 9 (c) were held valid, *it would be idle to pretend that anything would be left of limitations upon the power of the Congress to delegate its law-making function.* (emphases added)

The debate over the scope of the New Deal legislation was far from over, and the NIRA was again under fire in *A.L.A. Schechter Poultry Corporation v. United States,* 295 U.S. 495(1935). At issue in *Schechter* was the Live Poultry Code, a set of regulations promulgated under the law. Striking a second blow to the NIRA, Chief Justice Hughes again reiterated the Court's position that sweeping delegations of legislative power to the executive branch defied the separation of powers embodied in the Constitution. He wrote:

In view of the scope of [broad delegation of power in the statute], and of the nature of the few restrictions that are imposed, the discretion of the President in approving or prescribing codes [or "regulations," in common contemporary language], and thus enacting laws for the government of trade and industry throughout the country, is virtually unfettered. We think that the code-making authority thus conferred is an unconstitutional delegation of legislative power.

An additional blow to the New Deal came on January 6, 1936, when the Court, in a six-to-three decision, struck down a taxation provision in the Agricultural Adjustment Act in *United States v. Butler,* 297 U.S. 1 (1936). While Justice Owen Roberts recognized that Congress was granted the power to tax in Article I, Section 8, of the Constitution, the majority opinion challenged the range of the federal taxing power:

The power of taxation, which is expressly granted, may, of course, be adopted as a means to carry into operation another power also expressly granted. But resort to the taxing power to effectuate an end which is not legitimate, not within the scope of the Constitution, is obviously inadmissible.

The majority also stated what it viewed as its responsibility to the national government:

The Constitution is the supreme law of the land ordained and established by the people. All legislation must conform to the principles it lays down.

> When an act of Congress is appropriately challenged in the courts as not conforming to the constitutional mandate, the judicial branch of the Government has only one duty—to lay the article of the Constitution which is invoked beside the statute which is challenged and to decide whether the latter squares with the former. All the court does, or can do, is to announce its considered judgment upon the question.

The decision in *Butler* provoked "acrimonious criticism of the Court," according to historian William Leuchtenberg.[7] The scope of the criticism was wide ranging, from administration officials, newspaper columnists, and citizens who viewed the Court as usurping power from the elected branches of government.

While Roosevelt himself remained silent, Congress began initiatives to curb the power of the Supreme Court. According to Michael Nelson, "The years 1935–1937 saw more Court-curbing bills introduced in Congress than in any other three-year (or thirty-five year) period in history." Creating new vacancies on the US Supreme Court and establishing a mandatory retirement age were but two of the proposals considered. Senators discussed constitutional amendments that would limit the scope of judicial review. For example, "Senator George Norris proposed an amendment that would require the agreement of seven justices in order to declare a federal law unconstitutional."[8]

The landslide victory for FDR in the 1936 presidential contest gave him the opportunity to work with Congress in addressing the attack on the New Deal by the High Court. The president's Democratic base in the Senate and the House of Representatives was strengthened above and beyond the massive majorities he already enjoyed, with gains of seven and nine seats, respectively. Like many aspects of politics, timing is crucial—President Roosevelt was keenly aware that challenges to two pillars of the New Deal, the Social Security Act and the National Labor Relations Act, were on the Court's docket for early 1937.

Working with his advisers and academics, Roosevelt orchestrated the development of his "Court-packing" plan, which he announced on February 5, 1937. For each federal judge who had turned 70 years old and did not resign or retire within six months of reaching this age, the president would be empowered to nominate an additional member to the bench. Roosevelt rationalized that life tenure "was not intended to create a static judiciary";[9] his plan would reinvigorate not only the US Supreme Court, but also the lower federal courts, which he claimed were overburdened and inefficient. (If this had passed, Roosevelt could have potentially added six additional Supreme Court justices.)

FDR appealed to the American public for support of his proposal through a "fireside chat" on March 9, 1937, the evening before the Senate Judiciary Committee began hearings on what was called the Judiciary Reorganization Bill of 1937. The president implored listeners to restore the control to the elected branches of the national government:

> When the Congress has sought to stabilize national agriculture, to improve the conditions of labor, to safeguard business against unfair competition, to protect our national resources, and in many other ways, to serve our clearly national needs, the majority of the Court has been assuming the power to pass on the wisdom of these acts of the Congress—and to approve or disapprove the public policy written into these laws.[10]

The hearings before the Senate Judiciary Committee did not proceed as FDR had envisioned. In the roughly five weeks between his announcement and the start of the hearings, supporters and critics engaged in a wide-ranging debate about the merits of the proposal.

> The opponents made the most of the opportunity offered by the public hearings. . . . They led off with their most important witness, Senator [Burton] Wheeler [D-MT] . . . [who challenged] the Administration's contention that aged Justices were unable to keep abreast of their work. With a dramatic flourish, Wheeler . . . unfolded a letter from Charles Evans Hughes. The Chief Justice denied that the Court was behind in its business or that more Justices would increase efficiency.[11]

At the conclusion of the hearings, the Senate Judiciary Committee voted 10 to 8 to report the legislation out of committee "adversely"—meaning the bill was sent to the floor with an unfavorable recommendation. The committee report attacked the Court-packing plan as an effort to punish the Court and to trample the power of the federal judiciary established in the Constitution.

The full Senate began its consideration of the bill on July 2, 1937. Reports in the Washington press predicted a victory for Roosevelt, as Senate majority leader Joseph Robinson (D-AR) supported the legislation and was prepared to battle its opponents. Fate was not on the president's side. Robinson died less than two weeks into the debate. His death seemed to presage the fate of the Court-packing plan. On August 26, 1937, the legislation was passed *without the key provision to change the composition of the federal courts.*

Although Roosevelt may have lost the initial battles over the scope of Congress's power to regulate commerce, ultimately he won the war. Whether responding to political pressure, or because of the nuances of particular cases, or a real change of heart on the part of some justices, the Court had already begun ratifying major parts of the New Deal in the spring of 1937, including both the Social Security Act and the National Labor Relations Act,[12] as the Judicial Reorganization Act was being considered.

Most important, in cases in 1937 and subsequently in the early 1940s, the **Commerce Clause** of the Constitution, which gave Congress the power "to regulate [c]ommerce . . . among the several States," was reinterpreted. Prior to these cases, the Court had very strictly limited Congress's ability to regulate wages, working conditions, and other business activities, determining that strictly speaking, these were internal state matters. With *West Coast Hotel Co. v. Parrish,* 300 U.S. 379 (1937) and *U.S. v. Darby Lumber Co.,* 312 U.S. 100(1941), in effect the Court said that virtually any business activity could be regulated by Congress *as long as that business engaged in interstate commerce.*

In the wake of the New Deal period, then, the Court had established, at least broadly, the scope of Congress' power to regulate commerce. In the 1935 cases (*Schechter* and *Panama Refining Company*), the Court ruled that executive branch regulatory activity was invalid if it ranged too far from what was in statute. At the same time, the reinterpretation of the Commerce Clause just described made it possible for almost any business activity to be regulated so long as Congress was reasonably clear about its intentions.

The debate on the Commerce Clause in particular is important to understand, as it continues to be discussed and, in fact, litigated today. Liberals side with the idea that the Commerce Clause allows a very wide range of regulation of business in the interest of the public good. Conservatives tend to believe, as we shall see below, that the Constitution permits only regulations that clearly relate to commercial activity "among the several states."

## The Modern Era: The Court Strikes Down Major Legislation

While the US Supreme Court invalidated major legislation in some instances during the New Deal era, the middle decades of the 20th century—from the 1940s up to the 1970s—saw the Court commonly defer to the legislative branch.[13] But in more recent years, with more conservative courts, in particular those headed by Chief Justices William Rehnquist (1986–2005) and John Roberts (2005–present), Congress and executive branch agencies have occasionally been reined in.[14]

Two cases illustrate how the Supreme Court has inserted itself into contentious issues at the top of the partisan political agenda. In *United States v. Lopez,* 514 U.S. 549 (1995), the US Supreme Court considered the constitutionality of the Gun-Free School Zones Act of 1990, which used the Commerce Clause to justify regulating firearm possession near schools. In the initial paragraph of the five-to-four majority opinion, Chief Justice Rehnquist clearly stated the provision of the legislation in question and position of the more conservative members of the bench (Justices O'Connor, Scalia, Kennedy, and Thomas):

> In the Gun-Free School Zones Act of 1990, Congress made it a federal of-
> fense "for any individual knowingly to possess a firearm at a place that the
> individual knows, or has reasonable cause to believe, is a school zone. The
> Act neither regulates a commercial activity nor contains a requirement that
> the possession be connected in any way to interstate commerce. We hold
> that the Act exceeds the authority of Congress "[t]o regulate Commerce . . .
> among the several States."

Although the Court often considers report language attached to statutes, as well as proceedings from congressional committees, the majority in *Lopez* noted that the government in defending the law in court had even conceded that Congress had not expressly stated how gun possession in a school zone affects interstate commerce. Stepping back from almost six decades of expanding the powers of Congress under the Commerce Clause, the High Court under the conservative bloc led by Chief Justice Rehnquist started to check the power of Congress. In effect, it put some limits on what can be regulated using that particular clause as justification.

President Clinton reacted immediately to the *Lopez* decision, directing Attorney General Janet Reno to draft legislation that would pass constitutional muster. Working with a bipartisan group of senators, Senator Herbert Kohl (D-WI) introduced the legislation, noting that the bill addressed the Supreme Court's concerns by adding "a requirement that the prosecutor prove as part of each prosecution that the gun moved in or affected interstate or foreign commerce."[15] The changes to the Gun-Free School Zones Act were adopted; subsequent challenges in the US Courts of Appeal have upheld the revisions.

More recently, Chief Justice John Roberts wrote in *National Federation of Independent Business v. Sebelius*, 132 S.Ct. 603 (2012), that the Commerce Clause was not a permissible justification for the individual mandate to buy health insurance in the **Affordable Care Act (2010)**. While Roberts allowed that provision in the law to stand on other grounds, he explicitly stated that the Commerce Clause cannot be construed to permit requirements or regulations that are not directly related to commerce. Although the insurance industry obviously constitutes a major part of the US economy, Roberts suggested making people purchase health insurance is a regulation of personal behavior and not strictly speaking of commercial activity.[16]

In the area of campaign finance, in *Buckley v. Valeo*, 424 U.S. 1 (1976), the US Supreme Court weighed in on congressional efforts—the Federal Election Campaign Act (1974) in particular—to prevent the appearance of corruption from money in campaigns. In that instance (as noted in Chapter 4), while upholding some restrictions on campaign contributions, the Court began a consistent jurisprudence that equated expenditures of moneys in the course of campaigns as a form of free speech, sometimes striking down statutory provisions as violations of the First Amendment.

In this century, the Court weighed in on the Bipartisan Campaign Reform Act of 2002 (BCRA), or, as it was popularly known, McCain-Feingold. The BCRA was an attempt to limit the influence of "soft money" on campaigns as well as the timing of advertising by unions, corporations, or not-for-profit organizations. Although the bill's constitutionality was for the most part upheld in *McConnell v. Federal Election Commission,* 540 U.S. 93 (2003), it was a different story a few years later.

Subsequent challenges to provisions of the BCRA emerged during the 2008 election cycle after the composition of the Court had changed. Three new justices were serving, including Sonia Sotomayor, John Roberts, and, most important, Samuel Alito. Alito, a George W. Bush nominee, was approved by the Senate in 2006 to replace Sandra Day O'Connor, who had voted to uphold the BCRA in *McConnell.* Alito was widely anticipated to be a strong skeptic of some of the provisions of the law.

The Supreme Court ruled in another five-to-four decision that corporations and unions have the same political speech rights as individuals under the First Amendment, striking down some of the expenditures limits set in the Bipartisan Campaign Reform Act. The decision in *Citizens United v. Federal Election Commission,* 558 U.S. 310 (2010), effectively overruled *McConnell* and a related decision, *Austin v. Michigan Chamber of Commerce,* 494 U.S. 652 (1990), that had upheld restrictions on independent corporate expenditures. The decision also called into question laws on campaign financing in 24 states. The decision opened up the 2010 elections to new moneys for "electioneering communication" from corporations' and unions' general treasuries. Outside groups' spending soared by more than 400 percent in 2010 from the 2006 midterm level.

## The Modern Era: The Courts and Regulatory Policy

As we saw in the last chapter, one of the key elements of federal policy in the 21st century is the implementation of laws by executive branch agencies, which are often given wide latitude to put in force regulations to clean up rivers, inspect the food supply, ensure the safety of the workplace, and so on. We have also seen in earlier chapters that most laws addressing complex issues are open to interpretation.

A classic example of the courts weighing in on agency interpretations of federal statute involves the 1990 Clean Air Act. The Environmental Protection Agency under the George W. Bush administration interpreted the act narrowly when it came to regulating carbon dioxide emissions. The State of Massachusetts and other plaintiffs claimed it was harmed by the agency's refusal to limit emissions from the transportation sector. In a five-to-four decision, *Massachusetts v. Environmental Protection Agency*, 549 U.S. 497 (2007), the Court ruled that, in fact, the Clean Air Act should be interpreted to include carbon dioxide as a pollutant, stating that the "EPA identifies nothing suggesting that Congress meant to curtail EPA's power to treat greenhouse gases as air pollutants." The agency was then required to go back to the drawing board, coming up with new regulations to limit $CO_2$ emissions.

More recently, the US Court of Appeals for the District of Columbia tapped the brakes on some EPA actions in *EME Homer City Generation v. EPA*, 696 F.3d 7 (2012). The court of appeals determined that certain regulations limiting emissions in one state that crossed over into other states went beyond the scope of the Clean Air Act. In 2013, the EPA appealed the ruling to the Supreme Court.

The *Homer* case highlights the importance of the US Court of Appeals for the District of Columbia, which handles challenges to federal regulations. Many of these cases are either never appealed or simply not taken up by the Supreme Court, in effect giving the court of appeals the last say. Given the contentious nature of much regulatory policy—often a flash point for the two parties, with Democrats normally more supportive of environmental and some other forms of federal regulation and Republicans typically opposed—the makeup of that court gains a great deal of attention. The panel has 11 seats, although more often than not in recent years several remain open due to the difficulty of getting Senate approval for presidential nominations given the high stakes.

As noted in the *Hill* in 2013, "The Court is in a position to help decide crucial battles over the Affordable Care Act and the Dodd-Frank Wall Street reform law and Obama's quest to counter the effects of climate change."[17] In all of those areas, and many others, the perspectives of the people on the DC Court of Appeals will say a lot about the direction of policy.

## THE NOMINATION AND APPOINTMENT PROCESS

We have seen the tremendous impact the decisions of judges in the federal court system can have on the direction of public policy by weighing in on the constitutionality of legislation as well as whether agency actions are consistent with existing law. Because of this, the selection process for federal judges is tremendously consequential.

Article II of the Constitution sets forth the role for the president and the Senate in selecting members of the federal court system. Section 2 of that article provides that the president "shall nominate, and by and with the Advice and Consent of the Senate, shall appoint . . . judges of the Supreme Court."

Unlike the office of president or for members of Congress, the Constitution is silent on the formal qualifications for members of the Supreme Court. Over time, however, the justices who have served or are serving on the Court have developed into "an elite within an elite." The justices "come from upper- or upper-middle-class families that are politically active and that have a tradition of public, and often, judicial service."[18] The exceptions to this stereotype have largely come in the second half of the 20th century and into the current one. For example, Justice Thurgood Marshall, the first African American to be appointed to the High Court, was the son of a Pullman car steward and the great-grandson of a slave. One of President Obama's nominees, Sonia Sotomayor, was raised in modest circumstances in the Bronx by her mother following the death of her father when Sotomayor was nine years old.

The lack of formal qualifications has given rise to differing priorities among presidents, which has produced mixed results when looking toward Senate confirmations. Scholars Robert Carp and Ronald Stidham examine four informal factors that determine who becomes a federal judge: professional competence, political qualifications, self-selection, and the element of pure luck. Whereas self-promotion in politics would come as no surprise, nor would the element of pure luck, these two factors are not the focus of the vetting before the Senate for potential justices—or, for that matter, for lower federal court judges. Instead, the emphasis in the nomination and subsequent confirmation focuses on the first two factors, professional competence and political qualifications. Within the latter category, political ideology and judicial philosophy have moved to the forefront in the confirmation process.

The reason for this shift is simple. First, federal judges weigh in on major matters of policy and the interpretation of constitutional rights; second, they are effectively appointed for life. The Constitution's use of the term *good behavior* has given the members of the Supreme Court the ability to shape the constitutional landscape longer than any presidential administration. Indeed, presidents often view these appointments as a potential check on the legislative branch after their departure from the Oval Office (e.g., President John Adams's efforts in 1801 to pack the bench with Federalists in the wake of the election of Thomas Jefferson). Table 12.2 provides a listing of US Supreme Court justices who served during the 20th and 21st centuries. On average, these men and women served 15.6 years,[19] or about twice the length of time a president may serve.

Take the case of Chief Justice William Rehnquist as an example. Rehnquist was nominated by President Richard Nixon for a seat as an associate justice on the Supreme Court in 1972. After serving 14 years, he was then confirmed as chief justice during the second term of President Ronald Reagan. Rehnquist's conservative judicial philosophy, which reflected the values of both Nixon and Reagan, contributed to the Court's shift to the right for the better part of 30 years before his death in 2005.

**TABLE 12.2. US Supreme Court Justices and Their Length of Tenure (20th and 21st Centuries)**

| President | Justice | Tenure | Years |
|---|---|---|---|
| Roosevelt, T. | Oliver Wendell Holmes | 1902–1932 | 29.1 |
| | William Rufus Day | 1903–1922 | 19.7 |
| | William Henry Moody | 1906–1910 | 3.9 |
| Taft | Horace Harmon Lurton | 1910–1914 | 4.5 |
| | Charles Evans Hughes | 1910–1916 | 5.7 |
| | Edward D. White | 1910–1921 | 10.4 |
| | Willis Van Devanter | 1911–1937 | 26.4 |
| | Joseph Rucker Lamar | 1911–1916 | 5.0 |
| | Mahlon Pitney | 1912–1922 | 10.8 |
| Wilson | James Clark McReynolds | 1914–1941 | 26.3 |
| | Louis Dembitz Brandeis | 1916–1939 | 22.7 |
| | John Hessin Clarke | 1916–1922 | 5.9 |
| Harding | William H. Taft | 1921–1930 | 8.6 |
| | George Sutherland | 1922–1938 | 15.3 |
| | Butler Pierce | 1923–1939 | 16.9 |
| | Edward Terry Sanford | 1923–1930 | 7.1 |
| Coolidge | Harlan Fiske Stone | 1925–1941 | 16.3 |
| Hoover | Charles Evans Hughes | 1930–1941 | 11.4 |
| | Owen Josephus Roberts | 1930–1945 | 15.2 |
| | Benjamin Nathan Cardozo | 1932–1938 | 6.3 |
| Roosevelt, F. | Hugo Lafayette Black | 1937–1971 | 34.1 |
| | Stanley Forman Reed | 1938–1957 | 19.1 |
| | Felix Frankfurter | 1939–1962 | 23.6 |
| | William Orville Douglas | 1939–1975 | 36.6 |
| | Frank Murphy | 1940–1949 | 9.5 |
| | James Francis Byrnes | 1941–1942 | 1.2 |
| | Harlan Fiske Stone | 1941–1946 | 4.8 |
| | Robert Houghwout | 1941–1954 | 13.2 |
| | Wiley Blount Rutledge | 1943–1949 | 6.6 |
| Truman | Harold Hitz Burton | 1945–1958 | 13.0 |
| | Fred M. Vinson | 1946–1953 | 7.2 |
| | Tom Campbell Clark | 1949–1967 | 17.8 |
| | Sherman Minton | 1949–1956 | 7.0 |
| Eisenhower | Earl Warren | 1953–1969 | 15.7 |
| | John Marshall Harlan | 1955–1971 | 16.5 |
| | William J. Brennan, Jr. | 1956–1990 | 33.8 |
| | Charles Evans Whittaker | 1957–1962 | 5.0 |
| | Potter Stewart | 1958–1981 | 22.7 |
| Kennedy | Byron Raymond White | 1962–1993 | 31.2 |
| | Arthur Joseph Goldberg | 1962–1965 | 2.8 |
| Johnson, L. | Abe Fortas | 1965–1969 | 3.6 |
| | Thurgood Marshall | 1967–1991 | 24.0 |
| Nixon | Warren E. Burger | 1969–1986 | 17.3 |
| | Harry A. Blackmun | 1970–1994 | 24.2 |
| | Lewis F. Powell, Jr. | 1972–1987 | 15.5 |
| | William H. Rehnquist | 1972–1986 | 14.7 |
| Ford | John Paul Stevens | 1975–2010 | 34.5 |
| Reagan | Sandra Day O'Connor | 1981–2006 | 24.4 |
| | William H. Rehnquist | 1986–2005 | 18.9 |
| | Antonin Scalia | 1986–present | 27.1 |
| | Anthony M. Kennedy | 1988–present | 25.7 |
| Bush, G. H. W. | David H. Souter | 1990–2009 | 18.7 |
| | Clarence Thomas | 1991–present | 22.0 |
| Clinton | Ruth Bader Ginsburg | 1993–present | 20.2 |
| | Stephen G. Breyer | 1994–present | 19.2 |
| Bush, G. W. | John G. Roberts | 2005–present | 8.1 |
| | Samuel A. Alito, Jr. | 2006–present | 7.8 |
| Obama | Sonia Sotomayor | 2009–present | 4.2 |
| | Elena Kagan | 2010–present | 3.2 |

While building a legacy may be on the mind of the president when making a nomination, the job of the Senate is to vet the nominee. Given the lack of formal qualifications in the Constitution, the president has the ultimate plum of patronage with regard to seats on the federal bench and, in particular, on the Supreme Court. The Senate provides the check on the president's power and, in turn, supports the integrity of the federal courts as an institution. The Senate has not capitulated in the process, subjecting judicial nominees to a thorough and, increasingly, more public and political confirmation process.

## The Confirmation Process

Political machinations aside, the confirmation process for nominees to the Supreme Court has largely been routinized as the nation has moved into its third century of existence. As partisan and ideological battles shape the legislative process, these differences have a profound impact on the confirmation process, with increased attention from organized interests and the mass media.

A president should expect to make one nomination to the US Supreme Court during a four-year term of office.[20] Jimmy Carter has been the only president who did not have the opportunity to nominate a justice to the Supreme Court during a full four-year term. This contrasts with his successors: Reagan had three, two for George H. W. Bush (who served only one term), two for Clinton, two for George W. Bush, and two for Obama as of 2013.

Presidents, with the help of their inner circle of advisers, often prepare a short list of potential nominees. Following the tradition established by President Washington, the nominees typically are individuals who reflect the president's political views. Individuals who are seeking appointments to federal judgeships engage in varying types and degrees of self-promotion. Generally, self-promotion is considered unseemly at the Supreme Court level, so must be done very subtly; it is done more aggressively at the circuit and district levels, although it is still important to leave the work to well-placed surrogates.

With the short list in hand, the investigation of the individual's character and fitness for the position begins. The investigation proceeds on two tracks, with the FBI looking into the potential nominees' fitness from a security standpoint and the White House seeking to uncover more generically embarrassing information that might derail the nomination. The president's aides will scrutinize a prospective nominee's body of scholarship (articles they have written, speeches they have given), and, if they have served as a judge, their body of work on either a state or a lower federal court.

Reviewing a nominee's professional qualifications is not sufficient in the era where nominations play out like theater on C-SPAN and a host of other political news outlets. Well before the Internet era, the spectacle of the 1991 confirmation hearings for Clarence Thomas showed the need for greater scrutiny on nominees' personal lives during the investigation process. The uncovering of Thomas's allegedly inappropriate associations with subordinates in previous positions of authority led to a circus-like atmosphere at the hearing. Even before that, in 1987, President Reagan's nomination of Douglas Ginsburg was sent off track by revelations of his having smoked marijuana as a law professor.

One actor that has been important in this phase of the confirmation process is the American Bar Association. Starting in the Truman administration, the ABA has rated nominees for the High Court. In the early years, the ABA held what amounted to a veto power over nominees. In recent years, the organization has remained an important player, but its influence is no longer unchallenged.

Following the nomination by the president and the background investigation, the attention then shifts to the Senate Judiciary Committee. Whereas the task of the Senate Judiciary Committee is to determine the nominee's fitness for the bench, the vetting in recent years has, just like with the president's appointment process, emphasized the nominee's ideological position. This has had the effect of increasing partisan wrangling as the nomination proceeds.

Questioning from members of the Senate Judiciary Committee has taken on decidedly different tones in recent decades, with some nominees being subjected to fierce and often blistering attacks and others being treated in a more civil manner. The example of the exchange between Senator Leahy and US Supreme Court nominee Judge Samuel Alito at the beginning of this chapter illustrates the tenor of the proceedings when the Senate Judiciary Committee is controlled by the party out of power.

With its hearings concluded, the nomination moves to consideration by the full Senate. The majority leader makes the final determination on when to call for consideration by the full chamber. Strategic considerations affect the timing of the debate and the subsequent roll-call vote. It is rare that members of the Senate choose to employ a filibuster in the confirmation of nominees for the US Supreme Court, but contentious nominations (e.g., the nomination of Associate Justice Abe Fortas to the position of chief justice in 1971) can produce marathon sessions and occasionally negative results. Indeed, the Senate is hardly a rubber stamp in the confirmation process, rejecting 12 nominees since the Court's inception (see Table 12.3).

## Nomination Battles in the Modern Era

The modern era of contentious Supreme Court nomination battles could be said to begin with the announced retirement of Chief Justice Earl Warren (1953–1969) in

**TABLE 12.3. US Supreme Court Nominations Rejected by the US Senate**

| Nominee | President | Senate Vote (YEA/NAY) |
| --- | --- | --- |
| John Rutledge | George Washington | 10–14 |
| Alexander Wolcott | James Madison | 9–24 |
| John Spencer | John Tyler | 21–26 |
| George Woodward | James Polk | 20–29 |
| Jeremiah Black | James Buchanan | 25–26 |
| Ebenezer Hoar | Ulysses Grant | 24–33 |
| William Hornblower | Grover Cleveland | 24–30 |
| Wheeler Peckham | Grover Cleveland | 32–41 |
| John Parker | Herbert Hoover | 39–41 |
| Clement Haynsworth Jr. | Richard Nixon | 45–55 |
| G. HarroldCarswell | Richard Nixon | 45–51 |
| Robert Bork | Ronald Reagan | 42–58 |

1968. As he was running for the Republican nomination in 1968, Richard Nixon rejected the liberal activist judiciary exemplified by Warren and championed a return to "law and order." To many, Nixon was echoing the sentiment of a large segment of the public that wanted to impeach the chief justice and some of his brethren for decisions that in its view stretched the Constitution beyond its meaning. These began with *Brown v. Board of Education,* 347 U.S. 483 (1954), which ended legal segregation in the South (a decision some regarded at the time as an unconstitutional violation of states' prerogatives), and included a range of rulings that enhanced the rights of the accused in criminal proceedings—*Escobedo v. Illinois,* 378 U.S. 478 (1964), *Miranda v. Arizona,* 384 U.S. 436 (1965), and *Gideon v. Wainwright,* 372 U.S. 335 (1963), for example, as well as the decision that public school prayer was an unconstitutional violation of the First Amendment.

Warren announced his retirement in '68 in order to give outgoing liberal president Lyndon Johnson an opportunity to name his successor. He did not want to wait, which would mean taking the chance of a Republican winning the election that fall. Johnson decided to elevate Associate Justice Abe Fortas to the chief's position—a decision requiring Senate approval. Johnson and Fortas had been friends and political confidantes for almost three decades. When LBJ became president following the assassination of John Kennedy, Fortas was one of the first advisers who came to the White House to consult with him. As Bruce Allen Murphy wrote, "Fortas was more than just a political insider; in the new president's mind he was 'Lyndon Johnson's insider.'"[21]

The Fortas nomination grew increasingly contentious as hearings progressed before the Senate Judiciary Committee. Fortas, during his testimony, disclosed his interactions with the president and members of the White House staff even while he was serving on the High Court. The final straw for several senators who supported Fortas's nomination was the revelation that he had received a substantial private payment (about 40 percent of his Court salary) for teaching a law school class. President Johnson withdrew the nomination on October 4, 1968. With only thirty-two days until the presidential election, Johnson did not make another nomination. Fortas resigned from the Court on May 14, 1969.

Within his first six months in office, Richard Nixon now had two seats to fill on the US Supreme Court, the vacancy created by the retirement of Chief Justice Warren and the seat that had been held by Fortas.[22] Nixon's selection for chief justice, US Court of Appeals judge Warren Burger (1969–1986), faced little opposition during his Senate confirmation process, ultimately winning approval by a vote of 74–3 in June 1969.

But filling the other vacancy proved more problematic for Nixon, presaging an era of ideological struggles over the composition of the Court. His first nominee, Clement Haynsworth Jr., embodied the conservative values that President Nixon desired in his appointees—in particular, opposition to judicial activism on civil rights questions and the rights of accused criminals. Controversy swirled as the American Bar Association, the American Federation of Labor and Congress of Industrial Organizations, and the National Association for the Advancement of Colored People (NAACP) challenged his ethics for participating in decisions as a member of the Fourth Circuit Court of Appeals when there were alleged conflicts of interest.

Senator Walter Mondale (D-MN) offered the following statement after eight days of hearings before the Senate Judiciary Committee:

> Mr. President, I very much hope that President Nixon will withdraw his nomination of Judge Clement F. Haynsworth to the Supreme Court.
>
> Judge Haynsworth's record clearly indicates his insensitivity to the needs and aspirations of Americans who have spent the last 50 years struggling for equal rights and the opportunity to earn a decent living. Moreover, I believe the conduct of his personal financial affairs shows far less discretion than we should expect of a Supreme Court Justice.
>
> It is no accident that those most concerned about civil rights and economic justice—the civil rights movement and organized labor—have led the effort to prevent Judge Haynsworth's confirmation. To these groups and organizations, the nomination of a man with Judge Haynsworth's philosophy is a throwback to an America of a different age—when segregation was the law of the land and when working men were prevented from organizing for higher wages and better working conditions.

> If this nomination is not withdrawn, the Senate will have to make a deci-
> sion which may prove to be a turning point in American history.[23]

Although the Senate Judiciary Committee voted to confirm Haynsworth by a vote of 10–7, the confirmation vote before the full Senate on November 21, 1969, produced a defeat for President Nixon. Haynsworth's nomination was defeated by a vote of 55–45. An angry President Nixon vowed that he would find another nominee who met his criteria: a southern conservative who professed a strict-constructionist perspective with regard to constitutional interpretation.

On the eve of his first anniversary in office, President Nixon nominated George Harrold Carswell for the seat on the Court vacated by Fortas. Coming from the Fifth Circuit Court of Appeals, he had been confirmed by the Senate seven months earlier; he had also been confirmed by the Senate previously as a US attorney in 1953 and as a federal district court judge in 1958. The lack of a record on the appellate bench was undoubtedly attractive to President Nixon, as the nomination was less likely to draw criticism from civil rights and labor organizations. However, the media and the Senate were skeptical of President Nixon's choice, and intense scrutiny began to raise more questions about Carswell's fitness.

The five days of confirmation hearings before the Senate Judiciary Committee provided public insight into Carswell's actions and beliefs. Controversies ranged from Carswell's purported support for maintaining segregationist policies in public accommodations (at a municipal golf course) to his lack of judicial qualifications. Despite concerns, the Committee voted 13–4 in favor of Carswell's nomination.

Consideration by the full Senate produced more scrutiny and statements that would eventually derail the nomination:

> Senator Roman Hruska (R-NE), the president's floor manager of the nom-
> ination, made a pathetic fumbling attempt to convert the candidate's me-
> diocrity into an asset: "Even if he is mediocre there are a lot of mediocre
> judges and people and lawyers. They are entitled to a little representation,
> aren't they, and a little chance? We can't have all Brandeises, Cardozos, and
> Frankfurters, and stuff like that there."[24]

The Senate rejected Carswell's nomination by a vote of 51–45 on April 8, 1970.

The rejection of three nominations to the US Supreme Court in the Johnson-Nixon era showed the significant check that the Senate could exercise on presidential appointments. Each of the rejected nominees was plagued with questions about his past, many of which were raised by outside organized interests. The members of the Senate Judiciary Committee acted upon these reports and invited more input into the confirmation process. This was clearly evident in subsequent nominations for the High Court such as President Reagan's choice of Robert Bork.

Nearing the end of his second term of office, President Reagan was given the opportunity to name his fourth member of the US Supreme Court when Justice Lewis Powell announced his retirement in July 1987. While being keenly aware of the need to protect his conservative legacy, President Reagan wanted to avoid a confirmation fight like the one experienced only two years earlier with the elevation of William Rehnquist to chief justice of the Supreme Court. In announcing the selection of US Court of Appeals judge Robert Bork, the president "highlighted his nominee's unquestionably outstanding professional and scholarly qualifications as a means of placing him above the political fray."[25]

It did not matter. Organized interests like the NAACP, the National Education Association, and the National Abortion Rights Action League immediately denounced the Bork nomination. Even before hearings began before the Senate Judiciary Committee, senators publicly expressed their concerns about how this nomination would change the direction of the Court. In October 1987, the Senate Judiciary Committee voted 9–5 to send the nomination to the full Senate with a recommendation that it be rejected. Neither Judge Bork nor President Reagan would withdraw the nomination despite the negative recommendation from the Judiciary Committee or the public criticism.

When the full Senate was called to order to vote, there was little expectation that Bork would be confirmed. The nomination was defeated 58–42, the largest margin of defeat for a nominee in the nation's history. Following the defeat of his nomination, Judge Bork commented on the nature of the confirmation process at the time: "There is now a full and permanent record by which the future may judge not only me but the proper nature of a confirmation proceeding."[26]

President Reagan received his notice that most Democrats in the Democratically controlled Senate, as well as many moderate Republicans, would not support another nominee like Bork. Senator Edward Kennedy (D-MA) stated: "If we receive a nominee who thinks like Judge Bork, who acts like Judge Bork, who opposes civil rights and civil liberties like Judge Bork, he will be rejected like Judge Bork." Senator John Warner (R-VA) expressed the views of some Republicans when he said, "I searched the record. I looked at this distinguished jurist, and I cannot find in him the record of compassion, of sensitivity and understanding of the pleas of the people to enable him to sit on the highest Court of the land."[27]

In addition to the dozen rejections, presidents have had to withdraw 11 nominations before the Senate concluded its decision-making process. Looking at Table 12.4, the contentious relationship that existed between the Senate and the president with regard to judicial confirmations is particularly evident with Presidents John Tyler and Ulysses Grant. Arguably, these nominations, five in total, would have ended with rejections by the full Senate if the president had not tried to save political face by withdrawing his choice. President Lyndon Johnson, a master at counting votes from his days as Senate majority leader, withdrew the Fortas nomination in the waning days of his presidency. President George W. Bush withdrew the nomination of John Roberts as associate justice when Chief Justice William Rehnquist died unexpectedly and renominated him as chief justice, taking advantage of his relative youth to have an impact on the Court for decades to come.

President Bush was not as strategic with his selection of White House counsel Harriet Miers. Miers had a distinguished career, serving as an elected member of

**TABLE 12.4 US Supreme Court Nominations Withdrawn Before a Vote by the US Senate**

| NOMINEE | PRESIDENT | REASON FOR WITHDRAWAL |
| --- | --- | --- |
| William Patterson | George Washington | Nomination withdrawn because Patterson was serving in the US Senate and there was a conflict with the Incompatibility Clause in the US Constitution (Article I, Section 6); nomination and subsequent appointment as associate justice upon his retirement from the Senate |
| Reuben Walworth (two separate occasions) John Spencer Edward King | John Tyler | Nominations were continually tabled by senators who did not support President Tyler; Tyler eventually withdrew the nominations |
| Millard Fillmore | George Badger | Nomination tabled by the Senate; Fillmore was a lame duck, and senators preferred to allow incoming president Franklin Pierce to make the nomination |
| George Williams | Ulysses Grant | Nomination withdrawn due to a scandal involving the purchase of a carriage from Justice Department funds while Williams served as attorney general of the United States |
| Caleb Cushing | Ulysses Grant | Nomination as chief justice withdrawn due to increased scrutiny of political statements made by Cushing when serving as a diplomat |
| Abe Fortas | Lyndon Johnson | Nomination withdrawn after revelations of close association with President Johnson and significant payments for activities based upon his position as associate justice |
| John Roberts Jr. | George W. Bush | Nomination as associate justice withdrawn; nomination and subsequent appointment as chief justice |
| Harriet Miers | George W. Bush | Nomination withdrawn at the request of Miers |

the Dallas City Council, as president of the Texas State Bar, and as a member of the Texas Lottery Commission. The relationship between President Bush and Miers was a close one, with Miers acting as Bush's personal attorney when she was a partner at Locke Lord, one of Dallas's leading law firms. She subsequently followed Bush to Washington, DC, to serve as staff secretary and chief of staff before moving to the role of counselor to the president.

However, unlike the eight sitting justices, Miers had never served as a judge at either the state or federal level. President Bush did not hide this fact, and in fact trumpeted it, noting that many previous justices (Rehnquist, Byron White, and others) served with distinction in part *because* they had different backgrounds.

But the battle over the Miers nomination was significant not because of her alleged lack of qualifications; instead, it developed into a question of her commitment to conservative ideals in the interpretation of the law and the Constitution. Even with a Republican Senate, conservative President Bush did not get a pass. Questions arose about Miers's positions on controversial issues, such as abortion. Speeches she had made while serving as the president of the Texas Bar Association provided more fodder for conservatives, who accused Miers of being a liberal judicial activist in the mold of Earl Warren and then sitting justices, such as Ruth Bader Ginsburg and David Souter. As the criticism mounted, Miers asked President Bush to withdraw her nomination. In the end, in the 21st century it is the ideology of the nominees that matters the most. Presidents are under intense pressure from their political bases—mostly made up of groups with strong policy preferences, liberal ones for Democrats and conservative ones for Republicans—to put up nominees who will reflect their views for years and even decades to come.

## CONCLUSION: THE FEDERAL COURTS IN THE 21ST CENTURY

The importance of the federal judiciary in shaping public policy is considerable. As we have seen, the courts weigh in on the interpretation of the Constitution and the actions of federal agencies in the implementation of the law. This puts the courts in a position to make their mark on an incredibly wide range of issues. This is true even though the courts are not in a position to "take the initiative," as Congress and the president are.

On public policy, it is Congress that provides the statutory authority for federal programs to exist and agencies to act. Congress passes the law, and then agencies implement it. The implementation often requires interpretation and regulatory decisions that have the force of law. Presidents can take the initiative by promoting their policy agenda and encouraging Congress to pass laws to make their agenda real; presidents also have the opportunity to put their stamp on policy by issuing executive orders that direct agency actions where the law gives them wiggle room, as well as through their influence over the regulatory process. Meanwhile, the courts have to sit back and wait for aggrieved parties to come to them with cases that challenge the constitutionality of laws or the way the law is being implemented.

Having said that, there is always plenty for the Supreme Court and the lower federal courts to do. Even a cursory look at the cases the Supreme Court agreed to decide in 2013 is revealing. The Court is set to decide whether DNA swabs of people arrested for serious crimes violates 4th Amendment privacy rights, the constitutionality of parts of the Voting Rights Act, whether university racial preference policies run afoul of the Equal Protection Clause (14th Amendment); different aspects of the same-sex marriage issue, including the constitutionality of the Defense of Marriage Act; and many other matters. The DC Court of Appeals will be asked to rule on a wide range of regulatory matters in the coming years. Especially controversial among them will be whether regulatory actions by the EPA are within the bounds of the Clean Air Act and other statutes, whether Health and Human Services is acting in ways consistent with the Affordable Care Act, and whether the Security and Exchange Commission, the Consumer Financial Protection Bureau, and other agencies are promulgating regulations that comport with the Dodd-Frank financial regulation reform bill.

With health care, environmental regulation, energy policy, financial policy, and controversial social issues coming to the attention of the federal court system for final resolution, the nomination and approval process for positions on these courts become political footballs. Democrats, when they hold the White House, look to fill the courts with people who are open to a broad regulatory role for the federal government and who hold a view of the Constitution as a "living document" that has to be reinterpreted based on changing circumstances in order to stay relevant. Conservative Republicans, on the other hand, believe that Congress is unwise when regulating commercial activity too vigorously and sometimes even goes beyond what the Constitution allows. In addition, they see the constant reinterpretation of the Constitution as a subjective enterprise that essentially allows a person to have the Constitution say whatever they wish it said. They prefer judges who will rely on a stricter interpretation based on what the words of the Constitution meant when they were written.

These views—the liberal "living document" approach and the conservative "strict-constructionist" philosophy—inevitably animate the debate in the Senate over Supreme Court and many lower-court nominations. But it is really the whole Congress that pays attention to the decisions of the federal courts. Bills often have to be written (or rewritten if struck down) with an eye to whether they will stand up to judicial scrutiny. In addition, the details in ambitious legislation need to be carefully considered for the possibility that down the line, agency actions will be challenged in court. In the separated system of government in the United States, the judicial branch has become a major player.

## Questions for Discussion

1. Some of the framers of the Constitution thought the judicial branch would be "the least dangerous" in terms of its threat to the liberty of the citizens. Why did they think so? Why do you think many people in contemporary America think that, in fact, the Supreme Court poses a threat to the people's rights and liberties, while at the same time many people think that it is the Court that is most important in protecting rights?

2. The interpretation of the Commerce Clause of the Constitution has been a point of great contention for much of our history. Why do you think this is so? How does Congress fit into the debate? Find and read the article by James B. Stewart below. Which side do you come down on?

## Suggestion for Further Reading

Coyle, Marcia. *The Roberts Court: The Struggle for the Constitution.* New York: Simon and Schuster, 2013.

Pacelle, Richard L., Jr. *The Role of the Supreme Court in American Politics: The Least Dangerous Branch?* Boulder, CO: Westview Press, 2008.

Stewart, James B. "In Obama's Victory, a Loss for Congress." *New York Times,* June 29, 2012. www.nytimes.com/2012/06/30/us/conservatives-see-silver -lining-in-health-ruling.html?pagewanted=all&_r=0.

## NOTES

1. "US Senate Judiciary Committee Hearing on Judge Samuel Alito's Nomination to the Supreme Court," *Washington Post,* January 10, 2006.

2. Robert A. Carp and Ronald Stidham, *Judicial Process in America,* 2nd ed. (Washington, DC: CQ Press, 1993), 35.

3. Sheldon Goldman, *Constitutional Law and Supreme Court Decision-Making: Cases and Essays* (New York: Harper & Row, 1982), 43.

4. In addition, *Dred Scott* earned its reputation as the worst decision in history by denying the right of *even free black citizens* to sue in federal court.

5. Peter Irons, *A People's History of the Supreme Court* (New York: Penguin Putnam, 1999), 245.

6. See *Hammer v. Dagenhart,* 247 U.S. 251 (1918); and *Bailey v. Drexel Furniture Co.,* 259 U.S. 20 (1922).

7. William E. Leuchtenberg, *The Supreme Court Reborn: The Constitutional Revolution in the Age of Roosevelt* (New York: Oxford University Press, 1995), 96.

8. Michael Nelson, "The President and the Court: Reinterpreting the Court-Packing Episode of 1937," *Political Science Quarterly* 103, no. 2 (1988): 273.

9. Leuchtenberg, *Supreme Court Reborn*, 134.

10. Transcript of the fireside chat, March 9, 1937, www.pbs.org.

11. Leuchtenberg, *Supreme Court Reborn*, 140.

12. See *National Labor Relations Board v. Jones & Laughlin Steel Corporation*, 301 U.S. 1 (1937); and the Social Security Act of 1935 (see *Helvering v. Davis*, 301 U.S. 619 [1937] and *Steward Machine Company v. Davis*, 301 U.S. 538 [1937]).

13. See the appendixes of Lori Ringhand's "The Rehnquist Court: A 'By the Numbers' Retrospective," *Journal of Constitutional Law* 9, no. 4 (2007): 1033–1081, for a comprehensive analysis of the statutes, both federal and state, overturned during the Warren, Burger, and Rehnquist Courts.

14. See Thomas Keck's "Party, Policy, or Duty? Why Does the Supreme Court Invalidate Federal Statutes?," *American Political Science Review* 101, no. 2 (2007): 321–338; and Ringhand, "Rehnquist Court."

15. *Congressional Record*, June 7, 1995, S7919–S7920.

16. For a useful discussion of the decision and different views of the interpretation of the Commerce Clause, see James B. Stewart, "In Obama's Victory, a Loss for Congress," *New York Times*, June 29, 2012, www.nytimes.com/2012/06/30/us/conservatives-see-silver-lining-in-health-ruling.html?pagewanted=all&_r=0.

17. Ben Goad, "Courts Cry "Court Packing" on Appeals Nominees," *Hill*, May 29, 2013, 1.

18. Carp and Stidham, *Judicial Process in America*, 223.

19. This calculation excludes the current members of the US Supreme Court (as of May 1, 2013).

20. S. Sidney Ulmer, "Supreme Court Appointments as a Poisson Distribution," *American Journal of Political Science* 26, no. 1 (1982): 113–116.

21. Bruce Allen, *Fortas: The Rise and Ruin of a Supreme Court Justice* (New York: William Morrow, 1988), 115.

22. For a thorough examination of the struggles between President Nixon and the Senate in the confirmation process, see Henry Abraham's *Justices, Presidents, and Senators: A History of the U.S. Supreme Court Appointments from Washington to Clinton*, rev. ed. (Lanham, MD: Rowman and Littlefield, 1999), chap. 2.

23. *Congressional Record*, October 2, 1969, 28211.

24. Abraham, *Justices, Presidents, and Senators*, 11.

25. Ibid., 297.

26. Linda Greenhouse, "Bork's Nomination Is Rejected, 58–42; Reagan 'Saddened,'" *New York Times*, October 24, 1987, A1.

27. Ibid.

# 13

# Interest Groups and
# Congressional Policy Making

On December 14, 2012, twenty children and six teachers and support personnel were killed by a lone gunman inside Sandy Hook Elementary School in Newtown, Connecticut. The Sandy Hook tragedy, where young children were targeted, seemed to galvanize more interest in congressional efforts at gun control than the mass shooting at an Aurora, Colorado, movie theater in July 2012, or even the targeting and grievous wounding of Congresswoman Gabrielle Giffords (D-AZ) at a forum in Tucson, Arizona, in January 2011.

In fact, the Newtown shooting moved gun control to the top of the legislative agenda of the 113th Congress.[1] This marked only the third time in a generation when a gun-control measure had made this much headway in the legislative process. In 1994 the controversial Violent Crime Control and Law Enforcement Act was signed into law by President Clinton. Among other provisions, it banned the sale of certain types of assault weapons. (The ban was not permanent—it was set to expire in 2004 and was in fact permitted to do so.) In 1999 a measure that would require background checks at gun shows did not receive support in the House of Representatives after the Senate passed the measure with the tie-breaking vote by Vice President Al Gore.[2]

The tragedy at Sandy Hook and public opinion polls showing increased support for gun-control legislation prompted Senators Joe Manchin (D-WV) and Pat Toomey (R-PA), both from states with long-standing support for gun owners' rights, to push for passage of the Public Safety and Second Amendment Rights Protection Act. The proposed legislation expanded the requirements for background checks and, according to its sponsors, was aimed at keeping guns out of the hands of criminals and the dangerously mentally ill. In their public messages, Toomey and Manchin stressed how its passage would improve public safety.

Organized interests on both sides of this issue unleashed their lobbying efforts using a range of tactics, including direct contact with members and staff, press conferences, mass media advertising, e-mail appeals, and social media outreach. Mayors Against Illegal Guns (a group formed in 2009 by wealthy New York City mayor Michael Bloomberg) spearheaded the gun-control groups and was joined by other groups, including former congresswoman Giffords's new group, Americans for Responsible Solutions, as well as the Sandy Hook parents (who hired a major Washington lobbying firm to aid the effort). The mayors' group spent more than $200,000 in direct lobbying of lawmakers in the first few months of 2013. On the other side, the long-standing National Rifle Association (NRA) spent about $800,000 in opposition to the bill.[3] It was joined by several other pro–gun rights groups, including Gun Owners of America and the National Association for Gun Rights.

Ultimately, the NRA and other advocates for gun ownership rights were successful, as the Manchin-Toomey bill went down to defeat. Although 54 senators supported it, a 60-vote threshold was required for passage. It is a certainty that groups on both sides of the issue will take the battle to the 2014 electoral cycle, spending many millions to elect supporters and defeat opponents of their positions.

This example illustrates the broad range of players and activities that may be involved in efforts to influence the voting decisions of members of Congress. It also points up something more fundamental. In a free society with constitutional protections on free speech and the right to petition the government, individual citizens will see it in their interest to organize around common goals in an effort to influence the policy-making process on issues they feel strongly about. In this chapter, we focus on this activity, specifically the actions of **interest groups** and their paid employees, the lobbyists.

The chapter begins by examining the scope of interest group activity in Washington as it has developed in the last many decades. As we have seen in earlier chapters, federal government programs expanded dramatically in the 20th century and into this century. Concomitantly, groups have formed to advance and protect their interests as the government reaches into nearly every aspect of American society.

The next section looks at the tactics employed in lobbying members of Congress and their staffs, including the recent evolution of social media campaigns. In general, efforts to gain influence over congressional policy making can be fitted into three categories: direct lobbying, indirect lobbying, and grassroots lobbying. Effective interest groups naturally need to convey their position and indeed the intensity of their feeling on the issue. But it is sometimes overlooked that interest groups are in the business of being helpful by providing reliable information in their areas of specialty to help guide members and staff.

We shift gears at this point to the efforts over the years to regulate lobbying to eliminate outright corruption—bribes in exchange for votes—and even regulate the appearance of corruption. Although lobbying restrictions have been in place for more than 70 years, scandals sometimes lead to more efforts to crack down on "influence peddling." We look at the regulations and where the courts stand on them when constitutional questions are raised.

Finally, we consider the most important question: how influential are organized interests? This is a complicated question with no easy answer. We look at what political scientists have found on the subject and discover that the political system's very complexity often makes it difficult for even powerful interests to get their way.

## THE UNIVERSE OF INTEREST GROUPS

Interest group lobbyists are, in fact, hugely important in the day-to-day activities in Congress. There were about 12,000 registered lobbyists in Washington in 2012[4] and probably far more than 100,000 people working in some capacity in the lobbying industry.[5] It is a multibillion-dollar industry. Every imaginable interest is represented, including corporations, unions, charitable organizations, issue and cause groups, trade associations, county and state governments, universities, and so on.

Interest group activity has mushroomed in the past 40 years in Washington. Although lobbyists for various corporate concerns had been fixtures in Washington for decades (as had lobbyists for unions), trying to secure government contracts, tax breaks, or favorable regulatory rulings, the scope of interest group activity was fairly circumscribed. The federal government was a major player in American life in the first half of the 20th century, but it tended to stay out of the affairs of the states in health, housing, education, social issues, and other areas.

As we have seen in previous chapters, the 1960s changed all that. Massive new government programs were put in place during the Great Society of President Lyndon Johnson and into the early years of Richard Nixon's presidency that involved a heavy federal presence in health care, education at all levels, housing, welfare, race relations, women's issues, consumer protection, the environment, the arts, science, and a host of other areas. Rather suddenly, there was not anything in American life that was not touched in a significant way by federal policies.

Many of the new government programs of that era affected corporate America—and, in the eyes of some sectors of the corporate world, often not in a good way. Businesses geared up in ways they never before had to in order to try to mitigate some of the effects of what they regarded as overly burdensome new government regulations and taxes. They established Washington offices (and hired lobbyists from established Washington firms) in order to lobby members of Congress to change the law, or at least take their concerns into consideration. Issue-oriented groups interested in the environment, consumer issues, women's rights, the rights of welfare recipients, and many other issues sprouted up and established a Washington presence. Universities and state and local governments also wanted a piece of the action.

Political scientists describe a kind of **hyperpluralism** that developed at that time.[6] The term **pluralism** describes a political system in which no one particular group dominates the decision-making processes. Instead, numerous groups—economic, cultural, and ethnic—share power, in a sense, in a process of shifting coalitions depending on the issue. One particular group may hold the upper hand for a time in collaboration with some other group or groups, but their interests never coincide perfectly for long, so other combinations of groups coalesce to challenge for influence.

In a country as diverse as the United States, there are thousands of identifiable groups and interests vying to protect or advance their position in society. Not all of them had traditionally found it necessary to expend the time and effort to lobby decision makers in Washington. But as Washington's reach extended into practically every sphere of American life in the 1960s and 1970s, it became apparent that if you didn't want to get the short end of the stick in federal policy, you had to have a presence in Washington.

Hyperpluralism developed in the 1970s as all economic sectors, cultural groups, issue-oriented groups, universities, and the like recognized that in order to remain competitive and protect their interests, they had to be in Washington and had to be active trying to influence the board of directors and agency officials in the executive branch. Corporations realized that if they did not have a presence, their competitors would win the day in the competitive marketplace with tax breaks and favorable regulatory rulings. A state university system would lose out on federal grants if they were not in Washington making their case. People opposed to legal abortion feared the increasing influence of women's groups; they rapidly organized to agitate for more restrictions. Governors who did not have a Washington office would lose highway funding.

Total numbers are hard to measure accurately. Health analysts estimate that the number of health-related groups has increased more than twentyfold since the 1970s. Citizen groups have gone up roughly tenfold in that period. Five or six times as many corporations base their operations in Washington as did 40 years ago. All in all, the number of organized interests active in Washington has probably at least quintupled since the 1960s.[7] As depicted in Figure 13.1, in 2011 there were more than 16,000 interest groups that addressed federal concerns.

**FIGURE 13.1.  Interest Group Presence in Washington**

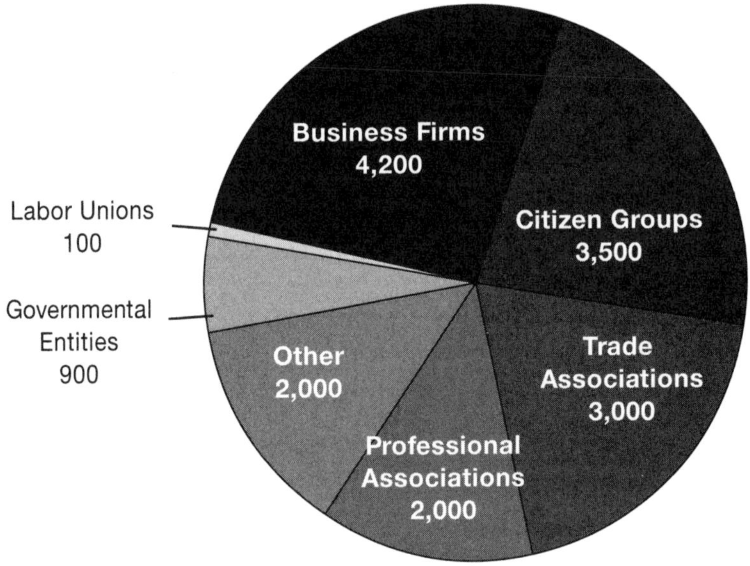

Source: Anthony J. Nownes, *Interest Groups in American Politics* (New York: Routledge, 2013.

Note: Nownes drew from various sources to arrive at the numbers above, as noted on page 29 of his book. It is hard to make exact estimates for a lot of reasons. The interest group community is fluid, and groups change names and associate on temporary and more permanent bases with other groups sometimes under different names. We have included the major groupings. We have not included Political Action Committees, which are technically interest groups but generally have associated groups fitting into the above categories.

## LOBBYING TACTICS

Organized interests of all sorts share the goal of influencing public policy. The tactics used by interest groups fall into three principal areas: direct lobbying, indirect lobbying, and grassroots lobbying.

### Direct Lobbying

**Direct lobbying** relies on access to the members of Congress or, more commonly staff members in personal and committee offices. Increasing access to policy makers is critical for an organized interest group's direct lobbying strategy. Some groups will hire specialists from Washington, DC, lobbying firms who can "open doors" for them. Two hundred thirty-eight clients would not have hired the law firm of Patton Boggs LLP in the first quarter of 2013 if it did not produce results.[8]

Organized interests sometimes use their members in their direct lobbying efforts. For example, the American Association of Retired Persons (AARP) mobilizes its membership for Advocacy Days on Capitol Hill. Members from across the nation arrive in Washington to talk with representatives and senators about issues on the interest group's agenda. In 2011, as budget cuts for Social Security and Medicare loomed, more than 500 members told legislators: "I am NOT a pushover—cut waste, not Medicare and Social Security benefits," according to the AARP website.[9]

But lobbying is about a lot more than just conveying your position. Lobbyists in fact are looking to develop relationships with policy makers. The key to doing this is to be helpful to congressional staff and members. "Being helpful" can take many forms. Members and staff need good information from a wide range of sources to make considered decisions on public policy. A lobbyist will go to great lengths to be the "go-to person" on a particular issue, providing reliable and verifiable information to Congress. Many go out of their way to give due to their opponents' arguments in order to bolster their credibility. Political scientist Anthony Nownes puts it this way: "Lobbying = The Provision of Information."[10] That way, the lobbyist has the ear of the decision makers, which of course is the key to getting their views heard. A lobbyist who is unreliable or provides bad information does not get in the door. Access is the essential ingredient to influence in Washington. By being useful, good lobbyists become integral parts of the legislative process, helping staff with crafting legislation, anticipating roadblocks to success, and building coalitions in support of mutually held objectives.

Who makes the ideal lobbyist? Who is going to be best at understanding the process and helping staff with legislative puzzles? One place to start is at the top. Interest groups heavily recruit among experienced former members and staff. Table 13.1 shows that, remarkably, 39 members who retired following their service in the 112th Congress (2011–2012) were employed as registered lobbyists by the first quarter of 2013.

Moving to the private sector from Capitol Hill may provide a staffer or member a much better salary than he or she can make staying in the public sector. (Members make $174,000 and staff usually much less, although the most experienced ones may make close to $170,000.) The effect of this is that these former insiders are able to be quite useful to congressional staff and members who often know less about the legislative process and lawmaking than they do. Trent Lott, formerly a Republican Senate leader, upon his retirement in 2007 joined with his former Senate colleague John Breaux (D-LA) to form one of the most formidable lobbying teams in Washington, taking on interest group clients interested in making connections on the Hill or better understanding what is likely to happen in their issue area. Billy Tauzin, a onetime Louisiana congressman, could write his own ticket after chairing the Energy and Commerce Committee in the House, signing on to head

**TABLE 13.1. Former Members of the 112th Congress Now Employed as Lobbyists**

| FORMER MEMBER | OFFICE HELD | CURRENT EMPLOYER |
|---|---|---|
| Altmire, Jason | PA-4 | Blue Cross/Blue Shield of Florida |
| Berman, Howard | L CA-28 | Covington & Burling |
| Bingaman, Jeff | NM-Sen | Stanford University |
| Bono Mack, Mary | CA-45 | Faegre BD Consulting |
| Boren, Dan | OK-2 | Chickasaw Nation |
| Brown, Scott | MA-Sen | Nixon Peabody LLP |
| Burton, Dan | IN-5 | Azerbaijan America Alliance |
| Cardoza, Dennis | CA-18 | Manatt, Phelps & Phillips |
| Conrad, Kent | ND-Sen | Campaign to Fix the Debt |
| Critz, Mark | PA-12 | EIS Solutions |
| Davis, Geoff | KY-4 | Republic Consulting LLC |
| DeMint, Jim | SC-Sen | Heritage Foundation |
| Dreier, David | CA-26 | Annenberg Foundation |
| Filner, Bob | CA-51 | San Diego City |
| Gallegly, Elton | CA-24 | California Lutheran University |
| Gonzalez, Charlie | A TX-20 | Via Metropolitan Transit |
| Harman, Jane | CA-36 | Newsweek Daily Beast |
| Hochul, Kathleen | NY-26 | M&T Bank |
| Hutchison, Kay | B TX-Sen | Bracewell & Giuliani |
| Inslee, Jay | R WA-1 | State of Washington |
| Kildee, Dale | E MI-5 | Akin, Gump et al. |
| Kohl, Herb | WI-Sen | Milwaukee Bucks, NBA |
| Kucinich, Dennis | OH-10 | News Corp |
| Kyl, Jon | AZ-Sen | Covington & Burling |
| LaTourette, Steve | OH-14 | McDonald, Hopkins et al. |
| Lieberman, Joe | CT-Sen | American Enterprise Institute |
| Lugar, Richard G. | IN-Sen | Indiana University |
| Mack, Connie | IV FL-14 | Liberty Partners Group |
| Manzullo, Don | IL-16 | Korean Economic Institute of America |
| Nelson, Ben | NE-Sen | National Assn of Insurance Commissioners |
| Pence, Mike | IN-6 | State of Indiana |
| Rehberg, Denny | MT-1 | Mercury/Clark & Weinstock |
| Ross, Mike | AR-4 | Southwest Power Pool |
| Rothman, Steven | R NJ-9 | Sills, Cummis et al. |
| Shuler, Heath | NC-11 | Duke Energy |
| Snowe, Olympia | ME-Sen | Bipartisan Policy Center |
| Stearns, Cliff | FL-6 | APCO Worldwide |
| Walsh, Joe | IL-8 | WIND-AM (560) |
| West, Allen | FL-22 | PJ Media |

*Source:* "Revolving Door: Former Members of the 112th Congress" www.opensecrets.org/revolving /departing.php?cong=112

the Pharmaceutical Research and Manufacturers of America, one of the most powerful lobbies, and eventually moving on to set up his own for-hire lobbying firm.

The most effective lobbyists can go so far as to present complete packages of legislation to lawmakers in order to advance or protect their interests. Organized interests do not try to hide their influence in this portion of the legislative process. According to Kenneth E. Bentsen Jr., the president of the Securities Industry and Financial Markets Association and former representative (D-TX), "We will provide input [to staffers] if we see a bill and it is something we have interest in."[11]

After the Dodd-Frank financial reform bill passed in 2010, banking interests took their pleas for more leniency to the executive branch as it drafted proposed regulations under the new law. According to Michael Beckel, from the Center for Responsive Politics, "More clients who lobbied on Wall Street reform mentioned targeting the Securities and Exchange Commission and the Commodity Futures Trading Commission during the fourth quarter of 2010 than at any other point of the past two years, with more than 100 clients naming each in their lobbying reports."[12] As we saw in Chapter 11, the agencies had implemented far fewer than half of the regulations three years after the bill had passed, even though *all* were meant to be in place by then.

As public interest in the reform efforts waned, the lobbyists returned their attention to members of Congress to repeal portions of Dodd-Frank. Beyond the corporate contributions to support lawmakers' campaign war chests, banking interests also drafted specific legislation to weaken the controls imposed only three years earlier. In fact, according to the *New York Times*, "one bill [HR 992, 113th Congress, first session] that sailed through the House Financial Services Committee [in 2013]—over the objections of the Treasury Department—was essentially Citigroup's. . . . Citigroup's recommendations were reflected in more than 70 lines of the House committee's 85-line bill. Two crucial paragraphs, prepared by Citigroup in conjunction with other Wall Street banks, were copied nearly word for word. (Lawmakers changed two words to make them plural.)"[13]

For organized interest groups, the ability to engage directly with members of Congress (or their senior staff members) is essential. And because of the potential for abuse of these relationships, they have become highly scrutinized in the American political system. Scandals in the forms of bribes and conflicts of interest receive front-page headlines and may prompt legislative responses—a topic we get into later in the chapter.

## Indirect Lobbying

In the case of **indirect lobbying**, groups try to influence broader public opinion to create a better environment for their issues. Sometimes the aim is to achieve a kind of lobbying "bank shot"—create an advertising campaign highlighting issues that encourages citizens to contact lawmakers.

When the federal government began to regulate business more vigorously in the 1960s and 1970s, corporations recognized that they needed to bolster their public image if they were to have any chance to turn back these efforts. Oil companies in particular initiated ad campaigns touting their "corporate responsibility"—basically, how they were giving back to the communities in the states where they had refineries.[14] Similarly, in recent years British Petroleum has gone to great lengths to publicize the contributions it has made to clean-up efforts after the 2010 oil spill in the Gulf of Mexico. In these types of cases, the companies are not looking for citizens to take any action; rather, they are simply trying to improve the political climate in the hopes of preventing future regulations of their activities. Famously, the major health insurers undertook a major campaign in the mid-1990s to turn public opinion against the Clinton administration's plan to reform the health care system. This effort generated thousands of citizen contacts to congressional offices (as well as the White House) and was credited with helping to prevent the consideration of major legislation in Congress.

These days groups—like the gun-rights and gun-control advocacy groups described at the beginning of the chapter, as well as many others—rely on much more than television and radio ads. In the social media era, Facebook, Twitter, and other such platforms are used to gain attention to issues of the day. Firms have sprouted up in Washington, and, in fact, around the country, that specialize in integrating a wide range of indirect (sometimes in tandem with direct) lobbying techniques using old and new media alike. These efforts often take the long view and can bear fruit. For example, some have credited the National Right to Life Committee with moving public opinion in the direction of more conservative positions on abortion through a variety of indirect lobbying techniques.[15] Even more dramatically, swift changes of opinion on gay marriage[16] have been attributed in part to a range of public efforts by the Human Rights Campaign, a gay rights organization, including encouraging millions of people to publicize their attitudes through a red "equal" sign on Facebook.

## Grassroots Lobbying

Activating citizens as lobbyists can also fit into the definition of **grassroots lobbying**. Grassroots lobbying occurs when organizations "mobilize [their own] members to contact a policymaker to influence a specific policy outcome."[17] Before the emergence of the range of communication technologies that we have today, grassroots lobbying focused on having group members write letters or make telephone calls to their members of Congress. The challenge with these efforts is that the specifics of the organization's message were potentially lost in the transmission. Today the group's specific message can essentially be forwarded on by the membership—although it is also true that lawmakers and their staff are frequently skeptical of these campaigns. They find that constituents may not be fully aware of what they are participating in; furthermore, because simply forwarding a message takes virtually no effort, members may not be persuaded that people actually care about the issue.

Still, grassroots lobbying of this sort can make a statement that members pay attention to if the message is clear, emphatic, and widely held. A key advantage of grassroots methods is that they can be much cheaper than hiring lobbyists or orchestrating major multimedia campaigns. Expensive and well-connected lobbyists and television advertising is too pricey for some groups.

## Lobbying Tactics and the Constituent Connection

With both grassroots lobbying and direct lobbying, it is important to show members of Congress the impact of a particular piece of legislation on the people who "hired" them—the constituents back home. The grassroots campaign is most effective when people are sending their views to the House members and senators who represent them. Similarly, lobbyists from the National Association of Counties (NACo) report that they do not need a campaign contribution to get access for direct lobbying. Federal regulatory decisions on land use frequently vex county officials, especially in the western states. And counties across the country are interested in federal legislation in a wide range of areas, from Medicaid to transportation spending to educational requirements. NACo lobbyists bring county officials and sometimes ordinary citizens to Washington to meet their representatives and senators. The members of Congress know full well that they are meeting leaders in the communities they serve and are almost always attentive to their concerns on pending legislation.[18]

If you are on Capitol Hill from the Parkinson's Action Network advocating for stem-cell research money, bring afflicted constituents to the Hill to meet their representatives to press the case. If Congress is considering decreasing the number of F-22 Raptors (a fighter aircraft) it funds for the US Air Force, the manufacturer will make sure members and their staff know how many jobs will be lost in their district—and they will probably bring a local worker or two to put a human face on the issue. (In fact, the principal manufacturer, Lockheed Martin, makes a point of producing parts for the plane in as many states and congressional districts as possible in order to bolster the constituent connection to members of Congress.)

The point is that the most effective strategy for interest groups may be to show the district and state effects of policy to the representatives and senators. Most members see policy first and foremost in terms of the impact on their constituency. Interest groups do not rely on abstract arguments; they rely on tangible effects. If jobs in the district, educational opportunities, or health care access are at stake, the advocate has to make clear the local impact. That gets the member's attention.

## CORRUPTION AND THE REGULATION OF LOBBYING

Most lobbying involves the conveyance of information to lawmakers and their staff for the purposes of developing good relations and persuading people to take certain actions. Normally, this raises few eyebrows. However, when groups and individual lobbyists that contribute money to political campaigns are the ones in the office providing information, the suspicion level rises. Few people dispute that being a campaign contributor increases the opportunity for access to policy makers, which is the first step toward being able to persuade someone that a particular provision in law should be passed. Having said that, as we saw above with the National Association of Counties (which does not have a PAC and does not contribute to campaigns), there are other ways to get your foot in the door. Still, just because a person or group has contributed money and a member votes in accord with their views does not necessarily mean a quid pro quo arrangement (when a member's vote comes in exchange for the contribution—a federal felony) has been made.

Many, if not most, campaign contributions go to members of Congress who already support the interest's position—what the interest group is doing is, in effect, helping an ally stay in office—and those who may be undecided and thus open to persuasion. The *Washington Post* depicted the relationship this way:

> W. J. "Billy" Tauzin, a former Republican House member from Louisiana who runs the Pharmaceutical Research and Manufacturers of America (PhRMA), said campaign contributions from his industry simply reflect participation in American democracy.
>
> "We do what most people do in political systems: We support people with whom we agree and with whom we believe in," Tauzin said, adding, "We also support other people who don't always agree with us but are honest and fair and open-minded."[19]

Simply put, a correlation between a contribution and a vote does not necessarily imply that the contribution *caused* the member to vote that way. A member like former senator Ben Nelson (D-NE) received contributions from the health insurance industry and worked to protect its interests while in Congress. We cannot know for sure whether Nelson intellectually supported the industry's position (nor for that matter whether there was a causal link between the contributions and his votes), but we can know for sure that Nelson and virtually every member will support industries that employ their constituents, which was certainly the case with health insurers in Nebraska.

Having said all that, corruption does exist, including the classic 2005 case involving Representative Duke Cunningham (R-CA) depicted in Box 13.1. So-called Koreagate was a major scandal in the 1970s involving numerous Democratic members who took contributions from a well-connected Korean businessman in what appeared to be an exchange for support for legislation. Several members chose to retire rather than face the bad publicity in a reelection campaign, three were reprimanded by the House, and one spent time in jail. Similarly, in the first decade of the 21st century, some Republicans in the House accepted trips and gifts from lobbyist Jack Abramoff. House minority leader Tom DeLay was convicted of money laundering in association with the scandal after leaving office. (The case is on appeal.) Another member and some staffers spent time in jail.

The fact is the potential for corruption has always been there, and, when it exists (or perhaps even just appears to exist), it obviously undermines public trust in government. As a result, efforts to regulate lobbying are common.

Although states began efforts to monitor the lobbyists' activities as early as 1890, regulations did not come into the national picture until the New Deal era. Under the Public Utilities Holding Company Act of 1935, lobbyists for these industries were required to register with the Securities and Exchange Commission if they operated in multiple states.[20] Similarly, under the Merchant Marine Act of 1936, shipbuilders and related concerns were required to register with the Maritime Commission. The Foreign Agents Registration Act of 1938 "requires persons acting as agents of foreign principals in a political or quasi-political capacity to make periodic public disclosure of their relationship with the foreign principal, as well as activities, receipts and disbursements in support of those activities."[21]

These efforts were specific and directed to perceived abuses by organized interests of their open relationship with members of the legislative branch. The first comprehensive effort at regulating lobbying was still 10 years away.

### The Federal Regulation of Lobbying Act (FRLA) of 1946

As part of the Legislative Reorganization Act of 1946, the Federal Regulation of Lobbying Act required any person who sought "to influence, directly or indirectly, the passage or defeat of any legislation by the Congress of the United States" to register with the clerk of the House of Representatives and the secretary of the Senate each calendar quarter. The act provided that each filing would include:

---

## BOX 13.1
### Congressman Cunningham Caught Taking Bribes

Representative Duke Cunningham (R-CA), a member of the influential Appropriations Committee, had a precipitous fall from grace in 2005 due to a widely publicized lobbyist scandal.

For years Cunningham had arranged to direct federal funds, a process frequently called "earmarking," for government contractors in the defense and intelligence industries. In and of itself, this is neither necessarily illegal nor at all unusual. Most members try to earmark funds to address particular needs, both in the private and in the public sectors. Usually, members do this to enhance services or create jobs in their districts or states. In Cunningham's case, there was an ulterior motive.

Cunningham insisted on a cut for each earmark he put into federal legislation on a sliding scale depending on the size of contract. All told, Cunningham was discovered to have received about $2.4 million in bribes and numerous extravagant gifts, as well as the use of a yacht while in Washington, all courtesy of corporate lobbyists. He pleaded guilty to conspiracy to commit bribery, tax evasion, and other charges. He is currently in federal prison serving out an eight-year, four-month term and was required to forfeit his multimillion-dollar home and $1.8 million in cash and other items.*

*"Foggo Pleads Guilty to Fraud," signonsandiego.com (San Diego Union-Tribune), www .signonsandiego.com/news/politics/cunningham/index.html; Gig Conaughton, "Congressman, War Hero, Found Guilty of Bribes," nctimes.com (North County Times), November 28, 2005, http://nctimes.com/articles/2005/11/29/news/top_stories/112805193248.txt.

---

(1)  the name and address of each person who has made a contribution of $500 or more not mentioned in the preceding report; except that the first report filed pursuant to this title shall contain the name and address of each person who has made any contribution of $500 or more to such person since the effective date of this title;

(2)  the total sum of the contributions made to or for such person during the calendar year and not stated under paragraph (1);

(3)  the total sum of all contributions made to or for such person during the calendar year;

(4)  the name and address of each person to whom an expenditure in one or more items of the aggregate amount or value, within the calendar year, of $10 or more has been made by or on behalf of such person, and the amount, date, and purpose of such expenditure;

(5)  the total sum of all expenditures made by or on behalf of such person during the calendar year and not stated under paragraph (4);

(6)  the total sum of expenditures made by or on behalf of such person during the calendar year.

The penalty for being found in violation of FRLA was a fine of up to $5,000 or a jail sentence of up to 12 months, together with a three-year prohibition on lobbying Congress.

Robert Harriss and Ralph Moore were charged with six counts of violating the registration and disclosure requirements under FRLA. The US District Court for the District of Columbia determined the statute was unconstitutional because it restricted individuals' First Amendment constitutional right to petition Congress. On direct appeal, the Supreme Court evaluated the rationale for the legislation as found in the report issued by the Joint Committee on the Organization of Congress. Writing for the six-justice majority in *United States v. Harriss,* 347 U.S. 612 (1954), Chief Justice Earl Warren concluded that the registration and disclosure requirements were within the scope of Congress's authority and were essential for the protection of the institution. However, the Court did limit the scope of the act.

> We believe this language should be construed to refer only to "lobbying in its commonly accepted sense"—to **direct communication** with members of Congress on pending or proposed federal legislation. The legislative history of the Act makes clear that, at the very least, Congress sought disclosure of such direct pressures, exerted by the lobbyists themselves or through their hirelings or through an artificially stimulated letter campaign. It is likewise clear that Congress would have intended the Act to operate on this narrower basis, even if a broader application to organizations seeking to propagandize the general public were not permissible.

Congress turned its attention away from regulating lobbying efforts to the regulation of campaign financing in the early 1970s. These regulations did not directly affect the operation of existing registration and disclosure requirements, but they did have a major impact on the operations of interest groups in the electoral sphere. At the federal level, the Supreme Court handed down multiple decisions on various aspects of the 1974 Federal Election Campaign Act. Whereas some key provisions were ruled unconstitutional, limits on interest groups' direct contributions to campaigns through political action committees remained in force. (See Chapter 4 for more details on campaign finance limits.)

Attention shifted back to the regulation of lobbying following the release of a 1991 report by the General Accounting Office on the efficacy of FRLA. The report's title summarizes the findings succinctly: "Federal Regulation of Lobbying Act of 1946 Is Ineffective."

Tackling the questions of registration by lobbyists and their reporting of receipts and expenditures, the GAO concluded that approximately 9,800 individuals and organizations who were engaged in lobbying Congress were not registered. Even if an individual or organization attempted to comply with the Federal Regulation of Lobbying Act, "85 percent of a random sample of initial registrations and 94 percent of quarterly reports were incomplete."[22] Finally, the GAO reported there was little to no oversight or audit of the filings.

## The Lobbying Disclosure Act of 1995

In order to address the inadequacies of existing legislation, Congress enacted the Lobbying Disclosure Act of 1995, which repealed the 1946 FRLA. The LDA addressed the inadequacies pointed out by the GAO. To create a more effective system for monitoring lobbying activities and dispel the public's negative perception of lobbying, the LDA started by providing clear definitions of three crucial terms: *lobbyist, lobbying activities,* and *lobbying contracts.*

The LDA defines a lobbyist in terms of activities on behalf of a client who is paying a fee for services. Under the LDA, an individual is considered a lobbyist if "he or she makes more than one lobbying contact and his or her 'lobbying activities' constitute at least 20 percent of the individual's time in services for that client over any three-month period." To provide further clarification, the statute defines the phrase *more than one lobbying contact* to mean more than one communication to an official as specified in the LDA. In its guidance about compliance with the LDA, the clerk of the House offered two examples about the need for filing the requisite disclosure forms:

- *Example 1:* Lobbyist "A" telephones Covered Official "B" in the morning to discuss proposed legislation. In the afternoon she telephones Covered Official "C" to discuss the same legislation. Lobbyist "A" has made more than one lobbying contact.
- *Example 2:* Under some circumstances a series of discussions with a particular official might be considered a single communication, such as when a telephone call is interrupted and continued at a later time. Discussions taking place on more than one day with the same covered official, however, should be presumed to be more than one lobbying activity.[23]

Just as there was need for clarification of the 1946 act, the LDA required amendments that provided additional clarity of the scope of its coverage (executive branch officials were placed under the LDA in 1998) and the limitations on not-for-profit organizations in accordance with the Internal Revenue Code. Congress also amended the act to enhance reporting requirements and disclosure provisions for lobbyists and lobbying firms.

## The Honest Leadership and Open Government Act of 2007

While the Lobbying Disclosure Act of 1995 provided more monitoring of the activities of organized lobbying, scandals still dominated the news and provided a less than savory appearance of the relationship between paid lobbyists and members of Congress. In particular, the Cunningham (Box 13.1) and Abramoff scandals referred to earlier prompted Senate majority leader Harry Reid (D-NV) and a bipartisan group of senators to introduce the **Honest Leadership and Open Government Act (HLOGA) (2007).**

The legislation was designed to close—or at least regulate—the revolving door where members and staff move back and forth between Congress and the lobbying world. HLOGA increased the length of time senators and their staff were prohibited from lobbying former colleagues from one to two calendar years. The act further enhanced reporting requirements and provided for criminal and civil penalties associated with nonreporting and reporting false information. Furthermore, conviction also disqualified an individual from holding any office of honor, trust, or profit in the United States. HLOGA also strictly limited gifts and travel for members of Congress and their staffs (see Box 13.2).

Public disclosure and the promotion of transparency were the two critical elements of HLOGA. These sorts of provisions in the bill were meant both to curtail quid pro quo arrangements as well as, more broadly, to promote trust in the system. If reporters and average citizens could access what lobbyists were doing, the thinking goes, the policy-making process would be less prone to corruption. Section 209 of the legislation addressed the public availability of lobbying disclosure information. To that end, the secretary of the Senate has developed a searchable online database that tracks registrations and the amounts spent on lobbying. Table 13.2 shows registrations by Washington lobbying firms recorded for the first quarter of 2013 with the clerk of the Senate related to firearms, guns, and ammunition. The form includes the firms and the client interest group that hired them. Furthermore, HLOGA directed the secretary of the Senate to notify members and employees who were leaving public service about the length of time they were barred from lobbying activities and to disclose this information to the public (see the Public Disclosure website for the United States Senate at www.senate.gov).

On September 14, 2007, President George W. Bush signed HLOGA into law. In his signing statement expressing his views on the bill, the president took Congress

## BOX 13.2

### Fancy Restaurants, Expensive Watches, and Golf Trips . . . Not Anymore!

Contrary to popular perception, it is not legal for outside groups to ply members of Congress and their staff with expensive gifts. The 2007 HLOGA even put strict limits on favors coming from ordinary citizens, who may not offer a gift (defined as a meal, loan, transportation, ticket, lodging, and so on) if it is worth $50 or more.

The situation is much stricter concerning gifts from registered lobbyists, people working for an organization that employs a lobbyist, or an agent of a foreign government. In these cases, no gifts at all are permitted. One exception is that members may accept free attendance at a charity event (and room and board if it is needed, provided it is paid for by the charity). Members and staff also may not solicit charitable contributions from lobbyists or foreign agents.

The situation gets somewhat more complicated with potential gifts exchanged between relatives or personal friends who happen currently to be members or staff and lobbyists. HLOGA defines what constitutes a relative—a fairly easy thing to do—but it also defines what constitutes a personal friend, something far trickier. The friendship must be substantially preexisting the individuals' current situation, and members and staff may be required to consult the respective Ethics Committee to get a ruling when accepting a gift from someone they believe to be their friend. A potential gray area involves people who are dating or engaged to be married who have not been friendly for a long time. Congress saw fit in the bill to address these relationships as well.*

*See www.cleanupwashington.org/lobbying/page.cfm?pageid=43 for a full rundown of congressional ethics rules pertaining to gifts.

to task, providing explicit examples of areas where the legislation could be strengthened. President Bush noted that the standards for senators and executive branch employees were heightened as compared to members of the House of Representatives. The president continued, expressing concern about "loopholes in some of the earmark reforms included in this bill . . . such as ending the practice of putting earmarks in report language."[24] While HLOGA was being criticized for not going far enough by President Bush, organized interests were prepared to challenge the regulations in court.

The National Association of Manufacturers (NAM) sought to challenge provisions of the HLOGA, specifically Section 207, which changed disclosure

**TABLE 13.2 Lobbyist Registrations with the Clerk of the Senate Related to Firearms, Guns, and Ammunition (First Quarter 2013)**

| REGISTRANT | CLIENT |
|---|---|
| The Majority Group, LLC | Americans for Responsible Solutions |
| Ferguson Group | Brady Center and Campaign to Prevent Gun Violence |
| Robison International, Inc. | Colt Manufacturing Company, LLC |
| Monument Policy Group, LLC | Dick's Sporting Goods, Inc. |
| The OB-C Group, LLC | Mayors Against Illegal Guns |
| Mayors Against Illegal Guns Action Fund | Mayors Against Illegal Guns Action Fund |
| The JBH Group, LLC | Mayors Against Illegal Guns Action Fund |
| Thorsen French Advocacy LLC | Mayors Against Illegal Guns Action Fund |
| The Hoffman Group | National Law Enforcement Partnership to Prevent Gun Violence |
| Greenberg Traurig, LLP | National Rifle Association, Institute for Legislative Action |
| FTI Government Affairs | National Rifle Association-Institute for Legislative Action |
| Remington Outdoor Company Inc. | Remington Outdoor Company Inc. |
| Mehlman Vogel Castagnetti, Inc. | Sandy Hook Promise |
| Patton Boggs LLP | SST, ShotSpotter, Inc. |
| Bob Adams | TheTeaParty.net |

*Source:* US Senate, 2013.

requirements under the 1995 LDA. Section 207 requires registration that includes the following:

> the name, address, and principal place of business of any organization, other than the client, that—
>
> (A) contributes more than $5,000 to the registrant or the client in the quarterly period to fund the lobbying activities of the registrant; and
>
> (B) actively participates in the planning, supervision, or control of such lobbying activities.

Although on its face these changes do not appear onerous, for umbrella organizations (groups that include numerous similarly situated smaller groups) like NAM, the second provision was troublesome because NAM's membership list is confidential. In challenging the specific disclosure provision of HLOGA, NAM relied on the First Amendment and the impact that legislation had on free speech. The District Court and then the US Court of Appeals for the District of Columbia rejected NAM's arguments in *National Association of Manufacturers v. Taylor*, 582 F.3d 1 (2009), noting that, although the regulations requiring disclosure do burden First Amendment rights, Congress was simply requesting that lobbyists provide "a modicum of information." Relying on the decades-old precedent in *Harriss*, the court of appeals adhered to the intent of Congress and, for the time being, ended questions about lobbying disclosure.

## CONCLUSION: HOW INFLUENTIAL ARE INTEREST GROUPS?

There is a common belief that politicians in Washington are controlled by **special interests** with slick lawyer-lobbyists. Instead of putting the interest of the ordinary person first and foremost, lawmakers are thought to side with powerful interests, especially those that have political action committees that contribute to campaigns. In effect, the complaint is that members, in directing the work of the federal government, address the needs of those with access and power instead of serving the public interest. But in fact, the reality is much more complicated than that. Political science offers some insights about the extent of influence interest groups and lobbyists have on the policy-making process.

### Interest Groups: They Will Always Be with Us

First, it is critical to stress that, in a free society, citizens will choose to organize to advance and protect their interests. The defenders of the Constitution in *The Federalist Papers* recognized this fact explicitly. In fact, James Madison, the author of *Federalist*, No. 10, wrote: "Liberty is to faction what air is to fire." What he meant was that it was inevitable in a complex and free society that people would divide up into "factions" or interest groups, based on property distinctions and differences in viewpoint. The Constitution included a provision that reflected that idea: the First Amendment includes the right "to petition the Government for a redress of grievances"—in effect the right of citizens to come to policy makers with their arguments. So interest groups and lobbyists will always be with us. (And at the same time, we can be confident that scandals and corruption will be part of the landscape from time to time—as well as periodic legislative efforts to respond to the latest ones.)

In modern America, it is not a stretch to say that interest groups are us—they are not an alien force. They range across the political spectrum and include almost any imaginable interest—they represent us in our occupations, they represent our communities and local governments, they represent universities, they represent corporations that provide jobs, and the list goes on. Of course, this does not mean that every organization has equal resources to effect change in Washington. But it is true that, although certain groups may have built-in advantages, there may be more than one way to get the attention of policy makers. And it cannot be overstated how important it is for any group, corporate or otherwise, to bring home to members, literally, the impact of what they are planning to put in law. It is an essential part of the representative role to listen to constituents—members' popularity and reelection depend on it—and constituents' voices are often most effectively presented through the efforts of lobbyists.

### Interest Groups and the Policy-Making Process

However, gauging exactly how effective interest groups are is a complicated task. One of the foremost scholars on the subject, Matt Grossmann, stresses that expertise matters. Groups are more or less successful in integrating into the policy-making system—including lawmaking and oversight in Congress, presidential actions, the agency regulatory process, and the courts—in part based on their ability to provide good and usable information. In addition, groups that have stronger connections to their membership communities are more likely to be effective in the policy-making arena.[25] The bottom line: having a sustained, informed, and engaged presence in Washington is crucial. For example, gun owners have this through the NRA, trial lawyers through the American Association for Justice (once known as the Association of Trial Lawyers of America), and seniors through the AARP—all long-standing fixtures in Washington that know how to deliver the kind of information policy makers need.

Grossmann contends that the representativeness of the groups that succeed depends on where the policy making is happening. In general, groups representing broader swaths of the public do better inserting themselves into the more political parts of our government, Congress and the presidency itself, and less well when it comes to the decision-making processes in the regulatory agencies and the courts.

Having said that, it may be surprising to learn that making change happen is hard for almost any group, regardless of its resources and expertise. A rigorous study of 98 issue areas, conducted by Frank Baumgartner and several other scholars, found that the status quo was tough to budge even for well-connected groups.[26] The bias in our system of separated powers seems to be against change. However, the authors of this study did find that, when change happened, it can be dramatic, and, consistent with Grossmann's view, it was the groups that had worked to be a part of the process that had the most success. These groups tended to be the ones that had the resources to develop connections and expertise. It is reasonable to conclude that major policy victories involve a long slog in the American system—a lesson that the gun-control advocates we looked at in the beginning of the chapter, some of which are very new to the policy-making arena, are learning.

In the end, it is not news that the American system is hard to move for radical change. The framers intended it that way; that is why they put in a system of checks and balances. This brings to our attention a key aspect of lobbying: it is not all about making change happen; it can instead be about preserving a satisfactory status quo for a particular group by preventing change that may be damaging to their interests. In that sense, it matters a lot how a particular group defines *success*.

## Questions for Discussion

1. Take a particular policy issue of interest to you—farm policy, abortion, greenhouse gas emissions, surveillance of phone and e-mail records, or any other—and try to identify through journalistic sources interest groups that are lobbying on the subject. Are there groups on both or all sides of the issue? Which groups do you think have an advantage? Why?

2. If political scientists are right, it is the status quo that wins the day most of the time in the policy debates. Exactly why do you think this is so? Identify the specific aspects of the political system that produce this result.

3. If you were trying to persuade a policy maker—a member of Congress or an important staffer—to support your position, how would you go about it? How would you design your materials to have the most impact? How would you identify the people you most needed to persuade?

## Suggestions for further reading

Andres, Gary. *Lobbying Reconsidered.* New York: Pearson/Longman, 2009.

Baumgartner, Frank, J. M. Berry, M. Hojnacki, D. C. Kimball, and B. L. Leech. *Lobbying and Policy Change: Who Wins, Who Loses, and Why.* Chicago: University of Chicago Press, 2009.

Grossmann, Matt. *The Not-So-Special Interests.* Stanford, CA: Stanford University Press, 2012.

## NOTES

1. See Michael Memoli, "Senate Poised to Debate Gun Control Measure," *Los Angeles Times,* April 10, 2013.

2. See Helen Dewar and Juliet Eilperin, "Senate Backs New Gun Control, 51–50," *Washington Post,* May 21, 1999, A1.

3. See www.opensecrets.org.

4. Ibid.

5. Testimony of Dr. James A. Thurber, Distinguished Professor and Director, Center for Congressional and Presidential Studies, American University, Washington, DC, before the US Senate Committee on Rules and Administration, "Lobbying Reform: The Importance of Enforcement and Transparency," February 8, 2006.

6. See Jack L. Walker, "The Origins and Maintenance of Interest Groups in America," *American Political Science Review* 77, no. 2 (1983): 390–406; Kay Lehman Schlozman and John T. Tierney, *Organized Interests and American Democracy* (New York: HarperCollins, 1986); Robert Salisbury, "The Paradox of Interest Groups in Washington: More Groups, Less Clout," in *The New American Political System,* edited by Anthony King, 2nd ed. (Washington, DC: AEI Press, 1990), 203–229; and Jonathan Rauch, *Demosclerosis* (New York: Three Rivers Press, 1994).

7. See Rauch, *Demosclerosis,* chap. 3 and esp. p. 39; and Anthony Nownes, *Pressure and Power* (Boston: Houghton Mifflin, 2001), chap. 2.

8. Office of the Clerk of the House of Representatives, Lobbying Disclosure Database.

9. See www.aarp.org/politics-society/advocacy/info-10-2011/aarp-urges-congress-to-protect-social-security-medicare.html.

10. Anthony Nownes, *Interest Groups in American Politics,* 2nd ed. (New York: Routledge, 2013), chap. 5.

11. Eric Lipton and Ben Protess, "Banks' Lobbyists Help in Drafting Financial Bills," *New York Times,* May 23, 2013, http://dealbook.nytimes.com/2013/05/23/banks-lobbyists-help-in-drafting-financial-bills/.

12. Michael Beckel, "Lobbyists Aggressively Targeted Democrats' Top Legislative Priorities During President Barack Obama's First Two Years: A Center for Responsive Politics Report," March 10, 2011, www.opensecrets.org/news/2011/03/lobbyists-aggressively-targeted-dem-legislation.html.

13. Lipton and Protess, "Banks' Lobbyists Help in Drafting Financial Bills."

14. Nownes, *Pressure and Power,* chap. 6.

15. Ibid., 197–198.

16. Nate Silver, "How Opinions on Same-Sex Marriage Is Changing, and What It Means," *New York Times,* March 26, 2013, http://fivethirtyeight.blogs.nytimes.com/2013/03/26/how-opinion-on-same-sex-marriage-is-changing-and-what-it-means/.

17. Daniel E. Bergan, "Does Grassroots Lobbying Work? A Field Experiment Measuring the Effects of an E-mail Lobbying Campaign on Legislative Behavior," *American Politics Research* 37 (2009): 337–352.

18. E-mail correspondence with James E. Phillips, media relations manager, National Association of Counties, September 11, 2008.

19. Dan Eggen, "Health Sector Has Donated Millions to Lawmakers," *Washington Post,* March 8, 2009, A9.

20. Heavy lobbying by utility interests and a lack of enforcement of its provisions by the SEC prompted the repeal of the Public Utilities Holding Company Act in 2006. See "We Mourn the Death Today," www.citizen.org/documents/Dead%20PUHCA.pdf.

21. Department of Justice, Foreign Agents Registration Act, www.fara.gov.

22. See www.gao.gov/products/T-GGD-91-56.

23. http://lobbyingdisclosure.house.gov/amended_lda_guide.html#section4.

24. The president did ultimately win the war on earmarks—after he left office. In 2011 both houses of Congress put in place an earmark moratorium in their respective rules.

25. Matt Grossmann, *The Not-So-Special Interests* (Stanford, CA: Stanford University Press, 2012).

26. F. R. Baumgartner et al., *Lobbying and Policy Change: Who Wins, Who Loses, and Why* (Chicago: University of Chicago Press, 2009).

# 14

# Congress in the 21st Century

The political institutions in a nation as dynamic and diverse as the United States reflect that dynamism and diversity and are ever changing. This has been true throughout American history.

Having said that, in many ways Congress looks a lot like it did in the 20th century and even, in many ways, like it did before that. As we learned in Chapters 2 and 3, the fundamental nature of Congress was established more than 200 years ago in the Constitution, and very little in that document relevant to Congress has been changed.

A lot of critics of the contemporary Congress wistfully recall the day when Congress was a problem-solving, productive, bipartisan, and downright chummy place. Usually, they are thinking of a post–World War II "era of consensus" that existed sometime from about the late 1940s to the mid-1960s or even into the 1980s. Most of the gauzy reminiscences of this era conspicuously leave out Senator Joseph McCarthy's controversial efforts in trying to root out Communists from the US Army and the State Department (and his subsequent censure by the US Senate); the intensely contentious debates over the federal role in education and other areas, the hardball tactics used by President John Kennedy and Speaker of the House Sam Rayburn in 1961 to give the newly elected president even a slim chance to pass his top agenda items, the filibusters in the Senate opposing basic equality for African Americans, and so on.

Congress is what it is: a rough-and-tumble place whose members search for advantage in order to serve their constituents and help their party gain or retain majority status. It is no use pretending it can be anything else. In the final analysis, understanding Congress involves, first and perhaps most important, understanding its limitations.

The first section of this chapter covers those limitations, which can be summed up succinctly: the institution is inherently slow, parochial, and unable to plan. We have seen throughout the book (and review here) the impact of these characteristics on the lawmaking process. Given these limitations, it is almost unimaginable to see how an institution so constituted could serve the needs of a vast country in changing times. As the central lawmaking institution, if it performed as badly as the polls suggest people think, how could the nation have prospered and developed into the superpower it has?

It is probably more accurate to suggest that Congress cannot be as bad as it seems. The answer is that the institution is flexible enough to "make things work," however imperfectly. Here we review some of the key ways Congress has adjusted to stay relevant and enable the nation to address new challenges.

Having said that, Congress just in the past 20 years has developed serious problems—but not the ones usually alleged. Most critics suggest Congress, an institution set up to be slow and deliberative, simply cannot get things done in fast-paced, changing modern times.[1] It is, some say, in short a "do-nothing" institution at a time when serious issues need to be addressed with dispatch.

But that criticism is actually off base. Congress in the last few years of the 20th century and into the new century has in fact been rather productive, at levels not seen since the spate of legislation from the mid-1960s into the 1970s that saw the creation of massive entitlement programs, the federal role in education and science dramatically enhanced, civil rights and voting rights guarantees, and many other things.

Congress has been doing a lot of big things these past 20 years or so. What it is not able to do anymore are the basics: in particular, as we have seen in earlier chapters, updating agency program authorizations and finishing the bills that fund the federal government every year. The disease may not be the equivalent of stage IV cancer, but it is certainly serious and chronic.

What has changed? Why can't Congress do its most important, basic tasks in directing the work of the federal government? The answer is that, although the basic genome of the institution has stayed the same, the environment the members work in has not. And a couple of aspects of that environment have made it very difficult for Congress to do its central legislative and oversight tasks adequately.

First, the political parties and the electoral context evolved in the second half of the 20th century in ways that have exacerbated the partisanship on Capitol Hill. Although it has always been the case that Congress has been one of the venues for intense and even violent struggles on the major issues of the day, it has not always been the case that Congress has been organized along the lines of these disagreements.[2] Through much of the 20th century the major issues of the day found both parties on both sides; in the 21st century we are seeing the parties taking opposing positions on energy policy, health, taxes, the size of government, and controversial social issues. This, together with highly competitive biennial campaigns for control of the chambers, has rendered the atmosphere too toxic for regular productive legislating. At the same time, the communications revolution has made Congress more accessible to more people and groups, making it extremely difficult for members to balance their legislative and representative responsibilities.

The goal of this chapter, and the subject of the last section, is to answer this question: can an institution set up like Congress work in the 21st century? At this writing, the United States, while winding down its involvement in the War in Afghanistan, is still very active—often covertly—in that part of the world and in other hot spots, is still digging its way out of the most severe economic crisis since the 1930s and faces a daunting challenge in addressing what are unsustainable budgetary commitments. It is an open question whether Congress is up to the task.

Clearly, just as in therapy, accurately identifying the problematic behavior is a good first step. Next, you have to pinpoint the root causes, which boil down to the increased partisanship and mounting pressures members face related to their representative responsibilities, fundraising, and campaigning. What does Congress need to do to avoid partisanship that paralyzes and right the imbalance between their legislative and representative roles? Are there any models out there that offer hope? Ultimately, politicians' ability to take productive steps will go a long way toward determining how effective an institution Congress will be in the 21st century.

## CONGRESS'S INHERENT LIMITATIONS

Understanding Congress is to a significant degree a matter of understanding the consequences of what is imprinted on the institution's genome. The framers of the Constitution did not work from an efficiency model in developing the branches of government. They wanted a government that would put into law (Congress's job) and carry out (the job of the executive branch agencies) good public policy. But their primary concern was establishing a republic that would have built-in safeguards against the abuse of power. Protecting the liberties of the people was job one in their eyes.

Political scientist James Sundquist says that Congress is by its very nature slow, parochial, and unable to plan.[3] Left to its own devices, the institution tends toward inaction, is more likely to legislate in the service of state and local concerns than national ones, and has a great deal of difficulty pursuing an agenda in a concerted and systematic way.

## The Slow Nature of the Legislative Process

Speaking to the first point, *the legislative process is by its nature plodding.* A good lawmaking process is a thorough one; the work of the expert staff on the committees and the subcommittees necessarily takes time. Speed and efficiency usually come at the cost of thoroughness. A hastily considered bill is usually one that needs to be revisited before long.

On complex legislation, often more than one committee in each chamber weighs in with hearings and markups. The requirement that a bill, in order to be passed, must be approved, in identical form, by two chambers with profoundly different perspectives—stemming from different term lengths and different types of constituencies—throws another wrench in the works. Time-consuming effort is required to forge the compromises necessary to win enough votes in both chambers to pass the final version of a bill.

In addition, government programs ordinarily necessitate both an authorization in law and a subsequent appropriation to be put into operation. Congress has, in effect, divided the process of thinking through what should be done (the authorization process) from the funding (the appropriations process) of the actual activity. Because that funding decision—made annually for most programs—is often affected by each year's new budgetary circumstances, it can be harder to fund certain activities up to the authorized level.

No discussion of the deliberate nature of the legislative process can proceed without focusing on the Senate. The Senate was created by the Great Compromise to give every state equal representation. Senators have always taken that equality principle very seriously. Each and every one values the numerous prerogatives they have in Senate procedure to defend and advance the interests of their state. The chamber has always tended to move very deliberately, providing the brake to the House of Representatives' accelerator.

As a practical matter, Senate rules afford every senator the ability to bring the chamber to a halt for at least a few days, and supermajorities are usually needed to pass significant legislation. (The House runs on an almost purely majority-rule principle, which enables its leadership, assuming it has the votes, to move legislation on a very swift timetable. The concerns of the minority simply do not always have to be taken into account.) Savvy senators know how to use every prerogative to their advantage. One Capitol Hill reporter says that Senator Mary Landrieu of Louisiana is particularly adroit at stalling Senate action to her advantage. Her strategy is to wait until a holiday is coming up, when senators head back to their home states for an extended period of time. As the holiday approaches and senators are getting anxious about making their flights, she objects to consideration of a crucial bill—in effect placing a hold on the business of the Senate. The process to break that hold may take days if she utilizes every avenue available to her. Senate leadership is forced to consider her immediate needs if they want to move the important bill.[4] These needs usually involve funding for infrastructure in her state.

There is another reason Congress fails to act swiftly (and sometimes fails to act at all): it is often more advantageous to keep an issue alive than to resolve it with decisive legislative action. In short, winning a legislative battle is not always good politics. For example, Congress's *failure* to forge a compromise on raising the minimum wage enables Democrats to keep an issue they can exploit on the agenda for the next campaign.

A good example of legislative success coming at a political cost occurred in the summer of 1996. As described in Chapter 6, that year congressional Republicans spearheaded the passage of welfare reform legislation, which ended no-strings-attached government payments to poor single mothers. Republicans had for years been able to capitalize on Democrats' support of the program, charging them with providing a steady stream of taxpayer money to people who were making no effort to get out of poverty.[5] In some areas of the country, the issue was a linchpin of successful GOP campaigns. Fixing the program (forcing recipients to take steps toward finding jobs or eventually be cut off) had the political effect of taking a very useful issue off the table.

Having said all this, it is certainly not impossible for Congress to move with alacrity, even on major items. It can and does more frequently that people usually understand.

Crisis conditions sometimes drive the board of directors to move bills rapidly, short-circuiting much of the process, especially the committee deliberations that are so crucial to bringing expertise to bear on the issues. In March and April 1933, Congress passed in short order several major bills that created new agencies and dozens of new programs, at the behest of President Franklin Roosevelt, in an attempt to deal with the worsening Great Depression. In many cases, no hearings were held, and the bills themselves were mere outlines.

After the September 11, 2001, attacks on New York City and the Pentagon, Congress moved very quickly to authorize military action and give the president enhanced law enforcement tools with the so-called PATRIOT Act. Essentially, the president got all the tools he wanted to counter terrorism in the United States. Congress had second thoughts and rescinded some of the more controversial provisions in 2006.

In 2009 President Obama, citing the deepening recession and the urgent need to get more money into the economy to generate jobs and spending, persuaded Congress to pass the $787 billion American Recovery and Reinvestment Act (ARRA).

Just four weeks into his administration, the bill was ready for his signature. It represented more overall stimulus, in the form of domestic spending and tax cuts and credits, than any other legislation in at least 70 years.[6]

Quick action comes at a cost. Invariably, the normal deliberative process is short-circuited—there are few or no hearings, little careful consideration is given at the subcommittee or even committee level, and sometimes even floor debate is sharply limited. (Members had little opportunity to amend the ARRA.) Decisions made in haste do not always stand up well to the test of time. The creation of the Department of Homeland Security in 2002 involved relatively little deliberation considering the scope of the task of bringing 22 disparate agencies together into a coherent whole. The new department has undergone numerous overhauls in the years since its establishment.

## Parochialism

*The second of Congress's immutable traits is its parochialism.* This is another way of saying that members of Congress look after their own. The members are elected by the people in discrete districts and states—Congress was created to represent us where we live, not just as a nation. Voters have always held representatives and senators accountable for how well they are able to address constituent needs. As we have seen, it is this principle of accountability that is the bedrock of a republican system of government. The idea is that people in power are less likely to abuse their authority if they have to stand for election on a regular and frequent basis.

One cannot overstate the importance of the constituency connection for members of Congress. Nearly everything the board of directors does in carrying out its lawmaking and oversight powers is influenced by the local and state perspective. Political scientist Garry Young puts it this way: there is a certain grain to the policy-making tendencies of Congress, and, as with cutting a piece of wood, going with that grain is a lot easier than going against it.[7] What he means is that legislation that addresses particular local and state concerns stands a better chance of passing than legislation that does not.

A federal education program that guarantees funding for every congressional district is much more likely to pass than one that sends taxpayer money only to needy areas. The second program may be more defensible from a policy standpoint on the grounds that it saves taxpayers money by focusing resources where they are needed the most, but the first is the more likely legislative success story because every member would see a benefit for his or her district or state.

When Congress was contemplating the distribution of homeland security funding for states in the aftermath of the September 11, 2001, attacks, proposals that "shortchanged" sparsely populated states based on threat assessments (some government assessments recommended pouring funds into the big cities and other likely targets) were attacked by small-state senators who wanted their first responders to receive a good share of federal funds.[8] It goes without saying that senators from Alaska, Wyoming, and other states not high on the threat-assessment list made sure their states got what they viewed as a fair shake.

The committee system in Congress, set up to provide for specialization and policy analysis, in many ways tends to reinforce the parochial perspective of the membership. Although members get on committees for all kinds of reasons—power within the chamber, policy interests, ideology—early in their careers, most do everything they can to secure an assignment on a committee that addresses the economic needs of their constituents. Farm-state senator John Thune (R-SD) pulled out all the stops to make sure he got on the Agriculture Committee; Susan Davis's (D-CA) first job after getting elected in 2000 was to persuade her party's Steering Committee that she needed a slot on the Armed Services Committee to address the needs of the thousands of navy families in her San Diego–area district.

It should be noted that the often-reviled but undeniably influential "special interest groups" are most effective when they can demonstrate to members of Congress the local impact of their agenda. If jobs are at stake or numerous constituents are mobilized, the group, whether it is an advocacy organization, a local government, or a corporate concern, is much more likely to get what it wants.

The Obama administration's efforts in 2009 to scale back some of the big-ticket weapons systems that were developed decades ago to counter the Soviet threat ran into vigorous opposition for just this reason. A single weapon system or fighter jet is likely to be manufactured in numerous states (the F-22 fighter jet has component parts made in 44 states) and sometimes hundreds of congressional districts; scaling back production can cost thousands of jobs. Former Office of Management and Budget official Gordon Adams says, "The thing about weapons and bases is they are backyard issues for members of Congress. It's not like foreign aid. It's about contracts in my district, contributors to my campaign, things that directly affect my prospects of staying in office and my ability to say to my constituents, 'I got one for you!'"[9]

## Congress's Inability to Plan

*Third, Congress is unable to plan.* The very cumbersomeness of the legislative process makes planning by Congress problematic. It is very difficult to follow through on a concerted agenda when there are so many veto points in the path of a bill. Legislation can be stalled in committees and subcommittees by clever members in opposition. Interest groups watch Congress's mostly open deliberations very carefully and have often successfully waylaid seemingly popular measures by waging extensive campaigns to drum up a public outcry. Senators can put holds on legis-lation to gum up the process.

Ultimately, Congress, when viewed as a single entity, cannot plan *because it is not actually a single entity*. Time and again, we return to the institution's bicameral nature. Even if leadership can make one or the other chamber work efficiently (usually the House), there is no guarantee that the other chamber will go along. The chambers were formed, by design, with different interests and needs. It is rare that the two will see eye to eye on major legislation and move in a swift and timely manner. The fact is that Congress does not have the equivalent of a central ner-vous system. Our bodies have the built-in capacity to coordinate the left and right sides, making it possible for us to hit a softball or juggle, but Congress's two sides have only ad hoc means to forge compromises. These days conference committees have fallen out of favor, and instead the leadership of the two chambers, usually in conjunction with White House negotiators, work informally to cobble together agreements on many major pieces of legislation. These efforts require a great deal of political capital and do not always bear fruit.

Newt Gingrich learned this the hard way. When he became Speaker of the House after the stunning landslide Republican takeover of Congress in the 1994 elections, he assumed that, by a massive show of political, oratorical, and legislative force, he could dominate the whole Congress, building so much popular support for his programs that the Republican-controlled Senate and even the Democratic president would be forced to sign on to it. He moved swiftly on the ten-point "Contract with America" agenda, passing nine of the ten agenda items in fewer than 100 days. Many of the bills garnered large majorities that included dozens of Democrats. But then there was the Senate. Most of the contract items were either delayed or altered substantially there; the majority did not make it into law at all. In addition, the president was able to sustain a veto on one item. The lesson was clear: a bicameral legislature arranged like ours puts nearly insuperable obstacles in the way of the implementation of a concerted congressional agenda.

The upshot is that the branch of the federal government that the framers saw as the most important is constitutionally slow, narrowly focused, and unable to plan. But what if a crisis requires a comprehensive solution? Sometimes complex, major issues must be resolved in the interest of the whole nation—with parochial concerns taking a back seat. What then? What if there *must be* a plan? How does the board of directors respond?

## CONGRESS ADMITS ITS WEAKNESSES

Congress has at times openly acknowledged its shortcomings, sometimes by show-ing a willingness to find a way to compensate for its natural weaknesses. There are three common approaches: delegating responsibility to the executive branch, setting up a commission to find a solution, and legislating reform.[10] Essentially, what Congress is trying to do when addressing its own weaknesses is to find a way to remain relevant in the important policy debates of the day. We are likely to see Congress continue to rely on these approaches in the future as it attempts to grapple with the challenges of the 21st century.

## Delegating Responsibility to the Executive Branch

The congressional history of the middle decades of the 20th century—from roughly 1920 to 1970—was one of voluntary abdication of decision-making responsibility to the executive branch in a whole host of areas.[11] There were various reasons the board of directors abdicated when it did. First, in the early part of the 20th century, scientific public management theories came into vogue. The idea was that, with the increased complexity of modern life and the growing role of government, many things were too important to leave to the hurly-burly of partisan politics and the parochial deal making of legislative bodies. Legislatures were seen as corrupt and prone to pork-barrel spending and favoritism. Instead, the idea was to have professional civil servants who would not be beholden to one party or the other and who, as specialists in their fields, would make rational, data-driven decisions on allocating resources for addressing problems and improving infrastructure.

At the county and municipal levels, these ideas took hold in much of the nation. But Congress never gave up its most important power—the power of the purse. Nor did it give up its authority to authorize in law what the government does. It did, however, increasingly delegate regulatory and other key decisions to the bureaucrats in executive branch agencies, particularly when highly technical, sensitive, or scientific matters were involved. The Securities and Exchange Commission was given the authority to regulate the stock market, the Environmental Protection Agency was made responsible for regulations on pollutants, the Nuclear Regulatory Commission was established to ensure the safety of nuclear power plants, and so on.

The board, at times, has even allowed agency officials a great deal of leeway in allocating resources for government programs and even in deciding where to locate agency offices that hire numerous people for secure government jobs. In addition, the members increasingly ceded management responsibilities to the president, who was given the Executive Office of the President in 1939 so that he could better coordinate all of the far-flung activities of the fast-growing federal government. At the time, the president was given considerable authority by Congress to reorganize executive agencies and define missions.

Of particular note, in 1921 Congress required the president, with the passage of the Budget and Accounting Act, to submit to it a budget—basically an agenda—for the upcoming fiscal year. This gave him the opportunity to suggest legislative proposals to fix big problems. He always had had the right to offer up legislation—the Constitution authorizes the president to report to Congress on the state of the Union and suggest any legislative measures he deems necessary. (President Woodrow Wilson was the first regularly to do so, beginning in 1913.)[12] The 1921 law gave the president an institutionalized process by which to propose legislation in a more comprehensive way and the resources to follow through. Essentially, this law was an admission of weakness by members of Congress—they desperately needed *someone* to look at the big picture for them.

In fact, as we saw in Chapter 7, Congress's budget process begins with an assessment of the president's request in his budget plan. Thus, in a formal way via this act, the board of directors gave the president the ability to look at the big picture and potentially set the agenda. And every president since Franklin Roosevelt has tried to do so. If a plan for action on big-picture issues is going to be on the table, it is more likely than not going to come from the president. The expression "the president proposes, and the Congress disposes" derives from this tradition of deference on agenda setting that came about in the middle decades of the 20th century.

None of this is to say that Congress is acquiescent. Usually, it is not. To the extent that there is action on major issues, it usually happens at a deliberate pace, and Congress leaves an indelible mark on the final product. Sometimes, when a president is in a weakened political position, it is Congress that gets the bulk of what it wants on the major issues. It is fairly rare—although it does happen—for even strong presidents to have their way with Congress.

Earlier chapters have touched on those times when presidents have moved an agenda with little resistance. One of those times was in the 1930s. For an unprecedented period lasting more than three years, Franklin Roosevelt got what he wanted passed, and mostly in the form he wanted. He was a highly skilled politician and persuader, he had an electoral mandate that included huge congressional majorities for his party, and the Great Depression was a crisis of unmatched severity.

Similarly, Lyndon Johnson capitalized on a time of unease after the assassination of John Kennedy to pass rafts of important legislation in 1964 and 1965. He was aided by a landslide triumph for his party in the 1964 elections and his own tremendous political skills. No one was better than Johnson at knowing what motivates members of Congress and doing what it takes to get their votes.

To a somewhat lesser degree, another talented politician, Ronald Reagan, capitalized on a great political victory in 1980 (his party took over the Senate and replaced thirty-three Democrats in the House to give a conservative cross-party coalition, if not Republicans alone, a working majority on key issues) and an economic crisis to move his agenda through Congress in speedy fashion in 1981. Similarly, Barack Obama was, over a two-year period in 2009–2010, able to put nearly

$800 billion into the economy in one fell legislative swoop as well as reform the financial regulatory apparatus of the government and the health care system. A pathbreaking electoral triumph and a great crisis were key drivers.

A couple of things are notable. One is that these times of congressional acquiescence are fairly rare. Another is that when times are dire—during severe economic downturns especially—Congress often does follow the presidential lead, even though these productive presidencies eventually run into congressional roadblocks, usually sooner rather than later. The bottom line is that Congress looks to the executive branch for guidance and frequently gives top-ranking officials a great deal of delegated authority to address new issues and problems. This is wise; after all, Congress has put in place a great body of expertise in the executive branch in all the agencies established through its authorizations and appropriations laws. It would be silly to ignore this enormous resource—and in fact there are times, especially during crises, when Congress *must* rely on the executive branch to compensate for its own shortcomings. But the board retains its power to come back at the executive if it does not like what it sees. It relies on hearings and other forms of oversight to persuade agency officials to do things its way. It may pass new legislation providing clearer guidance on policy matters or more restrictions on how money is spent. In particular, it is through the annual appropriations process, in which the most regular and rigorous assessment of government programs takes place, that Congress exerts itself as the board of directors of the federal government.

## The Commission Solution

A lot of major issues are very difficult for the locally focused Congress to handle, particularly those that are highly intricate and apt to bring pain to the people back home. The time-tested solution: form a bipartisan commission, made up largely of former public officials, to come up with a solution that is relatively free from politics and focused on the national interest.

At the end of Chapter 8, we saw that a bipartisan commission was formed in the early 1980s, headed by Alan Greenspan, to address the approaching insolvency of Social Security. (In fact, Social Security had run out of dedicated funds one year, and Congress had to authorize it to poach from general revenue to meet its commitments.) A small and select group, composed of leading Democrats and Republicans, met out of the public eye and formed a plan. With President Reagan and Democratic speaker Thomas P. "Tip" O'Neill signing off, it passed Congress, despite having decreased old-age benefits and raised taxes on many elderly. Congress seemed to know that it could not have had productive, open deliberations on such a sensitive and important program in the normal legislative process and still have managed to produce a workable solution.

Similarly, Congress has recognized that closing and realigning military bases (the economic engines of many communities across the country) is both necessary in the aftermath of the Cold War and too difficult to handle in the regular legislative process. Instead, Congress set up the Base Realignment and Closure Commission (BRAC) in the late 1980s. Five rounds of closures and realignments have been passed into law since then. The latest round was initiated in 2005. Here is how BRAC described its activities that year:

> Welcome to the 2005 Defense Base Closure and Realignment (BRAC) Commission's official website. Our goal is to assist the American public, including interested stakeholders, to fully understand the open and transparent process through which our work is conducted. The website will also serve as a means by which you may share your thoughts, concerns, or suggestions with the Commissioners. Your input is appreciated.
>
> The Congress established the 2005 BRAC Commission to ensure the integrity of the base closure and realignment process. As directed by law, the Commission will provide an objective, non-partisan, and independent review and analysis of the list of military installation recommendations issued by the Department of Defense (DoD) on May 13, 2005. The recommendations provided by DoD are extremely complex and interrelated and will require in-depth analysis and careful attention to detail. The Commission will follow a fair, open, and equitable process, as set forth by statute. The Commission's mission is to assess whether the DoD recommendations substantially deviated from the Congressional criteria used to evaluate each military base. While giving priority to the criteria of military value, the Commission will also take into account the human impact of the base closures and will consider the possible economic, environmental, and other effects on the surrounding communities.[13]

After BRAC made its final decisions as to what closures and realignments to recommend, it was up to Congress to vote on whether to accept the report. *Congress did not permit itself, by statute, to amend the report in any way.* The recommendation would come to an up-or-down vote, with no opportunity for individual members to pick it apart on either chamber floor, as would surely have happened if they had been free to do so in the normal amending process or if the report had been subject to subcommittee and committee markups. A great deal is at stake in these decisions, from jobs to whole local economies. Congress, knowing that its innate inability to plan and its tendency to protect narrow constituent concerns would prevent it from agreeing to a comprehensive realignment of military facilities without dispensing with the regular process, in effect tied its own hands by forcing a vote on the whole lot of commission recommendations.

The procedures followed by the 9/11 Commission, as described in Chapter 6, were different. Although that commission was also bipartisan and was to present the Hill with a comprehensive proposal (dealing with the intelligence lapses that came to light after the 9/11 attacks), Congress did not require itself to take or leave the commission's plan as a whole. Instead, members implemented some suggestions but not others. In fact, they passed 39 of the 41 official recommendations.

More commonly, commissions are established to avoid directly addressing major issues that are too politically difficult to tackle. Several commissions have been established to tackle the entitlement and national debt crisis—going back to the Grace Commission in the 1980s and the Kerrey-Danforth Commission in the 1990s and the Bowles-Simpson Commission in this century—but their recommendations were never adopted. Some commissions can be very helpful in breaking the gridlock on Capitol Hill, but others serve just to further it.

## Legislating Reform

From time to time, Congress comes clean. It publicly recognizes its inherent tendency to serve narrow special interests and to avoid addressing bigger issues in a decisive way. A common solution: corrective surgery by means of "reform." The approach of choice is usually campaign finance reform.

The theory is that big corporations and other powerful entities have outsized influence over the legislative process and that this influence is largely traceable to their campaign donations. By reforming the campaign finance system and limiting the amount of special interest money in politics, members of Congress will be free to focus, undistracted by pesky campaign donors, on the big issues—such as streamlining the tax code, cutting off subsidies for wealthy farmers and oil companies, and other controversial matters that affect the wealthy and big business.[14]

The two most significant efforts to do just that were the Federal Elections Campaign Act (1972, substantially amended in 1974) and the Bipartisan Campaign Reform Act (or McCain-Feingold, 2002). The 1970s acts required full disclosure of candidates' funding sources and put strict limits on interest group donations to campaigns. PAC contributions were limited to $5,000 per election (primary and general) to a candidate. Individual donations were capped at $1,000.

BCRA adjusted some of those amounts to keep up with inflation and put an end to a major loophole that special interests had used to funnel unlimited amounts of money to the political parties—the "soft-money" loophole. It restricted campaign activities by special interests in other ways as well, many of which have been contested successfully in the federal courts, in effect opening up avenues for campaign spending that cannot be restricted. (See Chapter 4 for a full discussion of these changes.)

Although reform efforts may be defensible on their merits, they have been nowhere near the panacea that their advocates believed them to be. Interest groups have always influenced members of Congress *whether or not they form PACs and contribute to campaigns.* They do this by bringing the local effects of policy to members' attention. Members have always been locally focused. The fact is that corporate interests will have the opportunity to make their views known to members and exert influence as long as the companies in question continue to employ people and contribute to the larger community. Campaign contributions help interest groups gain access to make their case, but they are not an absolutely necessary component of effective lobbying.

There are also periodic reform efforts aimed at special interest influence that focus on the dispensing of favors to members. These happen after a spate of ethics scandals in which members are found taking bribes or otherwise abusing the public trust.

In the past 15 years or so, Congress has gradually put more and more restrictions on the kinds of gifts (meals, sports tickets, and so on) that members may accept from individual lobbyists or groups, to the point where almost no favors are permitted. Significant restrictions were put in place by the new Republican majority in 1995 on the heels of a series of embarrassing revelations and a few indictments largely involving Democrats in the years leading up to the Republican takeover, followed by Democrats imposing yet stricter rules when they took control of Congress in 2007 after several Republicans came under investigation or were indicted for accepting bribes or other bad behavior.

Members of Congress also focused on earmark reform in the aftermath of the scandal involving Representative Randy "Duke" Cunningham (R-CA), who received sizable kickbacks from corporate interests in exchange for inserting earmarks in appropriations bills to funnel federal money to those companies for various projects. As of 2011, there has been a comprehensive earmark ban.

Unfortunately, however right thinking these reforms are, they, like campaign finance reform efforts, are oversold. Shining a light on shady behavior is certainly a good thing, but such efforts do not end the influence of interest groups or enable members to focus in a disinterested fashion on controversial issues. The influence of outside groups, while enhanced by campaign donations, is to a significant degree based on their ability to bring useful information to the attention of members, especially information about the effects of legislative proposals on local economies or the larger American economy; the ability of these groups to wine and dine members and staff is not really the key. Members want to serve their districts and states, and interest groups that are worth their salt help them do it.

What should be clear is that regardless of the value of reforming the campaign finance system, or putting more restrictions on the favors that outside groups can do for members, or shining a light on the earmarking process, Congress cannot legislate away its inherent tendencies. The rhetoric of campaign finance reform and ethics reform is intoxicating, but it cannot alleviate Congress's parochial focus or its difficulty in dealing speedily with big, intractable problems. Having said that, it is a safe bet that members of both parties will continue to push for more reforms, arguing that reforms hold the potential to "solve" the problem of special interest influence on the legislative process—because it is good politics to do so.

* * *

The lesson from this discussion is that Congress does attempt to manage its inherent limitations, even if they cannot be removed. Campaign finance and ethics reform cannot remove those limitations (despite the claims of some proponents), and neither can commissions—but they can help, and, indeed, the **commission solution** has at times been essential to addressing some otherwise intractable problems.

In addition, the board of directors will continue to delegate responsibility to the executive branch. It is wise to do so; furthermore, it is simply impossible for Congress not to, given the size and scope of the federal government. Congress regularly cedes quasi-legislative authority to the agencies in areas where technical or controversial regulations must be promulgated to implement the law.

All of these methods have, however imperfectly, helped Congress maintain its prominent place in the policy-making process. Ultimately, it should go without saying that Congress will never give up its essential authorizing and funding powers. It is these that give it the leverage to change agency behavior through oversight or, of course, by changing the law and taking back the delegated powers.

## CONGRESS'S FATAL FLAWS: NOT WHAT PEOPLE THINK

Congress is not popular. We looked at the numbers on this question in Chapter 2. Things have been particularly bad in terms of congressional popularity in the 21st century, with support for the institution coming in at barely into double figures. Furthermore, the institution and its members are simply not trusted.

A lot of people think all Congress does is spin its wheels as problems fester and that the situation is worse than ever. The sniping and the partisanship are undeniably considerable, but in fact recent Congresses have been quite productive when it comes to legislating in comprehensive ways on major issues. The laundry list of major initiatives to pass into law since the mid-1990s is quite impressive, irrespective of the merits of the solutions.

- *Personal Responsibility and Work Opportunity Act of 1996* ("Welfare Reform"): ended the federal entitlement for Aid to Families with Dependent Children, the only major entitlement ever terminated
- *Balanced Budget Act of 1997*: an omnibus bill incorporating spending cuts in both discretionary and mandatory programs, increasing spending in some social programs (net reduction of more than $100 billion in spending over five years), creating the Child Health Insurance Program (paid for by an increase in tobacco taxes), and numerous tax provisions, all meant to put the government on a path to balance the budget by 2002
- *Transportation Equity Act for the 21st Century (1998)*: the biggest surface transportation (roads, bridges, bike paths, and so on) bill in the nation's history
- *Economic Growth and Tax Relief Reconciliation Act of 2001* and *Job Growth and Tax Relief Reconciliation Act of 2003*: broad-ranging tax relief, including lowering marginal rates, lowering the tax on capital gains and dividends, relief for the so-called marriage penalty, the child credit, an estate-tax overhaul, and many other provisions
- *USA PATRIOT Act of 2001*: provided for wide-ranging authorities for government agencies in domestic surveillance or investigation of people and organizations suspected of plotting terrorism
- *No Child Left Behind Act of 2001*: comprehensive restructuring and enhancement of the federal role in elementary and secondary education
- *Authorization of the Use of Military Force Against Terrorists (2001)* and *Authorization of the Use of Military Force Against Iraq (2003)*: these two laws authorized military action in Afghanistan and other places, in the first instance, and against Iraq, in the second
- *Sarbanes-Oxley Act of 2002*: set new federal standards for all corporate accounting
- *Homeland Security Act of 2002*: established a new federal department composed of 22 federal agencies drawn from several departments
- *Medicare Prescription Drug, Improvement, and Modernization Act of 2003*: made seniors eligible for assistance in paying for prescription drugs, establishing the biggest entitlement program since the larger Medicare program was established in 1965

- *Bipartisan Campaign Finance Reform Act of 2003* ("McCain-Feingold"): first comprehensive campaign finance reform since the 1970s, putting in place restrictions on advertising and the use of "soft money" (although many of the restrictions were subsequently struck down in the courts)
- *Intelligence Reform and Terrorism Prevention Act of 2004:* created the Office of the Directorate of National Intelligence to provide coordination of the 16 agencies involved in foreign intelligence
- *Bankruptcy Abuse Prevention and Consumer Protection Act of 2005:* rewrote the nation's bankruptcy laws
- *Emergency Economic Stabilization Act of 2008* (which set up the *Troubled Asset Relief Program*): a massive effort to underwrite losses by major financial institutions to continue the flow of capital in the system
- *American Recovery and Reinvestment Act of 2009:* the so-called Recovery Act provided a total of nearly $600 billion in mostly infrastructure and research spending, plus another $200 billion in tax cuts and credits, easily the largest single spending bill in at least 70 years
- *Patient Protection and Affordable Care Act of 2010:* greatly expanded Medicaid and provided a new federal health care entitlement
- *Dodd-Frank Wall Street Reform and Consumer Protection Act of 2010:* overhauled the regulatory apparatus for the financial industry
- *Food Safety Modernization Act of 2010:* the first overhaul of the nation's food-safety regime since the 1930s

These laws were passed in all sorts of circumstances—by a unified Republican Congress and president, by a unified Democratic Congress and president, and during divided government. Some received wide bipartisan support; others were nearly or strictly party line. And it is worth stressing the scope of some of these laws. Major functions of the government were fully restructured (homeland security and intelligence), massive new entitlements were instituted (prescription drugs in 2003 and the 2010 health reform), and an array of wide-ranging reforms were put in place in the financial realm and other areas. All of it was done during a period of a supposedly "dysfunctional" Congress.

What is going on here? First of all, major events such as the Great Recession and the attacks on September 11, 2001, created the political conditions where lawmakers had to do something. The PATRIOT Act is an example of this, as was the authorization for the use of force against al-Qaeda. The development of the Department of Homeland Security and the Intelligence Reform Act in 2004 were responses to the dangers of terrorism, but were more discretionary in nature. TARP, in particular, was needed when the financial system seemed on the brink of freezing up in

2008. The Recovery Act was more discretionary but directly tied to the economic situation, and Dodd-Frank was as well.

But it is striking the extent to which other major legislation was shepherded through the supposedly "do-nothing Congress." And it is important to give Congress its due credit in being able to act quickly and comprehensively.

There are a couple of factors that explain why Congress has been so productive when it comes to the big things.[15] One is that the leaders of the institution have seen fit to focus the time and energies of the chambers on completing these major legislative packages. The interesting thing is that the highly competitive partisan environment motivates leaders to accomplish big things when they can. Shortly, we shall see exactly how this dynamic works. Suffice it to say for now that congressional leadership has not only responded to the urgency of major events like 9/11, but also moved the institution to respond to the *political* needs of the parties.

This focus on major legislation has to some degree come at the expense of other business, *which gets us to the real problem with Congress in the 21st century. It is that it fails to get done the regular authorizations and appropriations bills that it needs to in order to keep the government running on something like a rational and planned basis.* It is important to note the complete overhaul of the elementary and secondary education programs in No Child Left Behind, but one cannot lose sight of the fact that the authorization expired in 2007 and no law has been passed to fix what has not worked. Both parties agree a new law is needed, but no agreement has been reached. The intelligence community has been reorganized, but the once annual authorizations are now next to impossible to get enacted. Appropriations bills almost never get done on time, with federal agencies stuck with continuing resolutions for months, or even for an entire year, that lead to inefficient operations. And the list goes on.

Congress can do big things, but cannot complete its basic responsibilities—a serious problem that wastes taxpayer money and leads to programmatic failures. That is what is wrong with Congress. We move to an analysis of the root causes.

### The Working Environment on Capitol Hill

In recent years, things have changed in the working environment in Congress in a couple of ways that contribute to the institution's difficulties in completing its basic legislative and oversight responsibilities. Both developments are decades in the making, with a kind of tipping point reached in the past 20 years or so. The representative side of the members' job is much more onerous than ever before due to a host of factors, much of it related to changes in communications technology. Also, as many observers have noted,[16] partisanship is at a level that makes the cooperation needed for most legislation almost impossible to rely upon.

## The Increasing Burdens on the Representative Role

A politician running for office 100 or more years ago took a very different approach from the way politicians run today—and the process was nowhere near as taxing or as time-consuming. Nominations for office were controlled by local and state party leaders. Any potential candidate for Congress had to have had inside connections, usually gained by having been active in party politics. The party organizations would also normally take care of most of the business of running the general election for their candidates.

But this began to change in the first few decades of the 20th century with the advent of **primary elections** as a means to choose nominees for the parties. Increasingly, candidates for office might have to win two elections—the primary and the general—in order to gain a seat.

The primary presented a new challenge for aspiring politicians. In the **general election**, candidates could easily differentiate themselves from their opponent just by virtue of their party label, but in a primary some other tack had to be taken. A Democrat running against other Democrats had to convince voters that he or she was the better individual to represent the party. This was the beginning of what political scientists now call **candidate-centered politics**.

What was rapidly developing was a campaign politics based on personality, which was aided and abetted by the advent of television and sophisticated advertising techniques. By the mid-20th century, candidates often ran away from their party label and appealed directly to the broader electorate, many of whom did not neatly fit into the Democratic or Republican box. With candidate-centered politics, it also took more time and effort for a person to get elected to a high-profile position such as one in Congress. Candidates had to establish their name to get the nomination, then start over again in the general election campaign.

In Chapter 4, we saw in detail what it takes to run for Congress in the 21st century. Candidates have to set up what amounts to a small or medium-size business. In many respects, House and Senate candidates, Democrat or Republican, are on their own in setting up the campaign enterprise. They may get vital help from their party, but it is *their* campaign, and they have to put in tremendous time and effort in order to be competitive and even to get their name on the ballot.

It is the fundraising that presents the biggest challenge. The cost of running for office has skyrocketed. A competitive House race is about four or more times as expensive as it was just 15 years ago, with competitive races often requiring at least $3 million. Fundraising for Senate races is even more burdensome, with costs hitting $10 million or more. These figures do not include money spent by outside interests and the political parties that are, for all intents and purposes, on behalf of those candidates.

The reform impulses that resulted in changes in the campaign finance laws in 1974 made fundraising a more burdensome and labor-intensive task than it had been. With the contribution limits that were part of that legislation, more people have to be contacted in order to raise enough money.

The demands on members' time to raise the requisite cash are incredible. One member of the House who was running for a Senate seat in 2008 spent nearly every working day in Washington in the first half of that year, from 9:00 a.m. to 6:00 p.m., in a cubicle in his party's senatorial campaign committee offices making fundraising phone calls, leaving only for floor votes. Members attend breakfast fundraisers before work and go to evening fundraisers after work. Most sitting members of the Senate retain permanent campaign fundraising offices near Capitol Hill, as do more and more House members.

The pressure to spend time back in the district, whether for fundraising or more generally for meetings and politicking, is also strong. There are constant demands from constituent groups and donors for face time. So not only do members have to spend more time than ever before raising money, but they also face a much more organized electorate as well. Technological advances have made citizen organizing around shared interests easier than ever. Contact time with the senators and representatives is very important to attentive constituencies and very time-consuming for the members.

The related growth of the lobbying industry, covered in Chapter 13, contributes to the pressures on members. The tremendous expansion of interest groups began after the explosion of government activism in the period from about 1965 to 1971. At that point, the federal government became involved, through programs and regulatory measures, in literally every aspect of American life. No area of business, no occupation, no state or local government unit, no educational establishment, not even any area of citizens' personal lives, was untouched by federal law or agency regulations.

As a result, businesses that did not want to be at a competitive disadvantage had to try to influence policy makers in Congress. County, city, and state governments that did not want to miss out on their fair share of federal program dollars had to make their presence felt—in Washington and back home. Blind people, old people, dentists, electricians, artists, social workers, real estate agents, auto dealers, and many other categories of people had to organize in order to protect what they got from the government or, better yet, to promote and advance their interests. Universities had to meet with members of Congress or miss out on research grants. People who believed strongly in women's rights, gay rights, affirmative action, the rights of the unborn, school prayer, or the need to protect the environment had to press their case.

Because of all this, representatives' and senators' scarce staff resources are stretched more thinly than ever. First the fax machine and now e-mail, Facebook, and Twitter have made contacting members of Congress a snap. The staff in the district or state and in Washington are inundated with messages. Most offices have a policy of responding to every communication in at least a perfunctory manner. The more thoughtful inquiries require more detailed responses. It is highly embarrassing to be confronted at a town hall meeting or another venue by constituents or group representatives who have not received a satisfactory response from the office or, worse yet, have received no response at all. Members from competitive districts sometimes find that they have few resources and less time to do much more than address constituent questions and needs.

Members rarely lose reelection campaigns, but this happy situation for them does not happen by accident. They must tend to constituent needs, bring home the bacon in appropriations legislation, raise money in the hopes of discouraging potential opposition, and help the party fund operations for more vulnerable colleagues. Pitching in by raising money for the party serves the purpose of enhancing one's own chances for a better committee assignment, committee or subcommittee chair, or leadership position, which in turn enables one to deliver more for constituents. (As we have seen, party leaders require members to pitch in in this way.)

As a result of this changed environment, members are not in Washington as much as they used to be. There was a tipping point sometime in the 1970s or early 1980s when they began to demand more time at home. Larger social and economic forces were also at work.

First, by that time commercial jets had made it possible to travel regularly to almost anywhere in the country. Members could now get home every weekend (which most do, especially in the House).

As members felt compelled to go home more often, it became the norm for them not to have their family with them in Washington. Why bring the family to the capital city when it would be less unsettling for the children and less expensive to raise them back home in the district—where members were spending a good bit of their time anyway? It was also good politics for members to have their district home truly be their primary residence.

The social changes of the time reinforced this trend. More and more members had a spouse (usually a wife) with a career. Women's liberation had opened up more opportunities for talented women, and many were unwilling to leave their career to follow their husband to Washington.

In the 21st century, members' representative role puts a great deal more pressure on them than in the past. The lawmaking environment in Washington has changed as a result. There is a substantial potential cost when members have to focus so much effort on their constituent service, fundraising, and other reelection efforts, and one is that the board-of-director duties get short shrift. The fact is that members are not in Washington to work on legislation and oversight as much as they used to be.[17]

The American Enterprise Institute's Congress watcher, Norman Ornstein, has noted the drop in days at work in Washington in the current era, declining close to 20 percent in the House and 15 percent in the Senate when comparing the 1960s and 1970s to the 1990s and the new century. And hearings, one of the mainstays of congressional oversight, happen far less frequently than they used to—to the tune of a 50 percent drop over the past 40 years.[18]

Why do these statistics matter? It takes a lot of work to direct something as large, complex, and multifaceted as the $3.5 trillion federal government. Certainly, it is a full-time job for the 535 elected representatives of the people. But of course, this is only one of their jobs. As a practical matter, getting reelected has to be priority number one for the members—after all, what good can a lawmaker do for the people if he or she loses the election? The problem is that what is required to run for reelection and address the requests and needs of constituents and organized interests has cut into the time needed to serve the legislative role and establish policy for the agencies of government.

## A More Partisan Place

The political party system was not envisioned by the framers of the Constitution, although something resembling a party system developed not too long after the founding period. In the 19th century, Congress began to organize much of its business along party lines, to the point where the parties were officially recognized in the rules of the House and Senate. And as developed in Chapter 3, today parties are in charge of committee assignments and the development of the legislative agenda in the two chambers. As such, the party system is the most important noninherent characteristic of the institution.

The journalistic and "inside-the-Beltway" conventional wisdom is that over the past 30 years, Congress and American politics in general have become much more divided along party lines than they had been. In fact, there is little doubt that the two parties in Congress have become more polarized. Political scientists point to various ways to measure this phenomenon. Data show that members of Congress are more likely to vote with the majority of their party on the floor of the House or Senate today than they were 20, 30, or 40 years ago.[19] Also, the voting behavior of members of the two parties in Congress has become more liberal on the Democratic side and more conservative on the Republican side. There is less ideological variation within the parties than there was several decades ago.[20]

**FIGURE 14.1. Disappearing Ideological Overlap Between the Parties**

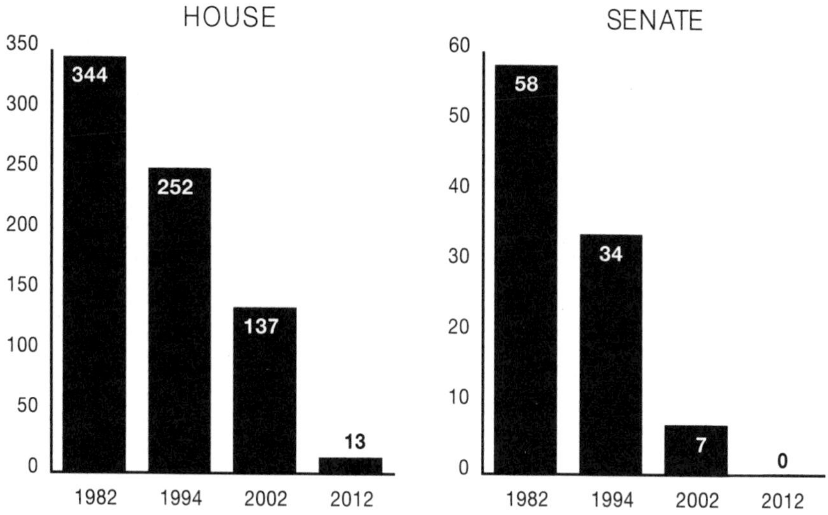

Note: Members of Congress whose vote rating according to the National Journal falls between their chamber's most conservative Democrat and most liberal Republican.

Amazingly, as can be seen in Figure 14.1, in 1982 fully 344 of the 435 House members fitted somewhere on the ideological spectrum between the most liberal Republican and the most conservative Democrat. In 2012 only 13 members fell in that range. In the Senate, 57 members were between the most liberal Republican and the most conservative Democrat—in 2012 no senator met that description. There was no ideological overlap on the controversial issues of the day. This development has major ramifications for the workings of the institution—but first a short detour to explain how and why the parties have changed.

### A Short History of the Parties

The key factors leading to the increased ideological homogeneity within the congressional delegations of the Democratic and Republican Parties were the rise of polarizing social issues in the middle decades of the 20th century and the consequent change in the makeup of the party coalitions. The evolution of the two parties' coalitions, particularly in the past 40 years or so, has gone unmistakably in the direction of what is called **ideological sorting**. A short history lesson is required to understand exactly what has happened.

The Democratic Party's history goes further back than the Republicans' (even though the Republican Party is often called the Grand Old Party, or GOP).

Democrats trace their lineage to Thomas Jefferson and Andrew Jackson. In fact, most state parties still have Jefferson-Jackson dinners to bring supporters together for fundraising and other purposes. The party was rooted in two principles: promoting the cause of the workingman (originally thought of as a small farmer or tradesman) and permitting states to have control over their domestic affairs free of federal interference, sometimes called *states' rights*.

In the South (the 11 states that were part of the Confederacy, sometimes expanded to include border states such as Kentucky, Oklahoma, and Missouri), the Democratic Party became the political force behind slavery, and after slavery was abolished it became the force behind the segregated system of legal apartheid dividing the races that lasted from its start in the 1880s and 1890s until the civil rights movement overturned it in the mid-1960s. Southern Democrats tended to hold very conservative positions across the board, and not just on racial issues: They were prodefense, antiunion, and generally opposed to federal intervention in local affairs.

In other parts of the country, the Democrats evolved very differently as the 20th century progressed. State and local party units in the industrial North and Midwest were very likely to be prounion and very strongly in favor of a range of government services. In some major cities—Chicago, for example—the party was instrumental in assimilating masses of immigrants from Poland, Ireland, and other European countries. In some places, African Americans played a role in the party machines. With Catholics and Jews often serving in important leadership roles, Democrats in some parts of the country were diverse, especially as compared to the overwhelmingly white Protestant southern members of the party.

The party held together despite its profound differences at the state level because of the shared belief that, in the end, states should run their own affairs. The party had some tumultuous conventions in the late 1890s and into the 1920s because of the widely varying views of the different state parties, but as long as the more liberal members of the party did not meddle with the South's segregationist system, accommodations could usually be reached.

Things began to get trickier in the 1930s when a Democrat—in fact, a big-government, prounion liberal, Franklin Roosevelt—dramatically expanded the reach of the federal government into states' affairs. This was a change that many leading southern Democrats had feared, as they believed it would be the first step toward the federal government trying again to desegregate the region—an effort that had failed, as undertaken by Republicans, after the Civil War. But Roosevelt was very careful not to get into the internal affairs of southern states when it came to race relations. He had won all those states easily, but he knew that meddling in racial matters might well cost him and his party at the ballot box in future elections.

What had developed in the first several decades of the 20th century was a Democratic Party at the congressional level that had some of the most liberal people in Congress (followers of Roosevelt who supported an expanded federal role) and some of the most conservative (most of the 125 or so southern Democrats in the House and Senate who were strict segregationists and suspicious of the federal government).

Republicans, for their part, also have a mixed ideological heritage. The party was formed in the 1850s from the remnants of the disintegrating Whig Party and various social movements and smaller parties. The driving force was opposition to slavery—or at least opposition to its spread to the territories and new states. The various fragments of smaller parties and movements that formed the Republican Party were favorably disposed toward a stronger central government to achieve their ends. More broadly, many Republicans also supported federal action in the service of promoting a better business environment for American industry.

With the successful prosecution of the Civil War by Republican president Abraham Lincoln, the party was dominant and intent on enforcing its views on the formerly Confederate states. This initially took the form of a military occupation of the South; eventually, after the occupation was ended in 1877, the party acted on its interest in securing the rights of the freedmen in the region. The party in Congress wished to use the federal government as an instrument for social change in the recently occupied areas. But the white South—represented by the Democrats—resisted. And it won out. The generation of so-called Radical Republicans who were willing to fight for civil rights for newly freed slaves and other black Americans either became weary from the struggle or passed on. They were gradually replaced by other Republicans who, while sometimes liberal on questions of racial equality, were more interested in using government in less controversial ways, mainly to promote business.

By the middle of the 20th century, the party was characterized by a similar if somewhat less dramatic version of the schism within the Democratic Party. The Republican Party included some very liberal members in the Northeast and parts of the Midwest (so-called Progressives) who wanted to see the federal government do much more than just protect and encourage industry, as well as some members in the Midwest and the growing West who advocated a laissez-faire approach to the economy—lower taxes and a smaller government. Although Republicans in midcentury had no prosegregation wing to speak of, they did have large internal differences on the role of government in addressing social problems, including racial injustice, and regulating the economy; consequently, by this time, Republican members in Congress spanned the political spectrum.

In the 1950s and into the 1960s, Congress had many contentious debates on the major issues of the day, including the role of the federal government in education and in regulating the economy and the status of civil rights for African Americans. But these debates typically did not break neatly along party lines. Both parties had a lot of people on both sides of these and other major issues. Each party had both strong conservatives and strong liberals. The coalitions in support of this or that specific policy shifted constantly as a result. Congress and the country were polarized on many important questions, but that polarization was not principally along party lines.

## Sorting Begins

There are disagreements on exactly when the change that resulted in the more ideologically consistent, polarized parties of today began to take hold, but most people point to sometime in the 1960s. The decisive year was probably 1964, during which:

1. Lyndon Johnson, a Democratic president—and a southern one at that (he was from Texas)—put his considerable political capital and skills behind the Civil Rights Act, legislation that would end once and for all legal segregation in the South. He told aides privately that, by supporting this bill, he had lost the South for the Democratic Party for a generation. (As it turned out, he underestimated the length of time.)
2. The Democratic Party, traditionally the party of states' rights, moved for the first time as a national party at its national convention to penalize a state party for refusing to seat an African American in its delegation. (The all-white Mississippi delegation was challenged by a rump group, the Mississippi Freedom Democratic Party, which protested the segregation policies of the state party.) This was a crucial break from past practice. Up until that time, the party had heeded each state's right to choose freely its own delegation without national interference.
3. The Republicans nominated a resolutely small-government, anti–New Deal, pro–states' rights conservative for president, Senator Barry Goldwater of Arizona.

The result of these events was that the national Democratic Party moved unmistakably in the liberal direction, upstaging the conservative wing of the party at the convention and in Congress. Conversely, the Republican Party went full force against its liberal elements by nominating an anti–federal intervention conservative for president. These changes proved lasting. Ever since, at the national level in presidential campaigns, Democrats have been pro–civil rights, liberal on social issues (abortion, the rights of the accused, gay rights, and so on), and strongly in

**TABLE 14.1 Ideological Sorting of the Parties on Major Issues**

|  | PRE-1964 | POST-1964 |
|---|---|---|
| Democrats | Party split, with southern Democrats opposed to desegregation and often resistant to government regulation of the economy; the rest of the partyt ended to be pro–civil rights, pro-union, and in favor of government regulation. | Party becomes increasingly uniform in support of affirmative action, liberal on other social issues, and in favor of government regulation and social programs. |
| Republicans | Party split, with largely northeastern faction for desegregation and favorably disposed to government regulation of the economy; the rest of the party was more likely to oppose government regulation and was mixed on the question of desegregation. | Party becomes increasingly uniform, with conservative positions on social issues and in opposition to more taxes, government regulations, and social programs. |

favor of government intervention in the economy. Successful Republicans at the national level have opposed affirmative action and forced integration, attempts to liberalize on social issues, and any increased federal role in the economy. Table 14.1 depicts these changes in the two parties.

It took some time, however, for these developments to filter down below the presidential level. At the congressional level, it is hard to defeat an **incumbent**, and voters are not necessarily tied to party labels as long as their representative is attuned to and delivers for the district. In some of the most conservative parts of the South, amazingly enough, there were hardly any qualified Republicans available to run for House seats or even Senate seats in the 1960s, and there was not a deep bench into the 1980s. In fact, in the 1980s, although the South was stronger than any region for the Republican presidential candidates (Ronald Reagan in 1984 and George H. W. Bush in 1988), it remained the strongest for the Democrats in the House of Representatives.

Similarly, many liberal Republicans remained in Congress, especially from the Northeast. Many southern Democrats were far more conservative than their presidential candidates (and would not campaign with them), and most northeastern congressional Republicans were far more liberal than their presidential candidates.

Having said that, gradual change at lower levels was happening, and grander change was in the offing. The 1994 elections were the tipping point in the South. Moderate or conservative southern Democrats were replaced in large numbers by conservative Republicans in the House and Senate. (Some conservative Democrats who survived that year switched parties to become Republicans.) As a result, the Democrats became a much more uniformly liberal party in Congress in short order. In 2006 and 2008, Republicans lost the bulk of what remained of their liberals and moderates, leaving the party more uniformly conservative in Congress than it had ever been. The *New York Times* described moderate Republicans at that time as "an endangered species."[21] (The 2012 election left the GOP with no representation in the House in all of New England.) Now the vast majority of members line up with their party on most issues of the day.

As noted earlier, Congress has always had contentious issue debates. The difference in the modern era is that these debates split Congress along party lines. Congress has long been *organized* along party lines; now the party in control is in a much better position to use its power in an attempt to pursue an ideological agenda. When the parties were more ideologically diverse, the party leaders could not do that. The imperative on most issues in those days was to build cross-party coalitions.

The other factor that has contributed to bitter partisanship in this era is the relative narrowness of the margins between the parties in the two chambers since 1994. Every election cycle, both parties have believed that they have a fighting chance to take over one or both of the chambers, or at least close the gap considerably.

It was not always so. In the 1930s and '40s, as well as from 1958 to 1994, Democrats normally had commanding majorities in the House. Through much of this time, Republicans had become resigned to the fact that they were unlikely to take back the chamber anytime soon. This was often the case in the Senate as well, although the 1980 surprise takeover of the Senate by the Republicans changed that thinking.

Republican resignation to minority status in those days led them to a more accommodating stance. They felt their interests were best served by attempting to work with Democrats and helping to smooth Democrats' interactions with Republican administrations in exchange for help with projects for their districts and certain concessions on major legislation. Democrats were open to this, as it is always easier to pass legislation, especially in the Senate, when it is presented in a bipartisan way. Relations between the leadership of the two parties at the time were characterized by a spirit of relative comity.

The closer margins that became a permanent feature beginning in 1994 changed the calculus in Congress. When your party's hold on power is precarious, you are much less likely to help members of the minority; you do not want them to be able to return to their districts or states touting legislative accomplishments. The minority, for its part, tends not to cooperate to help the majority with its agenda items, preferring to maintain a united front in accusing the majority of "overreach." Plus, and most important, if the minority provides few if any votes to the majority, then the majority has to lean on some of its vulnerable members to support controversial agenda items. Democratic moderates were pummeled (and defeated in many cases) in the 2010 elections for supporting liberal legislation, including health care reform, a climate change bill, and the Recovery Act—a circumstance made possible by the nearly 100 percent united opposition to these bills by Republicans. (Health care got no Republican votes in either chamber; the Recovery Act got one in the House and three in the Senate.)

The ideological sorting of the parties means that clear partisan divisions are here to stay for the foreseeable future. The effect of this change in the party system on Congress almost cannot be exaggerated. When the two sides have very different views on the major issues of the day, the odds for cooperation and comity go down. And sometimes, even when there can be a meeting of the minds across party lines, members of the minority party choose not to cooperate for fear of assisting the majority party's electoral prospects.

## Party Leadership Ascendant

As the parties began to sort themselves out ideologically in the 1960s and 1970s, Congress—Democrats in the House, that is—implemented rules changes that had the potential to enhance the power of party leaders. By the mid-1990s, a sea change had occurred in the way Congress went about its business directing the work of government.

In some ways, this new system resembled the one that existed in the late 19th and early 20th centuries, when party leaders often were able to exert their will, controlling the agenda of the House and sometimes even the Senate. The leadership in those days ran roughshod over the prerogatives of the committees and the whims of rank-and-file members.

Eventually, this heavy-handed control proved too much for many members. Such a system restricted their freedom and control over the issues that mattered to them. Many found themselves in regular disagreement with their leadership and chafed at having to kowtow to those leaders in order to secure good committee assignments and chairmanships. By about 1920, a system that rewarded seniority and insulated committees from outside pressures from the caucus or the leadership had developed, and this system would flourish throughout the middle decades of the 20th century.

Democratic reformers in the late 1960s and early 1970s wanted to change all that. They felt that the party in power should be able to pursue an ideologically coherent, party-based agenda and not be hamstrung by the whims of a few senior members who chaired committees and who were out of step with the caucus. At the time, the reformers were targeting the conservative southerners in their midst, whom the majority of the party saw as thwarting the will of the people. Leadership was given the tools to make the House work the majority's will, especially by giving the speaker control of the Rules Committee and the caucus the power to ignore seniority in picking committee chairs. But change happened slowly. Democratic leaders in the 1970s through the early 1990s were not always assertive in the use of their newfound powers.

As we saw in Chapter 5, it was the Republican leadership in the House that took full advantage of the 1970s-era rules changes after the Republican Revolution of 1994. For most of its 12-year reign from 1994 to 2006, the leadership had its way on the floor, where it controlled the agenda, and in naming committee chairs. Democratic speaker Pelosi followed up in kind in the 110th and 111th Congresses by taking full control of the agenda.[22] Internal disharmony has hampered the GOP House leadership since the 2010 Tea Party–inspired elections added numerous uncompromising conservatives to their new majority. Even so, party leadership certainly has not allowed Democrats a role in agenda setting.

Even in the Senate, the party leaders on both sides have been more active.[23] They assert themselves in negotiations over legislation in ways that would have been unthinkable a generation ago, and they have been vigorous in promoting their respective interests in the public relations realm (which often means criticizing the other party). But the Senate is still the Senate—the majority leader cannot move an agenda the way it is done in the House, and the seniority system still determines the selection of committee chairs.

In many respects, the rank and file have acquiesced in the accretion of power by party leaders in both chambers, if more so in the House. Members are well aware of the stakes in each upcoming electoral cycle. Losing the majority means losing control of the distribution of federal funds and the agenda more broadly; conversely, for the minority, gaining control comes with those valuable perks. The rank and file have been willing, in both parties, to give up some prerogatives at the committee and subcommittee levels in order to further the broader aims of their party. The mantra is to stay on message, do not help the other side, and stick with the party on legislation if at all possible. Someone has to manage this process, and it makes sense to give elected leadership that authority.

What has developed is a much more tightly managed legislative process—tightly managed by the leadership. As Barbara Sinclair says, and as we saw in Chapter 5, "unorthodox lawmaking" has become the norm.[24] If the regular process—major legislation being examined in one or more committees and subcommittees by dozens of members—is too slow or yields an unacceptable result, the leadership steps in to engineer a solution more friendly to the majority. This may involve skipping stages on the "how a bill becomes a law" chart and including only relatively few members in the discussions (and often few, if any, minority party members). The regular process can be too messy and fraught with too much uncertainty.

Many members, and certainly the leadership, believe that the old ways are not suited to the modern media environment. Congress is a complex and confusing place that too often moves slowly. Someone needs to try to streamline it and translate it to the new media. The leadership takes on this task.

The resurgence of leadership and the resultant use of unorthodox lawmaking are in large part products of the increase in partisanship in congressional politics and in American politics more broadly. Leaders are granted the power to assert themselves when members understand that the fate of their party is at stake.

### The New Environment and Congress's Failure to Do Its Job

A highly charged partisan environment, with the parties staking out opposing positions on taxes, health care, energy, and other major issues, results both in a Congress that strives to accomplish big things (see the laundry list of major bills passed in the past 20 years) and a Congress that fails to do the basics. How can that be?

First, as noted, each party is united behind a policy platform—less regulation, less taxation, and smaller government for Republicans, an enhanced federal role in education, health, and the environment for Democrats. The members genuinely want to accomplish their respective ends and receive a great deal of pressure from their electoral bases to do so. And often the time is short. On the partisan issues, things have to be done when your party's president is in office and has the political capital to hold some sway. These factors create an urgency to accomplish things when you have the levers of power. Bills are passed by any means necessary, sometimes using highly unorthodox tactics and taking full advantage of reconciliation procedures, when available, to get around the de facto supermajority requirement in the Senate.

But keeping the government running and updating agency authorities means passing many bills every year—the 12 appropriations bills plus perhaps another dozen or more policy authorizations that may be expired or expiring. These bills usually require a certain amount of cooperation between the parties to pass in the House and always require that in the Senate, as reconciliation is not available for these types of measures. Extraordinary means that were used to pass the health reform in 2010 and the tax cuts in 2001 and 2003 simply cannot be used for updating education policy, the defense authorization, or any of the appropriations bills. In addition, the leadership does not have the political capital to force party-line votes on that many bills.

The bottom line: *bipartisanship is required to get most of the work done on Capitol Hill.* But what happens now is that these bills are hijacked, in effect, by the minority party in both chambers. Doing this is all too easy. Amendments are offered to embarrass the majority with the aim of enhancing the political position of the minority for the next election. This often kills bills or at least delays passage. (In the Senate, in particular, many bills are simply not brought to the floor in order to prevent the minority from scoring points through the amendment process.) It is literally impossible to pass all that needs to pass on time—or even close to it. Congress spins its wheels when it comes to reauthorizing vital agencies of government and keeping the funding stream for government programs in place.

And to make matters worse, a highly partisan atmosphere creates another problem for Congress. In recent decades, oversight has gotten short shrift when Congress and the White House are controlled by the same party.

This was not always the case. As noted in Chapter 9, Democratic senator Harry Truman conducted vigorous and often embarrassing investigations of Democratic president Roosevelt's administration in the early years of World War II. The Republican Congress did not lay off President Eisenhower in the early to mid-1950s. Lyndon Johnson's conduct of the Vietnam War eventually received intense scrutiny from the Democratically controlled Congress of the day. And Jimmy Carter was not let off easily either by the Democratic Congresses with which he served.

In more recent years, the trend has been for Congress to conduct only perfunctory oversight during times of unified government, the fear being that criticism of one's own party's administration could have adverse electoral consequences. The attitude: we all rise and fall together. Before the 1990s, it was not the case that members of Congress necessarily saw their electoral fates linked to the president of their party.

On the other hand, in times of divided government in the past two decades, the party in charge in Congress has hired dozens of investigators to go after alleged wrongdoing in the executive branch, and they have inundated the White House and agency personnel with subpoenas demanding documents and testimony.[25] Sometimes it seemed as though key officials spent more time trying to cope with congressional demands than actually doing the work of the agencies.

Oversight has too often become more about scoring political points than about ensuring the efficient implementation of government programs and the wise stewardship of taxpayer money. Of course, oversight has always had a political element to it—lawmakers are always trying to look good by exposing waste, fraud, and abuse in the government. But members of Congress seem to have lost sight of their institutional responsibility to oversee the executive. Most observers do not think the prospects for a turnaround are good.

## CONCLUSION: CAN CONGRESS WORK IN THE 21ST CENTURY?

Anyone looking for Congress to move expeditiously and harmoniously on the major issues of the day, while at the same time giving careful consideration to expert opinion and a wide variety of views, is living in a fantasyland. The institution's fundamental nature makes it impossible for it to achieve some idealized level of performance.

It is better to grade Congress on a curve. Given its inherent limitations, how does Congress do? Is it obviously better or worse than other democratically elected legislatures around the world at tackling complex issues?

There is no consensus answer. Most political scientists would say that the US Congress does not fare too badly by comparison, although in one sense there are not too many comparable counterparts. Very few legislatures around the world have the kind of responsibilities that Congress has. Our legislative body is the board of directors, with funding and authorizing authority over a vast government; most legislatures do not have that level of power and responsibility. The branches are usually not coequal in other democracies—typically, the executive has more unchecked authority than is the case in the United States.

As we have seen, Congress's enhanced responsibilities compared to other legislatures compel it to be creative in dealing with difficult issues. The board of directors has chosen to delegate power and responsibility to the executive branch, and it often employs commissions in an attempt to get past its parochial nature. But Congress has always retained its ability to reclaim delegated authority or reject commission proposals, even as it chooses to delegate. It is exactly this flexibility that has allowed Congress to retain its place at the center of our political system.

However, in the 21st century, the institution is simply not meeting its basic responsibilities. It uses all or nearly all of its bandwidth reorganizing swaths of the government and instituting grand new programs, but cannot update key authorizations, pass appropriations bills, and conduct useful oversight.

## Is There a Workable Model Out There?

It is instructive to consider the legislation that does regularly make it through Congress in a timely fashion: the yearly reauthorization of the activities of the Defense Department. This massive bill sets the policies for a more than $600 billion entity entrusted with defending the security of the nation, and, as such, it is about as important as any other single thing Congress does. Each year—51 in a row as of 2012—it gets done, even while immigration reform and other ambitious plans may stall and appropriations bills get shoveled together into omnibus packages months into the new fiscal year.

How does Congress do this? Some people point to the strong imperative that members feel when working on legislation that affects the men and women who put their lives at risk in defense of the country. And that is certainly a factor. From a procedural standpoint, however, the key is the tradition of bipartisanship practiced by the Armed Services Committees in the two chambers. Bipartisanship happens on the Hill, but it is episodic and not deeply ingrained in very many other places. Sometimes a bipartisan process is claimed when the majority is able to persuade a few members of the minority to join them. President Bush claimed bipartisanship when a handful of Democrats signed on to his tax-cut bill in 2001. President Obama did the same when three Republicans came on board to vote for the Recovery Act in 2009. But this is not the real thing.

Consider that the whole of the Armed Services Committees' membership and staff share information and work together on the defense authorization bill. Everyone understands that the majority has the upper hand at the end of the day, but the internal processes are cooperative. That is true bipartisanship, and it explains why the final product that these committees come up with passes by overwhelming margins most years. And keep in mind that the Senate *can work if and only if real efforts are made at developing consensus,* given the ability of the minority to prevent legislation from coming up for a vote.

Not only is national defense policy made on a bipartisan basis, but so is legislation in some other areas, such as farming and infrastructure improvements. The Farm Bill and transportation reauthorizations usually move through Congress on a bipartisan basis, with divisions more likely to be drawn on regional than partisan lines, although even these are tougher and tougher to pass on time these days. Bipartisanship is the sine qua non of productive legislating. Recognizing that reality is the first step toward addressing Congress's failings. Cooperative processes are required if the board of directors is to get its legislative work done on a timely and consistent basis.

The defense authorization also highlights the fact that total harmony is not required for the process to work. There are important disagreements on defense policy, and both parties try to add amendments that score political points. But the committees of jurisdiction have been successful in minimizing the damage by productive compromise and getting "buy-in" from both sides. Members have shown they can and do tone down the partisanship when they get to have a say in the final product.

Whether this model can work more broadly is debatable. Maybe the defense bill is the proverbial exception that proves the rule. But having a goal or a working model to draw upon certainly cannot hurt.

## The Serious Business of Directing the Work of Government

The Constitution set up Congress as a powerful player in our separated system of government. As we look ahead, there is a lot for it to consider.

The 21st century presents major policy challenges that we can anticipate and surely some equally as daunting that we cannot. The baby-boom generation is retiring and claiming full Medicare and Social Security benefits. Everyone recognizes that this could bankrupt the government in the not too distant future if dramatic reforms are not enacted. The key component of the problem is the health care system, which, while delivering miracles on a daily basis, is inefficient and tremendously costly. A growing consensus is developing that global climate change presents a host of profound domestic policy dilemmas. The Defense Department and the intelligence agencies also list it as one of the top national security challenges in the new century. In these areas and many more, the government *has* to act.

This chapter has been an exercise in identifying Congress's failings and then looking at the root causes. In tandem with that effort, we have tried to tamp down expectations. Congress will never be perfect; solutions have to be realistic.

What is reasonable to expect from Congress? Congress is naturally slow, parochial, and unable to plan, but it must continue to find ways to improvise and adjust when circumstances demand concerted action. And partisanship will always be with us, but leaders in Congress cannot allow it to destroy the working relationships between members of the two parties that have to be there in order to move legislation.

In addition, some action also needs to be taken to readjust the balance between the members' legislative and representative roles. Much too much is at stake for the problem to be ignored. Agencies do an incredibly broad and complex range of things—from the intelligence and national security realm; to scientific research on cancer, AIDS, and mental health; to inspecting nuclear power plants; and the list goes on. In our system it is only Congress that can provide the legal framework and the funding for government programs. It is essential that the board of directors does so carefully and well, and in a timely manner.

The vast majority of members of Congress are hardworking and talented people trying to do the right thing as they see it. But they have, in essence, two very difficult jobs. Directing the federal government while being available to constituents and doing what needs to be done to get reelected is a tremendous, perhaps overwhelming, challenge, especially the way the system is structured now. As a result, it is no surprise that authorizations of major agencies lapse and fall out of date. It is also no surprise that the board has trouble finding the time each year to consider carefully the funding requirements of every agency of the government when they have so much on their plate. Both of those responsibilities carry with them the need to conduct oversight to determine which programs are working, which ones need more funding, and what changes need to be made so that agencies can better serve their missions and the American people. But oversight is done unsystematically and is too often undertaken to score political points in anticipation of the next election rather than to ensure good government.

To do the job will require more time in Washington and marginally less time focused on reelection and constituent service. Congressional scholars Norman Ornstein and Tom Mann suggest that "the best reform would be to require Congress to hold sessions five days a week for a minimum of 26 weeks a year, with members spending two weeks on, in Washington, and two weeks off, in their home districts. Members of Congress should not be distracted by permanent campaigning; accordingly, fundraising in the capital should be banned when the legislature is in session."[26]

In addition, Mann, Ornstein, and other observers—notably Donald Wolfensberger of the Woodrow Wilson Center—provide a range of steps that could be taken in reforming the electoral system and fundraising, opening up the legislative process to more amendments, and reducing filibusters in the Senate.[27] Whether their proposals are feasible is debatable. But the direction we need to go in is not.

At the end of the day, Congress is a work in progress. Meaningful reform can come about only after the players, the members themselves, recognize and acknowledge the problems we have talked about and take genuine steps to find solutions. In particular, there needs to be an attitude adjustment on the part of party leaders, who must refrain from trying to control every legislative outcome and, instead, do what they can to encourage cooperative, bipartisan processes in the development of legislation.

With the need to pass laws to address the challenges of the 21st century, Congress will remain a central player. The quality of its work will determine the kind of future we have.

## Questions for Discussion

1. In dealing with the many problems facing the nation in the coming years, would it be wise for the board of directors to delegate more to the president on the big issues? Should it rely on commission recommendations more? Or is there some way Congress can restructure how it does its legislative work in order to help it cope with complex, large-scale problems?

2. Can you think of any practical solutions for Congress to deal with its imbalance that has developed between its legislative and representative roles?

3. There are good reasons people are partisan—after all, political parties are the main vehicles in a democratic political system for pursuing strongly held beliefs and viewpoints. Is there a point where partisanship goes too far? If so, can you identify that point? Have you seen it in action?

## Suggestions for Further Reading

Brownstein, Ronald. *The Second Civil War*. New York: Penguin Press, 2007.

Dodd, Lawrence C., and Bruce I. Oppenheimer. "Party Polarization and Policy Productivity in Congress: From Harding to Obama." In *Congress Reconsidered,* edited by Bruce I. Oppenheimer and Lawrence C. Dodd, 437–463. 10th ed. Washington, DC: CQ Press, 2013.

Mann, Thomas E., and Norman J. Ornstein. *It's Even Worse than It Looks*. New York: Basic Books, 2012.

Sundquist, James L. *The Decline and Resurgence of Congress*. Washington, DC: Brookings Institution Press, 1981.

Volden, Craig, and Alan E. Wiseman. "Legislative Effectiveness and Representation." In *Congress Reconsidered,* edited by Bruce I. Oppenheimer and Lawrence C. Dodd, 237–264. 10th ed. Washington, DC: CQ Press, 2013.

Wolfensberger, Donald R. "Getting Back to Legislating: Reflections of a Congressional Working Group." Bipartisan Policy Center, November 27, 2012. www.wilsoncenter.org/sites/default/files/Culture_Congress_Report_0.pdf.

## NOTES

1. For example, see Robert Dahl's *How Democratic Is the American Constitution?*, 2nd ed. (New Haven, CT: Yale University Press, 2003).

2. Ronald Brownstein, *The Second Civil War* (New York: Penguin Press, 2007).

3. James L. Sundquist, *The Decline and Resurgence of Congress* (Washington, DC: Brookings Institution Press, 1981), chap. 7.

4. Joe Schatz of *Congressional Quarterly,* interview with the author, April 23, 2009.

5. For a good description of how welfare and other racially tinged issues played politically in the 1980s, see E. J. Dionne, *Why Americans Hate Politics* (New York: Simon & Schuster, 1991), chap. 3.

6. David M. Herszenhorn and Carl Hulse, "Deal Reached in Congress on $789 Billion Stimulus Plan," *New York Times,* February 11, 2009, A1.

7. Garry Young, interview with the author, October 24, 2007.

8. See Veronique de Rugby, "What Does Homeland Security Spending Buy?," American Enterprise Institute Papers and Studies, June 5, 2009, www.aei.org/paper/21483.

9. Quoted in R. Jeffrey Smith and Ellen Nakashima, "Pentagon's Unwanted Projects in Earmarks," *Washington Post,* March 8, 2009, A1.

10. See David Mayhew, *Congress: The Electoral Connection* (New Haven, CT: Yale University Press, 1974), chap. 2.

11. Sundquist, *Decline and Resurgence of Congress,* chaps. 3–6.

12. Sidney Milkis and Michael Nelson, *The American Presidency: Origins and Development, 1776–2007* (Washington, DC: CQ Press, 2007).

13. See "2005 Defense Base Closure and Realignment Commission Report," www.brac.gov/.

14. David Mayhew, *Congress: The Electoral Connection* (New Haven, CT: Yale University Press, 1974), 178–179.

15. See E. Scott Adler and John D. Wilkerson, *Congress and the Politics of Problem Solving* (New York: Cambridge University Press, 2012), for an analysis of Congress's ability to focus on bigger, nonparticularistic issues.

16. Thomas E. Mann and Norman J. Ornstein, *It's Even Worse than It Looks* (New York: Basic Books, 2012).

17. A good overview with links to data can be found in Marian Currinder's "What Congressional Recesses Mean for the Federal Agencies," *GAI on the Hill*, April 1, 2013, www.gairegistration.org/newsletter.aspx?nl=59&bt=1.

18. The average Congress in the 1960s and '70s had 5,372 committee and subcommittee meetings; in the 1980s and 1990s, the average was 4,793. In the 108th Congress, the number was 2,135. See Norman J. Ornstein, Thomas E. Mann, and Michael J. Malbin, *Vital Statistics on Congress, 2008* (Washington, DC: Brookings Institution Press, 2009), 125.

19. Mark Brewer, *Parties and Elections in America,* 5th ed. (Lanham, MD: Rowman and Littlefield, 2007), 403, 405.

20. Probably the definitive work on this topic is Keith T. Poole and Howard Rosenthal, *Ideology and Congress* (Piscataway, NJ: Transaction, 2007). See also Gary C. Jacobson, *The Politics of Congressional Elections,* 8th ed. (Boston: Pearson, 2013), chap. 7.

21. Claudia Dreifus, "A Science Advocate and an 'Endangered Species,' He Bids Farewell," *New York Times,* May 9, 2006, www.nytimes.com/2006/05/09/science/09conv.html.

22. See Gary W. Cox and Matthew D. McCubbins, *Legislative Leviathan: Party Government in the House* (Berkeley: University of California Press, 2007).

23. See Nathan W. Monroe, Jason M. Roberts, and David W. Rohde, *Why Not Parties? Party Effects in the United States Senate* (Chicago: University of Chicago Press, 2008).

24. Barbara Sinclair, *Unorthodox Lawmaking,* 3rd ed. (Washington, DC: CQ Press, 2007).

25. Alexis Simendinger of the *National Journal,* speech delivered September 12, 2007.

26. Norman J. Ornstein and Thomas E. Mann, "When Congress Checks Out," *Foreign Affairs,* November 30, 2006.

27. Donald R. Wolfensberger, "Getting Back to Legislating: Reflections of a Congressional Working Group," Bipartisan Policy Center, November 27, 2012, www.wilsoncenter.org/sites/default/files/Culture_Congress_Report_0.pdf.

# APPENDIX: A CENTURY OF CONGRESS

# A Century of Congress

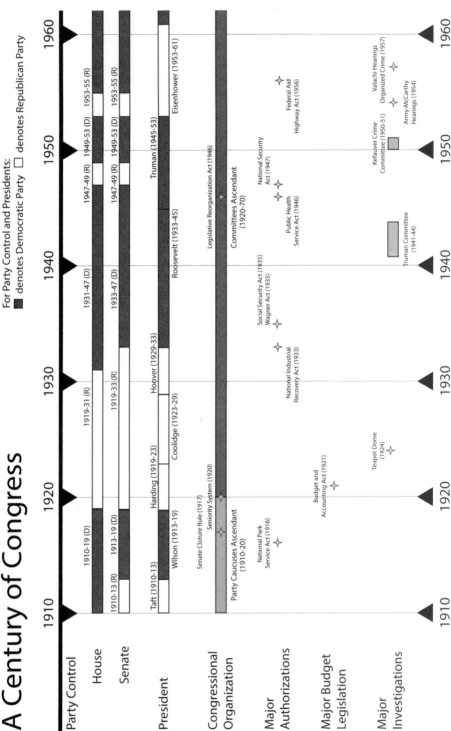

For Party Control and Presidents:
■ denotes Democratic Party   □ denotes Republican Party

**Party Control**

House
- 1910-13 (R)
- 1913-19 (D)
- 1919-31 (R)
- 1931-47 (D)
- 1947-49 (R)
- 1949-53 (D)
- 1953-55 (R)

Senate
- 1910-13 (R)
- 1913-19 (D)
- 1919-33 (R)
- 1933-47 (D)
- 1947-49 (R)
- 1949-53 (D)
- 1953-55 (R)

**President**
- Taft (1910-13)
- Wilson (1913-19)
- Harding (1919-23)
- Coolidge (1923-29)
- Hoover (1929-33)
- Roosevelt (1933-45)
- Truman (1945-53)
- Eisenhower (1953-61)

**Congressional Organization**
- Party Caucuses Ascendant (1910-20)
- Senate Cloture Rule (1917)
- Seniority System (1920)
- Committees Ascendant (1920-70)
- Legislative Reorganization Act (1946)

**Major Authorizations**
- National Park Service Act (1916)
- National Industrial Recovery Act (1933)
- Social Security Act (1935)
- Wagner Act (1935)
- Public Health Service Act (1946)
- National Security Act (1947)
- Federal Aid Highway Act (1956)

**Major Budget Legislation**
- Budget and Accounting Act (1921)

**Major Investigations**
- Teapot Dome (1924)
- Truman Committee (1941-44)
- Kefauver Crime Committee (1950-51)
- Army-McCarthy Hearings (1954)
- Valachi Hearings Organized Crime (1957)

Timeline axis: 1910, 1920, 1930, 1940, 1950, 1960

# A Century of Congress (continued)

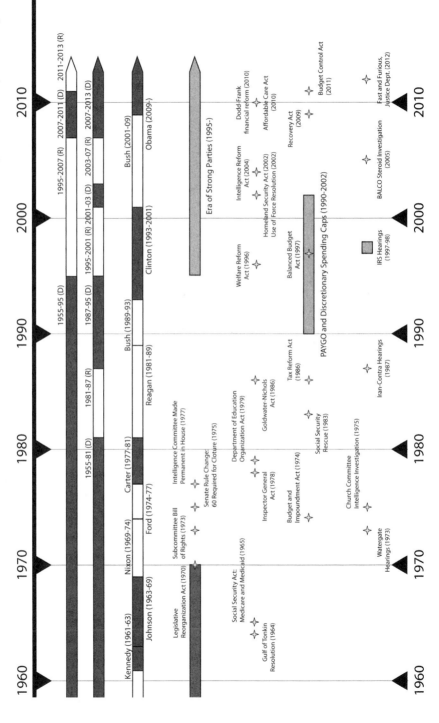

For Party Control and Presidents:
■ denotes Democratic Party   □ denotes Republican Party

1960   1970   1980   1990   2000   2010

Kennedy (1961-63)
Johnson (1963-69)
Nixon (1969-74)
Ford (1974-77)
Carter (1977-81)
Reagan (1981-89)
Bush (1989-93)
Clinton (1993-2001)
Bush (2001-09)
Obama (2009-)

1955-95 (D)
1981-87 (R)   1987-95 (D)
1995-2007 (R)   2007-2011 (D)   2011-2013 (R)

1955-81 (D)
1995-2001 (R)   2001-03 (D)   2003-07 (R)   2007-2013 (D)

Era of Strong Parties (1995-)

PAYGO and Discretionary Spending Caps (1990-2002)

Legislative
Reorganization Act (1970)

Social Security Act:
Medicare and Medicaid (1965)

Gulf of Tonkin
Resolution (1964)

Subcommittee Bill
of Rights (1973)

Intelligence Committee Made
Permanent in House (1977)

Senate Rule Change:
60 Required for Cloture (1975)

Department of Education
Organization Act (1979)

Inspector General
Act (1978)

Goldwater-Nichols
Act (1986)

Budget and
Impoundment Act (1974)

Social Security
Rescue (1983)

Tax Reform Act
(1986)

Welfare Reform
Act (1996)

Intelligence Reform
Act (2004)

Homeland Security Act (2002)
Use of Force Resolution (2002)

Dodd-Frank
financial reform (2010)

Affordable Care Act
(2010)

Recovery Act
(2009)

Budget Control Act
(2011)

Church Committee
Intelligence Investigation (1975)

Watergate
Hearings (1973)

Iran-Contra Hearings
(1987)

Balanced Budget
Act (1997)

IRS Hearings
(1997-98)

BALCO Steroid Investigation
(2005)

Fast and Furious,
Justice Dept. (2012)

1960   1970   1980   1990   2000   2010

# GLOSSARY OF KEY TERMS

**302(a) allocation**  The section of the budget resolution that determines each committee's spending allocation for legislation pertaining to the next fiscal year. Most attention is paid to the allocation for the Appropriations Committees covering discretionary spending.

**302(b) allocation**  The subdivision of the 302(a) allocation made by the Appropriations Committees. In each chamber, the Appropriations Committee allots a portion of the 302(a) to each of its 12 subcommittees (constituting the 302[b] allocations) to fund the agencies in each subcommittee's jurisdiction for the next fiscal year.

**accounts**  The unnumbered paragraphs in appropriations bills that provide budget authority to the agencies. Each account usually covers a broad range of programs and expenses in a given agency.

**"A" committees**  A subset of Senate committees including most authorizing committees. Senators are guaranteed one A committee assignment and may have as many as two.

**Affordable Care Act (2010)**  Major legislation that expanded Medicaid and put in place health care exchanges with the aim of expanding health care coverage to the uninsured.

**amendment in the nature of a substitute**  An amendment offered as a replacement to the bill being considered on the floor.

**amendments between the chambers**  The process of passing a bill back and forth until one chamber agrees to the version passed in the other chamber. One of the principal methods of resolving the differences between the two chambers on pending legislation.

**apportionment**  The process of distributing the 435 House seats among the states after the decennial census. The "method of equal proportions" is currently used by the Census Bureau to determine how many representatives each state gets.

**Appropriations Committees**  The committees in the House and Senate that write the bills that control the funding for the discretionary portion of the federal government.

**assistant leader**  The second-ranking party leader in the Democratic and Republican Parties in the Senate. Sometimes called the "majority whip" or the "minority whip."

**authorization of appropriations**  The section of authorizing legislation that sets a funding ceiling for discretionary programs.

**authorizing committees** The committees in the House and Senate that write legislation that sets agency policies. These committees also have oversight responsibilities for the agencies in their jurisdiction.

**authorizing power** One of Congress's three powers as the board of directors of the federal government, this power, granted in Article I of the Constitution, gives Congress the authority to determine the policies of executive branch agencies.

**Bipartisan Campaign Reform Act (BCRA)** Legislation signed into law in 2002 that updated and revised existing campaign finance law and, among other things, put an end to unlimited so-called soft-money contributions and adjusted the contribution limits for individual donors to campaigns for federal office. Often called "McCain-Feingold" in honor of the two senators—Russ Feingold (D-WI) and John McCain (R-AZ)—who were its principal sponsors.

**budget authority** The authority provided in law that enables agencies to obligate money in order to carry out government programs.

**Budget Control Act (BCA) (2011)** Major legislation that put in place statutory caps on discretionary spending through 2021 and also required sequestration of mostly discretionary spending in that time period if additional deficit reduction were not achieved through major reforms on the spending and revenue side.

**budget request** See "president's budget."

**budget resolution** See "Concurrent Budget Resolution."

**candidate-centered politics** Campaign politics focused on individual candidates rather than parties. Candidate-centered politics developed in the 20th century as parties began using primaries to select nominees, forcing candidates to distinguish themselves based on personal characteristics.

**caucus** The official meeting of the members of one party in either the House or the Senate for the purposes of conducting official business, such as selecting members for leadership positions or discussing legislative strategy. House Republicans call their meeting of party members a "conference."

**caucus chair** Member chosen by the Democrats or Republicans in the House or Senate to lead meetings of the party members and to take on other duties. House Republicans call this member the "conference chair."

**chairman's mark** The version of a bill developed by the chair of a subcommittee or committee that is brought up for discussion, amendment, and vote in that subcommittee or committee.

**chief of staff** The staff member who is in charge of a senator's or representative's personal office. Sometimes referred to as "administrative assistant (AA)."

**circuit courts** Appellate-level courts in the federal system situated between the district or trial courts and the Supreme Court.

*Citizens United v. Federal Elections Commission* **(2010)** Supreme Court ruling invalidating parts of the BCRA. It allowed corporations and unions to spend unlimited amounts of money on independent expenditures and issue advocacy.

**closed rule** A type of special rule governing debate on the House floor that permits no amendments to the legislation under consideration. See "structured rule."

**cloture**  A Senate procedure that puts a limit on floor debate and nongermane amendments. Cloture requires 60 votes to be "invoked," after which a vote takes place after thirty hours on the motion or bill under consideration.

**commander-in-chief power**  The power granted to the president, in Article II of the Constitution, over the armed forces and over the state "militias" "when called into the actual service of the United States."

**Commerce Clause**  Provision in Article I, Section 8, of the Constitution that gives Congress the power to regulate interstate commerce. Its interpretation has been and continues to be the source of considerable controversy.

**"commission solution"**  The term coined here for Congress's practice of establishing commissions—panels of experts who study pressing or long-term problems facing the nation. A commission is usually required to report its findings or provide a legislative solution, which Congress may or may not be required to act upon.

**committee jurisdiction**  The policy domain (including the operations of the relevant federal agencies) given each congressional committee by the parent chamber.

**Committee of the Whole**  A committee whose membership includes the whole House of Representatives. Most important legislation in the House is handled by the Committee of the Whole before it is voted on by the House of Representatives. The Committee of the Whole offers a streamlined method to handle most debate and amendments on the floor of the chamber.

**committee referral**  The process, managed by the parliamentarian of the House or Senate, that determines which committee should receive the bills introduced by members of Congress. Parliamentarians make this decision based on the established committee jurisdictions.

**committee report**  Nonstatutory language attached to a bill as it is reported out of committee, giving the committee's views of the intent of the proposed legislation.

**committee staff**  See "professional staff."

**Concurrent Budget Resolution**  A resolution agreed to by the full House and Senate that sets the parameters for all budget-related legislation to be handled that year. Also called the "budget resolution," it includes spending and revenue targets, sets the limits on discretionary spending, and may include instructions for tax bills or mandatory spending legislation.

**conference chair**  The term used by House Republicans for their party equivalent of a "caucus chair."

**conference committee**  An ad hoc panel comprising members from both chambers and selected to iron out the differences between similar legislation passed by the House and Senate. Often simply called a "conference."

**conference report**  The final version of conference committee deliberations to iron out the differences between similar legislation passed by the House and Senate. The conference report must be agreed to by the majority of each chamber's delegation to the conference and is subsequently sent to both chambers for final approval.

**continuing resolution (CR)**  The legislation that keeps government agencies running when Congress has failed to pass appropriations bills by the beginning of the fiscal year.

**cracking** A process sometimes used by majority partisans in a state legislature when they redraw congressional district lines. Its purpose is to distribute the minority party's supporters more thinly across congressional districts so that the majority party can maximize its representation from the state in the House of Representatives. Historically has referred to the process, now unconstitutional, by which voters of a racial or ethnic minority are distributed in such a way as to minimize their chances of electing one of their own to office.

**debt ceiling** Statutory limit placed on federal borrowing.

**deficit** The difference between government revenues and government expenditures when expenditures outpace those revenues.

**direct lobbying** Direct face-to-face contact between citizens or groups—or their paid advocates or "lobbyists"—and members of Congress and their staff in efforts to influence policy making.

**direct spending** The program funding provided, usually by formula, in authorizing law. Also called "mandatory spending."

**discretionary program** A government program that receives its funding in an annual appropriations bill.

**discretionary spending** Spending that is controlled annually in appropriations legislation, including program funds and, more generally, agency operating funds.

**district courts** The trial stage in the federal system. Every state has at least one federal district court.

**district office** Member offices set up in districts and states to address directly constituent needs and concerns, usually those related to federal government programs and services.

**Dodd-Frank financial regulatory reform (2010)** Major legislation meant to rein in the excesses by large banks and other financial institutions that led to the Great Recession and the near meltdown of the financial system.

**earmark** A specification by Congress, usually in an appropriations bill or report language attached to an appropriations bill, of the location or recipient of federal funding, thus circumventing the established merit-based formulas or competitive allocation processes handled by the executive branch.

**entitlements** See "mandatory program."

**exclusive committees** The five House committees—Appropriations, Energy and Commerce, Financial Services, Rules, and Ways and Means—that are given special status by the rules of one or both parties. Members who secure membership on one of these committees may not serve on any other committees unless granted a waiver by the party leadership.

**Executive Office of the President (EOP)** Agencies, including the White House Office staff, that help the president manage and keep track of the vast federal government.

**executive order** Presidential action setting agency policy (or providing authority to high-ranking agency officials) usually pursuant to delegated authority from Congress. Executive orders may also be put forward in areas where Congress has been silent.

**executive power**  The broad grant of power given the president at the beginning of Article II of the Constitution.

**executive privilege**  The doctrine that asserts that the president and other high officials of the executive branch should be able to keep certain communications private if disclosing those communications would disrupt the functions or decision-making processes of the executive branch.

**favorable report**  Action taken by a committee giving approval to legislation under its jurisdiction with the hope that such legislation will be taken up for floor consideration.

**Federal Elections Campaign Act (FECA)**  A law passed in 1974 that put strict limits on campaign donations and instituted rigorous reporting requirements for congressional campaigns.

**"fencing off" (funds)**  Action by Congress (through a provision in appropriations law) to prohibit an agency from using some portion of appropriated funds until certain administrative plans to implement a program are approved by the Appropriations Committees. Such a provision constitutes an unconstitutional "legislative veto" but is nonetheless commonly used by Congress and not contested by agencies.

**filibuster**  A delaying tactic that may be used by members of the Senate to stop legislation from coming to a vote. A supermajority of 60 senators is required (see "cloture") to limit debate and move toward a vote.

**"fire-alarm" system**  Political science term referring to the web of oversight of federal programs. On the basis of the monitoring of federal programs by congressional staff, the GAO, inspectors general, and interested parties in the public, key members and staff in Congress are more likely to be aware of problems and malfeasance in the federal government.

**fiscal year (FY)**  For accounting purposes, the federal government year begins on October 1 and goes 12 months through September 30 of the following calendar year.

**franking**  The allowance given to each member of Congress, through his or her chamber, to send mail to constituents free of charge; often called the "franking privilege." Congress reimburses the Postal Service through its legislative branch appropriation.

**functional categories**  Broad categories of federal spending included in the Concurrent Budget Resolution. The functional categories do not align perfectly either with the government departments and agencies or with congressional committee jurisdictions. They are meant to facilitate discussion in Congress on the goals and purposes of federal spending.

**funding power**  One of Congress's three powers as the board of directors of the federal government; often called "the power of the purse." Congress is given this power to determine the budgets for the federal agencies in Article I, Section 9, of the Constitution.

**general election**  The final election in a campaign, usually between a Democrat and a Republican, that determines the winner of a House or Senate seat.

**general provisions**  A component of appropriations law, identifiable by section numbers, that gives specific instructions to agencies on a wide range of matters.

**germaneness** The House has a general rule that amendments must be directly related ("germane") to the legislation under consideration. In the Senate, germaneness applies to appropriations bills (although it is not uncommon for the rule to go unenforced) and to bills under consideration after cloture has been invoked or by unanimous consent agreement.

**gerrymandering** The process of drawing House district lines to benefit an incumbent or a particular party or to improve the chances that a candidate from a racial or ethnic minority will win the seat.

**grassroots lobbying** Efforts by interest groups to generate contacts from their membership to congressional offices, often using e-mail, phone calls, or other forms of communication.

**Great Compromise** The deal struck between big and small states at the Constitutional Convention that led to the establishment of a bicameral Congress.

**Great Society** Major programs implemented during the Lyndon Johnson administration in the 1960s that led to a dramatic expansion in federal government activities.

**hearings** Public committee or subcommittee meetings (initiated by the chair) that are intended to gather information from witnesses on pending legislation, to look into the operations of agencies and programs, or to investigate potential wrongdoing at agencies or in the private sector. Senate committees hold hearings on nominations to the federal courts and the top-level executive branch positions. Hearings involving classified information are not held in public.

**hold** Action by a senator to deny the majority leader unanimous consent to proceed with legislative business. The hold delays that business until it is withdrawn (often after a deal is negotiated with the senator or senators placing the hold) or until the leader successfully forces action by invoking cloture.

**Honest Leadership and Open Government Act (HLOGA) (2007)** Law passed to impose stricter reporting requirements on lobbyists, with the intention of increasing transparency to the public for their activities. It also placed stricter limits on gift giving to members of Congress and staff.

**hotlining** A tool of the Senate majority leader to apprise the entire chamber (by e-mail and phone) of legislative business he would like to bring up on the floor, usually the next day, by unanimous consent. Hotlining enables the leader to expedite that business. Members may notify the leader of their objections, thus denying unanimous consent.

**hyperpluralism** A term coined by Jonathan Rauch referring to the dramatic proliferation of interest group activity beginning in the 1970s.

**ideological sorting** The process by which the adherents of the two parties began to divide increasingly along ideological lines, to the point where the Democratic Party is now more uniformly liberal and the Republican Party more uniformly conservative than they have been in the past. Sorting by ideology became especially noticeable beginning in the 1960s.

**incumbent** The current occupant of a political office.

**independent expenditure (IE)**  Money that may be spent on an unlimited basis by the political parties on behalf of congressional candidates. Independent expenditure campaigns must not be coordinated in any way with the candidate campaigns.

**indirect lobbying**  Describes advertising campaigns in different media, orchestrated by corporations or interest groups, that are intended to improve the political climate for specific issues or influence attitudes about groups or corporations.

**interest group**  A group of people that bands together in order to pursue common aims. In particular, interest groups use many methods to influence public policy, including hiring lobbyists, public relations tactics, and forming political action committees to contribute to candidates for public office.

**interest on the debt**  The money spent by the Treasury to service the accumulated debt owed by the federal government.

**joint explanatory statement (JES)**  Nonstatutory language added to the final version of legislation to explain how the two chambers came to agree on the final version. Part of the "conference report," the JES often includes instructions from Congress on how to implement the law, requests for reports on the ongoing conduct of government programs, and earmarks. The generic term *report language* encompasses the joint explanatory statement.

**judicial review**  Power of the federal courts to decide the constitutionality of laws or whether executive agency actions comport with the law.

**Judiciary Act of 1789**  Established the three-tier federal court system, at least in its basic form, that we have today.

**leadership PACs**  Political action committees set up by federal politicians as a means to contribute to their fellow party members' campaigns and their party committees and to support their own campaign-related expenses.

**leadership staff**  Congressional staff hired by party leadership to assist in their duties.

**legislative assistant (LA)**  The staff position in a representative's or senator's Washington office that is responsible for researching and tracking a certain set of policy issues.

**legislative correspondent (LC)**  The staff position in a representative's or senator's office that is responsible for drafting responses to constituent correspondence.

**legislative director (LD)**  The staff position in a representative's or senator's Washington office that is responsible for overseeing the legislative interests of the member.

**legislative role**  One of two central roles that the Constitution gives to members of Congress. The legislative role is the congressional responsibility to direct the work of government through authorizing and appropriations legislation and by conducting oversight of agencies and programs.

**legislative sunset**  Statute that gives a specific end date for authorities to agencies granted in law. Those authorities expire if the statute is not renewed.

**legislative veto**  The provision in legislation that enables a committee or chamber of Congress to reject an executive branch plan of action. Legislative vetoes were ruled unconstitutional in 1983; nonetheless, Congress continues to put them in legislation. See "fencing off (funds)" for the most common type.

**limitation language**  The provision in appropriations law that prohibits an agency from spending money for a particular purpose.

**lobbyist**  A person who is hired to persuade members of Congress to support the legislative concerns of a particular interest group.

**majority leader**  In the Senate, the senator selected by the majority party to schedule legislation and otherwise pursue the majority party's agenda in the chamber. In the House, the member selected by the majority party to develop and plan legislative strategy. The majority leader in the House is second in command to the speaker.

**majority whip**  The House member selected by the majority party to count votes and marshal support for the legislative agenda. The equivalent position in the Senate is usually referred to as the "assistant leader."

**mandatory program**  A government program that is established and funded based on criteria set forth in authorizing legislation. Mandatory programs are not subject to the annual appropriations process.

**mandatory spending**  Spending on programs for which formulas or criteria are set forth in authorizing legislation. Mandatory spending is not under the control of the appropriations committees.

**marginal district**  A district that a US House candidate wins in a close election, typically with less than 55 percent of the vote. Unlike safe Democratic or Republican districts, marginal districts are considered competitive.

**markup**  The process of considering legislation (see "chairman's mark") in subcommittee or committee meetings. Most markups are held in public, and members on the panel are given the opportunity to offer and vote on amendments and the entire bill.

**members' representational allowance (MRA)**  The allotment given to House members to pay for all office-related expenses. The MRA for the 111th Congress was about $1.4 million per year, with some variation depending on travel costs for individual members. Senators also get an allowance (not called MRA) that is based on population but not strictly proportional.

**minority leader**  In the Senate, the senator selected by the minority party to lead negotiations with the majority leader on legislative agenda items. The minority leader is also usually the chief spokesperson for the party. In the House, the member selected by the minority party to speak for the party and sometimes devise strategies to thwart the majority party's agenda.

**minority whip**  The House member selected by the minority party to keep tabs on the views of the minority members on pending legislation. The minority whip is also often the member who tries to keep the party together in opposition to the majority's agenda. The equivalent position in the Senate is usually referred to as the "assistant leader."

**modified open rule**  See "open rule."

**motion to recommit**  A motion put forward on the floor by the minority party, after debate has been completed on a bill, to send the bill back to committee for reconsideration. A successful motion normally results not in reconsideration but rather in the bill's failure. Motions to recommit may include instructions to the relevant committee to make particular changes.

**necessary and proper clause** The provision in Article I of the Constitution that has the effect of giving Congress wide latitude to do legislatively what is "necessary and proper" to carry out the powers given to it in the article.

**New Deal** Program put in place by President Franklin Roosevelt and Congress that was meant to address problems associated with the Depression in the 1930s. It involved the creation of dozens of new programs and federal agencies.

**obligations** Contractual arrangements made by government agencies for services rendered by nonfederal entities (often in the private sector) or other agencies of the federal government.

**Office of Information and Regulatory Affairs (OIRA)** Component of the Office of Management and Budget that serves as a clearinghouse for most executive branch agency regulations.

**Office of Management and Budget (OMB)** The agency within the Executive Office of the President that has the principal duty of putting together the president's budget, based on the input of all federal agencies. The OMB also monitors the progress of the president's priorities on Capitol Hill.

**ombudsman** The person who serves the public by looking into their problems with government agencies. Members of Congress serve this function for their constituents.

**omnibus appropriations** When multiple appropriations bills are packaged together as one bill to facilitate passage, often well after the beginning of a new fiscal year.

**open rule** A type of special rule governing debate on the House floor, an open rule permits any germane amendments to the legislation under consideration. A "modified open rule" normally permits any amendments as long as they have been submitted to the Rules Committee in advance.

**outlays** Payments made by the government for services rendered (see "obligations").

**oversight** One of the three key powers held by Congress in its role as the board of directors of the federal government, this implied power gives Congress the right to look into the performance and conduct of government programs and agencies. Congress cannot effectively do its legislative work of authorizing and funding the government without the ability to get information from the executive branch agencies as to how programs are working.

**packing** Sometimes used by majority partisans in a state legislature as they are redrawing congressional district lines, packing is a way of putting as many minority party supporters in as few districts as possible, thereby giving the majority party a near-lock on the state's other congressional districts.

**passback** Action by the Office of Management and Budget, usually in late November or early December, in which it "passes back" to the federal departments and agencies a draft presidential budget for the next fiscal year (the one starting approximately ten months later). The agencies can appeal the OMB draft budget.

**personal office** The offices of representatives and senators in Washington and in their districts and states. The personal offices deal with legislative matters (in the Washington office) and address the concerns of constituents (see "ombudsman").

**personal staff** Aides hired by members of Congress to deal with legislative matters and more generally address the concerns of constituents.

**pluralism** The idea that political power in society is not held by a defined narrow elite but rather is distributed among a wide range of overlapping groups, any one of which is not in ascendance permanently or even for a long period of time.

**pocket veto** If a bill passes Congress within the last ten days of a congressional session and the president chooses not to sign it or veto it, the bill dies when Congress adjourns, and the president can thus, in effect, veto legislation without taking any action.

**political action committee (PAC)** The fundraising and campaign-contributing arm of an interest group (a business, labor union, or other sort of association or advocacy organization). A PAC raises money from its members or employees and contributes those funds to the election campaigns of candidates it wishes to support.

**postcommittee adjustments** Action by party leadership in Congress to alter legislation after it is reported out of committee.

**prerogative view** The theory that the president has an "undefined residuum" of power, implied by the "executive power" provision at the beginning of Article II of the Constitution, and that this enables him to take actions in a time of crisis that, although not always strictly legal, are in the nation's best interest.

**presentment clause** The Article I constitutional provision that requires legislation to pass the House and Senate in identical form before it is sent to the president for his consideration.

**president's budget** The comprehensive document developed at the president's direction every year stating his budgetary and legislative priorities for the coming fiscal year and beyond. Delivered to Congress in early February, it kicks off the congressional budget process.

**primary election** An election held to determine a party's candidate for the general election.

**professional staff** The people who are hired by and work for the chair or ranking member of a committee to do research on legislation, set up hearings, and attend to other business of the committee.

**ranking member** The top-ranking minority party member on a committee given the power to hire professional staff to support his or her legislative priorities. Normally, the ranking member becomes chair when his or her party wins the majority in the chamber.

**reconciliation instructions** An optional provision in the Concurrent Budget Resolution that directs authorizing committees to report out legislation related to taxes or mandatory programs or both. That legislation is subsequently protected from filibuster on the Senate floor.

**redistricting** Action taken at the state level to draw House district lines based on the results of the decennial census.

**report language** Nonstatutory provisions attached to a bill as it goes through the legislative process. Report language is intended to make clearer to agency officials and other interested parties Congress's intentions in the law and may include earmarks, requirements for reports, and suggestions regarding the implementation of government programs.

**representative role** One of two central roles that the Constitution gives to members of Congress. The representative role is derived from a member's connection to the voters of the district or state that put him or her in office. The American republic was based on the notion that the elected representatives would be *accountable* to the people who put them in office.

**republic** A government in which sovereignty is vested in a voting citizenry that elects representatives to exercise power on its behalf.

**"right-eye-dominant"** A term coined here to describe the tendency of members to vote on legislation consistent with their constituents' views even if their own analysis or ideology might lead them to vote differently.

**Rules Committee** The House committee that determines the guidelines for consideration—including the amending process and the time allotted for debate—of most important legislation on the floor.

**select committees** Committees of Congress whose membership is determined by the leadership of the parties in a particular chamber rather than by the parties' Steering Committees.

**self-executing provision** The provision in a special rule that, if that special rule is approved by the full House, has the effect of amending the pending legislation before it comes to the floor; often used to implement postcommittee adjustments.

**sequestration** Process of automatic budget cuts set to go into effect as prescribed by law. Gramm-Rudman (1985) and the Budget Control Act (2011) both instituted sequestration in order to force deficit reduction.

**Speaker of the House** The position established in the Constitution that serves as the presiding officer of the House of Representatives. The speaker also serves as the leader of the majority party overseeing the legislative agenda of the chamber.

**special rule** A resolution developed by the Rules Committee that determines the guidelines for consideration—including the amending process and the time allotted for debate—of most important legislation on the floor. A special rule guiding debate is subject to a vote before the pending legislation is brought up for consideration.

**split referral** One method of referring legislation to committees in the House, the split referral may be employed by the majority party leadership to send a bill to more than one committee when the bill does not fit neatly into one committee's jurisdiction. Usually, leadership sets a deadline for each committee to complete consideration of the relevant portion of the legislation.

**stacking votes** A common method of handling voting on amendments in the Committee of the Whole in the House of Representatives. Debate is conducted on several amendments with no votes taken. When debate is complete, members are summoned to the floor to vote serially on the amendments.

**staff director** A common term for the top aide to the chair or ranking member of a committee.

**Steering Committee** The party committees in the House and Senate that handle committee assignments and other important business.

**structured rule**  A type of special rule governing debate on the House floor that permits only certain types of amendments; sometimes called a "modified closed rule." See "closed rule."

**"super A" committees**  The Armed Services, Appropriations, Finance, and Foreign Relations Committees, which are considered the most important committees in the Senate. Members are guaranteed by their party an assignment on one super A committee. Democrats have an additional committee in the super A category—the Commerce, Science, and Transportation Committee.

**Supremacy Clause**  Term used to describe the clause in Article VI of the Constitution that establishes the supremacy of federal statutes over state laws, among other things.

**Supreme Court**  The only federal court specified in the Constitution. It has nine justices, including the chief justice, and has the last say on the constitutionality of legislation passed by Congress as well as whether executive agency actions comport with the law.

**suspension of the rules**  A method in the House to expedite consideration of (usually) noncontroversial legislation. Passing a bill under "suspension" requires a two-thirds vote. Debate and amendments are strictly limited.

**unanimous consent**  In this procedure meant to expedite consideration of legislation, usually in the Senate, every member agrees to proceed regardless of whether rules of the chamber are being violated.

**unanimous consent (UC) agreement**  Carefully crafted agreement in the Senate, usually negotiated by the majority and minority leaders, that limits debate and structures the amendment process. As the term implies, all members are party to the arrangement.

**unitary theory**  The theory that the Constitution strictly limits Congress's power to be involved in executive branch decision making, including setting criteria for hiring agency officials and developing administrative plans.

**unorthodox lawmaking**  A term coined by political scientist Barbara Sinclair to describe the increasingly common practice in Congress of using creative approaches to the legislative process.

**whistleblowers**  Agency officials who report wrongdoing at the workplace, usually to Congress or to agency inspectors general. Whistleblowers usually have some statutory protections from retribution.

**writ of mandamus**  A court order directing a governmental official to take an action required within the scope of official duties.

# INDEX